Jaffey on the Conflict of Laws

Second edition

C M V Clarkson BA, LLB, LLM
Professor of Law,
University of Leicester

Johnathan Hill LLB, LLM
Professor of Law
University of Bristol

OXFORD
UNIVERSITY PRESS

Great Clarendon Street, Oxford OX2 6DP

Oxford University Press is a department of the University of Oxford.
It furthers the University's objective of excellence in research, scholarship,
and education by publishing worldwide in

Oxford New York
Auckland Cape Town Dar es Salaam Hong Kong Karachi Kuala Lumpur
Madrid Melbourne Mexico City Nairobi New Delhi Taipei Toronto
Shanghai

With offices in
Argentina Austria Brazil Chile Czech Republic France Greece
Guatemala Hungary Italy Japan South Korea Poland Portugal
Singapore Switzerland Thailand Turkey Ukraine Vietnam

Published in the United States
by Oxford University Press Inc., New York

First published 2002

British Library Cataloguing in Publication Data
Data available

Library of Congress Cataloging in Publication Data
Data available

ISBN 0-406-94287-0

3 5 7 9 10 8 6 4 2

Printed in Great Britain by
William Clowes Ltd,
Beccles, Suffolk

Preface

Five years have passed since the publication of the previous edition of this work. During those five years, the Conflict of Laws has not stood still, with the subject becoming increasingly dominated by legislation. Since the last edition, legislative developments at the European and international levels have become more and more important. This is particularly evident in relation to jurisdiction and the recognition and enforcement of foreign judgments, both in the commercial and family law areas.

The structure and emphasis of this edition follows that of the previous one. After the first two chapters, which deal with introductory matters, chapters 3 to 7 address the most important commercial topics (civil jurisdiction, the recognition and enforcement of foreign judgments, choice of law in contractual and non-contractual obligations, and arbitration); family questions are considered in chapters 8 to 10 (marriage, matrimonial causes and children); chapter 11 examines questions relating to property; some theoretical questions which are introduced in the first chapter are considered in greater detail in chapter 12.

As a result of the replacement of the Brussels Convention by the Council Regulation (EC) No 44/2001 (the 'Brussels I Regulation') large parts of chapters 3 and 4 have had to be rewritten. Even more radical changes brought about by Council Regulation (EC) No 1347/2000 (the 'Brussels II Regulation') have meant that chapter 9 has had to be completely restructured and rewritten. A new Council Regulation on matters relating to parental responsibility is imminent. Chapter 10 has been somewhat rewritten in anticipation of this Regulation. Similarly, and in the same chapter, the text has been rewritten on the assumption that the Adoption and Children Bill will shortly be enacted and brought into force. Most of the remaining chapters have required significant redrafting to accommodate important, albeit less far-reaching, changes since 1997.

The aim of this book (like the previous edition) remains to provide a clear account of those topics in private international law which are covered in typical undergraduate courses. Consistent with that aim, some topics have been excluded and the coverage of others is far from comprehensive. Where appropriate the reader is referred to more encyclopedic works, in particular Dicey and Morris, *The Conflict of Laws* (13th edn, 2000) and Cheshire and North, *Private International Law* (13th edn, 1999).

For the sake of simplicity, throughout the text we have used 'he', 'his' and 'him' to signify 'he or she', 'his or her' and 'him or her'.

We are indebted to our wives, Barbara Clarkson and Sheila Hill, for their patience, understanding and support during the writing of this book.

As far as possible, we have attempted to state the law as on 1 March 2002, though it has been possible to incorporate some later material.

Chris Clarkson
Jonathan Hill
May 2002

Contents

Table of Statutes

References in this Table to *Statutes* are to Halsbury's Statutes of England (Fourth Edition) showing the volume and page at which the annotated text of an Act may be found.

Table of Conventions

List of cases

B

Decisions of the European Court of Justice are listed below numerically. These decisions are also included in the preceding alphabetical list.

Chapter 1

Introduction

I NATURE OF THE SUBJECT

The part of English law called the conflict of laws or private international law deals with cases before the English court which have connections with foreign countries. The foreign elements in the case may be events which have taken place in a foreign country or countries, or they may be the foreign domicile, residence or place of business of the parties. For example, the case may involve a contract between an English and a French person, made by correspondence, and to be performed partly in England and partly in France or in a third country. Alternatively, the English court may be hearing a tort case in which an English defendant's conduct in New York caused injury to a Mexican visitor there. Another example is a case in which the English court has to decide on the validity of a marriage celebrated in France between an English woman and an Egyptian man. In short, any case involving a foreign element raises potential conflict of laws issues.

A Overview

This requisite foreign element can arise in one of three ways, or, to put it differently, the conflict of laws is concerned with the following three questions.

1. Jurisdiction

The first point which may have to be decided in a case having foreign elements is whether the English court has power to deal with the case at all. This raises the issue of when should foreigners or persons having little or no link with England be able to sue or be sued in the English courts. For example, in *Maharanee of Baroda v Wildenstein*[1] the plaintiff, a French resident, purchased a painting from the defendant,

1 [1972] 2 QB 283, [1972] 2 All ER 689.

an international art dealer also resident in France. The painting was allegedly by Boucher. When the Maharanee discovered that the painting was probably not by Boucher at all, she commenced an action for rescission of the contract of sale by serving a writ on the defendant while he was on a brief visit to England. In many ways the most appropriate jurisdiction for this litigation was France: the contract was made in France between two French residents and was governed by French law. However, the Maharanee wished to sue in England because there might have been problems in having her expert evidence admitted in France and there would have been severe delays in having the action heard there. The problem for the conflict of laws is whether the English court should exercise jurisdiction to hear such a case that involved only the most tenuous connection with England.

2. Choice of law

If the English court does exercise jurisdiction, the next question is whether in deciding the case it will apply the rules of English law or those of a foreign country with which the case has connections. For instance, when the English court decided it had jurisdiction in *Maharanee of Baroda*[2] (as it did, under the law as it then stood), it then had to decide whether the legal issue (misrepresentation leading to rescission) was to be governed by English law (the law of the forum) or by French law.

While the novice to this area of law might assume that English courts can apply only English law, the reality is that in appropriate cases the English court can apply a foreign law to resolve the legal issue. The rules that direct the court which law to apply in a case involving foreign elements are called choice of law rules. Examples of such rules, to show their characteristic form, are: the formal validity of a marriage is governed by the law of the country in which the marriage was celebrated; the material validity of a contract is governed by the law expressly or impliedly chosen by the parties; questions of title to immovable property are governed by the law of the country in which the property is situated.

3. Recognition and enforcement of foreign judgments

The question here is the determination as to when the judgments of foreign courts will be given effect in England. Suppose a claimant having obtained a judgment against an English defendant in a New York court for damages for breach of contract, wishes to have the judgment satisfied out of the defendant's assets in England. Will the

2 *Maharanee of Baroda v Wildenstein* [1972] 2 QB 283, [1972] 2 All ER 689.

New York judgment be enforced, or will the claimant have to bring fresh proceedings in the English court to establish the claim? Alternatively, the question may be the recognition of a foreign divorce. A husband and wife living in England are Muslims; the husband pays a visit to a Muslim country of which he is a citizen where he divorces his wife under the Islamic law prevailing there by declaring three times that he divorces her. Will the divorce be effective in England? Answering these questions is the third and final task of the conflict of laws.

B Terminology

This subject has two alternative titles, the conflict of laws and private international law. The reason for the first of these is obvious. It is concerned with cases in which the parties or other relevant issues are connected with more than one country. Different countries have different laws and there can be a 'conflict' in the sense that more than one country might have jurisdiction and more than one law can be applied. Conflict of laws rules are designed to eliminate these conflicts by indicating which court should have jurisdiction and which of the 'conflicting' laws should be applied. So far as the second title is concerned, the subject is 'international' because the facts of the case or the parties to it are connected with a country or countries other than England. It is 'private' as opposed to 'public' international law because it is not concerned with the relations of states with each other, but with the disputes of persons[3] arising out of their marriages, contracts, wills, torts and other private law matters. It is not international in the sense of being a body of law shared by the different countries.

The English conflict of laws (or private international law) is just as much a part of English law as is the law of contract or the law of tort, but at a different level of classification. For present purposes, English law can be divided into two parts, English conflict of laws and English domestic law.[4] The conflict of laws can be subdivided into jurisdiction, choice of law and recognition of foreign judgments, as was seen above. English domestic law can be subdivided into contract, tort, family law, property law and so on. Domestic law, then, consists of the substantive rules defining and regulating people's rights and duties, the application of which directly decides the case. If a case before the English court has no foreign elements, then the court simply applies the appropriate rules of English domestic law. But if the case does have foreign

3 Which may, of course, include legal persons, such as companies, and governments and other public authorities.

4 Synonyms for 'domestic law' include 'internal law', 'municipal law' and 'local law'.

elements, then the court must turn to the English conflict of laws. The first question will be whether the court has jurisdiction. If not, the claimant must find a foreign court which has jurisdiction under its law. If the English court does have jurisdiction, however, then the English choice of law rules come into play. They will direct the court whether to apply English domestic law or the domestic law of one or more foreign countries in deciding the case.

English law therefore includes English conflict of laws as well as English domestic law. Similarly, French law includes French conflict of laws as well as French domestic law. Very often, however, the expression 'English law' is used to mean English domestic law only, excluding English conflict of laws. When it is said that a particular issue is governed by 'French law', that normally means French domestic law only, excluding the French conflict of laws, although occasionally, as shall be seen, the reference is to French conflict of laws.

C Meaning of country

For the purposes of the conflict of laws, a 'country' is any territorial unit having its own separate system of law, whether or not it constitutes an independent state politically. So in the conflicts context, England,[5] Scotland and Northern Ireland are separate countries because they have separate legal systems. The United Kingdom cannot be the relevant country for the purposes of those branches of private law for which there is no such thing as the law of the United Kingdom. Similarly, each of the states of the United States, each Canadian province and Australian state is a separate country. One needs to know, for instance, whether a tort was committed in Ontario, not whether it was committed in Canada. Of course, it does not follow that a country, for conflicts purposes, cannot coincide with a sovereign independent state for the purposes of public international law. Indeed, usually they will coincide, for many states have a uniform legal system throughout their territory.

In the United States and other federal countries, the convenient expression 'law district' is often used to denote a country in the conflict of laws sense.

II THE CONFLICTS PROCESS

In order to obtain a clear overview of the subject, it is important in this introductory chapter to trace the consecutive stages of a conflict of laws

5 Throughout the text 'England' is used to signify 'England and Wales'.

action. Most of the topics and issues raised will be explored more fully in subsequent chapters. What matters here is that the component elements of the subject are seen in relation to each other and to the whole and that some understanding is gained as to how and why the system operates as it does.

Tracing the various stages of a conflicts action involves examining the problems of jurisdiction and choice of law. A brief further word will be added concerning the recognition and enforcement of foreign judgments.

A Jurisdiction

The first issue for resolution in any conflicts case is whether the English court has jurisdiction. There is an argument that the English courts should be open to anyone. It is good for commerce, lucrative for English lawyers and the standards of British justice are internationally acclaimed, especially in commercial fields. This argument is particularly forceful when the parties to an international contract have agreed in their contract that the English courts should have jurisdiction. On the other hand, there is a formidable case that proceedings should be heard only in *appropriate* courts, that is, courts having some genuine connection with either the parties or the cause of action. Defendants and witnesses should not have to undergo the expense and inconvenience of having to travel round the world to defend legal proceedings. Opening one's courts to the whole world encourages forum shopping (the process of shopping round the world's courts until one finds a court where one is likely to obtain the most successful outcome) which is not conducive to settled international business. Further, if judgment is obtained in an inappropriate forum, the defendant may well not have any assets in that jurisdiction against which the judgment can be enforced and it may be necessary to commence further proceedings elsewhere to enforce the judgment. One of the objects of a modern and coherent system of conflict of laws ought to be the avoidance of such a multiplicity of proceedings.

Accordingly, before an English court assumes jurisdiction in a case involving foreign elements, there needs to be a careful investigation of all the relevant considerations, such as the interests of the parties and whether, having regard to the events and the evidence, the English court is an appropriate forum to decide the dispute.

It is, of course, important to bear in mind here that different degrees of connection (and thus different jurisdictional rules) might be required for different areas of law. For example, in an action for breach of contract the connection with England need not be particularly strong and it could suffice that the contract is governed by English law. On the other hand, in a divorce case a stronger connection with England may be required because a divorce will have a significant impact on British society if, for example, one of the parties and their children are living here. Accordingly, there is a good argument for saying that only those belonging here in the sense of being, at least, resident here, should be permitted to obtain a divorce from the English courts.

The central problem is thus one of ascertaining whether the parties and/or the cause of action have a sufficiently close connection with England to justify the English court assuming jurisdiction. As shall be seen shortly, the issue of choice of law involves similar considerations. The choice of law rules are structured to lead to the application of a law of close connection with either the parties or the cause of action. At first this would seem to indicate that if a court is sufficiently closely connected to the parties or the cause of action to justify the assumption of jurisdiction, its law would be a closely connected law, meaning all courts could apply their own law. This would be simpler, cheaper and more certain than trying to apply foreign laws. Indeed, there is something to be said for this approach. Under present jurisdictional rules it is likely that an English court today would decline jurisdiction in a case such as *Maharanee of Baroda*[6] meaning it would not have to concern itself with French law. Equally, continuing with the contract example, by assuming jurisdiction only in cases where it is an appropriate and closely connected court, there is a good chance that English law will be the applicable law.

Accordingly, there can be little doubt that in some senses it is the jurisdictional rules that are of most importance today. Once the jurisdiction question is resolved, that is the end of the contentious issues in the majority of cases; English law can be applied and there might be little or no dispute as to the outcome. However, it must be stressed that there is no perfect symmetry between jurisdictional and choice of law rules. While both are structured to tease out a country or law of close connection, the policy considerations underlying each are rather different. In particular, the jurisdictional rules are designed to ensure that England is *an* appropriate forum; there might be others equally appropriate. Indeed, as shall be seen, there might be another country that is far more appropriate but nevertheless the English court will proceed to hear the case if it feels that justice will not be done in the foreign court.[7] Choice of law rules, on the other hand, are designed to be more exclusive in the sense of leading to only one applicable law, generally the *most* appropriate law.

Finally, it should be stressed that while the jurisdictional hurdle always has to be overcome in every conflicts case, in practice, in very

6 *Maharanee of Baroda v Wildenstein* [1972] 2 QB 283, [1972] 2 All ER 689.
7 See pp 124–128.

many cases, it is not a live issue because the parties have agreed on the English court having jurisdiction. It is fairly common in international commercial disputes in the High Court for there to have been an agreement to jurisdiction in England.

B Choice of law

Once it has been determined that it possesses jurisdiction, the court is in a position to apply the relevant choice of law rule that can lead to the applicable law (lex causae). As noted above, this applicable law could be English law or a foreign law.

1. Why apply foreign law?

At this point an obvious question presents itself. *Why* should an English court apply foreign law? If the parties have chosen litigation in England, surely it is not unreasonable that English law be applied. While this question will be answered more fully in chapter 12, it is important here to sketch the two main reasons why a foreign law may be applied by the English courts.

The first explanation is that it may be necessary to apply foreign law in order to achieve justice between the parties and to reach a realistic result. Simply applying English law could lead to a highly inappropriate outcome that would defeat the reasonable expectations of the parties. Some simple examples will illustrate this point. In *Maharanee of Baroda*[8] two French residents entered into a contract in France. In these circumstances it is appropriate that French law should be applied by the English court; it is the law which the parties would reasonably have expected to apply and the law of the country by reference to which they can be deemed to have contracted. It is the law with which they can be presumed to have been familiar or, at any rate, if they had sought legal advice at the time of contracting, it would have been French legal advice. Applying French law is applying a law with which they could have complied. Accordingly, the English choice of law rule in contractual situations where the parties have not chosen the applicable law is that the contract is governed by the law of the country with which it is most closely connected[9] – which in this case would have been French law.

Another example can be taken from the field of family law. It is becoming increasingly common for English couples to take package holidays to exotic locations, such as Jamaica, and there to go through

8 [1972] 2 QB 283, [1972] 2 All ER 689.
9 Rome Convention, art 4(1), implemented by the Contracts (Applicable Law) Act 1990.

a marriage ceremony followed by a honeymoon with all costs included in the price of the package. Marriages in Jamaica can be conducted with a minimum of formalities. No banns are necessary and the marriage ceremonies are often conducted on the beach against a picturesque backdrop of palm trees and pounding surf. If the validity of such a marriage were to be tested some years later in the English courts it would be highly unjust to apply English law, which insists on more elaborate formalities for a marriage. The parties got married in the only way they could in Jamaica – by relying on Jamaican law and formalities. Their reasonable expectations would be frustrated by the application of anything other than Jamaican law. Accordingly, the rule is that the formalities of a marriage are governed by the lex loci celebrationis (the law of the place where the marriage ceremony was conducted). One final example will suffice. Suppose a British person emigrates to Spain and lives there for 50 years before dying without having made a will. Which law should govern the question of intestate succession if that issue should arise in English proceedings? The obvious answer is the law of the country in which the deceased was domiciled – in the sense of having a settled home and living permanently – at the time of death. This is the law which the deceased might reasonably have expected to be the applicable law. Such a person can either be presumed to be familiar with this law, or, if seeking legal advice as to whether to draft a will or not, it would have been Spanish legal advice that would have been sought. Application of English law – the law of the forum – in this case would result in the inappropriate and unjust result that the deceased's property would devolve according to the laws of a country with which the deceased was no longer connected. Accordingly, a clear choice of law rule has developed to meet such cases: intestate succession to movables is governed by the law of the deceased's domicile at the date of death.

It must not be thought that the most appropriate foreign law is necessarily the one that the parties would have *wanted* to apply. If an Englishman goes to Saudi Arabia and there marries two women in polygamous form, he might want and hope that the law of Saudi Arabia would apply and that these marriages would be regarded as valid. However, such a person should reasonably *expect* that English law would be applicable to such an important matter (which is concerned with the essential validity of a marriage, rather than simply its formal validity). This is not on a par with matters of formality such as getting married on a beach. In this case, if the man is domiciled in England, his reasonable expectations would have to be that English law would apply to the marriage. He would have to recognise (or be deemed to recognise) that on fundamental matters such as capacity to contract a polygamous marriage, the policy interests of England, a country committed to monogamy for English domiciliaries, will be held to prevail over the particular interests of the parties in question. Accordingly, a choice of law rule has been developed to reflect this: capacity to marry is governed by the law of domicile.[10]

A related advantage of applying foreign laws or, at least, of not always applying one's own law is that this can lead to uniformity of decision irrespective of where the litigation is actually brought. In a case with international connections, the courts of two or more countries may each have jurisdiction under their own law. If these courts each applied their own law to decide the case, the outcome of the case might depend purely on where the case was brought. The claimant would have the advantage of being able to choose to sue in the court whose law would be most favourable (a simple example of forum shopping), which is arguably unfair to the defendant. In matrimonial cases, if the courts of different countries each applied their own laws, parties might be regarded as married to each other in some countries, but single in others (a situation known as a 'limping marriage'), hardly an ideal state of affairs. On the other hand, if courts in different countries were to apply conflict rules with some of them applying foreign laws, these problems could be overcome. If, in a factual situation like the one that arose in *Maharanee of Baroda*, both French and English courts would apply French law, one reason for forum shopping would be removed.

It must be emphasised that the willingness of courts to apply foreign laws does not guarantee uniformity of decision because each country has its own choice of law rules, whose content may differ. Thus the English choice of law rule might direct the English court to apply the law of France in a case in which the French choice of law rule would require the French court to apply English law. Attempts have been made to harmonise the choice of law rules (and the jurisdictional and recognition rules) of different countries by means of international conventions (particularly those concluded under the auspices of the Hague Conference on Private International Law) and regional conventions and legislation (particularly within the European Union). While the former have had only limited success, European legislation has achieved significant uniformity at a regional level. Also, a doctrine known as renvoi is sometimes used, in rather a haphazard way, to achieve uniformity, as shall be seen.

It should be noted that the fact that different countries have different choice of law rules is only one reason why litigation may be brought in a seemingly inappropriate forum. Even when both countries adopt the same choice of law rule, there might still be procedural advantages

10 The problem of whose domicile and what this term means in this context is considered in chapter 8.

for the claimant to bring proceedings in one country rather than another which means that forum shopping will still continue. For example, in *Maharanee of Baroda* it was questions of admissibility of evidence and possible delay that prompted the Maharanee to sue in England.

2. How can foreign law be applied?

Having accepted that justice might best be served by the application of a foreign law, another question nevertheless presents itself. How can an English judge apply foreign law? Is it not an abdication of sovereignty for an English judge sitting in an English court to apply, say, Mexican law? This question is easily answered. While one constantly refers to judges 'applying' foreign law, this is not technically correct. The truth is that the only law the judge applies is the English conflict of laws rule, which is clearly as much a part of English law as any other. That English rule might refer the matter to a foreign law. The judge, however, being untrained in foreign laws, cannot 'apply' that foreign law, but rather relies on an expert who gives evidence on that foreign law as a matter of *fact* and the judge then applies that foreign fact solution to decide the case. In a sense this is no different from what happens in every domestic case. In an English murder prosecution the relevant law that is applied is that the defendant must have acted with intent to kill or cause grievous bodily harm. Whether the defendant actually possessed such an intention is a matter of fact which needs to be established by evidence. That finding of fact resolves the case. So too with the conflict of laws. In *Maharanee of Baroda*[11] the English conflicts rule at that time was that matters of contract should be governed by the law of closest connection, which would have been French law. That rule is the law applied in the case. To reach an outcome, however, the facts need to be applied to the law. The French solution to the problem is part of the relevant facts. Evidence must be given as to what that French fact solution would be and the case can then be decided.

3. Mechanics of the process

Having established the rationale of, and justification for, choice of law rules that can lead to the application of either English or a foreign law, it is now necessary to explain the mechanics of this process. This raises several important and sometimes complex issues. While most of these will be examined in more detail in chapter 12, it is necessary at this stage to highlight some of the main features of this process.

11 *Maharanee of Baroda v Wildenstein* [1972] 2 QB 283, [1972] 2 All ER 689.

(A) CLASSIFICATION OF CAUSE OF ACTION

The conflict of laws still remains highly compartmentalised. For example, there are different choice of law rules for movables and immovables. If a British person living in Mexico were to die intestate, the rule for determining how the deceased's property should devolve is as follows: intestate succession to movables is governed by the law of the deceased's domicile at the date of death (lex domicilii ultimi). The court has to ascertain where the deceased was domiciled at the relevant time and then, using expert evidence, has to ascertain what the relevant intestate succession rules of that country are so that it can dispose of the case according to those rules. If, however, this same intestate person were to leave an estate consisting of land, the appropriate rule would be: intestate succession to immovable property is governed by the law of the place where the land is situated (lex situs). This compartmentalisation is also evident in relation to the validity of marriage. To determine the validity of a marriage there are two rules to be applied: formal validity of marriage (details relating to the marriage ceremony such as the number of witnesses and how the ceremony needs to be performed) is governed by the law of the place where the marriage took place (lex loci celebrationis) and essential validity of marriage (the important matters relating to the parties themselves such as the age at which they can marry) is normally governed by the law of the parties' domicile at the date of the marriage.

As a result of having different choice of law rules for such closely related areas of law the first step in the choice of law process is to categorise the factual situation into a precise legal category.[12] For example, if an English manufacturer sells defective goods to an English retailer who sells them to a French consumer who is injured by the goods in France, the court will not know what law to apply until it has decided whether it is dealing with an issue in contract or in tort. If it is the former it will apply the law governing the contract, which would normally be English law; if it is the latter it will apply the rule governing torts committed abroad which will lead it to French law as the law of the place where the claimant was injured. This process of allocating the relevant facts into a legal category is known as classification or characterisation.

The main problem that arises at this stage is one of determining by which law the process of classification is to be effected. If English and French law are agreed that the matter relates to tort, there is no problem. But what if French law would regard the matter as raising a contractual claim but English law would regard the issue as tortious?

12 Whether it is actually the factual situation or a rule of law that is classified, along with alternative analyses of the process of classification, is considered in chapter 12.

Which law must be used to classify the facts into a legal category? The answer is clear. Classification of facts into legal categories is normally effected by English law, the lex fori. The reason for this is that until one has a legal category, no choice of law rule can be attached to lead to a foreign law. One can only consider the application of the substantive law of France after one has settled on a legal category and attached a choice of law rule. At the stage of allocating facts into legal categories there is generally no law that can possibly be applied other than the law of the forum. In the above example it must be left to English law to decide whether the issue is contractual or tortious. Once that decision has been made the correct choice of law rule can be applied which will lead to the applicable law.

While this approach is not without its problems,[13] and indeed has been rejected in a few limited areas,[14] there is little doubt that it represents the current English common law. For example, in *Apt v Apt*[15] an English domiciled woman accepted a marriage proposal from an Argentinian domiciliary. Unable to attend her marriage ceremony she executed a power of attorney authorising a friend to stand in for her at the ceremony which was duly celebrated by proxy in Argentina. In assessing the validity of this marriage, the English court had to classify the issue as being one relating to essentials or formalities. If it had decided that the issue of proxy marriages affected essentials, the marriage would have been held void: essential validity is governed by the law of domicile; the woman was domiciled in England and by English law proxy marriages are not valid. On the other hand, if this were simply a matter relating to formal validity, the lex loci celebrationis, Argentinian law, could be applied, under which the marriage was valid. The English court, without any reference to the Argentinian classification of the issue, decided that under English law this was a matter of formal validity and therefore the marriage was valid.

One other matter relating to classification, again to be explored more fully in chapter 12, needs brief mention here. Laws can broadly be divided into substantive and procedural rules. While in other areas of law this classification is seldom decisive, it is critical in the conflict of laws because of a clear rule that matters of procedure are governed by the lex fori. Procedural matters such as rules of evidence and court procedures must be governed by English law as it is simply not

13 See p 525.

14 A well-known exception is that whether property is to be regarded as movable or immovable is determined by the lex situs (the law of the country where the property is situated). See p 534. Also, for the purposes of jurisdiction under the Brussels regime, whether the claimant's claim is a matter relating to a contract or a matter relating to tort is to be determined by reference to European law. See pp 81–82.

15 [1948] P 83, [1947] 2 All ER 677.

practicable to expect an English court to conduct trials according to foreign procedures with which it is not familiar. However, once one gets beyond the obvious instances, one soon strikes the problem of classification. How, and by which law, does one decide whether a particular rule is procedural or not? For example, in *Re Cohn*[16] a mother and her daughter, both German domiciliaries, were killed together in an air raid in London during the Second World War. In order to decide the question of succession it was necessary to determine which of them died first. In English law there is a presumption in section 184 of the Law of Property Act 1925 that in such circumstances the deaths are presumed to have occurred in order of seniority. If this presumption were procedural, it would have been applied as part of the lex fori. However, using English law to effect the classification, it was decided that the rule was a substantive one, that is, part of the substantive law of succession. The court was then able to apply its succession choice of law rules which led to the application of German law according to which the rule was that both parties were presumed to have died simultaneously. (The problem of classifying foreign legal rules after the choice of law rules have led to a foreign law is discussed in chapter 12.)

(B) CONNECTING FACTORS

The characteristic form of choice of law rules is to identify the governing law by means of a connecting factor, consisting of a link between an event, a thing, a transaction or a person, on the one hand, and a country, on the other. For example, in the rule that the essential validity of marriage is governed by the law of domicile, domicile is the connecting factor; it provides the connection or link with a country. Connecting factors may be quite precise: for example, title to land is governed by the law of the country in which the land is situated; the formal validity of a marriage is governed by the law of the country in which the marriage was celebrated. Some connecting factors are, however, rather vague: for example, in the absence of choice by the parties, the validity of a contract is governed by the law of the country with which the contract has its closest connection.

As shall be seen, the rules of jurisdiction and recognition of foreign judgments also make use of connecting factors in determining the circumstances in which the English court should exercise jurisdiction or recognise a foreign judgment. For example, an English court has jurisdiction to grant a divorce if, inter alia, both spouses are habitually resident or domiciled in England[17] and many foreign divorces can be recognised, inter alia, if either party was domiciled or habitually

16 [1945] Ch 5. See pp 529–530.
17 See p 383.

resident in the foreign country at the date of the divorce.[18] A potential problem is that some common connecting factors, such as domicile, can be interpreted differently in different countries. For example, the concept of domicile is widely used in the United States but has there acquired a rather different meaning from that adopted under English law. If one were trying to decide whether a person had acquired a domicile in Texas, should one adopt the English or the Texan meaning of domicile? Or, to put the matter more technically, by which law should the connecting factor, domicile, be classified? Again, the answer is for most purposes clear. Any such classification must be made by English law, the lex fori. Until one has applied the English rules on domicile one cannot possibly have been referred to Texan law. Having used the English concept of domicile and having found oneself referred to Texan law, it would make little sense then to decide the same matter afresh using the foreign concept of domicile.

(C) RENVOI

Once the factual issue has been classified, a choice of law rule containing a connecting factor can be attached which will lead to the lex causae. This law might be, and indeed often is, English law. In such cases the role of the conflict of laws is complete and the matter can simply be decided according to domestic English law. However, when the lex causae is a foreign law, a further problem arises. Take a simple example of intestate succession to movables (the factual issue) which is governed by the law of the deceased's domicile at the date of death (the choice of law rule) and suppose that the deceased was a British national who dies domiciled in Mexico. The choice of law rule leads to the application of Mexican law. Does this mean the domestic (non-conflict) Mexican law of intestate succession which will describe how the property should devolve, or does it mean Mexican law in its entirety, including the Mexican conflicts rule? If it is the latter, one might find (as is common in civil law systems) that the Mexican conflicts rule would refer the question of intestate succession, not to the law of domicile, but to the law of nationality. In other words, under Mexican law this might be a conflicts case that would result in the application of British law. Leaving aside for the moment the problem that there is no such thing as 'British law' and making a chauvinistic assumption (which English courts tend to make[19]) that this means English law, what is meant by English law? Does this mean the English domestic

18 Different rules apply to the recognition of divorces granted by the courts of most member states of the European Union. See p 398.

19 See p 549.

rules on intestate succession, or does it mean the whole of English law, including English conflicts rules? If it means the latter, it has already been seen that the English choice of law rules would refer to Mexican law. In short, if this approach were adopted one would have an impasse with the case being continually referred back and forth between English and Mexican law. This process of taking account of foreign conflicts rules which refer the case back to its starting-point is called remission. Where the foreign law's conflicts rules would refer the case to the law of a third country, the process is called transmission.

The problem of renvoi (both remission and transmission) raises important theoretical issues which will be explored more fully in chapter 12. For present purposes, all that needs be said is that the doctrine is seldom employed in modern conflicts cases. It can only ever be raised if one of the parties expressly pleads it and, given the expense and difficulty of ascertaining foreign countries' conflicts rules including their rules on renvoi, this is hardly ever done. Further, in most of the important commercial areas of the conflict of laws that now dominate the subject, the use of renvoi is expressly outlawed. For example, article 15 of the Rome Convention, incorporated into English law by the Contracts (Applicable Law) Act 1990, stipulates that the doctrine of renvoi has no place in the English conflicts rules on contract. The doctrine of renvoi is also excluded in tort cases by section 9(5) of the Private International Law (Miscellaneous Provisions) Act 1995. Finally, even in those areas where the doctrine has been employed in the past, such as family law and succession, there is a growing recognition that utilising renvoi amounts to a subordination of English choice of law rules. These rules were developed in order to identify the law which is the most appropriate to govern a particular issue. For example, the rules on domicile are based on a premise that the domestic law of a person's permanent home is the most appropriate law to be applied to certain questions. This rationale is significantly undermined if our concept of domicile, enshrined in so many conflicts rules, does no more than lead to the application of another country's conflicts rules which could result in our having to apply the law of that person's nationality, a connecting factor that English law has largely rejected as leading to inappropriate results.

However, despite its relative lack of importance today, the reader must be aware of the potential for the application of renvoi in non-commercial fields. Indeed, in one of the more modern House of Lords cases, *Quazi v Quazi*,[20] both Lord Diplock and Lord Scarman stated obiter that they were not prepared to rule on the validity of a Thai divorce because they had not heard satisfactory evidence on the

20 [1980] AC 744, [1979] 3 All ER 897.

Thai doctrine of renvoi. It would thus be premature to assert the doctrine was dead, but as there is not much life left in its body further consideration can be postponed until later in this book.

(D) PROOF OF FOREIGN LAW

Before an English court will apply foreign law, it is necessary not only for the relevant choice of law rule to indicate that an issue in the case is to be decided by a foreign law, but also for a party to the case to plead and prove that law. Otherwise the court will simply apply English law. It will not apply a foreign law of its own motion. For example, in *Aluminium Industrie Vaassen BV v Romalpha Aluminium Ltd*[21] a contract contained a provision that it was to be governed by Dutch law but as neither party chose to plead Dutch law before the English courts the case was simply decided according to English law.

As seen earlier,[22] the only *law* that is applied is the relevant conflicts rule. If that rule indicates that a foreign law is applicable, that foreign law must be proved as a matter of *fact*. Because foreign laws are regarded as mere facts of which judges have no *judicial* knowledge, they have to be proved in court by the party alleging that they are applicable. This means that the normal rules of civil evidence for proof of facts are applicable. The foreign law has to be proved by the testimony of experts, who give evidence in the case in the same way as other expert witnesses. This expert must be someone who is qualified on account of 'knowledge or experience' of the foreign law.[23] Although it is possible to obtain evidence from non-legal specialists such as bankers, in most cases it is lawyers, whether practising or not, who provide the expert testimony.

Because foreign law is proved as a matter of fact, and not law, it used to be clear that any finding as to foreign law could not operate as a precedent. Even if the identical point arose the next day in a different case, the foreign law would need to be proved afresh. In order to avoid the expense and inconvenience involved in such cases, section 4(2) of the Civil Evidence Act 1972 provides that any such decision on foreign law, if reported or recorded in citable form, is admissible as evidence in any later case as establishing the relevant foreign law unless the contrary is proved. This effectively raises a presumption that the earlier decision is correct. While the presumption may be rebutted, the desirability of consistency renders the previous decision 'a weighty piece of evidence in itself'.[24] This provision,

21 [1976] 2 All ER 552, [1976] 1 WLR 676.
22 See p 10.
23 Civil Evidence Act 1972, s 4(1).
24 *Phoenix Marine Inc v China Ocean Shipping Co* [1999] CLC 478 at 481.

along with the fact that appellate courts are far more willing to disturb these particular findings of fact by the trial judge, underlines the statement in *Parkasho v Singh* that while foreign law must be proved as a question of fact it is nevertheless 'a question of fact of a peculiar kind'.[25]

If there is a conflict in the evidence of the experts, then the English court will have to decide, on the basis of that evidence and the statutes, cases and other materials cited by the experts, what the foreign law correctly is, and it may even have to do so on a point which is not yet settled in the foreign country itself.[26]

As mentioned above, the onus is on the person alleging that the foreign law is applicable to prove that foreign law. In the absence of such proof, the court will simply apply English law. It is often stated that this is because there is a presumption that the foreign law is the same as English law.[27] An alternative and more modern analysis is that English law is always the applicable law unless and until the relevant foreign law is proved.[28] For instance, in *Szechter v Szechter*[29] the choice of law rules on validity of marriage indicated that Polish law was the applicable law. However, at the critical moment the expert witness had to go into hospital for an operation and was thus not available for oral examination. In such circumstances the court felt obliged to apply English law. Failing to prove foreign law has the same effect as choosing not to plead foreign law and in such cases the only law before the court is English law.

Finally, it ought to be noted that these rules apply only to the proof of foreign law. Thus the House of Lords does not need to have Scots law or the law of Northern Ireland proved to it, even when hearing an English appeal. Similarly, European Community law does not have to be proved in the United Kingdom courts; it is not foreign law.

(E) EXCLUSION OF FOREIGN LAW

Despite its choice of law rules leading to a foreign law, English courts will not apply certain foreign laws: (a) foreign revenue laws; (b) foreign penal laws; (c) other public laws; and (d) laws contrary to public

25 [1968] P 233 at 250.

26 *Re Duke of Wellington* [1947] Ch 506 at 515.

27 For a recent example, see *Royal Boskalis Westminster NV v Mountain* [1997] 2 All ER 929 at 976.

28 Fentiman, 'Foreign Law in English Courts' (1992) 108 LQR 142 describes the old presumption as 'a cumbersome and inaccurate fiction' (at 148) in that it suggests that courts will go through the unrealistic process of ascertaining the applicable law and then just apply English law. See, generally, Fentiman, *Foreign Law in English Courts* (1998) pp 143–153, 183–186.

29 [1971] P 286, [1970] 3 All ER 905.

policy. These matters will be developed more fully in chapter 12. By way of introduction, however, a few points in relation to public policy need to be noted.

An English court always possesses a residual discretion to refuse to apply a foreign law or recognise a foreign judgment if to do so 'outrages its sense of decency or justice'.[30] The conflict of laws involves applying the laws of many different countries, some of whose rules are strange and alien to English lawyers. If the doctrine of public policy were to be used to deny application to all such laws, the result would be a complete emasculation of the conflicts process. Public policy has been described as an 'unruly horse' which if left uncontrolled would trample over the whole field of the conflict of laws.[31] Accordingly, public policy is invoked in only the most extreme cases where an application of the foreign law would have an undesirable impact in England and on English institutions. For example, in *Saxby v Fulton*[32] a contract for the loan of money to be spent on gambling in Monte Carlo was enforced. If this contract were to have been performed in England there can be no doubt that it would have been declared unenforceable as touching too closely on English interests. Similarly, it is well established that it is not contrary to public policy to recognise polygamous marriages; rights and obligations can be attached to such married couples provided the marriages took place abroad. On the other hand, polygamous marriages cannot be contracted in England. Such a purported marriage taking place here is felt to threaten our institution of monogamous marriage. Of course, in extreme cases where a foreign law is totally repugnant to us, for example a prohibition on marriages between persons of different races, the English court will refuse to enforce the rule.[33] Such cases are, however, truly exceptional.

The doctrine of public policy is thus kept on a tight rein and is exceedingly sparingly used. However, this is not entirely attributable to English judges exercising a proper internationalist restraint and tolerance. The truth is that, in comparison with many other countries, our conflict of laws rules are structured in such a way as to lead all too often to English law as the lex causae (a phenomenon known as forum preference). For example, English law is routinely applied in important family law matters such as divorce, adoption and maintenance. Until recently no claim in tort could succeed unless the conduct was actionable as a tort by English law and many important rules are classified as being procedural which means that foreign law is not

30 *Re Fuld's Estate (No 3)* [1968] P 675, [1965] 3 All ER 776.
31 Lord Hodson in *Chaplin v Boys* [1971] AC 356 at 378.
32 [1909] 2 KB 208.
33 But see pp 560–561.

referred to. Finally, while the doctrine of public policy is seldom applied as such, many of the conflicts rules to be examined are in fact crystallisations of public policy considerations. Take, for instance, the rule that no polygamous marriage can take place in England. While there is no overt public policy discretion here, it is clear that public policy has been critical in the formation of this rule. Similarly, it shall be seen that there is a common law rule that a foreign judgment obtained by fraud can be denied recognition. Again, this rule is an overt manifestation of public policy. The important difference between excluding foreign laws on grounds of public policy and applying these crystallised public policy rules is that with the former there is always a discretion, whereas rules, where applicable, are mandatory.

C Recognition and enforcement of foreign judgments

The problem here is one of laying down criteria as to when foreign judgments should be recognised. Clearly one could adopt a view that all foreign judgments should be recognised provided they were granted by the courts of an internationally recognised country. This approach is being adopted increasingly within the European Union; most commercial and matrimonial judgments granted by the courts of a member state are entitled to automatic recognition with only limited exceptions. However, with certain courts exercising extraordinarily wide jurisdiction, such an approach would be inappropriate on a worldwide basis. For example, in some central American countries a divorce can be obtained after an extremely short presence there. While tour operators might organise marriage-packages from this country, it is not uncommon for divorce packages to be organised by United States attorneys in conjunction with travel agents whereby a weekend package to a Caribbean island secures flights, a hotel and a divorce. English courts are understandably not prepared generally to recognise such 'quickie divorces'. However, once one moves away from the proposition that all judgments should be recognised to the more limited version whereby only some are recognised, one needs carefully to circumscribe the circumstances in which judgments will be recognised. Generally, as with matters of jurisdiction and choice of law, the issue is one of appropriateness and degree of connection. English law is not prepared to recognise a 'quickie divorce' because it is felt that the parties had no connection with the foreign country, making its court an inappropriate forum.

Is the criterion for appropriateness for recognition the same as that required for the exercise of jurisdiction? The answer to this depends on the area of law involved. In the commercial sphere there is a strong case for demanding that the foreign court have the same degree of connection with the parties and/or the cause of action as would be required for the exercise of jurisdiction in England. If an English court today would not regard itself as an appropriate forum in *Maharanee of Baroda v Wildenstein*,[34] there would be little justification in recognising a Mexican judgment if the only connection with Mexico was that Mr Wildenstein had been temporarily present there when the proceedings were commenced. In the commercial sphere the recognition rules should be premised largely on the same basis as the jurisdictional rules, namely, that defendants should not have to trouble themselves with defending actions in inappropriate fora. The policy considerations dictating when a court should exercise jurisdiction apply with equal force to the recognition and enforcement of foreign judgments. A degree of symmetry between jurisdictional and recognition rules is part of the scheme of protection to which defendants are entitled.

On the other hand, in some areas of law it could be justifiable to have a more flexible criterion of appropriateness for recognition than for jurisdictional purposes. With divorce jurisdiction, for example, the English court has to decide whether to become involved with the parties' marriage at all. This decision could have a profound effect; it would result in a change of status for the parties; matters affecting property distribution, financial relief and arrangements for children would often need determination. Assuming jurisdiction too readily could encourage forum shopping. Accordingly, a fairly close connection between the parties and England will often be required before jurisdiction is exercised. With recognition of foreign divorces, on the other hand, the forum shopping, if any, has already taken place. A foreign court of competent jurisdiction (according to its rules) has heard the case and adjudicated upon it. The parties may have relied on the foreign divorce and remarried. Particularly now that the English court is empowered to grant financial relief when recognising foreign divorces,[35] there is usually little to be gained by a denial of recognition. Accordingly, it could be justifiable to have more flexible criteria for the recognition of foreign divorces than for the exercise of divorce jurisdiction.

34 [1972] 2 QB 283, [1972] 2 All ER 689.
35 Matrimonial and Family Proceedings Act 1984, Pt III.

Chapter 2

Domicile and other personal connecting factors

I INTRODUCTION

In the previous chapter it was seen that the object of jurisdictional rules is to determine the appropriate forum and that choice of law rules are designed to lead to the application of the most appropriate law, the law that generally the parties might reasonably expect to apply. The test for recognition of foreign judgments is not dissimilar. A judgment granted by an appropriate forum should normally be recognised. The problem is one of ascertaining the connecting factor (or factors) which would best satisfy the criterion of appropriateness.

The test of appropriateness, and therefore the required link with a country, varies in different areas of law. For example, in the fields of status, marriage and succession the traditional view is that a much closer connection between a person and a country is required than in the commercial sphere. Laws on marriage and the family are intimately connected with the culture and the moral and religious standards of the community. It is appropriate that, in the conflict of laws, a person's legal position in these fields should be wholly or partly determined by the courts of their own country in accordance with the law of that country. However, even in these personal areas of law, the test of appropriateness will vary depending on the purpose for which the connecting factor is being employed. It was seen in chapter 1 that the policy considerations underlying jurisdictional, choice of law and recognition rules are somewhat different and, accordingly, different, or a different range of, connecting factors might be appropriate for each purpose. With regard to jurisdiction the rules are designed to ensure that England is an appropriate forum. For example, England has a legitimate interest in divorces granted here because financial and custody arrangements can have an impact upon British society. However, this does not mean that only persons with a 'permanent home' in England should be afforded access to our courts for this purpose. Where persons are living and working in England, albeit not permanently, it is clear that English law has an interest in their marriage and its dissolution and the consequences that flow from a divorce decree. Accordingly, the connecting factor or factors utilised for divorce jurisdiction need to be flexible enough to encompass all such persons. Similar considerations apply to connecting factors employed for recognition of foreign personal judgments, such as divorce decrees. If English law deems certain connecting factors to be appropriate for founding English jurisdiction, it should be prepared to recognise foreign decrees in similar circumstances. However, as seen in chapter 1, one could adopt an even broader range of connecting factors for purposes of recognition than for jurisdiction so that recognition would be given in any case where the parties had some legitimate connection with the country in which the judgment was obtained.

In contrast, with regard to choice of law in the fields of status, marriage and succession, the prevailing view has been that the applicable law should be the law of the country with which the parties have a reasonably substantial connection on the basis that people should be subject to the law of the country to which they primarily belong. This law is known as the personal law. Wherever a person goes in the world this personal law accompanies him and governs his status and personal relationships. Thus if a man's personal law is English, he cannot go to Saudi Arabia and contract a polygamous marriage there which is valid in the eyes of English law. English law, which does not permit polygamous marriages, will continue to be applicable. However, even with regard to choice of law, it is clear that different degrees of connection might be appropriate for different personal areas of law. For example, in relation to the formal validity of wills, policy considerations in favour of upholding the validity of wills militate against insisting on compliance with the law of the country to which a person most closely belongs. In respect of such matters a more flexible approach is appropriate and accordingly different, or a wider range of, connecting factors can be employed.

Bearing in mind these different purposes for which personal connecting factors are used, it is hardly surprising that there is little international agreement as to the appropriate test of 'belonging'. In England and most common law countries the traditional personal connecting factor is *domicile*, which loosely translates as one's permanent home. One of the problems here is that domicile is a connecting factor which is interpreted differently in various parts of the world. In the United States, for instance, domicile is given a significantly different meaning from that ascribed by English law. In contrast, most of continental Europe and other civil law countries use *nationality* as the basic connecting factor, especially for choice of law purposes; the personal law is the law of the country of which the person is a citizen. An alternative approach for choice of law is adopted in yet other countries such as India and Cyprus where the personal law is based on *adherence to a particular religion*. In these countries what matters is whether one is a Muslim, Hindu or Christian. In Cyprus, for example, the marriage law of the Orthodox, Roman Catholic, Maronite and Armenian Churches, Moslem marriage law, and the received English law, modified by local statutes, each apply, depending on the religion, origin and nationality of the parties. Of course, Cypriot law has rules prescribing which of these laws is to be applicable in particular circumstances. Finally, in some countries, including England, another connecting factor, *habitual residence*, has emerged. This is increasingly being used for the purposes of jurisdiction rules and in the law relating to recognition of foreign judgments and even in some choice of law rules, for example, in relation to the formal validity of wills.

Each of these personal connecting factors will be examined. Primary emphasis will be laid on domicile and habitual residence as the two main connecting factors employed by English law.

II DOMICILE: INTRODUCTION

A A variable meaning

Unfortunately the term 'domicile' has a variable meaning in English law and, indeed, within the conflict of laws. The traditional concept that will be discussed in this chapter has a relatively long history, but it was during the Victorian era that it developed most of its essential characteristics. However, the use of domicile is not restricted to the conflict of laws; it is also employed in tax law where it generally bears the same meaning.[1] Indeed, several of the leading authorities on the meaning of domicile are, in fact, tax cases. This is somewhat regrettable and has perhaps impeded the rational development of the concept for conflicts purposes. When significant reforms to the law of domicile were proposed in the Domicile Bills of 1958 and 1959, it was concern over the tax implications that led to the abandonment of the proposed reforms.

Further problems resulted from developments at the European level in the field of jurisdiction and the recognition of judgments in civil and commercial matters. The Brussels regime,[2] dealing with civil and commercial matters, utilises the continental concept of

1 There are some statutory modifications which are limited to the field of tax. See, for example, Inheritance Tax Act 1984, s 267.

2 The Brussels Convention of 1968, the Lugano Convention of 1988 and Council Regulation (EC) No 44/2001. See Ch 3.

'domicile' which is markedly different from the traditional English one. It might have been preferable, and less confusing, if the connecting factor used by the Brussels regime had been given a different name. Domicile for the purposes of the Brussels regime is discussed in chapter 3. This chapter is only concerned with the traditional concept as employed mainly in the fields of family law and succession. The reader must always be alert as to which concept of domicile is being used.

B General principles

In general terms, domicile means 'permanent home'. A person is domiciled in the country where he has his permanent home. The rationale of this is that people are deemed to 'belong' to the community where they have made their home. This is their 'centre of gravity'.[3] As permanent members of that community it is only right that its laws be applied to them. Further, domicile is supported as a connecting factor on the ground that it allows respect to be shown to the freedom of individuals who can choose where they wish to live and, thus, indirectly, choose the law to which they are to be subject.

There are three kinds of domicile: domicile of origin, domicile of dependence and domicile of choice. At any given time, a person's domicile will be one of these. The *domicile of origin* is the domicile which a person obtains at birth. A *domicile of dependence* is the domicile which a dependent person, such as a child, has by virtue of being dependent on another person. A *domicile of choice* is a domicile which an independent person acquires by residing in a country with the intention of settling there permanently or indefinitely.

Several general introductory points in relation to the law of domicile need to be made.

1. Only one domicile

Because so many important areas of law are governed by the law of domicile, it is crucial that every person have a domicile, and only one domicile. A person could not have two competing laws governing the same status or relationship. However, in reality, there are some people who might not actually have a home anywhere or who might have more than one home. In order to ensure that a domicile, and only one domicile, is attributed to all such people, detailed rules have been developed. As shall be seen, these rules are structured in such a way that a domicile can always be assigned to every person.

3 *Re Flynn* [1968] 1 All ER 49, [1968] 1 WLR 103.

The rule that one cannot have two domiciles is perhaps an over-simplification. It would be more accurate to say that one cannot have more than one domicile for the same purpose. It has already been seen that a country for the purposes of the conflict of laws is a law district, a territorial unit having a separate legal system, which may for political purposes be part of a larger composite state. It is the law district, not the composite state, in which a person is domiciled. A person is domiciled in England, Scotland or Northern Ireland, not in the United Kingdom as a whole.[4] However, some federal states such as Australia[5] have introduced rules that for the purpose of matrimonial proceedings a person can be domiciled in the federal state. Thus, for purposes of divorce a person could be domiciled in Australia while being domiciled in, say, Queensland for other purposes.

A further point that ought to be stressed at the outset is that while, apart from the above exception, a person can have only one operative domicile it might well be that the way in which the court applies the rules – and the conclusion which it reaches – is coloured by the context in which the question of a person's domicile arises.[6] For example, in *Ramsay v Liverpool Royal Infirmary*[7] George Bowie, domiciled in Scotland, left there and moved to Liverpool where he lived for the last 36 years of his life sponging off his brother and sister. During that whole period he never set foot in Scotland. The House of Lords concluded that Bowie was still domiciled in Scotland at the date of his death. However, it is crucial to note that the issue before the court was the formal validity of Bowie's will and that, by holding him domiciled in Scotland, the court was able to uphold the validity of his will. Had the court concluded that he was domiciled in England, the will would have been invalid. In short, it seems likely that the nature of the issue before the court strongly influenced the court's interpretation of the rules on domicile. If the issue had been the capacity of Bowie to marry or a question of domicile for the purpose of taxation, it is quite possible that the court would have concluded that he was domiciled in England.

2. *Classification by lex fori*

English courts will normally apply their own rules of domicile to determine where a person is domiciled.[8] The connecting factor,

4 For tax purposes one can be domiciled in the United Kingdom. See, for example, Inheritance Tax Act 1984, s 267.

5 Australian Family Law Act 1975, s 39(3); *Lloyd v Lloyd* [1962] VR 70.

6 Cook, *The Logical and Legal Bases of the Conflict of Laws* (1942); Fawcett, 'Result Selection in Domicile Cases' (1985) 5 OJLS 378.

7 [1930] AC 588.

8 *Re Annesley* [1926] Ch 692.

domicile, must be classified according to English law, the lex fori. There is one statutory exception to this rule. Under section 46(5) of the Family Law Act 1986 a foreign divorce (or other matrimonial decree) is entitled to recognition on the basis that one of the parties is domiciled in the country where the divorce is obtained. For the purpose of this rule, domicile may mean either domicile according to English law or domicile according to the law of the country in which the divorce was obtained.

While domicile must normally be classified initially according to English law, if this results in a reference to a country where the law is not territorially based it is necessary to adopt that country's criterion of the personal law to lead to the applicable law. For instance, in determining the essential validity of a marriage English choice of law rules will normally lead to the law of domicile of the parties. If one is dealing with a country such as Cyprus or India where the personal law is based on adherence to a religion, there is no such thing as a general Cypriot or Indian law of marriage. The solution to this problem is that having used the English concept of domicile and having been referred to the law of Cyprus, one then has to adopt the Cypriot test of the personal law which will refer to the appropriate religious law. This is not really an exception to the proposition that domicile must be construed according to English law. One is utilising the English concept of domicile and then applying 'Cypriot law'. It just so happens that Cypriot law in this case will mean one of a number of religious laws and Cypriot law indicates which religious law is, in the circumstances, the relevant law.

Finally, it has been argued that there is another exception here in that a person's capacity to acquire or change a domicile should be governed by the law of the existing domicile.[9] Thus if it were alleged that a Ruritanian domiciliary aged 15 had acquired a domicile elsewhere and Ruritanian law allows a domicile to be acquired at that age, this question should be governed by Ruritanian law. The argument is that capacity is a matter of status and questions of status are governed by a person's existing domiciliary law. However, such an approach cannot be accepted. Ascertaining the domicile of a 15-year-old involves the application of the English rules on domicile of dependence. It would only be through an application of these rules that one would have been referred to Ruritanian law. One cannot then regard the person as having the capacity to acquire an independent domicile because this would necessitate a re-examination of the whole issue according to the English rules on domicile of choice under which the person might be domiciled in a completely different country. Further, section 3(1) of the Domicile

9 Graveson, *Conflict of Laws: Private International Law* (7th edn, 1974) p 193.

and Matrimonial Proceedings Act 1973 is explicit: a person has the capacity to acquire a new domicile by attaining the age of 16. The age of capacity by any other law is irrelevant.

3. Presumption in favour of existing domicile

There is a presumption in favour of the continuance of an existing domicile. The burden of proving a change of domicile lies on the person alleging the change.[10] While the standard adopted is the normal civil one of proof on a balance of probabilities, in reality the standard required when alleging that a domicile of origin has been lost appears to be somewhat higher.[11] In all the reported cases that have reached the House of Lords, in only one case has it been held that a domicile of origin has been replaced by a domicile of choice.[12] However, it should be stressed that there has not been a House of Lords decision on the subject since 1932[13] and, as will be seen, a greater degree of flexibility has been introduced into this area of law. Although 'the acquisition of a domicile of choice is a serious matter not to be lightly inferred'[14] the burden of proving a loss of domicile of origin today is perhaps not quite as onerous as it was in the past.

III SPECIES OF DOMICILE

A Domicile of origin

The domicile which a person acquires at birth is called the domicile of origin. Apart from the exceptional case of the foundling whose domicile of origin is the place where he was found,[15] the domicile of origin is conferred on the basis of parentage. Accordingly, in most cases it does not matter where a child is born. The domicile of origin is that of the parents at the date of the child's birth. If the child is legitimate the domicile of origin is that of the father;[16] if the child is illegitimate the domicile of origin is that of the mother;[17] if the

10 *Winans v A-G* [1904] AC 287; *Re Fuld's Estate (No 3)* [1968] P 675, [1965] 3 All ER 776.
11 *Henderson v Henderson* [1967] P 77, [1965] 1 All ER 179.
12 *Casdagli v Casdagli* [1919] AC 145.
13 *Wahl v A-G* (1932) 147 LT 382.
14 *Re Fuld's Estate (No 3)* [1968] P 675 at 686.
15 *Re McKenzie* (1951) 51 SRNSW 293 (illegitimate child whose mother's domicile was unknown was treated as found in its country of birth and therefore having its domicile of origin there).
16 *Udny v Udny* (1869) LR 1 Sc & Div 441 at 457.
17 Ibid.

child is a posthumous legitimate child (born after the death of the father), the domicile of origin is that of the mother;[18] if an illegitimate child is later legitimated[19] it would appear that the domicile of origin remains that of the mother;[20] and, finally, an adopted child probably acquires a new domicile of origin from the adoptive parents because such a person is treated as if he had been born in lawful wedlock.[21]

These rules are archaic and unsatisfactory. First, the rule that domicile depends on legitimacy overlooks the fact that in many cases legitimacy depends upon domicile. One cannot ascertain whether a child is legitimate until one has established its domicile, but the domicile cannot be established until the question of legitimacy has been resolved. As there is no logical way out of this impasse, perhaps the best solution would be to regard the child as legitimate if it is so regarded by the law of either parent's domicile. However, as shall be seen, there is authority favouring the application of the father's domiciliary law at the date of the child's birth.[22] Secondly, there is no longer any rational basis for the rule that a legitimate child takes the domicile of the father. The historical explanation for this rule was that on marriage a woman took her husband's domicile as a domicile of dependence. This rule was abolished in the 1970s largely because of its sexist assumptions. To abolish the basic rule but allow its manifestations to continue makes little sense. Finally, as shall be seen, when parents are living apart, children take the domicile of the parent with whom they have a home.[23] If a married mother and father are living apart when their child is born, it makes little sense to assert that the child takes the domicile of origin of the father which could then instantly be replaced by a domicile of dependence on the mother.

In view of these objections there is a strong case for a substantial overhaul of these rules. The Law Commission has proposed that dependent children should be regarded as domiciled in the country

18 Dicey and Morris, *The Conflict of Laws* (13th edn, 2000) p 115.

19 By English law this can only occur by the subsequent marriage of the parents. In some other countries a child may be legitimated by parental recognition or acknowledgement. See *Re Luck's Settlement Trusts* [1940] Ch 864. It need hardly be added that it is irrelevant that the foreign law might retrospectively alter the child's domicile. Domicile is interpreted according to English law (see p 25–27).

20 Cheshire and North, *Private International Law* (13th edn, 1999) p 154.

21 Adoption and Children Act 2002, s 65(1)(a). This point is, however, by no means settled. See Law Commission No 168, *Private International Law, The Law of Domicile* (1987) para 2.4.

22 See pp 440–442.

23 Domicile and Matrimonial Proceedings Act 1973, s 4(2).

with which they are most closely connected.[24] If the concept of domicile of origin is to be retained[25] there should be a coincidence of domicile of origin and dependence at birth and the Law Commission's proposals should be followed.

There are two distinctive features relating to a domicile of origin. The first, as already noted, is that it is more difficult to lose a domicile of origin than any other form of domicile. The burden of proof in such cases goes 'beyond a mere balance of probabilities'.[26] For example, in *Ramsay v Liverpool Royal Infirmary*[27] it was held that a Scottish domicile of origin had not been lost despite the fact that the propositus (as the person whose domicile is in question is referred to) had lived in England for the last 36 years of his life without expressing any intention to return to Scotland and despite even having made arrangements to be buried in England. In *Winans v A-G*[28] it was similarly held that a man who resided primarily in England for the last 37 years of his life had not lost his domicile of origin despite not having visited that place for the last 47 years of his life. In *IRC v Bullock*[29] a man who had lived in England for the past 44 years was also held not to have abandoned his domicile of origin. When one recalls that domicile is meant to indicate a person's permanent home, this excessive importance attached to a domicile of origin can only be regarded as out of touch with the realities of today, where people are far more mobile and establish permanent homes in new countries with greater ease and readiness than in the mid-Victorian era when these rules were developed. However, there is some evidence that the courts have started adopting a more flexible approach. In *Brown v Brown*[30] it was held that a person had lost his domicile of origin in a state in the United States and acquired an English domicile 14 years after leaving the United States, despite the fact that six of those years had been spent working in Rome. It was emphasised that there is 'no warrant for ... using the words "heavy burden"'[31] when dealing with the displacement of a domicile of origin. The Law Commission has endorsed this approach, recommending that there should be no 'special tenacity' given to the domicile of origin.[32]

24 Law Com No 168, paras 4.13–4.20. Several rebuttable presumptions for determining this country of closest connection are suggested. See p 35.
25 See p 31.
26 *Henderson v Henderson* [1967] P 77 at 80.
27 [1930] AC 588.
28 [1904] AC 287.
29 [1976] 3 All ER 353, [1976] 1 WLR 1178.
30 (1981) 3 FLR 212.
31 At 218.
32 Law Com No 168, para 4.24.

The second distinctive feature of the domicile of origin is that while it can be replaced by a different domicile of dependence or choice it is never totally lost, but rather held in abeyance. If a domicile of choice is abandoned without being replaced by a new domicile of choice, then the domicile of origin revives. In fact, this revival rule is the only reason why the concept of domicile of origin is needed; apart from that, the domicile of a child at birth could be a domicile of dependence, just as it is thereafter until the age of 16.[33]

The rule that a domicile of choice can be abandoned without a new one being acquired, the domicile of origin reviving to fill the gap, was settled by the House of Lords in 1869 in *Udny* v *Udny*.[34] A more recent example is *Tee v Tee*,[35] where a man whose domicile of origin was English acquired a domicile of choice in one of the states of the United States. Later he went to work in Germany, but did not become domiciled there. At first, his intention was to return to the United States, but then he decided to make his permanent home in England. While still living in Germany,[36] he started divorce proceedings in the English court. As the law then stood, the court would have had jurisdiction only if he was domiciled in England. It was held that he was. When, while living in Germany, he decided that he would not after all return to the United States, he lost his domicile of choice there. He did not, however, acquire a new domicile of choice in Germany because he did not intend to live there permanently. Accordingly, his English domicile of origin revived.

This revival of the domicile of origin rule, conceived and developed in Victorian England, assumes that if ever a person ceases to have a permanent home, the most appropriate personal law to allocate to him is the law of the original native home. Rather like elephants who allegedly return to their birthplace to die, British colonists, for whom these rules were primarily designed, would naturally return to Britain to see out their final days. These rules were designed for the class of person who might have an ancestral home to which they would long feel a commitment.[37] However, in the more migratory modern world it would normally be more sensible to attribute to a person the law of the country which was most recently the home, rather than that of a

33 See p 34.
34 (1869) LR 1 Sc & Div 441.
35 [1973] 3 All ER 1105, [1974] 1 WLR 213.
36 Accordingly, no domicile of choice had been acquired in England. See pp 37-38.
37 It has been suggested that the rules on revival of the domicile of origin were developed as a response to the growing rise and popularity of nationality in the middle of the nineteenth century; it was a mechanism for endowing domicile with enduring qualities similar to those attached to nationality. See Carter, 'Domicil: The Case for Radical Reform in the United Kingdom' (1987) 36 ICLQ 713 at 716.

country which has been abandoned, perhaps very many years previously. A person may have few, or no connections with the domicile of origin, and even may never have been there. Suppose the propositus is born in Ontario when his father, domiciled in England, is working temporarily in Ontario. After his birth his father decides to settle in Ontario permanently. Although the propositus has a domicile of dependence in Ontario, his domicile of origin is still English. If in later life he leaves Ontario for good, but dies before settling in another country, the succession to his movable estate will be governed by English law – rather than the law of Ontario – even though he may never have set foot in England, and until shortly before his death had lived his whole life in Ontario.

In many countries, such as the United States, the doctrine of the revival of the domicile of origin has been abolished. Instead, a domicile of choice continues until a new one is obtained. While it might previously have been argued that this divergence of approach was explicable on the basis that the population in the United States was more migratory and less influenced by birth, locality and the local history of families than in Britain, such an explanation can no longer be accepted. Accordingly, the Law Commission has proposed that the doctrine of revival of the domicile of origin be abolished and that an existing domicile should continue until a new one is established. This recommendation, along with the proposal that it should be no harder to lose a domicile acquired at birth than any other domicile, means that there would be no special significance to be attached to such a form of domicile and, accordingly, it should be abolished as a separate species of domicile.[38]

B Domicile of dependence

A domicile of dependence is the domicile conferred on legally dependent persons by operation of law. The domicile of such a dependent person is the same as the person upon whom he is dependent and will change with any change in the latter's domicile. The underlying rationale here (apart from being another mechanism for ensuring that every person always has an operative domicile) is two-fold. First, certain classes of person are regarded as being incapable of forming the necessary intention to acquire a domicile of choice. A young child, for instance, cannot intend to reside permanently anywhere; his home will generally be with his parents and, accordingly, the law directs that he follows their domicile as one of dependence. Similarly, a mentally incapable person is regarded as unable to form

38 Law Com No 168, para 4.24.

the necessary intention for acquisition of a domicile of choice and is therefore assigned a domicile of dependence. Secondly, there are advantages in preserving a unity of domicile for all members of a family. The potential for further conflict between laws is exacerbated when different members of the same family have separate domiciles. Thus, a child's domicile is dependent on that of his parents and before the Domicile and Matrimonial Proceedings Act 1973, a wife was regarded as having a domicile of dependence on her husband.

1. Children

It has already been seen that at birth all children are assigned a domicile of origin, normally on the basis of parentage. This domicile can never be completely lost as it may revive at some later stage in life, but it may be temporarily replaced by a domicile of dependence until the child reaches the age of 16 or marries under that age. Any change in the domicile of the parent upon whom the child is dependent will generally automatically be communicated to the child even if the child does not in fact follow the parent to the new country. The law is a combination of common law principles and rules contained in the Domicile and Matrimonial Proceedings Act 1973.

First, if the child is illegitimate he takes the domicile of his mother.[39] Secondly, if the child is legitimate and his parents are alive and living together, the child takes the domicile of his father. (In such a case the mother may have a different domicile from the father and the child, even though they are all living together.) Thirdly, if, in this latter situation, the father then dies, the child thereafter normally takes the domicile of the mother.[40] However, in these circumstances, the child does not always automatically follow a change in the mother's domicile. Where the child lives with the mother when she acquires a new domicile, the child's domicile will follow the mother's. It has been decided, however, that if she changes her domicile, but leaves the child permanently resident in the former country (for example, in the care of a relative), the child's domicile does not change with the mother's. In *Re Beaumont*[41] a widow, domiciled in Scotland, remarried an English domiciliary thereby acquiring an English domicile (of dependence). She moved to England with her new husband leaving one daughter in Scotland. It was held that the daughter's domicile remained Scottish because the change of a child's domicile is the 'result of the exercise by [the mother] of a power vested in her for the

39 *Udny v Udny* (1869) LR 1 Sc & Div 441 at 457; Domicile and Matrimonial Proceedings Act 1973, s 4(4).

40 *Potinger* v *Wightman* (1817) 3 Mer 67 at 79.

41 [1893] 3 Ch 490.

welfare of the infants, which in their interest she may abstain from exercising, even when she changes her own domicile'.[42] It has even been suggested that a mother in such cases can confer a domicile on her child in a third country by placing the child there under the care of a competent person.[43] Such an interpretation seems implausible. Why should a widow have such extensive powers not possessed by anyone else? A father who sends a child to another country has no such power. The underlying rationale behind the decision in *Re Beaumont* was the desire to prevent a child effectively obtaining a domicile of dependence on a stepfather. As a married woman no longer acquires a domicile of dependence on her husband, there seems little point any longer in singling out widows for special treatment.

Fourthly, if a legitimate child's parents are 'alive but living apart', then as long as the child has a 'home' only with the mother he takes her domicile, but if he has a home with the father alone, or a home with each parent, then he takes the father's domicile.[44] If the child ceases to have a home with the parent whose domicile he shares, that domicile continues unless and until he has a home with the other parent.[45] These statutory provisions, designed to introduce a correlation between the legal rules on domicile of dependence and the factual realities of a child's dependence on a parent, present certain problems of interpretation. What is the meaning of 'home'? A 'home' clearly combines notions of both physical presence and an emotional link. It is appropriate here to consider the duration and regularity of the residence and whether the child regards the parent's house as his 'home ... or ... proper abode'.[46] Also, do these rules apply to amicable arrangements where the parents have two separate homes, or do they apply only to situations where the marriage has broken down? There is a strong argument for saying that the Domicile and Matrimonial Proceedings Act 1973 should be applicable to all cases of parents living apart. The rules are designed to mirror reality. If a happily married couple choose to maintain separate homes in different countries – for, say, employment reasons – the child's domicile should be the same as that of the parent with whom he has his home. In such situations, however, it is likely that it would be held that the child has a home with each parent and would therefore follow the father's domicile.

42 At 497.
43 Blaikie, 'The Domicile of Dependent Children: A Necessary Unity' [1984] Jur Rev 1 at 7; Cheshire and North, *Private International Law* (13th edn, 1999) p 156.
44 Domicile and Matrimonial Proceedings Act 1973, s 4(1) and (2).
45 S 4(2)(b).
46 Law Com No 168, para 4.20; *Re Y* [1985] Fam 136 at 140.

Fifthly, if a legitimate child has, during the father's lifetime, the mother's domicile, and then the mother dies, the child's domicile remains that of the mother on her death, unless and until he has a home with his father.[47] If the child, however, has the father's domicile when the parents are alive but living apart and the father then dies, it appears that the child will follow the mother's domicile (and will be subject to her powers under *Re Beaumont*).

Sixthly, an adopted child is for all purposes to be treated as if he were the natural legitimate child of his adoptive parents.[48] While, as already seen, it is uncertain whether the child's domicile of origin is retrospectively altered, there is no doubt that from the moment of adoption, the child follows the domicile of his parents under the above rules.

Finally, after the death of both parents of a legitimate child, or of the mother of an illegitimate child, the child's domicile remains unchanged until he is old enough to have an independent domicile.[49]

How is a child's domicile of dependence lost? Section 3(1) of the Domicile and Matrimonial Proceedings Act 1973 provides that a child becomes capable of acquiring an independent domicile upon reaching the age of 16 or by marrying under that age. Prior to the 1973 Act an independent domicile could be acquired only at the age of majority. However, as one can leave school, marry and live an independent life at the age of 16, it was thought that this was the appropriate age for an emancipated child to acquire an independent domicile.[50] As a domicile of dependence 'cannot survive the destruction of the factors essential to its creation and continued existence'[51] it will be lost immediately the minor turns 16 and replaced by a domicile of choice (if the person is already in that country with the requisite intention of remaining there indefinitely) or, alternatively, by the domicile of origin. This can be illustrated by the case of *Harrison v Harrison*.[52] Harrison was born with an English domicile of origin. When he was 18 (the age of majority at which an independent domicile could be acquired was then 21) his parents emigrated to South Australia and acquired a domicile there, leaving him in England. Under the rules described above he therefore acquired a South Australian domicile of dependence. When he was 20 he emigrated to

47 Domicile and Matrimonial Proceedings Act 1973, s 4(3).
48 Adoption and Children Act 2002, s 65(1)(a).
49 Dicey and Morris, *The Conflict of Laws* (13th edn, 2000) p 139.
50 Law Com No 48, *Report on Jurisdiction and Matrimonial Causes* (1972) para 33. For a view that this age limit should be lowered, or even abandoned, see Carter, 'Domicil: The Case for Radical Reform in the United Kingdom' (1987) 36 ICLQ 713 at 720–721, 725.
51 Wade, 'Domicile: A Re-Examination of Certain Rules' (1983) 32 ICLQ 1 at 17.
52 [1953] 1 WLR 865.

New Zealand, intending to remain there permanently, and married a New Zealander. Shortly thereafter he returned to England, where he turned 21. His wife petitioned the English court for a divorce and at that time the English court could have exercised jurisdiction only if Harrison were domiciled in England. It was held that the court did have jurisdiction. When Harrison turned 21 he lost his South Australian domicile of dependence. As he had not yet acquired a New Zealand domicile of choice (because he had not resided there since turning 21) his English domicile of origin revived.

Despite the reforms effected by the Domicile and Matrimonial Proceedings Act 1973, these rules are highly artificial. If the facts of *Harrison* were to recur today (with Harrison being under 16) he would still acquire a South Australian domicile of dependence in a country in which he had never set foot. Thirty years ago judges in other jurisdictions were questioning this approach. For example, Wilson J in the New Zealand case of *Re G* stated that 'the true position may now be that a dependent person's domicile changes when his parent intends it to change and the change is for his benefit, irrespective of whether the domicile of the parent also changes'.[53] The Law Commission, conscious of the artificiality of the present law, proposed that a child under the age of 16 should have a domicile 'in the country with which he is for the time being most closely connected'.[54] In order to introduce a degree of certainty this test would be combined with rebuttable presumptions that the child would have the same domicile as his parents where they are both domiciled in the same country and he has his home with either of them, or, where the parents are domiciled in different countries, the child would share the domicile of the parent with whom he has his home.[55] In other cases, for example, where the child has a home with both parents or with neither parent, the basic test of closest connection would be applied without the aid of any presumption.[56]

2. *Married women*

Until 1 January 1974 the domicile of a married woman was necessarily the same as that of her husband.[57] On the death of the husband or on divorce, the woman's former domicile of dependence continued as her domicile of choice[58] (if it was not her domicile of origin) unless and until she abandoned it (which, however, would happen at the very

53 [1966] NZLR 1028 at 1031.
54 Law Com No 168, para 4.13.
55 Law Com No 168, paras 4.15, 4.16.
56 Law Com No 168, para 4.17.
57 *Lord Advocate v Jaffrey* [1921] 1 AC 146; *A-G for Alberta v Cook* [1926] AC 444.
58 *Re Wallach* [1950] 1 All ER 199. For a criticism of this approach see Wade, 'Domicile: A Re-Examination of Certain Rules' (1983) 32 ICLQ 1 at 17.

moment of the death or divorce, if she had previously ceased to reside in, and did not intend to return to, the country in question).[59]

The Domicile and Matrimonial Proceedings Act 1973 provided that from 1 January 1974 a married woman should have her own independent domicile.[60] The Act is not retrospective,[61] so if the domicile of a married woman has to be ascertained as at a date before 1974 the common law applies. A woman who was already married on 1 January 1974 retains her former domicile of dependence as her domicile of choice (or origin), unless and until she changes it by acquisition or revival of another domicile on or after that date.[62] This means that the independent domicile of a married woman when the Act came into effect was not necessarily the domicile she would have had if her domicile had never been dependent on her husband. Her domicile of choice might be a country in which she had never decided to settle permanently if that was her husband's domicile and she was resident there on 1 January 1974. In *IRC v Duchess of Portland*[63] the propositus, who had a domicile of origin in Quebec, married an English domiciliary in 1948, thereby acquiring an English domicile of dependence. Despite the fact she had always planned to return to Canada with the consequence that an acquisition of an English domicile of choice under the normal rules would have been 'an impossibility in the real world'[64] it was held that on 1 January 1974 her English domicile of dependence became converted into an English domicile of choice which she could lose only by satisfying the strict rules on abandonment of a domicile of choice. She could 'only free herself from the shackles of dependency by choosing to leave her husband for permanent residence in another country'.[65] A more realistic approach that would enable such women to avoid this 'last barbarous relic of a wife's servitude'[66] would be to hold that in such cases where the woman, according to the normal rules, does not herself acquire a domicile of choice on 1 January 1974, her domicile of origin should revive on that date.[67]

3. *Mentally incapable people*

It seems that a mentally disordered person who is incapable of forming the necessary intention to acquire a domicile of choice retains whatever

59 *Re Scullard* [1957] Ch 107, [1956] 3 All ER 898.
60 S 1(1).
61 Ibid.
62 S 1(2).
63 [1982] Ch 314, [1982] 1 All ER 784.
64 At 318.
65 At 320.
66 *Gray v Formosa* [1963] P 259 at 267.
67 Wade, 'Domicile: A Re-Examination of Certain Rules' (1983) 32 ICLQ 1.

domicile he had immediately before becoming incapable.[68] The Law Commission has proposed that such a person should be domiciled in the country with which he is for the time being most closely connected.[69]

C Domicile of choice

1. Acquisition of domicile of choice

A domicile of choice in a country is acquired by residing there with the intention of remaining permanently or indefinitely. There are thus two requirements to be satisfied: the objective one of residence (or, perhaps, presence) and the subjective one of intention. The two factors must co-exist for a domicile of choice to be acquired.

(A) RESIDENCE

Residence is the easier factor to establish. The test of residence for the purpose of acquiring a domicile is a qualitative one rather than a quantitative one.[70] The residence need be of no particular duration, and may indeed be only momentary.[71] So, if the propositus has firmly decided before he arrives in the country to settle there permanently, then the residence factor will be satisfied as soon as he arrives, and the domicile will immediately be acquired. In such cases it seems more apt to say that only presence in a country is required for acquisition of a domicile of choice. Indeed, because of such cases, the Law Commission has proposed that 'presence' is a more appropriate term than 'residence'. In the United States it has been suggested that where a person sends his family and belongings ahead of him to establish a home in a new state, a domicile might be vicariously acquired even before the propositus himself arrives there.[72] In view of the somewhat stricter nature of our rules on domicile, it is unlikely that such a notion would be accepted by an English court.

In less clear-cut cases, it has been held that 'residence' for these purposes means physical presence 'as an inhabitant'.[73] This excludes presence merely as a visitor. In *IRC v Duchess of Portland*,[74] the propositus with a domicile in England spent between ten and twelve weeks every year in Quebec and maintained her links with Canada with

68 *Urquhart v Butterfield* (1887) 37 Ch D 357.
69 Law Com No 168, para 6.6.
70 *Ramsay v Liverpool Royal Infirmary* [1930] AC 588 at 595, 598.
71 *Bell v Kennedy* (1868) LR 1 Sc & Div 307.
72 Scoles and Hay, *Conflict of Laws* (2nd edn, 1992) pp 178–179.
73 *IRC v Duchess of Portland* [1982] Ch 314 at 319.
74 [1982] Ch 314, [1982] 1 All ER 784.

a view to retiring there. This was not sufficient to make her an inhabitant of Quebec and accordingly she could not acquire a domicile there. (The same result could have been reached – even if it were accepted that mere presence always amounts to residence – on the ground that at the relevant time the propositus had the intention of residing permanently in Quebec only at some future time.)

In *Plummer v IRC*[75] it was held that as regards a person with two homes, a person is an inhabitant of the country in which he has his chief residence. The propositus in this case had a home in England where she finished school, did a secretarial course and went to university, and a home in Guernsey where her family lived and she spent many weekends and some holidays. It was concluded that Guernsey was not her place of chief residence and, accordingly, a domicile had not been acquired there.

A domicile will not be acquired in England if the residence here is prohibited by English law. The reason is said to be that 'a court cannot allow a person to acquire a domicile in defiance of the law which the court itself administers'.[76] In *Puttick v A-G*[77] the propositus, a fugitive from justice from Germany, came to England on a forged passport. It was held that even if she had the necessary intention to remain in England permanently, she had not acquired an English domicile because her residence, having been obtained by fraud, was illegal. This rule seems to assume that a domicile in England is a privilege, which should be denied to a person who has no right to be here. Domicile, however, gives rise to liabilities as well as rights – for instance, the liability, in some circumstances, to be sued in the English court or a liability to tax. Would a person who is in fact permanently resident in England be held free of such liabilities on the ground that his residence is illegal? Further, it is uncertain whether this rule extends to the acquisition by illegal residence of a domicile in a foreign country.[78]

(B) INTENTION

For a domicile of choice to be acquired, the propositus's residence must be accompanied by the intention to remain permanently or indefinitely. It is the intention requirement that is most likely to lead to dispute for, from the legal point of view, it is imprecise, and, on the facts, it may be difficult to prove.

75 [1988] 1 All ER 97, [1988] 1 WLR 292.
76 Dicey and Morris, *The Conflict of Laws* (13th edn, 2000) p 118.
77 [1980] Fam 1, [1979] 3 All ER 463.
78 Dicey and Morris, *The Conflict of Laws* (13th edn, 2000) pp 118–119. See generally, Pilkington, 'Illegal Residence and the Acquisition of a Domicile of Choice' (1984) 33 ICLQ 885.

What is meant by the intention to remain permanently? Sometimes the word 'indefinitely' is used instead, but that makes the notion little clearer. If the propositus's intention is to remain only temporarily, say for the duration of a job,[79] then however long that is, a domicile will not be acquired. At the other extreme, if the propositus has decided to make the country his home, having no intention ever to leave, nor having in mind any circumstances which may cause him to leave, then clearly he has the requisite intention.

The difficult cases are those where the propositus intends to remain in the country unless and until the happening of some event, which may or may not happen; if it does happen, then he will, or may, leave. Older cases suggested that no domicile could be acquired in such circumstances. If the propositus foresaw any event that would cause him to leave, no matter how remote or unlikely that event, the intention required by law was lacking.[80] However, in the latter half of the twentieth century a more flexible and realistic approach was adopted so that today the fact that the propositus has in mind such a contingency does not necessarily mean that he does not have the intention to remain permanently. In *Re Fuld's Estate (No 3)* Scarman J stated that:

> ... if a man intends to return to the land of his birth upon a clearly foreseen and reasonably anticipated contingency, eg, the end of his job, the intention required by law is lacking; but, if he has in mind only a vague possibility, such as making a fortune (a modern example might be winning a football pool), or some sentiment about dying in the land of his fathers, such a state of mind is consistent with the intention required by law.[81]

Accordingly, it is necessary to distinguish between two types of contingency that might cause a person to leave the country of residence. If the contingency is vague and uncertain, or not at all likely to happen, then a domicile of choice may be acquired. Where the propositus's intention was to remain in England, but to return to France if he 'made his fortune', this vague contingency did not prevent him from acquiring a domicile of choice in England.[82] Similarly, where the intention was to leave England if the propositus ceased to be capable of leading an active life on his farm, the contingency was sufficiently vague and uncertain (especially as whether or not it occurred would

79 In *Irvin v Irvin* [2001] 1 FLR 178 a man worked in the Netherlands for 25 years but always intended to return to England on retirement. It was held that he had not acquired a Dutch domicile.

80 *Udny v Udny* (1869) LR 1 Sc & Div 441; *Ramsay v Liverpool Royal Infirmary* [1930] AC 588.

81 [1968] P 675 at 684–685.

82 *Doucet v Geoghegan* (1878) 9 Ch D 441.

depend on the propositus's own assessment) and so a domicile was acquired in England.[83] In *Lawrence v Lawrence*[84] the propositus loved Brazil but was prepared to leave if there were to be a revolution there and things got 'badly out of hand'. It was held that this contingency was too vague to prevent him acquiring a domicile in Brazil.

If, on the other hand, it is a definite event that the propositus has in mind, and this contingency is 'clearly foreseen and reasonably anticipated'[85] and the propositus firmly intends to leave if it does happen, then he will not have the requisite intention. For example, in *IRC* v *Bullock*[86] the domicile of origin of the propositus was in Nova Scotia. In 1932 he had come to England to join the RAF and England was his home for the next 44 years. At first, his intention had been to return to Canada when he retired from the Air Force. However, in the meantime, he had married an English woman and when he retired in 1959 he remained in England. His wife disliked Canada and was not willing to live there. Thereafter, his intention was to remain in England unless his wife died before him, in which event he would return to Canada. The Court of Appeal held that he had not acquired a domicile of choice in England, for he had in mind a definite, not a vague, contingency – the death of his wife before him – and there was a 'sufficiently substantial possibility of the contingency happening' and he firmly intended to leave if it happened.

This approach raises several questions. First, while the *Fuld (No 3)* test asked whether the contingency was 'clearly foreseen and reasonably anticipated', in *Bullock* this was rephrased as 'was there a sufficiently substantial possibility of the contingency happening?' These two tests are not the same. Although in *Bullock* it was clear that there was a substantial possibility of his wife dying before him (there was a fair chance that this would happen), it seems unlikely that the propositus would reasonably anticipate or expect his wife (who was three years younger than him) to die before him. The test in *Fuld (No 3)* is clearly preferable. Had it been applied in *Bullock*, the propositus would have been held to have acquired a domicile in England, which after 44 years' residence here would have been a more realistic result.

Secondly, must the contingency be subjectively foreseen as reasonably likely to occur, or is it enough that it is objectively likely to occur or objectively a sufficiently substantial possibility? In *Cramer v Cramer*[87] a French domiciliary came to England with the hope of marrying her lover and establishing a home here. Her intention to remain was,

83 *Re Furse* [1980] 3 All ER 838.
84 [1985] 1 All ER 506 at 508.
85 *Re Fuld's Estate (No 3)* [1968] P 675.
86 [1976] 3 All ER 353, [1976] 1 WLR 1178.
87 [1987] 1 FLR 116.

however, conditional upon her being able to marry him (he was already married) and their relationship lasting until then. While she hoped to remain in England, it was decided that an objective assessment of the situation had to be made. A mere desire to remain would not suffice. Her intentions were too speculative and, accordingly, no domicile was acquired in England. While there are also dicta in *Bullock* suggesting that the test was whether the wife was in fact likely to die before the propositus,[88] the better test is that favoured in *Fuld (No 3)* of examining the 'contingencies in the contemplation of the propositus, their importance to him, and the probability, in his assessment, of the contingencies he has in contemplation being transformed into actualities'.[89] This was confirmed in *Bheekhun v Williams*[90] where it was stated that 'the relevant enquiry is what was in his mind; not what a person who was better informed would have appreciated the position to be'.

However, as subjective intentions are often impossible to ascertain, objective considerations are important *evidence* from which intentions can be inferred. If a person claims he intends to return to his country of origin upon the happening of an outlandish contingency – for example, the British National Party winning a general election in the United Kingdom – it would be virtually impossible for him to establish that he foresaw this as reasonably likely to occur. Judges can do little other than draw inferences from conduct and the objective likelihood of contingencies occurring. They are forced to apply their own standards: 'If I had been in that situation, what would I have foreseen?' The only realistic circumstances in which it could be concluded that the propositus foresaw a bizarre contingency as reasonably likely to occur would be where there was clear evidence that the propositus's state of mind was in some material way different from that of the reasonable person – say, because he was mentally retarded. In such a situation, however, it is unlikely that the propositus would be regarded as sufficiently mentally capable to change his domicile.[91] However, while it will make little practical difference in most cases whether an objective or subjective test is applied, the test ought ultimately to be a subjective one. As already seen,[92] one of the underlying rationales of the concept of domicile of choice is that it allows full autonomy to persons to choose where they wish to make their home and thus, indirectly, to choose the law to which they are to be subject. Such a principle can only find expression in rules that take full account of

88 [1976] 3 All ER 353 at 359, 360.
89 [1968] P 675 at 685.
90 [1999] 2 FLR 229.
91 See p 36.
92 See p 24.

a person's subjective hopes, wishes and expectations. If a person genuinely expects a contingency to occur which will cause him to leave (and the court can be persuaded that this is his genuine belief), then, as the rules are presently structured, he cannot be said to have made a permanent home in the new country.

Thirdly, and flowing directly from the last point, what is the position of a person who wants to remain in a country, but realistically will have little prospect of being able to do so – say, for immigration reasons? In *Szechter v Szechter* it was stated that if a person wished to remain permanently in a country a domicile would be acquired and it was 'immaterial that their intentions were liable to be frustrated by the decision of the Secretary of State for the Home Department as to permission for their continued residence here'.[93] This seems to suggest that intention here is to be equated with an aim or desire to remain. The more realistic approach, however, adopted in *Cramer* and *Fuld (No 3)*, is that simply desiring to remain is not sufficient. If the propositus realises that there is a clear contingency, such as a refusal to extend residence rights in a country, that could cause him to leave (whether he wants it to occur or not), the issue becomes whether he anticipates that contingency as reasonably likely to occur. Under this approach the expectations of the propositus are crucial. The issue is whether he foresees himself remaining permanently in a country, rather than whether he wishes to remain there. To adapt terminology employed in other areas of law, the type of intention required here is not direct intention (what one wants or hopes will happen), but rather oblique intention (what one foresees as reasonably likely to happen). Any other approach could result in the totally unrealistic situation of a person acquiring a domicile in a country in which he would have no prospect of being able to reside permanently.

(i) Evidence of change of domicile

How does a court decide where a person was domiciled at a given time? There is a presumption against a change of domicile, so that once it has been shown, or is admitted, that the propositus was domiciled in a particular country, the onus of proving any subsequent change of domicile lies on the party alleging it. This onus may be difficult to discharge because the evidence that must be adduced relates to the intention rather than to the residence factor. The most direct evidence of the propositus's intention is his own statements. Even if such evidence is available, however, it may well not be conclusive or even reliable.[94] For the most part, the intention of the propositus must be

93 [1971] P 286 at 294.

94 *Wahl v A-G* (1932) 147 LT 382; *Buswell v IRC* [1974] 2 All ER 520, [1974] 1 WLR 1631.

judged from his conduct. Since the state of mind in question is whether at the relevant time he regarded a given country as his permanent home, there is a very wide range of facts which may be relevant. As Kindersley VC said in *Drevon v Drevon*:

> ... there is no act, no circumstance in a man's life, however trivial it may be in itself, which ought to be left out of consideration in trying the question whether there was an intention to change the domicile. A trivial act might possibly be of more weight with regard to determining this question than an act which was of more importance to a man in his lifetime.[95]

It is not surprising then that contested domicile cases may be lengthy and expensive, involving a minute analysis of the significance to be attached to the activities of a person over many years.

The fact that a person has resided in a country for a substantial time is in itself some evidence that he has made it his permanent home, but however long such residence lasts it does not raise any presumption that he is domiciled there. The quality of the residence, and all other indications of the propositus's intention, must still be considered in deciding whether a change of domicile has been proved. The courts have taken into account a wide variety of factors in assessing whether a person possesses the requisite intention. One of the more important factors is naturalisation. Becoming a naturalised citizen of the new country is strong evidence that a person intends to remain there permanently, but it is never decisive and is simply 'one of the totality of facts'.[96] In *Fuld (No 3)* the propositus changed his nationality, but was held not to have changed his domicile. In *Bullock*, on the other hand, the fact that the propositus had not changed his nationality was regarded as relevant in deciding he had not changed his domicile. In *Bheekhun v Williams*[97] the propositus had come from Mauritius to live in England. When Mauritius became an independent country he was required to choose whether to retain British nationality or to become a national of Mauritius. His decision to obtain a British passport was regarded as a 'clear pointer' to his intention.

Another factor is the purchase of real property. The fact that a person has purchased a house or a flat in a country rather than renting accommodation used to be regarded as important.[98] Today, however, not much weight is attached to this factor, given that the acquisition of a second home or a holiday home is more common than was once the case and in view of the fact that, when the property market is buoyant,

95 (1864) 34 LJ Ch 129 at 133.
96 *Wahl v A-G* (1932) 147 LT 382.
97 [1999] 2 FLR 229.
98 *Re Flynn* [1968] 1 All ER 49, [1968] 1 WLR 103.

a person might sensibly decide to purchase a house or a flat with the intention of selling after a few years rather than to rent accommodation.[99]

Also significant are a person's family ties in the new community. The fact that the propositus has married a person from the new country[100] and established a matrimonial home there[101] can in some situations be regarded as evidence of an intention to remain. However, with greater mobility today, this factor is unlikely to assume much importance.[102] More relevant, perhaps, is the degree of social integration into the new community. Details of the daily life of the propositus in the new country are commonly regarded as indicators of whether or not he had the requisite intention to remain. Factors that have been considered include membership of churches and clubs,[103] exercising rights to vote,[104] newspapers read,[105] whether the language of the country has been learnt[106] and general lifestyle in the local community.[107] Also relevant here is the congeniality of the local customs. In older cases it was asserted that stronger evidence was required to establish that a westerner had acquired a domicile in an Oriental country.[108] Even in more modern times a similar approach has been applied in relation to people from Pakistan coming to England.[109] However, given the multi-cultural nature of British society today, it is doubtful whether too much weight would be attached to this factor. Other relevant factors that have been taken into account include a person's career prospects, answers to income tax questionnaires,[110] age[111] and the motive for moving to the new country.[112]

99 *Qureshi v Qureshi* [1972] Fam 173, [1971] 1 All ER 325 (no account taken at all of fact that property had been purchased in England).

100 *Re Fuld's Estate (No 3)* [1968] P 675, [1965] 3 All ER 776.

101 At first instance in *IRC v Bullock* [1975] 3 All ER 541 Brightman J thought it an 'attractive proposition' that because marriage is intended to be a permanent institution, the establishment of a matrimonial home should be evidence of a permanent home (at 551). This is a non sequitur. A 'permanently married' couple can move around the world establishing a succession of matrimonial homes.

102 *IRC v Bullock* [1976] 3 All ER 353.

103 *Re Craignish* [1892] 3 Ch 180.

104 *IRC v Bullock* [1976] 3 All ER 353. For the purposes of tax law, the fact one registers as an overseas elector to vote in United Kingdom elections will not be taken into account in determining the domicile of that individual (Finance Act 1996, s 200).

105 Ibid; *Irvin v Irvin* [2001] 1 FLR 178.

106 *Irvin v Irvin* [2001] 1 FLR 178.

107 *Re Furse* [1980] 3 All ER 838.

108 *Casdagli v Casdagli* [1919] AC 145. See also *Steel v Steel* (1888) 15 R 896 at 909 ('Nobody in his senses ever goes to Burma sine animo revertendi').

109 *Qureshi v Qureshi* [1972] Fam 173, [1971] 1 All ER 325.

110 *Buswell v IRC* [1974] 2 All ER 520, [1974] 1 WLR 1631.

111 Graveson, *Conflict of Laws: Private International Law* (7th edn, 1974) p 202: 'permanence is necessarily relative to the individual's expectation of life.'

112 *Wood v Wood* [1957] P 254, [1957] 2 All ER 14.

(ii) Intention freely formed

It is often said that in forming the intention necessary for the acquisition or loss of a domicile of choice the propositus must make a free choice, formed independently of external pressures.[113] This proposition, however, seems to have little practical significance. One unlikely case in which it could arise is that of the prisoner under a sentence likely to last his lifetime who is moved to a prison in a different country (say, from England to Scotland). He might then believe that he will spend the rest of his days in Scotland; even if that were regarded as an intention to remain permanently,[114] the prisoner would not acquire a domicile of choice in Scotland, for the intention was not freely formed.[115]

Lesser pressures, such as those motivating fugitives from justice, refugees and people migrating for the sake of their health, do not normally negate intention.[116] For example, in *Donaldson v Donaldson*[117] it was held that an officer with the RAF who was stationed in Florida and liable to be posted elsewhere (and indeed was posted back to England) acquired a domicile in Florida. Any inference that he lacked the necessary intention because of the 'involuntary' nature of his presence there was rebutted by the fact that he married a local woman and clearly intended to return to Florida to make a permanent home as soon as he was free to do so.

Whether a person changes his domicile depends on the answers to the usual questions: does the propositus intend to return to his former country? Does he intend to remain permanently in the new country? The fact that he is, for instance, a refugee will, depending on the circumstances of his plight, help to show that he does, or does not, have in mind a sufficiently definite and likely contingency on which he will return home. In *Re Martin*[118] it was stated that what mattered was whether the person (in this case a fugitive from justice) was free to return home after a specified number of years. If the fugitive remains perpetually liable to prosecution or punishment, this is a factor which suggests that he does not intend to return and so thereby acquires a domicile in the new country.

113 *Udny v Udny* (1869) LR 1 Sc & Div 441 at 458; *Re Fuld's Estate (No 3)* [1968] P 675 at 684.
114 As it would be under the test of expectation or oblique intention. See p 42.
115 *Re late Emperor Napoleon Bonaparte* (1853) 2 Rob Eccl 606.
116 See *Puttick v A-G* [1979] 3 All ER 463; *Moynihan v Moynihan (Nos 1 and 2)* [1997] 1 FLR 59 (fugitives); *May v May and Lehmann* [1943] 2 All ER 146 (refugees); *Hoskins v Matthews* (1856) 8 De GM & G 13; *Re James* (1908) 98 LT 438 (invalids).
117 [1949] P 363.
118 [1900] P 211.

2. Abandonment of domicile of choice

A domicile of choice will be lost if the propositus both ceases to reside in the country in question and ceases to intend to reside there permanently. So while a domicile of choice can be acquired only by the concurrence of residence and intention, it continues as long as either one of them remains.

(A) CESSATION OF RESIDENCE

Even when the propositus has ceased to intend to reside permanently, he will not lose his domicile merely through absence from the country. He must cease to reside there as an *inhabitant.* In *IRC v Duchess of Portland*[119] the question was whether the propositus abandoned her English domicile of choice in 1974. At the relevant time, the intention factor for the loss of the domicile was already satisfied, for, though she lived in England, she did not intend to remain there permanently. She had a house in Quebec, where she spent ten or twelve weeks each year. It was argued that when she made her annual visit there in 1974 she lost her English domicile on the basis that her absence from England meant that she ceased to reside in England and that she did not have the intention of residing permanently in England. It was held, however, that she retained her English domicile, for, despite her temporary absence, her residence as an inhabitant in England continued. Where a person has two homes residence in the old country will only be abandoned when a chief residence is established in the new country.[120]

(B) CESSATION OF INTENTION

If the propositus has ceased to reside in the country in question, what precisely is the intention requirement for loss of the domicile of choice? The law here is not settled. Certainly, if the propositus positively intends not to return to live in his former country, the domicile will be abandoned. Equally, if he positively intends at some time in the future to resume his residence in the former country, he will retain his domicile there. It is the case in between that causes difficulty, where the propositus is undecided whether or not he will return. The intention needed to acquire a domicile of choice is to remain in the country permanently. Does it follow that all that is required for its abandonment is that the propositus should cease to intend to reside there permanently? If so, the domicile of choice will be lost if the propositus is undecided whether or not to return;

119 [1982] Ch 314, [1982] 1 All ER 784.
120 *Plummer v IRC* [1988] 1 All ER 97, [1988] 1 WLR 292.

in such a case he no longer has the intention of residing permanently (even though, of course, he does not have the intention of not doing so). There is support for this view. In *Re Flynn*[121] it was indicated that there need not be a departure with the intention of not returning permanently, but rather a domicile of choice could be lost where there was a departure without a specific intention of returning. This view was endorsed in *Qureshi v Qureshi* where it was stated that a domicile of choice could be lost if the propositus went to a new country without an intention of returning to the old country of domicile: 'the animus that must be shown is not necessarily non revertendi; it is sufficient that the residence in the new country is sine animo revertendi.'[122] In this respect it was added that an intention to return could 'wither away'.[123]

On the other hand, in *Re Lloyd Evans*[124] the domicile of choice of the propositus had been Belgium. During the German occupation in the Second World War, he had escaped to England (which was his domicile of origin). While in England he was undecided whether, after the war, he would return to Belgium or go to Australia. He died before he could make up his mind. It was held that he had not lost his Belgian domicile, for he had not definitely decided not to return there as his home. This supports the view that a domicile of choice will not be lost unless there is a positive intention not to return (except temporarily). Similarly, in *Re S (No 2) (Hospital Patient)* it was held that a person living in England had not lost his Norwegian domicile because 'he wanted to keep his eventual options (of returning) open although for the time being the die was cast (and he did not anticipate leaving England)'.[125]

As long as the doctrine of revival of the domicile of origin remains part of English law the approach taken in *Re Lloyd Evans* seems preferable. Where a person is in a state of some indecision it is not desirable that the old domicile of choice be lost and, because there is insufficient intention for acquisition of a new domicile of choice, replaced by the domicile of origin. Had the *Re Flynn* approach been applied in *Re Lloyd Evans*, since the propositus did not positively intend to return to Belgium, he would have lost his domicile there, with the consequence that his English domicile of origin (the one country in which it was clear he did not intend to remain) would have revived.

121 [1968] 1 All ER 49, [1968] 1 WLR 103.
122 [1972] Fam 173 at 191.
123 Ibid. See also *Maples v Melamud* [1988] Fam 14.
124 [1947] Ch 695.
125 [1996] 1 FLR 167.

3. Reform of domicile of choice

The central problem with the law here relates to the nature, and difficulty of proof, of the requisite intention requirement. Despite developments in cases such as *Fuld (No 3)*,[126] the law still remains rooted in its Victorian origins when the establishment of a home was an affair of a lifetime. It is simply unrealistic in the modern world to assert that people like the propositus in *Bullock*, who have lived in this country for over 40 years, are not domiciled here. The function of domicile is to connect people to the legal system to which they belong and whose laws are most appropriate to apply to them. For all practical purposes (other than purely emotional and sentimental considerations) the propositus in *Bullock* had made his home in England and should have been held domiciled here. Further, because of the infinite range of factors that can prevent a person from acquiring a domicile in a country, and the difficulty of proving a person's state of mind, trials involving domicile of choice tend to be lengthy and expensive with the outcome difficult to predict.

In an attempt to address these problems there have been several proposals to reform the law on domicile of choice. As long ago as 1954, reforms were recommended by the Private International Law Committee,[127] the main one being the introduction of a rebuttable presumption that a person should be presumed to intend to live permanently in the country in which he has his home. This proposal was carried forward into the Domicile Bill 1958, which foundered after its second reading in the House of Lords because of intense opposition from United States and Commonwealth businesspeople who feared they would become liable to United Kingdom income tax and estate duty.[128] A revised Domicile Bill in 1959 was similarly abandoned because of opposition in the House of Commons.[129] In 1963 the Private International Law Committee again proposed similar reforms which were never implemented.[130] In 1985 the Law Commission published a consultation document suggesting that, subject to evidence to the contrary, a person should be presumed to

126 See Fentiman, 'Domicile Revisited' [1991] CLJ 445 who argues that cases such as *Re Furse* [1980] 3 All ER 838, *Brown v Brown* (1981) 3 FLR 212 and *Plummer v IRC* [1988] 1 All ER 97 represent a more realistic move in the direction of utilising a real and substantial connection test as the measure of domiciliary intent.

127 First Report of the Private International Law Committee, 1954 (Cmd 9068).

128 Graveson, *Conflict of Laws: Private International Law* (7th edn, 1974) p 189; Carter, 'Domicil: The Case for Radical Reform in the United Kingdom' (1987) 36 ICLQ 713 at 724.

129 Ibid.

130 Seventh Report of the Private International Law Committee, 1963 (Cmnd 1955).

intend to make his home indefinitely in a country in which he has been habitually resident for seven years.[131] In its final Report in 1987 the Law Commission, responding to criticisms that such a presumption could be difficult (and expensive) to rebut, abandoned the use of presumptions and simply proposed that a domicile of choice should be acquired if a person was present in a country and intended to settle there for an indefinite period.[132] This proposal is little more than a restatement of the present law on domicile of choice and would mean that persons such as the propositus in *Bullock* will continue to be domiciled in a country that they left 40 or more years ago. While several of the Law Commission's proposals are to be welcomed,[133] it is regrettable that the opportunity was not taken to try to modernise the somewhat antiquated rules on domicile of choice.[134]

IV NATIONALITY

In most civil law systems, such as those operating in continental Europe and the former colonies of those countries, the test of 'belonging' to a country for conflict of laws purposes is not domicile, but nationality. For example, such countries would regard French law as the most appropriate law to govern the personal transactions and relationships of a French citizen. In England the use of nationality as a connecting factor has been extremely limited. With regard to choice of law it is used as one of a range of alternative connecting factors compliance with the law of which can render a will formally valid.[135] It is also employed as a basis for the recognition of a foreign divorce or other matrimonial decree. If one of the parties to the marriage was a national of the country in which the divorce or other decree was obtained the decree is prima facie entitled to recognition in England.

The advantages of nationality over domicile are that it can easily be ascertained and is therefore more certain: whereas most people know what their nationality is, fewer can be certain as to where they are domiciled; it is difficult to change one's nationality, making evasion of the law more difficult; in times of crisis a person may turn to his state

131 Law Com Working Paper No 88 (1985) para 5.15. See Carter, 'Domicil: The Case for Radical Reform in the United Kingdom' (1987) 36 ICLQ 713.
132 Law Com No 168, cl 2(2) of the Draft Bill.
133 See pp 31 and 35.
134 The government announced that it has abandoned any intention of implementing the Law Commission's reform proposals (*Hansard*, (HC) vol 269, col 488–489w, 16 January 1996; see (1996) 146 NLJ 371).
135 Wills Act 1963, s 1.

of nationality for protection and so it is only appropriate that he should be subject to its laws for conflict of laws purposes.[136]

On the other hand, there are distinct disadvantages to utilising nationality instead of domicile as a connecting factor. First, there is the problem posed by stateless persons or those with dual nationality. Secondly, the concept does not work efficiently when dealing with composite states, such as the United Kingdom or the United States, comprising more than one legal system. Finally, as with domicile, it can lead to highly unrealistic results in that persons who have long since left a country, but failed to become naturalised elsewhere, will continue to be subject to the law of their former country. The propositus in *Bullock* would still be subject to Canadian law as, despite 44 years' residence in England, he had still retained his Canadian nationality. Accordingly, the Law Commission has recommended against replacing domicile by nationality because while it 'is a proper test of political status and allegiance, domicile being based on the idea of the country where a person has his home is a more appropriate concept for determining what system of law should govern his civil status and certain aspects of the administration of his property'.[137]

One possible compromise, not explored by the Law Commission, that would bring our law more in line with the laws of other European Union member states, is the solution adopted in Singapore whereby a person who is a citizen of Singapore is presumed, until the contrary is proved, to be domiciled in Singapore.[138] This approach, assuming it were elevated into a general presumption that a person is domiciled in the country of his nationality, would introduce a great measure of certainty and simplicity into the law and, as the presumption would be rebuttable, would allow nationality to be displaced in cases where its application would be inappropriate. The disadvantage of this approach is that it would solve little, as in all the difficult cases there would need to be the same full inquiry as at present in order to ascertain whether the presumption has been rebutted.

V HABITUAL RESIDENCE

A Introduction

The operation of the conflict of laws depends upon choice of law rules containing connecting factors that lead to realistic and appropriate

136 See generally, Nadelman, 'Mancini's Nationality Rule and Non-Unified Legal Systems: Nationality versus Domicile' (1969) 17 Am J Comp Law 418.
137 Law Com No 168, para 3.11.
138 Women's Charter (Ch 353) (revd edn, 1985) s 3(4).

laws. With regard to the personal law, connecting factors should lead to the law that is most appropriate for governing and controlling the personal transactions of an individual. Also, with regard to jurisdiction and the recognition of foreign judgments, the system depends on the employment of connecting factors that ensure that appropriate courts have jurisdiction and that the judgments of appropriate foreign courts are recognised.

As has been explored, the major problem with the concepts of domicile and nationality is that they can lead to unrealistic, unpredictable and inappropriate laws or jurisdictions. If domicile or nationality were the sole connecting factor employed by English law for choice of law and jurisdictional purposes, the propositus in *Bullock* would not have been able to obtain a divorce in England and, in any choice of law dispute, the law of Nova Scotia would have been applicable to him, despite 44 years' residence in England.

Accordingly, over the last 30 years a new connecting factor, habitual residence, has emerged. Initially this was a concept developed by the Hague Conference on Private International Law as a compromise between the common law concept of domicile and the civil law notion of nationality. When uniform jurisdictional rules for divorce, separation and annulment were introduced throughout the European Union, habitual residence was adopted as the main connecting factor.[139] The concept has been widely employed in English statutes, even those not implementing international conventions. For example, in cases not governed by the EC Regulation, it is used as a connecting factor for jurisdiction with regard to divorce,[140] separation[141] and nullity of marriage,[142] the recognition of foreign divorces,[143] the formal validity of wills,[144] international adoptions[145] and child abduction.[146] Even in commercial areas of law the concept is now being utilised – most importantly in relation to contractual obligations as a result of the Contracts (Applicable Law) Act 1990.

B Meaning of habitual residence

Over the last decade there has been a voluminous jurisprudence developing on the meaning of habitual residence. Most of the decisions

139 Council Regulation (EC) No 1347/2000 of 29 May, OJ 2000 L160/19.
140 Domicile and Matrimonial Proceedings Act 1973, s 5(2).
141 Ibid.
142 Domicile and Matrimonial Proceedings Act 1973, s 5(3)(b).
143 Family Law Act 1986, s 46(1)(b).
144 Wills Act 1963, s 1.
145 Adoption and Children Act 2002, s 47(3). See also pp 447–558.
146 Child Abduction and Custody Act 1985, Sch 1, art 4.

have concerned the habitual residence of children under the Child Abduction and Custody Act 1985, implementing the Hague Convention on Civil Aspects of International Child Abduction of 1980. Under this statute the English court has a prima facie duty to order the return of a child who has been wrongfully removed from a contracting state in which he is habitually resident. In determining such a child's habitual residence the courts have necessarily had to explore the habitual residence of the parents and have thus laid down principles capable of general application.

The House of Lords in *Re J (Abduction: Custody Rights)*[147] stressed that the ascertainment of habitual residence is a question of fact to be decided by reference to all the circumstances of the case. However, it is clear that several important legal principles have emerged from this case and others. Before examining the rules in detail, some general observations need to be made.

First, the burden of proving a change of habitual residence lies on the party alleging the change.[148] However, the burden is less onerous here than it is for establishing a change of domicile. Secondly, it is clear that in certain situations a person can have no habitual residence.[149] In *Nessa v Chief Adjudication Officer*[150] it was indicated by the House of Lords that in certain situations, in order to make particular legislation effective, it might be necessary to ensure that there is no 'gap' between habitual residences. While it has also been indicated that a child should, where possible, have a habitual residence for the purposes of the Hague Convention,[151] there have been cases where it has been concluded that a child may have no habitual residence.[152] Thirdly, a person can have more than one habitual residence at the same time.[153] In *Ikimi v Ikimi*[154] it was held that a couple who had consistently maintained matrimonial homes in both England and Nigeria could be habitually resident in both countries at the same time. Accordingly, it is not necessary to prove that a habitual residence has

147 [1990] 2 AC 562 at 578.
148 *Re R (Wardship: Child Abduction)* [1992] 2 FLR 481 at 487.
149 *Re J (Abduction: Custody Rights)* [1990] 2 AC 562.
150 [1999] 3 FCR 538, [1999] 2 FLR 1116.
151 *Re F (Child Abduction)* [1992] 1 FLR 548 at 555.
152 Balcombe LJ in *Re M (Residence Order: Jurisdiction)* [1993] 1 FLR 495 at 501; *D v D (Custody: Jurisdiction)* [1996] 1 FLR 574 at 582; *Al Habtoor v Fotheringham* [2001] EWCA Civ 186, [2001] 1 FLR 951. See, generally, Stone, 'The Habitual Residence of a Child' (1992) 4 JCL 170.
153 *Shah v Barnet London Borough Council* [1983] 2 AC 309, [1983] 1 All ER 226. In *Re V* [1996] 3 FCR 173 it was held that for the purposes of the Hague Convention a child who lived in two countries for different parts of the year had consecutive habitual residences rather than being concurrently habitually resident in both.
154 [2001] EWCA Civ 873, [2001] 2 FCR 385.

been lost and replaced by another. (It need hardly be added that there is no concept of revival of a habitual residence of origin.) The reason why a person does not need to have one, and only one, habitual residence is that, unlike domicile, habitual residence is used primarily for jurisdictional purposes or as an alternative to domicile for choice of law purposes (as in the Wills Act 1963). So, while it is essential that everyone have one, and only one, domicile – because it is only possible to have one law applying to questions such as succession to movable property – with matters such as divorce jurisdiction, there is no requirement that the courts of only one country should have jurisdiction. If, for example, a respondent has no habitual residence, the English court simply has no jurisdiction on that basis; if a respondent is habitually resident in England, the court does have jurisdiction and it is irrelevant that he might also be habitually resident elsewhere. Finally, habitual residence, like all connecting factors, is to be construed according to English law and not according to any foreign law under which it is alleged that a person has acquired a habitual residence.[155] It has been held that habitual residence bears the same meaning in all statutes.[156] It is, however, likely that the courts 'pay mere lip-service to this rule'[157] and that the meaning of habitual residence varies according to the context in which the issue arises. In particular, it has been suggested that the interpretation of habitual residence for abducted children should take account of the particular vulnerabilities of children in identifying a settled environment to which they should be returned.[158]

1. *Adults*

In order to prove habitual residence it is necessary to establish a concurrence of both the physical element of residence and a mental state of having a 'settled purpose' of remaining there.[159] However, the nature of these two requirements differs markedly from the superficially similar requirements of domicile.

(A) RESIDENCE

An examination of reported cases suggests that where there has been residence for a year or more, habitual residence is always held to be established.[160] In such cases the objective fact of the residence is

155 *Re A (Abduction: Habitual Residence)* [1996] 1 All ER 24 at 31; *Re B (Child Abduction: Habitual Residence)* [1994] 2 FLR 915 at 918.

156 *Re J (Abduction: Custody Rights)* [1990] 2 AC 562 at 578.

157 Rogerson, 'Habitual Residence: The New Domicile?' (2000) 49 ICLQ 86.

158 Beaumont and McEleavy, *The Hague Convention on International Child Abduction* (1999) pp 112–113.

159 *Shah v Barnet London Borough Council* [1983] 2 AC 309 at 344.

160 Clive, 'The Concept of Habitual Residence' [1997] Jur Rev 137.

decisive and the intentions of the person are of little importance – even if it is clear that the person has no desire to live in the country.[161]

More problematic are cases where the residence has endured for less than a year. How quickly can habitual residence be established? It is clear that, while a person can lose a habitual residence the moment he leaves a country for good, he does not acquire a new habitual residence as soon as he arrives in the new country. In *Re J* Lord Brandon stated that a person could never acquire a habitual residence within a single day but only after an 'appreciable period of time'.[162] In *Nessa v Chief Adjudication Officer*[163] the House of Lords interpreted this to mean that a person must have taken up residence and lived there for a period. It must be shown that the residence has become 'habitual' and is likely to continue to be habitual. In the *Nessa* case a woman from Bangladesh, who had a right of abode in the United Kingdom, arrived in England and applied for income support four days later. She was only entitled to income support if she was habitually resident in England. It was held that, even though she had come here for the settled purpose of remaining (and so could even be domiciled here), she had not acquired habitual residence within four days.

However, the period of residence may be short[164] and the amount of time needed to be spent in the new country depends on the degree of settled purpose. In *Re S (Custody: Habitual Residence)*[165] the House of Lords held that if there was an established intention of settling in the country permanently a new habitual residence may be acquired 'very quickly'. On this basis, in *Re F (Child Abduction)*[166] habitual residence was acquired within one month of a family moving to Australia with the intention of remaining there. In *V v B (Abduction)*[167] habitual residence was acquired after a little over two months' residence in Australia. On the other hand, in *A v A (Child Abduction)*[168] it was stated that if there were doubts over the requisite 'settled intention' eight months' residence in Australia would be insufficient for the acquisition of habitual residence there. Ultimately, it is a factual inquiry. For instance, a person resuming a habitual residence

161 *M v M (Abduction: England and Scotland)* [1997] 2 FLR 263. See Rogerson, 'Habitual Residence: The New Domicile?' (2000) 49 ICLQ 86 at 94.
162 [1990] 2 AC 562 at 578.
163 [1999] 3 FCR 538, [1999] 2 FLR 1116.
164 Lord Slynn in *Nessa v Chief Adjudication Officer* [1999] 2 FLR 1116 approved *Re F (Child Abduction)* [1992] 1 FLR 548 where it was stated that 'a month can be an appreciable period of time' (at 555).
165 [1997] 4 All ER 251.
166 [1992] 1 FLR 548.
167 [1991] 1 FLR 266.
168 [1993] 2 FLR 225 at 235.

previously held can acquire habitual residence in a relatively short period of time.[169] The residence need not be continuous. Occasional absences, such as for holidays, will not affect a person's habitual residence. In *Re H (Abduction: Habitual Residence: Consent)*[170] it was held that a student studying abroad for a finite one-year course would not lose her habitual residence.[171] Finally, the residence must be lawful. If a person is an illegal immigrant he cannot rely on this unlawful residence as constituting habitual residence.[172]

(B) SETTLED INTENTION

Residence must be accompanied by a 'settled purpose'[173] or 'settled intention'[174] of remaining 'as part of the settled order of [a person's] life for the time being'.[175] The intention need only be to remain for a relatively short or limited period of time.[176] Thus a person who goes to a country for the purpose of obtaining a degree or of taking up employment under a fixed-term business contract can become habitually resident there. In *Kapur v Kapur*[177] a man who came to England to study for the English Bar exams was held to be habitually resident here for the purposes of divorce jurisdiction. In *Re B (No 2)*[178] a couple living in Scotland went to Germany (the wife's place of origin) in order to resolve their matrimonial difficulties and plan their future lives. Despite being there for only six months it was held that they had a sufficient settled purpose to become habitually resident in Germany. As stated in *Shah v Barnet London Borough Council*: 'All that is necessary is that the purpose of living where one does has a sufficient degree of continuity to be properly described as settled.'[179] On the other hand, in *Re B (Child Abduction)*[180] two months' residence in Canada trying to effect a marital reconciliation did not indicate a sufficient settled purpose for habitual residence to be acquired.

It is necessary that the residence be voluntarily adopted. However, as with domicile, it seems that this is less a rule of law than an evidential proposition that where residence is involuntary, it is unlikely that the

169 *Nessa v Chief Adjudication Officer* [1999] 3 FCR 538, [1999] 2 FLR 1116.
170 [2000] 3 FCR 412, [2000] 2 FLR 294.
171 Following *Kapur v Kapur* [1984] FLR 920 it is possible that such a person could also acquire a habitual residence in the country of study.
172 *Shah v Barnet London Borough Council* [1983] 2 AC 309 at 343.
173 Ibid.
174 *Re J (Abduction: Custody Rights)* [1990] 2 AC 562.
175 *Re B (Abduction) (No 2)* [1993] 1 FLR 993 at 995.
176 *Al Habtoor v Fotheringham* [2001] EWCA Civ 186, [2001] 1 FCR 385, [2001] 1 FLR 951.
177 [1984] FLR 920.
178 [1993] 1 FLR 993.
179 [1983] 2 AC 309 at 344.
180 [1994] 2 FLR 915 at 918.

propositus would have the requisite settled intention to remain. In *Shah* Lord Scarman instanced kidnapping, imprisonment and being stranded on a desert island with no opportunity of escape as factors that may be so overwhelming 'as to negative the will to be where one is'.[181] In *Re A (Abduction: Habitual Residence)*[182] it was argued that a member of the United States forces stationed in Iceland could not become habitually resident there because of the compulsory nature of the posting. This argument was swept aside on the basis that joining the army involved a 'voluntary election' that was no different from joining a business firm knowing one could be required to work in another country. It was, however, added that a new habitual residence would not be acquired by a member of the armed forces who is posted to a foreign country on active service.

2. *Children*

There is no concept of habitual residence of dependence.[183] In *N v N (Abduction: Habitual Residence)*[184] an argument that the rules on the habitual residence of children should mirror the law of domicile was specifically rejected. How then is the habitual residence of a child to be determined? One possible approach is the 'child-centred' model under which children are treated as autonomous individuals with their habitual residence being determined by their objective connections with a country. It is argued[185] that this model best fits the philosophy of the children's rights movement.

While this approach has been adopted in some jurisdictions,[186] English law has preferred the 'parental rights' model. Under this, the habitual residence of a child under the age of 16[187] is largely determined by the parent or parents who have parental responsibility for him. This rule operates in the following manner.

Where the parents, who have joint parental responsibility, and the child are living together the child has the same habitual residence as

181 [1983] 2 AC 309 at 344. In the Scottish case of *Cameron v Cameron* 1996 SC 17 the opposite view was adopted: it was stated that Nelson Mandela would have been habitually resident on Robben Island where he was imprisoned (at 20).

182 [1996] 1 All ER 24 at 31.

183 *Al Habtoor v Fotheringham* [2001] EWCA Civ 186, [2001] 1 FLR 951; Beaumont and McEleavy, *The Hague Convention on International Child Abduction* (1999) p 91.

184 [2000] 3 FCR 84, [2000] 2 FLR 899.

185 Schuz, 'Habitual Residence of Children under the Hague Child Abduction Convention: Theory and Practice' (2001) 13 CFLQ 1.

186 Ibid.

187 Family Law Act 1986, s 41; Stone, *The Conflict of Laws* (1995) pp 37–38. In *Re O (Abduction: Habitual Residence)* [1993] 2 FLR 594 at 599 it was indicated that a child could acquire an independent domicile when old enough to form his own intentions relevant to acquiring habitual residence.

them and neither parent can change that without the consent of the other or an order of the court.[188] Where the parents and children move to a new country but only one parent becomes habitually resident there, the habitual residence of the children remains unchanged.[189] One parent may acquiesce in the change of a child's habitual residence where he takes no steps to prevent a change in the child's home over a period of time.[190] Where the parents separate, the child's habitual residence will follow that of the principal carer with whom he resides.[191] A mere change in custodial rights, without an accompanying change in actual physical control, is not enough to alter a child's habitual residence. In *Re O (Abduction: Habitual Residence)*[192] a child habitually resident in England was taken to Nevada for a custody hearing where custody was granted to the father. The mother who had had custody immediately prior to the hearing brought the child back to England. It was held that, as no transfer of actual physical control had occurred, the child's habitual residence remained the same as that of the mother.

A person who does not have parental rights cannot immediately change a child's habitual residence by taking him to a new country – although the longer the actual residence there without challenge, the more likely a child would acquire a habitual residence there. In *Re S (Custody: Habitual Residence)*[193] an Irish mother, who had full parental rights over her child, was habitually resident in England. She was not married to the father who had no parental rights. The mother died and the maternal grandmother and aunt took the child to Ireland without the father's knowledge or consent. It was held that after only one week in Ireland the child had not lost his English habitual residence or acquired an Irish habitual residence.

Finally, a parent may change a child's habitual residence without changing his own. Merely sending a child abroad to boarding school will not suffice to effect a change of habitual residence.[194] However, if the child is sent abroad for more than educational or cultural purposes (for example, to live with grandparents), the child may acquire a habitual residence in the new country. In *Re M (Residence Order: Jurisdiction)*[195] a mother, habitually resident in England, who had sole parental responsibility for her children, sent them to Scotland to attend school and live with their grandparents for at least a year. During this

188 *Re B (Abduction) (No 2)* [1993] 1 FLR 993 at 995; *D v D (Custody: Jurisdiction)* [1996] 1 FLR 574; *Re C (Abduction: Consent)* [1996] 1 FLR 414.
189 *N v N (Abduction: Habitual Residence)* [2000] 3 FCR 84, [2000] 2 FLR 899.
190 *Re F (Child Abduction)* [1992] 1 FLR 548.
191 Ibid.
192 [1993] 2 FLR 594.
193 [1997] 4 All ER 251.
194 *Re A (Wardship: Jurisdiction)* [1995] 1 FLR 767 at 773.
195 [1993] 1 FLR 495. See also *F v F* [1993] Fam Law 199.

period the children became habitually resident in Scotland. However, a 'strong burden' is placed upon a parent who wishes to establish that their child's habitual residence is different from theirs.[196] That parent must show a settled intention that the child should take up 'long-term' residence in the other country.[197] If the parents have made a joint agreement that a child be sent abroad in circumstances where he acquires a habitual residence there, it is possible for either parent to revoke that agreement at any time and bring the child back, thereby terminating his habitual residence in that country.[198] However, a unilateral decision by a parent, without a physical change in the child's place of residence, cannot alter the habitual residence of the child. In *Re KM (A Minor: Habitual Residence)*[199] the parents, both habitually resident in England, agreed that their child should live with grandparents in India and be brought up there until adulthood. After the child had been in India for over a year, the mother changed her mind and sought to have the child returned to England. The jurisdiction of the High Court depended on whether her change of mind was sufficient to make the child habitually resident in England. It was held that such a unilateral decision (even by a parent with sole parental responsibility) could not alter the child's habitual residence. Such a notion would clothe habitual residence with 'some metaphysical or abstract basis more appropriate to a legal concept such as domicile'.[200] The mother's change of mind could not alter the fact that the child remained resident in India. It was possible (though 'very much doubt[ed]'[201]) that her decision could alter the 'habitual' nature of the residence in India thus rendering the child habitually resident nowhere. Her decision, however, could certainly not make the child 'resident' in England and so he was not habitually resident in England at the relevant time.

C Conclusion

The concept of habitual residence is one clearly suited to modern conditions where people move around the world with greater ease than in the past and is ideally suited for purposes such as divorce jurisdiction or child abduction where the aim is not to establish a 'real home' but rather to identify a jurisdiction with which a person has a legitimate connection (although he may be more closely connected with some other country). The concept is, however, unsuitable for general choice

196 *Re A (Wardship: Jurisdiction)* [1995] 1 FLR 767.
197 *Re V (Jurisdiction: Habitual Residence)* [2001] 1 FLR 253.
198 *Re A (Wardship: Jurisdiction)* [1995] 1 FLR 767 at 773.
199 [1996] 2 FCR 333.
200 At 342.
201 Ibid.

of law purposes as it generates a link with a country that can be too tenuous. An English domiciliary working on a one or two-year contract can become habitually resident in Saudi Arabia. If habitual residence were to replace domicile as a general connecting factor for choice of law purposes this would mean that questions such as his capacity to marry more than one wife would be governed by Saudi Arabian law. Such an approach would be inappropriate and could encourage people to engage in deliberate evasion of the law that would normally be applicable to them.[202] Further, one could not countenance habitual residence as a general connecting factor when it is possible to have no, or more than one, habitual residence. Accordingly, the Law Commission has rejected the employment of habitual residence as a general substitute for domicile.[203] The road forward seems clear. Habitual residence can, and should, be utilised in many areas of law, particularly in the context of jurisdiction and the recognition of foreign judgments. For most family choice of law purposes, however, the concept of domicile is more appropriate. That concept, however, as has been seen, is somewhat outdated and, accordingly, efforts should be redoubled to reform it. With a more modern and realistic concept of domicile, one could then engage in a functional analysis to determine which connecting factor, domicile or habitual residence (or even, perhaps sometimes, nationality), is most suitable for each conflicts rule.

202 Law Com No 168, para 3.6.
203 Law Com No 168, paras 3.5–3.8.

Chapter 3

Civil jurisdiction

I INTRODUCTION

A General considerations

This chapter deals with the English court's jurisdiction other than in matrimonial causes (which is dealt with in chapter 9) and excluding a few other kinds of proceeding.[1]

Broadly speaking, questions of jurisdiction may be looked at from two angles – one positive, the other negative. Looked at positively there are various reasons why the English court may be a suitable forum to decide a dispute that has foreign elements. One is that the parties have agreed or submitted to its jurisdiction. If both parties are content for litigation to proceed in England there can be little objection to the exercise of jurisdiction by the English court. A second ground is a connection between the defendant and England; it will seldom be an injustice to a person to have to defend a case in the court of his own country. Thirdly, the English court may be appropriate because there is a connection between the cause of action and England. While it may cause a foreign defendant great expense and inconvenience to defend proceedings in England, it may nevertheless be reasonable for the English court to deal with the case if relevant events occurred here. For example, if the defendant is alleged to have committed a tort against the claimant while on a visit to England, both fairness to the English claimant and the ready availability of the witnesses and other evidence make the English court an appropriate forum.

These positive considerations are only one half of the equation. Situations arise in which, although it is plausible to regard England as a suitable forum, there are even stronger grounds for the courts of another country to try the case. There are a variety of reasons why a

1 Such as administration of estates and bankruptcy.

foreign court may be a more appropriate forum, notwithstanding the fact that there is a sufficient connection with England to justify the exercise of jurisdiction by the English court. For example, it may be more convenient for the claim against the defendant to be joined to related proceedings which have already been commenced in a foreign forum at the time when the claimant seeks to invoke the English court's jurisdiction. A jurisdictional inquiry involves not only an investigation of the potential bases on which the English court may exercise jurisdiction, but also a consideration of countervailing factors which may point towards the English court staying the proceedings or declining jurisdiction in favour of the courts of another country.

It has been suggested that certain aspects of English law relating to the exercise of jurisdiction may have to be reconsidered in light of the Human Rights Act 1998, which implements the European Convention on Human Rights (ECHR). In *Lubbe v Cape plc*[2] the House of Lords was presented with the argument that, if the English proceedings were stayed, the claimants would be deprived of their right to a fair trial under article 6 of the ECHR. As the House of Lords refused to grant a stay under normal principles,[3] the argument did not have to be directly addressed. Nevertheless, Lord Bingham did not think that 'article 6 supports any conclusion which is not already reached on application of [the usual] principles'.[4] Although, in particular circumstances, the ECHR may become relevant, its role is unlikely to be other than marginal. Article 6 of the ECHR protects the right to a 'fair and public hearing before an independent and impartial tribunal established by law', but it says nothing about where that right has to be capable of being exercised.[5] Accordingly, only in exceptional circumstances will jurisdiction rules designed to determine where litigation is to take place (rather than whether or not it can take place at all) run the risk of falling foul of the Human Rights Act 1998.

In the context of the current discussion there are two types of claim which may be commenced in England: claims in personam and Admiralty claims in rem. A claim in personam is one in which the claimant seeks a judgment requiring the defendant to pay money, deliver property or do, or refrain from doing, some other act. A claimant who wishes to commence proceedings in personam must be able to serve a claim form[6] on the defendant – either in England or abroad. In certain circumstances a claimant is able to serve process on

2 [2000] 4 All ER 268, [2000] 1 WLR 1545.
3 As laid down in *Spiliada Maritime Corpn v Cansulex Ltd* [1987] AC 460, [1986] 3 All ER 843. See pp 119–129.
4 [2000] 1 WLR 1545 at 1561.
5 See Atkins J in *The Kribi* [2001] 1 Lloyd's Rep 76 at 87.
6 Formerly, a writ.

the defendant as of right; in others the claimant requires the permission of the court. Typical proceedings in personam include claims for an injunction or damages in tort and claims for damages or specific performance for breach of contract.

Admiralty proceedings in rem are directed against property, usually a ship.[7] Although it is not uncommon for the ship to be referred to as the defendant in a claim in rem,[8] the reality is that the claim is brought against the owner of the ship.[9] A typical case is where the claimant has a claim against a shipowner in respect of his ship – for example, where the claimant's cargo has been damaged as a result of the negligent navigation of the vessel. Proceedings in rem are commenced by process being affixed to the mast or any suitable part of the superstructure of the ship. The claimant will normally also seek to arrest the ship so that it can be sold to meet any judgment granted to the claimant. The owner of the vessel will, however, often avoid the arrest of vessel (or obtain the vessel's release after its arrest) by giving security for the claim. In that case the proceedings assume a hybrid character; the claim proceeds in rem (notionally) against the ship and in personam against the shipowner who has submitted to the English court's jurisdiction by giving security. In proceedings which proceed solely in rem the claimant is confined to the proceeds of sale of the ship for the satisfaction of his judgment, but where a claim proceeds both in rem and in personam the claimant is not so limited.

B The structure of English law on jurisdiction in personam

There are three main regimes governing the in personam jurisdiction of the English court. The first, which has a European origin, is the Brussels regime (which is derived from the Brussels Convention on Jurisdiction and the Enforcement of Judgments in Civil and Commercial Matters). The second regime is a modified version of the European jurisdiction rules, which in certain circumstances allocates jurisdiction within the United Kingdom. These regimes are contained in European legislation, the Civil Jurisdiction and Judgments Act 1982 (as amended) and the Civil Jurisdiction and Judgments Order 2001.[10] Thirdly, there are the traditional rules which apply in cases not regulated by the Brussels regime and/or the

7 A claim in rem may also be directed at cargo or freight and, in certain circumstances, against aircraft: Supreme Court Act 1981, s 21(5).

8 See, for example, Cheshire and North, *Private International Law* (13th edn, 1999) p 326.

9 *Republic of India v India Steamship Co (No 2)* [1998] AC 878. See Teare, 'The Admiralty Action In Rem and the House of Lords' [1998] LMCLQ 33.

10 SI 2001/3929.

modified version which allocates jurisdiction within the United Kingdom. A brief introductory description of these regimes will be given before treating the law in more detail.

1. *The Brussels regime*

(A) THE DEVELOPMENT OF THE BRUSSELS REGIME

In the 1960s the original six member states of the EEC (Belgium, Germany, France, Italy, Luxembourg and the Netherlands) started negotiating a convention to provide for uniform rules of jurisdiction in civil and commercial matters and for the reciprocal recognition and enforcement of judgments in such matters. These negotiations led to the signing of the Brussels Convention in 1968. As the EC expanded the new member states acceded to the Brussels Convention. In 1978 an Accession Convention, making some amendments to the original text of the Brussels Convention, was signed by the original contracting states, Denmark, Ireland and the United Kingdom. The Greek Accession Convention was concluded in 1982. A further opportunity to amend provisions of the Brussels Convention was taken on the accession of Spain and Portugal in 1989. Austria, Finland and Sweden acceded to the Brussels Convention in 1996.

In 1988 the EC member states negotiated a parallel convention with the countries which were then members of EFTA. The Lugano Convention, the main provisions of which were almost identical to those of the Brussels Convention, was concluded in 1988; it regulates the relationship between, on the one hand, the EC member states and, on the other, Iceland, Norway and Switzerland and Poland.[11]

The next step in the development of the Brussels regime was the replacement of the Brussels Convention by the so-called 'Brussels I Regulation'[12] (to distinguish it from the 'Brussels II Regulation'[13]), which came into force on 1 March 2002. The first three Chapters of the Regulation[14] define its scope (Chapter I), set out detailed rules on jurisdiction (Chapter II) and make provision for the reciprocal recognition and enforcement of judgments (Chapter III).[15] The Regulation is based

11 The Lugano Convention was extended to Poland in 2000: SI 2000/1824.
12 Council Regulation (EC) No 44/2001, OJ 2001 L12/1. Denmark, however, chose not to participate in the adoption of the Regulation.
13 Council Regulation (EC) No 1347/2000, OJ 2000 L160/19, which deals with jurisdiction and the recognition and enforcement of judgments in matrimonial matters and in matters of parental responsibility for children of both spouses. See chapters 9 and 10.
14 The equivalent provisions of the Lugano Convention are found in Titles I, II and III.
15 This chapter considers Chapters I and II of the Brussels I Regulation; Chapter III is considered in chapter 4.

on the recommendations of a working party that was set up to consider reform of the Brussels and Lugano Conventions.[16] The Regulation made a number of amendments to the text (as a result of which many of the articles had to be renumbered[17]). It is anticipated that, as soon as practicably possible, the Lugano Convention will be amended with a view to bringing it into line with the Regulation.[18]

(B) INTERPRETATION

Questions of interpretation under the Regulation may be referred to the Court of Justice in accordance with the terms of article 234 of the Treaty establishing the European Community.[19] Under article 234 EC, a court against which there is no judicial remedy under national law shall make a reference if a ruling on a point of European law is necessary to enable the court to make its decision. In the context of English civil proceedings, the House of Lords is, for nearly all practical purposes, the only court against which there is no judicial remedy.

In the context of the Brussels and Lugano Conventions, it is provided that, when ascertaining the meaning of provisions of the Conventions the court may consider the official reports which accompanied the Conventions and the various subsequent Accession Conventions,[20] of which the most important are the Jenard Report[21] and the Schlosser Report.[22] These reports remain relevant when the provisions of the Regulation derived from the Conventions are under consideration as does the extensive case law of the Court of Justice.

The Court of Justice has adopted a teleological style of interpretation; the Regulation must be interpreted having regard to both its principles

16 See *Proposal for a Council Regulation (EC) on jurisdiction and the recognition and enforcement of judgments in civil and commercial matters* (hereafter '*Proposal*'), COM (1999) 348, which sets out some of the thinking behind the amendments made by the Regulation.

17 Unless otherwise indicated, the text uses the numbering employed in the Brussels I Regulation; where appropriate, the number of the article of the Brussels Convention from which the provision in question is derived is indicated in a footnote.

18 This chapter considers, in detail, only the position under the Brussels I Regulation. For consideration of the Brussels Convention (as amended) and the original Lugano Convention of 1988, see the 1997 edition of this work.

19 As limited by arts 65 and 68 EC. Under the Brussels Convention references to the Court of Justice are made under the Luxembourg Protocol, which was implemented by the Civil Jurisdiction and Judgments Act 1982 and is set out in Sch 2.

20 Civil Jurisdiction and Judgments Act 1982, ss 3(3), 3B(2).

21 OJ 1979 C59/1.

22 OJ 1979 C59/71.

and objectives.[23] Because each of the different language versions is equally authoritative an ambiguity in the English text may be resolved by reference to other language versions.

The Court of Justice has been required to consider on numerous occasions whether a specific concept should be given an autonomous interpretation or a national one. This is a question of policy which has to be resolved by reference to the regime's objectives. Because the Brussels regime aims to produce uniformity in the allocation of jurisdiction the Court of Justice has tended to impose an autonomous interpretation in relation to the terms used in Chapter I, which defines the material scope of the regime, and the conceptual categories which determine the scope of the specific jurisdiction provisions in Chapter II. For example, whether a particular dispute concerns 'matters relating to a contract' for the purposes of article 5(1) has to be decided by reference to a supranational conception of 'contract' rather than a purely national one.[24] It is not, however, the aim of the regime to harmonise the systems of civil procedure of the member states. Accordingly, matters which relate to procedural consequences or the detailed operation of legal concepts are normally to be interpreted by reference to the relevant national law.

(C) OUTLINE

The material scope of the Brussels regime – as defined by article 1 – extends to civil and commercial matters. The regime does not apply to revenue, customs or administrative matters. Problems surrounding the scope of civil and commercial matters are likely to arise most frequently in cases involving a public authority – whether as claimant or defendant. The Court of Justice has ruled that proceedings fall outside the ambit of article 1 where they involve a public authority acting in the exercise of its public authority powers.[25]

It is also provided that various matters are excluded from the regime's scope. Article 1 excludes matters relating to the status or legal capacity of natural persons, rights in property arising out of a matrimonial relationship, wills or succession. Except to the extent that it is expressly provided otherwise, the intention of the drafters was that family law matters should be excluded. In addition, the regime does not apply to bankruptcy, proceedings relating to the winding up of insolvent companies or other legal persons, judicial arrangements,

23 Case 33/78 *Somafer SA v Saar-Ferngas AG* [1978] ECR 2183.
24 See pp 81–82.
25 Case 814/79 *Netherlands State v Rüffer* [1980] ECR 3807; Case C-172/91 *Sonntag v Waidmann* [1993] ECR I-1963.

compositions and analogous proceedings,[26] to social security or to arbitration.[27] When deciding whether or not proceedings fall within the regime's scope reference must be made solely to the subject-matter of the dispute; if, by virtue of its subject-matter a dispute falls outside the regime's scope, the existence of a preliminary issue which the court must resolve in order to determine the dispute does not bring the proceedings within the scope of the Brussels regime.[28]

As regards the allocation of jurisdiction under the Brussels regime, the defendant's domicile[29] is 'the point on which the jurisdiction rules hinge'.[30] A defendant who is domiciled in a member state may normally be sued in the courts of that state.[31] This means that a person domiciled in France may usually be sued in France. However, the Brussels regime specifies circumstances in which a person domiciled in one member state may be sued in other member states. For example, where a person domiciled in England commits a tort in France the claimant has a choice whether to bring proceedings in England or France; where an English company and a German company agree to refer a dispute to the jurisdiction of the German courts the German company may sue the English company in Germany.

A person domiciled in a member state may be sued in the courts of another member state only in accordance with the terms of the Regulation.[32] For example, a claimant cannot invoke the jurisdiction of the English court on the basis of the traditional rules in a case where proceedings are brought against a defendant domiciled in France; the court's jurisdiction must be derived from the rules set out in the Regulation. Where proceedings are commenced in England against a person domiciled in another member state and the defendant does not enter an appearance, if the Regulation does not confer jurisdiction on the English court, the court must decline jurisdiction of its own motion.[33]

26 As between European Union member states private international law aspects of insolvency proceedings are dealt with by Council Regulation (EC) No 1346/2000, OJ 2000 L160/1.

27 Of these exceptions the only one which has posed significant difficulties is the one relating to arbitration. See Case C-190/89 *Marc Rich & Co AG v Società Italiana Impianti, The Atlantic Emperor* [1991] ECR I-3855.

28 Case C-190/89 *Marc Rich & Co AG v Società Italiana Impianti, The Atlantic Emperor* [1991] ECR I-3855 at 3902 (para 26).

29 For the purposes of the Brussels regime 'domicile' has a special meaning and is different from the common law concept considered in chapter 2. See pp 69–70.

30 Jenard-Möller Report, OJ 1990 C189/65.

31 Art 2.

32 Art 3. Where the English court has jurisdiction under the Brussels I Regulation, the claim form may be served on the defendant out of the jurisdiction without the permission of the court: CPR 6.19 (replacing RSC Ord 11, r 1(2)).

33 Art 26(1) (formerly art 20(1) of the Brussels Convention).

If the defendant is not domiciled in a member state the general rule is that the court may apply its traditional rules on jurisdiction.[34] It must be emphasised, however, that there are certain bases of jurisdiction which apply regardless of domicile. For example, the effect of article 22(1)[35] is that a dispute relating to the ownership of immovable property in Italy is within the exclusive jurisdiction of the Italian courts, whether the defendant is domiciled in Italy, another member state or a non-member state. It is a mistake to think that the Regulation does not apply to parties who are not domiciled in a member state.

The Brussels regime also includes provisions that are designed to reduce the incidence of conflicting judgments by preventing situations where the courts of two or more member states may exercise jurisdiction in relation to the same or related issues. According to these rules, where parallel proceedings involving the same parties and the same cause of action are brought in more than one member state (lis pendens) any court other than the court 'first seised' must stay the proceedings or decline jurisdiction; where related proceedings are brought in different member states, a court other than the court 'first seised' may, in the exercise of its discretion, stay the proceedings or, if certain conditions are fulfilled, decline jurisdiction.

2. Schedule 4 to the Civil Jurisdiction and Judgments Act 1982

Schedule 4, which is modelled on the jurisdiction provisions of the Regulation, applies when the defendant is domiciled in the United Kingdom (or the proceedings come under article 22 of the Regulation dealing with exclusive jurisdiction) and the proceedings are within the material scope of the Regulation.[36] However, the Court of Justice has no jurisdiction under article 234 EC to rule on the interpretation of Schedule 4, even in relation to those of its provisions which are identical to the equivalent provisions of the Regulation.[37] Schedule 4 operates in two main ways.

First, it supplements the Regulation in those cases where the rules in the Regulation allocate jurisdiction to the United Kingdom but without specifying any particular part of the United Kingdom.[38] For example, the effect of article 2 of the Regulation is simply that a person domiciled in the United Kingdom may be sued in the United Kingdom. Rule 1 of

34 Art 4.
35 Formerly art 16(1) of the Brussels Convention.
36 Civil Jurisdiction and Judgments Act 1982, s 16.
37 Case C-346/93 *Kleinwort Benson Ltd v City of Glasgow District Council* [1995] ECR I-615, [1995] All ER (EC) 514.
38 Where the Brussels regime allocates jurisdiction to a 'place' rather than to a member state (for example, where art 5(1) or art 5(3) applies) Sch 4 to the Civil Jurisdiction and Judgments Act 1982 does not have to be invoked.

Schedule 4 identifies the particular part (or parts[39]) of the United Kingdom in which proceedings may be brought by providing that a person domiciled in a part of the United Kingdom may be sued in that part.

Secondly, Schedule 4 allocates jurisdiction in cases which are internal to the United Kingdom but which have connections with more than one part of it.[40] The effect, so far as the English court is concerned, is that Scotland and Northern Ireland are (subject to modifications) treated as if they were member states. If the defendant is domiciled in another part of the United Kingdom the English court will have jurisdiction only if it would have had jurisdiction if the defendant had been domiciled in another member state. The consequence of Schedule 4 is that, as regards disputes that fall within the material scope of the Brussels regime, the English court cannot exercise jurisdiction on the basis of the traditional rules if the defendant is domiciled in another part of the United Kingdom.

3. *The traditional rules*

At common law the basis of the English court's jurisdiction in claims in personam is that the defendant is amenable to the court's jurisdiction in the sense that he is present in England so that the claim form commencing the proceedings can be served on him here or, if he is not present in England at the commencement of the proceedings, that he has submitted to being sued in England. If the defendant cannot be served with process in England, and does not submit to the jurisdiction, then the court may have the power under CPR 6.20[41] to exercise jurisdiction by giving permission for process to be served out of the jurisdiction. This power arises where, notwithstanding the fact that the defendant is foreign, the events or subject-matter of the dispute are connected with England.

An important feature of the traditional rules is that the outer limits of the court's jurisdiction are fixed by a number of discretions. Where a defendant is served with process in England as of right (because he is physically in England at the time of service) the court may nevertheless grant a stay of the English proceedings at the request of the defendant on the basis that there is a more appropriate forum abroad (forum non conveniens). Similarly, in exercising its powers to give permission for service of process out of the jurisdiction under

39 *Daniel v Foster* 1989 SLT 90.

40 Unless jurisdiction is allocated by the Brussels I Regulation. See the discussion of art 22(1) at p 73 and art 16(1) at p 98.

41 The Civil Procedure Rules 1998 superseded the Rules of the Supreme Court; CPR 6.20 replaced (with amendments) RSC Ord 11, r 1(1).

CPR 6.20 the court has a discretion and will permit service only if it is shown that England is the appropriate forum (forum conveniens).

When the traditional rules are compared with the Brussels regime the obvious difference in approach is that under the Brussels regime the exercise of jurisdiction is, for the most part, mandatory whereas under the traditional rules the scope of the court's jurisdiction is determined to a large extent by the exercise of discretion on the basis of an assessment of whether the English court is the appropriate forum.

4. The meaning of 'domicile'

Under the Brussels regime the English court's jurisdiction may depend on whether the defendant is domiciled in England, in another part of the United Kingdom, in another member state or in a non-member state. It is provided that, as regards individuals, the courts of each member state are to apply their own law in deciding whether a person is domiciled in that state.[42] For the purposes of the Brussels regime, 'domicile' is given a special meaning, which is different from its meaning at common law and closer to the continental usage of this term. For the purposes of the Regulation, an individual is domiciled in the United Kingdom if he is resident in the United Kingdom and the nature and circumstances of his residence indicate that he has a substantial connection with the United Kingdom, which will be presumed to be so (unless the contrary is proved) if he has been resident in the United Kingdom for the last three months or more.[43] A person will be regarded as resident in a particular part of the United Kingdom if that place is his settled or usual place of abode.[44] If an individual is not domiciled in the forum state according to its law, then a court of that state must decide the question whether he is domiciled in another member state by applying the law of the latter state.[45] So, if an English court wishes to determine whether someone is domiciled in France (for the purposes of the Regulation) it must apply French law.

As regards the domicile of companies and other legal persons, the Regulation lays down a uniform rule. A company or other legal person (or association of natural or legal persons) is domiciled at the place

42 Art 59(1).

43 Civil Jurisdiction and Judgments Order 2001, SI 2001/3929, Sch 1, para 9(2), (6). To determine whether an individual is domiciled in England, the same test applies (mutatis mutandis): Sch 1, para 9(3), (6). An individual is also to be regarded as domiciled in England if he is domiciled in the United Kingdom and resident in England and the nature and circumstances of his residence do not indicate that he has a substantial connection with any particular part of the United Kingdom: Sch 1, para 9(5).

44 *Bank of Dubai Ltd v Abbas* [1997] IL Pr 308.

45 Art 59(2).

where it has its statutory seat or its central administration or its principal place of business.[46]

Through the operation of these rules, it is possible for an individual be regarded as domiciled in more than one member state (where, for example, an individual is domiciled in England under the Civil Jurisdiction and Judgments Order 2001 and domiciled in Germany under German law). It is equally possible for a company to have more than one domicile (where, for example, its central administration is in Italy, but its principal place of business is in Spain). Conversely, it is possible for an individual who is physically present in Europe or a company which does business in Europe not to be regarded as domiciled in any of the member states.

C The structure of English law on jurisdiction in rem

The kinds of case in which the claimant may invoke the court's Admiralty jurisdiction in rem are based on international conventions[47] and set out in the Supreme Court Act 1981.[48] The Act provides, for example, that the English court may exercise jurisdiction in a case involving 'any claim for damage done by a ship'[49] or 'any claim for loss of or damage to goods carried in a ship'[50] or 'any claim arising out of any agreement relating to the carriage of goods in a ship or to the use or hire of a ship'.[51] It should be noted that the terms of the 1981 Act are, in certain respects, broader than the international conventions from which the domestic legislation is derived. As a general rule where a claim falls within the scope of the court's Admiralty jurisdiction proceedings in rem may be brought against the ship or property in connection with which the claim arises.[52] It is also provided that in certain circumstances a claim in rem can be brought against a sister ship of the ship in connection with which the claim arises.[53]

The Admiralty jurisdiction of the English court in rem is strictly territorial. Although there is no requirement that the cause of action

46 Art 60(1). In the United Kingdom the statutory seat means the registered office, or if there is no such office, the place of incorporation or, if there is no such place, the place under the law of which the formation took place: art 60(2).

47 There are two important conventions which date from 1952: the International Convention for the Unification of Certain Rules relating to the Arrest of Seagoing Ships and the International Convention for the Unification of Certain Rules concerning Civil Jurisdiction in Matters of Collision.

48 Ss 20–24.

49 S 20(2)(e).

50 S 20(2)(g).

51 S 20(2)(h).

52 S 21(2) and (3).

53 S 21(4).

or the parties should have any connection with England, the claimant may invoke the jurisdiction of the English court only if, first, the claim falls within one of the bases of jurisdiction outlined in the 1981 Act and, secondly, the ship in question can be served with the claim form in English territorial waters. However, just as with a claim in personam where jurisdiction is based on the defendant's presence in England, the court has a discretion to grant a stay of proceedings on the ground of forum non conveniens. Indeed, many of the cases in which the principles regulating the granting of stays have been formulated and applied were commenced as Admiralty proceedings in rem.[54]

It is important not to forget the potential application of the Brussels regime to cases involving Admiralty claims in rem. Although the impact of the Brussels regime is limited by provisions which preserve the effect of special conventions in the field of jurisdiction and the recognition and enforcement of judgments,[55] there are two important points to note.

First, where the claim falls within the material scope of the Brussels regime and the person who is interested in contesting the claim in rem is domiciled in a member state the English court has jurisdiction only if the exercise of jurisdiction under the Supreme Court Act 1981 is consistent either with the special conventions preserved by article 71[56] or with the provisions of Chapter II of the Regulation.[57] Where, for example, cargo-owners bring English proceedings in rem against a vessel chartered by a German defendant, but refrain from arresting the vessel because the defendant puts up security for the claim, the English court does not have jurisdiction.[58] This is because, in such circumstances, the exercise of jurisdiction under Supreme Court Act 1981 is authorised neither by the Regulation (because the defendant is domiciled in Germany rather than England) nor by the Arrest Convention (because the application of the Arrest Convention depends on the ship having been arrested). The fact that the court would have jurisdiction under the Supreme Court Act 1981 if the defendant were not domiciled in a member state is irrelevant.

Secondly, where parallel or related proceedings are commenced in two or more member states the provisions of the Regulation concerning lis pendens and related actions are relevant whether the proceedings are in personam or in rem.[59]

54 For example, *The Atlantic Star* [1974] AC 436, [1973] 2 All ER 175; *The Abidin Daver* [1984] AC 398, [1984] 1 All ER 470.
55 Such as the 1952 Arrest and Collision Conventions.
56 Formerly art 57 of the Brussels Convention.
57 *The Po* [1991] 2 Lloyd's Rep 206; *The Nordglimt* [1988] QB 183, [1988] 2 All ER 531; *The Deichland* [1990] 1 QB 361, [1989] 2 All ER 1066; *The Prinsengracht* [1993] 1 Lloyd's Rep 41.
58 *The Deichland* [1990] 1 QB 361, [1989] 2 All ER 1066.
59 Case C-406/92 *Owners of the cargo lately laden on board the ship Tatry v Owners of the ship Maciej Rataj* [1994] ECR I-5439, [1995] All ER (EC) 229.

II BASES OF JURISDICTION IN PERSONAM

When considering the bases on which the court may exercise jurisdiction in personam it is important to distinguish those cases that are governed by the Brussels regime from those which fall within the scope of the traditional rules. Whether the case falls to be determined by the Brussels regime or the traditional rules, the territorial connections of the claimant – in terms of nationality, domicile or residence – are generally irrelevant when deciding whether or not the claim falls within the particular jurisdictional basis invoked by the claimant.[60]

A Bases of jurisdiction under the Brussels regime

Although the domicile of the defendant is the point on which the jurisdiction rules in Chapter II hinge, it is appropriate in cases falling within the material scope of the Brussels regime – as determined by article 1 – to start by considering those bases of jurisdiction which apply in relation to all defendants, regardless of their domicile.

1. General bases of jurisdiction which do not depend on the defendant being domiciled in a member state

Article 4 provides that, except in cases where articles 22 and 23[61] are effective to confer jurisdiction on the courts of a member state, where the defendant is not domiciled in a member state jurisdiction is to be determined by the traditional rules.[62]

(A) EXCLUSIVE JURISDICTION

Article 22 allocates exclusive jurisdiction, regardless of the defendant's domicile, in circumstances where the courts of a particular member state are thought to be uniquely appropriate to adjudicate upon the subject-matter of the dispute. The five paragraphs of article 22 concern: (1) certain proceedings relating to immovable property; (2) certain proceedings concerning the formation and dissolution of companies and the decisions of their organs; (3) certain proceedings

60 Other than in relation to a few specific provisions, the Brussels regime applies whether or not the claimant is domiciled in a member state: Case C-412/98 *Universal General Insurance Co (USIG) v Group Josi Reinsurance Co SA* [2000] ECR I-5925.

61 Formerly arts 16 and 17 of the Brussels Convention.

62 It is also established that arts 27 to 31 (formerly arts 21 to 24 of the Brussels Convention) apply regardless of domicile. These provisions are discussed at pp 111–119 and 138–141.

concerning entries in public registers; (4) certain proceedings concerning intellectual property rights; and (5) proceedings concerning the enforcement of judgments.

The jurisdiction rules in article 22 are mandatory and exclusive; they may not be departed from either by an agreement purporting to confer jurisdiction on the courts of another member state or by submission. If the claimant seeks to invoke the jurisdiction of the English court in a matter which, by virtue of the provisions of article 22, falls within the exclusive jurisdiction of the courts of another member state, the English court must of its own motion decline jurisdiction.[63] Of the various provisions of what is now article 22 only the first paragraph has been regularly referred to the Court of Justice and, accordingly, the discussion which follows is limited to that paragraph.[64]

The general rule contained in article 22(1) provides that the courts of the member state in which immovable property is situated have exclusive jurisdiction in proceedings which have as their object rights in rem in, or tenancies of, such property. So, if the immovable property is in England, the English court has jurisdiction irrespective of where the defendant is domiciled.[65] On the other hand, if the property is situated in another member state (or in another part of the United Kingdom), the English court may not exercise jurisdiction, even if the defendant is domiciled in England.[66]

Article 22(1) encompasses claims which seek to determine the extent, content, ownership or possession of immovable property or the existence of other rights in rem therein and to provide the holders of those rights with the protection of the powers which attach to their interest.[67] For example, if land is occupied by squatters a claim by the paper owner to evict the squatters and recover possession would clearly fall within the scope of article 22(1).

By contrast, neither a claim based on a contract for the transfer of ownership or other rights in rem affecting immovable property[68] nor a claim for rescission of a contract for the sale of land and consequential damages[69] is covered by the exclusive jurisdiction rules. Where a defendant occupies immovable property for nine years under a transfer

63 Art 25 (formerly art 19 of the Brussels Convention).
64 For consideration of the other paragraphs of what is now art 22, see Dicey and Morris, *The Conflict of Laws* (13th edn, 2000) pp 374–378.
65 Art 22(1) of the Brussels I Regulation allocates jurisdiction to the courts of the United Kingdom; rule 11(a) of Sch 4 to the Civil Jurisdiction and Judgments Act 1982 gives exclusive jurisdiction to the English court.
66 See, for example, *Re Hayward* [1997] Ch 45, [1997] 1 All ER 32.
67 Case 115/88 *Reichert v Dresdner Bank* [1990] ECR I-27 at 41–42 (para 11).
68 Schlosser Report, OJ 1979 C59/122, para 172.
69 Case C-518/99 *Gaillard v Chekili* [2001] IL Pr 474.

from the claimant which is subsequently declared by the courts to be void, a claim to recover compensation for use of the property during the nine-year period is not covered by article 22(1) and therefore is not within the exclusive jurisdiction of the courts of the member state in which the property is situated.[70] In addition, article 22(1) does not apply to a claim by a creditor to have a disposition of immovable property declared ineffective as against him on the ground that it was made in fraud of his rights by the debtor.[71] Similarly, English proceedings for a declaration that the defendant holds an apartment in the south of France on trust for the claimant and for an order that the defendant should execute such documents as are required to vest legal ownership in the claimant is not within the scope of article 22(1); as the claimant is not claiming that he already enjoys rights in relation to the property which are enforceable against the whole world, but is seeking only to assert rights as against the defendant, his claim is a claim in personam rather than a claim in rem within the meaning of article 22(1).[72] The application of this reasoning leads to the conclusion that the English court has jurisdiction to make an order for the sale of a villa situated in Portugal in a case where, following the bankruptcy of one of the owners, that person's trustee in bankruptcy applies for such an order.[73]

In *Rösler v Rottwinkel*[74] the Court of Justice ruled that proceedings which have as their object tenancies of immovable property (even a short holiday lease) include disputes as to the existence or interpretation of a lease, claims by the landlord for recovery of the premises, for rent and other charges, or for compensation for damage caused by the tenant. The Court of Justice has also held that what is now article 22(1) covers any proceedings which involve rights and obligations arising under a tenancy of immovable property (such as a claim for compensation against a tenant for causing damage to rented accommodation), whether or not the proceedings are based on a right in rem.[75] Article 22(1) does not to apply to a dispute arising from an agreement by which one party is to take over from the other a business carried on in immovable property which the latter leases from a third party.[76] Nor does it apply to disputes which are only indirectly related to the use of the property let, such as those concerning the loss of holiday enjoyment and travel expenses,[77] nor to holiday contracts which include not only

70 Case C-292/93 *Lieber v Göbel* [1994] ECR I-2535.
71 Case C-115/88 *Reichert v Dresdner Bank* [1990] ECR I-27.
72 Case C-294/92 *Webb v Webb* [1994] ECR I-1717 at 1738 (para 15). For a criticism of this decision see Briggs, (1994) 14 YBEL 557.
73 *Ashurst v Pollard* [2001] Ch 595, [2001] 2 All ER 75.
74 Case 241/83 [1986] QB 33, [1985] ECR 99.
75 Case C-8/98 *Dansommer A/S v Götz* [2000] ECR I-393.
76 Case 73/77 *Sanders v van der Putte* [1977] ECR 2383.
77 Case 241/83 *Rösler v Rottwinkel* [1986] QB 33, [1985] ECR 99.

accommodation, but also other services, such as information and advice, the reservation of transport, reception on arrival and insurance against cancellation.[78] It would also seem that, in principle, timeshare contracts should normally be regarded as consumer contracts within the scope of article 15, rather than article 22(1).[79] Proceedings relating to disputes which arise out of financing arrangements concerning leases covered by article 22(1) fall outside the scope of the exclusive jurisdiction provisions.[80]

The practical significance of *Rösler v Rottwinkel* with regard to short leases is limited by the fact that article 22(1) also provides that, in certain circumstances, the claimant may bring proceedings in the court of the member state in which the defendant is domiciled. Where proceedings involve a tenancy for temporary private use for a maximum period of six consecutive months, the courts of the member state in which the defendant is domiciled have jurisdiction, provided that the tenant is a natural person and that the landlord and the tenant are both domiciled in the same member state. It should be emphasised that the forum designated by the rule relating to short leases is an alternative to the courts of the member state in which the property is situated. If a cottage in England is let by its French owner to a French tenant for a period of three months, a dispute arising out of the tenancy may be litigated either in England or in France.

(B) PROROGATION OF JURISDICTION

As a general rule a person may confer jurisdiction on a court by consent. A party may consent to the jurisdiction of a court by a formal agreement concluded within the context of a wider contractual relationship (such as a jurisdiction clause in a printed contract) or by submitting to the jurisdiction of a court after the commencement of proceedings by the claimant. The Brussels regime refers to both of these situations as examples of 'prorogation of jurisdiction'; by the parties' agreement or submission the jurisdiction of the courts of a member state is thereby extended. Article 23,[81] which is concerned with the effects of jurisdiction agreements, potentially applies to all defendants;[82] article 24,[83] which enables the parties to confer jurisdiction

78 Case C-280/90 *Hacker v Euro-Relais GmbH* [1992] ECR I-1111.
79 See *Proposal*, COM (1999) 348, p 16. Cf *Jarrett v Barclays Bank plc* [1999] QB 1, [1997] 2 All ER 484.
80 *Jarrett v Barclays Bank plc* [1999] QB 1, [1997] 2 All ER 484.
81 Formerly art 17 of the Brussels Convention.
82 It should be noted that Chapter II also includes specific rules relating to jurisdiction agreements in insurance contracts, consumer contracts and individual contracts of employment. See pp 96–99.
83 Formerly art 18 of the Brussels Convention.

by submission and applies only to defendants domiciled in a member state, is considered in a later section.[84]

Under article 23(1), if the parties, one or more of whom is domiciled in a member state, have agreed that a court or the courts of a particular member state shall have jurisdiction, then such court or courts will have jurisdiction, provided that the agreement satisfies certain formal requirements. There is, however, no requirement that there should be any objective connection between the relationship in dispute and the designated court.[85] It should be stressed that this provision applies even if the defendant is not domiciled in a member state, so long as the claimant is; it has no application, however, to cases where the parties have chosen the courts of a non-member state.[86] Although a jurisdiction agreement will normally take the form of a provision in a contract, a clause conferring jurisdiction which appears in a company's articles of association is to be regarded as an agreement for the purposes of what is now article 23.[87] It is not necessary for the parties' agreement to identify directly the chosen court; a jurisdiction clause in a bill of lading which indirectly identifies the chosen courts (by referring disputes to the courts of the carrier's principal place of business) falls within article 23.[88]

Article 23(1) applies only if the jurisdiction agreement satisfies one of a range of alternative formal requirements.[89] To be effective a jurisdiction agreement must be (a) in writing or evidenced in writing;[90] or (b) in a form which accords with practices which the parties have established between themselves; or (c) in international trade or commerce in a form which accords with a usage of which the parties are or ought to have been aware and which in such trade or commerce is widely known to, and regularly observed by, parties to contracts of the type involved in the particular trade or commerce concerned. The purpose of these requirements is to ensure that there really is consensus between the parties.

As a general rule, a jurisdiction agreement is 'in writing' only if it is contained in a document that is signed by both parties.[91] Furthermore, where a clause conferring jurisdiction is included in general conditions

84 See pp 79–80.

85 Case C-159/97 *Trasporti Castelletti Spedizione Internazionali SpA v Hugo Trumpy SpA* [1999] ECR I-1597 at 1656 (para 50).

86 Case C-387/98 *Coreck Maritime GmbH v Handelsveem BV* [2000] ECR I-9337.

87 Case C-214/89 *Powell Duffryn plc v Petereit* [1992] ECR I-1745.

88 Case C-387/98 *Coreck Maritime GmbH v Handelsveem BV* [2000] ECR I-9337.

89 National courts cannot impose additional requirements, over and above those contained in art 23(1) itself: Case 150/80 *Elefanten Schuh v Jacqmain* [1981] ECR 1671; Case C-159/97 *Trasporti Castelletti Spedizione Internazionali SpA v Hugo Trumpy SpA* [1999] ECR I-1597.

90 Any communication by electronic means which provides a durable record of the agreement is treated as 'writing': art 23(2).

91 Case 71/83 *Partenreederei ms Tilly Russ v NV Haven & Vervoerbedrijf Nova* [1984] ECR 2417 at 2432 (para 16).

printed on the back of the contract, the agreement is not 'in writing' unless the contract signed by both parties contains an express reference to the general conditions.[92] Where, having reached an oral agreement on jurisdiction, one of the parties sends written confirmation of that agreement to the other and the latter raises no objection the agreement is to be regarded as 'evidenced in writing'.[93] Where, however, the parties conclude a contract orally without expressly agreeing on jurisdiction, if one party subsequently confirms the contract by sending to the other printed terms and conditions which contain a jurisdiction clause that clause is not 'in writing or evidenced in writing' unless the party receiving the written confirmation accepts the standard terms and conditions in writing.[94]

An agreement which is not 'in writing or evidenced in writing' may, nevertheless, be effective under paragraph (b) or (c) of article 23(1). Where, for example, the parties orally conclude a contract for the carriage of goods, which is subsequently confirmed in writing when the carrier issues a bill of lading (which includes a jurisdiction clause), the requirements of article 23(1)(b) are satisfied, notwithstanding the absence of express written agreement by the shipper, if the carrier and the shipper have a continuing business relationship which is governed as a whole by the carrier's general conditions which contain the jurisdiction clause.[95] Even in the absence of a continuing trading relationship such a jurisdiction clause may be effective if it conforms to trade usages. However, for the purposes of article 23(1)(c) it is not sufficient that, in international trade or commerce, a jurisdiction agreement is in a form which accords with practices in such trade or commerce of which the parties are or ought to have been aware; the usage must also be widely known in international trade or commerce and regularly observed by parties to contracts of the type involved in the particular trade or commerce concerned.[96] If the requirements of subparagraph (c) are satisfied, consensus between the contracting parties as to a jurisdiction clause is presumed to exist.[97]

92 Case 24/76 *Estasis Salotti di Colzani Aimo v RÜWA Polstereimaschinen GmbH* [1976] ECR 1831. See also *Crédit Suisse Financial Products v Société Générale d'Entreprises* [1997] IL Pr 165.

93 Case 221/84 *F Berghoefer GmbH & Co KG v ASA SA* [1985] ECR 2699.

94 Case 25/76 *Galeries Segoura SPRL v Bonakdarian* [1976] ECR 1851.

95 Case 71/83 *Partenreederei ms Tilly Russ v NV Haven & Vervoerbedrijf Nova* [1984] ECR 2417. Cf *Lafarge Plasterboard Ltd v Fritz Peters & Co KG* [2000] 2 Lloyd's Rep 689.

96 See Case C-159/97 *Trasporti Castelletti Spedizione Internazionali SpA v Hugo Trumpy SpA* [1999] ECR I-1597.

97 Case 106/95 *Mainschiffahrts-Genossenschaft eG (MSG) v Les Gravières Rhénanes Sarl* [1997] ECR I-911.

Article 23(1) provides that the jurisdiction which is derived from the parties' agreement 'shall be exclusive unless the parties have agreed otherwise'. In a simple case where contracting parties agree on French jurisdiction, the claimant cannot bring proceedings in England even if, in the absence of the agreement, the English court would have been competent on the basis of the defendant's domicile in England. However, where the parties have concluded a non-exclusive jurisdiction agreement the claimant has the option of relying either on the agreement or on other provisions of Chapter II. So, where two parties domiciled in Germany conclude a non-exclusive jurisdiction agreement in favour of the English courts either party may sue the other in England (on the basis of article 23) or in Germany (on the basis of article 2). Whether a jurisdiction agreement is exclusive or non-exclusive is a question of construction which, in principle, ought to be answered by reference to the law governing the agreement.[98]

There are a number of other points concerning article 23 which should be noted. First, the courts of a member state which have been designated in a jurisdiction clause validly concluded under article 23(1) also have exclusive jurisdiction where the proceedings are for a declaration that the contract containing the jurisdiction clause is void.[99] Secondly, article 23 yields both to article 22 and, as regards defendants domiciled in a member state, to article 24. So, if the dispute between the parties involves rights in rem relating to immovable property situated in France, the French courts have mandatory and exclusive jurisdiction, notwithstanding an agreement by the parties in favour of the courts of another member state.[100] Similarly, in a case where the parties have agreed on the jurisdiction of the Italian courts, if the claimant issues proceedings in England and the defendant acknowledges service of process, the English court has jurisdiction; the defendant's submission – which is in effect a waiver of the jurisdiction clause – supersedes the earlier contractual agreement.[101]

Thirdly, the parties may, by their agreement, confer jurisdiction on the courts of more than one member state. The parties may, for example, agree that if A sues B the German courts are to have jurisdiction, but that if B sues A the French courts are to have jurisdiction.[102]

98 For consideration of the position under English law (and the problems of interpretation to which the text of art 17 of the Brussels Convention, which differs from art 23 of the Regulation, gives rise) see Fawcett, 'Non-Exclusive Jurisdiction Agreements in Private International Law' [2001] LMCLQ 234.
99 Case C 269/95 *Benincasa v Dentalkit Srl* [1997] ECR I-3767.
100 Art 23(5).
101 Case 150/80 *Elefanten Schuh GmbH v Jacqmain* [1981] ECR 1671.
102 Case 23/78 *Meeth v Glacetal* [1978] ECR 2133.

Fourthly, even if neither party is domiciled in a member state a jurisdiction clause which satisfies the other requirements of article 23 is effective to prevent any member state court, other than the courts chosen by the parties, from exercising jurisdiction unless the chosen courts have declined jurisdiction.[103] So, where two parties, neither of whom is domiciled in a member state, agree to the jurisdiction of the Dutch courts, the English court may not exercise jurisdiction in accordance with the traditional rules unless the Dutch courts decline jurisdiction.

2. General bases of jurisdiction with regard to defendants domiciled in a member state

If jurisdiction is not allocated by the above provisions, which apply both to defendants who are domiciled in a member state and to defendants who are not so domiciled, the domicile of the defendant becomes of crucial importance. If the defendant is domiciled in a member state the court may exercise jurisdiction only by virtue of the provisions of Chapter II; if the defendant is not domiciled in a member state the traditional rules are applicable.

(A) SUBMISSION

Although the Regulation does not expressly state that article 24[104] applies only to defendants who are domiciled in a member state, this conclusion follows from article 4 which states that, if the defendant is not domiciled in a member state, the jurisdiction of the courts of each member state is, subject to articles 22 and 23 (but not article 24), to be determined by that state's traditional rules.[105] As far as English law is concerned, it makes little difference whether article 24 or the equivalent traditional rules apply since it is well established under the traditional rules that a defendant may confer jurisdiction on the English court by submission.[106]

Article 24 provides that the court of a member state has jurisdiction if the defendant enters an appearance in that court, unless the appearance was entered to contest the court's jurisdiction. By virtue of article 24 the court will have jurisdiction if the defendant empowers a solicitor in England to accept service on his behalf and the solicitor

103 Art 23(3).
104 Formerly art 18 of the Brussels Convention.
105 Under the Brussels Convention it was unclear whether or not what is now art 24 applied regardless of the defendant's domicile: see Advocate-General Darmon in Case C-318/93 *Brenner and Noller v Dean Witter Reynolds Inc* [1994] ECR I-4275 at 4280 (para 15).
106 See pp 102–103.

does so. If, however, the defendant appears, not to defend the claim on the merits, but merely to contend that the court has no jurisdiction, that is not a submission. The defendant's contention that the court does not have jurisdiction cannot confer jurisdiction.

For the purposes of article 24 a defendant should not be regarded as having submitted even if at the same time as contesting the court's jurisdiction he raises in the alternative a defence on the merits.[107] Article 24 cannot override the exclusive jurisdiction provisions of article 22. If the English court has jurisdiction in relation to a dispute concerning immovable property situated in England the defendant cannot confer jurisdiction on the French courts by submitting to proceedings commenced by the claimant in France. However, a submission by appearance in England is effective to confer jurisdiction on the English court even if the parties had agreed, prior to the dispute, that the courts of another member state were to have jurisdiction.[108]

(B) DEFENDANT DOMICILED IN ENGLAND

Under article 2 a person domiciled in a member state may be sued in the courts of that state. Where a defendant is domiciled in England article 2 of the Regulation provides that the claimant may bring proceedings in the courts of the United Kingdom. The Civil Jurisdiction and Judgments Act 1982, through rule 1 of Schedule 4, allocates jurisdiction to England – the part of the United Kingdom in which the defendant is domiciled. The relevant time at which the defendant's domicile in England must be established is when the claim form is issued, rather than when it is served.[109] This ground of jurisdiction is applicable even if neither the claimant nor the dispute has a connection with any member state.[110]

(C) 'SPECIAL JURISDICTION': ALTERNATIVES TO THE DOMICILE RULE

The basic rule that a defendant shall be sued in the member state in which he is domiciled must be considered in conjunction with the 'special jurisdiction' provisions of Chapter II – notably, articles 5 and 6[111] – according to which a person domiciled in a member state may be sued in an alternative member state.

107 Case 150/80 *Elefanten Schuh GmbH v Jacqmain* [1981] ECR 1671.

108 Idem.

109 *Canada Trust Co v Stolzenberg (No 2)* [2002] 1 AC 1; *Petrotrade Inc v Smith* [1999] 1 WLR 457. This rule is supported by art 30 of the Brussels I Regulation, under which English proceedings will normally be deemed to be definitively pending when the claim form is issued: see p 113.

110 Whether the English court may stay the proceedings in such circumstances on the basis of forum non conveniens is discussed at pp 131–134.

111 Art 7, the third article which confers 'special jurisdiction', concerns claims relating to the limitation of liability for the use or operation of a ship.

Jurisdiction under article 5 is premised on the existence of a close connection between the cause of action and the forum (unlike article 2 which is based on the defendant's connections with the forum). Article 5 contains seven paragraphs of which the most important are paragraph (1), which concerns 'matters relating to a contract', and paragraph (3), which allocates jurisdiction in 'matters relating to tort, delict or quasi-delict'. Paragraph (5) is concerned with disputes 'arising out of the operations of a branch, agency or other establishment'.[112] Article 6, which deals with cases involving multiple defendants, is based on the simple idea that it is often convenient for related proceedings involving two or more defendants to be heard by the same court. The bases of jurisdiction in articles 5 and 6 are derogations from the general principle contained in article 2 and the Court of Justice has indicated that these derogations should be interpreted restrictively.[113]

Articles 5 and 6 are similar to CPR 6.20 in inspiration. Their operation is, however, very different. In cases where the claimant relies on any of the jurisdiction rules contained in Chapter II, process can be served on the defendant without the court's permission;[114] the claimant does not have to demonstrate that the forum in which the proceedings are commenced is the most appropriate one. In a situation where the courts of a member state in which the defendant is not domiciled have special jurisdiction the claimant may bring proceedings in the member state in which the defendant is domiciled, on the basis of article 2, or sue the defendant in the alternative forum which has special jurisdiction (under article 5 or article 6). The choice is entirely for the claimant; there is no mechanism whereby the defendant can require the claimant to opt for one jurisdiction rather than another.

(i) Matters relating to contract and tort: introduction

Article 5 draws a distinction between 'matters relating to a contract' (article 5(1)) and 'matters relating to tort, delict or quasi-delict' (article 5(3)). The Court of Justice has ruled that for the purposes of article 5 'contract' and 'tort' are autonomous concepts which must be interpreted by reference principally to the system and objectives of the

112 The other paragraphs of art 5 deal with the following matters: (2) 'matters relating to maintenance'; (4) 'a civil claim for damages or restitution which is based on an act giving rise to criminal proceedings'; (6) certain proceedings relating to trusts; (7) 'a dispute concerning the payment of remuneration claimed in respect of the salvage of a cargo or freight'.

113 Case 189/87 *Kalfelis v Bankhaus Schröder, Münchmeyer, Hengst & Co* [1988] ECR 5565.

114 CPR 6.19 (replacing RSC Ord 11, r 1(2)).

Brussels regime, rather than in accordance with the law of the forum.[115] This means that a situation which according to English law would not be regarded as tortious may have to be classified as such for jurisdictional purposes. For example, it has been held that, in the context of a case involving a breach of trust, a constructive trust claim based upon dishonest assistance is within the scope of article 5(3).[116]

Paragraphs (1) and (3) are mutually exclusive.[117] If the proceedings concern 'matters relating to a contract' the claimant cannot, in reliance on English law, invoke the English court's jurisdiction under article 5(3) by framing the claim in tort rather than contract. Equally, if the proceedings concern 'matters relating to tort, delict or quasi-delict' the French courts may not exercise jurisdiction under article 5(1) on the basis that the claim is contractual according to French law.[118] Where a claimant has a claim against a defendant part of which is based in tort and another part of which is based in contract a court which has jurisdiction under article 5(3) over the claim in so far as it is based on tort does not have jurisdiction over that claim in so far as it is not so based.[119]

There is some controversy over whether paragraphs (1) and (3) necessarily encompass claims which are restitutionary, rather than contractual or tortious. The Court of Justice, in the course of its judgment in *Kalfelis v Bankhaus Schröder, Münchmeyer, Hengst & Co*, stated that article 5(3) must be regarded as covering 'all actions which seek to establish the liability of a defendant and which are not related to a "contract" within the meaning of article 5(1)'.[120] Although this statement would appear to endorse the view that paragraphs (1) and (3), taken together, cover all situations in which the claimant seeks to establish the civil liability of the defendant, the judgment as a whole seems to accept the possibility of a situation in which an obligation is excluded from the scope of paragraph (3) (because it is not tortious) and is not within paragraph (1) (because it is not contractual either).

115 Case 9/87 *SPRL Arcado v SA Haviland* [1988] ECR 1539; Case 189/87 *Kalfelis v Bankhaus Schröder, Münchmeyer, Hengst & Co* [1988] ECR 5565.

116 *Casio Computer Co Ltd v Sayo* [2001] EWCA Civ 661, [2001] IL Pr 694; *Dexter Ltd v Harley* (2001) Times, 2 April.

117 Case 189/87 *Kalfelis v Bankhaus Schröder, Münchmeyer, Hengst & Co* [1988] ECR 5565.

118 Case C–26/91 *Jakob Handte & Co GmbH v Traitements Mécano-chimiques des Surfaces SA* [1992] ECR I-3967.

119 Case 189/87 *Kalfelis v Bankhaus Schröder, Münchmeyer, Hengst & Co* [1988] ECR 5565.

120 [1988] ECR 5565 at 5585 (para 17). See also Case C-51/97 *Réunion Européenne SA v Splietoff's Bevachtingskantoor BV* [1998] ECR I-6511 at 6543 (para 22).

In the context of Schedule 4 to the Civil Jurisdiction and Judgments Act 1982 it has been decided in Scotland that proceedings which raise questions of the defendant's liability may fall outside both article 5(1) and article 5(3) – on the basis that they concern neither matters relating to a contract nor matters relating to tort, delict or quasi-delict.[121] Similarly, in *Kleinwort Benson Ltd v Glasgow City Council*[122] the House of Lords held that a claim for restitution of moneys paid under a purported contract which was void fell neither within article 5(1) nor within article 5(3). In policy terms, there is no compelling reason why claims based on unjust enrichment should fit somewhere within article 5: 'If a claim cannot be brought within article 5, it can always be pursued in the courts of the defendant's domicile.'[123]

(ii) Jurisdiction in matters relating to a contract[124]

Article 5(1)(a) provides that in matters relating to a contract a person who is domiciled in a member state may be sued in another member state if that is the place of performance of the obligation in question. This general principle is fleshed out by subparagraph (b), which indicates how the place of performance is to be determined in certain types of case. There are two questions which need to be considered.

First, what are matters relating to a contract? The Court of Justice has expressed the view that article 5(1) 'is not to be understood as covering a situation in which there is no obligation freely assumed by one party towards another'.[125] So, where a manufacturer sells defective goods to a wholesaler, who sells them to a retailer, the retailer's claim against the manufacturer is to be classified, for jurisdictional purposes, as tortious, even if the claim is regarded as contractual under the law of the forum. In *Source Ltd v TUV Rheinland Holding AG*[126] the Court of Appeal held that where the alleged facts give rise to parallel claims in contract and tort (for negligence), article 5(1) covers the tortious claim as well as the contractual one. However, in a different context, the House of Lords emphasised that article 5(1) allocates jurisdiction by reference to the place of performance of a *contractual* obligation[127]

121 See *Davenport v Corinthian Motor Policies at Lloyd's* 1991 SLT 774.
122 [1999] 1 AC 153.
123 Millett LJ in *Kleinwort Benson Ltd v Glasgow City Council* [1996] QB 678 at 698.
124 For consideration of the rules that apply to matters relating to insurance, consumer contracts and individual contracts of employment see pp 96–99.
125 Case C-26/91 *Jakob Handte & Co GmbH v Traitements Mécano-chimiques des Surfaces SA* [1992] ECR I-3967 at 3994 (para 15) (discussed by Hartley, (1993) 18 ELRev 506). See also Case C-51/97 *Réunion Européenne SA v Spliethoff's Bevachtingskantoor BV* [1998] ECR I-6511.
126 [1998] QB 54.
127 *Kleinwort Benson Ltd v Glasgow City Council* [1999] 1 AC 153.

and, on the basis of this decision, the correctness of the decision in the *Source* case has been questioned.[128]

Article 5(1) is not rendered inapplicable merely by the fact that the defendant denies the existence of the contract on which the claim is based.[129] It has been held in England that article 5(1) is applicable even in a case where it is the claimant who asserts that no contract exists between the parties. In *Boss Group Ltd v Boss France SA*[130] the French defendants had alleged that the English plaintiffs were in breach of the terms of an exclusive distribution agreement. The plaintiffs applied for a declaration from the English court that there was no contract between the parties and sought to establish that the case concerned a matter relating to a contract for the purposes of article 5(1) by relying on the defendants' contentions against them. The Court of Appeal held that the case fell within the scope of article 5(1); the defendants could not contend both that the plaintiffs were in breach of contract and that article 5(1) was inapplicable because there was no contract between the parties. However, the decision has been doubted by commentators[131] and is not easy to reconcile with the jurisprudence of the Court of Justice, according to which the basis of proceedings under article 5(1) is an obligation which has allegedly been broken by the defendant.[132]

In *Agnew v Lansförsäkringsbølagens AB*[133] it was held that article 5(1) extends to certain pre-contractual obligations. The plaintiff sought to avoid a contract of reinsurance on the ground that the defendant had failed to comply with the duty to make fair presentation of the risk. The House of Lords, by a majority, held that the proceedings involved 'matters relating to a contract' for the purposes of article 5(1) of the Lugano Convention, notwithstanding the fact that, as a matter of English law, the defendant's obligation arose extra-contractually.

The extent to which article 5(1) extends to restitutionary obligations is not entirely free from doubt. Although in *Kleinwort Benson Ltd v Glasgow City Council*[134] the House of Lords accepted the proposition that normally restitutionary claims fall outside the scope of article 5(1), Lord Goff suggested that certain types of proceedings, which would be regarded as restitutionary in nature according to English law (such as

128 *Raiffeisen Zentralbank Osterreich Aktiengesellschaft v National Bank of Greece SA* [1999] 1 Lloyd's Rep 408.
129 Case 38/81 *Effer SpA v Kantner* [1982] ECR 825.
130 [1996] 4 All ER 970.
131 Dicey and Morris, *The Conflict of Laws* (13th edn, 2000) p 346.
132 The authority of the *Boss* case is also weakened by the decision of the House of Lords in *Kleinwort Benson Ltd v Glasgow City Council* [1999] 1 AC 153. See, however, *USF Ltd v Aqua Technology Hanson NV/SA* [2001] 1 All ER (Comm) 856.
133 [2001] 1 AC 223.
134 [1999] 1 AC 153.

a claim to recover, on the ground of failure of consideration, money paid under a valid contract), might come within article 5(1).[135]

There is a degree of tension between the decisions in the *Agnew* and *Kleinwort Benson* cases. Whereas in *Kleinwort Benson* one of the reasons for holding that restitutionary claims normally fall outside article 5(1) was that, in such cases, there is no contractual obligation (breached by the defendant) which can serve as the basis of the claim, in the *Agnew* case it was held that a pre-contractual obligation imposed by the general law may qualify as the 'obligation in question' for the purposes of article 5(1). The solution to this tension may be to confine the decision in the *Kleinwort Benson* case to situations in which the invalidity of the contract is not in dispute.[136]

Secondly, how is the place of performance of the obligation in question to be identified? Under the version of article 5(1) introduced by the Regulation two different types of situation need to be distinguished.

In the commercial context, a significant number of contractual disputes arise out of contracts for the sale of goods and contracts for the provision of services. Jurisdiction in these cases falls to be determined primarily by article 5(1)(b). As regards contracts not falling within these categories,[137] article 5(1)(a) applies; under this provision jurisdiction turns on, first, designation of the obligation in question and, secondly, identification of the place of performance of that obligation.[138]

For the purposes of article 5(1)(a), the relevant obligation is, as a general rule, the obligation (allegedly breached by the defendant) on which the claim is based.[139] So, where A contracts with B to exchange a ton of potatoes for a ton of carrots, if A sues for B's failure to deliver the carrots, the obligation in question is B's obligation to deliver, even if B's non-performance is a response to the fact that the potatoes

135 At 171.

136 Somewhat exceptionally, prior to the commencement of the *Kleinwort Benson* litigation, it had already been established, in related proceedings raising identical issues, that the contract in question was void ab initio (because it was ultra vires the local authority): *Hazell v Hammersmith and Fulham London Borough Council* [1992] 2 AC 1, [1991] 1 All ER 545.

137 Other than insurance contracts, consumer contracts and employment contracts, which are covered by specific provisions, rather than by article 5(1). See pp 96–99.

138 In relation to intra-United Kingdom cases, rule 3(a) of Sch 4 to the Civil Jurisdiction and Judgments Act 1982 contains no counterpart to art 5(1)(b) and (c).

139 Case 14/76 *Ets A de Bloos SPRL v Société en commandite par actions Bouyer* [1976] ECR 1497. This ruling has been confirmed in subsequent cases such as Case C-288/92 *Custom Made Commercial Ltd v Stawa Metallbau GmbH* [1994] ECR I-2913.

delivered by A are not of satisfactory quality. In the context of a contract under which A hires a car from B, if B sues A for the unpaid hire, the obligation in question is A's obligation to pay the hire charge. Where the claim is based on more than one obligation the court should be guided by the maxim 'accessorium sequitur principale'; jurisdiction under article 5(1)(a) should be determined by the principal obligation.[140] Where, for example, the claimant wishes to sue the defendant on the basis not only of the latter's failure to perform the principal obligation in England but also of a failure to perform an accessory obligation abroad, article 5(1)(a) allocates jurisdiction to the English court with regard to the entire claim. For example, in *Union Transport plc v Continental Lines SA*[141] the plaintiff brought proceedings in England against a Belgian company for failure, under the terms of a tbn[142] charterparty agreement, to nominate and provide a vessel to carry a cargo of telegraph poles from Florida to Bangladesh. Although Florida was the place of performance of the obligation to provide the vessel, the House of Lords held that the English court had jurisdiction over the entire claim under article 5(1) on the basis that the principal obligation was the obligation to nominate a vessel and that nomination should have been made in England.[143]

Where the defendant is in breach of two independent obligations of equal significance – rather than a principal obligation to which another is accessory – jurisdiction with regard to each obligation must be determined by the general rule.[144] This means that where two independent obligations are to be performed in two different member states, there is a danger that there will be a fragmentation of related proceedings. It must be remembered, however, that special jurisdiction under article 5 is an alternative to the general jurisdiction which is conferred by article 2; the claimant has the option of relying on article 2 and litigating the entire claim in the courts of the member state in which the defendant is domiciled.

If the parties agree in their contract on the place of performance of the obligation on which the claim is based, article 5(1)(a) normally allocates jurisdiction to the courts for that place.[145] If, however, the agreed place of performance is fictitious (or abstract) – in the sense that it has no actual

140 Case 266/85 *Shenavai v Kreischer* [1987] ECR 239.
141 [1992] 1 All ER 161, [1992] 1 WLR 15.
142 To be nominated.
143 See also *AIG Europe (UK) Ltd v The Ethniki* [2000] 2 All ER 566; *Barry v Bradshaw* [2000] CLC 455; *MBM Fabri-Clad Ltd v Eisen-und Huttenwerke Thale AG* [2000] IL Pr 505.
144 Case C-420/97 *Leathertex Divisione Sintetici SpA v Bodotex BVBA* [1999] ECR I-6747.
145 Case 56/79 *Zelger v Salinitri* [1980] ECR 89.

connection with the subject-matter of the contract – and is designed solely to establish jurisdiction (rather than to determine the real place of performance), the agreement is not effective to confer jurisdiction on the courts for that place unless it satisfies the requirements as to form laid down in article 23.[146] In the absence of such agreement, the court whose jurisdiction is invoked must fix the place of performance by applying the law which, according to its own choice of law rules, governs the contract.[147] So, if the claimant seeks to proceed in England under article 5(1)(a), the court must decide, by reference to English choice of law rules, which law is applicable to the contract and determine the place of performance of the obligation in question in accordance with that law.

The potential scope of the general principle in article 5(1)(a) is significantly curtailed by article 5(1)(b), which expressly identifies the place of performance in relation to contracts for the sale of goods and contracts for the provision of services. As regards these contracts, the Regulation adopts the 'characteristic obligation' theory – that is to say jurisdiction is determined by reference to the place of performance of the obligation which determines the nature of the contract, namely the seller's obligation to deliver the goods (in a contract for the sale of goods) and the obligation to provide the services (in a contract for the provision of services).[148] So, where the proceedings relate to a contract for the sale of goods, the place of performance of the obligation in question is, unless otherwise agreed, the place in a member state where, under the contract, the goods were delivered or should have been delivered; where the proceedings relate to a contract for the provision of services, the place of performance is, unless otherwise agreed, the place in a member state where the services were or should have been provided. Article 5(1)(b) does not expressly indicate the solution if, under the contract, goods are to be delivered to (or services provided in) more than one place. The jurisprudence spawned by the original version of article 5(1) suggests that the English court has jurisdiction under article 5(1)(b) only in relation to disputes arising out of goods which were (or should have been) delivered in England, even if similar goods were (or should have been) delivered in another place and the same legal issues arise in relation to both deliveries.[149] Although the effect of article 5(1)(b) may be to fragment proceedings which involve identical issues, the claimant can always avoid such

146 Case C-106/95 *Mainschiffahrts-Genossenschaft eG (MSG) v Les Gravières Rhénanes Sarl* [1997] ECR I-911.

147 Case 12/76 *Industrie Tessili Italiana Como v Dunlop AG* [1976] ECR 1473; Case C-440/97 *GIE Groupe Concorde v Master of the Vessel Suhadiwarno Panjan* [1999] ECR I-6307.

148 For further consideration of the characteristic obligation (which is also relevant in the choice of law context) see pp 215–217.

149 See *Viskase Ltd v Paul Kiefel GmbH* [1999] 3 All ER 362, [1999] 1 WLR 1305.

fragmentation by relying on article 2 and suing in the member state in which the defendant is domiciled.

The purpose of article 5(1) is to allocate jurisdiction by reference to a connecting factor which identifies a place which has a close connection with the dispute.[150] Where, for example, an Irish company agrees to provide services in England for a Belgian client, in the event of the client's failure to pay for the services (for example, because the standard of the service is unsatisfactory), the English court may exercise jurisdiction in relation to the Irish company's claim for payment. In these circumstances, it is the claimant's obligation to provide the services (not the defendant's obligation to pay for them) which localises the contract and determines jurisdiction for the purposes of article 5(1)(b). To this extent, the Regulation is an improvement upon the much-criticised article 5(1) of the Brussels Convention[151] (as interpreted by the Court of Justice) which adopted the 'specific obligation' theory – according to which jurisdiction in contractual matters is determined by reference to the specific obligation (of the defendant) on which the claim is based. In proceedings relating to a dispute arising out of a contract for the sale of goods, the place of performance of the seller's obligation to deliver the goods is more likely to be the factual centre of gravity of the dispute than the specific obligation on which the claim is based. Where, for example, defective goods are delivered to D in Germany and D refuses to pay for them, the dispute underlying C's claim for recovery of the price will normally have a closer connection with the place of delivery than the place of payment. However, it should not be assumed that the Regulation will always allocate jurisdiction in contractual matters to a closely connected forum – for three reasons.

First, article 5(1)(b) applies not only to cases of defective performance (in which the place of performance will normally have a close connection with the subject-matter of the dispute – at least in cases involving a contract for services) but also to cases of non-performance (in which it is less certain that the intended place of performance will have a close factual connection with the dispute).

Secondly, as regards contracts for the sale of goods, the place designated by article 5(1)(b) is where, *under the contract*, the goods were (or should have been) delivered; it by no means follows that the contractual place of delivery is the place where the goods are actually delivered.[152]

150 Jenard Report, OJ 1979 C59/22.

151 See Hill, 'Jurisdiction in Matters Relating to a Contract under the Brussels Convention' (1995) 44 ICLQ 591; Kennett, 'Place of Performance and Predictability' (1995) 15 YBEL 193.

152 See Case C-288/92 *Custom Made Commercial Ltd v Stawa Metallbau GmbH* [1994] ECR I- 2913; *Viskase Ltd v Paul Kiefel GmbH* [1999] 1 WLR 1305.

Thirdly, article 5(1)(b) applies only where the place of delivery (or of the provision of services) is in a member state. If article 5(1)(b) does not apply, article 5(1)(a) applies.[153] Consider, for example, a case in which C, an English seller, contracts with D, a German buyer, to deliver goods to premises in New York. If D fails to pay for the goods, can C sue D in England? As article 5(1)(b) does not apply (because the agreed place of delivery is not in a member state), C is able to rely on article 5(1)(a). Under article 5(1)(a) the obligation in question is D's obligation to pay and, if the contract is governed by English law (which is very likely[154]), the place of performance is England (since under English law, as a general rule, the debtor must seek out the creditor at his place of business and pay him there[155]).

(iii) Jurisdiction in matters relating to tort

Article 5(3) provides that in matters relating to tort a person who is domiciled in a member state may be sued in another member state in the courts for the place where the harmful event occurred or may occur. Where all the elements constituting the tort occur in the same member state (where, for example, the claimant is injured in a road accident caused by the defendant's negligent driving) the application of article 5(3) is generally unproblematic.

The position is slightly more difficult in a situation where the defendant's wrongful act is committed in one place and the claimant is injured in another. In *Bier v Mines de Potasse d'Alsace*[156] it was alleged that the defendant, a French mining company, had discharged harmful chemicals into the Rhine in France as a result of which the plaintiff, a nursery gardener in the Netherlands, who used polluted water from the Rhine, suffered damage to his property. The question was whether the plaintiff was permitted, in reliance on article 5(3), to sue the defendant in the Netherlands. The Court of Justice ruled that the harmful event occurs either at the place where the damage occurs or at the place of the event giving rise to it. Article 5(3) gives the claimant the option of suing at either place. At first glance, the interpretation favoured by the Court of Justice seems to allow the claimant an excessively wide choice. However, as the Court of Justice pointed out in its judgment, 'the place of the event giving rise to the damage no less than the place where damage occurred can, depending on the case, constitute a significant connecting factor from the point of view of

153 Art 5(1)(c).
154 See p 216.
155 *Robey & Co v Snaefell Mining Co Ltd* (1887) 20 QBD 152; *Rein v Stein* [1892] 1 QB 753.
156 Case 21/76 *Handelskwekerij GJ Bier BV v Mines de Potasse d'Alsace SA* [1976] ECR 1735.

jurisdiction'.[157] Furthermore, in most cases involving a transnational tort, the place of the event giving rise to the damage is likely to coincide with the defendant's domicile.

The application of the ruling in *Bier v Mines de Potasse d'Alsace* to the case of a libel by a newspaper article distributed in several member states gives the claimant a wide choice of jurisdictions in which to sue.[158] The claimant may bring proceedings in the place where the publisher is established because that is the place of the event giving rise to the damage. If successful, the claimant will recover damages for all the loss he has suffered. Alternatively, the claimant may sue in any of the places where the publication is distributed, because that is where the damage occurs. However, in such a case, the claimant may recover damages only for the loss of reputation suffered in the particular member state in which the publication is distributed. Suppose a publishing company which is domiciled in Belgium produces a newspaper which is distributed in France and England. A person who is defamed by the publication may sue the publisher in England for the damage to his reputation in England and may sue the publisher in France for the damage to his reputation in France. The potential disadvantage of having different courts ruling on various aspects of the same dispute can be avoided if the claimant litigates his entire claim in Belgium, the place where the publisher is established.

The Court of Justice has been called upon to give further guidance on the significance of the phrase 'the place where the damage occurs'. It is important, particularly where economic loss is involved, not to confuse the place where the injury is suffered with the place where the harm is inflicted. Although the ruling of the Court of Justice in *Bier v Mines de Potasse d'Alsace* allows the claimant to sue in the place where the damage occurs, article 5(3) cannot be construed to confer jurisdiction on the courts for the place where the claimant feels the adverse consequences of an event that has already caused actual damage elsewhere.[159] Where, for example, a French company suffers loss when its German subsidiaries become insolvent as a result of the negligent advice of the defendant, a German bank, the French courts do not have jurisdiction under article 5(3); Germany, which is the place where the event giving rise to the damage directly produces its harmful effects upon the immediate victims, is also the place where

157 At 1746 (para 15).

158 Case C-68/93 *Shevill v Presse Alliance SA* [1995] 2 AC 18, [1995] ECR I-415.

159 Case C-51/97 *Réunion Européenne SA v Spliethoff's Bevachtingskantoor BV* [1998] ECR I-6511 at 6545 (para 30). See Takahashi, 'Jurisdiction over Direct Action against Sub-Carrier under the Brussels Convention' [2001] LMCLQ 107.

the damage occurs, even though it is in France that the claimant suffers injury.[160] Similarly, where an Italian claimant suffers financial loss in Italy consequential upon initial damage arising from the defendant's refusal to return promissory notes which the claimant has deposited in England, article 5(3) does not confer jurisdiction on the Italian courts; England is the place where the damage occurs, notwithstanding the fact that Italy is the place where the loss is suffered.[161] The distinction between the place where the damage occurs and the place where the loss is suffered may also be relevant in cases not involving pure economic loss. For example, in a case where the claimant is injured in a road accident in France, the English courts do not have jurisdiction under article 5(3) even if the claimant can establish that he suffered an aggravation of his injuries in England and even if the worsening of his condition constitutes a fresh cause of action under French law; in these circumstances, the deterioration which occurs in England is a consequence of the original harmful event in France, rather than a new harmful event occurring in England.[162] Similarly, where goods are transported in sealed containers, if the owner of the goods, in reliance on article 5(3), brings a claim in tort against the carrier of the goods, the place where the harmful event occurred is the place where the carrier was to deliver the goods, rather than the place where the owner actually discovers that the goods are damaged.[163] Of course, in this type of case it is normally impossible to determine exactly where the goods were damaged. If, however, the place where the damage was discovered were treated as the relevant place for the purposes of article 5(3), it would mean that, in any case where the ultimate place of delivery is the claimant's place of business, the claimant would be able to bring proceedings in his home forum.

There are also questions surrounding the notion of 'the place of the event' giving rise to the damage, although these problems have not yet been addressed by the Court of Justice. The most recent English authorities indicate that, in a case involving a fraudulent or negligent misrepresentation contained in (say) a letter posted in France to a recipient in England, the place of the event giving rise to the damage occurs in France (where the misstatement originates) rather than in

160 Case 220/88 *Dumez France SA v Hessische Landesbank* [1990] ECR 49. See also *Modus Vivendi Ltd v British Products Sanmex Ltd* [1996] FSR 790.

161 Case C-364/93 *Marinari v Lloyd's Bank plc* [1995] ECR I-2719, [1996] All ER (EC) 84.

162 *Henderson v Jaouen* [2002] EWCA Civ 75, [2002] 2 All ER 705.

163 Case C-51/97 *Réunion Européenne SA v Spliethoff's Bevachtingskantoor BV* [1998] ECR I-6511.

England (where the misstatement is received).[164] What are the implications of this decision for a case where, for example, the defendant, having manufactured a machine in Germany, puts it on the market in England with no warning as to its defects and the claimant is injured by the machine in Ireland? There is an argument for saying that the claimant should be able to proceed against the defendant in England on the basis that England is the place of the event giving rise to the damage (although Ireland would be the place of the damage).[165]

A question may arise as to which law determines whether or not a particular event is to be regarded as 'harmful' for the purposes of article 5(3). In *Shevill v Presse Alliance SA*[166] the defendant argued that the plaintiff could not invoke the jurisdiction of the English court in a libel case because the plaintiff had sought to rely solely on the presumption of harm and therefore had failed to establish that a harmful event had occurred. The House of Lords rejected this argument. On the basis of the Court of Justice's opinion that 'the criteria for assessing whether the event in question is harmful ... are ... governed by ... the substantive law determined by the national conflict of laws rules of the court seised',[167] it was held that it was purely a question of English law whether the publication was a harmful event. So, where English law presumes that the publication of a defamatory statement is harmful that is sufficient for the application of article 5(3).

Finally, article 5(3) applies to cases of threatened wrongs as well as committed wrongs, thereby providing a clear ground of jurisdiction for preventive measures. Where, for example, a claimant seeks an injunction to prevent the publication of defamatory material, article 5(3) confers jurisdiction on the court for the place where the harm would occur if the publication were not prevented.

(iv) Branch, agency or other establishment

Under article 5(5) a defendant domiciled in a member state may, as regards a dispute arising out of the operations of a branch, agency or other establishment, be sued in another member state in the courts for the place in which the branch, agency or other establishment is

164 *Domicrest Ltd v Swiss Bank Corpn* [1999] QB 548; *Alfred Dunhill Ltd v Diffusion Internationale de Maroquinerie de Prestige SARL* [2001] CLC 949. Cf *Minster Investments Ltd v Hyundai Precision & Industry Co Ltd* [1988] 2 Lloyd's Rep 621. In this type of case, the place of the damage will often be where the communication is received and relied upon by the claimant. See, however, *Alfred Dunhill Ltd v Diffusion Internationale de Maroquinerie de Prestige SARL* [2001] CLC 949.

165 See *Castree v E R Squibb & Sons* [1980] 2 All ER 589, [1980] 1 WLR 1248 (a case decided under RSC Ord 11, r 1(1)).

166 [1996] AC 959, [1996] 3 All ER 929.

167 Case C-68/93 *Shevill v Presse Alliance SA* [1995] ECR I-415 at 464 (para 41).

situated. So, a natural or legal person domiciled in France can be sued in England if it has a branch in England, provided that the dispute arises out of the branch's operations.[168]

The words 'agency or other establishment' add little to 'branch', which normally displays the following characteristics: it is subject to the direction and control of the parent body; it has a place of business which has the appearance of permanency; it is able to transact business with third parties.[169] These characteristics seem not, however, to be of universal application. The Court of Justice has ruled that, for the purposes of article 5(5), a parent company may be regarded as a branch of one of its subsidiary companies – notwithstanding the fact that, from the point of view of company law, the two companies are independent of each other – if it appears to third parties that the parent is acting on behalf of the subsidiary.[170]

Although the matter is not free from doubt, it would seem that article 5(5) exists solely to enable a third party who deals with the parent through a branch or agent to sue the parent at the place where the branch or agent is established.[171] There is no reason why, in a dispute between the parent and an agent, the agent should be able to rely on article 5(5) to sue the parent in the place where the agency is situated.

The rationale of article 5(5) is the presumed existence of a close connection between the dispute and the country in which the branch is located. However, if its conditions are satisfied, article 5(5) is effective to confer jurisdiction on the courts for the place where the branch is situated, whether or not the dispute is connected in a meaningful way with that place. Where, for example, an English company undertakes (through its French branch) to perform services in Spain (through its Spanish branch) the French courts have jurisdiction under article 5(5) in relation to the claim for damages based on the defendant's defective performance of the services in Spain.[172]

(v) Multiple parties

Where a dispute involves more than two parties it is often just and convenient for all the claims and the defences to them to be decided

168 For the meaning of 'operations' see Case 33/78 *Somafer SA v Saar-Ferngas AG* [1978] ECR 2183.

169 Case 14/76 *Ets A de Bloos SPRL v Société en commandite par actions Bouyer* [1976] ECR 1497; Case 33/78 *Somafer SA v Saar-Ferngas AG* [1978] ECR 2183; Case 139/80 *Blanckaert and Willems PVBA v Trost* [1981] ECR 819.

170 Case 218/86 *SAR Schotte GmbH v Parfums Rothschild SARL* [1987] ECR 4905.

171 See the opinion of Advocate-General Reishl in Case 14/76 *Ets A de Bloos SPRL v Société en commandite par actions Bouyer* [1976] ECR 1497 at 1519.

172 Case C-439/93 *Lloyd's Register of Shipping v Société Campenon Bernard* [1995] ECR I-961, [1995] All ER (EC) 531.

at the same time by the same court. Article 6 seeks to mitigate the effects of those provisions of Chapter II which would tend towards the fragmentation of the various disputes which may arise out of a single set of facts. Nevertheless, article 6 cannot be used to undermine the effectiveness of exclusive jurisdiction agreements under article 23. In a case where the court has jurisdiction over D1 (under article 2) and prima facie jurisdiction over D2 (under article 6), jurisdiction over D2 cannot be exercised if that would conflict with a jurisdiction agreement (either between the claimant and D2 or between D1 and D2).[173] There are three paragraphs of article 6 to be considered.[174]

First, article 6(1) deals with the situation where the claimant wishes to sue two (or more) defendants in the same proceedings – for example, because they are each liable to him or they are liable in the alternative. Under article 6(1) each of a number of defendants domiciled in different member states may be sued in the courts for the place where any one of them is domiciled. Where, for example, there are two joint debtors – one domiciled in England, the other domiciled in France – the claimant may sue both in either country. Where, however, proceedings are brought against a defendant who is not domiciled in a member state, a second defendant who is domiciled in a member state cannot be joined to those proceedings under article 6(1).[175]

Article 6(1) provides that jurisdiction can be exercised over co-defendants who are domiciled in other member states only if the claims are so closely connected that it is expedient to hear and determine them together to avoid the risk of irreconcilable judgments resulting from separate proceedings.[176] According to the Court of Justice, the conditions of article 6(1) are not satisfied in a case involving two claims directed against different defendants and based in one instance on contractual liability and in the other on liability in tort.[177] It would also seem that where the first defendant is domiciled in England and the second defendant is domiciled in another member state the claimant cannot rely on article 6(1) to proceed against the second defendant in England

173 *Hough v P & O Containers Ltd* [1999] QB 834, [1998] 2 All ER 978.

174 Art 6(4) allows a mortgagee of immovable property to combine, in the member state in which the property is situated, an action concerning the personal liability of the owner with an action for the enforced sale of the property.

175 Case C-51/97 *Réunion Européenne SA v Spliethoff's Bevachtingskantoor BV* [1998] ECR I-6511 at 6548 (para 46).

176 The text of art 6(1) of the Brussels I Regulation effectively incorporates the ruling in Case 189/87 *Kalfelis v Bankhaus Schröder, Münchmeyer, Hengst & Co* [1988] ECR 5565.

177 Case C-51/97 *Réunion Européenne SA v Spliethoff's Bevachtingskantoor BV* [1998] ECR I-6511 at 6549 (para 50). See, however, *Watson v First Choice Holidays and Flights Ltd* [2001] EWCA Civ 972, [2001] 2 Lloyd's Rep 339.

if the claimant has no seriously arguable claim against the first defendant.[178]

Secondly, article 6(2) deals with the case where it is a defendant, rather than the claimant, who wishes to join a further party to the proceedings. For example, a case may arise in which A sues B and B wishes to join C as a party to the proceedings so that if B is held liable he can shift liability (either in whole or in part) to C.[179] Article 6(2) provides that a person domiciled in a member state may be joined as third party in the court of another member state which is seised of the original proceedings (unless these were instituted solely with the object of removing him from the jurisdiction of the court which would otherwise be competent). For example, where a German manufacturer sells defective goods to a Belgian wholesaler who sells them to an English retailer, if the English retailer sues the Belgian wholesaler in Belgium, the Belgian wholesaler can use article 6(2) to join the German manufacturer to the Belgian proceedings.

Although the text of article 6(2) is potentially ambiguous, it should be possible for jurisdiction to be exercised under article 6(2) only in cases where jurisdiction against the first defendant is derived from the provisions of Chapter II. Where, for example, C invokes the jurisdiction of the English court against D1, a New York defendant, under CPR 6.20, D1 should not be able to use article 6(2) to join D2, domiciled in Germany, as third party. There is, however, no requirement under article 6(2) that the original proceedings should be brought in the member state in which the first defendant is domiciled. Where, for example, the claimant relies on article 5(1) to bring proceedings in the Netherlands against the first defendant, a German company, the latter can invoke article 6(2) to join the second defendant, another German company, as third party.[180]

Thirdly, article 6(3) provides that a person domiciled in a member state may be sued on a counterclaim in the court in which the original claim is pending as long as the counterclaim arises from the same contract or facts on which the original claim was based. The Court of Justice has ruled that article 6(3) applies only to claims by defendants which may lead to the pronouncement of a separate judgment.[181] The effect of article 6(3) is that the court which has jurisdiction over the claim also has jurisdiction over the defendant's counterclaim.

178 *The Xing Su Hai* [1995] 2 Lloyd's Rep 15.

179 See, for example, *Kinnear v Falconfilms NV* [1994] 3 All ER 42, [1996] 1 WLR 920.

180 Case 365/88 *Kongress Agentur Hagen GmbH v Zeehaghe BV* [1990] ECR I-1845.

181 Case C-341/93 *Danvaern Production A/S v Schuhfabriken Otterbeck GmbH & Co* [1995] ECR I-2053.

Article 6(3) does not, however, deal with the situation where the defendant pleads, as a defence, the existence of a claim which he allegedly has against the claimant and which would have the effect of wholly or partially excluding the claim, but which would not lead to a separate judgment; the defences which may be raised and the conditions under which they can be raised are determined by the law of the forum in which the claimant is proceeding.[182] Where, for example, A sues B for the recovery of a sum of money and B raises set-off as a defence, article 6(3) has no application; the defence is an integral part of the proceedings initiated by the claimant and does not involve the claimant being 'sued' within the meaning of article 6(3).

3. *Jurisdiction in matters relating to insurance, consumer contracts and employment contracts*

Chapter II contains detailed provisions dealing with jurisdiction in matters relating to insurance, consumer contracts and employment contracts. These detailed provisions create self-contained and exclusive codes in relation to the matters within their scope; it is not possible for litigants to fall back on the other provisions of the Brussels regime (unless expressly authorised by the relevant provisions).[183] There are two important aspects of these special rules in these fields. First, the primary aim of the rules is to protect the party who from the socio-economic point of view is weaker – that is, the policyholder, the consumer or the employee. As a general rule the weaker party is able to ensure that any litigation will take place in his home forum. Secondly, a jurisdiction clause in an insurance contract, a consumer contract or an employment contract may be enforced against the weaker party only in limited circumstances.

(A) MATTERS RELATING TO INSURANCE

Under articles 8 to 14,[184] in a matter relating to insurance,[185] an insurer domiciled in a member state may be sued not only in the courts of the

182 Ibid, at 2075–2076 (paras 12–14).

183 *Jordan Grand Prix Ltd v Baltic Insurance Group* [1999] 2 AC 127. Note that the rules dealing with insurance, consumer contracts and employment contracts are 'without prejudice' to art 5(5) and, as regards defendants not domiciled in a member state, art 4: arts 8, 15(1), 18.

184 Formerly arts 7–12A of the Brussels Convention. For intra-United Kingdom cases, there are no special provisions in Sch 4 to the Civil Jurisdiction and Judgments Act 1982 dealing with insurance.

185 Proceedings relating to contracts of reinsurance do not fall within the scope of the insurance provisions: *Agnew v Lansförsäkringsbolagens AB* [2001] 1 AC 223; Case C-412/98 *Universal General Insurance Co (USIG) v Group Josi Reinsurance Co SA* [2000] ECR I-5925. However, claims brought by policyholders against reinsurers should fall within these provisions: see *Proposal*, COM (1999) 348, p 15.

member state in which he is domiciled, but also in the member state in which the weaker party (that is, as the case may be, the policyholder, the assured or a beneficiary) is domiciled.[186] Moreover, an insurer, who is not domiciled in any member state but has a branch or agency in a member state, is, in relation to disputes arising out of the operations of the branch or agency, deemed to be domiciled in that state.[187] In respect of liability insurance or insurance of immovable property, the insurer (whether or not domiciled in a member state[188]) may be sued in the courts for the place where the harmful event occurred.[189] As a general rule, the insurer may bring proceedings only in the member state in which the defendant is domiciled.[190]

The effectiveness of a jurisdiction agreement in an insurance contract is determined by articles 13 and 14. Such an agreement will be enforced in only five alternative situations: (1) it was entered into after the dispute arose; (2) the agreement allows the weaker party a wider choice than that permitted by the other provisions of the Regulation; (3) the agreement confers jurisdiction on the courts of the member state in which both the policyholder and the insurer are domiciled; (4) the policyholder is not domiciled in a member state (unless the insurance is compulsory or relates to immovable property situated in a member state); and (5) the agreement forms part of a contract of insurance dealing with major risks as defined by article 14 (such as a contract of marine insurance).

Although the rules relating to insurance were designed for the protection of the small policyholder against the more powerful insurer, the application of articles 8 to 14 does not depend on it being shown that the policyholder is weak and in need of protection.[191]

(B) CONSUMER CONTRACTS

Articles 15 to 17[192] set out provisions for the protection of consumers in cases where either the supplier is domiciled in a member state or the supplier has a branch in a member state and the dispute arises out of the operations of the branch. A consumer contract is defined as one made by a person for a purpose outside his trade or profession[193] if it

186 Art 9(1).
187 Art 9(2).
188 *Jordan Grand Prix Ltd v Baltic Insurance Group* [1999] 2 AC 127.
189 Art 10.
190 Art 12(1).
191 *New Hampshire Insurance Co v Strabag Bau AG* [1992] 1 Lloyd's Rep 361.
192 Formerly arts 13–15 of the Brussels Convention.
193 See *Standard Bank London Ltd v Apostolakis* [2000] IL Pr 766. A person who enters a contract with a view to pursuing a trade or profession, not at the present time but in the future, is not a consumer: Case C-269/95 *Benincasa v Dentalkit Srl* [1997] ECR I-3767.

is (a) a contract for the sale of goods on instalment credit terms,[194] or (b) a contract for a loan repayable by instalments, or for any other form of credit, made to finance the sale of goods, or (c) any other contract[195] concluded with a person who pursues commercial or professional activities in the member state of the consumer's domicile or, by any means, directs such activities to that member state and the contract falls within the scope of such activities.[196] The purpose of subparagraph (c) is to ensure that consumer contracts concluded via an interactive (rather than passive) website accessible in the state of the consumer's domicile are covered by the special provisions.[197]

If the supplier is domiciled in a member state (or is deemed to be so domiciled by virtue of having a branch in a member state[198]) the consumer may sue the supplier either in the courts for the place in which he is domiciled or in the courts of the member state in which the supplier is domiciled.[199] However, the consumer may be sued only in the member state in which he is domiciled.[200]

These rules are subject to the provisions which regulate jurisdiction agreements in consumer contracts. A jurisdiction agreement will be effective in only three alternative situations: (1) it was concluded after the dispute arose; (2) the agreement gives the consumer a wider choice of jurisdictions in which to sue than that permitted by the other provisions of the Regulation; and (3) the agreement is in favour of the courts of the member state in which both the consumer and the supplier are domiciled.[201]

These provisions are relevant only to the extent that a consumer is personally the claimant or defendant in proceedings; if A, a consumer, contracts with B and then assigns his rights under the contract to C, who is not a consumer, C is not able to rely on the consumer contract provisions even though A would have been able to do so.[202]

194 See Case C-89/91 *Shearson Lehman Hutton v TVB Treuhandgesellschaft für Vermögensverwaltung und Beteiligungen mbH* [1993] ECR I-139; Case C-99/96 *Mietz v Intership Yachting Sneek BV* [1999] ECR I-2277.

195 Including contracts which, for an inclusive price, provide for a combination of travel and accommodation (package holidays), but excluding other contracts of transport: art 15(3).

196 Art 15(1).

197 See Walden, 'Regulating Electronic Commerce: Europe in the Global E-conomy' (2001) 26 ELRev 529, 540–541.

198 Art 15(2).

199 Art 16(1). See Case C-318/93 *Brenner and Noller v Dean Witter Reynolds Inc* [1994] ECR I-4275, [1995] All ER (EC) 278. Under art 16(1) of the Brussels I Regulation an English consumer may sue a Scottish supplier in England, notwithstanding the fact that both parties are domiciled in the same member state: see *Proposal*, COM (1999) 348, p 17.

200 Art 16(2).

201 Art 17.

202 Case C-89/91 *Shearson Lehman Hutton v TVB Treuhandgesellschaft für Vermögensverwaltung und Beteiligungen mbH* [1993] ECR I-139 at 188 (para 23).

(C) EMPLOYMENT CONTRACTS

Articles 18 to 21[203] set out provisions for the protection of employees in cases where either the employer is domiciled in a member state or the employer has a branch in a member state and the dispute arises out of the operations of the branch, in which case the employer is deemed to be domiciled in that member state.[204] If the employer is domiciled (or is deemed to be domiciled) in a member state, the employee may sue the employer either in the member state of the employer's domicile or in the courts for the place where the employee habitually carries out his work[205] (or for the last place where he did so); if, however, the employee does not carry out his work in any one country, jurisdiction is conferred on the courts for the place where the business which engaged the employee is (or was) situated.[206] By contrast, the employee may be sued only in the member state in which the employee is domiciled.[207]

These provisions may be departed from only where the parties have concluded a jurisdiction agreement which was entered into after the dispute arose or where the jurisdiction agreement allows the employee to bring proceedings in courts other than those designated by the other employment contract provisions in Chapter II.[208]

B Bases of jurisdiction under the traditional rules

An important difference between the jurisdiction of the English court under the traditional rules and under the Brussels regime is that the exercise of the former jurisdiction is discretionary, depending on whether the English court is the appropriate forum, whereas the latter is, in the main, mandatory, the court not normally being free to decline jurisdiction. The traditional rules apply not only in cases which are not within the scope of article 1 of the Regulation but also in situations falling within the scope of article 1 where the defendant is not domiciled in a member state and jurisdiction is not allocated by any of the rules which apply regardless of domicile. Accordingly, the traditional rules apply both to cases involving arbitration (because the subject-matter of the dispute is outside the Regulation's scope) and to a simple claim for breach of contract brought against, say, a Japanese corporation.

203 These provisions replace the second sentence of art 5(1) and art 17(5) of the Brussels Convention.
204 Art 18.
205 See Case C-383/95 *Rutten v Cross Medical Ltd* [1997] ECR I-57.
206 Art 19.
207 Art 20.
208 Art 21.

Under the traditional rules the English court has jurisdiction in three situations: first, if the defendant is present is England (though the court may stay the proceedings on the ground that another court is a more appropriate forum); secondly, if the defendant submits to the court's jurisdiction; and, thirdly, if the claim falls within CPR 6.20 (though jurisdiction in this third situation depends on the court giving permission for service of the claim form abroad, which it will do only if England is the most appropriate forum).

1. *Presence*

(A) INDIVIDUALS

If a natural person is not domiciled in a member state (and jurisdiction is not determined by the provisions of the Brussels regime which apply regardless of domicile) the English court has jurisdiction if the claim form is served on the defendant in England. Jurisdiction on the basis of presence is potentially very wide; it allows the claimant to bring proceedings in England merely because the defendant happens to be temporarily present in England when process is served. For example, in *Maharanee of Baroda v Wildenstein*[209] process was served on the defendant, who was resident abroad, while he was briefly visiting England in order to attend the Ascot races. If, however, the claimant fraudulently induces the defendant to come to England – with the aim of serving a claim form on him here – the claim may be struck out as an abuse of process.[210]

(B) COMPANIES

It has already been seen that, as regards matters within the Brussels regime's scope, a company which is domiciled in England may be sued in England and a company which is domiciled in another member state may be sued in England only if the English court has jurisdiction under Chapter II of the Brussels I Regulation. A company which is not domiciled in a member state, but which has a place of business in England, may be sued in England in accordance with the provisions of the Companies Act 1985 or CPR 6.5.

A company registered in England may be served at its registered office in England.[211] A company outside the United Kingdom which has a 'branch'[212] in England is required to register certain information

209 [1972] 2 QB 283, [1972] 2 All ER 689.
210 *Watkins v North American Land and Timber Co Ltd* (1904) 20 TLR 534.
211 Companies Act 1985, s 725.
212 For the meaning of branch, see the discussion of art 5(5) of the Brussels I Regulation at pp 92–93.

with the Registrar of Companies, including 'a list of the names and addresses of all persons resident in Great Britain authorised to accept on the company's behalf service of process in respect of the business of the branch'.[213] Such a company may be sued in England – in respect of the carrying on of the business of the branch – by serving process on any of the persons authorised to accept service.[214] If the company fails to provide the required information the company may be served by the claim form being left at, or posted to, any place of business established by the company in England.[215]

A company which does not have a branch in England, but which establishes or has established a place of business in England, may also be served at an address filed for that purpose with the Registrar of Companies in accordance with the requirements of the Companies Act 1985.[216] Where the company has filed an address for service the claimant may serve process at that address even if the company no longer has a place of business in England at the time of service.[217] If no such address is filed, process may be served at a place of business which the company has established in England.[218]

These rules under the Companies Act 1985 are supplemented by CPR 6.5, as a consequence of which the court's jurisdiction is effectively extended to almost any case in which a foreign company has a business presence in England.[219] Under CPR 6.5(6), as regards a company or corporation which is not incorporated or registered in England, process may be served at any place within the jurisdiction where the corporation carries on its activities or any place of business of the company within the jurisdiction. It has been held not only that this rule is in addition to the rules in the companies legislation which prescribe methods of service but also that there is no requirement that the dispute should have any connection with the defendant's activities

213 Companies Act 1985, s 690A(2); Sch 21A, para 3(e). For the purposes of this rule, it is sufficient if the process is partly in respect of the carrying on of the business (as long as the connection is more than de minimis): *Saab v Saudi American Bank* [1998] 4 All ER 382, [1998] 1 WLR 937.

214 S 694A(2).

215 S 694A(3).

216 Ss 691 and 695.

217 *Rome v Punjab National Bank (No 2)* [1990] 1 All ER 58, [1989] 1 WLR 1211.

218 Ss 691 and 695. For the courts' interpretation of these provisions see *Re Oriel Ltd* [1985] 3 All ER 216, [1986] 1 WLR 180; *South India Shipping Corpn Ltd v Export-Import Bank of Korea* [1985] 2 All ER 219, [1985] 1 WLR 585; *Cleveland Museum of Art v Capricorn Art International SA* [1990] 2 Lloyd's Rep 166.

219 For criticism see Enonchong, 'Service of Process in England on Overseas Companies and Article 5(5) of the Brussels Convention' (1999) 48 ICLQ 921; Rogerson, 'English Courts' Jurisdiction over Companies: How Important Is Service of the Claim Form in England?' (2000) 3 CFILR 272.

in England.[220] On the basis of CPR 6.5(6) a claimant would be able to serve a claim form on a foreign company which occupied a stand for a few days at a trade fair in England.[221]

(C) FORUM NON CONVENIENS

Where jurisdiction is based merely on the defendant's presence within the jurisdiction, it is quite possible that the dispute will have only a limited connection with England. In such circumstances it hardly seems reasonable for a foreign defendant to have proceedings in the English court forced upon him. In cases involving both natural and legal persons the court has a discretion, under the doctrine of forum non conveniens, to stay the proceedings if the defendant is able to show that there is another more appropriate forum.

The doctrine of forum non conveniens is potentially misleading in two respects. First, the basis of the doctrine is appropriateness rather than simply convenience. When deciding whether to stay proceedings litigational convenience is only one of the factors which the court takes into account. Secondly, to obtain a stay of proceedings the defendant must satisfy the court that there is another forum which is more appropriate than England, rather than show that England is an inappropriate forum. It is theoretically possible for English proceedings to be stayed, notwithstanding the fact that England is an appropriate forum, because another forum is more appropriate.[222]

2. *Submission*

Under the traditional rules, the defendant's submission is sufficient to confer jurisdiction on the English court. Whereas any step taken voluntarily by the defendant to defend the claim on the merits amounts to submission, a defendant who appears to contest the court's jurisdiction does not thereby submit.[223] Any jurisdictional challenge must be made prior to submission. A defendant who has submitted to the court cannot subsequently change his mind and obtain a stay of English proceedings on the basis of forum non conveniens, even if the case has little connection with England and a much stronger connection with another country.

It is not uncommon for foreign defendants to instruct solicitors in London to accept service on their behalf. Where a defendant agrees to

220 *Sea Assets v PT Garuda Indonesia* [2000] 4 All ER 371.

221 As in *Dunlop Pneumatic Tyre Co Ltd v Actien-Gesellschaft für Motor und Motorfahrzeugbau Vorm Cudell & Co* [1902] 1 KB 342.

222 The doctrine of forum non conveniens is considered further at pp 119–129.

223 *Re Dulles' Settlement (No 2)* [1951] Ch 842, [1951] 2 All ER 69; *Williams and Glyn's Bank plc v Astro Dinamico Cia Naviera SA* [1984] 1 All ER 760, [1984] 1 WLR 438.

submit to English jurisdiction and the agreement stipulates a method whereby process can be served in England, if the claimant complies with the terms of the agreement (for example, by sending the claim form to the defendant's English solicitors), the defendant will be regarded as having submitted.[224] A contract which contains a jurisdiction clause but does not specify the method whereby process can be served in England is not to be regarded as a submission to the English court. In such a case, however, either the court will have jurisdiction under the Brussels regime[225] or jurisdiction may be exercised on a discretionary basis.[226]

3. *Service out of the jurisdiction with the permission of the court*

(A) INTRODUCTION

As regards a defendant who is not domiciled in a member state, the English court may exercise 'long-arm' or 'exorbitant' jurisdiction under the Civil Procedure Rules. CPR 6.20 is based on the idea that there are certain situations in which it is appropriate for proceedings to be conducted in England notwithstanding the fact that jurisdiction cannot be based on the defendant's presence in England or on his submission. Such situations arise most commonly in cases where there is a connection between the cause of action (rather than the defendant) and England. In functional terms, CPR 6.20 is similar to articles 5 and 6 of the Brussels regime.

Jurisdiction under CPR 6.20, which is discretionary, enables the court to give the claimant permission to serve process on the defendant out of the jurisdiction. The court will not give permission unless satisfied that England is 'the proper place in which to bring the claim'.[227] In *Seaconsar Far East Ltd v Bank Markazi Jomhouri Islami Iran*[228] the House of Lords confirmed that there are three issues to be considered, the third of which is derived from *Spiliada Maritime Corpn v Cansulex Ltd*.[229] Unless the claimant satisfies the court on all three issues permission will not be given.

224 CPR 6.4(2).
225 In particular, under art 23 of the Brussels I Regulation. See pp 75–79.
226 Under CPR 6.20(5)(d). See p 107.
227 CPR 6.21(2A).
228 [1994] 1 AC 438, [1993] 4 All ER 456.
229 [1987] AC 460, [1986] 3 All ER 843. Where, in proceedings falling outside the scope of art 1 of the Brussels regime, the application is for permission to serve process in Scotland or Northern Ireland and the claimant may also be entitled to a remedy in Scotland or Northern Ireland (as the case may be) the court must also have regard to: (i) the relative cost and convenience of proceeding in the other jurisdiction and (ii) the powers of the courts of the other jurisdiction: CPR 6.21(3).

First, as regards the merits, the claimant must show that there is a serious issue to be tried. This requirement will be satisfied if there is a substantial question of fact or law which the claimant bona fide desires to have tried.[230] Conversely, this requirement is not satisfied if the facts alleged by the claimant, if proved, would not provide a sufficient foundation for the alleged cause of action.

Secondly, the claimant must show that his claim falls within one of the paragraphs of CPR 6.20. If the second issue turns on the proper interpretation of the text of CPR 6.20 the court must be satisfied that the interpretation favoured by the claimant is the correct one.[231] If there is ambiguity in the construction of the rules, such ambiguity should be resolved in the defendant's favour.[232]

Where the second issue turns on a disputed question of fact, the claimant is required to show merely a 'good arguable case' that his claim falls within the paragraph of CPR 6.20 being relied on. Where, for example, the claimant seeks permission under CPR 6.20(6) – on the basis that the defendant committed a breach of contract in England – the claimant must have a good arguable case that there was a contract between the claimant and the defendant, that the contract was breached by the defendant and that the breach was committed in England. It is not enough for the claimant to show that if there was a contract and it had been broken the breach would have been committed within the jurisdiction.

Thirdly, the court must be satisfied that England is the forum conveniens, that is the forum in which the case can most suitably be tried in the interests of the parties and the ends of justice.[233] The factors which are relevant in deciding whether England is the forum conveniens are the same as those which the court must consider when deciding whether to stay proceedings on the ground of forum non conveniens in a case which is brought against a defendant who is present in England when process is served. The determination of the appropriate forum is conducted in two stages.

At the first stage the court must consider the nature of the dispute, the legal and practical issues involved, such questions as local knowledge, availability of witnesses and their evidence and expense.[234] Regard should also be had to the ground of CPR 6.20 invoked by the

230 [1994] 1 AC 438 at 452.
231 *EF Hutton & Co (London) Ltd v Mofarrij* [1989] 2 All ER 633, [1989] 1 WLR 488.
232 *The Hagen* [1908] P 189; *Siskina (Owners of cargo lately laden on board) v Distos Compania Naviera SA* [1979] AC 210, [1977] 3 All ER 803.
233 *Spiliada Maritime Corpn v Cansulex Ltd* [1987] AC 460, [1986] 3 All ER 843.
234 Lord Wilberforce in *Amin Rasheed Shipping Corpn v Kuwait Insurance Co* [1984] AC 50 at 72.

claimant. In some cases the ground is such that permission will normally be granted. For example, the English court will normally be regarded as the natural forum in a claim in tort if the tort was committed in England.[235] In other cases, the ground relied on will carry less weight in relation to the appropriateness of the English forum. If England is the centre of gravity of the dispute permission will be granted; if the factual and legal connecting factors do not suggest that England is the appropriate forum, permission should normally be refused.

Whether England is the forum conveniens, however, is not simply a question of practical convenience; the question is whether the English court is appropriate, having regard to all the circumstances. Even if England is not the natural forum, the court may give permission if the claimant establishes that justice will not be done in the appropriate foreign forum. Nevertheless, the mere fact that the claimant will be deprived of a legitimate personal or juridical advantage if the English court does not exercise jurisdiction is not decisive.

It is important to stress that, in the context of an application for permission to serve a claim form out of the jurisdiction under CPR 6.20, the burden is on the claimant to establish that England is the forum conveniens. If the claimant makes an application under CPR 6.20 and the court gives permission for process to be served out of the jurisdiction, the defendant is entitled to contest the court's jurisdiction and to apply for service of process to be set aside. This stage of the procedure should not be confused with an application for a stay of proceedings in a case where process is served on the defendant in England as of right. In the latter case the burden rests on the defendant to satisfy the court that there is another forum which is more appropriate than England; in the former, however, the burden remains on the claimant to show that England is the appropriate forum.[236]

(B) BASES OF JURISDICTION UNDER CPR 6.20

CPR 6.20 contains 19 paragraphs listing the various circumstances in which the court may grant permission to serve a claim form out of the jurisdiction. Only the most important and commonly relied on are considered in any detail.

235 *The Albaforth* [1984] 2 Lloyd's Rep 91; *Schapira v Ahronson* [1998] IL Pr 587; *Berezovsky v Michaels* [2000] 1 WLR 1004. If, in a libel case, the claimant is unable to satisfy the court that he has a sufficient reputation to protect in England permission to serve out may be refused: *Chadha & Oiscom Technologies Inc v Dow Jones & Co Inc* [1999] IL Pr 829.

236 The doctrine of forum conveniens is considered in more detail at pp 119–129.

(i) Contract

CPR 6.20(5) sets out four types of case in which the English court may exercise jurisdiction where 'a claim is made in respect of a contract'. The contract in question must be between the claimant and the defendant.[237]

First, permission may be granted if the contract was made within the jurisdiction.[238] Where the parties' acts in making the contract take place in different countries, the contract is regarded as made in the country where the last act occurred which was necessary for the conclusion of the contract – that is, the country in which the acceptance takes effect. A problem may arise because the laws of different countries have different rules on this matter. For example, in a contract concluded by correspondence the moment at which the acceptance is effective (whether, for example, on despatch by the offeree or on receipt by the offeror) differs in different laws. For the purposes of CPR 6.20, the rules of the English law of contract are applicable for determining the place where the contract was concluded, whether or not the contract is governed by English law. So, in a postal case, the contract is made in the country where the acceptance is posted,[239] whereas if virtually instantaneous means of communication are used, such as telephone, the contract is made in the country where the acceptance is received.[240] Where a contract is made partly in England and partly abroad it would seem that it is sufficient if the contract which is the subject-matter of the proceedings was 'substantially made' within the jurisdiction.[241]

Secondly, jurisdiction may be exercised if the contract was made by or through an agent trading or residing within the jurisdiction.[242] This head of jurisdiction is not confined to the case where the English agent concludes the contract on behalf of a foreign principal (when, in any event, the contract is likely to be made within the jurisdiction) but also includes the case where the agent in England solicits an order from the English customer and sends it on to the principal abroad, who concludes the contract by accepting the order.[243] This basis of

237 *Finnish Marine Insurance Co Ltd v Protective National Insurance Co* [1990] 1 QB 1078; *Bastone & Firminger Ltd v Nasima Enterprises (Nigeria) Ltd* [1996] CLC 1902.

238 CPR 6.20(5)(a).

239 *Benaim & Co v Debono* [1924] AC 514.

240 *Entores Ltd v Miles Far East Corpn* [1955] 2 QB 327, [1955] 2 All ER 493; *Brinkibon Ltd v Stahag Stahl und Stahlwarenhandelsgesellschaft mbH* [1983] 2 AC 34, [1982] 1 All ER 293.

241 Kerr J in *BP Exploration Co (Libya) Ltd v Hunt* [1976] 1 WLR 788 at 798.

242 CPR 6.20(5)(b).

243 *National Mortgage and Agency Co of New Zealand Ltd v Gosselin* (1922) 38 TLR 832.

jurisdiction is limited, however, to cases where the contract is concluded through the defendant's agent; the fact that the claimant concludes the contract through an agent in England is irrelevant.[244]

Thirdly, the claimant may seek to invoke the court's jurisdiction where a claim relates to a contract which is governed by English law.[245] Whether a contract is governed by English law has to be determined in accordance with English choice of law rules.[246]

Fourthly, it is provided that jurisdiction may be exercised where the contract contains a term to the effect that the court shall have jurisdiction to determine any claim in respect of the contract.[247] This provision has been largely superseded by the equivalent provisions of the Brussels regime[248] which, in many cases involving an English jurisdiction clause, allocate exclusive (and mandatory) jurisdiction to the English court.[249] In a case involving an English jurisdiction clause the traditional rules are generally of significance only if the subject-matter of the dispute falls outside the material scope of the Brussels regime, as determined by article 1, or if none of the parties to the contract is domiciled in a member state.

It is also provided by CPR 6.20(7) that permission to serve process on a defendant out of the jurisdiction may be given in a case involving a claim for a declaration that no contract exists where, if the contract was found to exist, it would comply with the conditions set out in CPR 6.20(5).[250]

(ii) Breach of contract in England

By virtue of CPR 6.20(6) the English court may exercise jurisdiction over an absent defendant where the claim is made in respect of a breach of contract committed within the jurisdiction. A breach is committed within the jurisdiction if the obligation not performed was, according to the terms of the contract or under the law applicable to the contract, required to be performed in England or if defective performance occurred in England. If the breach relied upon took the form of repudiation, that must have occurred in England.

244 *Union International Insurance Co Ltd v Jubilee Insurance Co Ltd* [1991] 1 All ER 740, [1991] 1 WLR 415.
245 CPR 6.20(5)(c).
246 See chapter 5.
247 CPR 6.20(5)(d).
248 Art 23 of the Brussels I Regulation; art 17 of the Lugano Convention.
249 See pp 75–79.
250 This paragraph provides a simple answer to a question which had troubled the courts in the context of RSC Ord 11, r 1(1)(d). See, for example, *DR Insurance Co v Central National Insurance Co* [1996] 1 Lloyd's Rep 74; *Finnish Marine Insurance Co Ltd v Protective National Insurance Co* [1990] 1 QB 1078, [1989] 2 All ER 929.

(iii) Tort

Permission may be granted under CPR 6.20(8) if the claim is made in tort where (a) damage was sustained within the jurisdiction; or (b) the damage sustained resulted from an act committed within the jurisdiction. To determine whether a claim is made in tort for the purposes of this rule the court will apply exclusively English law.

The form of words used in paragraph (8) – which expressly adopts the approach of article 5(3) of the Brussels Convention as interpreted by the Court of Justice – is designed to avoid the theoretical difficulties associated with trying to determine the place where a tort is committed in a case where the defendant commits the wrongful act in one country and the claimant suffers loss or damage in another. Paragraph (8) allows the English court to exercise jurisdiction if either some 'significant damage' was sustained in England or the damage resulted from 'substantial and efficacious acts' committed by the defendant in England (whether or not other substantial and efficacious acts were committed elsewhere).[251]

The problems of interpretation which arise in relation to article 5(3) of the Brussels regime are likely to be replicated under the traditional rules. In particular, the same difficulties may well arise in cases involving economic loss.[252]

(iv) Restitution

CPR 6.20(15) provides that permission to serve out may be granted where a claim is made for restitution where the defendant's alleged liability arises out of acts committed within the jurisdiction. There was no counterpart to paragraph (15) under RSC Order 11, rule 1(1) and there is, as yet, no case law on the relationship between paragraph (15) and paragraph (5). It is reasonable to suppose that, given that the implied contract theory of restitution is rejected by modern commentators,[253] claims for restitution should not normally be regarded as falling within the scope of paragraph (5).[254] However, there is no reason to think that a claim for restitution which is founded on the rescission or discharge of a contract does not fall within paragraph (5) as well as paragraph (15).

251 Slade LJ in *Metall und Rohstoff AG v Donaldson Lufkin & Jenrette Inc* [1990] 1 QB 391 at 437. See also *Arab Business Consortium International Finance and Investment Co v Banque Franco-Tunisienne* [1997] 1 Lloyd's Rep 531.

252 See pp 89–92.

253 See Briggs, 'Jurisdiction under Traditional Rules' in Rose (ed), *Restitution in the Conflict of Laws* (1995) p 49ff.

254 *Bowling v Cox* [1926] AC 751 and *Re Jogia* [1988] 2 All ER 328, [1988] 1 WLR 484, both of which rely on the now discredited implied contract theory, are of questionable authority in the context of CPR 6.20.

CPR 6.20(14) is primarily designed to enable proceedings to be brought in fraud cases against a foreign company which has not participated directly in the fraud, but which has been used by the persons who control it as a receptacle for the proceeds of the fraud. Under paragraph (14) the court may exercise jurisdiction in a case where, first, the claim is made for a remedy against the defendant as constructive trustee and, secondly, the defendant's alleged liability arises out of acts committed within the jurisdiction. A claimant is able to bring his claim within the scope of paragraph (14) by showing that some of the relevant acts of the defendant were committed in England; the fact that the factual matrix also has connections with other countries does not automatically take the case outside CPR 6.20.[255] For example, it is not essential that the defendant acquired the knowledge upon which a claim to enforce an alleged constructive trust is based within the jurisdiction.[256]

(v) Multiple defendants

Under CPR 6.20(3), where a claim is brought against a person on whom the claim form has been or will be served (the first defendant), permission may be granted to serve process on a person out of the jurisdiction (the second defendant) if (a) there is between the claimant and the first defendant a real issue which it is reasonable for the court to try and (b) the claimant wishes to serve the claim form on the second defendant, who is a necessary or proper party to that claim. So, if the first defendant is served in England or abroad, the court may grant permission for process to be served on the second defendant abroad, even though the case would not come under any other rule. Where claims against a number of defendants arise out of the same series of transactions and involve common questions of fact, each defendant is to be regarded as a necessary or proper party for the purposes of CPR 6.20(3).[257]

The requirement that there should be a real issue between the claimant and the first defendant is to enable the court to refuse permission where it appears that the claim against the first defendant is not brought bona fide, but merely as a pretext to get the second defendant before the English court.[258] In addition, CPR 6.20(3A) provides for permission to serve out in a Part 20 claim (third party proceedings) where the third party is a necessary or proper party to the

255 *ISC Technologies Ltd v Guerin* [1992] 2 Lloyd's Rep 430.

256 *Polly Peck International plc v Nadir* (1992) Independent, 2 September.

257 *United Film Distribution Ltd v Chhabria* [2001] EWCA Civ 416, [2001] 2 All ER (Comm) 865.

258 *Witted v Galbraith* [1893] 1 QB 577 (a case decided under a former rule which required the proceedings to have been 'properly brought' against the first defendant).

claim. Paragraph (3A) is the equivalent, under the traditional rules, of article 6(2) of the Brussels regime.[259]

Paragraphs (3) and (3A) are different from the other important bases of jurisdiction contained in CPR 6.20 because they are not founded on a connection between the claim and the forum. For this reason the courts should exercise 'caution' or 'special care' in cases falling within the scope of these provisions.[260] Paragraphs (3) and (3A) – like article 6 of the Brussels regime – are based on the practical consideration that it is more convenient and economical for a dispute involving multiple parties to be litigated in a single forum rather than to be fragmented between a number of different courts.[261]

(vi) Other bases of jurisdiction

Under the numerous other bases of jurisdiction in CPR 6.20 the English court may exercise jurisdiction over an absent defendant in relation to claims relating to property located within the jurisdiction,[262] claims brought against a defendant domiciled in England,[263] claims to enforce foreign judgments and arbitral awards,[264] claims in respect of United Kingdom taxes[265] and claims under various statutes.[266]

III DECLINING JURISDICTION AND STAYING PROCEEDINGS

The fact that there exists a basis on which the English court may exercise jurisdiction (whether under the Brussels regime or under the traditional rules) does not necessarily mean that the litigation will proceed in England. There may be countervailing factors which mean that the English court should decline jurisdiction or grant a stay of the proceedings. Under the traditional rules the English court may grant a stay on the basis of forum non conveniens; this involves consideration

259 See p 95.
260 *Multinational Gas and Petrochemical Co v Multinational Gas and Petrochemical Services Inc* [1983] Ch 258; *Petroleo Brasiliero SA v Mellitus Shipping Inc* [2001] EWCA Civ 418, [2001] 1 All ER (Comm) 993.
261 See *Barings plc v Coopers & Lybrand* [1997] IL Pr 576.
262 CPR 6.20(10). See *In re Banco Nacionel de Cuba* [2001] 1 WLR 2039. This basis of jurisdiction is not relevant in cases where the English court has exclusive jurisdiction under the Brussels regime (art 22(1) of the Brussels I Regulation; art 16(1) of the Lugano Convention).
263 CPR 6.20(1). This paragraph applies only in cases which fall outside the scope of art 1 of the Brussels regime (such as where proceedings relate to arbitration).
264 CPR 6.20(9).
265 CPR 6.20(16).
266 CPR 6.20(18). The statutes, which are listed in the relevant practice direction (CPR PD6B), include the Financial Services Act 1986 and the Banking Act 1987.

of the same factors as those which determine whether the court will allow service of a claim form out of the jurisdiction under CPR 6.20 on the basis of forum conveniens. The Brussels regime contains provisions dealing with parallel and related proceedings which are designed to reduce the possibility of the courts of two (or more) member states rendering irreconcilable judgments.

Whereas declining jurisdiction is a definitive step which brings the proceedings to a close, a stay merely places the proceedings on hold. In practice, it will normally make little difference whether the court stays proceedings or declines jurisdiction; while the stay is maintained the proceedings cannot continue. There are, however, situations in which the court may be justified in lifting a stay. Where, for example, English proceedings are stayed on the basis that there is another more appropriate forum abroad, if it subsequently transpires that the claim cannot be brought in the foreign forum the court may lift the stay to enable the claimant to pursue his claim in England.[267]

When considering whether or not the court should stay proceedings or decline jurisdiction it is important, once again, to draw a distinction between cases which fall within the relevant provisions of the Brussels regime and situations which are governed by the common law.

A The effect of parallel or related proceedings in another member state

1. Introduction

It has been seen that cases may arise under the Brussels regime where the courts of more than one member state have jurisdiction. For example, in a dispute arising out of a contract, proceedings may be brought either in the member state in which the defendant is domiciled (under article 2) or in the court for the place of performance of the obligation in question (under article 5(1)). Similarly, as a defendant may be domiciled in more than one member state, more than one court may have general jurisdiction under article 2.

The primary objective of the Brussels regime is to facilitate the free flow of judgments between the member states. If the courts of different member states may issue conflicting judgments on the same or related questions the free flow of judgments is impeded. Accordingly, the Brussels regime contains provisions which are designed to reduce the possibility of such conflicts. The Brussels I Regulation draws a distinction between two types of situation. First, there are cases within

267 See *Baghlaf Al Zafer Factory Co BR for Industry Ltd v Pakistan National Shipping Co (No 2)* [2000] 1 Lloyd's Rep 1.

article 27[268] concerning parallel proceedings or lis pendens – where the same parties are involved in litigation on the same issues in two or more member states. Secondly, article 28[269] deals with situations where related proceedings are being pursued in two or more member states. The general approach of the Brussels regime is to give precedence to the court 'first seised'.[270] Before turning to consider specific aspects of articles 27 and 28 a number of general points which are applicable to both provisions should be mentioned.

First, it is important to remember that the material scope of the Brussels regime is restricted to civil and commercial matters. If parallel or related proceedings are brought in two member states articles 27 and 28 are relevant only if both sets of proceedings fall within the scope of article 1. The Court of Justice has ruled that what are now articles 27 and 28 do not apply to proceedings, or issues arising in proceedings, concerning the recognition and enforcement of judgments given in civil and commercial matters in non-member states.[271] So, if a claimant starts proceedings to enforce a New York judgment in Italy and in England, articles 27 and 28 have no application even though the same issues (such as whether the judgment was procured by fraud) may be raised by the defendant in both sets of proceedings.

Secondly, although there is no indication as to whether or not the provisions relating to parallel and related proceedings apply to parties who are not domiciled in a member state, the Court of Justice has ruled that what is now article 27 applies regardless of the domicile of the parties and regardless of the basis of jurisdiction on which the proceedings are founded.[272] So, article 27 is relevant in the case where A, a Brazilian company, brings proceedings in England against B, a French national domiciled in Senegal (relying on CPR 6.20), and B brings proceedings against A in France (relying on article 14 of the French Civil Code). For the purposes of article 27 it is irrelevant that neither party is domiciled in a member state and that, as regards each set of proceedings, the claimant seeks to invoke the court's jurisdiction under traditional rules.

268 Formerly art 21 of the Brussels Convention.

269 Formerly art 22 of the Brussels Convention.

270 Art 29 of the Brussels I Regulation (formerly art 23 of the Brussels Convention) provides that where proceedings fall within the exclusive jurisdiction of the courts of more than one member state (for example, where the courts of two member states have exclusive jurisdiction under the different parts of art 22) any court other than the court first seised is required to decline jurisdiction.

271 Case C-129/92 *Owens Bank Ltd v Bracco (No 2)* [1994] QB 509, [1994] ECR I-117.

272 Case C-351/89 *Overseas Union Insurance Ltd v New Hampshire Insurance Co* [1992] 1 QB 434, [1991] ECR I-3317.

Thirdly, central to the operation of articles 27 and 28 is the idea of the court 'first seised'. Whereas the Brussels Convention left the question of when a court is 'seised' to the law of the state in question,[273] article 30 of the Regulation lays down a uniform rule for determining the moment at which a court is deemed to be seised. As a general rule, a court will be seised when the document instituting the proceedings is lodged with the court; however, the court will not be regarded as having been seised at this time if the claimant subsequently fails to take the steps he was required to take to have service effected on the defendant.[274] Furthermore, if under the procedural law of the court in question, the document has to be served before being lodged with the court, the court will be regarded as having been seised at the time when the document is received by the authority responsible for service – though the court will not be regarded as having been seised at this time if the claimant subsequently fails to take any necessary steps to have the document lodged with the court.[275]

Fourthly, articles 27 and 28 apply only in circumstances where there are concurrent proceedings. If, for example, proceedings are commenced in England and in Belgium the court second seised must consider the application of articles 27 and 28. If, however, the proceedings in the court first seised are properly discontinued, articles 27 and 28 cease to be applicable.[276]

2. *Parallel proceedings*

(A) THE FRAMEWORK OF ARTICLE 27

Article 27 deals with the situation where proceedings involving the same cause of action and between the same parties are brought in the courts of different member states. It is provided that any court other than the court first seised shall stay its proceedings until such time as the jurisdiction of the court first seised is established; if the jurisdiction of the court first seised is established any other court is required to decline jurisdiction. In the situation where A sues B in France and B challenges the jurisdiction of the French court and starts proceedings against A in England, the English court must stay the proceedings. If B's challenge to the French court's jurisdiction is successful, there is

273 Case 129/83 *Zelger v Salinitri (No 2)* [1984] ECR 2397.

274 Art 30(1). In the context of English proceedings, this means that the court will be seised when the court issues a claim form at the request of the claimant: CPR 7.2(1). A claim form is issued on the date entered on the form by the court: CPR 7.2(2).

275 Art 30(2).

276 *Internationale Nederlanden Aviation Lease BV v Civil Aviation Authority* [1997] 1 Lloyd's Rep 80.

no obstacle to the continuation of the English proceedings and the stay may be lifted. If, however, B's challenge to the jurisdiction of the French court is rejected, the English court must decline jurisdiction.

Although the English language version of article 27 refers only to 'the same cause of action ... between the same parties', the Court of Justice has held that, having regard to other language versions, what is now article 27 must be understood to require the parallel proceedings to involve three elements: the proceedings must have the same subject-matter (or the same object), as well as the same cause of action and the same parties.[277]

(B) THE SAME CAUSE OF ACTION AND THE SAME SUBJECT-MATTER (OR OBJECT)

Parallel proceedings have the same subject-matter (or object) where, for example, the question whether a contract is binding lies at the heart of the two sets of proceedings or where the issue of liability is central to both sets of proceedings; parallel proceedings are to be regarded as involving the same cause of action where they are both based on the same contractual relationship or where the same facts and the same rule of law are relied on as the basis of each claim.[278]

In *Gubisch Maschinenfabrik KG v Palumbo*[279] a German 'seller' started proceedings in Germany against an Italian 'buyer' to enforce the terms of a disputed contract and the 'buyer' subsequently started proceedings in Italy with a view to obtaining a declaration that the alleged contract was not binding on him. The Court of Justice ruled that the conditions of what is now article 27 were satisfied and that the Italian court was required to decline jurisdiction. Had the Italian proceedings been commenced first, however, the German court would have had to decline jurisdiction. Article 27 lays down a strict 'first come, first served' rule; it makes no difference whether the proceedings in the court first seised involve a positive claim by A to establish the liability of B or a claim for a declaration of non-liability by B against A.[280]

Where proceedings are brought in one member state for provisional measures (under article 31[281]) and substantive proceedings are subsequently commenced in another member state, the parallel proceedings do not involve the same cause of action. In these circumstances, there can be no obligation on the court second seised

277 Case 144/86 *Gubisch Maschinenfabrik KG v Palumbo* [1987] ECR 4861.
278 Idem.
279 Case 144/86 [1987] ECR 4861.
280 Case C-406/92 *Owners of the cargo lately laden on board the ship Tatry v Owners of the ship Maciej Rataj* [1994] ECR I-5439, [1995] All ER (EC) 229.
281 See pp 138–143.

to stay its proceedings or decline jurisdiction.[282] Equally, the commencement of substantive proceedings in one member state cannot bar an application for provisional measures in another member state.[283]

(C) THE SAME PARTIES

In a situation involving only two parties the requirement that the parallel proceedings should involve the same parties is simple enough to apply. The position is potentially more difficult where more than two parties are involved. What is the position, for example, where as a result of disputes arising out of a joint venture agreement between four parties (A, B, C and D), A sues B and C in France and B sues D and A in England? In *The Tatry*[284] the Court of Justice ruled that the obligation of the court second seised to decline jurisdiction applies only to the extent to which the parties to the proceedings pending before it are also parties to the proceedings before the court first seised; it does not prevent the proceedings from continuing between the other parties. So, in the above example, provided the parallel proceedings involve the same cause of action and the same object, the English court is required to decline jurisdiction as regards A, but not D. This approach obviously involves the danger that proceedings involving the same issues will be fragmented between the courts of different member states. This danger can, however, be averted, to some extent, by the application of article 28.

Article 27 raises difficult questions in multiparty cases where the interests of different parties overlap. For example, does article 27 apply in a case where, following a road accident involving cars driven by A and B, A sues B for negligence in France and C (B's insurer) sues A in England? It would seem that if the interests of B (the insured) and C (the insurer) are identical, the two sets of proceedings are to be regarded as involving the same parties; if, however, the interests of B and C are not entirely congruent the same parties are not involved in both sets of proceedings and article 27 does not apply (though, in all probability, article 28 does).[285] In any particular situation it may be difficult to determine whether or not the interests of the parties are congruent. It seems clear, however, that where a judgment rendered against B would have the force of res judicata as against C, B and C are to be regarded as one and the same party for the purposes of article 27.

282 *The Winter* [2000] 2 Lloyd's Rep 298.
283 *Republic of Haiti v Duvalier* [1990] 1 QB 202.
284 Case C-406/92 [1994] ECR I-5439, [1995] All ER (EC) 229.
285 See Case C-351/96 *Drouot Assurances SA v Consolidated Metallurgical Industries (CMI Industrial Sites)* [1998] ECR I-3075.

Questions surrounding the applicability of article 27 have also arisen in cases involving proceedings in rem. If A starts proceedings in rem in the Netherlands against a vessel owned by B and B starts proceedings in personam in England against A are the two sets of proceedings between the same parties or not? It used to be thought that, since proceedings in rem are (notionally) brought against specific property (usually a ship) rather than a person, article 27 could not apply.[286] However, this view has been rejected and the older cases overruled; for the purposes of article 27, the person who has an interest in defending proceedings in rem (typically, the shipowner) is a party to those proceedings.[287] So, if the claimant starts proceedings in rem against a vessel in Belgium and then starts proceedings in personam in England against the shipowner the two sets of proceedings are to be regarded as involving the same parties.

(D) THE RELATIONSHIP BETWEEN THE COURT FIRST SEISED AND THE COURT SECOND SEISED

As a general rule, it is not permissible for the court second seised to review the basis on which the court first seised exercised jurisdiction. As the Court of Justice stressed in *Overseas Union Insurance Ltd v New Hampshire Insurance Co*[288] in no case is the court second seised in a better position than the court first seised to determine whether the latter has jurisdiction; either the jurisdiction of the court first seised is determined directly by the Brussels regime, which is common to the member states, or jurisdiction is derived, by virtue of article 4, from the traditional rules of the state of the court first seised, in which case that court is clearly better placed to rule on the question of its own jurisdiction.

There is, however, an argument for saying that article 27 does not apply in cases where the court second seised has exclusive jurisdiction under article 22. If the court first seised exercises jurisdiction contrary to the terms of article 22, the judgment of that court is not entitled to recognition and enforcement under Chapter III.[289] If proceedings are commenced in another member state in a matter, which by virtue of article 22 falls within the exclusive jurisdiction of the English court, it makes no sense to apply article 27 to prevent one of the parties from starting proceedings in England on the same issue.

286 *The Nordglimt* [1988] QB 183.

287 Case C-406/92 *Owners of the cargo lately laden on board the ship Tatry v Owners of the ship Maciej Rataj* [1994] ECR I-5439, [1995] All ER (EC) 229; *Republic of India v India Steamship Co (No 2)* [1998] AC 878.

288 Case C-351/89 [1992] 1 QB 434, [1991] ECR I-3317.

289 Arts 35(1), 45(1).

There is also an argument, but a much weaker one, for the proposition that article 23 prevails over article 27. In *Continental Bank NA v Aeakos Compania Naviera SA*[290] the defendant brought proceedings in Greece against the plaintiff. The plaintiff, believing that the dispute fell within the scope of an English jurisdiction clause which satisfied the requirements of what is now article 23, started proceedings against the defendant in England. The defendant argued that, because the conditions laid down in what is now article 27 were satisfied and the Greek court was the court first seised, the English proceedings should be stayed. The Court of Appeal refused to grant the stay on the basis that, as long as the jurisdiction clause satisfies the requirements laid down in the Brussels regime, jurisdiction derived from the parties' agreement takes precedence over the provisions relating to parallel and related proceedings.

A central element in the Court of Appeal's rejection of the defendant's application is the perceived illogicality of requiring the court chosen by the parties to stay proceedings simply because of the commencement of proceedings in the courts of another member state. According to Steyn LJ, if the defendant's argument were accepted, 'a party who is in breach of the contract will be able to set at naught an exclusive jurisdiction agreement which is the product of the free will of the parties'.[291] The reasoning of the Court of Appeal is premised on the view that the court first seised has made (or will make) an error in the application of the relevant jurisdiction provisions. In a situation such as that which arose in the *Continental Bank* case, if the dispute falls within the scope of a valid jurisdiction clause, the court first seised is normally obliged to decline jurisdiction, thereby enabling the proceedings in the agreed forum to continue. If the court first seised does not decline jurisdiction, notwithstanding the jurisdiction clause, it can only be on the basis that, for one reason or another, article 23 does not confer exclusive jurisdiction on the English court. The court first seised may conclude, for example, that the proceedings fall within its exclusive jurisdiction by virtue of article 22, that the defendant has submitted to its jurisdiction under article 24, that the dispute does not fall within the scope of the jurisdiction clause or that the jurisdiction clause does not satisfy the formal requirements of article 23. The logic of the Regulation is to allow the court first seised to decide on its own jurisdiction (whether under Chapter II or under its traditional rules). The decision of the Court of Appeal in the *Continental Bank* case flies in the face of the general principle endorsed by the Court of Justice in the *Overseas Union Insurance* case that the court second seised is not

290 [1994] 1 WLR 588. See also *Glencore International AG v Metro Trading International Inc* [1999] 2 Lloyd's Rep 632; *The Kribi* [2001] 1 Lloyd's Rep 76.

291 At 597.

better placed than the court first seised to rule on the latter's jurisdiction. It is unfortunate both that the *Overseas Union Insurance* case seems to have been ignored by the Court of Appeal and that the Court of Appeal did not think it was appropriate to seek a ruling from the Court of Justice.

3. Related actions

Article 28 is designed to deal with those situations which do not fall within the strict confines of article 27. Where related actions are brought in the courts of two member states the court second seised has a discretion to stay the proceedings (or in certain circumstances decline jurisdiction). For the purposes of article 28 actions are deemed to be related where they are so closely connected that it is expedient to hear and determine them together to avoid the risk of irreconcilable judgments resulting from separate proceedings.[292] Under article 28 the concept of related actions is a broad one; two actions may be related – on the basis that there is a risk of irreconcilable judgments – even if it would be perfectly possible for the judgments resulting from the two actions to be separately enforced. The concept of related actions is broad enough to cover the situation where there is a risk that the courts of two member states may reach contradictory conclusions on questions of fact. For example, proceedings (in one member state) brought by an owner of cargo which has been damaged while being carried by the defendant's ship are related to proceedings (in another member state) brought by the shipowner to obtain exoneration from or limitation of liability for damage to a similar cargo owned by others.[293] Whether actions pending in different courts are related should not turn on a sophisticated and difficult exercise of legal analysis; rather there should be a broad commonsense approach to whether the actions in question are related.[294] In *The Tatry* Advocate-General Tesauro suggested that the court second seised should rely on what is now article 28 whenever it considers that the reasoning of the court first seised may concern issues likely to be relevant in the proceedings before the court second seised.[295]

Where there are related actions in the courts of two or more member states any court other than the court first seised may stay its proceedings.[296] Furthermore, on the application of one of the parties, the court second seised may decline jurisdiction if both actions are

292 Art 28(3).
293 Case C-406/92 *Owners of the cargo lately laden on board the ship Tatry v Owners of the ship Maciej Rataj* [1994] ECR I-5439, [1995] All ER (EC) 229.
294 Lord Saville in *Sarrio SA v Kuwait Investment Authority* [1999] 1 AC 32 at 40–41.
295 C-406/92 [1994] ECR I-5439 at 5457–5458 (para 28).
296 Art 28(1).

pending at first instance and, under the law of the court first seised, the two actions can be consolidated.[297]

Article 28 does not indicate how the courts should exercise their discretion. The traditional understanding is that where article 28 applies the first duty of the court is to stay its proceedings.[298] Where, however, the risk of irreconcilable judgments is very small[299] or where the risk is dependent on a range of contingent matters[300] the court second seised may be justified in refusing to stay its proceedings or to decline jurisdiction. In principle, when the court is considering whether or not to stay proceedings under article 28, the degree of risk of irreconcilable judgments should be the major factor. However, it seems that the appropriateness of the competing fora is also a factor which may be taken into account.[301]

Article 28 does not expand the jurisdiction of the court first seised; it is a negative rule, which enables a court other than the court first seised to stay proceedings in a situation in which it has prima facie jurisdiction.[302] Where, for example, A sues B in France, C sues A in England and the English court grants a stay under article 28 on the basis that the English proceedings are related to the earlier French proceedings, the fact that the English court has granted a stay does not confer jurisdiction on the French court in relation to C.

B Staying proceedings on the basis of the doctrine of forum non conveniens

1. *The development of the doctrine*

An important difference between the jurisdiction of the English court under the traditional rules and that under the Brussels regime is that the exercise of the former jurisdiction is discretionary, depending on whether the English court is an appropriate forum, while the latter is largely mandatory, the court not normally being free to decline jurisdiction.

Where the claimant invokes the jurisdiction of the English court on the basis of the defendant's presence in England, or the claimant is

297 Art 28(2).

298 Jenard Report, OJ 1979 C59/41.

299 *The Maciej Rataj* [1991] 2 Lloyd's Rep 458, revsd on other grounds [1992] 2 Lloyd's Rep 552.

300 *Centro Internationale Handelsbank AG v Morgan Grenfell Trade Finance Ltd* [1997] CLC 870.

301 See Advocate-General Lenz in Case C-129/92 *Owens Bank v Bracco (No 2)* [1994] ECR I-117 at 144 (para 76).

302 Case 150/80 *Elefanten Schuh GmbH v Jacqmain* [1981] ECR 1671; Case C-51/97 *Réunion Européenne SA v Spliethoff's Bevachtingskantoor BV* [1998] ECR I-6511.

seeking permission under CPR 6.20 for process to be served abroad, the court has discretion whether or not to exercise jurisdiction. Originally, the approaches in the two classes of case were very different. For much of the twentieth century the court would not stay proceedings brought against a defendant who was present in England unless the bringing of the proceedings was vexatious or oppressive, which usually required proof of an intention by the claimant to harass the defendant.[303] Short of that, the claim would be tried in England without regard to the court's appropriateness as a forum: the claimant as well as the defendant might be a foreigner and the facts of the dispute might have no connection at all with England. If the claimant believed he would enjoy some advantage by suing in England, he was free to do so, as long as process could be served on the defendant in England. The traditional attitude of the English courts – which necessarily encouraged forum shopping – was summed up by Lord Denning's observation that 'if the forum is England, it is a good place to shop in, both for the quality of the goods and the speed of service'.[304] By contrast, in cases brought under what is now CPR 6.20 it has been established since the nineteenth century that permission to serve out requires the claimant to show that England is the appropriate forum.[305]

The differences between these two categories of case have been largely reduced, though not entirely eliminated. In a series of cases decided in the 1970s and 1980s the House of Lords moved from the position that a stay would be granted only if the English proceedings were vexatious or oppressive to the modern position that a stay should be granted if there is an available forum which is more appropriate than the English court.[306] The culmination of this development is the speech of Lord Goff in *Spiliada Maritime Corpn v Cansulex Ltd*,[307] which forms the cornerstone of the modern law.

2. *General principles*

(A) THE FUNDAMENTAL QUESTION

Although in *Amin Rasheed Shipping Corpn v Kuwait Insurance Co*[308] Lord Wilberforce expressed the view that the principles which had

303 *St Pierre v South American Stores (Gath and Chaves) Ltd* [1936] 1 KB 382.
304 *The Atlantic Star* [1973] QB 364 at 382.
305 *Société Générale de Paris v Dreyfus Bros* (1885) 29 Ch D 239.
306 *The Atlantic Star* [1974] AC 436, [1973] 2 All ER 175; *Rockware Glass Ltd v MacShannon* [1978] AC 795, [1978] 1 All ER 625; *The Abidin Daver* [1984] AC 398, [1984] 1 All ER 470.
307 [1987] AC 460, [1986] 3 All ER 843. For a policy-based evaluation of the law see Fawcett, 'Trial in England or Abroad: The Underlying Policy Considerations' (1989) 9 OJLS 205.
308 [1984] AC 50 at 72.

been formulated as regards the staying of proceedings were of little assistance in deciding cases under what is now CPR 6.20, the *Spiliada* case[309] establishes that the same fundamental principles apply where the defendant seeks a stay of proceedings which have been started as of right in England (forum non conveniens) and where the claimant seeks permission to serve a claim form on the defendant out of the jurisdiction (forum conveniens). The fundamental principle is to identify the court in which the case can be most suitably tried for the interests of the parties and the ends of justice.

The question which the court is required to consider runs a real risk of drawing the court into a consideration of the merits and demerits of foreign systems for the administration of justice. In the past, English judges were criticised for displaying 'judicial chauvinism', a feature of 'the good old days, the passing of which many may regret, when the inhabitants of this island felt an innate superiority over those unfortunate enough to belong to other races'.[310] More recently, however, a number of senior judges have gone out of their way to deprecate such chauvinism and to indicate that it has been replaced by 'judicial comity'.[311] When applying the test of appropriateness the English court should not pronounce upon the advantages and disadvantages of the system of administering justice in foreign countries as compared with the system of administering justice in England. To make such invidious comparisons 'is not consistent with the mutual respect which the courts of friendly states, each of which has a well developed system for the administration of justice, owe, or should owe to each other'.[312]

(B) THE DETERMINATION OF THE APPROPRIATE FORUM

A stay will be granted on the ground of forum non conveniens if the defendant satisfies the court that there is another available forum, having competent jurisdiction,[313] which is clearly or distinctly a more appropriate forum than the English court. In cases where the court's jurisdiction under CPR 6.20 is invoked the burden is on the claimant to establish that England is the most appropriate forum. If there is no foreign forum which is available to the claimant as an alternative forum for resolution of the dispute the court will refuse to grant a stay (or will

309 *Spiliada Maritime Corpn v Cansulex Ltd* [1987] AC 460, [1986] 3 All ER 843.
310 Lord Reid in *The Atlantic Star* [1974] AC 436 at 453.
311 See, in particular, the speech of Lord Diplock in *The Abidin Daver* [1984] AC 398 at 411.
312 Brandon LJ in *The El Amria* [1981] 2 Lloyd's Rep 119 at 126.
313 In relation to the question whether or not a foreign forum is 'available', the basis on which the foreign court may exercise jurisdiction is irrelevant: *Lubbe v Cape plc* [2000] 4 All ER 268, [2000] 1 WLR 1545.

give permission to serve out). Assuming, however, that there is another available forum, the court applies a two-stage test to determine whether the English court or the alternative forum is more appropriate.

(i) The first stage

At the first stage, the judge must consider which forum – the English court or a foreign one – is, prima facie, the more appropriate forum. The court must have regard to connecting factors which point towards one forum or the other as that which has the most real and substantial connection with the dispute. Relevant factors include the law governing the substance of the dispute and the places where the parties reside or carry on business as well as factors which affect convenience and expense (such as the availability of witnesses). In a case where proceedings are brought in England on the basis of the defendant's presence within the jurisdiction, if the court concludes at this stage that there is no other forum which is clearly more appropriate than England, it will refuse a stay.

There is no finite list of connecting factors which the court must consider at the first stage; much depends on the circumstances of each particular case. A factor which is of special significance in one case may be regarded as largely irrelevant in another. In principle, at the first stage, the court is seeking to identify the centre of gravity of the dispute so that inconvenience and expense can be reduced. The decided cases suggest that the court will pay special regard to six factors.

First, the court will always consider the territorial connections of the parties and the location of the evidence. If both the parties are resident in a foreign country and all the evidence is abroad, England is not, prima facie, the appropriate forum.

Secondly, where proceedings between the same parties arising out of the same dispute are also pending in a foreign court (lis alibi pendens) the English court will often be a less appropriate forum than would have been the case in the absence of the foreign proceedings. The additional inconvenience and expense which results from allowing two sets of proceedings to be pursued concurrently in two different countries – where the same facts are in issue and the testimony of the same witnesses required – adds weight to the argument that the foreign court is the appropriate forum. The court must also bear in mind the danger that parallel proceedings in two countries may lead to conflicting judgments.[314] In *The Abidin Daver*,[315] for example, Turkish shipowners

314 *The Varna (No 2)* [1994] 2 Lloyd's Rep 41; *Chase v Ram Technical Services Ltd* [2000] 2 Lloyd's Rep 418.

315 [1984] AC 398, [1984] 1 All ER 470.

had started proceedings in Turkey, claiming compensation from Cuban shipowners for damage arising from a collision between their ships in Turkish waters. The Cuban shipowners then started proceedings in England claiming damages from the Turkish shipowners in respect of the collision. The House of Lords took the view that the English proceedings should be stayed.

It should be stressed that the traditional rules – unlike article 27 of the Brussels I Regulation – do not endorse a simple 'first come, first served' approach.[316] Where proceedings in the foreign court have been started only a few days before the commencement of English proceedings, the existence of a lis alibi pendens is of little or no significance. Where, however, the foreign proceedings are well advanced and judgment is imminent the argument that the foreign court is the appropriate forum is a very strong one.[317]

Thirdly, where the factual matrix from which the dispute arises involves a multiplicity of parties the court will have regard to the desirability of ensuring that, as far as possible, all the disputes between the parties are resolved in one set of proceedings in a single forum. For example, in a dispute involving A, B and C, the English court may regard itself as being the appropriate forum for the trial of A's claim against B, even though England is not the centre of gravity of that particular dispute, because England is the only forum in which C can also be joined as a party.[318] Conversely, if a foreign court has jurisdiction to determine all the claims in multiparty proceedings – and the English court does not – this is an argument in favour of the foreign court being regarded as the appropriate forum.[319]

Fourthly, the balance of convenience may be tilted in favour of one forum rather than another because of the existence of other proceedings in that forum involving different parties but raising the same factual and legal issues. This is known as the *Cambridgeshire* factor. In the *Spiliada* case[320] the dispute arose out of a contract made between the plaintiff shipowners and the defendants, who carried on business in British Columbia. The contract was governed by English law. The plaintiffs claimed that damage had been caused to the ship by the defendants having loaded a cargo of sulphur when it was wet. A similar cargo had been loaded at the same time on another ship, the *Cambridgeshire*. When the plaintiffs sought to invoke the jurisdiction

316 *EI du Pont de Nemours & Co v Agnew and Kerr* [1987] 2 Lloyd's Rep 585.
317 *Cleveland Museum of Art v Capricorn Art International SA* [1990] 2 Lloyd's Rep 166.
318 See, for example, *The Kapetan Georgis* [1988] 1 Lloyd's Rep 352; *Smyth v Behbehani* [1999] IL Pr 584.
319 *The Oinoussin Pride* [1991] 1 Lloyd's Rep 126.
320 [1987] AC 460, [1986] 3 All ER 843.

of the English court the owners of the *Cambridgeshire* had already commenced proceedings against the defendants in England. These proceedings involved a similar cause of action and the same solicitors and insurers. The House of Lords held that the judge was justified in holding that England was the appropriate forum.

Fifthly, although the first stage of the *Spiliada* doctrine is usually dominated by a consideration of factual connections, the court will also have regard to the applicable law. While it is perfectly possible for the English court to apply a foreign law and for a foreign court to apply English law, where the dispute centres on legal rather than factual questions it is preferable that the dispute should be tried in the country whose law governs.[321] Although English judges are better placed than others to rule on questions of English law, the weight to be attached to the applicable law depends on the circumstances of the case. If the dispute is essentially one of fact, the applicable law is of little significance. If, however, an issue of English public policy arises in the context of a dispute concerning a contract governed by English law that issue should be decided by the English court. Not only would proceedings in a foreign forum involve the extra expense and inconvenience of expert evidence from English lawyers, but also a question of English public policy is not 'capable of fair resolution in any foreign court, however distinguished and well instructed'.[322]

Finally, if documentary evidence is an important element in the equation the language of the documents is relevant. Where there is a dispute as to whether England or Mexico is the appropriate forum, the fact that the dispute centres on documents which are drawn up in Spanish is an argument in favour of regarding the Mexican court as the appropriate forum; if the relevant documents were in English, this would be a factor pointing towards England as the appropriate forum.[323]

(ii) The second stage

The second stage has to be considered only if, having regard to the relevant connecting factors at the first stage, the court thinks that, prima facie, it is more appropriate for the dispute to be heard by a foreign court. Where proceedings are brought in England as of right (because the defendant was present in England when the claim form was served), if the court would incline towards granting a stay on the

321 See *Gan Insurance Co Ltd v Tai Ping Insurance Co Ltd* [1999] IL Pr 729; *Zivlin v Baal Taxa* [1998] IL Pr 106.

322 Bingham LJ in *EI du Pont de Nemours & Co v Agnew* [1987] 2 Lloyd's Rep 585 at 594.

323 *The Magnum* [1989] 1 Lloyd's Rep 47; *The Al Battani* [1993] 2 Lloyd's Rep 219.

basis that there is, prima facie, another forum which is clearly more appropriate than the English court, the claimant may still seek to resist a stay at the second stage. (Similarly, in cases under CPR 6.20, a claimant who fails at the first stage – because the court is not satisfied that England is the country with which the dispute is most closely connected – may succeed at the second stage.)

Notwithstanding the fact that England is not the country with which the dispute is most closely connected, the court will not grant a stay (or will give permission to serve out under CPR 6.20) if the court is satisfied that justice requires that the claimant should not be required to litigate abroad. At the second stage the burden is on the claimant. The court will consider all the circumstances of the case, including circumstances which go beyond those taken into account at the first stage. If the claimant can establish that he will not obtain justice in the foreign jurisdiction, that is a very relevant consideration. To succeed at the second stage it is not enough for the claimant to show merely that he has a legitimate personal or juridical advantage in proceedings in England. The fact that the claimant will be deprived of such an advantage if the dispute is not determined in England is not a sufficient reason for the court to exercise jurisdiction, provided that the court is satisfied that substantial justice will be done in the available appropriate forum.

Perhaps the most difficult issue at the second stage is to determine the dividing line between, on the one hand, a factor which is merely an advantage to the claimant and, on the other, a factor which is so important that, if denied to the claimant, there will be a denial of justice. A number of factors have been discussed by the courts.

First, if the claim is time-barred in the alternative forum, the court may decide that England is the forum conveniens, notwithstanding the fact that England is not the centre of gravity of the dispute. If the claim is time-barred in the foreign court, but would not be time-barred under the law applicable in the English court, and if the claimant did not act unreasonably in failing to commence proceedings in time in the foreign court, it would probably not be just for the English court to stay the proceedings (or refuse to give permission to serve out), unless the defendant agrees to waive the time-bar in the foreign court.[324]

Secondly, although Lord Goff made it clear in the *Spiliada* case[325] that, as a general rule, an advantage to the claimant of proceeding in England, rather than abroad, should not be regarded as decisive, there are a number of cases where the court has decided that the fact that a particular advantage to the claimant is not available in the natural

324 See Lord Goff in *Spiliada Maritime Corpn v Cansulex Ltd* [1987] AC 460 at 483.
325 *Spiliada Maritime Corpn v Cansulex Ltd* [1987] AC 460, [1986] 3 All ER 843.

forum means that justice would not be done if the English proceedings are stayed (or if permission to serve out is refused). For example, in *The Vishva Ajay*,[326] which involved a dispute arising out of a collision between two ships in Indian waters, the court refused to stay the proceedings on the basis that delay in India was likely to be at least six years and that a successful litigant in India would not be awarded costs on a realistic basis. By contrast, in *Radhakrishna Hospitality Service Private Ltd v EIH Ltd*,[327] another case in which India was the country with which the parties' dispute was most closely connected, less weight was given to the possibility that Indian proceedings would be significantly slower than English proceedings and a stay was granted. In *Roneleigh Ltd v MII Exports Inc*,[328] a case in which New Jersey was plainly the forum with which the dispute had its most real and substantial connection, the Court of Appeal upheld the judge's decision to allow service out of the jurisdiction. The basis of the decision was that, since the law of New Jersey does not allow a successful claimant to recover costs, substantial justice would not be done in the foreign forum.

As a general rule, the mere fact that the claimant, if successful, would recover higher damages in English proceedings than in proceedings abroad is not enough to justify the conclusion that the grant of a stay should be refused (or permission to serve out granted).[329] Nevertheless, there are cases in which it has been held that, where the difference between the damages which could be recovered in England and abroad is very considerable, it would amount to an injustice if the defendant were required to pursue his claim abroad.[330] It has also been held that, where a foreign judgment is more difficult to enforce internationally than an English judgment (which is enforceable in other member states under the Brussels regime), it may be unjust to deprive the claimant of the advantage of proceeding in England.[331] Finally, the court may regard the fact that the claimant cannot afford to pursue his claim abroad to be decisive. Where the claimant's financial predicament means that there is no possibility of the claim being litigated in the natural forum, but litigation can be pursued in England (for example, because of the availability of legal aid or a

326 [1989] 2 Lloyd's Rep 558.

327 [1999] 2 Lloyd's Rep 249. See also *Konamaneni v Rolls-Royce Industrial Power (India) Ltd* [2002] 1 All ER 979.

328 [1989] 1 WLR 619.

329 *Herceg Novi v Ming Galaxy* [1998] 4 All ER 238.

330 *The Vishva Abha* [1990] 2 Lloyd's Rep 312 (damages limited to £367,500 under South African law; potential liability of £1.5 million under English law); *Baghlaf Al Zafer Factory Co BR for Industry Ltd v Pakistan National Shipping Co* [1998] 2 Lloyd's Rep 229.

331 *International Credit and Investment Company (Overseas) Ltd v Shaikh Kamal Adham* [1999] IL Pr 302.

conditional fee agreement between the claimant and his English solicitors) the court may decide that, in the interests of justice, English proceedings should not be stayed.[332] Similarly, in a case where the claim is being brought by a large number of claimants and the natural forum does not have either experience of or adequate facilities for dealing with such proceedings, the court may refuse to grant a stay on the basis that the English court (which does have the necessary experience and facilities) provides the most appropriate forum.[333]

Thirdly, if the defendant will not receive a fair hearing in the alternative forum – for example, because of political or ideological reasons – this is a significant factor which is likely to tilt the balance in favour of England as the appropriate forum. In *Oppenheimer v Louis Rosenthal & Co AG*[334] leave was sought in 1937 for process to be served in Germany. Although in other circumstances the German court might well have been the more appropriate forum, leave was granted because the plaintiff, being a Jew, would probably not have got a fair trial in the German court and, indeed, might have been put in a concentration camp if he visited Germany. However, it is not unjust to refuse a stay in a case where the principal reason for the claimant wanting to avoid litigation in a more appropriate foreign forum is to avoid being exposed to criminal charges in that country.[335]

It should not be thought that the court will simply accept an allegation by the claimant that he will not get a fair trial abroad. A litigant's fears as to the quality of justice in the alternative forum are not relevant[336] and the claimant who wishes to resist a stay (or obtain permission to serve out) on the basis that even-handed justice may not be done abroad 'must assert this candidly and support his allegations with positive and cogent evidence'.[337]

Fourthly, the court may conclude that justice will not be done abroad in circumstances where it is shown that the foreign court, applying its own choice of law principles, will reach a conclusion which is opposed to that which would be reached by the English court through the application of English conflicts rules.[338] For example, in a case where the rival jurisdictions are England and the United Arab Emirates, if the courts of the United Arab Emirates would apply the local law, under which the claimant is bound to fail, but the English

332 *Connelly v RTZ Corpn plc* [1998] AC 854. See also *Carlson v Rio Tinto plc* [1999] CLC 551.
333 *Lubbe v Cape plc* [2000] 4 All ER 268, [2000] 1 WLR 1545.
334 [1937] 1 All ER 23.
335 *Askin v Absa Bank Ltd* [1999] IL Pr 471.
336 *Jeyaretnam v Mahmood* (1992) Times, 21 May.
337 Lord Diplock in *The Abidin Daver* [1984] AC 398 at 411.
338 *Irish Shipping Ltd v Commercial Union Assurance Co plc* [1991] 2 QB 206, [1989] 3 All ER 853; *Tiernan v Magen Insurance Co Ltd* [2000] IL Pr 517.

court would – on the basis of English choice of law principles – apply Spanish law, according to which the claimant has an arguable claim, the English court is likely to exercise jurisdiction, even though the United Arab Emirates is the natural forum.[339] These decisions are based on the courts' view that it is not conducive to justice to require the claimant, who has – in the eyes of English private international law – an arguable claim, to litigate in a forum where his claim would inevitably be rejected. Such a view might be thought to be hard to reconcile with judicial comity. As one commentator has noted: 'It is a little difficult to see why, if ... restraint is (very properly) to be exercised with regard to adjectival matters, it should not be similarly appropriate with regard to substantive matters.'[340]

(iii) Weighing the factors

At the first stage, where the connecting factors point in different directions, the court has to weigh them against each other to decide where the balance of convenience lies. In *Amin Rasheed Shipping Corpn v Kuwait Insurance Co*,[341] for example, the plaintiff, a Liberian company resident in Dubai, had entered a contract of marine insurance with the defendant, a Kuwaiti insurance company. When a dispute arose between the parties the plaintiff wished to bring proceedings in England. The House of Lords, although holding that the parties had impliedly chosen English law as the applicable law, held that the judge had been right to conclude that England was not the appropriate forum. The factual issues 'could be determined as well in Kuwait as in England, possibly better, and with no clear overall balance of convenience'.[342] Although any legal questions were to be decided by English law, there was no reason to suppose that a Kuwaiti judge would have any difficulty in applying the applicable rules.

The problems of weighing the relevant factors are considerably greater at the second stage in cases where the court has to weigh the fact that England is not the country with which the parties' dispute is most closely connected against the claimant's assertion that justice will not be done abroad. The range of factors which the court is entitled to consider is very wide and the authorities do not give any guidance as to how these factors are to be weighed in any particular case. Inevitably, the test of appropriateness is rather open-textured and its application is unpredictable.[343]

339 *Banco Atlantico SA v British Bank of the Middle East* [1990] 2 Lloyd's Rep 504.
340 Carter, (1989) 60 BYIL 482 at 484–485.
341 [1984] AC 50, [1983] 2 All ER 884.
342 Lord Wilberforce at 66.
343 See Hill, 'Jurisdiction in Civil and Commercial Matters: Is There a Third Way?' [2001] CLP 439.

The English doctrine is open to the criticism that it unduly favours the English forum by giving the claimant two bites at the cherry. If England is the natural forum the English court will refuse to grant a stay (or will give permission to serve out); if England is not the natural forum the court may still refuse to grant a stay (or give permission to serve out) on the basis that justice will not be done in the foreign forum. As has been seen, the fact that the claimant has a significant advantage in suing in England rather than abroad may be regarded as of such importance that the court concludes that there would be a denial of justice if the case were not heard here. However, the court will invariably exercise jurisdiction in cases where England is the natural forum. In such cases it is unlikely that the second stage of the *Spiliada* test has any application as this would involve the defendant challenging jurisdiction in England on the basis that if the case is tried in England justice will not be done. If a claimant can resist a stay of proceedings on the basis that damages abroad are derisory, why is a defendant not able to obtain a stay on the basis that English damages are much lower than those which would be awarded by the alternative forum? Since the *Spiliada* doctrine is asymmetrical in this way the boast that 'judicial chauvinism has been replaced by judicial comity'[344] should not be accepted too uncritically.

3. *The effect of a jurisdiction clause*

(A) CASES INVOLVING A JURISDICTION CLAUSE IN FAVOUR OF THE ENGLISH COURTS

In many cases where the parties choose English jurisdiction the English court has jurisdiction by virtue of article 23 of the Regulation.[345] In those cases where article 23 does not confer jurisdiction (for example, in situations falling outside the scope of article 1 of the Brussels regime or where neither party is domiciled in a member state) whether the court is entitled to exercise jurisdiction is determined by the traditional rules. It would also seem that, even as regards cases within the scope of article 1, a claimant who is domiciled in a member state may invoke the traditional rules against a defendant who is not domiciled in a member state in a case where, although the parties agree to English jurisdiction, the agreement does not comply with the formal requirements of article 23.[346]

In cases involving an English jurisdiction clause in which the traditional rules apply, the court has a discretion whether or not to exercise jurisdiction. A defendant who, having agreed to English

344 Lord Diplock in *The Abidin Daver* [1984] AC 398 at 411.
345 Whether the court may stay proceedings in such cases is discussed at pp 133–134.
346 Art 4.

jurisdiction, is served with a claim form in England, may apply for a stay of proceedings. There is no reported case in which a stay has been granted in this situation.[347] If the defendant cannot be served with process in England, the court will – in the absence of strong reason to the contrary – hold the parties to their bargain and give permission to serve out of the jurisdiction under CPR 6.20(5)(d).[348]

(B) CASES INVOLVING A JURISDICTION CLAUSE IN FAVOUR OF THE COURTS OF A NON-MEMBER STATE

Where a dispute arises out of a contract which contains a provision conferring exclusive jurisdiction on the courts of a non-member state the English court will normally not permit proceedings to be conducted in England in breach of the terms of the agreement. If the defendant is served with the claim form in England the defendant is normally entitled to a stay;[349] if the claimant seeks permission to serve out of the jurisdiction under CPR 6.20 permission will normally be refused.[350] A non-exclusive jurisdiction clause also creates a strong prima facie case that the chosen forum is the appropriate one.[351]

Nevertheless, the court retains a discretion. The court may refuse a stay (or may give permission to serve out of the jurisdiction) if strong cause is shown by the claimant.[352] The court may decide to exercise jurisdiction, notwithstanding the foreign jurisdiction clause, if there are related proceedings already being conducted in England and there will be significant advantages – in terms of convenience and expense – if the claimant is permitted to sue the defendant in England.[353] The mere fact that the claimant has failed to bring proceedings in the agreed forum within the limitation period is not a sufficient cause to allow proceedings to be brought in England.[354] However, it has been

347 There is, however, one reported case where English proceedings were stayed on the plaintiff's application, notwithstanding an English jurisdiction agreement: *Bouygues Offshore SA v Caspian Shipping Co (Nos. 1, 3, 4 & 5)* [1998] 2 Lloyd's Rep 461.

348 *The Chaparral* [1968] 2 Lloyd's Rep 158.

349 *The Nile Rhapsody* [1994] 1 Lloyd's Rep 382; *The Pioneer Container* [1994] 2 AC 324, [1994] 2 All ER 250.

350 *Mackender v Feldia AG* [1967] 2 QB 590, [1966] 3 All ER 847; *Ingosstrakh Insurance Co Ltd v Latvian Shipping Company* [2000] IL Pr 164.

351 *The Rothnie* [1996] 2 Lloyd's Rep 206.

352 *The Eleftheria* [1970] P 94, [1969] 2 All ER 641; *Evans Marshall & Co Ltd v Bertola SA* [1973] 1 All ER 992, [1973] 1 WLR 349. See Peel, 'Exclusive Jurisdiction Agreements: Purity and Pragmatism in the Conflict of Laws' [1998] LMCLQ 182.

353 *The El Amria* [1981] 2 Lloyd's Rep 119; *Citi-March Ltd v Neptune Orient Lines Ltd* [1996] 2 All ER 545, [1996] 1 WLR 1367. See also *The MC Pearl* [1997] 1 Lloyd's Rep 566.

354 *The Pioneer Container* [1994] 2 AC 324, [1994] 2 All ER 250.

held that, if the limitation period has expired in the agreed forum and it was not unreasonable for the claimant not to have started proceedings before the limitation expired, a stay of proceedings may be refused (unless the defendant undertakes to waive the time bar in the agreed forum).[355]

If the claimant can establish that he will not receive a fair trial in the agreed forum – such as for political or racial reasons – the English court may allow the claimant to sue in England in breach of the terms of the jurisdiction agreement. For example, in *Carvalho v Hull, Blyth (Angola) Ltd*[356] the parties entered a contract which conferred exclusive jurisdiction of the courts of Angola. At that time Angola was still a province of Portugal, the courts applied Portuguese law and litigants had a final right of appeal to the Supreme Court in Lisbon. Soon after the start of the civil war in Angola the plaintiff, having received threats against his life, fled the country, leaving all his property there. A dispute arose and the plaintiff, who feared returning to Angola, started proceedings in England. The court refused to grant a stay of the English proceedings on two grounds. First, the post-revolution Angolan court was completely different from the court contemplated by the parties at the time of the contract. Secondly, there was a question as to whether the plaintiff would be treated fairly by the Angolan courts in view of the fact that the plaintiff 'was the sort of the person who would be anathema to the [new] government in Angola'.[357]

4. *Forum non conveniens and the Brussels regime*

Apart from the specific provisions of the Brussels regime which set out the circumstances in which proceedings must (or may) be stayed,[358] the court has no general discretion under the Brussels regime to stay proceedings. One possible conclusion from the Brussels regime's silence on this issue is that, where the English court has jurisdiction under the Brussels regime, the court never has discretion to stay its proceedings. However, the better view is that such silence should be interpreted as leaving the English courts free to stay proceedings on the basis of forum non conveniens if the grant of a stay would not be inconsistent with the Brussels regime itself.[359] Before the more difficult issues are discussed, there are a number of relatively uncontroversial points which should be noted.

355 *Baghlaf Al Zafer Factory Co BR for Industry Ltd v Pakistan National Shipping Co* [1998] 2 Lloyd's Rep 229.

356 [1979] 3 All ER 280, [1979] 1 WLR 1228.

357 Geoffrey Lane LJ at 1241.

358 As regards arts 27 and 28 of the Brussels I Regulation, see pp 111–119.

359 See Civil Jurisdiction and Judgments Act 1982, s 49 (which expressly applies in relation to the Brussels and Lugano Conventions, but not the Brussels I Regulation).

(A) CASES WHERE THE GRANT OF A STAY IS INCONSISTENT WITH THE BRUSSELS REGIME

If the jurisdiction of the English court is founded on the Brussels regime the English court is not entitled to stay the proceedings on the basis that another member state is more appropriate. Where, for example, an English defendant is sued in England in relation to a road accident which occurred in France, the court cannot stay the proceedings on the basis that France is the natural forum. This type of case is governed solely by the Brussels I Regulation.[360]

(B) CASES WHERE THE GRANT OF A STAY IS NOT INCONSISTENT WITH THE BRUSSELS REGIME

First, it seems reasonably clear that in a case which is internal to the United Kingdom and is governed entirely by Schedule 4 to the Civil Jurisdiction and Judgments Act 1982, the Brussels regime does not inhibit in any way the discretion of the English court to stay proceedings in favour of the courts of Scotland or Northern Ireland. Although in *Foxen v Scotsman Publications Ltd*[361] Drake J decided that the English court had no discretion to stay English proceedings on the ground that Scotland was the more appropriate forum, the same judge reached the opposite conclusion in *Cummings v Scottish Daily Record & Sunday Mail Ltd.*[362] The decision in the latter case is clearly the correct one.

Secondly, where the jurisdiction of the English court is based on the traditional rules a stay may be granted on the basis of forum non conveniens whether the alternative forum is another member state or a non-member state.[363] Of course, if parallel or related proceedings have already been commenced in another member state the English court must apply articles 27 and 28.

Thirdly, it is reasonable to suppose that there are two situations in which, although the court has jurisdiction under the Brussels regime, the court's discretion to stay the proceedings is not inhibited: where the parties have agreed that the courts of a non-member state are to have exclusive jurisdiction;[364] and where proceedings relate to title to, or possession of, immovable property situated in a non-member state.[365]

360 Mance J in *Sarrio SA v Kuwait Investment Authority* [1996] 1 Lloyd's Rep 650 at 654.

361 [1995] EMLR 145.

362 [1995] EMLR 538.

363 *The Xin Yang* [1996] 2 Lloyd's Rep 217; *Sarrio SA v Kuwait Investment Authority* [1997] 1 Lloyd's Rep 113.

364 This is supported by the Schlosser Report, OJ 1979 C59/124, para 176 and the decision of Potter J in *Arkwright Mutual Insurance Co v Bryanston Insurance Co Ltd* [1990] 2 QB 649, [1990] 2 All ER 335.

365 *Re Polly Peck International plc (No 2)* [1998] 3 All ER 812 at 829–830.

(C) THE MOST DIFFICULT CASES

The main area of controversy is whether the English court has a general discretion to stay proceedings in a case where, notwithstanding the fact that jurisdiction is derived from the Brussels regime, the court of a non-member state provides a more appropriate forum. At first the English courts took the view that, since the Brussels regime is designed (subject to article 4) to achieve uniformity and to harmonise the relevant procedural and jurisdictional rules of the courts of the member states, there is no room for the application of the doctrine of forum non conveniens in this situation.[366] However, when the question came for the first time before the Court of Appeal a different approach was adopted.

In *Re Harrods (Buenos Aires) Ltd*,[367] although the court had jurisdiction under article 2 of the Brussels Convention (on the basis of the defendant company's domicile), the Court of Appeal held that the proceedings could be stayed if the defendant satisfied the court that a non-contracting state (in this case Argentina) was a more appropriate forum. In the opinion of the Court of Appeal, the English court's refusal of jurisdiction in such circumstances does not in any way impair the object of the Brussels regime of establishing an expeditious, harmonious and certain procedure for the enforcement of judgments; if the English court refuses jurisdiction there will be no judgment of the English court to be enforced in other states.[368] Furthermore, although there is no reported case in which the defendant has obtained a stay of English proceedings in a situation where the court has jurisdiction under what is now article 23 of the Regulation, it has been held (obiter) that the court may grant a stay of its proceedings in favour of a non-member state in such circumstances.[369]

The decision in the *Harrods* case and its reasoning has been the subject of much criticism. Most fundamentally, it has been argued that the approach of the Court of Appeal misunderstands the Brussels regime, whose objective is not simply the allocation of jurisdiction between the member states, and that the decision is misguided, if not downright wrong.[370] One of the recitals to the Brussels I Regulation

366 *S & W Berisford plc v New Hampshire Insurance Co* [1990] 2 QB 631, [1990] 2 All ER 321; *Arkwright Mutual Insurance Co v Bryanston Insurance Co Ltd* [1990] 2 QB 649, [1990] 2 All ER 335.

367 [1992] Ch 72, [1991] 4 All ER 334.

368 See also *The Po* [1991] 2 Lloyd's Rep 206; *The Nile Rhapsody* [1994] 1 Lloyd's Rep 382; *Ace Insurance SA-NV v Zurich Insurance Co* [2001] EWCA Civ 173, [2001] 1 Lloyd's Rep 618; *Haji-Ioannou v Frangos* [1999] 2 Lloyd's Rep 337.

369 See, for example, *UBS AG v Omni Holding AG* [2000] 1 WLR 916; *Sinochem International Oil (London) Co Ltd v Mobil Sales and Supply Corpn* [2000] 1 Lloyd's Rep 670. The approach adopted in these cases is controversial: see Cheshire and North, *Private International Law* (13th edn, 1999) p 265.

370 Cheshire and North, *Private International Law* (13th edn, 1999) p 266.

states that '[t]he rules of jurisdiction must be highly predicable';[371] the attainment of this objective is not assisted by the application of the doctrine of forum non conveniens in cases where the English court has jurisdiction under the provisions of Chapter II of the Regulation. Even if it is accepted that the power to stay proceedings may be exercised in a case where all the connections are either with England or with non-member states, it is unclear whether the power is exercisable in a situation where there are factual connections with England, another member state and a non-member state. Although the decision in the *Harrods* case seems to have been premised on the fact that no other contracting state was in any way concerned,[372] in *The Po*[373] the Court of Appeal considered that it had the power to stay proceedings in favour of the courts of Brazil, notwithstanding the fact that one of the parties was domiciled in Italy. The controversy and uncertainty surrounding the *Harrods* case is unlikely to be resolved until the matter is considered by the Court of Justice.[374] In *Lubbe v Cape plc*[375] the House of Lords decided that, had it been required to determine whether or not *Re Harrods (Buenos Aires) Ltd* had been correctly decided, it would have been necessary to seek a ruling from the Court of Justice – on the basis that the answer to the question raised by that case is not clear.[376]

There is no easy solution to the problems posed by cases such as *Re Harrods (Buenos Aires) Ltd.*[377] The simple fact is that, as regards jurisdictional issues, Chapter II of the Regulation contains no provision which directly seeks to regulate the relationship between the courts of member states and those of non-member states. The provisions of Chapter II are inward-looking, in that they are focused exclusively on disputes which are internal to the member states. This is in marked contrast to the provisions of Chapter III which expressly provide a solution to the problem posed by conflicting judgments given by the courts of member and non-member states.[378] It is unfortunate that the member states have not taken the opportunity to amend the Brussels regime with a view to providing a framework for the resolution of jurisdictional disputes which involve connections with member states and non-member states.

371 Recital 11.
372 [1992] Ch 72 at 98.
373 [1991] 2 Lloyd's Rep 206.
374 *Re Harrods (Buenos Aires) Ltd* was appealed to the House of Lords which referred a number of questions to the Court of Justice (Case C-314/92). Before the reference was heard the dispute was settled.
375 [2000] 4 All ER 268, [2000] 1 WLR 1545.
376 Lord Bingham at 1562.
377 See Briggs, 'Some Points of Friction between English and Brussels Convention Jurisdiction' in Adenas and Jacobs (eds), *European Community Law in the English Courts* (1998) p 277.
378 Art 34(4). See pp 195–196.

C Cases involving immovable property not regulated by the Brussels regime

It has been seen that in a situation which falls within the scope of the Regulation, article 22(1) provides that proceedings relating to rights in rem in, or tenancies of, immovable property are within the exclusive jurisdiction of the courts of the member state in which the property is situated. However, the Brussels regime has no application to cases in which either the subject-matter of the dispute is not within the scope of article 1 or the immovable property in question is not situated in a member state. These situations are governed by the traditional rules.

At common law the English court will not adjudicate on questions relating to the title to, or the right to the possession of, immovable property[379] out of the jurisdiction.[380] Accordingly, in a case involving title to land in Brazil, the English court will not exercise jurisdiction even if the claimant can serve the Brazilian defendant with the claim form in England or can invoke some other basis of jurisdiction recognised by the traditional rules.

Although the origin of the common law rule may have lain in procedural requirements, the justification for it today is, first, that as immovable property is under the control of the authorities of the country where it is situated, whose law may refuse to recognise an English judgment relating to the property, such an exercise of jurisdiction would quite possibly be ineffective and, secondly, that the courts of the situs are the ones best able to apply their own often technical and complex rules about title to land.

In *Norris v Chambres*[381] the plaintiff had contracted to buy foreign land and paid a deposit to the vendor. The vendor repudiated the contract and sold the land to the defendant. The plaintiff brought proceedings against the defendant in England claiming that he was entitled to a lien over the land in respect of the deposit he had paid. The court held that it had no jurisdiction to decide whether the plaintiff had such a right over foreign land. The same approach is illustrated by *Deschamps v Miller*.[382] The plaintiff's father had acquired lands in India and subsequently transferred them to the defendant. The plaintiff claimed that his mother had been entitled, by virtue of the proprietary consequences of her marriage, to a half-share in the property and that, on his mother's death, he was entitled to succeed to this half-share. The court held that it lacked jurisdiction to decide the question.

379 For the distinction between movable and immovable property see pp 478–480.
380 *British South Africa Co v Companhia de Moçambique* [1893] AC 602.
381 (1861) 29 Beav 246; affd 3 De GF & J 583.
382 [1908] 1 Ch 856.

Until relatively recently the law was that the English court would not exercise jurisdiction in respect of a tort affecting foreign land.[383] Section 30 of the Civil Jurisdiction and Judgments Act 1982 provides that the court is not deprived of jurisdiction in such a case 'unless the proceedings are principally concerned with a question of the title to, or the right to possession of' the property.[384]

While the court will not exercise jurisdiction on a question as to the title to or a right to possession of a foreign immovable, it does not follow that it must not deal with any case having a connection with such property. For example, the court may exercise jurisdiction in rem against a ship to enforce a claim for damage done to foreign land.[385] More importantly, if the court has jurisdiction in contractual proceedings, that jurisdiction will not be ousted because the contract relates to foreign land. Moreover, the court will enforce an obligation arising from such a contract, or from a trust or some other source, not merely by an award of damages or other monetary relief, but even by ordering a party to transfer or create a right in foreign land. In such a case, the court is not adjudicating on the present title to the land, on which its decision may be ineffective; its order to transfer or create a title can be enforced in personam[386] – by committing the defendant for contempt if he does not comply with the order. However, the court will not order a party to do in relation to foreign land something which the law of the foreign country would not permit or enable him to do.[387]

A court may make a decree of specific performance in relation to the sale of foreign land[388] and may order a party to execute a mortgage over foreign land in fulfilment of a contractual promise to do so.[389] The court may also enforce an obligation to transfer or create a right in foreign land arising from 'a fiduciary relationship or fraud, or other conduct which, in the view of the Court of Equity in this country, would be unconscionable'.[390] For example, in *Razelos v Razelos (No 2)*[391] a husband had bought in his own name certain land in

383 *British South Africa Co v Companhia de Moçambique* [1893] AC 602; *Hesperides Hotels Ltd v Muftizade* [1979] AC 508, [1978] 2 All ER 1168.

384 See, for example, *Re Polly Peck International plc (in administration) (No 4)* [1998] 2 BCLC 185.

385 *The Tolten* [1946] P 135, [1946] 2 All ER 372.

386 *Penn v Lord Baltimore* (1750) 1 Ves Sen 444.

387 *Re Courtney* (1840) Mont & Ch 239.

388 *Richard West & Partners (Inverness) Ltd v Dick* [1969] 2 Ch 424, [1969] 1 All ER 289.

389 *Re Smith* [1916] 2 Ch 206.

390 *Deschamps v Miller* [1908] 1 Ch 856 at 863.

391 [1970] 1 All ER 386n, [1970] 1 WLR 392. See also *Hamlin v Hamlin* [1986] Fam 11, [1985] 2 All ER 1037.

Greece, using his wife's money. In proceedings under the Married Women's Property Act 1882 brought by the wife, who was living in England, it was held that the husband was under an obligation in equity to transfer the land to her, for otherwise he would be fraudulently depriving her of it. The court order to the effect that the wife was entitled to the property could not, of course, actually affect the title of the land in Greece; if, however, the husband returned to England the order could be enforced in personam against him.

An interesting feature of such cases in which the court enforces an obligation relating to foreign land arising from an equity is that in determining whether there is an equity the court has regard to English law, rather than to the foreign law; if according to English law there is an equity the court will enforce it, even though the equity may be one not recognised by the law of the place where the property is situated.[392] In such a case, an overriding effect is given to English rules relating to fraud, the abuse of fiduciary relationships and other unconscionable conduct. In effect, public policy is thought to require the application of these rules, whatever law would otherwise govern.

The cases just considered are not exceptions to the rule that the English court will not adjudicate on the title to or right to possession of foreign immovables, but rather fall outside its scope. There are, however, a number of true exceptions. First, where the court has jurisdiction over a deceased's estate which includes property in England the court will also determine entitlement to immovable property situated outside England which is part of that estate.[393] The basis of this jurisdiction, which is far from obvious, has not been satisfactorily explained by the courts, but the jurisdiction seems to be established. It should be noted that, because such proceedings fall outside the scope of the Brussels regime (which does not apply to wills and succession), this jurisdiction applies equally to immovable property in member states and non-member states. Secondly, 'in the exercise of the undoubted jurisdiction of the courts it may become necessary incidentally to investigate and determine the title to foreign lands'.[394] It is not clear what cases would fall within this category.[395]

392 *Re Anchor Line (Henderson Bros) Ltd* [1937] Ch 483, [1937] 2 All ER 823.

393 *Re Ross* [1930] 1 Ch 377; *Re Duke of Wellington* [1948] Ch 118, [1947] 2 All ER 854.

394 *British South Africa Co v Companhia de Moçambique* [1893] AC 602.

395 An example might be *Adams v Clutterbuck* (1883) 10 QBD 403 (which concerned a document executed in England conveying shooting rights over moorland in Scotland).

IV PROVISIONAL MEASURES[396]

A Introduction

One of the significant developments in the latter part of the twentieth century was the evolution of certain types of provisional measure designed to maintain the status quo pending the outcome of the dispute between the parties. For example, the English court may grant the claimant a freezing order (commonly referred to as a Mareva injunction), the purpose of which is to prevent the defendant from moving his assets or dissipating them, so that if the claim is successful there will be assets available to satisfy the judgment. By such orders the courts aim to frustrate the efforts of defendants who seek to make themselves immune from the court's final judgment.

Where the main proceedings are being conducted in England, plainly the English court has jurisdiction to grant such provisional measures as may be appropriate in the context of those proceedings.[397] More problematic, however, are cases where the main proceedings are being conducted in another country: may the English court grant provisional measures in support of those proceedings? Even more contentious is whether the English court may make orders requiring the defendant to do something or refrain from doing something not in England but in another country.

B Jurisdiction to grant provisional measures in support of foreign proceedings

Common sense would suggest that if proceedings are pending in one country and the defendant's assets are situated in another, the claimant ought to be able to obtain protective or interim relief by way of attachment in the country where the assets are to be found.[398] After a lengthy period of uncertainty and development, English law finally achieved this position in the 1990s.

1. Proceedings in another member state (or another part of the United Kingdom)

Article 31 of the Brussels I Regulation provides that application may be made to the courts of a member state for such provisional, including protective, measures as may be available under the law of

396 Collins, 'Provisional and Protective Measures in International Litigation' in *Essays in International Litigation and the Conflict of Laws* (1994) pp 1–188.
397 Case C-391/95 *Van Uden Maritime BV v Firma Deco-Line* [1998] ECR I-7091.
398 See Collins, 'The Siskina Again: An Opportunity Missed' (1996) 112 LQR 8.

that state, even if the courts of another member state have jurisdiction as to the substance of the matter.[399] Of course, this provision is relevant only in matters coming within the ambit of the Brussels regime. Article 31 applies to measures which are intended to preserve a factual or legal situation in one member state so as to safeguard rights which are the subject matter of litigation in the court of another member state which has jurisdiction as to the substance of the matter.[400] Article 31 may also be invoked by a claimant who is seeking provisional measures in support of arbitration proceedings (rather than court proceedings in another member state) as long as the rights which the claimant is seeking to safeguard are civil or commercial in nature.[401] A measure does not come within the scope of article 31 if its provisional character is not guaranteed; a court order requiring the defendant to make an unconditional interim payment cannot be a provisional measure for the purposes of article 31 unless, if the claimant is unsuccessful, the defendant can obtain repayment.[402] Mareva injunctions are measures falling within the scope of article 31.

Article 31 does not in itself confer jurisdiction on an English court to grant a Mareva injunction in support of foreign proceedings. It is, however, provided by section 25 of the Civil Jurisdiction and Judgments Act 1982 that the court may grant interim relief in cases where the subject matter of the litigation falls within the scope of article 1 of the Brussels regime and the proceedings have been commenced or are to be commenced in a member state other than the United Kingdom (or in another part of the United Kingdom), whether or not the defendant is otherwise amenable to the jurisdiction of the court. Where proceedings have been commenced in France, the claimant may apply to the court in England for a Mareva injunction freezing the defendant's assets, even though the court does not have jurisdiction over the claimant's substantive claim.[403] The power to grant interim relief in support of proceedings in another member state exists regardless of whether the defendant is domiciled in a member state.

399 Sch 4 to the Civil Jurisdiction and Judgments Act 1982 (rule 16) lays down the same rule for cases where the courts of another part of the United Kingdom have jurisdiction as to the substantive proceedings.

400 Case C-261/90 *Reichert v Dresdner Bank AG (No 2)* [1992] ECR I-2149 at 2184 (para 34).

401 Case C-391/95 *Van Uden Maritime BV v Firma Deco-Line* [1998] ECR I-7091.

402 Case C-391/95 *Van Uden Maritime BV v Firma Deco-Line* [1998] ECR I-7091; Case C-99/96 *Mietz v Intership Yachting Sneek BV* [1999] ECR I-2277.

403 See *Republic of Haiti v Duvalier* [1990] 1 QB 202, [1989] 1 All ER 456.

2. Proceedings in a non-member state and proceedings outside the scope of article 1 of the Brussels regime

At common law, the English court does not have jurisdiction to order provisional measures in support of foreign proceedings.[404] Towards the end of the twentieth century the position at common law came under considerable criticism and, in due course, section 25(1) of the Civil Jurisdiction and Judgments Act 1982 was extended not only to cases falling outside the scope of the Brussels regime but also to cases falling within the Brussels regime's scope in which the relevant foreign proceedings are being (or will be) conducted in a non-member state.[405]

3. Procedural issues

CPR 6.20(4)[406] provides that a claim form may be served out of the jurisdiction with the permission of the court if a claim is made for an interim remedy under section 25(1) of the Civil Jurisdiction and Judgments Act 1982. There is no requirement that the foreign proceedings in respect of which an interim remedy is sought should be international in nature; where a French claimant sues a French defendant in France, the English court is not prevented from giving permission to serve out under CPR 6.20(4).[407]

4. Discretion

When considering whether or not to grant interim relief under section 25(1) of the Civil Jurisdiction and Judgments Act 1982, the first issue is whether the conditions for the grant of the relief would have been satisfied if the main proceedings had been pending in England. A Mareva injunction will not be granted unless the claimant can establish that he has a good arguable case on the merits and that the refusal of a Mareva injunction would involve a real risk that a judgment (or arbitral award) in favour of the claimant would remain unsatisfied.[408] If the necessary conditions are satisfied the court has to consider whether the fact that the court does not have jurisdiction other than under section 25 makes it inexpedient to grant the interim

404 *Siskina (Owners of cargo lately laden on board) v Distos Compania Naviera SA* [1979] AC 210, [1977] 3 All ER 803.

405 The power to extend s 25(1) was provided by s 25(3) of the 1982 Act, which was exercised by the introduction of the Civil Jurisdiction and Judgments Act 1982 (Interim Relief) Order 1997, SI 1997/302.

406 This replaced RSC Ord 11, r 8A.

407 *Alltrans Inc v Interdom Holdings Ltd* [1991] 4 All ER 458.

408 *Ninemia Maritime Corpn v Trave Schiffahrtsgesellschaft mbH und Co KG* [1984] 1 All ER 398, [1983] 1 WLR 1412.

relief.[409] It would be inexpedient to exercise jurisdiction under section 25 if the grant of interim relief would obstruct or hamper the management of the case by the foreign court seised of the substantive proceedings.[410]

C Extraterritorial orders

As a matter of principle there is no reason why provisional measures granted by the court should be limited to acts performed in England or to assets located in England. If a defendant who is amenable to the court's jurisdiction commits an act in breach of the terms of an injunction the act amounts to a contempt regardless of whether the act was committed in England or abroad. The court has the power under section 37(1) of the Supreme Court Act 1981 to appoint a receiver over assets which are abroad,[411] to make a search order (frequently referred to as an Anton Piller order) in respect of foreign premises,[412] and to grant a Mareva injunction in relation to the defendant's assets, regardless of their location.[413]

The fact that the court has the power to grant provisional measures which seek to restrain the defendant from performing certain acts abroad does not mean, however, that such a power should be liberally exercised. The propriety of granting extraterritorial provisional measures has been considered most frequently by the courts in the context of applications for a 'worldwide' Mareva injunction. Although it is firmly established that the English court's jurisdiction to grant a Mareva injunction against a person depends not on the court's territorial jurisdiction over assets located in England but on the court's unlimited jurisdiction in personam against any person who is properly made a party to English proceedings,[414] an extraterritorial Mareva injunction will be granted only in exceptional circumstances.[415]

The court will only consider the grant of extraterritorial relief if the defendant has insufficient English assets to satisfy the claimant's claim. In an appropriate case the court may even order the transfer of foreign assets from one foreign country (where the final judgment will

409 Civil Jurisdiction and Judgments Act 1983, s 25(2).

410 *Crédit Suisse Fides Trust SA v Cuoghi* [1998] QB 818; *Refco Inc v Eastern Trading Co* [1999] 1 Lloyd's Rep 159.

411 *Duder v Amsterdamsch Trustees Kantoor* [1902] 2 Ch 132.

412 *Cook Industries Inc v Galliher* [1979] Ch 439, [1978] 3 All ER 945. See also *Protector Alarms Ltd v Maxim Alarms Ltd* [1978] FSR 442; *Altertext Inc v Advanced Data Communications Ltd* [1985] 1 All ER 395, [1985] 1 WLR 457.

413 The power to grant a Mareva injunction in relation to foreign assets was first recognised in *Babanaft International Co SA v Bassatne* [1990] Ch 13, [1989] 1 All ER 433.

414 See Dillon LJ in *Derby & Co Ltd v Weldon (No 6)* [1990] 1 WLR 1139 at 1149.

415 See, for example, May LJ in *Derby & Co Ltd v Weldon* [1990] Ch 48 at 55.

not be entitled to recognition) to another (where a judgment in the claimant's favour will be recognised).[416] As a matter of discretion, an extraterritorial Mareva injunction is more likely to be made after judgment than before[417] and the court will also be more inclined to grant Mareva relief in cases where the claim is proprietary rather than personal.[418] Although it has been said that the court should not normally grant an extraterritorial Mareva injunction in cases where the claimant is seeking to enforce a foreign judgment or arbitral award in England,[419] the correctness of this view has been doubted.[420]

In *Van Uden Maritime BV v Firma Deco-Line*,[421] in the context of what is now article 31 of the Regulation, the Court of Justice ruled that the granting of provisional measures in support of substantive proceedings in another member state is conditional on the existence of 'a real connecting link' between the subject-matter of the measures sought and the territorial jurisdiction of the court before which those measures are sought.[422] As a general rule, unless England is the forum for the substantive dispute between the parties, the court should confine itself to assets within the jurisdiction.[423] In a suitable case, however, the court may grant a worldwide Mareva injunction in support of proceedings abroad; such an order is most likely to be made in cases where the defendant is amenable to the in personam jurisdiction of the English court (such as where the defendant is domiciled in England).[424]

Somewhat exceptionally, extraterritorial relief was granted in *Republic of Haiti v Duvalier*,[425] a case in which the defendants neither were domiciled in England nor had assets in England. The Republic started proceedings in France against the defendants, who comprised Baby Doc Duvalier and various members of his family, who – it was alleged – had embezzled significant sums of money belonging to the Republic prior to their flight from Haiti. The Republic applied to the English court for a worldwide Mareva injunction and a disclosure order requiring the defendants to reveal the whereabouts of their assets, wherever located. The Court of Appeal decided that it was an appropriate case for the grant of a worldwide Mareva injunction,

416 *Derby & Co Ltd v Weldon (No 6)* [1990] 3 All ER 263, [1990] 1 WLR 1139.
417 *Babanaft International Co SA v Bassatne* [1990] Ch 13, [1989] 1 All ER 433.
418 *Republic of Haiti v Duvalier* [1990] 1 QB 202, [1989] 1 All ER 456.
419 *Rosseel NV v Oriental Commercial Shipping (UK) Ltd* [1990] 3 All ER 545, [1990] 1 WLR 1387.
420 *Crédit Suisse Fides Trust SA v Cuoghi* [1998] QB 818.
421 Case C-391/95 [1998] ECR I-7091.
422 At 7135 (para 40).
423 Lord Donaldson MR in *Rosseel NV v Oriental Commercial Shipping (UK) Ltd* [1990] 1 WLR 1387 at 1389.
424 *Crédit Suisse Fides Trust SA v Cuoghi* [1998] QB 818.
425 [1990] 1 QB 202, [1989] 1 All ER 456.

notwithstanding the fact that the substantive proceedings were being conducted in France, where the defendants were domiciled. Opinion is divided as to whether the requirement to show a real connecting link with England could have been satisfied in these circumstances. Although it has been suggested that the ruling in *Van Uden* does not necessitate a reconsideration of the *Republic of Haiti* case (because a real connecting link was provided by the fact that the defendants had solicitors in England who held assets for them abroad),[426] the link with England was, in objective terms, very weak. It is at least possible that the effect of the ruling in the *Van Uden* case is to deprive the English courts of the power to grant extraterritorial measures in circumstances like those which arose *Republic of Haiti v Duvalier*.[427]

Where the court exercises its discretion in favour of granting extraterritorial relief, it is important that steps should be taken to ensure that oppression of the defendants by way of exposure to a multiplicity of proceedings and the misuse of information is avoided and that the position of third parties is protected. Where the court grants extraterritorial relief the claimant will normally be required to give an undertaking not to take any action abroad in respect of the defendant's assets without the court's permission. Furthermore, a worldwide Mareva injunction will normally contain appropriate provisions for the protection of third parties.[428] This is of particular importance to banks which might otherwise find themselves in contempt of court for dealing with the defendant's assets in accordance with the defendant's instructions.

V RESTRAINING FOREIGN PROCEEDINGS: ANTISUIT INJUNCTIONS

A Introduction

While the English court cannot stay proceedings in a foreign court, it can grant an injunction restraining a party from instituting or pursuing such proceedings. An antisuit injunction is most likely to be sought by a defendant in foreign proceedings who claims that the matter should be decided in the English court rather than abroad. Often in such cases

426 Dicey and Morris, *The Conflict of Laws* (13th edn, 2000) p 193.

427 Peel, (1998) 18 YBEL 689, 698.

428 For consideration of the 'Babanaft proviso', the mechanism whereby the courts have sought to provide protection for third parties, see Lord Donaldson MR in *Derby & Co Ltd v Weldon (Nos 3 and 4)* [1990] Ch 65 at 84; *Baltic Shipping v Translink Shipping Ltd* [1995] 1 Lloyd's Rep 673; *Bank of China v NBM LLC* [2002] 1 WLR 844.

the defendant in the foreign proceedings will have already started proceedings in England. The general principles which determine the court's jurisdiction apply to applications for an antisuit injunction. If the defendant in the English proceedings is not amenable to the court's substantive jurisdiction (whether on the basis of the Brussels regime or the traditional rules[429]) the court cannot grant the relief sought by the claimant.

The major area of controversy as regards antisuit injunctions is the exercise of the court's discretion. An antisuit injunction is a measure which is designed to have an extraterritorial effect. It is recognised that, since an injunction which orders a litigant to discontinue proceedings abroad involves an indirect interference with the process of justice in the foreign court, the court's approach should be cautious.[430]

At one time the courts took the view that the principles to be applied to an application for an antisuit injunction were the same as those which governed the staying of English proceedings.[431] This approach has since been rejected by the courts. There are two broad categories of case in which the courts are entitled to grant injunctive relief: first, where a person has behaved, or threatens to behave, in a manner which is unconscionable; and secondly, where a litigant has invaded, or a litigant threatens to invade, a legal or equitable right of another.[432]

B Unconscionable behaviour

Where a remedy for a particular wrong is available both in England and in a foreign forum, the court will, as a general rule, only restrain the claimant from pursuing proceedings in the foreign court if England is

429 If the defendant cannot be served with process in England, the claimant may apply for permission to serve process abroad, for example, under CPR 6.20(5)(d), on the basis that the claim is in respect of a contract governed by English law: *Schiffahrtsgesellschaft Detlev von Appen GmbH v Voest Alpine Intertrading GmbH* [1997] 2 Lloyd's Rep 279; *Shell International Petroleum Co Ltd v Coral Oil Co Ltd* [1999] 1 Lloyd's Rep 72; *Youell v Kara Mara Shipping Co Ltd* [2000] 2 Lloyd's Rep 102; *The Ivan Zagubanski* [2002] 1 Lloyd's Rep 106. However, an antisuit injunction is not one of the types of provisional measure which fall within the scope of art 31 of the Brussels I Regulation and an application for an antisuit injunction falls neither within CPR 6.20(2) (which applies only to injunctions relating to conduct in England) nor within CPR 6.20(4) (because the claim is not within s 25 of the Civil Jurisdiction and Judgments Act 1982).

430 See Lord Diplock in *British Airways Board v Laker Airways Ltd* [1985] AC 58 at 95.

431 *Castanho v Brown & Root (UK) Ltd* [1981] AC 557, [1981] 1 All ER 143.

432 Lord Brandon in *South Carolina Insurance Co v Assurantie Maatschappij De Zeven Provincien NV* [1987] AC 24 at 40.

the natural forum and the pursuit of the foreign proceedings would be vexatious or oppressive.[433] It is, of course, notoriously difficult to define concepts such as 'vexatious or oppressive'. The fact that the foreign proceedings are not being conducted in the natural forum does not mean that such proceedings are vexatious or oppressive; the court should not grant an injunction if, by doing so, it would deprive the claimant of advantages in the foreign forum of which it would be unjust to deprive him.[434] Where proceedings are brought abroad in a forum which is not the natural one there is a dividing line to be drawn between, on the one hand, situations where the proceedings are brought with the purpose of obtaining an unfair advantage (which is vexatious or oppressive) and, on the other, proceedings which are brought to obtain an advantage of which it would be unjust to deprive the claimant. The drawing of this dividing line is not easy. It is clear, however, that the court will decide that it is oppressive for a litigant to pursue a claim in the United States if England is overwhelmingly the natural forum and the only advantages to the claimant in the United States proceedings are the contingency fee system or the more generous United States rules on the pre-trial disclosure of documents.[435]

In *Société Nationale Industrielle Aérospatiale v Lee Kui Jak*[436] the Privy Council, sitting on appeal from the Court of Appeal of Brunei, held that an injunction should be granted to restrain the plaintiff from continuing proceedings in Texas. The Brunei court was the natural forum and the continuance of the Texas proceedings would be oppressive or vexatious because the defendants would suffer serious injustice in being unable in those proceedings to claim an indemnity from a third party, which they would be able to claim in the Brunei court (because the third party was willing to submit to Brunei but not to Texas jurisdiction). Because of undertakings given by the defendants in relation to the litigation in Brunei, there would be no injustice to the plaintiff in not being able to continue with the proceedings in Texas.

Although in the *Société Nationale Industrielle Aérospatiale* case the Privy Council indicated that an antisuit injunction should not normally be granted unless England is the natural forum, the cases indicate that in certain situations an injunction may be granted even if the substance of the dispute between the parties cannot (or will not) be determined by the English court.

First, situations arise in which there would be no remedy on the cause of action in the English court but, if the facts alleged were

433 *Société Nationale Industrielle Aérospatiale v Lee Kui Jak* [1987] AC 871.
434 Lord Goff at 896.
435 *Simon Engineering plc v Butte Mining plc (No 2)* [1996] 1 Lloyd's Rep 91.
436 [1987] AC 871.

proved, the claimant would have a good cause of action in the foreign court. In an appropriate case the English court may grant an antisuit injunction even though the foreign court is the only forum in which the claimant is, in any meaningful sense, able to pursue his claim. Such cases are rare. But, in *Midland Bank plc v Laker Airways Ltd*,[437] an injunction was granted to restrain an English plaintiff from pursuing proceedings against an English defendant in the United States claiming damages under the United States anti-trust legislation (which operates extraterritorially). It was unconscionable and unjust for the plaintiff to invoke the United States jurisdiction against a defendant whose dealings with the plaintiff had taken place entirely in England and who had no relevant presence in, or business connections with, the United States.[438]

Secondly, an antisuit injunction may be granted, notwithstanding the fact that the English court is not the natural forum, in a case where 'the conduct of the foreign state is such as to deprive it of the respect normally required by comity'.[439] That such cases are unlikely to arise frequently (if ever) is illustrated by the House of Lords decision in *Airbus Industrie GIE v Patel.*[440] In this case, the plaintiff sought an injunction to restrain the English defendants from pursuing litigation in Texas in respect of a claim arising out of an aircrash in India. The House of Lords held that the English forum did not have a sufficient interest in, or connection with, the matter in question to justify interfering in the foreign proceedings. Even though the exercise of jurisdiction by the Texan courts was oppressive and the Indian courts were powerless to do anything about it, the Court of Appeal's decision to grant an antisuit injunction[441] was reversed.

C Infringement of a legal or equitable right

A defendant in foreign proceedings may apply for an antisuit injunction in a case where the bringing of those proceedings involves the breach of the legal or equitable rights of the defendant. A right not to be sued abroad may be contractual (for example, where there is an arbitration clause or a clause conferring exclusive jurisdiction on the English courts) or may arise by virtue of an equitable defence to the claim (such as estoppel). Most of the recent cases have involved foreign proceedings brought in breach of the terms of a contractual dispute-resolution clause.

437 [1986] QB 689, [1986] 1 All ER 526.
438 See also *British Airways Board v Laker Airways Ltd* [1985] AC 58, [1984] 3 All ER 39.
439 Lord Goff in *Airbus Industrie GIE v Patel* [1999] 1 AC 119 at 140.
440 [1999] 1 AC 119.
441 [1997] 2 Lloyd's Rep 8.

Traditionally, the courts have at least paid lip-service to the principle that an antisuit injunction should be regarded as an exceptional remedy.[442] More recently, it has been held that where proceedings abroad involve the breach of a jurisdiction or arbitration agreement the court should not feel reticent about granting an antisuit injunction; in such a case damages are not an adequate remedy for the breach of contract. Where the foreign proceedings involve the breach of an exclusive jurisdiction clause or an arbitration clause, an injunction should be granted unless there are 'special countervailing factors',[443] or unless good reason is shown why the court's discretion should not be exercised in the applicant's favour.[444] The fact that the claimant in the English proceedings, instead of seeking to rely on the jurisdiction clause or arbitration agreement to contest the foreign court's jurisdiction, submitted in the foreign proceedings will normally provide a good reason for the court to refuse to grant an antisuit injunction.[445] The court may also refuse an injunction, notwithstanding an exclusive jurisdiction clause in favour of the English courts, if, in a case involving a multiplicity of parties, foreign proceedings provide the best means of submitting the whole dispute to a single tribunal which is able to make a comprehensive judgment on all issues between the parties.[446]

It is important that a party who is sued abroad in breach of the terms of a dispute-resolution clause should apply promptly for an antisuit injunction from the English court. If the application is made at the last minute in an attempt to frustrate foreign proceedings which have been ongoing for an appreciable period of time, an antisuit injunction will be refused, notwithstanding the fact that the claimant in the foreign proceedings acted in breach of contract by commencing those proceedings.[447]

D Antisuit injunctions and the Brussels regime

Although the court's general jurisdiction to grant equitable remedies exists regardless of whether the proceedings are brought in a member

442 *Tracomin v Sudan Oil Seeds Co Ltd (No 2)* [1983] 3 All ER 140, [1983] 1 WLR 1026; *Sohio Supply Co v Gatoil (USA) Inc* [1989] 1 Lloyd's Rep 588.

443 Steyn LJ in *Continental Bank NA v Aeakos Compania Naviera SA* [1994] 1 WLR 588 at 598.

444 *The Angelic Grace* [1995] 1 Lloyd's Rep 87. See also *National Westminster Bank v Utrecht-America Finance Co* [2001] EWCA Civ 658, [2001] 3 All ER 733.

445 *A/S D/S Svendborg v Wansa* [1997] 2 Lloyd's Rep 183, affirming [1996] 2 Lloyd's Rep 559.

446 *Donohue v Armco Inc* [2001] UKHL 64, [2002] 1 All ER 749. See also *Bouygues Offshore SA v Caspian Shipping Co (Nos 1, 3, 4 and 5)* [1998] 2 Lloyd's Rep 461.

447 *Toepfer International GmbH v Molino Boschi SRL* [1996] 1 Lloyd's Rep 510.

state in accordance with the terms of the Brussels regime or in a non-member state, it might be supposed that the courts would be extremely unwilling, in a case falling within the scope of the Brussels regime, to interfere with the process of justice in another member state. If a litigant invokes the jurisdiction of the court of a member state in a matter falling within the scope of article 1 (either directly through the provisions of Chapter II or indirectly through article 4) the grant of an antisuit injunction by the English court to restrain the foreign proceedings hardly seems appropriate. It must also be remembered not only that article 27 of the Regulation provides that where proceedings between the same parties concerning the same cause of action are brought in the courts of more than one member state any court other than the court first seised must stay its proceedings or decline jurisdiction but also that the Court of Justice ruled, in *Overseas Union Insurance v New Hampshire Insurance*, that the court second seised is not normally in a better position than the court first seised to rule on the latter's jurisdiction.[448]

Where, for example, a claimant brings proceedings in France against a defendant who is domiciled in England for breach of contract (on the basis that France is the place of performance of the obligation in question) there should be no question of the English court granting an antisuit injunction restraining the claimant from pursuing the French proceedings, even if the defendant will be deprived of advantages which he would have enjoyed had the proceedings been brought in England.

Despite the formidable arguments against antisuit injunctions being granted in cases where jurisdiction is conferred by the Brussels regime, it has been held in England that the court may in appropriate circumstances grant an antisuit injunction in relation to proceedings in another member state notwithstanding the fact that the foreign proceedings concern civil and commercial matters within the scope of the Brussels regime.

In *Continental Bank NA v Aeakos Compania Naviera SA*[449] parallel proceedings involving a bank and a debtor were brought in Greece and England. The bank alleged that the debtor was in breach of an English jurisdiction clause by commencing proceedings in Greece and applied for an injunction restraining the debtor from continuing with the Greek proceedings; the debtor argued that the Greek court was the court first seised and that the proceedings which had been commenced

448 Case C-351/89 [1991] ECR I-3317 at 3350 (para 23).

449 [1994] 2 All ER 540, [1994] 1 WLR 588. See Asariotis, 'Antisuit Injunctions for Breach of a Forum Agreement: A Critical Review of the English Approach' (1999/2000) 19 YBEL 447.

by the bank in England should be stayed under the terms of what is now article 27. The Court of Appeal, having decided that the jurisdiction clause was valid and effective under what is now article 23, concluded that the English proceedings should not be stayed (on the basis that the jurisdiction clause provision takes precedence over the lis pendens provision[450]) and then 'add[ed] insult to injury'[451] by granting an antisuit injunction (on the basis that the continuance of the Greek proceedings amounted to conduct which was vexatious or oppressive).[452] The ruling in *Overseas Union Insurance v New Hampshire Insurance* was not considered and the Court of Appeal's decision is not easily reconciled with the jurisprudence of the Court of Justice. The foundation of the Court of Appeal's decision to grant the injunction is a review of the basis on which the Greek court exercised jurisdiction; this is exactly what the Court of Justice has said the court second seised is not entitled to do.

In *Turner v Grovit*[453] the Court of Appeal went further in holding that, in cases involving the Brussels regime, the cases in which the court may grant antisuit injunctions are not limited to those where the parties have conferred exclusive jurisdiction on the English court under what is now article 23. The court has an inherent jurisdiction to prevent an abuse of process; where proceedings are brought in another member state for no purpose other than to harass and oppress a party who is already a litigant in England, the court may grant an injunction to restrain the claimant in the foreign proceedings from pursuing those proceedings. The argument that the foreign court should be left to decide for itself whether it should exercise jurisdiction or stay its proceedings or decline jurisdiction under what are now articles 27 and 28,[454] did not persuade the Court of Appeal. This decision, which is even more controversial than the decision in the *Continental Bank* case, was appealed to the House of Lords, which has sought a ruling from the Court of Justice on the compatibility of antisuit injunctions with the Brussels regime.[455]

450 For criticism of this aspect of the judgment see pp 117–118.
451 Hill, *International Commercial Disputes* (2nd edn, 1998) p 336.
452 See also *Banque Cantonale Vaudoise v Waterlily Maritime Inc* [1997] 2 Lloyd's Rep 347; *Gilkes v Venizelos ANESA* [2000] IL Pr 487; *The Kribi* [2001] 1 Lloyd's Rep 76.
453 [2000] 1 QB 345. Cf *First National Bank Association v Compagnie National Air Gabon* [1999] IL Pr 617.
454 This argument had been accepted at first instance by Judge David Donaldson QC: [1999] 1 All ER (Comm) 445.
455 [2001] UKHL 65, [2002] 1 WLR 107.

Chapter 4

Foreign judgments

I INTRODUCTION

A General considerations

Although the conflicts process can be broken down into three elements (jurisdiction, choice of law and the recognition and enforcement of judgments), the English court will rarely have to address all three elements in the same case. Where, for example, the court exercises jurisdiction and grants a judgment in the claimant's favour, there are no special conflicts aspects to the enforcement of the judgment against the defendant's assets in England. Where, however, the court does not have jurisdiction in relation to a particular dispute – which is then determined by a foreign court – a question may arise as to the effect of the foreign judgment in England. In considering the effect in England of foreign judgments it is important to draw a number of distinctions.

First, a distinction has to be drawn between recognition and enforcement. The enforcement of a judgment, which necessarily involves its recognition, will be sought by a judgment-creditor – that is, a litigant who has obtained a judgment in a foreign court which awards him some relief and who now wishes to obtain that relief in England. Where, for example, a claimant is awarded damages by a French court in an action for breach of contract and the defendant has no assets in France, if the claimant wishes to have the judgment satisfied out of the defendant's assets in England, the question arises as to whether the English court will enforce the French judgment or whether the claimant is required to start fresh proceedings in England.

Although there can be no enforcement without recognition, situations arise in which a litigant in English proceedings wishes to have a foreign judgment recognised only. For example, where, in a claim for breach of contract, a foreign court decides that there was no breach and gives judgment in the defendant's favour, if the claimant starts proceedings in England on the same cause of action, the defendant will want the English court to recognise the foreign judgment, but no question of enforcement arises. In this type of case, the defendant raises the foreign judgment as a defence to the claim. Whereas enforcement of a foreign judgment is essentially a positive process whereby the English court authorises the judgment-creditor to take the necessary steps so that the judgment is satisfied, recognition of a foreign judgment merely provides a barrier which prevents proceedings being pursued in England.

Secondly, a distinction must be drawn between judgments in personam and judgments in rem. A judgment in personam is a court order which determines the rights and obligations of the particular parties to the litigation. In a typical case – based on an allegation of a breach of contract or of the commission of a tort by the defendant – the judgment either will order the defendant to pay damages to the claimant (or may order the defendant to do, or refrain from doing, something) or will decide that the defendant is not liable.

A judgment in rem may affect the position of third parties as well as the parties to the litigation. Most judgments in rem involve questions of status and arise in the context of family proceedings; the court may, for example, declare that an alleged marriage is (or is not) void or that a foreign divorce is of no effect in England.[1] In the commercial sphere judgments in rem are most frequently found in the context of Admiralty proceedings, typically in cases involving the ownership or possession of a ship. In this type of case a judgment in rem determines not only the rights of the parties, but also ownership or possession of the ship and is effective against the whole world. At common law a foreign judgment in rem may be recognised or enforced in England if the ship or other property was situated in the country of origin at the time of the commencement of proceedings.[2] Recognition or enforcement may be refused, however, on the same grounds which apply to foreign judgments in personam.[3]

Thirdly, foreign judgments may be entitled to recognition and enforcement under one of a number of different legal regimes. Which set of rules is applicable depends primarily on the country of origin. The common law rules are still applicable to judgments given by the courts of many countries around the world, including most countries

1 The recognition of foreign divorces and nullity decrees is considered in chapter 9.
2 *Castrique v Imrie* (1870) LR 4 HL 414. Judgments in rem granted by the courts of member states may be entitled to recognition and enforcement under the Brussels regime.
3 See pp 173–181, 188–196.

in the Middle East, Eastern Europe and most non-Commonwealth countries in the Americas (including the United States), Africa and Asia. The Administration of Justice Act 1920 applies to the enforcement of some Commonwealth judgments. The Foreign Judgments (Reciprocal Enforcement) Act 1933, which is a virtual codification of the common law, governs the recognition and enforcement of the judgments of some Commonwealth countries and judgments given by some non-Commonwealth countries (including countries in Western Europe and Israel). As regards judgments given by the courts of many Western European countries, however, the 1933 Act has been superseded – at least in civil and commercial matters – by the Brussels regime (that is, the Brussels I Regulation and the Brussels and Lugano Conventions). As regards judgments within the material scope of article 1 of the Brussels regime,[4] Chapter III of the Regulation applies to judgments given by the courts of European Union member states[5] and Title III of the Lugano Convention (implemented by the Civil Jurisdiction and Judgments Act 1982) applies to judgments granted by the courts of Iceland, Norway, Poland and Switzerland.[6] Although many of the provisions are common both to the Regulation and the Lugano Convention, the English court cannot make a reference to the Court of Justice if faced with a problem of interpretation under the Lugano Convention. The Civil Jurisdiction and Judgments Act 1982 also provides for the recognition and enforcement in England of judgments granted by the courts of Scotland and Northern Ireland.

Whereas, at common law, foreign judgments are enforced by bringing ordinary proceedings on the judgment, under the various statutory regimes there are special procedures prescribed leading to registration of the judgment. Once registered, a foreign judgment may be enforced in the same way as a judgment of the English court. There is, however, no special procedure for the recognition of foreign judgments.

B The basis of recognition and enforcement

In theory, the English court could recognise and enforce all foreign judgments; alternatively, it would be possible for the English court

4 See pp 65–66.

5 Other than judgments granted by the Danish courts, which continue to be regulated by Title III of the Brussels Convention.

6 This chapter considers, in detail, only the position under the Regulation. For consideration of the Brussels Convention (as amended) and the Lugano Convention see the 1997 edition of this work.

not to recognise or enforce any foreign judgment. Such extreme positions are not very attractive from a practical point of view. As Slade LJ noted in *Adams v Cape Industries plc*, the law is based on 'an acknowledgement that the society of nations will work better if some foreign judgments are taken to create rights which supersede the underlying cause of action, and which may be directly enforced in countries where the defendant or his assets are to be found'.[7] The crucial question therefore is not *whether* foreign judgments should be recognised and enforced in England but *which* judgments should be recognised and enforced.

There are, broadly speaking, two theories. The first is the theory of obligation, which is premised on the notion that if the original court exercised jurisdiction on a proper basis the court's judgment should prima facie be regarded as creating an obligation between the parties to the foreign proceedings which the English court ought to recognise and, where appropriate, enforce. In effect, a foreign judgment which orders a defendant to pay damages is to be regarded as creating a debt which the claimant can enforce in England. The alternative theory is based on the idea of reciprocity: the courts of country X should recognise and enforce the judgments of country Y if, mutatis mutandis, the courts of country Y recognise and enforce the judgments of country X. The theory of obligation was adopted by the English courts in the nineteenth century[8] and still forms the basis of recognition and enforcement at common law (and the statutory regimes which are based on the common law). English law has, however, been radically affected by the Brussels regime, which – as regards civil and commercial matters – provides for the reciprocal recognition and enforcement of judgments granted by the courts of the member states.

It should be noted that, whichever theory is adopted, the recognition and enforcement of foreign judgments is limited by a range of defences which may be invoked by the party wishing to resist the judgment in question. It would be unrealistic to expect the English court to give effect to a foreign judgment which conflicts with English public policy or with fundamental notions of justice and fairness. The recognition and enforcement of foreign judgments is therefore a two-stage process. First, are the basic conditions for recognition or enforcement satisfied? Secondly, if so, is there a defence by reason of which the foreign judgment should nevertheless not be recognised or enforced?

7 [1990] Ch 433 at 552.
8 *Schibsby v Westenholz* (1870) LR 6 QB 155.

II RECOGNITION AND ENFORCEMENT AT COMMON LAW

A Conditions for enforcement

For a judgment to be entitled to enforcement at common law there are a number of conditions which must be satisfied: first, the original court must have been a court of competent jurisdiction; secondly, the judgment must be final and conclusive; thirdly, the judgment must be for a fixed sum of money, not being a tax or penalty. If the judgment-creditor can satisfy the court that these criteria are satisfied, the foreign judgment is prima facie entitled to enforcement. The burden then shifts to the judgment-debtor; the foreign judgment will be enforced unless the judgment-debtor establishes a defence which negatives the effect of the judgment in England.

1. A court of competent jurisdiction

(A) INTRODUCTION

The important question when considering whether the original court was a court of competent jurisdiction is not whether the foreign court was entitled to exercise jurisdiction according to the foreign law, but whether the foreign court had jurisdiction according to the English rules of private international law.[9] The decided cases indicate that there are, broadly speaking, two situations in which the original court will be regarded as a court of competent jurisdiction: first, where the judgment-debtor submitted to the jurisdiction of the foreign court; secondly, where there is a sufficient territorial connection between the judgment-debtor and the country of origin.

Other types of connection between the parties or the cause of action and the original court are not sufficient. It is clear that the fact that the cause of action arose in the country of origin is irrelevant.[10] Similarly, even though the English court may exercise jurisdiction over absent defendants under CPR 6.20 on the ground that England is the forum conveniens, a foreign judgment founded on a similar basis of jurisdiction will not be entitled to enforcement in England.[11] It has also been decided that the fact that the defendant has assets in the country of origin does not make the foreign court a court of competent jurisdiction.[12] There are dicta which suggest that the

9 *Buchanan v Rucker* (1808) 9 East 192.
10 *Sirdar Gurdyal Singh v Rajah of Faridkote* [1894] AC 670.
11 This follows from *Schibsby v Westenholz* (1870) LR 6 QB 155.
12 *Emanuel v Symon* [1908] 1 KB 302.

English court will prima facie enforce a foreign judgment if the judgment-debtor is a national of the country of origin.[13] However, since nationality is not a connecting factor which has traditionally been adopted by the common law it is not surprising that the correctness of such dicta has been doubted.[14]

(B) SUBMISSION

A foreign judgment is prima facie enforceable in England if the judgment-debtor submitted to the jurisdiction of the foreign court. Submission can take one of three forms.[15]

First, the foreign court will be regarded as a court of competent jurisdiction if the judgment-debtor consented to the jurisdiction of the forum in which the judgment was obtained.[16] Such consent will usually take the form of a contractual clause providing for the exclusive or non-exclusive jurisdiction of the foreign court. A doubtful question is whether the original court should be regarded as a court of competent jurisdiction in a case where an agreement to submit, although not expressly stated in the contract, can be implied into it. In *Blohn v Desser*[17] Diplock J decided, albeit obiter, that a defendant, an English resident, who had been a sleeping partner in a firm which carried on business in Austria, could be regarded as having impliedly agreed with all people who made contracts with the firm in the course of its business in Austria to submit to the jurisdiction of the Austrian courts in any dispute arising from such contracts. Later decisions, however, have diverged on the question of whether it is possible for an agreement to submit to the jurisdiction of a foreign court to be implied.[18] *Adams v Cape Industries plc*,[19] the most recent case in which the issue was considered, casts further doubt on the correctness of Diplock J's observations in *Blohn v Desser*. Scott J thought that the minimum that is required is 'a clear indication of consent to the exercise by the foreign court of jurisdiction'.[20]

A further issue which was considered by Scott J in *Adams v Cape Industries plc* is the extent to which consent to the jurisdiction of the

13 In particular, in *Emanuel v Symon* [1908] 1 KB 302.

14 Cheshire and North, *Private International Law* (13th edn, 1999) p 419; Dicey and Morris, *The Conflict of Laws* (13th edn, 2000) p 500.

15 *Emanuel v Symon* [1908] 1 KB 302 at 309.

16 *Feyerick v Hubbard* (1902) 71 LJKB 509.

17 [1962] 2 QB 116, [1961] 3 All ER 1.

18 *Vogel v R & A Kohnstamm Ltd* [1973] QB 133 (agreement must be express); *Sfeir & Co v National Insurance Co of New Zealand* [1964] 1 Lloyd's Rep 330 (agreement may be implied).

19 [1990] Ch 433.

20 At 466.

original court might amount to submission notwithstanding that such consent does not form part of a contractually binding agreement. As a matter of principle, there is no reason why, in appropriate circumstances, a defendant should not be estopped from denying that the original court was a court of competent jurisdiction. Where the defendant consents to the jurisdiction of the foreign court otherwise than by contractual agreement and, before the consent is withdrawn, the claimant relies upon it to his detriment, the defendant should be regarded as having submitted to the foreign court's jurisdiction. For example, if D, an English resident, orally assures C that he will submit to the jurisdiction of the Mexican courts and, in reliance on this assurance, C fails to commence proceedings against D in England within the relevant limitation period, if C, having obtained a judgment in Mexico, seeks enforcement in England D should be estopped from denying that the Mexican court was a court of competent jurisdiction. However, no such estoppel can arise if the defendant's consent is not acted upon by the claimant or if it is withdrawn before it is acted upon.

Secondly, a defendant who voluntarily participates in the foreign proceedings submits to the jurisdiction of the foreign court. A foreign judgment can be enforced against a defendant in England if he entered an appearance to defend the case (even if he took no further steps) or if he took any step designed to contest the action on the merits or even if he filed an appeal against the judgment to a higher court in the country of origin, not previously having taken any steps in the action.[21] Of course, it is not sufficient that the judgment-debtor submitted in the eyes of the foreign court; it must be shown that the judgment-debtor took part in the foreign proceedings in a way accepted by English law as amounting to a voluntary appearance.[22]

If D submits to proceedings brought by C1 in a foreign country this is not to be regarded as an implied submission to related proceedings commenced by C2 in the same court, even if the proceedings commenced by C1 and C2 involve almost identical issues. In *Adams v Cape Industries plc* an English company, which had been involved – through subsidiary and associated companies – in the mining and sale of asbestos, was the defendant in two sets of proceedings (the *Tyler 1* actions and the *Tyler 2* actions) brought by more than 600 asbestos workers in Texas. The defendant took part in the *Tyler 1* actions, which were settled, but contested the

21 *SA Consortium General Textiles v Sun and Sand Agencies Ltd* [1978] QB 279, [1978] 2 All ER 339.

22 Roch LJ in *Desert Sun Loan Corpn v Hill* [1996] 2 All ER 847 at 862. See also *Akande v Balfour Beatty Construction Ltd* [1998] IL Pr 110.

jurisdiction of the original court in relation to the *Tyler 2* actions and took no further part in those proceedings. Scott J rejected the argument that, by taking part in the *Tyler 1* actions, the defendant had submitted to the jurisdiction of the original court as regards the *Tyler 2* actions. Since the two sets of proceedings were not to be regarded as 'one unit of litigation', the steps taken by the defendant in the *Tyler 1* actions could not be regarded as constituting submission for the purposes of the *Tyler 2* actions.[23] However, where D submits in foreign proceedings brought by C, D is regarded as having also submitted to the foreign court's jurisdiction in relation to, not only further claims concerning the same subject-matter, but also claims which are connected or related to the original claim; whether a claim is connected or related is a question of degree to be decided by the English court.[24]

What if the defendant's appearance in the foreign court is to contend only that it lacks jurisdiction or to argue that the foreign court should not exercise its discretionary jurisdiction? What is the effect of the foreign judgment if the foreign court exercises jurisdiction and the defendant does not contest the case on the merits? It is provided by statute that a defendant shall not be regarded as having submitted to the jurisdiction of the foreign court only by reason of the fact that he appeared to contest the jurisdiction or to ask the court to dismiss or stay the proceedings on the ground that the dispute should be submitted to arbitration or to the determination of the courts of another country.[25] Provided the defendant makes it clear in his first defence, rather than in some subsequent defence, that he is contesting the foreign court's jurisdiction that will not amount to a submission even though the first defence contains some additional material which constitutes a plea to the merits of the case.[26]

The defendant will not be held to have submitted to the jurisdiction of the foreign court if his appearance in the original proceedings was not voluntary. Whether the defendant appeared voluntarily is to be determined by English law, rather than by the law of the country of origin.[27] An appearance will not be voluntary if it is due to duress or undue influence brought to bear by the other party.[28] It is also

23 See Scott J at 462–463.

24 *Murthy v Sivajothi* [1999] 1 All ER 721, [1999] 1 WLR 467.

25 Civil Jurisdiction and Judgments Act 1982, s 33(1)(a) and (b). For the position at common law prior to the entry into force of the 1982 Act see *Henry v Geoprosco International Ltd* [1976] QB 726, [1975] 2 All ER 702.

26 Neill LJ in *Marc Rich & Co AG v Societa Italiana Impianti PA (No 2)* C-190/89 [1992] 1 Lloyd's Rep 624 at 633.

27 *Desert Sun Loan Corpn v Hill* [1996] 2 All ER 847.

28 *Israel Discount Bank of New York v Hadjipateras* [1983] 3 All ER 129, [1984] 1 WLR 137.

provided by the legislation that a defendant shall not be regarded as having submitted to the jurisdiction of the foreign court by reason only of the fact that he appeared 'to protect, or obtain the release of, property seized or threatened with seizure in the proceedings'.[29] This rule safeguards a defendant who is sued in a foreign country whose courts exercise jurisdiction on the ground of the presence of the defendant's property in that country. In the absence of a sufficient territorial connection between the defendant and the country of origin, if the defendant does not appear in the proceedings the judgment will not be enforceable in England. This might well be of little comfort to the defendant if his property in the country of origin is seised in order to found the court's jurisdiction and he loses this property as a result of an adverse judgment. The effect of the law is that the defendant may enter an appearance to protect his property but that, since this is not regarded as a voluntary submission, the foreign judgment is not enforceable in England by virtue of the defendant's participation.

Thirdly, the judgment-debtor will be held to have submitted to the jurisdiction of a foreign court if he took part in the proceedings as claimant.[30] If, for example, C brings an action for breach of contract against D in New York and the New York court gives a judgment in D's favour and orders C to pay D's costs, the order for costs would be enforceable in England on the ground that C had submitted to the jurisdiction of the original court. Similarly, if D counterclaims in proceedings commenced by C and obtains a judgment in his favour, that judgment is, in principle, entitled to recognition and enforcement in England.

(C) A SUFFICIENT TERRITORIAL CONNECTION

(i) Individuals

It is well established that a foreign judgment is enforceable in England if there was a sufficient territorial connection between the defendant and the country of origin. As regards individuals there is some uncertainty as to whether the appropriate connecting factor is residence or presence. There are three types of case to consider.

The first situation is where the defendant is not only resident in the country of origin but also is present there when the proceedings are commenced. There is no doubt that in this case the foreign court is a court of competent jurisdiction.[31]

29 Civil Jurisdiction and Judgments Act 1982, s 33(1)(c).
30 *Emanuel v Symon* [1908] 1 KB 302.
31 *Adams v Cape Industries plc* [1990] Ch 433, [1991] 1 All ER 929.

The second case is where the defendant is present in the country of origin at the commencement of proceedings, but is not resident in that country. There is some ambiguity in the cases as to the correct solution to this situation. For many years the textbooks relied on Buckley LJ's judgment in *Emanuel v Symon*[32] in which it was stated that a foreign court is to be regarded as a court of competent jurisdiction if the defendant was resident in the country of origin at the time of the commencement of the foreign proceedings.[33] The law was, however, subjected to extensive review in *Adams v Cape Industries plc*.[34] The Court of Appeal expressed the view[35] that the jurisdiction of the foreign court – in the private international law sense – depends on the defendant's voluntary presence in the country of origin, rather than his residence. In reaching this conclusion the Court of Appeal placed particular emphasis on *Carrick v Hancock* in which Lord Russell of Killowen CJ stated that the jurisdiction of a court is based upon the principle of territorial dominion, and that 'all persons within any territorial dominion owe their allegiance to its sovereign power and obedience to all its laws and to the lawful jurisdiction of its courts'.[36] The Court of Appeal also sought to derive support from the principles governing the English court's jurisdiction, according to which service of process on the defendant during a temporary visit to England is sufficient to found the court's jurisdiction.[37]

The third situation is where the defendant is resident in the country of origin at the commencement of proceedings, but is not present there at that time. The Court of Appeal expressly left open this third situation.[38] If presence is properly regarded as a sufficient connection, residence – even if not accompanied by presence – should also be adequate since residence is a more substantial connection than mere presence.

(ii) Companies

Since a company is a legal person without a physical existence any test which is based on presence or residence has to be applied analogistically rather than literally. One approach would be to look at the activities of the company and ask whether the company was economically present in the country of origin – by doing business

32 [1908] 1 KB 302 at 309.
33 See, for example, Jaffey, *Introduction to the Conflict of Laws* (1987) p 224.
34 [1990] Ch 433.
35 At 518.
36 (1895) 12 TLR 59 at 60.
37 *Maharanee of Baroda v Wildenstein* [1972] 2 QB 283, [1972] 2 All ER 689.
38 [1990] Ch 433 at 518.

there.[39] The common law has not adopted this approach. Rather than looking for economic presence, the court applies a more physical test based on the notion of a place of business. There are two possibilities to consider with regard to companies: direct presence and indirect presence (through a representative).

A company is to be regarded as having direct presence in the country of origin if 'it has established and maintained at its own expense (whether as owner or lessee) a fixed place of business of its own in the other country and for more than a minimal period of time has carried on its own business at or from such premises by its servants or agents'.[40] The mere fact that a company carries on business in a foreign country is not enough to make its court a court of competent jurisdiction. In *Littauer Glove Corpn v FW Millington*,[41] for example, proceedings in New York were commenced against an English company, which carried on business in the United States. The originating process was served on one of the company's directors in New York while he was on a business trip to the United States. The company took no part in the proceedings and resisted enforcement of the New York judgment in England. The court held that the judgment was not enforceable in England; the company had not submitted to the jurisdiction of the original court and did not have a place of business in New York.

As regards indirect presence the position is more complex. The leading authority is *Adams v Cape Industries plc*[42] in which the Court of Appeal had to consider a case involving the defendant – an English company – which, it was alleged, transacted business in the United States (and elsewhere) through subsidiaries or associated companies, including a United States marketing company. When the defendant was sued in the United States, the question arose as to whether the defendant was indirectly present there – through the marketing company. The Court of Appeal held that it was not. A company will be indirectly present in a foreign country only if a representative of the company has for more than a minimal period of time been carrying on the company's business in the other country at or from some fixed place of business.[43] For the purposes of this rule it is of crucial importance that the *company's* business has been transacted at or from the fixed place of business. On the facts of the case the Court of Appeal held that the United States

39 See Fawcett, 'A New Approach to Jurisdiction over Companies in Private International Law' (1988) 37 ICLQ 645.
40 Slade LJ in *Adams v Cape Industries plc* [1990] Ch 433 at 530.
41 (1928) 44 TLR 746.
42 [1990] Ch 433.
43 At 530.

marketing company was carrying on its own business – rather than the defendant's business.

In considering whether a representative in the country of origin is carrying on the company's business a range of factors are relevant including: the extent to which the company contributes to the financing of the business carried on by the representative; the way in which the representative is remunerated (for example, by commission or by fixed regular payments); the degree of control the company exercises over the running of the business conducted by the representative; whether the representative displays the company's name at his premises or on his stationery; what business, if any, the representative transacts as principal exclusively on his own behalf; whether the representative makes contracts with customers or other third parties in the name of the company and, if so, whether the representative requires specific authority in advance before binding the company to contractual obligations.[44] Although no single factor is decisive, whether the representative is able to contract on behalf of the company is of particular significance. In *Vogel v R & A Kohnstamm Ltd*,[45] for example, the defendant, an English company, sold goods to the plaintiff in Israel. The defendant was assisted by an agent in Israel who acted as a channel of communication between the defendant and its Israeli customers. The plaintiff obtained a judgment against the defendant from the Israeli courts and sought to enforce it in England. The defendant had taken no part in the foreign proceedings and contended that the agency in Israel could not be regarded as its place of business. The court held that the Israeli judgment was not enforceable; it could not be said that the defendant was indirectly present in Israel through the agent who sought customers and transmitted correspondence but who 'had no authority whatever to bind the defendant in any shape or form'.[46]

(iii) A problem with federal states

Particular problems may arise in the context of cases involving foreign judgments granted by the courts of federal states which comprise a number of separate countries or law districts. The problem results from the fact that there may be two different types of judgment: the judgments of local courts and the judgments of federal courts. Whether a case is assigned to a local court or a federal court is a question of the constitutional law of the state in question.

Where the claimant seeks enforcement in England on the basis of the defendant's presence at the commencement of the proceedings,

44 At 530–531.
45 [1973] QB 133.
46 Ashworth J at 143.

does the claimant have to show that the defendant was present in the particular law district in which the judgment was granted or is it enough that the defendant was present in the larger political unit? In *Adams v Cape Industries plc*[47] the United States marketing company was incorporated in Illinois, but the proceedings against the defendant were conducted in Texas. Was the Texan court to be regarded as a court of competent jurisdiction only if the defendant had been present in Texas (the law district in which the original proceedings took place) or was it sufficient for the defendant to have been present somewhere in the United States of America (the political unit)? As already noted, the Court of Appeal disposed of the appeal by deciding that the defendant was not present – either directly or indirectly – anywhere in the United States. Accordingly, a consideration of what the position would have been if the court had concluded that the defendant was present in the United States was unnecessary. However, since the question had been argued, the Court of Appeal decided to express its view on the matter.

The defendant contended that, for the purposes of the English conflict of laws, the relevant territorial unit should be the law district rather than the larger political unit. On the basis of this analysis the original court could not have been regarded as a court of competent jurisdiction, since, if present anywhere, the defendant was present in Illinois, rather than in Texas. The plaintiffs, however, sought to place emphasis on the fact that the proceedings in Texas had been conducted in a federal court, rather than in a local court. It was accepted that if proceedings are conducted in a local court, the defendant's presence in the relevant law district must be established; it was argued, however, that if the original proceedings are conducted in a federal court, it has to be established only that the defendant was present somewhere in the political unit.

Although the Court of Appeal did not purport to reach a definitive conclusion on this point, it favoured the plaintiffs' analysis. As regards proceedings conducted in local courts, the defendant must have the appropriate territorial connection with the law district in which the court sits. In the words of Slade LJ: 'The fact that Chicago is in the United States does not make Texas any the less a foreign court for a resident in Illinois than if Chicago were in France.'[48] In federal matters, however, the political unit should be treated as a single country, so that any federal court should be regarded as a court of competent jurisdiction as long as the defendant was present somewhere within the political unit. On the basis of this approach,

47 [1990] Ch 433.
48 [1990] Ch 433 at 555.

if the plaintiffs had been able to establish the defendant's presence in Illinois through the marketing company, the Court of Appeal would have been inclined to regard the original judgment granted in Texas as prima facie enforceable.

The basic approach adopted by the Court of Appeal has much to recommend it; the distinction between local and federal matters seems to be a logical one. The analysis is, however, premised on the notion that, as regards federal matters, there is a single, national system of jurisdiction. All three members of the Court of Appeal thought, 'albeit with varying degrees of doubt',[49] that there is a national system of jurisdiction in federal matters in the United States of America. It has been questioned whether this is really the case: United States legislation provides for the registration of the judgments of federal courts in other states of the Union; and, for the purposes of enforcement, United States law treats the judgment of a federal court in the same way as the judgment of a local court.[50] The Court of Appeal's approach might lead to a situation in which a judgment of a federal court sitting in Texas would be enforceable in England but it would not be enforceable in other parts of the United States. Since the Court of Appeal's view was both tentative and obiter, a court in a subsequent case may feel free not to follow it.

(D) IMMOVABLE PROPERTY

Just as the English court will not adjudicate on questions relating to title to, or the right to the possession of, foreign immovable property outside England,[51] it will not regard a foreign court as a court of competent jurisdiction on such a question in respect of immovable property outside its country, even if the defendant was present in the country of origin at the commencement of the proceedings or submitted to the jurisdiction of its courts.[52]

(E) FORUM CONVENIENS?

The foundations of the common law rules relating to foreign judgments were laid in the second half of the nineteenth century when the primary bases of the English court's jurisdiction were presence and submission. At this time there was only a very limited form of 'long-arm' jurisdiction, introduced by the Common Law Procedure Act 1854, and the doctrine of forum non conveniens was not even a glimmer in the eye of the House of Lords. It is hardly

49 Slade LJ at 557.
50 See Carter, (1990) 61 BYIL 402; Collier, [1990] CLJ 416.
51 See pp 135–137.
52 Dicey and Morris, *The Conflict of Laws* (13th edn, 2000) pp 508–512.

surprising that, when deciding whether or not to enforce a foreign judgment, the courts in the nineteenth century looked to see whether the defendant had been present in the county of origin or had submitted to the jurisdiction of its courts.

The traditional rules on jurisdiction have undergone a profound transformation in the intervening years; exorbitant jurisdiction – now under CPR 6.20 – has been significantly extended and the test of appropriateness has come to dominate the jurisdictional inquiry. It is no longer true to say that the English court exercises jurisdiction on the grounds of presence and submission; the English court may exercise jurisdiction over an absent defendant if England is the forum conveniens and may decline jurisdiction against a defendant who is present in England if another forum is more appropriate.[53] There has not, however, been a similar shift in attitude to jurisdictional questions in cases concerning foreign judgments.

The decision of the Court of Appeal in *Adams v Cape Industries plc*[54] has only served to widen the gulf between the common law principles which determine the English court's jurisdiction and those which, at the enforcement stage, determine whether a foreign court is to be regarded as a court of competent jurisdiction. To a very significant extent the traditional rules fall into a pattern which has been described as a 'sort of law of the jungle' in that they display 'the twin vices of ... exorbitant national jurisdictional rules, and extremely narrow judgment recognition practices'.[55] If, for example, an English defendant, while visiting a foreign country, causes injury to a local inhabitant in a driving accident, the English court will not enforce a judgment against the defendant granted by the foreign court, unless the defendant submitted to the jurisdiction of the original court or was served with the originating process while abroad. To reach the defendant's assets the claimant must sue in the English court. This hardly seems just to the claimant who has been injured in his own country. Moreover, the foreign court is prima facie the more appropriate forum. (If the facts were reversed – a foreigner injures an English resident in a road accident in England – the English court would be prepared to exercise jurisdiction.[56]) There is something fundamentally suspect about a system of rules which

53 See pp 103–110 and 119–129.

54 [1990] Ch 433.

55 Borchers, 'Comparing Personal Jurisdiction in the United States and the European Community: Lessons for American Reform' (1992) 40 Am J Comp L 121 at 128.

56 CPR 6.20(8). The court will almost invariably conclude in such a case that England is the natural forum: *The Albaforth* [1984] 2 Lloyd's Rep 91; *Berezovsky v Michaels* [2000] 1 WLR 1004.

refuses to enforce a judgment given by a foreign court which is obviously the most appropriate forum for the trial of the action.

The current rules may also work an injustice on a person with assets in England who finds himself the defendant in foreign proceedings. If, for example, an English resident is served with process in New York while on holiday there, the ensuing judgment of the New York court is prima facie entitled to enforcement in England even if the defendant's presence in New York is fleeting and the cause of action has no connection at all with the country of origin. Since this is a situation in which the English court would, mutatis mutandis, stay the proceedings, it seems somewhat illogical to say that the New York judgment creates an obligation which the English court should enforce.

It might be concluded that if the English court exercises jurisdiction when it is the appropriate forum it ought to be prepared to recognise a foreign judgment when the original court was the appropriate forum (and should refuse to enforce a foreign judgment if the original court was not an appropriate forum).[57] There are, however, certain problems with this approach. The test of appropriateness is fundamentally open-textured and turns on the exercise of the court's discretion. It seems inevitable that there would be considerable uncertainty if the enforceability of foreign judgments at common law depended on the English court having to determine whether it would have exercised its jurisdiction in similar circumstances. There is no easy answer to the question of whether such uncertainty would be a price worth paying for a more coherent system of rules.

2. *Final and conclusive*

Even if the foreign court was a court of competent jurisdiction, the judgment cannot be enforced in England unless it is final and conclusive in the country of origin. This means that, so far as the foreign court is concerned, the judgment must conclusively and permanently decide the matter between the parties. If, according to the foreign law, the judgment can be challenged by the losing party in the same court with the possibility of its being varied or set aside, the judgment will not normally be regarded as final and conclusive and will not be enforced in England.[58] Nevertheless, a default judgment (which is valid unless and until it is set aside) may be final

57 See Briggs, 'Which Foreign Judgments Should We Recognise Today?' (1987) 36 ICLQ 240; cf Harris, 'Recognition of Foreign Judgments – the Anti-suit Injunction Link' (1997) 17 OJLS 477.

58 *Nouvion v Freeman* (1889) 15 App Cas 1; *The Irini A (No 2)* [1999] 1 Lloyd's Rep 189.

and conclusive for the purposes of this rule.[59] As long as the decision of the foreign court is not provisional or subject to revision it will be regarded as final and conclusive even if the decision is made on a procedural matter at a stage of the proceedings prior to the final determination of the cause of action.[60] Furthermore, the fact that a judgment is subject to appeal in the country of origin does not mean that it is not final and conclusive, although in such a case the English court might stay enforcement proceedings pending the outcome of the appeal.[61]

3. For a fixed sum of money, not being a tax or penalty

At common law a foreign order for the delivery of goods (or other specific performance) or for an injunction will not be enforced. The only judgments which can be enforced at common law are judgments for a fixed sum of money. A foreign judgment for a tax or for the payment of a fine or other penalty will not be enforced. This is an aspect of the general principle that the English court will not enforce the revenue or penal laws of foreign countries.[62]

As a general rule, if the defendant is ordered to pay a sum of money to a private person – rather than to the state – the judgment will be enforceable. A judgment which orders the defendant to pay exemplary or punitive damages is in principle enforceable.[63] Similarly, an order by a criminal court that the defendant must compensate his victim may be enforced in England.[64] The mere fact that a judgment orders the defendant to pay a sum to the state does not, in itself, mean that the judgment cannot be enforced in England; the question is whether the sum is a tax or is payable by way of punishment. In *United States of America v Inkley*[65] the United States government sought to enforce a judgment for the amount of an appearance bond given by the defendant. Although the judgment resulted from civil proceedings in Florida, the appearance bond had been required to encourage the defendant to answer various criminal charges. The Court of Appeal concluded that the payment was in the nature of a penalty and therefore the judgment was not enforceable.

59 *Vanquelin v Bouard* (1863) 15 CBNS 341. See also *Skaggs Companies Inc v Mega Technical Holdings Ltd* [2001] 1 WWR 359 (for consideration of the relevant cases).
60 Stuart-Smith LJ in *Desert Sun Loan Corpn v Hill* [1996] 2 All ER 847 at 863.
61 *Colt Industries Inc v Sarlie (No 2)* [1966] 3 All ER 85, [1966] 1 WLR 1287.
62 See chapter 12.
63 *SA Consortium General Textiles v Sun and Sand Agencies Ltd* [1978] QB 279, [1978] 2 All ER 339.
64 *Raulin v Fischer* [1911] 2 KB 93.
65 [1989] QB 255, [1988] 3 All ER 144.

B Conditions for recognition

The recognition of a foreign judgment is dependent on various conditions being fulfilled: first, the court must be a court of competent jurisdiction; secondly, the judgment must be final and conclusive; thirdly, the judgment must be on the merits; fourthly, the foreign proceedings must have between the same parties and have involved the same cause of action or the same issue. The first and second of these four requirements apply equally in enforcement cases and have already been discussed.[66] Where the relevant conditions are established a foreign judgment is prima facie entitled to recognition; the foreign judgment establishes either a cause of action estoppel (if the English and foreign proceedings involve the same cause of action) or an issue estoppel (if an issue raised before the English court is the same as an issue decided by the original court). The party wishing to deny the effect of a foreign judgment may, however, resist recognition of the judgment if he can establish one of the available defences.

Broadly speaking, there are three types of situation in which the recognition of a foreign judgment may arise. First, a defendant who is successful in foreign proceedings may wish to rely on a foreign judgment as a defence to English proceedings involving the same issue or cause of action. In such cases there is little difficulty in establishing that the foreign court was a court of competent jurisdiction. Where, for example, C sues D abroad and the foreign court gives judgment in D's favour, if C starts proceedings in England on the same cause of action the judgment is prima facie entitled to recognition as a judgment of a court of competent jurisdiction since C submitted to the original court by participating in the proceedings as claimant.

Secondly, the defendant may seek to rely on a foreign judgment, not only where the judgment has been given in his favour, but also where the judgment has been given in the claimant's favour. Section 34 of the Civil Jurisdiction and Judgments Act 1982 provides that no proceedings may be brought by a person in England on a cause of action in respect of which a judgment has been given in his favour in proceedings between the same parties[67] in a foreign court unless that judgment is not enforceable or entitled to recognition in England. As long as the conditions laid down in section 34 are

66 See pp 154–166.

67 For the purposes of s 34 of the 1982 Act, English proceedings in rem brought by C in relation to a ship owned by D involve the same parties as foreign proceedings in which C sued D in personam: *Republic of India v India Steamship Co Ltd (No 2)* [1998] AC 878. For further discussion of this case, see p 171.

satisfied a claimant who has been awarded a sum of money by a foreign judgment cannot sue in England on the original cause of action.

In *Black v Yates*[68] the plaintiff's husband had been killed in Spain in a road accident caused by the defendant's negligence. The defendant was prosecuted and, in the context of the criminal proceedings to which the plaintiff joined a civil claim for damages, the Spanish court awarded the plaintiff compensation. The plaintiff subsequently commenced proceedings against the defendant in England, in the hope of obtaining higher damages under the Fatal Accidents Acts. It was held that the plaintiff's action was barred by section 34, notwithstanding the fact that the Spanish proceedings started out as a criminal prosecution to which the plaintiff was not an original party. It has been held, however, that section 34 is not a mandatory provision. In *Republic of India v India Steamship Co Ltd*[69] the House of Lords decided that section 34 merely provides the defendant with a defence and that this defence may be defeated by estoppel, waiver or contrary agreement. If a claimant, having obtained a judgment in his favour abroad, starts proceedings in England on the same cause of action and the defendant consents to the jurisdiction of the English court section 34 does not bar the English proceedings.

Thirdly, a judgment-creditor may wish to raise issue estoppel as a means of limiting the grounds on which the judgment-debtor may challenge enforcement of a foreign judgment in England. Consider the situation where C seeks to enforce in England the judgment of a foreign court which exercised jurisdiction on the basis of D's submission. If in the course of its decision the original court determined that D authorised a local lawyer to accept service of process on his behalf the foreign judgment will prima facie create an issue estoppel in relation to that factual question. If the factual issues definitively determined by the original court establish that D submitted to the jurisdiction of the foreign court *according to English conflict of laws rules* D will effectively be estopped from arguing that the foreign court was not a court of competent jurisdiction.[70]

1. On the merits

For a foreign judgment to be a good defence to proceedings in England it must have been a judgment on the merits.[71] It is provided

68 [1992] QB 526, [1991] 4 All ER 722.
69 [1993] AC 410, [1993] 1 All ER 998.
70 See *Desert Sun Loan Corpn v Hill* [1996] 2 All ER 847.
71 *Harris v Quine* (1869) LR 4 QB 653; *Black-Clawson International Ltd v Papierwerke Waldhof-Aschaffenburg AG* [1975] AC 591, [1975] 1 All ER 810.

by statute that where a foreign court dismisses an action on the ground that it is time-barred the action is deemed to have been determined on its merits.[72]

As a general rule, if the foreign court dismisses an action on the basis that it lacks jurisdiction under its own law, that will not preclude the claimant from suing on the same cause of action in the English court. This general principle is qualified, however, by the decision of the House of Lords in *The Sennar*.[73] This case concerned a Dutch judgment which had been given in the context of litigation involving two foreign companies. Although there was a contract between the parties conferring exclusive jurisdiction on the courts of Sudan, the plaintiff had sought to avoid the impact of the jurisdiction clause by framing the action in tort. The Dutch courts dismissed the claim on the ground that the plaintiff was entitled to found the claim only in contract and was bound by the jurisdiction clause. When the plaintiff started proceedings against the defendant in England with a view to obtaining damages in tort, the defendant sought to rely on the Dutch judgment. The plaintiff argued, however, that, since the Dutch court had dismissed the claim on jurisdictional grounds, the judgment was not on the merits and therefore was not entitled to recognition in England. The House of Lords declined to adopt the plaintiff's argument. In the course of his speech Lord Brandon went some way towards clarifying what is meant by a decision 'on the merits': although a decision on procedure alone, if looked at negatively, is not a decision on the merits, if looked at positively 'a decision on the merits is a decision which establishes certain facts proved or not in dispute, states what are the relevant principles of law applicable to such facts, and expresses a conclusion with regard to the effect of applying those principles to the factual situation concerned'.[74]

On the basis of this analysis, it was clear that the Dutch judgment was 'on the merits' in a positive sense as regards two questions: first, the plaintiff's only claim against the defendant was for breach of contract; second, the plaintiff was bound by the jurisdiction clause in favour of the Sudanese courts. Accordingly, the defendant was entitled to rely on the Dutch judgment in support of its application for a stay.

It follows from *The Sennar* that a foreign judgment which, in general terms, decides a procedural or jurisdictional question may be regarded as determining an issue (or a number of issues) 'on the merits'. In order for the decision of a foreign court on such an issue

72 Foreign Limitation Periods Act 1984, s 3.
73 [1985] 2 All ER 104, [1985] 1 WLR 490.
74 At 499.

to be regarded as a decision 'on the merits' two conditions must be satisfied: first, there must have been an express submission of the procedural or jurisdictional issue in question to the foreign court; and, secondly, the specific issue of fact must have been raised before, and decided by, that court.[75]

2. *Cause of action and issue estoppel*

Where a foreign judgment operates as a defence, this is by way of estoppel per rem judicatam, just as where the prior judgment is given by the English court. There are two forms of such estoppel: cause of action estoppel (where the claimant is prevented from suing on the same action) and issue estoppel (where, although the cause of action is different, the claimant is estopped from contending that a particular issue should be decided differently from the way the identical issue was decided in an earlier case). It is important to emphasise that, whichever form the estoppel takes, there are two fundamental conditions which must be satisfied, in addition to those already considered: first, the parties to the foreign proceedings and the English proceedings must be the same; secondly, the cause of action (or issue) in the English proceedings must be the same cause of action (or issue) as was determined by the foreign court.

(A) IDENTITY OF THE PARTIES

In the straightforward case, where a foreign court gives judgment in proceedings involving C and D and C then starts proceedings against D on the same cause of action in England, there is no doubt that the foreign judgment gives rise to a cause of action estoppel. The position is more complicated, however, in cases involving multiparty litigation and in cases involving a foreign judgment in personam and English proceedings in rem (or a foreign judgment in rem and English proceedings in personam).

It is well established that a cause of action estoppel is effective not only as between the parties to the foreign proceedings but is also binding on the parties' 'privies'. There is a dearth of authority as to who are privies for the purposes of the doctrine of res judicata.[76] Two parties will be in a relationship of privity if there is privity of blood, title or interest.[77] Privies include, for example, a person who succeeds to the rights and liabilities of another on the latter's death.

75 *Desert Sun Loan Corpn v Hill* [1996] 2 All ER 847.

76 See Spencer Bower and Turner, *The Doctrine of Res Judicata* (2nd edn, 1969) pp 209–211.

77 *Carl Zeiss Stiftung v Rayner & Keeler Ltd (No 2)* [1967] 1 AC 853, [1966] 2 All ER 536.

In *Republic of India v India Steamship Co Ltd (No 2)*[78] the court had to consider the impact of a foreign judgment in personam on proceedings in rem commenced in England. The plaintiff sued the defendant in India and obtained damages for breach of contract. Subsequently, the plaintiff started proceedings in rem in England in respect of one of the defendant's vessels. The defendant applied for the claim to be dismissed under section 34 of the Civil Jurisdiction and Judgments Act 1982[79] on the ground that the English proceedings involved the same cause of action and the same parties as the Indian proceedings. The plaintiff argued, however, that the parties to the two sets of proceedings were different because, in proceedings in rem, the defendant is the vessel, rather than its owner. The House of Lords rejected the plaintiff's argument. The purpose of section 34 is to prevent the same cause of action being tried twice over between those who are, in reality, the same parties. So, where C obtains a judgment in personam against D in foreign proceedings and then starts proceedings in rem in England, section 34 bars the English action if D is the owner of the vessel on which process is served in the Admiralty action in rem.

(B) IDENTITY OF THE CAUSE OF ACTION OR THE ISSUE

(i) Identity of the cause of action

It is easy enough to state the principle that cause of action estoppel prevents a party to an action from asserting or denying, as against the other party, the existence of a particular cause of action, the non-existence or existence of which has been determined by a court of competent jurisdiction in previous litigation between the same parties.[80] What comprises, however, a cause of action? The general principle is that a cause of action consists of the minimum facts which a claimant has to plead and (if necessary) prove in order to obtain the relief claimed.[81] Where a set of facts gives rise to two types of loss the question facing the court is whether there are two causes of action or one cause of action involving two types of damage.

This question was considered by the House of Lords in *Republic of India v India Steamship Co*,[82] a case which involved litigation arising out of bills of lading under which the plaintiff's cargo was carried from Sweden to India in a ship owned by the defendant. During the course of the voyage there was a fire on board the ship; some of the cargo was jettisoned and the rest was damaged. The plaintiff sued

78 [1998] AC 878.
79 See pp 167–168.
80 *Thoday v Thoday* [1964] P 181, [1964] 1 All ER 341.
81 *Letang v Cooper* [1965] 1 QB 232, [1964] 2 All ER 929.
82 [1993] AC 410, [1993] 1 All ER 998.

the defendant in India and the Indian court awarded damages for short delivery. The plaintiff then started English proceedings claiming compensation for delivery of the cargo in a damaged condition. The defendant argued that the Indian judgment created a cause of action estoppel which barred the plaintiff's claim.[83] The House of Lords accepted that the same cause of action was involved in both the Indian and the English proceedings; in each action the plaintiff sought to rely on the same breach of contract.[84] The general principle is that a cause of action estoppel extends to matters which might have been raised (but were not raised) in the original proceedings; it was therefore irrelevant that the plaintiff pleaded in the English proceedings particulars of damage which were not pleaded in the Indian proceedings.[85]

There is every reason to think that the court would take the same approach to different types of loss and different heads of damage in a tort action. Where, for example, the victim of a road accident suffers property damage and loses both an arm and a leg, if the victim sues abroad and pleads only the loss of the leg, the foreign judgment will create a cause of action estoppel as regards not only the other physical injuries (the loss of the arm) but also the other head of damage (property damage).[86]

(ii) Identity of the issue

Even if a foreign judgment does not create a cause of action estoppel, it may give rise to an issue estoppel. As a general rule, once an issue has been determined between the parties neither party is allowed to fight that issue all over again.[87] The nature of an issue estoppel can be illustrated by the following simple example: a dispute having arisen out a contract between C and D, the parties enter a settlement agreement according to the terms of which C undertakes to pay specified sums to D; subsequently, C obtains a declaration from a foreign court that the original contract was illegal and void and refuses to honour the settlement agreement; when D seeks to enforce the settlement agreement in England C challenges its validity. It is clear that no cause of action estoppel can arise in this situation because the central question in the English proceedings (the validity of the settlement agreement) is different from the

83 Under Civil Jurisdiction and Judgments Act 1982, s 34.

84 It was also held that if the defendant consents to the jurisdiction of the English court the defence provided by s 34 of the 1982 Act is waived.

85 See *Buehler v Chronos Richardson Ltd* [1998] 2 All ER 960.

86 *Talbot v Berkshire County Council* [1994] QB 290, [1993] 4 All ER 9. Compare, however, *Brunsden v Humphrey* (1884) 14 QBD 141.

87 See Lord Denning MR in *Fidelitas Shipping Co Ltd v V/O Exportchleb* [1966] 1 QB 630 at 640.

central question in the foreign proceedings (the validity of the underlying contract). However, the issue decided by the foreign court is one which is relevant to the English action. On the assumption that the conditions necessary for the creation of an issue estoppel are satisfied, the effect of the foreign judgment is that, in the context of the English proceedings, D will be estopped from denying that the underlying contract was void for illegality.

There may be considerable difficulty in deciding whether a foreign judgment has already determined a particular issue which is raised in proceedings in England. Accordingly, the courts have tended to be rather cautious when questions of issue estoppel are raised. If in doubt, the court will refuse to recognise the foreign judgment as having conclusive effect.[88] Indeed, it seems to have become accepted that the court has a discretion not to recognise a foreign judgment if it would be unjust to do so, even if the technical criteria for the creation of an issue estoppel are satisfied.[89] Moreover, the principle of issue estoppel may be held not to operate in a case where, subsequent to the foreign judgment, further material, which could not by reasonable diligence have been adduced in the foreign proceedings, becomes available.[90]

C Defences to recognition and enforcement

As already noted, the positive conditions which must be satisfied by the party wishing to enforce or rely on a foreign judgment are only one half of the equation. Even if the foreign court was a court of competent jurisdiction and the other relevant conditions are satisfied, recognition or enforcement will be refused if the party seeking to deny the impact of the foreign judgment establishes one of a number of defences. There are two general points which should be mentioned before the specific defences are considered.

First, as a general rule, it is not possible to raise at the recognition or enforcement stage defences which were raised, or could have been raised, in the foreign proceedings. Secondly, it is not a defence to recognition or enforcement that the judgment was wrong on the merits, whether on the facts or the law. It is even immaterial that the foreign court misapplied English law in reaching its decision.[91]

88 *Desert Sun Loan Corpn v Hill* [1996] 2 All ER 847. See also *Baker v Ian McCall International Ltd* [2000] CLC 189.

89 *Carl Zeiss Stiftung v Rayner & Keeler Ltd (No 2)* [1967] 1 AC 853, [1966] 2 All ER 536.

90 *C (a minor) v Hackney London Borough Council* [1996] 1 All ER 973, [1996] 1 WLR 789 (a case involving a domestic judgment).

91 *Godard v Gray* (1870) LR 6 QB 139.

The court has to strike a difficult balance: on the one hand, defences should be kept within limits, otherwise the English court will assume the unacceptable role of a Court of Appeal in relation to the foreign proceedings; on the other hand, it is not reasonable to expect the English court to recognise or enforce a foreign judgment which conflicts with fundamental notions of justice and fairness. Whether English law manages to deal adequately with these competing tensions may be questioned.

1. Natural justice

The English court will not recognise or enforce a foreign judgment which was obtained in a manner contrary to natural justice. The traditional understanding of natural justice is that it requires two conditions to be satisfied: first, the litigant must have been given notice of the foreign proceedings; secondly, the litigant must have been given a proper opportunity of presenting his case before the court.[92] Whether either of these elements is lacking is a question which should be determined by English law, rather than by the law of the country of origin. It would seem that if a method of serving notice on the defendant was used which was in accordance with a contract between the parties (for instance, service at a stated address) that will be sufficient for the English court, even if the defendant did not in fact receive the notice with the consequence that the judgment was obtained against him by default.[93] Indeed, although there are many cases in which it has been confirmed that breach of the principles of natural justice is a defence to the recognition or enforcement of a foreign judgment, the English court will not be easily persuaded that natural justice has not been complied with and there seems to be no reported case in which the defence has succeeded. The fact that under the law of the country of origin the parties were not competent to give evidence themselves has been held not to preclude enforcement.[94]

There is also a strand in the cases which indicates that a foreign judgment will not be recognised or enforced if the original proceedings 'offend against English views of substantial justice'.[95] The question of 'substantial justice' was one of the many issues considered (obiter) by the Court of Appeal in *Adams v Cape Industries plc*.[96] Following the defendant's decision not to take part in the *Tyler 2*

92 *Jacobson v Frachon* (1927) 138 LT 386.
93 *Feyerick v Hubbard* (1902) 71 LJKB 509.
94 *Scarpetta v Lowenfeld* (1911) 27 TLR 509.
95 Lindley MR in *Pemberton v Hughes* [1899] 1 Ch 781 at 790.
96 [1990] Ch 433.

actions, the proceedings took – to English eyes – a slightly unusual turn. The proceedings in Texas did not involve a judicial investigation of the injuries of any of the individual plaintiffs; the judge simply directed that the average award for each of the plaintiffs should be $75,000 and counsel placed the plaintiffs in four bands according to the seriousness of their injuries. The defendant argued that, even if the plaintiffs could establish that the original court was a court of competent jurisdiction, the way in which the proceedings were conducted meant that the judgment was unacceptable.

The Court of Appeal asked itself the following question: did the proceedings in the foreign court offend against English views of substantial justice?[97] This question was answered in the affirmative; in cases involving a claim for unliquidated damages for a tortious wrong, the notion of substantial justice requires the amount of compensation to be assessed objectively by an independent judge, rather than subjectively by or on behalf of the claimant.[98]

The relationship between natural justice and substantial justice is far from clear. Although parts of the judgment in the Court of Appeal in *Adams v Cape Industries plc* seem to be couched in the language of public policy, the judgment does not suggest what the relationship between substantial justice and public policy might be. Furthermore, the content of substantial justice is inherently vague and there is no indication in the judgment in *Adams v Cape Industries plc* as to what are the principles of substantial justice. The approach adopted by the Court of Appeal invests the English court with a broad discretion and makes it difficult to predict how similar questions will be dealt with in subsequent cases.

2. Fraud

The English court will not recognise or enforce a judgment which was obtained by fraud. Fraud may take one of a number of forms. Most cases involve allegations by one party that the judgment was obtained by the presentation of evidence which the other party knew to be false. The defence of fraud also covers cases where a litigant has been deprived of the opportunity to take part in the foreign proceedings either by a trick of the other party[99] or as a result of threats of violence[100] and cases in which the defendant's objection relates to fraud by the foreign court (where, for example, the court has accepted a bribe).

97 Slade LJ at 564.
98 At 567. See also *Masters v Leaver* [2000] IL Pr 387.
99 *Ochsenbein v Papelier* (1873) 7 Ch App 695.
100 *Jet Holdings Inc v Patel* [1990] 1 QB 335, [1989] 2 All ER 648.

The defendant is normally entitled in the English proceedings to establish the fraud in the original proceedings even if the allegations of fraud were considered and rejected by the foreign court. Although this rule, which was formulated by the courts in the nineteenth century[101] (when the prevailing attitude was judicial chauvinism, rather than judicial comity), has been challenged in recent years, it has been confirmed by decisions of the Court of Appeal[102] and the House of Lords.[103] The defence of fraud is therefore an exception to the general rule that the English court will not question the merits of the foreign judgment. So, the defendant was entitled, in proceedings to enforce a Russian judgment for the value of the plaintiff's goods wrongly withheld by the defendant, to contend that the plaintiff had fraudulently testified in the Russian proceedings that the defendant had the goods when in fact they were in the plaintiff's own possession, even though the defendant had unsuccessfully alleged this in the Russian proceedings.[104] It has also been held that the defence of fraud may be invoked in English proceedings even if the defendant failed to raise the issue in the foreign proceedings when he could have done so.[105]

There is, however, one circumstance in which the defence of fraud cannot be raised – namely, where there have been separate proceedings abroad leading to a judgment which creates an issue estoppel between the parties on the question of fraud. In *House of Spring Gardens Ltd v Waite*[106] the plaintiff obtained a judgment in Ireland (the first judgment).[107] The defendant subsequently started separate proceedings in Ireland with a view to having the first judgment set aside on the basis of fraud. The Irish court dismissed the defendant's allegation of fraud (the second judgment). When the plaintiff brought proceedings in England to enforce the first judgment the defendant sought to raise the defence of fraud. The Court of Appeal held that the defendant was estopped: the second judgment, in which it had been decided that the first judgment had not been obtained by fraud, created an issue estoppel, thereby preventing the defendant from raising the question of fraud again.

101 *Abouloff v Oppenheimer & Co* (1882) 10 QBD 295; *Vadala v Lawes* (1890) 25 QBD 310.
102 *Jet Holdings Inc v Patel* [1990] 1 QB 335, [1989] 2 All ER 648.
103 *Owens Bank Ltd v Bracco* [1992] 2 AC 443, [1991] 4 All ER 833.
104 *Abouloff v Oppenheimer & Co* (1882) 10 QBD 295.
105 *Syal v Heyward* [1948] 2 KB 443, [1948] 2 All ER 576.
106 [1991] 1 QB 241, [1990] 2 All ER 990.
107 This was prior to entry in force of the Brussels Convention between the United Kingdom and Ireland.

3. *Public policy*

The court will not recognise or enforce a foreign judgment if to do so would be contrary to public policy. As elsewhere in the conflict of laws, there is no closed list of cases where public policy will be invoked. The most likely instance is where, if the original proceedings had been brought in England, the cause of action under the foreign law would have been rejected on the ground of public policy even though the foreign law would otherwise have been applicable. There are very few cases involving commercial judgments in which public policy has been successfully invoked. It is not, for example, contrary to public policy to enforce a foreign judgment which orders the defendant to pay exemplary damages.[108]

In *Re Macartney*,[109] a Maltese judgment under which personal representatives were ordered to pay maintenance to an illegitimate child of the deceased was refused enforcement on grounds of public policy, because the judgment entitled the child to receive maintenance even after her minority. The decision has been criticised,[110] for the only objection to the Maltese law on which the judgment was based was that it was different from English law, which should not be sufficient reason to reject the foreign law. In *Israel Discount Bank of New York v Hadjipateras*[111] the defendant sought to resist enforcement of a New York judgment on the basis that it was only as a result of his father's undue influence that he entered the contract of guarantee on which the judgment was based. The defendant argued that it would be contrary to public policy to enforce the judgment. The Court of Appeal rejected the defence on the ground that the defendant, having failed to raise the issue of undue influence in the New York proceedings, was unable to raise the matter in the English enforcement proceedings. More controversially, the Court of Appeal seems to have accepted the notion that a foreign judgment based on an agreement which contravenes public policy may be unenforceable on the ground of public policy. This aspect of the judgment is at best questionable; the traditional understanding of the public policy defence is that it relates to the substance of the foreign judgment, not to the underlying cause of action.[112]

108 *SA Consortium General Textiles v Sun and Sand Agencies Ltd* [1978] QB 279, [1978] 2 All ER 339.
109 [1921] 1 Ch 522.
110 Patchett, *Recognition of Commercial Judgments and Awards in the Commonwealth* (1984) p 159.
111 [1983] 3 All ER 129, [1984] 1 WLR 137.
112 Collier, [1984] CLJ 47.

4. Conflicting judgments

A prior English judgment is a defence not only to subsequent English proceedings, but also to the recognition or enforcement of a subsequent foreign judgment.[113] It could hardly be otherwise; it is not reasonable to suppose that the English court would give effect to a foreign judgment which conflicts with an English judgment. If there are two conflicting foreign judgments – both of which satisfy the conditions for recognition or enforcement – the earlier judgment will prevail unless the circumstances are such that the party wishing to rely on the earlier judgment is estopped from doing so.[114]

5. Judgment invalid under the foreign law

Will the English court recognise or enforce a judgment which otherwise qualifies for recognition or enforcement if it is invalid by the law of the country where it was granted – for example, because the court which granted it lacked jurisdiction under that law? Under the Family Law Act 1986 a foreign divorce decree will not be recognised in England unless it is 'effective under the law of the country in which it was obtained'.[115] So far as judgments in personam are concerned, the requirement that the judgment must be final and conclusive should mean that if the judgment is void under the foreign law, in the sense of being a nullity even without its having been set aside by the court, it cannot be recognised or enforced in England.[116] It has been held, however, that if the judgment is merely voidable under the foreign law, being valid unless and until it is set aside, it will be recognised or enforced. Thus the omission in a French default judgment to recite the steps taken to bring the summons to the defendant's knowledge, as required by French law, was held not to prevent the enforcement of the judgment in England, as it was at the most only voidable under French law.[117] This is perhaps the best explanation also of *Vanquelin v Bouard*,[118] where the English court enforced a judgment of a French commercial court, even though by French law such a court had jurisdiction only over defendants who were traders, and the defendant was not a trader.

113 *Vervaeke v Smith* [1983] 1 AC 145, [1982] 2 All ER 144; *ED & F Man (Sugar) Ltd v Haryanto (No 2)* [1991] 1 Lloyd's Rep 429.
114 *Showlag v Mansour* [1995] 1 AC 431, [1994] 2 All ER 129.
115 S 46(1)(a) and s 46(2)(a). See pp 404–405.
116 See, however, *Merker v Merker* [1963] P 283, [1962] 3 All ER 928 where the court recognised a German divorce decree even though it was a complete nullity in Germany.
117 *SA Consortium General Textiles v Sun and Sand Agencies Ltd* [1978] QB 279, [1978] 2 All ER 339.
118 (1863) 15 CBNS 341.

6. *Foreign judgment in breach of arbitration or jurisdiction clause*

By virtue of section 32 of the Civil Jurisdiction and Judgments Act 1982 if the claimant sues in a foreign country on a contract which contains a provision that the courts of some other country shall have exclusive jurisdiction, or that the dispute shall be submitted to arbitration (whether in England or abroad), the ensuing judgment shall normally be refused recognition or enforcement. A jurisdiction or arbitration clause cannot provide a defence to recognition or enforcement, however, if it was illegal, void, unenforceable or was incapable of being performed.[119] Similarly, a defendant cannot rely on such a clause if the proceedings in the original court were brought with the defendant's agreement or if he counterclaimed in those proceedings or otherwise submitted to the jurisdiction.[120]

Where a foreign court exercises jurisdiction over a dispute on the basis that an alleged jurisdiction or arbitration clause is void (or that the defendant submitted to the court's jurisdiction), the original court's decision on this point does not establish an issue estoppel. In the context of proceedings in England for the recognition or enforcement of the foreign judgment on the merits the English court is entitled to decide, according to its own conflicts rules, whether or not the alleged clause is void (or the defendant submitted).[121]

In *Tracomin SA v Sudan Oil Seeds*[122] the parties concluded a contract which contained a clause referring any dispute which might arise to arbitration in England. The plaintiff sued the defendant for breach of contract in Switzerland. Although the defendant contested the court's jurisdiction the Swiss court concluded that the arbitration clause was of no effect and handed down a judgment ordering the defendant to pay damages. When the plaintiff started enforcement proceedings in England, the defendant sought to rely on section 32 of the 1982 Act. The Court of Appeal refused to enforce the judgment, notwithstanding the fact that the Swiss court had decided that the arbitration clause was of no effect. According to English law, which was the law governing the contract, the arbitration clause was a valid clause which provided for the dispute to be settled otherwise than by proceedings in the Swiss courts. The defendant was therefore able to rely on the arbitration clause as a defence to the Swiss judgment.

119 S 32(2).
120 S 32(1)(b) and (c). *Marc Rich & Co AG v Società Italiana Impianti (No 2)* [1992] 1 Lloyd's Rep 624.
121 S 32(3).
122 [1983] 1 All ER 404, [1983] 1 WLR 662.

7. Multiple damages

The Protection of Trading Interests Act 1980 was passed to counteract, in particular, the extraterritorial effect of United States anti-trust laws. One of the features of the United States legislation is that, where the law requires the claimant to be compensated for losses caused by anti-competitive behaviour, the defendant is required to pay 'triple damages'. Section 5 of the 1980 Act provides that a judgment for multiple damages shall not be enforced by any court in the United Kingdom.[123] A judgment is also not to be enforced if it is based on a rule of law specified by an order made by the Secretary of State as being concerned with the prohibition or regulation of agreements, arrangements or practices designed to restrain, distort or restrict competition.[124]

III STATUTORY REGIMES BASED ON THE COMMON LAW

A Administration of Justice Act 1920

The Administration of Justice Act 1920 provides for the reciprocal enforcement of money judgments as between the United Kingdom and Commonwealth countries. It applies only to the judgments of Commonwealth countries to which the Act has been extended by Order in Council, on the basis that such countries have made reciprocal provision for the enforcement of United Kingdom judgments.[125] It cannot be extended to any further country since the enactment of the Foreign Judgments (Reciprocal Enforcement) Act 1933, which was intended to take its place for the future.

Enforcement is by means of registration of the foreign judgment by the English court, but there are few differences from the substantive requirements at common law. The foreign court must have been a court of competent jurisdiction,[126] the only difference in this regard being that it is sufficient that an individual defendant carried on business in the foreign country.[127]

123 Provision is also made in s 6 for the recovery in a United Kingdom court by certain defendants of the excess paid under a judgment for multiple damages.
124 See Protection of Trading Interests (Australian Trade Practices) Order 1988, SI 1988/569. The effect of this Order is that a judgment based on s 81(1A) of the Australian Trade Practices Act 1974 is not enforceable in the United Kingdom.
125 Although the 1920 Act applies to many Commonwealth countries it does not apply to Australia, Bangladesh, Canada, Gibraltar, Hong Kong (which is no longer part of the Commonwealth), India, Pakistan and South Africa.
126 S 9(2)(a).
127 S 9(2)(b) and (c).

A foreign judgment shall not be enforced in England under the 1920 Act in the following circumstances: if the defendant 'was not duly served with the process of the original court and did not appear';[128] if the judgment was obtained by fraud; if an appeal is pending in the country of origin; or if the judgment was in respect of a cause of action which for reasons of public policy or for some other similar reason could not have been entertained by the English court.[129] Defences are also provided by section 32 of the Civil Jurisdiction and Judgments Act 1982 and section 5 of the Protection of Trading Interests Act 1980. Presumably, a judgment would also be refused enforcement if it conflicts with an English judgment.

The 1920 Act does not abrogate the common law. It does not deal with recognition, as opposed to enforcement, and, as regards a judgment which falls within the scope of the Act, a claimant may choose to bring an action at common law instead of applying to register the judgment under the Act. If, however, the claimant does not proceed under the Act when he could do so, he will normally be deprived of his costs.[130]

B Foreign Judgments (Reciprocal Enforcement) Act 1933

The Foreign Judgments (Reciprocal Enforcement) Act 1933 provides for the recognition and enforcement of money judgments given by foreign courts (including those of Commonwealth countries). Like the Administration of Justice Act 1920, it applies only to judgments of countries to which it has been extended by Order in Council, on the basis of their having made reciprocal provision for the recognition and enforcement of United Kingdom judgments. The Act has in fact been extended to very few countries.[131]

The foreign court must have been a court of competent jurisdiction, the grounds being broadly similar to those recognised at common law.[132] There are two differences, however. First, the 1933 Act is in one respect more restrictive than the common law. The legislation

128 It was said in *Sfeir & Co v National Insurance Co of New Zealand* [1964] 1 Lloyd's Rep 330 that 'duly served' means duly served under the foreign rules of procedure, rather than by reference to the standards of the English court.

129 S 9(2)(d)–(f).

130 S 9(5).

131 The Act applies to judgments granted by the courts of Guernsey, Jersey, the Isle of Man, Australia (including the states and territories), Canada (including the provinces, other than Quebec), India, Pakistan, Tonga, Israel and Suriname. Although the Act was extended to a number of western European countries (Austria, Belgium, France, Germany, Italy, the Netherlands and Norway) it has since been largely superseded as regards these countries by the Brussels regime.

132 S 4(1)(a)(ii) and (2)(a).

refers to a defendant who was resident in or had its principal place of business in the country of origin;[133] the defendant's presence in the country of origin does not suffice. Secondly, the Act goes beyond the common law in that the original court will be regarded as a court of competent jurisdiction if the defendant had an office or place of business in the country of origin and the proceedings were in respect of a transaction effected through or at that office or place.[134] The other common law requirements apply: the judgment must be final and conclusive; only money judgments, not being for a tax or penalty, may be enforced;[135] a judgment which is not on the merits is not entitled to recognition.[136] Once the Act has been extended to a country, proceedings for the enforcement of a judgment from that country must be by way of registration under the Act and not by an action at common law.[137]

As regards defences, the 1933 Act largely follows the common law. A foreign judgment may be refused recognition or enforcement if it was obtained by fraud,[138] if its recognition or enforcement would be contrary to public policy,[139] or if the judgment is irreconcilable with an earlier judgment of the English court or another court of competent jurisdiction.[140] As regards natural justice, the legislation provides that a judgment shall be refused recognition or enforcement if the defendant 'did not (notwithstanding that process may have been duly served on him in accordance with the law of the country of the original court) receive notice of those proceedings in sufficient time to enable him to defend the proceedings and did not appear'.[141] Defences are also provided by section 32 of the Civil Jurisdiction and Judgments Act 1982 and section 5 of the Protection of Trading Interests Act 1980.

IV RECOGNITION AND ENFORCEMENT UNDER THE BRUSSELS REGIME

The Brussels I Regulation is directly effective in England; the Lugano Convention is implemented into English law by the Civil

133 S 4(2)(a)(iv).
134 S 4(2)(a)(v).
135 S 1(2)(a) and (b).
136 *Black-Clawson International Ltd v Papierwerke Waldhof-Aschaffenburg AG* [1975] AC 591, [1975] 1 All ER 810.
137 S 6.
138 S 4(1)(a)(iv).
139 S 4(1)(a)(v).
140 S 4(1)(b).
141 S 4(1)(a)(iii).

Jurisdiction and Judgments Act 1982 (as amended). The Brussels regime is divided into three Chapters or Titles: the first defines its scope; the second regulates jurisdiction; the third covers the recognition and enforcement of judgments. Although considerable energy was devoted to questions of jurisdiction,[142] it must not be forgotten that the fundamental purpose of the Brussels regime is to facilitate the free movement of judgments between the member states. The harmonisation of jurisdiction rules was not an end in itself; it was thought necessary in order to achieve the primary objective of the Brussels regime. As has been seen in the context of the common law rules, one of the main obstacles to the recognition and enforcement of foreign judgments in England is the fact that a foreign court may decide a question in relation to which, for the purposes of English conflicts rules, it was not a court of competent jurisdiction. The theory underlying the Brussels regime is that, if international agreement is achieved in relation to bases of jurisdiction, the recognition and enforcement of judgments can be significantly simplified.

A Judgments falling within the scope of the Brussels regime

To fall within the scope of the Brussels regime there are a number of conditions which must be satisfied. First, the judgment must have been given by a court of a member state. The Brussels regime applies only to international recognition; the recognition and enforcement in England of judgments given by the courts of Scotland and Northern Ireland is not governed by the Brussels regime.[143]

Secondly, the judgment must fall within the material scope of the Brussels regime ('civil and commercial matters') as defined by article 1. The issue whether a particular matter falls within the ambit of article 1 may arise both at the jurisdiction stage and at the stage of recognition or enforcement. For example, when a claimant applies to the English court to enforce a judgment given by the French courts, the English court must determine for itself whether the judgment is within the scope of the Regulation; the fact that the French court, prior to exercising jurisdiction under Chapter II, has already decided that the case is covered by article 1 does not preclude the English court from reconsidering the material scope of the Regulation. It is theoretically possible for the original court to exercise jurisdiction under Chapter II of the Regulation (on the basis that the case falls within the scope of article 1) and for the

142 See chapter 3.
143 See p 196.

English court to refuse enforcement under Chapter III (on the basis that it does not). This type of case is likely to generate a reference to the Court of Justice.[144] Although the scope of the Brussels regime has already been considered,[145] there is one further question which should be addressed at this point.

What is the correct solution in a case where, notwithstanding the defendant's argument that the dispute should be referred to arbitration, the foreign court exercises jurisdiction, decides that the arbitration clause is invalid and gives a judgment on the merits in the claimant's favour? If the claimant seeks to enforce the judgment in England the question is whether this judgment concerns 'arbitration' for the purposes of article 1(4). In the context of the Regulation, if the judgment does not concern 'arbitration' it falls within the scope of article 1 and, in principle, is enforceable under Chapter III; if the judgment does concern 'arbitration' it falls outside the scope of article 1 and, if the arbitration clause is valid according to English conflicts rules and the defendant did not submit to the jurisdiction of the foreign court, the judgment will be unenforceable.[146]

This issue has been the subject of extensive debate and the decision of the Court of Justice in the *Marc Rich* case[147] failed to resolve the disagreement.[148] The clearest English authority on the question is the decision of the High Court in *The Heidberg*[149] in which the judge accepted (i) that a decision as to the validity of an arbitration agreement falls within the ambit of article 1 and (ii) that a judgment given in defiance of an arbitration clause which, according to its proper law, is valid and binding between the parties is, in principle, entitled to recognition and enforcement under what is now Chapter III. As regards the first point, the correctness of the decision has been doubted.[150] Furthermore, in *Van Uden Maritime BV v Firma Deco-Line*[151] the Court of Justice seems to have accepted that the Brussels regime does not apply to judgments determining whether an arbitration agreement is valid or not. As for the second point, there is a strong argument for saying that, even if the view

144 Under art 234 EC.
145 See pp 65–66.
146 Civil Jurisdiction and Judgments Act 1982, s 32. This provision does not apply to judgments falling within the scope of the Brussels regime: s 32(4).
147 Case C-190/89 *Marc Rich & Co AG v Società Italiana Impianti, The Atlantic Emperor* [1991] ECR I-3855.
148 Compare, for example, Briggs (1991) 11 YBEL 527 at 529 and Cheshire and North, *Private International Law* (13th edn, 1999) p 509.
149 [1994] 2 Lloyd's Rep 287.
150 Dicey and Morris, *The Conflict of Laws* (13th edn, 2000) p 546; *The Ivan Zagubanski* [2002] 1 Lloyd's Rep 106.
151 Case C-391/95 [1998] ECR I-7091 at 7133 (para 32).

adopted in *The Heidberg* is correct, the recognition or enforcement of a judgment given by the court of a member state in defiance of an arbitration clause, which is valid and binding according to English private international law, is contrary to public policy for the purposes of article 34(1) of the Regulation.[152] The issues raised in *The Heidberg* will in all probability remain controversial until definitively resolved by the Court of Justice.[153]

Thirdly, article 32 defines 'judgment' as 'any judgment given by a court or tribunal of a member state, whatever the judgment may be called, including a decree, order, decision or writ of execution'. No distinction is made between judgments in personam and judgments in rem. Notwithstanding the breadth of the formulation in article 32 the provisions of Chapter III do not apply to (i) interlocutory decisions which regulate procedural matters only;[154] (ii) provisional measures either which are granted without notice – that is to say, where the defendant was not given an opportunity to take part in the original proceedings[155] – or which fall outside the range of provisional measures which may be granted under article 31;[156] or (iii) court settlements.[157] Judgments by consent are, however, within the scope of article 32.[158]

Fourthly, although the purpose of Chapter II (jurisdiction) is to simplify Chapter III (judgments), recognition and enforcement under Chapter III does not depend on the original court having exercised jurisdiction on the basis of the heads of direct jurisdiction laid down in Chapter II. The basic requirements of Chapter III are that the original court is the court of a member state and that the judgment falls within the material scope of article 1. The English court will therefore recognise and enforce judgments granted by the

152 *Philip Alexander Securities and Futures Ltd v Bamberger* [1997] IL Pr 72.

153 For further discussion see Hill, *International Commercial Disputes* (2nd edn, 1998) pp 68–71 and 696–697.

154 Schlosser Report, OJ 1979 C59/127, para 187; *CFEM Façades SA v Bovis Construction Ltd* [1992] IL Pr 561.

155 Case 125/79 *Denilauler v SNC Couchet Frères* [1980] ECR 1553. Even if, following the grant of an ex parte order, the defendant is given a reasonable opportunity to apply to have the order set aside, the order falls outside the scope of art 32: *EMI Records Ltd v Modern Music Karl-Ulrich Walterbach GmbH* [1992] QB 115, [1992] 1 All ER 616. But, provisional measures granted in the context of inter partes proceedings are within art 32: *Normaco Ltd v Lundman* [1999] IL Pr 381.

156 Case C-99/96 *Mietz v Intership Yachting Sneek BV* [1999] ECR I-2277 at 2318 (para 56).

157 Case C-414/92 *Solo Kleinmotoren GmbH v Boch* [1994] ECR I-2237. Special rules on the enforcement of court settlements are laid down in Chapter IV on authentic instruments and court settlements. See Case C-260/97 *Unibank A/S v Christensen* [1999] ECR I-3715.

158 *Landhurst Leasing plc v Marcq* [1998] IL Pr 822.

courts of other member states where the original court exercised jurisdiction on an exorbitant basis over a defendant who is not domiciled in a member state (as authorised by article 4). Where, for example, the French court gives judgment against a New Yorker – having exercised jurisdiction on the basis of article 14 of the Civil Code, which confers jurisdiction on the French court if the claimant is a French citizen – the ensuing judgment is enforceable even though the French court would not have had jurisdiction under Chapter II if the defendant had been domiciled in a member state.[159] There can be little doubt that the structure of the Brussels regime discriminates against defendants who are not domiciled in a member state.[160] As one commentator has noted:

> Not only does the Brussels [regime] continue to authorise unreasonable jurisdictional assertions against outsiders; it enhances their effect by requiring unquestioning recognition of such judgments in all of the [member] states.[161]

B Recognition

If a judgment falls within the scope of Chapter III, article 33 provides simply that it 'shall be recognised in the other member states without any special procedure being required'. There is no requirement that the person seeking to rely on the foreign judgment should establish that the original court was a court of competent jurisdiction. To obtain recognition the party relying on the foreign

159 Art 3(2).

160 For the United States reaction see Nadelmann, 'The Outer World and the Common Market Experts' Draft of a Convention on Recognition of Judgments' (1967–68) 5 CMLRev 409; Von Mehren, 'Recognition and Enforcement of Sister-state Judgments: Reflections on General Theory and Current Practice in the European Economic Community and the United States' (1981) 81 Col LR 1044.

161 Borchers, 'Comparing Personal Jurisdiction in the United States and the European Community: Lessons for American Reform' (1992) 40 Am J Comp L 121 at 132–133. Under art 59 of the Brussels Convention a contracting state could (subject to limitations) assume, in a convention with a third state, the obligation not to recognise judgments given in other contracting states against defendants domiciled or habitually resident in the third state where the judgment could be founded only on one of the grounds of jurisdiction specified in art 3(2) of the Convention (various grounds of 'exorbitant jurisdiction' not available against defendants domiciled in a contracting state). The United Kingdom entered into such conventions with Australia and Canada. These conventions are not affected by the Brussels I Regulation: art 72. However, following the adoption of the Regulation, the negotiation of further conventions of this type falls within the exclusive powers of the European Union (rather than the member states).

judgment need do no more than produce a copy of the judgment.[162] Recognition is, however, subject to a limited range of defences.[163]

Although article 33 states that judgments given by courts of the member states shall be recognised, questions of cause of action estoppel and issue estoppel are not addressed. It would seem that a judgment falling within Chapter III may create an estoppel of either type.[164] There are, however, a number of unresolved questions surrounding recognition under Chapter III. Where, for example, the defendant in English proceedings raises a French judgment as a defence, what criteria should the court apply to decide whether the cause of action (or issue) in the English proceedings is the same as the cause of action (or issue) in the French proceedings? Similarly, what principles determine whether the parties to the two set of proceedings are the same? Are these procedural questions to be decided by English law – as the law of the forum – or should these questions be looked at from a broader European perspective?[165] There is an argument for seeking to derive some assistance from rulings of the Court of Justice in related areas. The phrases 'the same parties' and 'the same cause of action' are used in article 27 and article 34(4).[166] There is, however, little case law except in relation to what is now article 27.[167]

C Enforcement

There is no requirement under the Brussels regime that the foreign judgment should be final and conclusive or for a fixed sum of money; it must, however, be enforceable in the country of origin.[168] As long as the foreign order is a 'judgment' within the scope of article 32,[169] a decree of specific performance or an injunction is as entitled to enforcement under Chapter III as a money judgment.[170] It is also

162 Art 53(1).
163 Arts 34 and 35 (formerly arts 27 and 28 of the Brussels Convention).
164 *Berkeley Administration Inc v McClelland* [1995] IL Pr 201.
165 Some aspects of these questions were considered in a rather confusing manner by the Court of Appeal in *Berkeley Administration Inc v McClelland* [1995] IL Pr 201. See also the later judgment of the Court of Appeal involving further aspects of the same case: [1996] ILPr 772.
166 The Court of Justice has recognised that there is a relationship between the doctrine of res judicata and what is now art 28: Case C-352/96 *Drouot Assurances SA v Consolidated Metallurgical Industries (CMI Industrial Sites)* [1998] ECR I-3075. See Handley, (2000) 116 LQR 191.
167 See pp 113–116.
168 Art 38 (formerly art 31 of the Brussels Convention). See Case C-267/97 *Coursier v Fortis Bank* [1999] ECR I-2543.
169 See p 185.
170 Case 143/78 *De Cavel v De Cavel* [1979] ECR 1055.

provided that a judgment which orders a periodic payment 'by way of a penalty' is enforceable, though only if the amount of the payment has been finally determined by the court of origin.[171] Where the payments accrue to the state, rather than to an individual or company, the likelihood is that the judgment will concern public law questions rather than 'civil and commercial matters' and will therefore fall outside the scope of the Brussels regime altogether.

Chapter III contains a detailed series of provisions regulating the procedure whereby enforcement is to be obtained.[172] In very general terms, the procedure can be broken down into a number of elements. First, the claimant makes an application for enforcement to the High Court. Secondly, as long as the necessary formalities are satisfied, the court orders enforcement without considering whether there are any defences available to the judgment-debtor. Thirdly, the enforcement order is served on the judgment-debtor, who may appeal against the court's decision; if the court refuses to order enforcement, the claimant may appeal against that decision. This first appeal is also heard by the High Court. Finally, either party may appeal to the Court of Appeal, but only on a point of law. Whereas the first two elements are entirely unilateral (and largely formal), the third and fourth elements involve procedures which are of an adversarial nature. A claimant who obtains a judgment in another member state may enforce it in England only through the procedure laid down in Chapter III; the claimant cannot choose to bring an action on the judgment at common law.[173] The grounds on which recognition may be refused are also grounds for refusing enforcement.[174]

D Defences to recognition and enforcement

Chapter III starts from the premise that a judgment falling within its scope is entitled to recognition and, where appropriate, enforcement. The conditions which must be satisfied by the person seeking to rely on a foreign judgment are minimal. It goes without saying that under no circumstances may a foreign judgment falling within Chapter III be reviewed as to its substance.[175] It is important, however, that the scales are not tilted too much in favour of the claimant. It is therefore not surprising that there are some defences to recognition and

171 Art 49.
172 Arts 38–52 and Annexes II–IV.
173 Case 42/76 *de Wolf v Harry Cox BV* [1976] ECR 1759.
174 Art 45.
175 Art 36 (formerly art 29 of the Brussels Convention); art 45(2) (formerly art 34(3) of the Brussels Convention).

enforcement.[176] If an appeal is pending in the original court, proceedings for the recognition of the judgment in another member state may be stayed.[177]

1. Limited review of jurisdiction

As a general rule, it is for the original court to ensure that it had jurisdiction, whether according to the bases of jurisdiction laid down in Chapter II or according to its traditional rules if the case fell within article 4. The English court is not normally entitled to question whether the original court was justified in exercising jurisdiction. Article 35(3) expressly provides that the test of public policy (which is one of the available defences to recognition and enforcement) may not be applied to the rules relating to jurisdiction.[178]

The fact that the original court was not a court of competent jurisdiction according to English common law notions is irrelevant. Where, for example, an English defendant visiting France injures someone in a motor accident, a French judgment ordering the defendant to pay damages is enforceable in England, even if the defendant chose not to defend the action. Of course, had the accident taken place in Texas, a judgment of the Texan court would not be enforceable at common law (unless the originating process was served on the defendant in Texas or the defendant submitted to the jurisdiction).

There is, however, an exception to the general rule that the jurisdiction of the original court may not be reviewed. A judgment shall not be recognised or enforced if the exercise of jurisdiction by the original court was contrary to the provisions governing jurisdiction in matters of insurance (articles 8 to 14), jurisdiction in relation to consumer contracts (articles 15 to 17) or exclusive jurisdiction (article 22).[179] When examining the grounds of the original court's jurisdiction in such a case, the English court is bound by the findings of fact on which the original court based its jurisdiction.[180]

The limits of this jurisdictional review should be noted. There is no defence to recognition or enforcement if the exercise of jurisdiction by the court of origin was contrary to the provisions dealing with employment contracts (articles 18 to 19). Moreover, the fact that

176 Arts 34, 35 and 45.

177 Art 37 (formerly art 30 of the Brussels Convention).

178 See Case C-7/98 *Krombach v Bamberski* [2000] ECR I-1935, [2001] All ER (EC) 584.

179 Art 35(1). There are further, limited jurisdictional defences under art 54B and art 57(4) of the Lugano Convention.

180 Art 35(2).

the original court exercised jurisdiction, notwithstanding an agreement between the parties to refer the dispute to the courts of another member state, is not a defence.[181] Accordingly, if a defendant wishes to rely on such an agreement he must challenge the jurisdiction of the court in the original proceedings; he cannot afford to ignore the foreign proceedings and hope to rely on the jurisdiction clause to resist enforcement of the ensuing default judgment in England. The general policy of the Brussels regime is to draw the defendant into the original proceedings so that any jurisdictional problems can be resolved as early as possible. If the original court declines jurisdiction, the claimant will have to try his luck elsewhere. If, however, the court exercises jurisdiction, the court's judgment on the merits will be effective throughout the member states.

2. *Public policy*

A judgment will not be recognised in England if such recognition is manifestly contrary to English public policy.[182] Some of the problems relating to the notion of public policy have already been considered.[183] Within the context of the Brussels regime, public policy is a concept which should be given a restricted interpretation[184] and should be invoked only in exceptional cases.[185] Public policy cannot be relied upon unless recognition of the foreign judgment would constitute a breach of a fundamental principle or of a rule of law regarded as essential in the legal order of the state in which recognition is sought.[186] Although the fact that the court of origin made a mistake in the application of European Union law is not enough to justify non-recognition of the judgment,[187] the defence of public policy may be applied in a situation where the law of the state of origin has failed to prevent a manifest breach of the defendant's rights under the European Convention on Human Rights (such as where the defendant's right to fair trial under article 6 of the Convention has been infringed).[188]

181 Civil Jurisdiction and Judgments Act 1982, s 32(4).
182 Art 34(1) (formerly art 27(1) of the Brussels Convention).
183 See p 177.
184 Case C-414/92 *Solo Kleinmotoren GmbH v Boch* [1994] ECR I-2237.
185 Case 145/86 *Hoffmann v Krieg* [1988] ECR 645; Case C-78/95 *Hendrikman v Magenta Druck & Verlag GmbH* [1996] ECR I-4943.
186 Case C-7/98 *Krombach v Bamberski* [2000] ECR I-1935, [2001] All ER (EC) 584; Case C-38/98 *Régie Nationale des Usines Renault SA v Maxicar SpA* [2000] ECR I-2973.
187 Case C-38/98 *Régie Nationale des Usines Renault SA v Maxicar SpA* [2000] ECR I-2973.
188 Case C-7/98 *Krombach v Bamberski* [2000] ECR I-1935, [2001] All ER (EC) 584; van Hoek, (2001) 38 CML Rev 1011. See also art 61.

Although there is no separate defence of fraud under articles 34 and 35 it is generally accepted that, in certain circumstances, a foreign judgment which has been obtained by fraud may be refused recognition or enforcement on the ground of public policy. However, the common law approach to fraud is not compatible with the Brussels regime, under which a judgment cannot be reviewed as to its merits.[189] To the extent that fraud is a defence under the Brussels regime it is significantly narrower than the defence at common law.

In *Interdesco SA v Nullifire Ltd*[190] the High Court considered whether fraud could be raised as a defence under the heading of public policy. A number of points emerge from the judgment of Phillips J.[191] First, where the foreign court has ruled on precisely the matters which the defendant seeks to raise when challenging the judgment on the ground of fraud, the court is not entitled to review the conclusion of the foreign court. Secondly, a defendant who believes that a foreign judgment has been obtained by fraud should pursue any available remedy in the country of origin. Thirdly, the English court should not normally entertain a challenge to a judgment in circumstances where it would not permit a challenge to an English judgment.[192]

On the basis of these principles it will be extremely rare for a judgment falling within the scope of Chapter III to be denied recognition or enforcement on the basis of fraud. The defendant would have to establish not only that further evidence of the fraud has come to light since the judgment was handed down by the original court but also that there is no means of recourse in the country of origin.

3. *Natural justice*

Article 34(2)[193] provides that a judgment shall not be recognised 'where it was given in default of appearance, if the defendant was not served with the document which instituted the proceedings or with an equivalent document in sufficient time and in such a way as to

189 Art 36; art 45(2).

190 [1992] 1 Lloyd's Rep 180.

191 The approach of Phillips J was approved by the Court of Appeal in *Société d'Informatique Service Réalisation Organisation v Ampersand Software BV* [1994] IL Pr 55. Although a number of issues were subsequently referred to the Court of Justice the fraud question was not: Case C-432/93 [1996] QB 127, [1995] ECR I-2269.

192 Under English law a domestic judgment cannot normally be challenged on the basis of fraud unless new evidence, which was not considered at the trial, is forthcoming: *Henderson v Henderson* (1843) 3 Hare 100, [1843–60] All ER Rep 378.

193 This provision replaces (and is different in a number of respects from) art 27(2) of the Brussels Convention.

enable him to arrange for his defence, unless the defendant failed to commence proceedings to challenge the judgment when it was possible for him to do so'. The equivalent provision of the Brussels Convention generated a significant body of case law and offered defendants the possibility of resisting recognition or enforcement on largely technical grounds.[194] Therefore, in the Regulation, this provision was modified with a view to avoiding abuses of procedure.[195] A number of points concerning article 34(2) should be noted.

First, a defendant may rely on article 34(2) notwithstanding the fact that the issues which are relevant – service and sufficiency of time – have already been considered by the original court under article 26.[196] Even if the original court concludes that the defendant was served in sufficient time, this conclusion is not binding on the court of the country in which recognition or enforcement is sought.[197]

Secondly, the defence provided by article 34(2) is available only if the judgment was given 'in default of appearance'. If the defendant took part in the proceedings on the merits reliance cannot be placed on article 34(2).[198] Indeed, it seems generally to be thought that a defendant will be regarded as having appeared if he plays any part in the proceedings – even if only to contest the court's jurisdiction or to ask for a postponement of the proceedings. However, the Court of Justice has ruled that where proceedings are initiated against a defendant without his knowledge and a lawyer appears on his behalf, but without his authority, the ensuing judgment is to be regarded as given in default of appearance even if, under the law of the state of origin, the original proceedings are regarded as being inter partes.[199]

Thirdly, whether a defendant can resist recognition or enforcement under article 34(2) appears to be primarily a question of fact, rather than a question of law. A mere formal irregularity in the service procedure will not debar recognition or enforcement if it has not prevented the defendant from arranging his defence.[200] So, a defendant should be able to resist recognition or enforcement if, though he was served with the document initiating the proceedings,

194 See, in particular, Case C-305/88 *Isabelle Lancray SA v Peters und Sickert KG* [1990] ECR I-2725.

195 See *Proposal for a Council Regulation (EC) on jurisdiction and the recognition and enforcement of judgments in civil and commercial matters* (hereafter '*Proposal*'), COM (1999) 348, p 23.

196 See p 66.

197 Case 228/81 *Pendy Plastic Products BV v Pluspunkt Handelsgesellschaft mbH* [1982] ECR 2723.

198 Case C-172/91 *Sonntag v Waidmann* [1993] ECR I-1963.

199 Case C-78/95 *Hendrikman v Magenta Druck & Verlag GmbH* [1996] ECR I-4943.

200 See *Proposal*, COM (1999) 348, p 23.

there was not enough time (between when process was served and when, in the event of the defendant's failure to take part in the proceedings, a default judgment could have been issued against him) in which to arrange for his defence.[201] Similarly, a judgment should not be entitled to recognition or enforcement if the method whereby process was served fails to give the defendant a reasonable opportunity to prepare his defence. For example, the defendant should be able to rely on article 34(2) if the claimant, not knowing the defendant's address, employed a form of fictitious or substituted service as a result of which the defendant was wholly unaware of the proceedings which led to the judgment against him.

Fourthly, it is for the court in which recognition or enforcement is sought to decide whether service was in sufficient time and effected in an appropriate way. In a straightforward case, where the originating process is served on the defendant in a standard way (for example, where process is sent by post to the defendant's business address), time should start to run from the moment of service, even if the defendant only has actual knowledge that proceedings have been commenced at some subsequent point. In this type of case, it should not be for the claimant to prove that the originating process was actually brought to the defendant's knowledge.[202] For the purposes of article 34(2) 'the document which instituted the proceedings' is the document which, when served on the defendant, enables him to assert his rights before an enforceable judgment is given in the country of origin.[203] In assessing whether the time available is sufficient, any period after the grant of a default judgment – during which the judgment might be set aside – should be ignored.

An illustration of the problems which the courts have to confront is provided by *Debaecker v Bouwman*[204] (a case decided under article 27(2) of the Brussels Convention). Shortly after taking a lease of premises in Belgium, the defendant, who was domiciled in the Netherlands, left without giving notice and without leaving a forwarding address. The plaintiff issued Belgian proceedings and, not knowing the defendant's address, served the originating process on the local Police Commissariat – in accordance with Belgian law. A few days later the defendant sent the plaintiff details of a post office box through which he could be contacted. The plaintiff made no attempt to inform the defendant of the proceedings and, in due

201 Case 166/80 *Klomps v Michel* [1981] ECR 1593. See also *TSN Kunststoffrecycling GmbH v Jurgens* [2002] 1 All ER (Comm) 282.

202 Case 166/80 *Klomps v Michel* [1981] ECR 1593.

203 Case C-123/91 *Minalmet GmbH v Brandeis Ltd* [1992] ECR I-5661; Case C-474/93 *Firma Hengst Import BV v Campese* [1995] ECR I-2113.

204 Case 49/84 [1985] ECR 1779.

course, the Belgian court gave a default judgment in the plaintiff's favour. When the plaintiff applied to enforce the judgment in the Netherlands, the defendant resisted enforcement of the ground that he had been given insufficient time to arrange for his defence. The Court of Justice ruled that, in examining whether service had been effected in sufficient time, the Dutch court was entitled to take account of exceptional circumstances which arose after service of the originating process. The exceptional circumstances included the conduct of the defendant (who had returned to the Netherlands without leaving a forwarding address) and the conduct of the plaintiff (who had failed to inform the defendant of the proceedings even after receiving details of the defendant's new postal address). The Court of Justice gave no indication, however, as to the relative importance of the competing factors. Ultimately, whether a defendant has been given enough time is a question of fact to be determined in the light of all the circumstances by the court of the member state in which recognition or enforcement is sought.

Finally, a defendant who was not able to arrange his defence prior to a judgment being made against him in the court of origin will lose the defence provided by article 34(2) if, after the judgment has been made, he fails to take an opportunity to challenge the judgment in the country of origin.[205] The idea behind this proviso is that, if the defendant can appeal in the state of origin on grounds of a procedural irregularity, he should not be able to invoke that procedural irregularity as a ground for resisting recognition or enforcement.[206] Of course, if there is no possibility of such a challenge, the proviso to article 34(2) has no application. In the context of the Brussels Convention, the Court of Justice ruled that a judgment is to be regarded as having been given in default of appearance even if, after an enforceable judgment has been issued in the country of origin, the defendant applies to the court of origin for the judgment to be set aside.[207] If this ruling is still good law for the purposes of the Regulation, it is reasonable to suppose that a defendant who makes an unsuccessful challenge against a default judgment in the country of origin will not be able to invoke article 34(2) in recognition or enforcement proceedings. There is no reason why a defendant who makes an unsuccessful challenge should be treated more favourably than a defendant who could have made a challenge, but failed to do so.

205 The text of art 34(2) effectively reverses the ruling, under art 27(2) of the Brussels Convention, in Case C-123/91 *Minalmet GmbH v Brandeis Ltd* [1992] ECR I-5661.

206 *Proposal*, COM (1999) 348, p 23.

207 Case 166/80 *Klomps v Michel* [1981] ECR 1593.

4. Irreconcilable judgments

The jurisdiction provisions of Chapter II go a long way towards reducing the incidence of conflicting judgments. There are, however, limits to what can be achieved by article 6 and articles 27 and 28 – even if they are applied consistently and correctly by the courts of all the member states. The Brussels regime regulates jurisdiction only as between the member states. Where proceedings are being conducted in a member state the Brussels regime cannot prevent parallel litigation involving the same issues being conducted in the courts of a non-member state. In addition, because the material scope of the Brussels regime is limited by article 1, it is possible for there to be a conflict between a judgment of one member state in a matter falling within the scope of article 1 and a judgment of another member state in a matter falling outside its ambit. Paragraphs (3) and (4) of article 34 deal with the problems posed by irreconcilable judgments.

Article 34(3) provides that a judgment shall not be recognised if the judgment is irreconcilable with a judgment given in a dispute between the same parties in the state in which recognition is sought. Two judgments are irreconcilable for the purposes of this provision if they entail legal consequences that are mutually exclusive. So, a German judgment ordering an estranged husband to pay maintenance to his wife – which is premised on the existence of a matrimonial relationship between the parties – is irreconcilable with a Dutch decree dissolving the marriage.[208]

Article 34(4) is a simple provision for dealing with two foreign judgments (whether granted by the courts of member or non-member states). Its effect is that the English courts shall not recognise a judgment if it is irreconcilable with an earlier judgment given in a member state or non-member state involving the same cause of action and between the same parties, provided that the earlier judgment fulfils the conditions necessary for its recognition under English law.

Suppose, for example, that the English court is faced by conflicting foreign judgments in civil and commercial matters, one granted by the courts of New York, the other by the Italian courts. In order to determine whether the Italian judgment is entitled to recognition or enforcement under Chapter III, the court must consider the effect of the New York judgment under the common law. If both judgments satisfy the conditions for recognition or enforcement (the New York judgment under the common law and the Italian judgment under the Regulation) the English court must give priority to the earlier

208 Case 145/86 *Hoffmann v Krieg* [1988] ECR 645.

judgment. If the New York judgment was granted first, article 34(4) provides that the Italian judgment shall be refused recognition. Similarly, if the English court is faced with two member state judgments, article 34(4) gives priority to the earlier judgment – as long as it satisfies the condition for recognition under the Regulation.

V UNITED KINGDOM JUDGMENTS

Provision is made by the Civil Jurisdiction and Judgments Act 1982 for the recognition and enforcement in one part of the United Kingdom of judgments obtained in another part.[209] Under this legislation, a judgment obtained in Scotland or Northern Ireland can be registered and enforced in England. No jurisdictional requirements need to be satisfied in respect of the proceedings in the original court; it is sufficient that the judgment was granted[210] and that the time for an appeal has expired or any appeal has been disposed of. Enforcement is not confined to money judgments; decrees of specific performance and injunctions are equally enforceable.

It would seem that the common law defences of fraud, natural justice and public policy do not apply to judgments given by the courts of other parts of the United Kingdom;[211] the aggrieved party must seek relief in the original court. It is also expressly provided that section 32 of the 1982 Act does not apply to such judgments.[212] However, a judgment of the courts of Scotland or Northern Ireland cannot be enforced in England if it conflicts with an English judgment.[213]

209 Ss 18 and 19; Schs 6 and 7.
210 S 19.
211 See *Clarke v Fennoscandia Ltd* 1998 SC 464 (a case concerning the enforcement of an English judgment in Scotland).
212 S 32(4).
213 Sch 6, para 10(b) and Sch 7, para 9(b).

Chapter 5

Contractual obligations

I INTRODUCTION

A dispute about a contract which comes before the English court may have foreign elements: one or both of the parties may be foreign; the making or performance of the contract may be connected with a number of foreign countries. For example, according to the terms of a contract of sale concluded by telephone, an English seller may undertake to deliver goods to a French buyer in Italy. In a claim for breach of contract brought by the French buyer in England, a question may arise on which the rules of English, French and Italian law are different. In this type of case which law is the court to apply? It would be possible, in theory, for the court to apply English law as the lex fori. This solution has the attraction of simplicity and certainty. It would not, however, be consistent with the objectives which the conflict of laws seeks to achieve. If each country were simply to apply the lex fori to cases with a foreign element there would be a significant likelihood that the outcome of many international disputes would depend solely on the location of the litigation. Even though one of the purposes of jurisdiction rules is to ensure that international litigation is conducted in an appropriate forum, it does not follow that the law of the country which exercises jurisdiction in relation to a contractual dispute is necessarily the most appropriate law to govern the contract. Certain factors which are relevant for the allocation of jurisdiction – in particular, questions of practical litigational convenience (such as the location of evidence and witnesses) – have no significance for the determination of the governing law.

The general principle is that every international contract has a governing law – known at common law as the 'proper law' and by statute as the 'applicable law' – by reference to which most of the significant issues arising out of the contract are to be determined. Subject to certain limitations, parties to a contract are free to choose the applicable law; if the parties fail to make a choice, the governing law will be the law of the country with which the contract is most closely connected.

During the nineteenth and twentieth centuries the English courts developed the doctrine of the 'proper law of the contract'. According to this doctrine, the choice of law process is broken down into three stages. First, the parties might make an express choice of law. At common law, the court will give effect to an express choice of law, as long as it is bona fide, legal and not contrary to public policy.[1] Secondly, in the absence of express choice the proper law of the contract may be 'the system of law by reference to which the contract was made'.[2] This formula allows for the possibility of an implied, rather than express, choice. At common law, the court may imply a choice of law from the form of the contract (such as use of a particular standard form[3]) or from an arbitration clause[4] or from a jurisdiction agreement.[5] Thirdly, in the absence of an express or implied choice, a contract should be governed by the 'objective' proper law – that is the law 'with which the transaction has its closest and most real connection'.[6]

These rules can be explained by reference to a number of objectives which the law seeks to achieve. First, the law promotes certainty by allowing the parties to choose the governing law. Secondly, the rule that effect will be given to an express or implied choice of law is consistent with the principle of party autonomy which underpins the whole of the law of contract. Thirdly, in cases where the parties have not made a choice, the application of the law of the country with which the contract is most closely connected gives effect both to the reasonable expectations of the parties and to the interests of the country which is likely to have the greatest interest in the outcome of the parties' dispute.

Although one of the aims of the choice of law process is to promote uniformity of result regardless of the country in which the litigation is brought, the conflict of laws cannot achieve such

1 *Vita Food Products Inc v Unus Shipping Co Ltd* [1939] AC 277, [1939] 1 All ER 513. There is no reported English case in which an express choice was disapplied on the basis of the proviso. See, however, *Golden Acres Ltd v Queensland Estates Pty Ltd* [1969] Qd R 378 (a decision of the Supreme Court of Queensland) and the discussion of the Singapore Court of Appeal in *Peh Teck Quee v Bayerische Landesbank Girozentrale* [2001] 2 LRC 23.

2 *Bonython v Commonwealth of Australia* [1951] AC 201 at 219.

3 *Amin Rasheed Shipping Corpn v Kuwait Insurance Co* [1984] AC 50, [1983] 2 All ER 884.

4 *James Miller & Partners Ltd v Whitworth Street Estates (Manchester) Ltd* [1970] AC 583, [1970] 1 All ER 796; *Compagnie Tunisienne de Navigation SA v Compagnie d'Armement Maritime SA* [1971] AC 572, [1970] 3 All ER 71.

5 *The Komninos S* [1991] 1 Lloyd's Rep 370.

6 *Bonython v Commonwealth of Australia* [1951] AC 201 at 219.

uniformity if different countries have different choice of law rules. Generally speaking, it is the claimant who benefits from the flexibility which results from the fact that the outcome of a contractual dispute may differ depending on the country in which the proceedings are brought. If the courts of more than one country have jurisdiction, the claimant will be able to choose the most advantageous forum in which to sue the defendant. There are various ways in which the balance may be tilted back in favour of the defendant. First, as a result of the operation of a sophisticated framework of jurisdiction rules the claimant may be deprived of choice at the jurisdiction stage. Secondly, attempts may be made to harmonise law at the substantive level. If, for example, the law of contract were the same throughout Europe, the choice of law process would be circumvented entirely as regards contractual disputes which had connections only with European countries; the domestic contract law of each country would be identical. However, harmonisation at a substantive level is fraught with difficulty. It is dependent not only on international agreement being reached on the substance of the law itself, but also on the implementation into domestic law of the internationally agreed rules. One of the most significant developments in recent years is the United Nations Convention on Contracts for the International Sale of Goods (often referred to as the Vienna Convention) of 1980. Although this Convention has been accepted by many countries it has not been implemented in the United Kingdom. Thirdly, an attempt may be made to harmonise choice of law rules. This third option has been pursued by the member states of the European Union. As a consequence of developments at the European level, for most practical purposes, the proper law doctrine has been superseded in England – although it still forms the foundation of the law in most other parts of the English-speaking world.

In 1980 the member states of the European Community concluded the Rome Convention on the Law Applicable to Contractual Obligations. This Convention was motivated by recognition of the fact that the harmonisation achieved by the Brussels regime in relation to jurisdiction and judgments was not sufficient to achieve uniformity in the commercial sphere. The original plan was to produce a convention harmonising the choice of law rules relating to contractual and non-contractual obligations. However, when it became apparent that agreement in the field of non-contractual obligations was likely to prove very difficult to achieve, negotiations centred on contractual obligations only.[7] The Rome Convention,

7 The possibility of the harmonisation of the rules relating to choice of law in non-contractual obligations at the European level was revived in the late 1990s: see the Vienna Action Plan, OJ 1999 C19/1.

which was implemented in the United Kingdom by the Contracts (Applicable Law) Act 1990, came into force on 1 April 1991. The common law rules continue to apply to contracts concluded before that date and to contracts and contractual questions which are not regulated by the Convention or other statutory provisions.

The Rome Convention has been widely deprecated by commentators in England. Not only have critics questioned the need to harmonise choice of law rules in the field of contract,[8] they have also suggested that the content of the Convention is inferior to the equivalent principles of the common law.[9] While even its strongest supporters would concede that the Convention is not perfect, some of the criticisms seem rather exaggerated, especially in view of the fact that the Convention's basic approach to the choice of law process is very reminiscent of the proper law doctrine.

II ROME CONVENTION: GENERAL CONSIDERATIONS

A The scope of the Convention

The Convention applies, subject to exceptions, to contractual obligations in any situation involving a choice between the laws of different countries.[10] The Convention does not indicate what is meant by 'contractual obligations'. Although, at common law, classification is to be determined by reference to the conceptual categories of the lex fori, it would seem that for the purposes of the Convention a broader, European approach should be adopted. It is certainly the case that the simple fact that a particular situation would not be regarded as contractual according to English law is not sufficient to exclude the situation from the Convention's scope. Indeed, it had been recognised at common law long before the Convention's entry into force that for conflict of laws purposes the conceptual category 'contract' includes some situations which do not give rise to enforceable contractual obligations according to English domestic law. Where, for example, a claimant sues a defendant in England to enforce a promise which is not supported by consideration, for conflict of laws purposes the dispute involves a contractual obligation.[11] Within the framework of the Convention,

8 Collins, 'Contractual Obligations – the EEC Preliminary Draft Convention on Private International Law' (1976) 25 ICLQ 35.
9 Mann, 'The Proper Law of the Contract – an Obituary' (1991) 107 LQR 353.
10 Art 1(1).
11 *Re Bonacina* [1912] 2 Ch 394.

gifts and promises to give are to be regarded as involving contractual obligations.[12]

Various matters are excluded from the Convention's scope even though they involve contractual obligations.[13] The excluded matters are a mixed collection with no internal consistency. First, the rules in the Convention do not apply to questions involving the status or legal capacity of natural persons. This is subject, however, to article 11, which lays down a limited, uniform rule with regard to contractual capacity.[14] Secondly, the Convention does not apply to contractual obligations relating to wills and succession or to family law issues. Thirdly, obligations arising under bills of exchange, cheques and promissory notes are excluded from the Convention's scope.[15] Fourthly, the Convention does not apply to arbitration agreements and agreements on the choice of court. This exclusion is said to be justified by the fact that such agreements lie within the sphere of procedure and are, to some extent, regulated by other provisions of an international nature – namely, the New York Convention of 1958 and the Brussels regime.[16] Fifthly, questions governed by the law of companies and other bodies corporate or unincorporate are excluded. Sixthly, although contracts of agency are not excluded entirely, the Convention does not apply to the question whether an agent is able to bind a principal (or whether an organ is able to bind a company or body corporate or unincorporate) to a third party. Seventhly, excluded matters cover the constitution of trusts and the relationship between settlors, trustees and beneficiaries. Eighthly, questions of evidence and procedure are excluded. This is consistent with the general principle that procedural questions are governed by the lex fori. Finally, the position as regards insurance contracts is somewhat complicated. If the contract is a contract of reinsurance the Convention applies.[17] Similarly, if a contract of insurance covers risks situated outside the territories of the member states of the European Community the Convention applies.[18] However, the Convention does not apply to contracts of insurance which cover risks situated in the territories of the member states of the European Community; these contracts are governed by other uniform rules

12 Giuliano-Lagarde Report, OJ 1980 C282/10.
13 Art 1(2)–(4).
14 See pp 245–246.
15 These matters are governed by the Bills of Exchange Act 1882.
16 Giuliano-Lagarde Report, OJ 1980 C282/11–12.
17 Art 1(4).
18 Art 1(3). See, however, n 19, below.

which have been enacted as part of the European Community's efforts to harmonise the law of insurance.[19]

Article 2 provides that the law specified by the Convention 'shall be applied whether or not it is the law of a contracting state'. Indeed, the Convention applies regardless of the territorial connections of the parties and whether or not the contract or the dispute has any connection with a contracting state. Where, for example, a contractual dispute between a Singaporean company and a Malaysian company is litigated in England, the applicable law is determined by the Convention, not by the common law proper law doctrine. In practice, of course, many cases in which the Convention is applicable will have a significant connection with a contracting state, since, for the Convention to apply, the court of a contracting state must have jurisdiction in relation to the dispute.

As noted earlier, the United Kingdom is made up of three legal systems: England, Scotland and Northern Ireland. Although the United Kingdom is not required to apply the Convention to disputes which are internal to it,[20] the implementing legislation states that the Convention rules are applicable 'in the case of conflicts between the laws of different parts of the United Kingdom'.[21]

B Interpretation

The contracting states agreed, in principle, that the Court of Justice should have jurisdiction to interpret the Rome Convention. The negotiations leading to the protocols on interpretation were very protracted and the protocols are not in force; nor are they ever likely to be, as the intention is that the Rome Convention (like the Brussels Convention) should be replaced by an EC regulation.[22]

When interpreting the Convention, a national court should have regard to three factors. First, the court should have regard to the international character of the Convention's provisions and to the desirability of achieving uniformity in their interpretation and application.[23] Accordingly, the English court should consider any

19 The relevant EC Directives are implemented in the United Kingdom by the Financial Services and Markets Act 2000 (Law Applicable to Contracts of Insurance) Regulations 2001, SI 2001/2653 (as amended by SI 2001/3542). The 2001 Regulations extend to insurance policies relating to risks situated in an EEA (European Economic Area) state. The general pattern of these rules is similar to that found in the Convention. See *Crédit Lyonnais v New Hampshire Insurance Co* [1997] 2 Lloyd's Rep 1.
20 Art 19(2).
21 Contracts (Applicable Law) Act 1990, s 2(3).
22 Dicey and Morris, *The Conflict of Laws* (13th edn, 2000) p 1201.
23 Art 18.

relevant decisions of the courts of other contracting states and, where appropriate, other language versions of the Convention, all of which are equally authentic.[24] Secondly, the court should have regard to any relevant decisions of, or expressions of opinion by, the Court of Justice.[25] In the absence of a body of case law from the Court of Justice this principle is without meaning. Thirdly, the 1990 Act provides that the court may consider the official report which accompanies the Convention – the Giuliano-Lagarde Report[26] – when considering the meaning or effect of any of its provisions.[27]

C Exclusion of renvoi

It is well established at common law that the doctrine of renvoi has no role to play in the field of choice of law in contract.[28] At common law, if Russian law is the proper law of the contract, the rights and obligations of the parties are to be determined by Russian domestic law, not by reference to the law which would be regarded as the governing law according to Russian choice of law principles. The same general principle is adopted by the Rome Convention which provides that where its choice of law rules require the application of the law of a country that means 'the application of the rules of law in force in that country other than its rules of private international law'.[29]

III DETERMINING THE APPLICABLE LAW

Central to the operation of the Convention is the identification of the applicable law. The Convention draws a distinction between cases in which the parties have made a choice (which fall within article 3) and cases where the parties have not made a choice (which are governed by article 4). However, three important qualifications should be made at this stage. First, the determination of the applicable law is only the first stage of the choice of law process. Certain elements of the applicable law may be displaced by the mandatory rules of other countries – or may be disapplied on grounds of public policy. Secondly, the general rules in articles 3 and 4 do not apply to consumer contracts and individual contracts

24 Art 33.
25 Contracts (Applicable Law) Act 1990, s 3(1), (2).
26 OJ 1980 C282/1.
27 S 3(3).
28 See, in particular, the speech of Lord Diplock in *Amin Rasheed Shipping Corpn v Kuwait Insurance Co* [1984] AC 50 at 61–62.
29 Art 15.

of employment, which are regulated by articles 5 and 6 respectively. Thirdly, some contractual questions are not governed by the applicable law or are not governed exclusively by the applicable law. These three further aspects of the choice of law rules are considered in later sections.

A Applicable law chosen by the parties

Subject to limits which are considered later, article 3 of the Convention gives effect to the principle of party autonomy. The parties are free to choose the law to govern their contractual relationship. Article 3(1) provides simply that the choice of the parties must be 'express or demonstrated with reasonable certainty by the terms of the contract or the circumstances of the case'.

1. *Express choice*

A choice of law is express when the contract contains a provision which specifies the law by which it is to be governed. For example, a contract may include a clause which provides that the contract 'shall be governed by the law of Brazil' or which states that 'any dispute arising out of this contract shall be decided according to Israeli law'. Parties to an international contract are wise to include such a clause in their agreement to avoid the uncertainty which may otherwise arise in ascertaining the applicable law.

Where the parties have directly identified the applicable law – such as English law or French law – the court will normally have no difficulty in giving effect to the parties' choice. More problematical, however, is the case where the parties attempt to select the applicable law indirectly. For example, a bill of lading may provide that it is governed by the law of the country in which the carrier's principal place of business is situated; a charterparty may be governed by the law of the flag of the vessel in question. As long as there are no problems identifying the carrier's principal place of business or the flag of the vessel, the parties' choice of law will be effective. In any particular case where the parties purport to select the applicable law indirectly, it is a question of construction of the clause in question as to whether the alleged choice is effective.

In *Companie Tunisienne de Navigation SA v Companie d'Armement Maritime SA*[30] – a case decided by the House of Lords under the common law – a contract was made in Paris between the defendant, a French company, and the plaintiff, a Tunisian company, for the carriage of a number of consignments of oil between Tunisian ports

30 [1971] AC 572, [1970] 3 All ER 71.

over a period of some months. Although performance of the contract would require at least 12 voyages, the parties adapted a single-voyage charterparty form, clause 13 of which provided that the charterparty was governed by the law of the flag of the vessel carrying the goods. At the time of the conclusion of the contract the parties seemed to have assumed that the defendant would be using its own ships, which flew the French flag. Before performance of the contract was completed, war broke out in the Middle East and the defendant, relying on French law as the governing law, alleged that the contract had been frustrated. One of the questions facing the court was whether clause 13 was an effective choice of French law, in view of the fact that for the first six voyages the defendant had employed ships flying five different flags.

A minority of the House of Lords thought that clause 13 was meaningless and approached the case on the basis that the parties had not made an express choice. The majority, however, decided that clause 13 was an effective choice of French law. The parties had envisaged that the defendant would use French vessels in performing the contract and it was reasonable to conclude that the parties had chosen French law as the governing law, even though the parties' assumptions at the time of contracting were erroneous.

2. *Choice demonstrated with reasonable certainty*

Although a well-drafted international contract will include an express choice of law, it is not uncommon for the parties to fail to select the applicable law – whether because they do not apply their minds to the question at all or because they are unable to agree on which law is to be the applicable law.

Article 3(1) of the Convention does not require a choice of law to be express in order to be effective. It is sufficient if a choice can be demonstrated with reasonable certainty by the terms of the contract or the circumstances of the case. The burden of proof is on the party who asserts that a choice has been made. If the court is not satisfied that the parties have chosen the applicable law, the case must be determined in accordance with article 4, which sets out the principles which apply in the absence of choice. Within the structure of the Convention it is important that a clear distinction is drawn between cases involving a choice and cases in which the parties have failed to make a choice. It is not legitimate for the court to determine the applicable law under article 3 on the basis that, had the parties thought about it, they would have chosen the law of a particular country. So, while the court must give effect to the parties' choice, whether or not express, the court is not entitled to impute a choice to the parties.

In what circumstances is it possible to say that the parties have made a choice, albeit not an express one? In answering this question some guidance is provided by the Giuliano-Lagarde Report. The Report gives a number of examples where a choice of law may be implied.[31]

(A) JURISDICTION AND ARBITRATION CLAUSES

A choice of jurisdiction is not, in itself, a choice of law. Similarly, the fact that parties agree to refer their disputes to arbitration in England does not necessarily entail a choice of English law. It is important to keep distinct – at least for analytical purposes – the question of forum (where is the dispute to be resolved, whether by litigation or arbitration?) from the question of the applicable law (which law determines the substantive rights and obligations of the parties?).

At common law, the strongest indication of an implied choice of governing law is a choice of forum clause or a clause providing that any dispute arising out of a contract shall be referred to arbitration in a particular country. At common law, where a contract includes a choice of jurisdiction in favour of the English courts or an agreement to refer disputes to arbitrators in England it is readily implied that the parties intended English law to govern,[32] on the basis that they are most likely to have in mind that the court or the arbitral tribunal would apply its own law.

In *The Komninos S*,[33] for example, a cargo belonging to the plaintiff was shipped on a vessel owned by the defendant. The plaintiff started proceedings in England for damages alleging that, as a result of the unseaworthiness of the vessel and the defendant's negligence, the cargo had been damaged during the voyage. Although neither the contract nor the parties had any connection with England the bill of lading, which was drawn up in the English language, provided that any dispute should be referred to 'British courts'.

On the one hand, the defendant argued that the bill of lading was governed by Greek law according to which the plaintiff's claim was time-barred. This argument succeeded at first instance.[34] Leggatt J held that the parties had not made a choice of law and that, given that the contract was made in Greece between Greek shippers and Greek managers to carry goods from Greece to Italy for freight payable in

31 OJ 1980 C282/17.

32 *Hamlyn & Co v Talisker Distillery* [1894] AC 202; *Companie Tunisienne de Navigation SA v Companie d'Armement Maritime SA* [1971] AC 572, [1970] 3 All ER 71.

33 [1991] 1 Lloyd's Rep 370.

34 [1990] 1 Lloyd's Rep 541.

Greece in Greek currency, Greece was the country with which the contract was most closely connected.

On the other hand, the plaintiff argued that the jurisdiction clause in favour of 'British courts' was an implied choice of English law, under which the limitation period had not expired. The Court of Appeal adopted the plaintiff's view. First, the choice of 'British courts' was to be interpreted as a choice in favour of English courts. Bingham LJ rejected the defendant's suggestion that the jurisdiction clause was ambiguous on the ground that the idea that the parties might have intended to confer jurisdiction on the courts of Scotland or Northern Ireland was 'far-fetched'.[35] Secondly, the Court of Appeal decided that it should be inferred that the parties intended their contracts to be governed by the law of the forum where disputes are to be tried unless there are strong indications that they did not intend or may not have intended that result.[36] In the absence of such strong indications the Court of Appeal concluded that English law was the proper law of the bill of lading.

The same approach is evident in cases involving arbitration clauses. In *The Parouth*,[37] for example, the contract had connections with, inter alia, Panama, Greece and Florida, but none at all with England. The Court of Appeal held that English law was the proper law on the basis of an agreement for arbitration in England.

It should be noted, however, that – at common law – a jurisdiction clause or arbitration agreement is not conclusive. In *Companie Tunisienne de Navigation SA v Companie d'Armement Maritime SA*[38] the House of Lords considered what the position would have been if clause 13 of the charterparty had not effected an express choice of law. The charterparty included a clause which provided that any dispute should be settled by arbitrators in London. The House of Lords decided that, although a choice of English law would normally be implied from an agreement to refer disputes to arbitrators in England, on the facts of the case French law – as the law of the country with which the contract was most closely connected – was the proper law. The parties and the contract were connected entirely with France and Tunisia (a former French protectorate whose legal system is based on the French system). The contract was negotiated in France in the French language; it was made in France through French brokers; it provided for payment in France in French francs; one party was a French company; the other was Tunisian and Tunisia was the place of performance of that party's obligations.

35 [1991] 1 Lloyd's Rep 370 at 374.
36 At 376.
37 [1982] 2 Lloyd's Rep 351.
38 [1971] AC 572. See pp 204–205.

It follows from these cases that, according to the common law, where the parties have agreed to litigation or arbitration in a particular country, this agreement raises a strong, but not conclusive presumption in favour of the law of that country. Even if the contract has no connections with England (apart from the jurisdiction clause or arbitration agreement) an implication in favour of English law is likely to be drawn even if there are substantial connections with another country. The mere fact that there are systems of law with which the contract has a closer connection is not sufficient to rebut the implication.

There is some doubt as to whether the traditional common law approach should be applied in cases governed by the Convention. The Giuliano-Lagarde Report states that although 'the choice of a particular forum may show in no uncertain manner that the parties intend the contract to be governed by the law of that forum, ... this must always be subject to the other terms of the contract and all the circumstances of the case'.[39] The tenor of this passage of the Report is very different from the language adopted by English judges in cases such as *The Komninos S*. It must always be remembered that, for the purposes of article 3(1), in the absence of an express choice, the choice must be demonstrated with reasonable certainty. In cases governed by the Convention, if the parties have agreed to litigation or arbitration in England it is not legitimate for the court simply to presume that the parties made a choice of English law.

Nevertheless, it does not appear that the Convention has produced a radical change in the practice of the English courts. In *Egon Oldendorff v Libera Corpn*[40] the plaintiff, a German company, sought leave to serve a writ on the defendant, a Japanese corporation, under what is now CPR 6.20(5)(c), alleging that the contract between the parties was 'by implication' governed by English law. The contract had no connections with England apart from a clause providing for arbitration in England. Leave was given to serve the defendant out of the jurisdiction on the basis that there was a good arguable case that the contract was governed by English law; Mance J found the suggestion that it was contemplated that the arbitration tribunal should apply a foreign law 'unconvincing'.[41] In subsequent proceedings Clarke J held that the contract was indeed governed by English law.[42] In considering the effect of the arbitration clause under article 3 of the Convention Clarke J concluded that, although the test is not the same under the Convention as at common law, it

39 OJ 1980 C282/17.
40 [1995] 2 Lloyd's Rep 64.
41 At 69.
42 [1996] 1 Lloyd's Rep 380.

is very similar and that the considerations set out by the House of Lords in the *Companie Tunisienne* case are relevant to the correct application of the test under the Convention just as they are at common law.[43] Clarke J considered that 'if [the Convention] involves a change in emphasis from the approach by the common law it is a small one'.[44]

(B) STANDARD FORMS

A common indication of an implied choice is the use of standard forms, in particular certain types of standard form which are drafted against the background of a particular system of law. For example, in *Amin Rasheed Shipping Corpn v Kuwait Insurance Co*[45] a marine insurance policy was issued in Kuwait by the defendant, a Kuwaiti insurance company, in respect of a ship owned by the plaintiff, a Liberian company which carried on business in Dubai. The policy was based on a Lloyd's form set out in a Schedule to the Marine Insurance Act 1906. The House of Lords held that English law was the law governing the contract. In view of the English form of the policy, which could only be interpreted in the light of English law, the parties must have intended English law to govern. Moreover, since at the time the contract was made Kuwait did not have any law of marine insurance (as opposed to a general law of insurance) it was legitimate to conclude that the parties must have had English law in mind. Although this case was decided under the common law prior to the implementation of the Convention, the application of the Convention to the particular facts should yield the same result.[46] It has also been held that where a reinsurance contract is placed in London on the London market and the contract is of a standard type, the implication is that the parties chose English law as the applicable law – unless the contract includes clear indications that a different law was intended.[47]

(C) PREVIOUS COURSE OF DEALING

According to the Giuliano-Lagarde Report 'a previous course of dealing between the parties under contracts containing an express choice of law may leave the court in no doubt that the contract in question is to be governed by the law previously chosen where the

43 At 389.
44 At 390.
45 [1984] AC 50, [1983] 2 All ER 884. See also *James Miller & Partners Ltd v Whitworth Street Estates (Manchester) Ltd* [1970] AC 583, [1970] 1 All ER 796.
46 Giuliano-Lagarde Report, OJ 1980 C282/17.
47 *Gan Insurance Co Ltd v Tai Ping Insurance Co Ltd* [1999] IL Pr 729.

choice of law clause has been omitted in circumstances which do not indicate a deliberate change of policy by the parties'.[48] Each case will turn on its own facts; it would be wrong for the court to conclude that the parties had impliedly chosen the law of a particular country simply because they had done so in an earlier transaction.

(D) EXPRESS CHOICE OF LAW IN RELATED TRANSACTIONS

Where contracts are related to each other it is not unreasonable to suppose that the parties intended that they should be governed by the same law. At common law, where a charterparty is expressly governed by English law a choice of English law may be implied into the related bills of lading;[49] similarly, where Y's obligations to X under a contract which is expressly governed by English law are guaranteed by Z it may be appropriate to imply a choice of English law into the contract of guarantee between X and Z.[50] By contrast, a letter of credit issued in connection with a commercial transaction is not necessarily to be regarded as governed by the law which governs the underlying transaction; a letter of credit is an autonomous contract which does not depend in any way on the performance or non-performance of the underlying transaction.[51] The Giuliano-Lagarde Report seems to endorse the approach adopted by the English courts at common law.[52]

(E) REFERENCE TO PARTICULAR RULES

Just as the use of a standard form which is drafted against the background of the law of a particular country may imply a choice of the law of that country, references to the law of a particular country in a contract may imply a choice of that law. The Giuliano-Lagarde Report suggests that 'references in a contract to specific articles of the French Civil Code may leave the court in no doubt that the parties have deliberately chosen French law, although there is no expressly stated choice of law'.[53]

It is important not to confuse choice of law with incorporation. Where the parties choose the law of a particular country they run the risk that the chosen law might change in a way which is advantageous to one party or the other. If the parties end up litigating a dispute the

48 OJ 1980 C282/17.
49 *The Njegos* [1936] P 90; *The Freights Queen* [1977] 2 Lloyd's Rep 140.
50 *Broken Hill Proprietary Co Ltd v Xenakis* [1982] 2 Lloyd's Rep 304; *Wahda Bank v Arab Bank* [1996] 1 Lloyd's Rep 470.
51 See *Attock Cement Co Ltd v Romanian Bank for Foreign Trade* [1989] 1 All ER 1189, [1989] 1 WLR 1147.
52 OJ 1980 C282/17.
53 Ibid.

court will apply the chosen law as it is at the time of the trial, not as it was when the contract was concluded.[54] Rather than choosing a particular law the parties may incorporate specific rules – usually statutory provisions – of the law of country X into a contract which is governed by the law of country Y. The English court will apply these provisions of the law of country X just as if they had been written out in extenso as clauses of the contract. For example, a contract for the carriage of goods by sea, whose applicable law is English law, may contain a clause that 'with respect to shipments from a port in the United States, all the terms and provisions of the Carriage of Goods by Sea Act 1936 of the United States are to apply to this contract'.[55]

Where foreign legal rules are incorporated into a contract by reference the incorporated provisions are to be interpreted in the same way as other contractual terms. The parties are taken to have intended the incorporated provisions to apply as they existed at the date of the contract, unaffected by any subsequent amendments.

(F) OTHER CONSIDERATIONS

At common law, where a contract – or a particular provision in a contract – is valid under the law of one country with which the contract is connected but invalid under another, the court may imply a choice of the validating law, on the basis that the parties must have intended their contract to be valid, not void. For example, in *Re Missouri Steamship Co*[56] the United States plaintiff made a contract in Massachusetts with English shipowners for the carriage of cattle from Boston to England. On the voyage the cattle were injured through the negligence of the crew. When sued in England, the defendants relied on a clause in the contract exempting them from liability in such circumstances. By the law of Massachusetts this exemption clause was void, but it was valid by English law. It was held that English law was the proper law, for the parties must have intended the provisions of their contract, including the exemption clause, to be valid.

There are three points which might be made. First, the implication in favour of the validating law at common law is not conclusive. It may be outweighed by the fact that there are factors pointing more strongly to an implied choice of an invalidating law.[57] Secondly, the

54 *R v International Trustee for Protection of Bondholders Akt* [1937] AC 500, [1937] 2 All ER 164.

55 *Stafford Allen & Sons Ltd v Pacific Steam Navigation Co* [1956] 2 All ER 716, [1956] 1 WLR 629.

56 (1889) 42 Ch D 321.

57 *Royal Exchange Assurance Corpn v Sjoforsakrings Aktiebolaget Vega* [1902] 2 KB 384.

implication in favour of the validating law is often a fiction, for it is likely that in many cases the parties have no idea that the contract is valid under one law and invalid under another. Thirdly, whatever the position may be at common law, there is nothing in the Giuliano-Lagarde Report to suggest that a choice in favour of a validating law may be implied. Nevertheless, it has been suggested that where the parties are aware that a contract (or a clause) is valid under one law but invalid under another a choice of the law under which the contract (or clause) is valid may be implied under article 3(1).[58]

3. The distinction between implied choice and no choice

It is something of an irony that one of the most uncertain aspects of the choice of law regime introduced by the Convention is the requirement that a choice of law – if not express – must be demonstrated with reasonable certainty. This uncertainty is not unique to the Convention; it is also part of the proper law doctrine which the Convention has largely superseded. Although the conceptual distinction between implied choice and an absence of choice is not difficult to understand, the dividing line is much harder to draw in practice. The truth is that, unless the parties have made an express choice, it is impossible to say whether or not the parties actually made a choice. The cases decided by the English courts under the proper law doctrine and the illustrations given by the Giuliano-Lagarde Report show that, although certain factors *may* be regarded as justifying the implication of a choice of law, no single factor is decisive.

An alternative and, it is submitted, preferable approach would be to do away entirely with the notion of implied choice.[59] In cases where the contract does not include an express choice very often the parties will have given no thought at all to the applicable law. The real significance of factors such as jurisdiction clauses and the language and form of the contract is not that they reveal the parties' subjective intentions, but that they point to a law with which the contract is connected. For example, a contract is more likely to give effect to the parties' reasonable expectations if it is governed by the law in whose terminology and concepts it is couched.

In the absence of an express choice of law a contract should be governed by the law of the country with which it is most closely connected. Of course, in determining the country with which a contract is most closely connected, the court would necessarily have regard to factors such as any dispute-resolution clause and the form

58 Mayer, *Droit International Privé* (4th edn, 1991) para 714.
59 See Cheshire and North, *Private International Law* (11th edn, 1987) p 461.

and language of the contract; the court would not, however, be tempted to glean the supposed intentions of the parties from flimsy evidence.

4. *Splitting the applicable law*

The logic of the principle of party autonomy leads to the idea that different parts of the same contract may be subjected to different laws. The Convention provides that the parties can, by their choice, 'select the law applicable to the whole or a part only of the contract'.[60] There are problems associated with splitting the applicable law. A legal system is intended to be a coherent whole, the rules of which are interrelated with, and influenced by, each other. To apply the rules of one legal system to one issue in a contract case, but the rules of a different legal system to another issue might distort the true effect of the rules in question, producing a decision which would not be reached under either law alone, and which is not consistent with the objectives of either law.

Although the Convention permits splitting the applicable law the Giuliano-Lagarde Report states that the parties' choice 'must be logically consistent, ie it must relate to elements in the contract which can be governed by different laws without giving rise to contradictions'.[61] Accordingly, the parties may decide to subject a particular contractual term (such as an index-linking clause) to a different law from that which governs the rest of the contract.[62] However, if a contract provided that one party's obligations were governed by the law of country X and the other's by the law of country Y the choice should be regarded as ineffective on the basis that 'the harmony between the obligations of the parties to a bilateral contract'[63] is disturbed if different laws are applied to each party's obligations. In such a case the applicable law should be determined by reference to article 4.

5. *Changing the applicable law*

Can the parties, after they have made their contract, by agreement change the applicable law? The principle of party autonomy suggests that this question should be answered in the affirmative. Article 3(2) of the Convention provides that the parties 'may at any time agree to subject the contract to a law other than that which previously governed it'. The freedom to change the applicable law applies both

60 Art 3(1).
61 OJ 1980 C282/17.
62 Ibid.
63 Lando, 'The EEC Convention on the Law Applicable to Contractual Obligations' (1987) 24 CML Rev 159 at 169.

to cases in which the parties made a choice at the time of contracting and to cases where no initial choice was made. However, an agreement changing the applicable law will normally be express and the court will be slow to imply any such agreement.[64] A change in the applicable law cannot render a contract formally invalid; nor can such a change adversely affect the rights of third parties.[65]

A related question is whether a contract can have a 'floating' applicable law to be determined by an event occurring after the making of the contract. At common law a clause which provides that a contract should, at the option of one of the parties, be governed either by the law of country X or the law of country Y is void.[66] However, where the event on which the selection of the proper law depends is not the unilateral choice of one party, but an external event, the clause is valid. In *The Mariannina*,[67] for example, the Court of Appeal held valid a clause which provided that if a provision for arbitration in London should be ruled unenforceable then the contract should be governed by Greek law.

The position under the Convention would appear to be different. The logic of article 3 is to allow the parties to choose the applicable law at any time. There is no obvious reason why a contractual term which gives one party the power to select the applicable law at some later point should not be regarded as a valid clause. The argument that, until the choice has been made, the alleged contract cannot exist – because it inhabits a legal vacuum – is unsound. Until the party who has been given the power to select the applicable law has exercised the power the contract will be governed by the law which applies in the absence of choice (as determined by article 4); a subsequent exercise of the power should simply be regarded as a variation for the purposes of article 3(2).

B Applicable law in the absence of choice[68]

1. Introduction

According to article 4(1), to the extent that the parties have made no choice of law, express or implied, a contract is governed by the law of the country with which it is most closely connected. Although the principle of closest connection is easy enough to state, its operation is more complicated. Under the Convention, the task of

64 *The Aeolian* [2001] EWCA Civ 1162, [2001] 2 Lloyd's Rep 641.
65 Art 3(2).
66 *Armar Shipping Co Ltd v Caisse Algérienne d'Assurance et de Réassurance* [1981] 1 All ER 498, [1981] 1 WLR 207; *The Iran Vojdan* [1984] 2 Lloyd's Rep 380.
67 [1983] 1 Lloyd's Rep 12.
68 See Jaffey, *Topics in Choice of Law* (1996) pp 32–39.

identifying the applicable law is assisted (or, depending on one's point of view, hindered) by the use of various presumptions, which are set out in paragraphs 2 to 4 of article 4. However, the presumptions are neither comprehensive nor conclusive. In some cases no presumption applies; in others the presumption may be disregarded.

2. *The general presumption*

Article 4(2), which sets out the presumption which is potentially applicable to all contracts falling within the Convention's scope other than those which are regulated by specific provisions,[69] provides as follows:

> Subject to the provisions of paragraph 5 of this article, it shall be presumed that the contract is most closely connected with the country where the party who is to effect the performance which is characteristic of the contract has, at the time of conclusion of the contract, his habitual residence, or, in the case of a body corporate or unincorporate, its central administration. However, if the contract is entered into in the course of that party's trade or profession, that country shall be the country in which the principal place of business is situated or, where under the terms of the contract the performance is to be effected through a place of business other than the principal place of business, the country in which that other place of business is situated.

This presumption is structured around two ideas: (i) the party who is to effect the performance which is characteristic of the contract (the 'characteristic performer'); and (ii) a territorial connection (which varies depending on the precise circumstances of the case). The general principle is that a contract is presumed to be most closely connected with the country with which the characteristic performer has, at the time of the conclusion of the contract, the relevant territorial connection. The circumstances of the case determine which of the four possible territorial connections – habitual residence, central administration, principal place of business or another place of business through which the characteristic performance is to be effected – is the relevant one.

(A) THE CHARACTERISTIC PERFORMER

The notion of characteristic performance is one which the drafters of the Convention adopted from Swiss law.[70] In an ordinary bilateral

69 The presumption in art 4(3) applies to contracts relating to rights in immovable property; art 4(4) applies to contracts for the carriage of goods; consumer contracts are governed by art 5 and individual contracts of employment by art 6.

70 D'Oliveira, '"Characteristic Obligation" in the Draft EEC Obligation Convention' (1977) 25 Am J Comp L 303.

contract under which one party is to pay money in return for the provision of goods or services, the characteristic performance is the provision of the goods or services, rather than the payment of the price.[71] So, in a contract for the sale of goods, the presumption identifies the seller's law as the governing law;[72] in a banking contract the applicable law is the law of the banker;[73] in a broking contract the broker is the characteristic performer.[74] Where there are two performances involving the payment of money, the characteristic performer is the party carrying the greater risk.[75] So, in a contract of reinsurance, the reinsurer, rather than the reinsured, is the characteristic performer.

By selecting the law of one of the parties (rather than, say, the law of the country of performance), the presumption gives priority to the convenience of the parties. The choice of the law of the party who is to provide the goods or services, rather than the one who is to pay the price, may be justified by the likelihood that that party's performance is the more active and complex as a consequence of which the characteristic performer is more likely to have to consult the law during the course of performance. There is also an argument based on economic efficiency. Many contracts are concluded on standard forms. Although a contract of sale may be concluded on the seller's standard conditions of sale or on the buyer's standard conditions of purchase it is more common for the seller to frame the contract. Where a seller sells goods to buyers in different countries the application of the seller's law may be supported on the ground that 'mass bargaining, like mass production, brings down the cost and the price'.[76]

The limits of the doctrine of characteristic performance should be noted. First, it is impossible to determine the characteristic performance in relation to a contract where both parties undertake to perform obligations of the same type. In a contract of exchange – as opposed to sale – the characteristic performance cannot be identified. Secondly, it is not easy to see how the notion of characteristic performance can be applied in a complex contract, such as a joint venture agreement. Thirdly, it would seem that the characteristic performance is not always the performance in return

71 Giuliano-Lagarde Report, OJ 1980 C282/20.

72 See *William Grant & Sons International Ltd v Marie Brizard Espana SA* 1998 SC 536.

73 *Raiffeisen Zentralbank Osterreich Aktiengesellschaft* v *National Bank of Greece SA* [1999] 1 Lloyd's Rep 408.

74 *HIB Ltd v Guardian Insurance Co Inc* [1997] 1 Lloyd's Rep 412.

75 D'Oliveira, '"Characteristic Obligation" in the Draft EEC Obligation Convention' (1977) 25 Am J Comp L 303, 314.

76 Lando, 'The EEC Convention on the Law Applicable to Contractual Obligations' (1987) 24 CML Rev 159 at 202.

for which money is paid. It has been suggested that in relation to a distributorship agreement (where the distributor undertakes to market the manufacturer's goods) or a publisher's contract (where the publisher undertakes to print, bind and market the author's work) the performance of the distributor or the publisher is the characteristic performance, since it is their performance which is the economic purpose of the contract.[77]

(B) THE TERRITORIAL CONNECTION

Within the context of article 4(2) the factor which localises a contract is a territorial link between the characteristic performer and a country. Depending on the circumstances the link may be the characteristic performer's habitual residence, its central administration, its principal place of business or a place of business other than the principal place of business.

If a contract is concluded in the course of the characteristic performer's trade or profession the contract is, as a general rule, presumed to be most closely connected with the country in which the characteristic performer's principal place of business is situated. So, for example, if an English shoe manufacturer contracts to sell a thousand pairs of shoes to a French buyer, the applicable law is presumed to be English law, as England is the country in which the seller's principal place of business is located. Where, however, the contract provides that the characteristic performance is to be effected through a place of business other than the principal place of business, the contract is presumed to be most closely connected with the country in which the other place of business is situated. So, where the contract in question is a bank account held at an English branch, English law is presumed to be the most closely connected law.[78] But, if an English bank contracts to provide a loan to a foreign customer through its New York branch, the presumption would point towards the law of New York as the applicable law.

In *Bank of Baroda v Vysya Bank*[79] the defendant, an Indian bank, issued a letter of credit in favour of an Irish company which had sold a quantity of iron to an Indian buyer. The credit was confirmed by the plaintiff, another Indian bank, through its branch in London. When the plaintiff sought leave to serve the defendant out of the jurisdiction under what is now CPR 6.20(5)(c), the question arose as to whether the contract between the parties was governed by

77 Ibid at 204.

78 *Sierra Leone Telecommunications Co Ltd v Barclays Bank plc* [1998] 2 All ER 821.

79 [1994] 2 Lloyd's Rep 87. See Morse, 'Letters of Credit and the Rome Convention' [1994] LMCLQ 560.

English law. Mance J decided that English law was the applicable law. The performance which characterised the contract was the plaintiff's confirmation of the letter of credit and its honouring of the obligations in relation to the seller, rather than the defendant's obligation to reimburse the plaintiff. As the plaintiff's confirmation was to be effected through its London branch – a place of business other than its principal place of business – it was to be presumed that the contract was most closely connected with England.

Most international contracts are concluded in the course of the characteristic performer's trade or profession. Where, however, a contract is concluded otherwise than in the course of that person's trade or profession the contract is presumed to be most closely connected with the country in which the characteristic performer is habitually resident or, if the characteristic performer is a body corporate or unincorporate, the country in which it has its central administration.

3. *Special presumptions*

The general presumption in article 4(2) applies neither to contracts relating to rights in immovable property nor to contracts for the carriage of goods. Special presumptions are set out in paragraphs 3 and 4.

(A) CONTRACTS RELATING TO RIGHTS IN IMMOVABLE PROPERTY

Article 4(3) provides that 'to the extent that the subject matter of the contract is a right in immovable property or a right to use immovable property it shall be presumed that the contract is most closely connected with the country where the immovable property is situated'.

(B) CONTRACTS FOR THE CARRIAGE OF GOODS

The presumption in article 4(4) applies to contracts for the carriage of goods, a concept which includes single voyage charterparties and other contracts whose main purpose is the carriage of goods. It is provided that a contract for the carriage of goods shall be presumed to be most closely connected with the country in which the carrier has, at the time the contract is concluded, his principal place of business, if that country is also the place of loading or the place of discharge or the principal place of business of the consignor. If the country in which carrier has his principal place of business does not coincide with any of the other connecting factors (the place of loading, the place of discharge, the consignor's principal place of business), the presumption in paragraph 4 cannot be applied.

4. No presumption

In those circumstances in which it is not possible to apply the presumptions in paragraphs 2 to 4 – for example, because there is no characteristic performance[80] – one is thrown back on the general principle: the applicable law is the law of the country with which the contract is most closely connected.[81]

How is the court to decide with which country the contract is most closely connected? The terms of the Convention do not provide any guidance and the Giuliano-Lagarde Report is of limited help. It seems not unlikely that in England the courts will turn to the cases decided under the proper law doctrine prior to the Convention's entry into force. In determining which law is the applicable law the court is likely to look for the 'centre of gravity' of the contract. The theory advocated by Cheshire is that, in cases where the parties fail to make a choice, the court should have regard to 'localising elements'[82] – that it is to say, the elements which connect the contract with the various countries involved; the governing law should be the law of the country in which the localising elements are most densely grouped.

This 'localisation' or 'centre of gravity' approach can be justified on the basis that it is the country in which the elements of the contract are most densely grouped whose interests and policy are most likely to be affected by the contract. To some extent this approach involves a mere enumeration of the links with the different countries; in many cases, the applicable law will be simply the law of the country with the greatest number of localising elements. Where, however, there is no clear preponderance of connections with one country, the weight or quality of the different elements must be assessed.

Particular significance may be given to the place of performance of the contract – especially when the whole performance of both sides is to be in the same country. Such emphasis on the place of performance may be explained on the basis that a contract is most likely to impinge on the interests of a country if it is to be performed in that country rather than elsewhere. If both parties have strong links with one country this is a significant factor in determining the country with which the contract is most closely connected.

The cases decided at common law show that, except in those cases where the connections with one country are clearly predominant, it is often far from clear why the court finally concludes

80 Art 4(5).
81 Art 4(1).
82 *International Contracts* (1948) pp 27–28.

that one country is more closely connected than another. In such cases there may be great uncertainty for the parties, as it is difficult for them to predict in advance which law will be held to be the governing law.

5. Disregarding the presumption

It has just been seen that the general principle in article 4(1) has to determine those cases in which no presumption arises. Article 4(5) also provides that the presumptions in paragraphs 2 to 4 'shall be disregarded if it appears from the circumstances as a whole that the contract is more closely connected with another country'. This provision is, perhaps, one of the most controversial features of the Convention. What is not clear from the terms of the Convention is the precise relationship between the presumptions and paragraph 5. If the presumptions may be disregarded, what is their purpose? A number of observations may be made.

Since the general principle in article 4(1) is that, if the parties fail to choose the applicable law, a contract should be governed by the law of the country with which it is most closely connected, it would not be appropriate for the presumptions to be applied in a wholly mechanical way so as to undermine the general principle. In a case in which the overwhelming connections are with country X the law of that country should be the applicable law even though the presumption points towards country Y. The Giuliano-Lagarde Report suggests, for example, that the presumption in article 4(3) may be disregarded in a case where two Belgian residents make a contract for renting a holiday home in Italy on the basis that the contract is more closely connected with Belgium than with Italy.[83]

However, the possibility of disregarding the presumptions offered by article 4(5) should not be allowed to undermine the positive contribution which the presumptions can make in the choice of law process. As noted in the previous section, a choice of law rule based purely on the notion of closest connection is open-textured and unpredictable. The merit of a presumption is that it provides clear guidance in cases where the various connecting factors are distributed between two or more countries. In a simple contract of sale under the terms of which an English seller agrees to deliver goods to a French buyer, who in return, undertakes to pay for the goods by transferring the agreed purchase price to the seller's bank account in England, article 4(2) makes it clear from the start that, in the absence of choice by the parties, English law is the applicable law. In this type of case, the presumption produces a more predictable

83 OJ 1980 C282/21.

result than a test based simply on closest connection, which requires a detailed evaluation of the various elements of the contract.

The structure of article 4 seeks to combine certainty with flexibility. It would be unfortunate if the courts were to allow paragraph 5 to dominate paragraphs 2 to 4, thereby rendering the presumptions largely redundant. The proper approach is to apply the presumptions 'unless there is a valid reason, looking at the circumstances as a whole, not to do so'.[84] The mere fact that, whereas the presumption under paragraph 2 points to country X, the place of performance of the contract is country Y is not sufficient to justify disregarding the presumption;[85] however, it is this type of case in which the presumption is most likely to be disregarded.[86] If an appropriate balance is struck between, on the one hand, the presumptions and, on the other, paragraph 5, article 4 can promote certainty and predictability in most cases. In particular, where the connecting factors are equally balanced between two countries the presumption avoids the need for the court to engage in the difficult task of weighing the various factors against each other and enables the applicable law to be easily identified.

It has been seen that in *Bank of Baroda v Vysya Bank*[87] it was held that the contract between the parties was governed by English law by virtue of the application of the presumption in article 4(2).[88] Although not strictly necessary for the decision Mance J also considered the law applicable to other contractual relationships which arose out of the same letter of credit. As regards the relationship between the Indian defendant and the Irish seller, the presumption pointed towards Indian law because the defendant was the characteristic performer. Nevertheless, Mance J thought that the presumption should be rebutted in favour of English law (as the law of the country with which the contract was most closely connected) on the basis that, as a general principle, closely related contracts should be governed by the same law. In subsequent cases, the English courts have been equally willing to disregard the presumption in paragraph 2.[89] For example, in *Definitely Maybe (Touring) Ltd v Marek Lieberberg Konzertagentur GmbH*[90] the claimant was an English company which provided the services of the pop group 'Oasis' to concert organisers; the defendant was a German-based company

84 Mance J in *Bank of Baroda v Vysya Bank* [1994] 2 Lloyd's Rep 87 at 93.
85 *Caledonia Subsea Ltd v Microperi SRL* 2001 SC 716.
86 See *Definitely Maybe (Touring) Ltd v Marek Lieberberg Konzertagentur GmbH* [2001] 4 All ER 283, [2001] 1 WLR 1745.
87 [1994] 2 Lloyd's Rep 87.
88 See pp 217–218.
89 See also *Kenburn Waste Management Ltd v Bergman* (2001) Times, 9 July.
90 [2001] 4 All ER 283, [2001] 1 WLR 1745.

which organised pop festivals in Germany. The defendant contracted with the claimant for live performances by 'Oasis', but, because of a rift between the Gallagher brothers, Noel Gallagher did not play in Germany. As a result, the defendant refused to pay the full price due under the contract. The claimant issued proceedings in England and invoked the English court's jurisdiction under article 5(1) of the Brussels Convention – on the basis that the contract was governed by English law and that, under English law, England was the place of performance of the defendant's payment obligation. The defendant contested the court's jurisdiction, arguing that the contract was governed by German law, under which the place of performance was Germany. It was held that the contract was governed by German law and, accordingly, that the court did not have jurisdiction. Although the presumption in article 4(2) of the Rome Convention pointed towards English law as the applicable law, this was an appropriate case in which to disregard the presumption: the contract, which provided for payment in German currency, required the performance of contractual obligations in Germany by both parties; apart from the location of the claimant and the group, there was no other connection between England and the contract.

A different approach is to be found in *Société Nouvelle des Papeteries de l'Aa SA v BV Machinefabrike BOA*,[91] a decision of the Dutch Supreme Court. The claimant, a Dutch company, sold a paper press to the defendant, a French company. The contract, which was drawn up in French, was negotiated in France. The machine was delivered to the defendant in France, where it was assembled by the claimant. The price was expressed in French francs. When the defendant failed to pay the purchase price the claimant started proceedings in the Netherlands. The defendant argued that the Dutch courts did not have jurisdiction under article 5(1) of the Brussels Convention because the contract was governed by French law, according to which the place of performance of the defendant's obligation to pay was France. The claimant's contention was that the Dutch court was entitled to exercise jurisdiction on the basis that the contract was governed by Dutch law, according to which the Netherlands was the place of performance of the defendant's obligation to pay. In order to decide whether or not it had jurisdiction the Dutch court had to decide whether the contract was governed by French law or by Dutch law.

The Dutch court adopted the claimant's contention. There was no doubt that the presumption in article 4(2) pointed towards

91 See Struycken, 'Some Dutch Judicial Reflections on the Rome Convention, Art 4(5)' [1996] LMCLQ 18.

Dutch law as the applicable law; the seller's principal place of business was situated in the Netherlands. The key question was whether the presumption should be disregarded under article 4(5) on the basis that the contract was more closely connected with France. The court thought that, as paragraph 5 is to be regarded as an exception to paragraph 2, it should be applied restrictively; the presumption in paragraph 2 'should be disregarded only if, in the special circumstances of the case, the place of business of the party who is to effect the characteristic performance has no real significance as a connecting factor'.[92] The court decided that, as the seller's place of business was not without significance, the presumption should prevail.

Since, apart from the fact that the seller was a Dutch company, all the elements of the contract were connected with France, this decision reveals that the Dutch court regarded the presumption in paragraph 2 to be a very strong one indeed. Whether an English court, faced by similar facts, would be inclined to reach the same conclusion must be open to question. The fact that article 4 is open-textured means that there is a risk that national courts will continue to apply their previous choice of law rules in the guise of the Convention. Since during the course of the twentieth century the English courts gradually abandoned the use of presumptions in the determination of the objective proper law, English judges may well be inclined to strike the balance between the presumptions (in paragraphs 2 to 4) and the exception (in paragraph 5) somewhat differently from their Dutch counterparts. It seems unlikely that article 18 – which exhorts national courts to have regard to the Convention's international character and to the desirability of achieving uniformity – will be sufficient to prevent the courts of the various contracting states going their separate ways.[93]

6. *Severance*

It is envisaged that the operation of article 4 might lead to different parts of a single contract being governed by different laws. If the parties choose the applicable law for only part of a contract, article 4 determines the law applicable to the remainder. It is, of course, possible for the applicable law as determined by article 4 to be different from the law chosen by the parties. Furthermore, article 4(1) provides that, where a contract is most closely connected with one country, a severable part of the contract which has a closer connection with another country may by way of exception be governed by the

92 Translated and quoted by Struycken, [1996] LMCLQ 18 at 20.
93 See Morison J in *Definitely Maybe (Touring) Ltd v Marek Lieberberg Konzertagentur GmbH* [2001] 1 WLR 1745 at 1749.

law of that other country. According to the Giuliano-Lagarde Report, severance should be employed 'as seldom as possible' and only 'for part of a contract which is independent and separable, in terms of the contract and not of the dispute'.[94]

IV THE LIMITS OF THE APPLICABLE LAW

A Introduction

1. Mandatory rules and public policy

Are there any limitations on the parties' power to choose the applicable law, whether expressly or impliedly? One justification for giving the parties complete freedom to select the applicable law is that it gives them the certainty of knowing from the start what the governing law is. Another is that in domestic systems of contract law the parties are largely free to choose the terms of their contract for themselves; the power to choose the governing law follows as an obvious and reasonable extension. Most domestic contract rules are optional, in the sense that their function is to fill gaps in the contract, but giving way to the parties' agreement to the contrary. Why should not the parties to an international contract, instead of making express provision for various matters, simply agree on which law should be applied to fill the gaps? The answer, of course, is that not all rules of contract law are optional; some are mandatory.

In cases where the parties fail to make a choice, should the law of the country with which the contract is most closely connected be the only source of rules governing the rights and obligations of the parties? Although it is not unreasonable to assume that the country with which a contract is most closely connected has, from a policy point of view, the greatest interest in the way in which the contractual relationship is regulated, this does not mean that other countries do not also have an interest when a particular contractual relationship impinges on their policies. Accordingly, a choice of law regime may well provide that in certain types of case the applicable law should yield to policies embodied in the law of another country.

Although the Convention allows the parties freedom to choose the applicable law and provides that the applicable law should play the predominant role in determining the rights and obligations of the parties, the drafters recognised that a balance has to be struck between the applicable law (whether chosen by the parties or determined in

94 OJ 1980 C282/23.

accordance with article 4) and the legitimate interests of those countries whose law is not the applicable law. This balance is implemented in two ways: first, a number of provisions allow for the application of the mandatory rules of countries whose law is not the applicable law; secondly, the applicable law may be limited by the public policy of the forum.

2. Two types of mandatory rule

The Convention contains a number of provisions which allow for the application of mandatory rules which do not form part of the applicable law. These provisions are complicated by the fact that not all mandatory rules are of the same type. In other language versions of the Convention a clear distinction is drawn between two categories of mandatory rule. For example, in the French text of the Convention article 3(3) refers to *dispositions impératives*, whereas article 7 uses the expression *lois de police*. The English text is more clumsy: article 3(3) gives effect to rules of law 'which cannot be derogated from by contract, hereinafter called "mandatory rules"'; article 7 concerns mandatory rules of law which 'must be applied whatever the law applicable to the contract' or rules which are 'mandatory irrespective of the law otherwise applicable to the contract'. The rules referred to in article 7 are obviously a subset of the mandatory rules which fall within the scope of article 3(3). For the purposes of the discussion which follows the narrow category of rules which fall within article 7 are referred to as 'overriding rules'.

Although many mandatory rules are statutory, there is no reason in principle why a common law rule cannot be mandatory. Whether a rule is optional, mandatory or overriding is a question of interpretation to be resolved by the law of the country of which the rule forms a part. It is for French law to decide whether or not a particular article of the French Civil Code is mandatory, just as it is for English law to decide which provisions of the Unfair Contract Terms Act 1977 are mandatory and overriding.

B Limits on freedom of choice

The main practical objection to allowing unrestricted choice of the applicable law by the parties is that it allows evasion of the mandatory rules of the country with which the contract is most closely connected, whose purpose may be to protect the public interest, or to protect the interests of a particular class – such as employees or consumers. Moreover, the choice may be in effect the choice of the stronger party – where, for example, a standard form contract includes a non-negotiable choice of law clause.

There is no requirement under article 3 of the Convention that there should be any objective connection between the country whose law is chosen as the applicable law and the parties or the contract. So, a choice of English law in a contract between a Greek seller and an Italian buyer is prima facie valid. Article 3(3), however, provides that where the parties choose the law of one country and 'all the elements relevant to the situation' are connected with another country the mandatory rules of that other country must be applied. For the purposes of this provision the choice of law clause itself and any jurisdiction clause are not to be regarded as 'relevant elements'. So, if a contract entirely connected with France contains a provision for disputes to be litigated in England under Brazilian law the English court, while applying Brazilian law generally, must nevertheless apply any relevant French mandatory rules. There are various points to consider.

First, article 3(3) defines mandatory rules as rules 'which cannot be derogated from by contract'. The distinction between mandatory and non-mandatory rules can be illustrated by a couple of simple examples. Section 39(1) of the Marine Insurance Act 1906 provides that in a 'voyage policy' there should be an implied warranty that at the commencement of the voyage the ship shall be seaworthy. This rule is not, however, mandatory; the implied warranty can be excluded by an appropriately drafted term of the contract[95] or may be waived by the insurer.[96] The implied warranty of seaworthiness may be contrasted with certain implied terms under the Landlord and Tenant Act 1985. In a lease of residential premises for a term of less than seven years, there is an implied statutory covenant by the landlord to keep the structure and exterior in repair.[97] This implied statutory covenant is a mandatory rule, as the 1985 Act also provides that an agreement which purports to exclude or limit the landlord's statutory obligations is void (unless authorised by the county court).[98] So, with regard to a short lease of residential premises in England which includes a choice of Italian law, as long as all the elements relevant to the situation are connected with England, the effect of article 3(3) is to enable the tenant to rely on the covenants implied by the 1985 Act, even though Italian law governs other aspects of the contract.

Secondly, the application of article 3(3) does not depend on the parties' motives. What triggers the operation of article 3(3) is a choice of the law of country X and the fact that all the elements

95 *Parfitt v Thompson* (1844) 13 M & W 392.
96 S 34(3).
97 S 11(1)(a).
98 S 12.

relevant to the situation are connected with country Y. Although the purpose of article 3(3) is to nullify an evasive choice, whether or not article 3(3) applies depends on a consideration of objective factors, rather than subjective ones.

Thirdly, there can be little doubt that article 3(3) gives the courts room to manoeuvre, since neither the text of the Convention nor the Giuliano-Lagarde Report gives much guidance as to which elements are 'relevant to the situation'. If an English manufacturer contracts to sell goods to an English buyer is it relevant – for the purposes of article 3(3) – where the goods are manufactured? As there is no simple answer to this question, the sphere of operation of article 3(3) is somewhat uncertain.

Finally, it should be stressed that the effect of article 3(3) is not to invalidate the choice of law in relation to non-mandatory rules. Where article 3(3) applies, the chosen law is superseded only to the extent that it is in conflict with the mandatory rules of the law of the country with which the situation is connected.

C Overriding rules

Whereas article 3(3) is concerned entirely with cases where the parties have made a choice of law, article 7 is potentially applicable in cases where the applicable law is determined in accordance with article 4 as well as cases falling within the scope of article 3. Article 7 is premised on the idea that the country whose law is the applicable law is not the only country which, from the point of view of policy, has an interest in how a contractual relationship is to be regulated. Article 7 defines a category of mandatory rules which are of such importance that they must be applied even in the case of an international contract which is governed by a foreign law; an overriding rule is one which is mandatory 'irrespective of the law otherwise applicable to the contract'. Whether or not a rule is overriding is a question of interpretation.[99]

1. Overriding rules of a third country

The effect of article 7(1) is that where the applicable law is the law of country X but the situation has a close connection with country Y, effect may be given to the overriding rules of the law of country Y. Article 7(1) goes on to say that the court, in considering whether to give effect to these overriding rules, should have regard to their nature and purpose and to the consequences of their application or non-application.

99 This issue is considered further at pp 228–232.

Article 7(1) is obviously rather open-textured. What degree of connection is required to bring article 7(1) into the picture at all? What factors should be taken into account – and what weight should be given to them – in a situation where article 7(1) is potentially applicable? Article 7(1) confers a discretion but gives no guidance on how that discretion is to be exercised; the requirement that the court, when considering whether to apply overriding rules under article 7(1), should have regard to 'their nature and purpose and to the consequences of their application or non-application' does not take the matter much further.

For good or ill, the questions arising out of article 7(1) are not ones which will trouble the English courts. Although the Convention was intended to lay down a uniform choice of law code for all the contracting states, each state was permitted to enter a reservation on article 7(1). The United Kingdom entered such a reservation and article 7(1) does not form part of English law.[100] As a result, English law avoids the uncertainties which are part and parcel of article 7(1). This does not mean, however, that the non-implementation of article 7(1) was the most sensible course to take. The Convention is designed to operate as an integrated set of rules; the balance which the Convention seeks to achieve between the applicable law and other laws is distorted if article 7(1) is taken out of the equation.[101]

2. *Overriding rules of the forum*

Article 7(2) provides that nothing in the Convention shall restrict the application of the overriding rules of the law of the forum. This provision is potentially relevant in cases where the applicable law is determined in accordance with article 4 as well as in cases when the parties have made a choice of law. In cases where the parties choose the applicable law, it is possible for both article 3(3) and article 7(2) to be relevant. Where, for example, a contract entirely connected with California contains a provision for disputes to be litigated in England under Mexican law, the English court must have regard to a number of different laws: first, according to article 3(1) Mexican law is the law which generally governs the contract; secondly, article 3(3) indicates that Mexican law yields to any mandatory rules of Californian law; thirdly, article 7(2) provides for the application of any overriding rules of English law. In the event of

100 Contracts (Applicable Law) Act 1990, s 2(2). The reservation in relation to art 7(1), which was also made by Germany, Ireland and Luxembourg, was primarily based on a fear that it would give rise to uncertainty: see Giuliano-Lagarde Report, OJ 1980 C282/28.

101 This issue is considered further at pp 249–250.

conflict between the mandatory rules of Californian law and the overriding rules of English law, something has to give. It seems clear that in such a case the overriding rules of the forum prevail.

As a general rule, if a statute makes no provision, express or implied, for the circumstances in which it is to apply, it will apply to a contract which has foreign elements only if English law is the applicable law. Where, for example, a contract of sale is, by virtue of article 4 of the Convention, governed by Italian law, there can be no question of the implied terms contained in the Sale of Goods Act 1979 applying. Although the non-excludable implied terms in the 1979 Act are mandatory according to article 3(3), they are not overriding rules for the purposes of article 7; they are not applicable to an international contract whose governing law is not English law.

A number of statutes which apply to contractual situations make complete or partial provision for their sphere of application. A statute may provide that it is to apply only if specified connections exist; if the territorial connections are not present the statute will not apply to the contract. What is the position if those territorial connections do exist, but English law is not the applicable law?

One possibility is that the statute expressly determines its scope of operation. For example, the Unfair Contract Terms Act 1977 includes provisions defining its scope of application. First, the Act determines the circumstances in which its provisions are not applicable even though English law is the law governing the contract.[102] Secondly, and, in the context of the current discussion, more importantly, the Act determines the circumstances in which it is applicable notwithstanding a choice of a foreign law. The 1977 Act contains provisions which invalidate exemption and similar clauses in certain contracts, in some cases automatically and in others unless they satisfy a test of reasonableness. Although much of the Act is directed at consumer contracts,[103] its ambit is wider than that. The Act contains provisions designed to ensure that its protective provisions apply in appropriate cases even if a foreign law is the applicable law.

The extent to which the controls in the 1977 Act are to be regarded as overriding for the purposes of article 7 is fixed by section 27(2). The effect of this provision is that the Act applies to a contract, notwithstanding the choice of a foreign law, if (a) such a choice was 'imposed wholly or mainly for the purpose of enabling

102 Under s 27(1) the Act's controls do not apply if English law is the applicable law only by the choice of the parties and, in the absence of such choice, a foreign law would have been the applicable law; s 26 excludes 'international supply contracts' from the Act's scope.

103 For consideration of consumer contracts see pp 235–236.

the party imposing it to evade the operation of the Act' or (b) 'in the making of the contract one of the parties dealt as a consumer, and he was then habitually resident in the United Kingdom, and the essential steps necessary for the making of the contract were taken there, whether by him or by others on his behalf'. The operation of section 27(2) can be illustrated by the following example: the claimant, an English resident, purchases a train ticket from the defendant, a foreign railway operator, for a journey between two foreign cities;[104] the claimant takes all the essential steps necessary for the making of the contract in England; the contract contains a clause which excludes the railway operator's liability for death or personal injury; the contract includes an express choice of a foreign law according to which the contractual exclusion is valid.[105] If the claimant is injured as a result of the defendant's negligence and brings proceedings in England for breach of contract, the defendant will not be able to rely on the exclusion clause in the contract. The effect of section 27(2) is that, for the purposes of article 7(2), the provisions of the Act (which render void any contract term which seeks to exclude or restrict liability for death or personal injury resulting from negligence[106]) are overriding in these circumstances.

The Unfair Terms in Consumer Contracts Regulations 1999,[107] which exist alongside the 1977 Act, implement rules which are common to all the European Union member states.[108] The regulations provide that certain types of contractual term are not binding on consumers.[109] It is expressly provided that the regulations apply notwithstanding any contract term which applies or purports to apply the law of a non-member state, if the contract has a close connection with the territory of the member states. Accordingly, for the purposes of the Convention, the regulations are overriding rules in cases where the contract has the appropriate degree of connection.

If the statute does not expressly identify the circumstances in which it applies, the court has to decide whether or not its provisions are overriding. It seems that the courts are quite likely to hold that, on its true construction, the statute was impliedly intended by the legislator to be applicable if a particular territorial connection exists, whether or not English law is the applicable law.

104 This contract is not a consumer contract for the purposes of the Convention: art 5(4).
105 This example is taken from Hill, *International Commercial Disputes* (2nd edn, 1998) pp 465–466.
106 Unfair Contract Terms Act 1977, s 2(1).
107 SI 1999/2083.
108 Council Directive (EEC) No 13/93, OJ 1993 L95/29.
109 Reg 5(1).

An example – decided under the common law, rather than the Convention – is *Boissevain v Weil*,[110] where statutory provisions laid down that no person should borrow foreign currency, the prohibition being expressed to apply to British subjects in various countries including Monaco. It was held that these statutory provisions, on their true construction, rendered void a contract under which a British subject borrowed foreign currency in Monaco, even if the law of Monaco was the law governing the contract. Similarly, in *The Hollandia*[111] – another case decided at common law – rules set out in a schedule to the Carriage of Goods by Sea Act 1971 provided that they should apply 'to every bill of lading relating to the carriage of goods between ports in two different states if: (a) the bill of lading is issued in a contracting state or (b) the carriage is from a port in a contracting state'. Commentators had disagreed as to the scope of the rules in question: one suggestion was that the rules applied only if English law was the governing law;[112] the opposing view was that the 1971 Act was in the nature of an overriding statute.[113] The House of Lords held that the rules applied to a bill of lading where the carriage was from a Scottish port (the United Kingdom being a contracting state) to a foreign port, even though the contract contained an express choice of a foreign law. Both *Boissevain v Weil* and *The Hollandia* would be decided in the same way under the Convention on the ground that the relevant statutory provisions are overriding rules to be applied under article 7(2).

Even if a statute does not expressly mention any territorial connections, the court may nevertheless hold that the legislature must have impliedly intended the statute to be applicable if some territorial connection identified by the court is present, whether or not English law is the applicable law. A good example is *English v Donnelly*,[114] a Scottish case decided before the entry into force of the Contracts (Applicable Law) Act 1990. An English company entered into a hire-purchase agreement in Scotland with a Scottish hirer. A clause of the contract provided that it should be governed by English law. The company sued in Scotland for breach of the agreement, but the hirer successfully relied on the provisions of the Hire-Purchase and Small Debt (Scotland) Act 1932 – a statute which was part of Scots law but not English law – under which the contract was void because the company had not delivered a copy of the agreement to the hirer within a specified period. It was held that, on its true

110 [1950] AC 327, [1950] 1 All ER 728.
111 [1983] 1 AC 565, [1982] 3 All ER 1141.
112 Mann, 'Statutes and the Conflict of Laws' (1972–73) 46 BYIL 117.
113 Morris, 'The Scope of the Carriage of Goods by Sea Act 1971' (1979) 95 LQR 61.
114 1958 SC 494.

construction, the statute applied to all hire-purchase contracts made in Scotland, irrespective of whether Scots law was the governing law. In effect, the court decided that the statutory provision relied upon by the hirer was an overriding rule.

In *Ingmar GB Ltd v Eaton Leonard Technologies Inc*[115] C, a United Kingdom company, was employed by D, a Californian company, as D's exclusive agent in the United Kingdom and Ireland. The contract contained an express choice of Californian law. When the agency contract was terminated, C started proceedings in England with a view to recovering payment of commission as provided by the Commercial Agents (Council Directive) Regulations.[116] The High Court rejected the claim on the basis that the regulations were not relevant as the contract was governed by the law of California. However, on a reference from the Court of Appeal under what is now article 234 EC, the Court of Justice ruled that the regulations, the purpose of which is to guarantee certain rights to commercial agents after the termination of agency contracts, apply regardless of the law applicable to the contract, where the commercial agent carries on his activity in a member state, even though the principal is established in a non-member country.

D Public policy

It has been seen that the Convention contains a number of provisions which seek to balance the interests of the parties and those of the various countries which may be concerned with the regulation of a particular contractual relationship. Even though article 7(2) provides for the application of the overriding rules of the law of the forum, the public policy of the forum may also have a role to play. Article 16 provides that '[t]he application of a rule of the law of any country specified by this Convention may be refused only if such application is manifestly incompatible with the public policy (*ordre public*) of the forum'.

Public policy in the conflicts sphere has a more restricted role than in the domestic sphere. The fact that a contract is void on grounds of public policy by English domestic law does not necessarily mean that public policy will be invoked to invalidate it if it has foreign elements and a foreign applicable law. It is intended that, under the Convention, public policy should have a very narrow scope.

115 Case C-381/98 [2001] 1 All ER (Comm) 329. Verhagen, 'The Tension between Party Autonomy and European Union Law' (2002) 51 ICLQ 135.
116 SI 1993/3053, implementing Council Directive (EEC) No 653/86, OJ 1986 L382/17.

According to traditional English notions there are two categories of case where the court may on grounds of public policy refuse to enforce a contract which is valid by its governing law. The first is where to enforce the contract would infringe fundamental English ideas of justice or morality. The best known case of this sort is *Kaufman v Gerson*.[117] The French defendant had promised in France to pay the French plaintiff a sum of money in consideration for the plaintiff refraining from instituting criminal proceedings against the defendant's husband in France. Though the agreement was valid by French law, the plaintiff failed in English proceedings to recover the money on the ground that under English law the agreement was illegal and had been made under duress. Romer LJ said that the English court will not enforce a contract which contravenes 'what by the law of this country is deemed an essential moral interest'.[118] Under this exceptional category, there is no requirement that the contract should have any connection with England.

In the second category of public policy it is not so much justice or morality but the public interest that is at stake. Enforcement of a contract may be refused if it would tend to injure the public interest in a way which an English invalidating rule is designed to prevent. At common law, public policy has been relied on to refuse enforcement of a contract between a solicitor and his client, valid by its governing law, but void by English law because the solicitor was to receive as his fee a proportion of the proceeds of English litigation.[119] It has also been held that a restraint of trade clause in a contract of employment, restraining competition in England, will not be enforced if it is void by English law, even though valid by its proper law.[120] In this class of case public policy will not be invoked unless the contract has relevant connections with England. In the two examples given above, the English public interest – in the conduct of litigation in the one case and free competition in the other – which English law was designed to protect, was liable to be injured. If in the first case the litigation had been in a foreign country, and in the second case the restraint of trade provision was to operate only abroad, there would have been no reason to invoke public policy. It should not be thought, however, that doing an act abroad can never be injurious to the public interest. For example, public policy will preclude the enforcement of a contract under

117 [1904] 1 KB 591. See also *Royal Boskalis Westminster NV v Mountain* [1999] QB 674, [1997] 2 All ER 929.
118 At 599–600.
119 *Grell v Levy* (1864) 16 CBNS 73.
120 *Rousillon v Rousillon* (1880) 14 Ch D 351.

which a British subject trades abroad with an enemy.[121] Similarly, as public policy may be invoked to protect the public or national image of the United Kingdom, the court may refuse to enforce a contract where the parties intend to circumvent or breach the laws of another country. In *Regazzoni v KC Sethia (1944) Ltd*[122] a contract provided for the sale of jute bags by Indian sellers to Swiss buyers. Although the contract provided for the goods to be shipped to Genoa, to the knowledge of the sellers, the buyers intended to reship the goods from Genoa to South Africa. Under Indian law the shipment from India of jute destined for or intended to be taken to South Africa was prohibited, as both parties well knew. When the sellers repudiated the contract it was held by the House of Lords that the contract should not be enforced by the English court.

Two points should be made by way of conclusion. First, in the commercial sphere, it is very unusual for the law governing a contract to be disapplied on the ground of public policy. If there is no express choice of a foreign law, public policy will not often need to be relied upon, for if the contract is sufficiently closely connected with England to affect the public interest, English law, as the law of the country with which the contract is most closely connected, is likely to be the applicable law. Where the parties have chosen a foreign law in a contract which is closely connected with England, the law chosen by the parties will yield to the overriding rules of English law as the law of the forum.

Secondly, within the context of the Convention, it is possible that some of the cases which have traditionally been considered as raising questions of public policy should be dealt with by reference to the provisions relating to overriding rules. In particular, it may be difficult to maintain a clear dividing line between article 7(2) and article 16. Whereas the effect of article 7(2) is positive (by providing that the applicable law should be displaced by the overriding rules of the forum), article 16 operates negatively (by excluding the applicable law). In practical terms, however, it is irrelevant whether an agreement is legally ineffective because it conflicts with the public policy of the forum or because an overriding rule of the law of the forum renders it unenforceable; whichever analysis is employed the result is the same.[123]

121 *Dynamit Act v Rio Tinto Co Ltd* [1918] AC 260.
122 [1958] AC 301, [1957] 3 All ER 286.
123 Lando, 'The EEC Convention on the Law Applicable to Contractual Obligations' (1987) 24 CML Rev 159 at 208.

V CONSUMER CONTRACTS AND INDIVIDUAL CONTRACTS OF EMPLOYMENT

Notwithstanding the possible application of mandatory rules which do not form part of the applicable law, the starting-point for the choice of law regime introduced by the Convention is the principle of party autonomy. It has come to be well recognised that freedom of contract should not be unrestricted in areas where there is a structural inequality between the parties. It is therefore not surprising that the Convention contains specific provisions dealing with consumer contracts and individual contracts of employment.

A Consumer contracts

1. Protecting the consumer

The purpose of article 5 is to ensure that, as regards contracts falling within the article's scope, a consumer is not deprived of the protection provided by the consumer legislation of the country in which he is habitually resident. This purpose is achieved by two basic rules. First, in cases where a consumer contract includes a choice of law, this choice cannot have the effect of depriving the consumer of the protection of the mandatory rules of the law of the country where he is habitually resident.[124] However, if the law chosen by the parties is more advantageous to the consumer than the law of the country in which the consumer is habitually resident, the chosen law should govern.[125] Secondly, where the contract does not include a choice of law, it is provided that the law of the consumer's habitual residence is the applicable law.[126] The choice of law rule which applies in the absence of choice by the parties is an inflexible one; the law of the country in which the consumer is habitually resident applies, even if the contract is more closely connected with another country.

2. The scope of article 5

It is important not to overestimate the significance of the consumer contract provisions. The ambit of article 5 is circumscribed by a number of factors. Most importantly, article 5 does not apply unless the object of the contract is 'the supply of goods or services to a

124 Art 5(2).
125 See Morse, 'Consumer Contracts, Employment Contracts and the Rome Convention' (1992) 41 ICLQ 1 at 8–9.
126 Art 5(3).

person ('the consumer') for a purpose which can be regarded as being outside his trade or profession'.[127] Although it is specifically provided that article 5 applies to 'a contract which, for an inclusive price, provides for a combination of travel and accommodation',[128] as a general rule article 5 applies neither to contracts of carriage nor to contracts for the supply of services 'where the services are to be supplied to the consumer exclusively in a country other than that in which he has his habitual residence'.[129] Furthermore, the consumer contract provisions do not apply unless one of a further set of conditions is satisfied: (i) the contract was preceded by a specific invitation addressed to the consumer or advertising in the country of the consumer's habitual residence and the consumer took in that country all the steps necessary on his part for the conclusion of the contract; or (ii) the other party or his agent received the consumer's order in the country of the consumer's habitual residence; or (iii) the contract is for the sale of goods and the consumer travelled from the country of his habitual residence to another country and there gave his order, provided that the consumer's journey was arranged by the seller for the purpose of inducing the consumer to buy.[130]

3. *Overriding rules of the forum*

It is important to note that consumer contracts are subject to the general provisions of the Convention concerned with mandatory rules and public policy. In principle, where litigation takes place in England, a consumer contract is, by virtue of article 7(2), subject to the overriding rules of English law. However, in many cases, article 7(2) will be redundant. If a contract falls within the scope of article 5, the consumer receives the protection of the mandatory rules (including the overriding rules) which form part of the law of the country where he is habitually resident. A consumer who is resident in England will therefore often receive the protection of English consumer legislation by virtue of article 5.[131]

127 Art 5(1).
128 Art 5(5).
129 Art 5(4).
130 Art 5(2).
131 There are circumstances in which, although art 5 does not apply, the Unfair Contracts Terms Act 1977 and/or the Unfair Terms in Consumer Contracts Regulations 1999 are overriding. For example, if a contract includes a choice of the law of a foreign country, the court may, relying on art 7(2), apply the Unfair Contract Terms Act 1977 if it appears that the purpose of the choice of law was to evade the operation of the Act. See also the example on p 230.

B Individual contracts of employment

Whereas article 5 defines what is meant by a consumer contract for the purposes of the Convention, article 6 which regulates individual contracts of employment contains no equivalent definition. Although the question has not yet been settled, there are strong arguments in favour of applying the governing law to determine whether or not a contract is an individual employment contract for the purposes of article 6: this approach is most likely to achieve uniformity and it has the added advantage of avoiding a situation where the court applies the employment law of a particular country to a contract which is not a contract of employment according to that law.[132]

If the parties to a contract of employment do not make a choice, the law applicable to an individual contract of employment is determined by article 6(2). Although article 6(2) does not use the language of presumption, the basic approach is similar to that adopted by article 4. Article 6(2) provides that a contract of employment is governed:

(a) by the law of the country in which the employee habitually carries out his work in performance of the contract, even if he is temporarily employed in another country; or
(b) if the employee does not habitually carry out his work in any one country, by the law of the country in which the place of business through which he was engaged is situated;
unless it appears from the circumstances as a whole that the contract is more closely connected with another country, in which case the contract shall be governed by the law of that country.

The interpretation of article 6(2) is fraught with difficulty. Although the Court of Justice ruled, in the context of article 5(1) of the Brussels Convention, that an employee is to be regarded as habitually carrying out his work at the place where he establishes the effective centre of his working activities,[133] a number of questions remain unresolved. If an employee is recruited by an agency can the reference in article 6(2)(b) to 'the place of business through which he was engaged' signify a place of business of the agent, or must that place of business be a place of business of the employer? In what circumstances will the rules in subparagraphs (a) and (b) yield to the proviso in favour of the law of the country with which the contract is most closely connected?[134]

132 See Morse, 'Consumer Contracts, Employment Contracts and the Rome Convention' (1992) 41 ICLQ 1 at 13.
133 Case C-383/95 *Rutten v Cross Medical Ltd* [1997] ECR I-57.
134 This question is essentially the same as the question concerning the relationship between the presumptions in art 4(2)–(4) and art 4(5).

If the parties make a choice of law, the chosen law prima facie governs the contract.[135] This rule is subject to an important limitation: a choice of law shall not have the result of depriving the employee of the protection afforded to him by the mandatory rules of the law which would be applicable in the absence of choice. So, if a French resident is employed to work in France under a contract which is expressly governed by German law, the mandatory provisions of French law prevail over German law. It would seem that if the applicable law gives the employee more protection than the law which would be applicable in the absence of choice, the employee should be given the benefit of the law which is more favourable.

Finally, it should be noted that, whether or not the parties have made a choice of law, the applicable law will have to give way to any relevant overriding rules of the law of the forum.

VI PARTICULAR ASPECTS OF THE CONTRACT

Although the applicable law, as identified by articles 3 to 6 (and modified by any relevant mandatory rules), is central to the determination of the rights and obligations of the parties, it cannot be assumed that all aspects which arise under a contract are governed exclusively by the applicable law. In the sections which follow the choice of law aspects of various contractual issues are considered.

A Material validity

Article 8 of the Convention identifies the law which determines whether a contract or a term of a contract is materially valid. One of the most important aspects of material validity is the formation of the contract. Have the parties reached an agreement by offer and acceptance? Is consideration required for the agreement to be enforceable? Did the parties have the necessary intention to create legal relations? Have the parties freely given their consent or is there a relevant factor – such as mistake or duress – which vitiates the consent of one or other of the parties? Is the alleged contract void for illegality? These are all questions of material validity which fall within the scope of article 8. Article 8 comprises two paragraphs: the first lays down a general rule; the second contains an exception.

135 Art 6(1).

1. The general rule

The general rule is that the existence and validity of a contract, or of any term of a contract, is determined by the law which would govern it if the contract or term were valid.[136] This rule is difficult to defend from the point of view of logic. As a matter of logic, questions of formation cannot be governed by the applicable law, for until such questions have been decided it is not clear that there is a contract at all. The Convention ignores these logical problems and lays down the rule that the putative applicable law governs these issues.[137]

The application of the general rule may be illustrated by a couple of simple examples. Suppose a Swiss seller sends by post an offer to sell goods to an English buyer, who posts back an acceptance which is lost in the post. By English law there is a contract, because acceptance is effective on posting; by Swiss law there is no contract because acceptance is effective only on receipt. Which law is to decide whether a contract was made? The putative applicable law approach adopted by the Convention requires the court to determine which law would be the applicable law on the assumption that a contract was made. In the absence of choice by the parties, this would be the law of the country with which the contract is most closely connected, which would be presumed to be the law of the country in which the seller had his principal place of business. So, unless the alleged contract is regarded as being more closely connected with England, Swiss law would be applied to decide whether there was a contract, with the result that there would not be.

A similar analysis can be applied in the situation in which an Italian donor promises to make a gift to an English donee. According to Italian law the promise is legally binding; under English law it is unenforceable because the donee gave no consideration for the promise. In the absence of choice the putative applicable law would be Italian law, the law of the country in which the donor was habitually resident. Accordingly, the promise would be enforceable.

The position is slightly more complicated if it is alleged that the supposed contract contains a choice of law clause. Article 3(4) provides that the existence and validity of the consent of the parties as to the choice of the applicable law is to be determined according to the general principles which apply to other questions relating to the existence and validity of contractual terms. It follows that whether a choice of law clause is materially valid is to be determined by the law which would govern it on the assumption that the clause

136 Art 8(1).
137 For criticism of art 8 see Jaffey, *Topics in Choice of Law* (1996) chapter 4.

is valid. So, the existence and validity of a choice of English law is to be determined by English law.

What is the position, as regards the substance of the contract, if according to its putative applicable law the alleged choice of law does not exist? Suppose that an English buyer offers to buy goods from a German seller on terms which include a choice of English law. Although the buyer purports to withdraw the offer before the seller replies, the seller accepts the offer. Under English law the revocation is effective; under German law it is not. Is there a valid contract?

There are two possible ways of looking at the problem. First, if the contract – including the alleged choice of law – is looked at as a single entity, the answer is that no contract comes into being: if the contract exists it will be governed by English law, but according to English law there is no contract. The logic of this approach is, however, rather questionable. Furthermore, both article 3(4) and article 8 suggest that the existence of the alleged choice of law clause should be considered independently, before the contract as a whole is examined.

According to the second approach, the first step is to consider the existence of the alleged choice of English law by reference to its putative applicable law. Under English law there is no effective choice because of the revocation prior to the seller's acceptance. Having disposed of the choice of law clause, the putative applicable law – as regards the remainder of the disputed contract – has to be determined by article 4, the presumption being that German law, being the seller's law, governs. According to German law the purported revocation is ineffective and, subject to the exception in article 8(2), the contract is validly created with German law as its applicable law.

2. *The exception*

One of the problems posed by the putative applicable law approach is that it could be unjust to hold a party bound under a foreign law in circumstances in which he is not bound by his own law. For example, an offeree might find himself bound under a contract even though he did not accept the offer on the basis that according to the putative applicable law – but not the offeree's law – silence can amount to consent. To deal with this problem the Convention contains an exception to the general rule: a party may rely upon the law of the country in which he has his habitual residence to establish that he did not consent if it appears from the circumstances that it would not be reasonable to determine the effect of his conduct in accordance with the law specified by the general rule.[138]

138 Art 8(2).

There are a number of points to make about this provision. First, its effect is entirely negative. The exception cannot be invoked to validate a contract which would be materially invalid under the general rule. Secondly, the exception allows a contracting party to invoke the law of the country in which he is habitually resident. Habitual residence, as a connecting factor, is easy enough to apply to individuals, but less so with regard to corporations. One might have expected the connecting factor for companies to be the principal place of business, rather than the place of habitual residence. Thirdly, the exception – which is based on a reasonableness test – is rather open-textured and the text of the Convention does not give any guidance as to how the test should be applied. The issue was considered by Mance J in *Egon Oldendorff v Libera Corpn.*[139] The case concerned an alleged charter agreement which, if it existed, was governed by English law. The Japanese defendant sought to invoke the exception in article 8(2) and to rely on Japanese law, according to which, it was argued, consent was not established. The question facing the court was whether or not it was reasonable to determine the effect of the defendant's conduct in accordance with English law, as the putative applicable law. Clearly this question could be answered neither from the viewpoint of the defendant's law nor entirely from the viewpoint of the putative applicable law. According to Mance J the question 'can only be answered by the court before which it comes adopting a dispassionate, internationally minded approach'.[140] The court decided that, in the circumstances, it was not unreasonable to apply the putative applicable law to the question of the defendant's consent. The alleged contract included an English arbitration clause from which the court implied a choice of English law. In Mance J's view, to ignore the arbitration clause would have been contrary to ordinary commercial expectations, given that the arbitration clause was precisely the sort of clause which would be expected in an international charter agreement and the circumstances suggested that the defendant must actually have considered and accepted the clause.

B Formal validity

Article 9 of the Convention lays down the choice of law rules which apply to questions of formal validity. Although the Convention does not attempt to define the scope of formal (as opposed to material) validity the Giuliano-Lagarde Report states that formal validity covers 'every external manifestation required on the part of a person

139 [1995] 2 Lloyd's Rep 64.
140 At 70.

expressing the will to be legally bound, and in the absence of which such expression of will would not be regarded as fully effective'.[141] So, for example, a requirement that certain types of contract – such as contracts for the sale of land[142] – must be made in writing is an aspect of formal validity.[143]

The regime set out in article 9 is very liberal with the consequence that in most cases an international contract will not be invalid as a result of a failure by the parties to comply with formal requirements. A number of rules should be noted.

First, a contract which is concluded by parties in the same country is formally valid if it satisfies the formal requirements of either the applicable law (as determined by articles 3 and 4) or the law of the country in which the contract is concluded (lex loci contractus).[144] Secondly, if the parties to the contract are in different countries, the contract is formally valid if it satisfies the requirements of the applicable law or of the law of either country. If, for example, an English resident and a French resident conclude by telephone a contract which contains a choice of German law, the contract will be formally valid if it satisfies the formal requirements of English law or French law or German law.[145]

Thirdly, where a contract is concluded by agents, the location of the agents (rather than the principals) determines whether the contract is one made by parties in the same country or by parties in different countries.[146] So, if an English seller and the Belgian agent of a French buyer conclude in Belgium a written contract which contains a choice of English law the relevant laws for the purposes of article 9 are English law (as the applicable law) and Belgian law (as the lex loci contractus).

Fourthly, article 9 also lays down rules for acts intended to have legal effect relating to an existing or contemplated contract as well as to concluded contracts. Such an act – for example, an offer or an invitation to treat – will be formally valid if it is formally valid according to the putative applicable law or the law of the country where the act was done.[147]

Finally, article 9 includes a special rule for consumer contracts. The formal validity of a consumer contract – within the scope of

141 OJ 1980 C282/29.
142 Law of Property (Miscellaneous Provisions) Act 1989, s 2.
143 For consideration of the classification questions raised by the Statute of Frauds and its interpretation in *Leroux v Brown* (1852) 12 CB 801, see pp 536–537.
144 Art 9(1).
145 Art 9(2).
146 Art 9(3).
147 Art 9(4).

article 5 – is governed by the law of the country in which the consumer has his habitual residence.[148]

C Capacity

Rules relating to capacity define classes of person who lack the power which people in general have to make or to be bound by a contract. (If it is contended that no person can validly make the contract in question, the issue is one of material validity, not capacity.) The commonest kind of incapacity to contract is that of the minor. Others who may lack capacity under a particular legal system are married women, corporations[149] and mentally disordered people.

In general, questions of capacity are excluded from the scope of the Convention on the ground that such issues are part of the law of persons, rather than the law of obligations. Accordingly, the relevant rules have to be located in the common law. There is, however, a specific rule in article 11 which provides that, in certain circumstances, an incapacity under the law governing that question should be disregarded.

1. Capacity rules at common law

The position at common law is not definitively settled, there being very few modern authorities. There are dicta in some older cases[150] that capacity to contract is governed by the law of domicile. By contrast, in the old case of *Male v Roberts*[151] it was held that Scots law, as the lex loci contractus, governed the capacity of a party to make a contract, even though that party was domiciled in England. At that time, however, it was generally assumed that contracts were governed by the law of the country where they were made and there are few commentators nowadays who favour the general application of the lex loci contractus to questions of capacity.

In the Canadian case of *Charron v Montreal Trust Co*[152] it was decided that the proper law, rather than the law of the domicile or the lex loci contractus, governed capacity to contract. The case is, however, weak authority.[153] The question was whether a Quebec

148 Art 9(5).

149 See *Merrill Lynch Capital Services Inc v Municipality of Piraeus* [1997] 6 Bank LR 241.

150 *Cooper v Cooper* (1888) 13 App Cas 88 at 99.

151 (1790) 3 Esp 163.

152 (1958) 15 DLR (2d) 240.

153 Nevertheless, it was followed by the New South Wales courts in *Homestake Gold of Australia Ltd v Peninsula Gold Pty Ltd* (1996) 131 FLR 447.

rule under which married people were not legally able to enter a separation agreement was applicable. The issue facing the court was one of material validity, however, rather than capacity. Since ex hypothesi a single person cannot enter a separation agreement, it was not a case where a class of people lacked a power to contract which other people enjoyed.

In *Bodley Head Ltd v Flegon*[154] it was held obiter that capacity is governed by the proper law. The author, Solzhenitsyn, had executed in Russia a power of attorney in favour of a Swiss lawyer, empowering him to deal with Solzhenitsyn's books outside Russia. It was contended that this contract of agency was void, as Solzhenitsyn lacked capacity under Russian law to make it. Russian law governed capacity, it was argued, either as the law of the domicile or the lex loci contractus. It was held, however, that the issue was not one of capacity, for the relevant rule of Russian law was that no Russian citizen was permitted to trade abroad, a rule not of capacity but of material validity. The question was therefore governed by the proper law, which was Swiss law. However, Brightman J went on to say that, even if it had been the case that Solzhenitsyn lacked capacity by Russian law, the contract would still have been valid, for capacity is also governed by the proper law.

In view of the confusion surrounding the authorities it is difficult to state the current law with confidence. One suggestion is that a party to an international contract should be regarded as having capacity if he has capacity either by his personal law or by the objective proper law.[155] This suggestion not only draws on the decided cases but also is defensible from the point of view of principle.

Even if a party lacks capacity by the law of the country with which the contract is most closely connected, he should still be bound if he has capacity by the law of his domicile. To the extent that an incapacity is protective of the party concerned, the law of the country to which a person belongs is best able to decide whether he needs such protection. There is no reason why a party who has capacity by his own law should be able to rely on any other law to avoid being bound.

However, to allow a party to rely on an incapacity under the law of his domicile could be unjust to the other party, who may have no reason to suppose that his contracting partner is domiciled in a foreign country, let alone to know what the rules of capacity in that country are.[156] Where both parties have capacity by the proper law,

154 [1972] 1 WLR 680.
155 Dicey and Morris, *The Conflict of Laws* (13th edn, 2000) pp 1271–1272.
156 *McFeetridge v Stewarts and Lloyds Ltd* 1913 SC 773 at 784.

it would be unfair to allow one party to avoid being bound by invoking an incapacity under his personal law. For the purposes of the capacity rules, the proper law should be objectively ascertained; the relevant law is the law of the country with which the contract is most closely connected. If the proper law were determined subjectively a person would be able to confer capacity on himself by his mere agreement to a contractual clause which selected a law according to which he had capacity.

2. The significance of article 11

Although capacity questions are, in general, excluded from the Convention's scope,[157] article 11 provides as follows:

> In a contract concluded between persons who are in the same country, a natural person who would have capacity under the law of that country may invoke his incapacity resulting from another law only if the other party to the contract was aware of this incapacity at the time of the conclusion of the contract or was not aware thereof as a result of negligence.

The Giuliano-Lagarde Report explains that the purpose of this provision is to protect a party who in good faith believed himself to be contracting with a person of full capacity and who, after the conclusion of the contract, is confronted by the incapacity of the other contracting party.[158] Nevertheless, article 11 is not without its difficulties.

First, it is not at all clear how the negligence test is to be applied. In what circumstances, if any, would it be negligent for a foreign trader not to know that an English youth of 17 does not have capacity to conclude a commercial contract? The Giuliano-Lagarde Report indicates only that the burden of proof is on the incapacitated party to prove that the other party knew or should have known of the incapacity.[159]

Secondly, care is needed when considering the possible application of article 11. Take, for example, the situation where X, an English youth of 17, agrees – while on holiday in France – to buy a motorbike from Y, a French seller; the youth has capacity under French law by virtue of the fact that, even though he is under the age of majority, he is married.[160] When Y seeks to enforce the contract in England can X rely on the fact that he does not have capacity under English domestic law? At first glance, this might appear to be the type of

157 Art 1(1).
158 OJ 1980 C282/34.
159 Ibid.
160 See French Civil Code, arts 476, 481, 1123 and 1124.

situation in which, on the assumption that the seller knew of the incapacity or was negligent in not knowing about it, article 11 allows an incapacitated person to invoke his incapacity. This would, however, be too superficial a view. According to the Giuliano-Lagarde Report, article 11 applies only if there is a conflict of laws: 'The law which, according to the private international law of the court hearing the case, governs the capacity of the person claiming to be under a disability must be different from the law of the country where the contract was concluded.'[161] So, if X has capacity not only under French law, but also according to English *conflicts rules* (because French law is the objective proper law of the contract), there can be no argument for allowing X to invoke his incapacity under English domestic law.

D The effect and construction of a contract

A question may arise as to the nature or extent of the parties' rights and obligations under a valid contract. As questions of substance are governed by the applicable law, it follows that this law governs the interpretation of contractual provisions.[162] Primarily, the court will be seeking to ascertain the intention of the parties, but to the extent that any rules of law or canons of construction are needed to determine what the terms are, the court will use those of the applicable law.

The applicable law also governs performance.[163] The Convention provides, however, that '[i]n relation to the manner of performance and the steps to be taken in the event of defective performance regard shall be had to the law of the country in which performance takes place'.[164] The precise significance of this provision is somewhat opaque; the Giuliano-Lagarde Report states that matters falling within the scope of the phrase 'manner of performance' include 'rules governing public holidays, the manner in which goods are to be examined, and the steps to be taken if they are refused'.[165] The Convention does not state that, as regards questions relating to the manner of performance, the law of the place of performance (lex loci solutionis) governs but simply provides that 'regard shall be had' to it. As a matter of principle, the position should be clear. Questions of substance are governed by the applicable law and the lex loci

161 OJ 1980 C282/34.
162 Art 10(1)(a).
163 Art 10(1)(b).
164 Art 10(2).
165 OJ 1980 C282/33.

solutionis should not, as a general rule, be allowed to impinge upon such questions so as to alter the rights and obligations of the parties.

The consequences of breach are within the province of the applicable law.[166] So, the applicable law determines whether a party is entitled to a particular type of loss (such as non-pecuniary losses) and whether or not such losses are too remote. Questions of causation and contributory negligence must also be for the applicable law. Whether the defendant can rely on a defence (such as set-off) as a means of limiting his liability is a substantive matter governed by the applicable law.[167]

E Discharge

The circumstances in which a contract, or obligation under it, comes to an end is for the applicable law to determine.[168] The applicable law therefore governs such matters as frustration, termination for breach or by agreement or as a result of any other factor (such as insolvency). The applicable law also determines whether a claim is barred by lapse of time.

F Illegality

There are no provisions of the Convention which deal with illegality as such. Problems of illegality have to be dealt with by applying those articles of the Convention which deal with material validity, the performance and discharge of contractual obligations and mandatory rules. Two issues can be dealt with simply. First, if a contract or contractual provision is invalid by virtue of its being illegal under the putative applicable law, then the English court will hold it invalid.[169] Secondly, the fact that a contract is illegal under a foreign law which is neither the applicable law nor the law of the place of performance (lex loci solutionis) will be ignored if the contract is valid according to the applicable law.[170]

The difficult cases are those in which the contract is prima facie valid by the applicable law, but is illegal under the lex loci solutionis. In considering problems of illegality under the lex loci solutionis it is vital to draw a number of distinctions: first, cases of initial illegality (where the contract is illegal at the outset) should be distinguished

166 Art 10(1)(c).
167 *Meridien BIAO Bank GmbH v Bank of New York* [1997] 1 Lloyd's Rep 437.
168 Art 10(1)(d).
169 Art 8(1).
170 This principle is illustrated by *Kleinwort Sons & Co v Ungarische Baumwolle Industrie Akt* [1939] 2 KB 678, [1939] 3 All ER 38, a case decided at common law.

from cases of subsequent illegality (where the contract is valid at the outset, but is rendered illegal by a change in the law); secondly, a distinction should be made between cases in which English law is the applicable law and cases in which a foreign law is the applicable law. While some difficult questions remain, the general principles are clear.

1. Contracts governed by English law

There is clear authority that, as regards a contract which is governed by English law, it will not be enforced if performance is illegal under the lex loci solutionis. This general principle applies equally to cases of initial and subsequent illegality.

So, for example, a contract of sale involving the export of goods from country X will not be enforced if by the law of country X such export is permitted only under licence and such licence has not been obtained.[171] The courts' refusal to enforce contracts which are illegal under the lex loci solutionis has been extended to cases in which the parties contemplate the commission of acts which are illegal by the law of the country in which the intended acts are to be performed, even though performance of the contract does not require the commission of such acts. For example, in *Foster v Driscoll*[172] the Court of Appeal refused to enforce an agreement to ship a cargo of whisky across the Atlantic during Prohibition; although the contract did not require performance in the United States, the parties' intention was to smuggle the cargo into the United States. This case, which involved a contract whose proper law was English law, would be decided the same way under the Convention.[173]

The leading case relating to subsequent illegality is *Ralli Bros v Compania Naviera Sota y Aznar*,[174] in which English charterers, by a charterparty made in London, chartered a Spanish ship to carry a cargo of jute from Calcutta to Barcelona at an agreed freight, part of which was to be paid in Barcelona on the arrival of the ship there. Spanish legislation passed after the making of the contract, but before the arrival of the ship at Barcelona, laid down that the freight payable on jute imported into Spain should not exceed a certain rate, and made it an offence to pay or receive freight above that amount. The freight agreed in the charterparty to be payable in

171 *AV Pound & Co Ltd v MW Hardy & Co Inc* [1956] AC 588.
172 [1929] 1 KB 470.
173 See also *S v A Bank* [1997] 6 Bank LR 163; *Ispahani v Bank Melli Iran* [1998] Lloyd's Rep Bank 133.
174 [1920] 2 KB 287.

Spain exceeded the statutory rate, and the issue for the English court was whether the shipowners were entitled to recover the excess. It was held by the Court of Appeal that in view of the Spanish legislation the excess was not recoverable; the contract, which was governed by English law, was not enforceable to the extent that it required a performance in Spain which was prohibited by Spanish law.

2. Contracts not governed by English law

While the position with regard to a contract whose applicable law is English law is unambiguous, the picture is less clear in cases where the contract is governed by the law of another country according to which the contract is valid. There are two questions to consider. First, are the principles laid down in cases such as *Foster v Driscoll* and the *Ralli Bros* case simply part of English domestic law or are they also part of the English conflict of laws? Secondly, if these principles are part of the conflict of laws, how do they fit within the framework established by the Convention?

The neatest and simplest way of dealing with problems posed by illegality under the lex loci solutionis would be through the application of article 7(1). Indeed, it would seem that this is what was envisaged by the drafters of the Convention.[175] Article 7(1) permits the application of the overriding rules of the law of a country with which the situation has a close connection. For the purposes of this provision, the place of performance may be regarded as having a close connection with the situation. Accordingly, a court might decide, having regard to the nature and purpose of the overriding rules of the lex loci solutionis, that the applicable law should yield to such overriding rules in a case where performance is illegal under the lex loci solutionis. However, since article 7(1) has not been implemented in the United Kingdom,[176] this avenue is not one which is open to the English courts. How, then, should the English courts deal with cases involving illegality under the lex loci solutionis?

Where the parties set out to engage in activity which involves performing an illegal act by the law of a friendly foreign country there is an argument for saying that, regardless of the applicable law, the English court should refuse to enforce the contract in order to protect the public or national interest or image of the United Kingdom.[177] With respect to cases of initial illegality, the operation

175 Giuliano-Lagarde Report, OJ 1980 C282/27.
176 Contracts (Applicable Law) Act 1990, s 2(2).
177 Carter, 'Rejection of Foreign Law: Some Private International Law Inhibitions' (1984) 55 BYIL 111 at 124.

of the principle applied in cases such as *Foster v Driscoll* does not depend on English law being the law governing the contract.[178] From this it follows that the principle, as applied in cases of initial illegality, should be regarded as an overriding rule for the purposes of article 7(2).

With regard to cases of subsequent illegality, the position is different. The judgments in the *Ralli Bros* case are somewhat ambiguous on the question of whether the relevant rule was a rule of English private international law or merely a rule of English domestic law, by which the contract was frustrated. Passages in the judgments veer between the two standpoints. In other cases, the rule has sometimes been stated in one way,[179] sometimes in the other.[180] It has been convincingly argued that the rule in *Ralli Bros* – as applied to cases of subsequent illegality – is a rule of English domestic law.[181] Whether or not a contract is frustrated is a question of substance which ought to be determined by the applicable law.[182] Subsequent illegality by the lex loci solutionis should be regarded as discharging the defendant's obligations only to the extent that those obligations are discharged under the applicable law.[183] If in *Ralli Bros* German law had been the applicable law, the effect under German law would have been that, because of the Spanish prohibition, the full freight would have become payable in London. The correct approach in such a case would be to apply the German rule, rather than to hold that the balance of the freight was not recoverable.

G Remedies and damages

The Convention expressly provides that 'evidence and procedure' are excluded from the material scope of the Convention.[184] Accordingly, the nature of the remedy which is to be granted for a breach of contract is to be determined by English law, as the lex fori, even if the contract is governed by a foreign law. In deciding whether or not to grant specific performance or an injunction the court will refer exclusively to the principles of English law.

178 *Royal Boskalis Westminster NV v Mountain* [1999] QB 674, [1997] 2 All ER 929.
179 As a conflicts rule: *Zivnostenska Banka National Corpn v Frankman* [1950] AC 57 at 79; *Sharif v Azad* [1967] 1 QB 605 at 617; *Euro-Diam Ltd v Bathurst* [1987] 2 All ER 113 at 119–120, 124–125; *Libyan Arab Foreign Bank v Bankers Trust Co* [1989] QB 728 at 743.
180 As a domestic rule: *Kahler v Midland Bank Ltd* [1950] AC 24 at 48.
181 Mann, 'The Proper Law of Contracts Concluded by International Persons' (1959) 35 BYIL 34 at 47.
182 Art 10(1)(d).
183 See Reynolds, 'Illegality by Lex Loci Solutionis' (1992) 108 LQR 553.
184 Art 1(2)(h).

At common law, the quantification of damages is treated as a procedural matter to be determined by the lex fori, rather than a substantive question for the proper law. So, if a particular type of loss is recoverable according to the proper law, it is for the English law, as the law of the forum, to determine how the amount of damages for that loss is to be assessed. The Convention provides, however, that 'within the limits of the powers conferred on the court by its procedural law' the applicable law governs 'the assessment of damages in so far as it is governed by rules of law'.[185] This provision seeks to locate a half-way house between the idea that quantification of damages is a matter for the lex fori and the view that quantification is to be determined by the applicable law. Even under the Convention, to the extent that the assessment of damages is not governed by rules of law, the measure of damages is procedural and is therefore subject to the law of the forum.

It remains to be seen what the courts will make of the Convention's approach. How, for example, should the courts treat the rules determining the following matters: whether tax that would have been payable on lost earnings is to be deducted; the time at which the loss is to be assessed; whether the claimant is entitled to the loss value of damaged property or the cost of repairing it; whether loss of value is to be assessed in relation to market value? Which, if any, of these rules are 'rules of law' for the purposes of the Convention? The suggestion has been made that these rules seem to be concerned with the extent of the rights of the party in the event of the contract being broken and hence should be decided by the applicable law, unless it is for some reason impracticable for the court to apply it.[186]

A further question to be considered relates to the currency in which the judgment should be expressed. Suppose that in an international contract of sale which is the subject of litigation in England the price of the goods sold is expressed in US dollars. Can the court give judgment for that amount in US dollars, rather than sterling? Can the court award a sum expressed in a foreign currency as damages for breach of contract? Until the 1970s the rule was that the court could give judgment only in sterling.[187] This led to injustice because of the further rule that the amount of the foreign currency had to be converted to sterling at the date when it was due – that is, the date of payment in the case of an agreed sum payable[188] and the date of breach in the case of a claim for damages.[189] If there

185 Art 10(1)(c).
186 Jaffey, *Introduction to the Conflict of Laws* (1988) p 169.
187 *Tomkinson v First Pennsylvania Banking and Trust Co* [1961] AC 1007, [1960] 2 All ER 332.
188 Ibid.
189 *Di Ferdinando v Simon, Smits & Co Ltd* [1920] 3 KB 409.

was a substantial change in the relative values of sterling and the foreign currency between the date of conversion and the judgment, one or other of the parties would be prejudiced.

The law in this respect was changed by the House of Lords in *Miliangos v George Frank (Textiles) Ltd*;[190] where a party is entitled to an amount under a contract which is expressed in a foreign currency the court will give judgment in that currency. Similarly, the court may give judgment for damages for breach of contract[191] (or for tort[192]) in a foreign currency in which the loss was sustained by the claimant. When judgment is given in a foreign currency the defendant may pay either in that currency or in the sterling equivalent at the date of actual payment. If the claimant has to enforce the judgment, the date of conversion into sterling is the date when the court authorises enforcement of the judgment.[193]

190 [1976] AC 443, [1975] 3 All ER 801.

191 *Services Europe Atlantique Sud (SEAS) v Stockholms Rederiaktiebolag Svea* [1979] AC 685, [1979] 1 All ER 421; *The Texaco Melbourne* [1994] 1 Lloyd's Rep 473.

192 *The Despina R* [1979] AC 685, [1979] 1 All ER 421.

193 *Miliangos v George Frank (Textiles) Ltd* [1976] AC 443, [1975] 3 All ER 801.

Chapter 6

Non-contractual obligations

I INTRODUCTION

The choice of law regime introduced by the Rome Convention on the Law Applicable to Contractual Obligations of 1980 applies to 'contractual obligations';[1] choice of law questions arising from non-contractual obligations are left to be answered by the national law of each of the contracting states.[2] Most cases involving non-contractual obligations are cases involving torts. Until the mid-1990s choice of law in tort was determined entirely by the common law. Part III of the Private International Law (Miscellaneous Provisions) Act 1995 introduced a statutory choice of law regime which, subject to some exceptions, applies to torts committed after the entry into force of the relevant provisions. However, not all cases involving non-contractual obligations involve tortious obligations. In English law a defendant may be personally liable by virtue of having committed an equitable wrong (such as a breach of confidence) or liability may arise through the application of the principle of unjust enrichment. While choice of law problems arising out of tortious claims have perhaps been discussed more frequently and more extensively than any other by commentators (especially by United States scholars), the conflicts aspects of equitable wrongs and the law of restitution have received the attention of courts and commentators only relatively recently.

1 Art 10(1)(e) of the Convention provides that the applicable law governs 'the consequences of nullity of the contract'. The United Kingdom entered a reservation on this provision (on the ground that the consequences of nullity are part of the law of restitution) and art 10(1)(e) was not implemented into English law: Contracts (Applicable Law) Act 1990, s 2(2).

2 One of the priorities laid down by the Action Plan drawn up in Vienna in December 1998 (OJ 1999 C19/1) concerned the feasibility and advisability of introducing European legislation on the law applicable to non-contractual obligations ('Rome II').

II CHOICE OF LAW IN TORT: INTRODUCTION

Before the development of the English choice of law rules is considered, the various possible approaches which the law might take should be outlined. The obvious starting-point in tort cases is the law of the country in which the tort occurs (lex loci delicti). In the simple case where an English motorist injures an Italian pedestrian in a road accident in Italy, it seems reasonable that the driver's liability should be determined by Italian law: when in Rome do as the Romans do. It is widely accepted that, as a general rule, a person's criminal liability should be determined by the law of the country in which the alleged crime occurs. Although the analogy between tort and crime is by no means exact, the law of the place where the tort was committed is the natural applicable law. In most cases both parties might, if they applied their minds to the question, reasonably anticipate that liability in tort would be governed by the lex loci delicti.

The basic appeal of the lex loci delicti does not mean, however, that the law of the country in which the tort occurs should invariably govern or that it should govern all aspects of a tortious situation. In most cases the application of the lex loci delicti will produce a just solution. It would perhaps always be right to apply the lex loci delicti in the usual case where one or both of the parties belong to the country where the tort is committed. Then a party who acts, or is injured, in his own country will not be deprived of the protection of his own law, while if he loses he can have no complaint of injustice if his own law is applied against him. Equally, a foreign party can have no cause for complaint if he is subjected to the lex loci delicti in such a case. Where, however, both parties belong to the same country, which is not that in which the tort was committed, justice may often be served better by applying the law of that country.

The idea that the lex loci delicti should normally be the applicable law, but that some other law might be more appropriate in particular cases, leads to the suggestion that issues in tort should be governed by the 'proper law of the tort' – that is, the law of the country with which the tort is most closely connected – just as issues in contract, in the absence of choice by the parties, are governed by the law of the country with which the contract is most closely connected.[3]

Flexible approaches to choice of law in tort have been widely adopted in the United States. Originally the rule in most states was simply that the lex loci delicti governed, but it came to be accepted that the automatic application of that law in all circumstances could

3 Morris, 'The Proper Law of the Tort' (1951) 64 Harv LR 881.

lead to inappropriate decisions. The general principle adopted by the Second Restatement of the Conflict of Laws is that:

> the rights and liabilities of the parties with respect to an issue in tort are determined by the local law of the state which, as to that issue, has the most significant relationship to the occurrence and the parties.[4]

It can be seen that the reference is not to a proper law which will necessarily govern all issues which may arise from a tort; rather, the significant relationship must be assessed with regard to the particular issue. For example, the same law would not necessarily be applicable both to the question whether the defendant's conduct was wrongful and to the question whether the claimant is entitled to recover for a particular type of loss.

As with contract, the difficulty with the proper law approach is to identify the criteria which make one law more appropriate than another in given circumstances. While there are many different views to be found among United States writers, a common emphasis is on the need to identify the purpose or policy of the relevant rules of the possibly applicable laws in deciding which of them should be applied. If, on analysis, it is found that the facts of the particular case do not come within the purpose or policy of the rule of one country, there is no good reason to apply it, even if it is a rule of the lex loci delicti; it is better in such a case to apply the rule of another country within whose policy the case does fall. United States courts and writers often speak in this context in terms of the 'interests' of states or governments; if the case comes within the policy of the relevant rule of a particular state, that state has an 'interest' in its rule being applied.[5]

A look at a few well-known cases will give an impression of United States approaches. The starting-point for the revolution in United States thinking about choice of law in tort was the celebrated case of *Babcock v Jackson*.[6] The plaintiff and the defendant were both residents of the state of New York. They went on a trip together to Ontario in the defendant's car and, while there, the plaintiff was injured as a result of the defendant's negligent driving. The plaintiff sued the defendant in New York. Under the law of Ontario the defendant was not liable because of Ontario's 'guest statute', under which a driver was not liable for injury caused negligently to a gratuitous passenger. The defendant was, however, liable under the law of New York, which had no such statute.

4 S 145.
5 See further pp 568–573.
6 12 NY 2d 473 (1963). The decision was also reported in England: [1963] 2 Lloyd's Rep 286.

The New York Court of Appeals rejected the traditional view that liability in tort is necessarily governed by the lex loci delicti, here the law of Ontario. It held instead that the issue whether the driver was liable to his gratuitous passenger should be decided by the law of the country which, in relation to that issue, had the most significant relationship with the events and the parties. Which country that was depended on the purposes and the relevant rules of the laws of Ontario and New York. What was the purpose of the Ontario guest statute? One purpose was to prevent the fraudulent assertion of claims by passengers, in collusion with drivers, against insurance companies. Another purpose was to protect drivers of cars from an unfair liability to passengers to whom they had given a free lift. Which insurance companies and which drivers would the Ontario statute have been concerned to protect? Those from Ontario, not those from New York, as the driver and his insurer were in this case. As Fuld J, who gave the leading judgment, said:

> Whether New York defendants are imposed upon or their insurers defrauded by a New York plaintiff is scarcely a valid legislative concern of Ontario simply because the accident occurred there, any more so than if the accident had happened in some other jurisdiction.[7]

The case did, however, fall within the policy of the New York rule, the purpose of which was to ensure that even gratuitous passengers were fully compensated. In the circumstances of the case there was every reason for applying New York law. So, the plaintiff succeeded, notwithstanding the fact the defendant was not liable according to the lex loci delicti. It should be added, however, that the court was at pains to stress that, had the issue been a different one, the law of Ontario might have had the most significant relationship. If, for example, the issue had been the manner in which the defendant had been driving the law of Ontario would have been the applicable law.

In *Reich v Purcell*[8] the plaintiff and his wife lived in Ohio. When driving her car through Missouri, the plaintiff's wife was killed in a collision caused by the negligence of the defendant, who lived in California. The plaintiff sued in California for damages for the wrongful death of his wife. By the laws of Ohio, Missouri and California the defendant was liable for such damages. However, a Missouri statute limited the damages recoverable for wrongful death to $25,000. Under the laws of Ohio and California the plaintiff was entitled to his full loss, which the court assessed at $55,000. The court held that the law of Ohio should be applied. The purpose of the statute of Missouri, where the tort was committed,

7 [1963] 2 Lloyd's Rep 286 at 290.
8 432 P 2d 727 (1967).

was to protect defendants, by avoiding the imposition of excessive financial burdens on them. However, Missouri's concern would be for Missouri defendants, not defendants from other states (such as California), so Missouri had no interest in its rule being applied. By contrast, Ohio did have an interest in its rule being applied, for the purpose of the rule was to secure full compensation for the surviving spouse of a person wrongfully killed and, in this case, the deceased and her husband came from Ohio. The purpose of the Californian rule was the same as the purpose of the Ohio rule, but California had no interest in the application of its rule, because neither the deceased nor the plaintiff had any connection with California. So, the plaintiff was awarded full compensation under the law of Ohio, which was the only state with an interest in the situation.

In *Babcock v Jackson* and *Reich v Purcell* no doubt the right result was reached on grounds which at first sight may seem plausible. In each case the court was able to hold that there was a 'false conflict' since only one state had an interest in the application of its rule. What, however, is to be done if it turns out that more than one country has an interest? One possibility would be to say that if one of the countries having an interest is the court's own country, the court should prefer the policies of its own law.[9] What if the forum state has no interest, but others do (as would have been the case in *Reich v Purcell* if the defendant had been a resident of Missouri) or if the court is not convinced that it should necessarily prefer the policy of its own law? Should the court apply the law of the country whose interest is the greater (on the basis of the 'comparative impairment' theory[10]) or the lex loci delicti or some other law?

The apparent simplicity of cases such as *Babcock v Jackson* hides the fact that there may be the greatest difficulty in deciding what the policy or purpose of a given rule is. Consider the converse of *Babcock v Jackson*: the driver and his gratuitous passenger (both from Ontario) are involved in an accident in New York. The passenger sues in New York. Ontario would have an interest in its guest statute being applied. Would New York have an interest in its rule, that the gratuitous passenger is entitled to compensation, being applied? If the purpose of the rule is regarded as being only to secure compensation for the victim of an accident, it could be argued that New York has no concern whether or not an Ontario plaintiff is compensated by an Ontario defendant. But perhaps it is also a

9 Currie, 'Notes on Methods and Objectives in the Conflict of Laws' in *Selected Essays on the Conflict of Laws* (1963).

10 Baxter, 'Choice of Law and the Federal System' (1963) 16 Stan LR 1. This approach was applied in *Bernhard v Harrah's Club* 16 Cal 3d 313, 546 P 2d 719 (1976).

purpose of the New York rule of liability to deter negligent driving. Then, of course, New York will have an interest in its rule being applied to an accident in New York, wherever the parties come from. Then both countries have an interest. On such facts the New York court in *Krell v Henderson*[11] applied New York law.

The opposite situation is where neither country is found to have an interest: the case comes within the purpose of neither country's rule. That would be the position if a New York driver gave a gratuitous lift to an Ontario passenger in Ontario – as long as it is assumed that the purposes of the Ontario statute are to protect drivers and insurers and of the New York rule to secure compensation for injured passengers and to promote safe driving in New York. In such a case, the New York court in *Neumeier v Kuehner*[12] applied Ontario law as the lex loci delicti.

Quite apart from the difficulties of discerning the purposes and policies of rules of law, the odd conclusion that the facts of a case may fall within the purpose of neither country's rule suggests the possibility that this whole way of looking at things may be misconceived. Apart from the purpose which a rule may have of protecting or advancing the public interest – for example, by deterring dangerous conduct – is it not the purpose of tort rules to achieve justice between the individuals involved in a dispute? To describe the purpose of a rule which, for example, limits the amount of damages recoverable as being to protect the defendant or a rule which imposes no such limit as protecting the claimant, is only a manner of speaking; such rules simply fix the balance between the parties in the particular circumstances in a particular way. On that basis, the case will of course come within the purpose of the relevant rule of every country. That is precisely why choice of law rules are needed to determine which country's domestic standards of justice are to be applied.

III CHOICE OF LAW IN TORT: THE COMMON LAW RULES

Notwithstanding the enactment of the Private International Law (Miscellaneous Provisions) Act 1995 there are two types of case which are still governed by the common law rules. First, the common law choice of law rules are applicable in cases involving defamation claims falling within the scope of section 13 of the 1995

11 270 NYS 2d 552 (1960).
12 286 NE 2d 454 (1972).

Act.[13] It is provided that the statutory choice of law rules do not apply to 'the determination of issues arising in any defamation claim'[14] which is defined as a claim 'for libel, slander, slander of title, slander of goods or other malicious falsehood' and 'any claim under the law of any other country corresponding to or otherwise in the nature of' such a claim.[15] Secondly, the statutory rules apply only to events which occurred after the entry into force of Part III of the 1995 Act; the common law still applies to any tort committed before 1 May 1996.[16]

The common law cases may well also have an indirect effect on the determination of some issues arising under the 1995 Act. For example, the basic structure of the common law (a general rule and an exception) is replicated by section 11 (a general rule) and section 12 (an exception); it is quite likely therefore that the common law authorities will help the courts in working out the relationship between sections 11 and 12 of the 1995 Act.

A The place of the tort

The English cases establish that, if the tort occurs in England, English law applies, irrespective of whether the case has strong connections with a foreign country.[17] If, however, the tort occurs abroad, the applicable law is determined in accordance with the rule in *Phillips v Eyre*[18] (as adapted by subsequent cases). Accordingly, the first issue to consider, at common law, is the place where the tort occurs (locus delicti).

In many situations the locus delicti is simple to determine: it is the country in which the defendant commits the wrongful act and in which the harm is suffered by the claimant. The position is slightly more complicated in a case where the defendant acts in one country and the victim suffers harm in another. A product manufactured in one country may cause injury to a consumer in another; financial advice given by the defendant in one country may be relied upon by the claimant in a different country. In this type of case the locus delicti is to be determined by answering the following question:

13 S 9(3). For consideration of why defamation claims were excluded from the 1995 Act see pp 270–271.
14 S 13(1).
15 S 13(2).
16 SI 1996/995.
17 *Szalatnay-Stacho v Fink* [1947] KB 1, [1946] 2 All ER 231; *Metall und Rohstoff AG v Donaldson Lufkin & Jenrette Inc* [1990] 1 QB 391, [1989] 3 All ER 14.
18 (1870) LR 6 QB 1.

where in substance did the cause of action arise?[19] Such an open-textured question gives the courts considerable room to manoeuvre as a consequence of which it is impossible to lay down hard and fast rules. Where, for example, a claimant is injured in England by machinery manufactured in Germany, the locus delicti is England on the ground that the substantial wrongdoing is putting a defective machine on the English market with no warning as to its defects;[20] if a United States bank gives negligent advice to a claimant, who receives and acts upon the advice in London, the locus delicti is England;[21] where a libel is contained in a letter written by the defendant abroad, but received by the addressee in London, the place of the tort is England, where the defamatory material is published.[22]

B The development of the common law rules

1. The nineteenth-century cases

In *The Halley*[23] a collision occurred in Belgian territorial waters between a ship owned by a Norwegian plaintiff and one owned by an English defendant. The collision was due to the negligence of a compulsory pilot on the defendant's ship. The plaintiff sued the defendant in England for damages. Under Belgian law, the lex loci delicti, the defendant was vicariously liable for the pilot's negligence, but under English law at that time the defendant was not. It was held that the defendant was not liable because liability was not imposed by English law. So, the rule was established that, whatever the foreign elements in the case may be, a defendant is not liable in tort in English proceedings unless his conduct was actionable by English law.

In *Phillips v Eyre*[24] the defendant was the Governor of Jamaica. In the course of putting down a rebellion there, he arrested and imprisoned the plaintiff. The actions would have amounted to battery and false imprisonment under Jamaican law, as well as English law, but for the fact that the Jamaican legislature subsequently

19 The question was formulated, in the context of a jurisdiction case, by Lord Pearson in *Distillers Co (Biochemicals) Ltd v Thompson* [1971] AC 458 at 468. It was subsequently applied both to jurisdiction and choice of law issues. See, in particular, *Metall und Rohstoff AG v Donaldson Lufkin & Jenrette Inc* [1990] 1 QB 391, [1989] 3 All ER 14.

20 *Castree v ER Squibb & Sons Ltd* [1980] 2 All ER 589, [1980] 1 WLR 1248.

21 *The Albaforth* [1984] 2 Lloyd's Rep 91.

22 *Bata v Bata* [1948] WN 366.

23 (1868) LR 2 PC 193.

24 (1870) LR 6 QB 1.

passed legislation which had the effect of retrospectively making the defendant's acts lawful. So, on the facts of the case, the defendant was liable according to English law, but not under the lex loci delicti. In the course of his judgment Willes J formulated the following proposition, which has come to be known as the rule in *Phillips v Eyre*:

> As a general rule, in order to found a suit in England for a wrong alleged to have been committed abroad, two conditions must be fulfilled. First, the wrong must be of such a character that it would have been actionable if committed in England. ... Secondly, the act must not have been justifiable by the law of the place where it was done.[25]

According to this rule, the wrong must be *actionable* by English law (the first branch of *Phillips v Eyre*) and *not justifiable* by the lex loci delicti (the second branch of *Phillips v Eyre*). In *Machado v Fontes*[26] (a case which has since been overruled) the Court of Appeal interpreted the rule to mean that the second branch is satisfied whether the defendant's act gives rise to civil or criminal liability. This interpretation led to the surprising conclusion that the plaintiff recovered damages in England for a libel published abroad even though, according to the law of the place of publication, libel was a criminal offence which did not give rise to civil liability.

If all that is necessary under the second branch of *Phillips v Eyre* is that the conduct should in some sense be legally wrongful by the lex loci delicti, it follows that liability is primarily governed by English law. The effect of *Machado v Fontes* was that, so long as the conduct was not justifiable by the lex loci delicti, all issues as to liability or defences were for English law to decide; they could hardly be for the lex loci delicti to decide given that civil liability by that law was not even necessary.

2. *Twentieth-century developments*

(A) INTRODUCTION: *CHAPLIN V BOYS*

In the 1960s the English courts were presented with an opportunity to reconsider the rule in *Phillips v Eyre*.[27] In *Chaplin v Boys*[28] the plaintiff and the defendant were both members of the British armed forces, resident in England. While both were temporarily stationed in Malta, they were involved in a road accident in which the plaintiff was injured as a result of the defendant's negligence. The plaintiff

25 At 28–29.
26 [1897] 2 QB 231.
27 (1870) LR 6 QB 1.
28 [1971] AC 356, [1969] 2 All ER 1085.

sued the defendant in England. Under the laws of England and Malta the defendant was liable to the plaintiff. Under Maltese law, however, the plaintiff was entitled to recover only pecuniary loss which amounted in this case to £53, whereas by English law the plaintiff was also entitled to recover damages for pain and suffering and loss of amenity, which the trial judge assessed at £2,250.

At first instance the plaintiff succeeded in recovering for his pecuniary and non-pecuniary losses. The defendant's conduct was actionable according to English law and was not justifiable under Maltese law; on the basis of *Machado v Fontes*,[29] the fact that the defendant was not liable for non-pecuniary losses was irrelevant. The Court of Appeal (by a majority) and the House of Lords (unanimously) concurred in the result, but for so many different reasons that it is not easy to determine the ratio decidendi of the case. A number of propositions are, however, reasonably uncontroversial.

First, a majority of the House of Lords overruled *Machado v Fontes* and reinterpreted the rule in *Phillips v Eyre*. Secondly, a differently constituted majority favoured the notion that the rule in *Phillips v Eyre* was a general rule to which there should be a flexible exception. However, the precise nature of the exception is less clear. Thirdly, a majority decided that whether or not the plaintiff could recover damages for non-pecuniary losses was a question of substance to be determined by the applicable law, rather than a question of procedure regulated by the law of the forum. Fourthly, whatever may technically be the ratio of *Chaplin v Boys*, in subsequent cases the courts have regarded the speech of Lord Wilberforce as setting out the approach to be followed.[30]

(B) THE GENERAL RULE: DOUBLE ACTIONABILITY

In *Chaplin v Boys* a majority of the House of Lords decided that, as a general rule, a plaintiff could recover damages for a tort committed abroad only if the defendant's conduct was actionable under English law and the lex loci delicti. According to Lord Wilberforce, at common law, the general rule requires 'actionability as a tort according to English law, subject to the condition that civil liability in respect of the relevant claim exists as between the actual parties under the law of the country where the act was done'.[31] Under this

29 [1897] 2 QB 231.

30 See, for example, *Church of Scientology of California v Metropolitan Police Comr* (1976) 120 Sol Jo 690; *Coupland v Arabian Gulf Petroleum Co* [1983] 3 All ER 226, [1983] 1 WLR 1136.

31 [1971] AC 356 at 389.

revised interpretation of the rule in *Phillips v Eyre*[32] the defendant is liable only to the extent that he is liable under both the law of the forum and the lex loci delicti; moreover, not only must the defendant be civilly liable to the claimant under both laws, he must also be liable in respect of the particular loss claimed by the claimant. In adopting this approach the House of Lords overruled *Machado v Fontes*[33] and followed the interpretation of the rule in *Phillips v Eyre* favoured by the Scottish courts.[34]

It is important to stress that, for the purposes of the double actionability rule, it is the position as between the actual parties in the particular circumstances of the case which determines whether or not the defendant's conduct is actionable. If the defendant has a defence under either the lex loci delicti or the lex fori this will have the effect of barring the claim. For example, if contributory negligence is a complete defence under the lex loci delicti the claimant will lose, even if the lex fori provides for apportionment.[35] Similarly, to succeed the claimant must be entitled under both laws and each kind of loss must be recoverable under both laws.

The interpretation of the *Phillips v Eyre* rule in *Machado v Fontes* was legitimately criticised on the basis that it encouraged forum-shopping and ran the risk of causing injustice to defendants, by imposing liability in cases where the defendant's conduct did not give rise to civil liability according to the lex loci delicti. Although the rejection of *Machado v Fontes* by the House of Lords is not difficult to understand, the adoption of the Scottish approach is not without its problems, since the double actionability rule goes to the other extreme and gives the claimant the worst of both worlds. If, for example, the limitation period has expired under either the lex loci delicti or the lex fori, the effect of the double actionability rule is to bar the claim for lapse of time. The classic illustration of the injustice to which the double actionability rule can give rise is the Scottish case of *M'Elroy v M'Allister*.[36] The pursuer's husband was killed when the lorry in which he was a passenger was involved in a road accident caused by the negligence of the defender. The parties were Scottish and, although England was the locus delicti, the accident occurred while the pursuer's husband was travelling

32 (1870) LR 6 QB 1.
33 [1897] 2 QB 231.
34 *M'Elroy v M'Allister* 1949 SC 110; *Mackinnon v Iberia Shipping Co* [1954] 2 Lloyd's Rep 372.
35 *Anderson v Eric Anderson Radio and TV Pty Ltd* (1966) 114 CLR 20 (an Australian case in which the lex fori denied recovery but the lex loci delicti provided for apportionment).
36 1949 SC 110.

between two Scottish towns. The pursuer sued the defender for damages in Scotland. By Scots law the pursuer had a claim for damages for her bereavement, but by English law, as it then stood, she did not. Accordingly, this claim failed under the second branch of the rule in *Phillips v Eyre*. By English law the pursuer, in her capacity as the deceased's executrix, had an action on behalf of his estate for loss of expectation of life, but by Scots law such a claim did not survive the death of her husband. So, this claim failed under the first branch of *Phillips v Eyre*. Under both laws, the pursuer had a claim for loss of support, but for the fact that under the English Fatal Accidents Acts the action was time-barred. This claim therefore failed under the second branch of the rule in *Phillips v Eyre*. The effect of the application of the double actionability rule was that the pursuer, who had a substantial claim under each law separately, recovered only a small amount for funeral expenses, the only head of damage which was common to both English and Scots law, for which the defender admitted liability.

The application of the double actionability rule to the facts of *Chaplin v Boys* would lead to the conclusion that the plaintiff's claim for non-pecuniary losses would fail because they were not recoverable by Maltese law, the lex loci delicti. The solution to this undesirable state of affairs was the formulation of an exception to the double actionability rule.

(C) THE EXCEPTION

Once it is decided that there should be an exception to the double actionability rule the question arises as to what form the exception should take. Perhaps not surprisingly, the House of Lords in *Chaplin v Boys*[37] was influenced, up to a point, by developments which had occurred in the United States. The exception which was envisaged was on the lines of the American Second Restatement: 'The rights and liabilities of the parties with respect to an issue in tort are determined by the local law of the state which, as to that issue, has the most significant relationship to the occurrence and the parties.'[38] There is no suggestion in the House of Lords that the proper law approach should become the general rule; rather the view was that, where the application of the double actionability rule would lead to an unjust decision, a particular issue may, by way of exception, be governed by a single law. Lord Wilberforce indicated that 'the general rule must apply unless clear and satisfying grounds are

37 [1971] AC 356.
38 S 145.

shown why it should be departed from'.[39] *Chaplin v Boys*, however, was a suitable case in which to apply the exception. The issue was whether a particular kind of loss was recoverable; it was appropriate to apply English law to that issue given that England was the country to which both parties belonged. Accordingly, the plaintiff was entitled to recover damages for non-pecuniary losses, even though such recovery was denied by Maltese law.

In the course of his speech in *Chaplin v Boys* Lord Wilberforce said:

> I think that the necessary flexibility can be obtained ... through segregation of the relevant issue and consideration whether, in relation to that issue, the relevant foreign rule ought, as a matter of policy ... to be applied. For this purpose it is necessary to identify the policy of the rule, to inquire to what situations, with what contacts, it was intended to apply; whether not to apply it, in the circumstances of the instant case, would serve any interest which the rule was devised to meet.[40]

There are two points to note about this passage. First, the exception seeks to identify the law appropriate to a particular issue; different laws could be applicable to different issues in the same case. Secondly, Lord Wilberforce seems to favour United States interest analysis rather than the 'centre of gravity' approach which has traditionally been applied in contract cases.[41] It can perhaps be gleaned from his speech that the general rule should not be departed from unless it is found that only one country's law has an interest to be applied. So, if in *Chaplin v Boys* the defendant, or both of the parties, had been Maltese the claim for non-pecuniary losses would have been rejected on the application of Maltese law.[42]

In subsequent cases the courts accepted that the position at common law is a rule of double actionability subject to a limited exception. In *Johnson v Coventry Churchill International Ltd*,[43] for example, the plaintiff was an English carpenter employed by the defendant, an English company, to work on a construction site in Germany. The plaintiff, who was injured while working in Germany, sought to recover compensation for his injuries and sued the defendant in England. The first branch of the rule in *Phillips v Eyre*[44] was satisfied: the alleged default of the defendant would have amounted to a tort under English law had the events occurred in England. The plaintiff's claim would have failed,

39 [1971] AC 356 at 391.
40 Ibid.
41 See p 198.
42 [1971] AC 356 at 379, 382.
43 [1992] 3 All ER 14.
44 (1870) LR 6 QB 1.

however, under the second branch of the general rule because German law provides that an employer is not normally civilly liable for injuries suffered by an employee at work, the employee being compensated through a system of social security payments. In these circumstances it was held that, given that both parties were English, the application of the German rule denying recovery would not serve any interest which the rule was devised to meet. Furthermore, England was clearly the country which had the most significant relationship with the occurrence and the parties. Accordingly, this was one of the limited number of cases envisaged by Lord Wilberforce in which justice dictated the application of English law to the issue before the court.

More significantly, some of the uncertainties surrounding the exception were considered by the Privy Council in *Red Sea Insurance Co Ltd v Bouygues SA*.[45] In *Chaplin v Boys* the application of the exception led to the segregated issue being governed by English law; English law also applied by way of exception in *Johnson v Coventry Churchill International Ltd*. In the *Red Sea Insurance* case the central question was whether a defendant can rely purely on the lex loci delicti to establish liability in tort when the lex fori does not recognise such liability. The Privy Council decided that, although the application of the lex loci delicti to the exclusion of the lex fori is a departure from the strict rule in *The Halley*,[46] in principle the exception can be applied in an appropriate case to enable a claimant to rely exclusively on the lex loci delicti.[47] Although the *Red Sea Insurance* case does not directly address the question whether the general rule can be displaced in favour of the law of a third country, the logic of the decision is that, in an appropriate case, it can.

The other question raised by *Red Sea Insurance Co Ltd v Bouygues SA* was whether the whole case, as opposed to an isolated issue, can be decided according to the lex loci delicti (or the lex fori), rather than by the general rule. The Privy Council decided that, although the application of the exception to the whole case is not likely to happen very frequently, the exception is not limited to specific isolated issues but may apply to the whole claim (for example, where all or virtually all of the significant factors point towards the locus delicti).[48]

45 [1995] 1 AC 190.
46 (1868) LR 2 PC 193.
47 At 206.
48 At 207.

IV CHOICE OF LAW IN TORT: THE 1995 ACT

A Introduction

1. Background of the statutory rules

Notwithstanding the reinterpretation of *Phillips v Eyre* by the House of Lords in *Chaplin v Boys*,[49] the common law choice of law rules display a strikingly parochial character. The double actionability rule gives the predominant role to English law, even though the tort was committed abroad, and regardless of whether either party is English; because of the first branch of the rule in *Phillips v Eyre*,[50] the defendant cannot be liable unless he is liable under English law. It is not obvious why this should be the case. Suppose an English driver, while on a visit to Germany, runs down a pedestrian. The driver was not at fault, but under German law the liability of the driver of a motor vehicle is strict. If the pedestrian sues the driver in England the application of the double actionability rule means that he will lose. But, it would not be unjust to the English driver to impose on him liability under the law of the country which he chose to visit, while it seems unjust to the pedestrian who was injured in his own country that he should be deprived of the remedy given by that law.

Dissatisfaction with the common law rules led to a review of choice of law in tort by the Law Commission in the 1980s[51] and led ultimately to the enactment of Part III of the Private International Law (Miscellaneous Provisions) Act 1995.[52] The essence of the Law Commission's proposals was to replace the double actionability rule with a general rule that the lex loci delicti alone should govern, but to retain an exception to the general rule along the lines of the 'proper law' exception. Section 11 of the 1995 Act sets out the general rule that a tort should be governed by the law of the country in which the events (or most significant events) constituting the tort occurred. By way of exception, section 12 provides that the general rule should be displaced in favour of the law of another country if it would be substantially more appropriate to apply the law of that other country.

49 [1971] AC 356.

50 (1870) LR 6 QB 1.

51 Law Com Working Paper No 87, *Choice of Law in Tort and Delict* (1984); Law Com No 193, *Choice of Law in Tort and Delict* (1990).

52 See Briggs, 'Choice of Law in Tort and Delict' [1995] LMCLQ 519; Morse, 'Torts in Private International Law: A New Statutory Framework' (1996) 45 ICLQ 888.

2. The scope of the statutory rules

(A) ISSUES RELATING TO TORT

The choice of law rules set out in the 1995 Act apply to determine the applicable law in relation to 'issues relating to tort'.[53] In accordance with the general rule that questions of classification are to be determined by the lex fori, the Private International Law (Miscellaneous Provisions) Act 1995 provides that the characterisation of issues arising in a claim as issues relating to tort is a matter for the courts of the forum.[54] What, then, are issues relating to tort for the purposes of the Act?

First, the Act obviously applies to those areas which are regarded as tortious for the purposes of English domestic law. The fact that there exists a contractual relationship between the parties to a dispute does not preclude the possibility of the claimant suing the defendant in tort, and relying on the relevant tort choice of law rules, if the alleged wrong amounts to a tort as well as a breach of contract.[55]

Secondly, the statutory scheme must also extend to wrongs which, although they do not give rise to tortious liability under English domestic law, are to be classified as torts for the purposes of English private international law. There is, of course, no common law authority on what types of wrong may fall within this category; under the double actionability rule if the alleged wrong is not actionable as a tort under English law the claim fails. It is therefore not easy to predict how the courts will deal with claims based on wrongs which are recognised by a foreign law but which have no obvious counterpart in English law. However, the statutory rules ought to apply, for example, to claims for damages for invasion of privacy or for seduction, notwithstanding the fact that there are no such torts in English law, on the basis that the claims are 'tort-like' and are obviously neither contractual nor founded on unjust enrichment.

Thirdly, there is uncertainty as to whether the statutory scheme applies to equitable wrongs which are not regarded by English domestic law as torts, but which are analogous to torts. It would, for example, not be unreasonable to apply the statutory scheme to a case involving an alleged breach of confidence. However, whether this is authorised by the Act, and what the choice of law rule would be if the Act does not apply, is not clear.[56]

53 S 9(1).
54 S 9(2).
55 *Matthews v Kuwait Bechtel Corpn* [1959] 2 QB 57, [1959] 2 All ER 345; *Coupland v Arabian Gulf Oil Co* [1983] 3 All ER 226, [1983] 1 WLR 1136. For the possible impact of the contract on the claim in tort see pp 281–284.
56 This issue is discussed further at pp 288–289.

(B) TORTS WHICH OCCUR IN ENGLAND

Does the statutory regime apply to torts committed in England? Section 9(6) of the Private International Law (Miscellaneous Provisions) Act 1995 provides as follows:

> For the avoidance of doubt (and without prejudice to the operation of section 14 below) this Part applies in relation to events occurring in the forum as it applies in relation to events occurring in any other country.

While, prime facie, this provision seems to indicate that the statutory choice of law regime applies regardless of where the alleged tort was committed, section 9(6) is expressly made subject to section 14 which provides, inter alia, that '[n]othing in this Part affects any rules of law (including rules of private international law) except those abolished by section 10 above'.[57] Whatever else may be obscure about the 1995 Act, section 10 is quite clear. It abolishes only two rules: the double actionability rule and the common law exception to it. Where does this leave the common law rule that, as regards torts committed in England, English law is invariably the applicable law?[58] There are two possible answers to this question.

One view is that, although section 9(6) states – as a general principle – that the Act applies to events wherever they take place, this principle is almost entirely negated by the combined effect of section 14, section 10 and the pre-Act common law rules. If this is the correct view, to determine whether or not the statutory scheme is applicable, the first question which has to be addressed is: did the tort occur in England?[59] If the question is answered affirmatively, English law applies; if negatively, the statutory choice of law rules determine the applicable law.

The alternative approach takes as its starting-point the view that the common law rule to the effect that English law governs torts which occur in England is not an independent rule but a necessary consequence of the double actionability rule. According to this approach, the abolition of the double actionability rule by section 10 also has the effect of abolishing its consequences – including the inflexible rule that torts committed in England are governed by the law of the forum. Notwithstanding these potential difficulties, the courts have accepted that the choice of law regime introduced by the 1995 Act applies to torts committed in England as well as to those committed abroad.[60]

57 Sub-s (2).
58 *Szalatnay-Stacho v Fink* [1947] KB 1, [1946] 2 All ER 231; *Metall und Rohstoff AG v Donaldson Lufkin & Jenrette Inc* [1990] 1 QB 391, [1989] 3 All ER 14.
59 For the relevant common law approach to this question see pp 259–260.
60 See *Roerig v Valiant Trawlers Ltd* [2002] EWCA Civ 21, [2002] 1 All ER 961.

(C) THE EXCLUSION OF DEFAMATION CLAIMS

It has already been noted that defamation claims are excluded from the scope of the statutory rules.[61] This exclusion is a result of pressure brought to bear by the press following the publication of the bill. When the bill first appeared it caused a furore in the newspapers; it even provoked a hostile editorial in *The Times*.[62]

The central plank of the reform was the replacement of the double actionability rule with the rule that the lex loci delicti is the law applicable to a tort. Because certain regimes are not adverse to using local libel laws as a means of stifling press criticism, the newspapers feared that the reform might expose them to liability for libel in English proceedings as a result of circulation in foreign countries.

Suppose an English newspaper, which is circulated in countries throughout the world, runs a story alleging that the president of Ruritania has unlawfully rigged the local parliamentary elections. The president brings proceedings in England alleging libel. Whereas under English law the newspaper may plead justification and fair comment, no such defences are available under Ruritanian law. Under the double actionability rule the newspaper has little to fear. Liability cannot be imposed for a tort committed abroad unless the defendant would be liable according to English law; as long as the newspaper has a good defence under English law the libel claim is bound to fail. What, however, would be the position under the Private International Law (Miscellaneous Provisions) Act 1995? The newspapers were concerned that, in this type of case, the statutory regime would require the court to apply Ruritanian law, as the lex loci delicti, with the consequence that defences provided by English law would not be available.

It might be questioned whether the newspapers' fears were fully justified. First, there is an argument for saying that, for the purposes of the 1995 Act, where a newspaper is produced in England and circulated in Ruritania, English law should be the applicable law on the basis that the most significant elements of the events constituting the tort occurred in England.[63] Secondly, even if Ruritanian law is the applicable law, the 1995 Act provides that the court shall not apply a foreign law if to do so would conflict with principles of public policy.[64] It is at least arguable that the application of a foreign law which has the effect of imposing civil liability for publishing the truth

61 Ss 9(3) and 13.

62 19 January 1995.

63 S 11(2)(c). At common law, however, there is authority for the proposition that the tort occurs where the defamatory statement is published: *Bata v Bata* [1948] WN 366.

64 S 14(3)(a)(i).

on questions of legitimate public concern would be contrary to English public policy.

It is understandable, however, that English newspapers preferred the certainties of the double actionability rule to the uncertainties of the proposed statutory regime. Because of the hostility demonstrated by the press the bill was hastily amended to exclude defamation claims from its scope.

(D) THE EXCLUSION OF THE DOCTRINE OF RENVOI

Just as the Rome Convention includes a provision which excludes the doctrine of renvoi from the choice of law regime which applies to contractual obligations, the Private International Law (Miscellaneous Provisions) Act 1995 includes a similar provision excluding the doctrine of renvoi from the tort regime. Section 9(5) provides that the applicable law to be used for determining the issues arising in a tort claim 'shall exclude any choice of law rules forming part of the law of the country or countries concerned'. So, if a claimant is injured in a road accident in Italy and, according to the 1995 Act, Italian law is the applicable law, the rights of the claimant as against the defendant are to be determined by Italian tort law, even if Italian choice of law rules would stipulate that the law of another country should be the applicable law.

B The general rule

The Private International Law (Miscellaneous Provisions) Act 1995 abolishes the double actionability rule and the common law exception.[65] As already noted, this abolition of the common law rules does not apply to defamation claims falling within section 13. The general rule is to be found in section 11. This provision draws a distinction between cases in which the events constituting the tort occur in a single country and cases in which those events occur in two or more countries. In effect, though not in form, the general rule in section 11 is that a tort is governed by the lex loci delicti.

The simplest situation is where the events constituting a tort occur in a single country. In this case the applicable law under the general rule is the law of that country.[66] So, if a French driver negligently runs down an English tourist in Scotland, the applicable law under the general rule is Scots law.

65 S 10.

66 S 11(1). See *Glencore International AG v Metro Trading International Inc* [2001] 1 Lloyd's Rep 284 (an interference with goods case).

In situations where elements of the events constituting the tort occur in different countries a choice has to be made between adopting a rigid rule based on a single connecting factor or a more flexible rule. If a rigid rule is adopted a further question arises: which connecting factor should be used – the place where the defendant committed the wrongful act or the place where the victim suffered the injury? The 1995 Act adopts different approaches to different types of claim. With regard to cases involving personal injury or property damage a rigid rule is adopted as the general rule; in other cases a more flexible general rule is advocated.

First, if the cause of action is 'in respect of personal injury caused to an individual or death resulting from such personal injury', the general rule is that the applicable law is 'the law of the country where the individual was when he sustained the injury'.[67] So, if the defendant, a chemical manufacturer, negligently releases poisonous fumes into the atmosphere as a consequence of which X suffers personal injury in Belgium and Y suffers personal injury in the Netherlands, the general rule provides that X's claim is governed by Belgian law, whereas Y's claim is governed by Dutch law.

Secondly, if the cause of action is 'in respect of damage to property', the general rule is that the applicable law is 'the law of the country where the property was when it was damaged'.[68] So, if a French manufacturer discharges pollution into the Rhine as a consequence of which a Dutch horticulturist's plants are damaged, the applicable law is, according to the general rule, Dutch law (rather than French law).

Thirdly, section 11(2)(c) provides that, in any other case, the applicable law under the general rule is 'the law of the country in which the most significant element or elements of [the events constituting the tort] occurred'. It is this third rule which is most likely to generate problems in practice. The fixed rule approach which is adopted for cases involving personal injury and property damage would be unlikely to produce satisfactory results when applied to cases of economic loss; the place where the economic loss is suffered may be somewhat fortuitous and may not represent the centre of gravity of the tort. There are, of course, difficulties in applying a test based on the location of the most significant elements of the events. The test is inherently vague and therefore permits considerable manipulation by the courts. However, the nature of the problems raised by section 11(2)(c) are not new.

There are various situations in which the courts have had to determine where a tort occurs. Under the pre-1987 version of what

67 S 11(2)(a).
68 S 11(2)(b).

is now CPR 6.20(8) the courts could allow service of a writ out of the jurisdiction where the claim was 'founded on a tort committed within the jurisdiction'. In deciding whether a tort was committed in England or abroad the court would ask itself the question: where in substance did the cause of action arise?[69] The same test was applied, at common law, for deciding whether a case involved an English tort (which was governed by English law) or a foreign tort (to which the double actionability rule applied).[70] On the basis of this approach it was held, for example, that as regards claims based on negligent statements the tort occurred where the statement was received and acted upon;[71] in *Metall und Rohstoff AG v Donaldson Lufkin & Jenrette Inc*[72] the Court of Appeal held that, in the particular circumstances of the case, the alleged tort of inducing breach of contract was committed in England, where the breaches of contract were induced and the resulting damage was suffered by the plaintiff.

It seems likely that the courts will have recourse to these cases when considering which law is the applicable law under section 11(2)(c). It is not implausible to suggest that the country in which the most significant elements of the events constituting the tort occurred is the country in which the cause of action arose.

C The exception[73]

In most cases the general rules set out in section 11 of the Private International Law (Miscellaneous Provisions) Act 1995will be both the beginning and the end of the inquiry as to the ascertainment of the applicable law. However, just as the double actionability rule is subject to an exception, section 11 is subject to an exception, which is contained in section 12. Although the drafting of section 12 is, perhaps, more complicated than it needs to be, its basic effect is simple enough: the applicable law under the general rule may be displaced by the law of another country with which the tort is more closely connected. Section 12(1) provides:

69 *Distillers Co (Biochemicals) Ltd v Thompson* [1971] AC 458 at 468.

70 *Metall und Rohstoff AG v Donaldson Lufkin & Jenrette Inc* [1990] 1 QB 391, [1989] 3 All ER 14.

71 *Diamond v Bank of London and Montreal Ltd* [1979] QB 333, [1979] 1 All ER 561; *The Albaforth* [1984] 2 Lloyd's Rep 91. See also *Armagas Ltd v Mundogas SA* [1986] AC 717, [1986] 2 All ER 385 (a case involving allegations of fraud).

72 [1990] 1 QB 391, [1989] 3 All ER 14.

73 See Jaffey, *Topics in Choice of Law* (1996) chapters 6 and 7.

> If it appears, in all the circumstances, from a comparison of –
> (a) the significance of the factors which connect a tort or delict with the country whose law would be the applicable law under the general rule; and
> (b) the significance of any factors connecting the tort or delict with another country,
> that it is substantially more appropriate for the applicable law for determining the issues arising in the case, or any of those issues, to be the law of the other country, the general rule is displaced and the applicable law for determining those issues or that issue (as the case may be) is the law of that other country.

The section goes on to say that the factors which may be taken into account include 'factors relating to the parties, to any of the events which constitute the tort or delict in question or to any of the circumstances or consequences of those events'.[74] This does not really take the matter much further.

The exception in section 12 is potentially far-reaching. The exception can apply to an issue or a number of issues arising out of a tortious situation, leaving other issues to be governed by the applicable law as determined by the general rule in section 11; alternatively, the exception might displace entirely the applicable law under the general rule.

Although there are no theoretical limitations as to the law which might be applied by way of exception, it is quite likely that, in the majority of cases in which the exception is invoked, the choice facing the court will be whether the lex loci delicti or the lex fori is the most appropriate law. One of the functions of jurisdiction rules is to channel litigation to the most appropriate forum, a forum with which the parties and the situation have a close connection. It is not surprising that many of the cases which have been at the forefront of the development of tort choice of law at common law – cases such as *Babcock v Jackson*[75] and *Chaplin v Boys*[76] – have involved situations in which the law of the forum has been held to be more appropriate than the lex loci delicti. However, the operation of the exception in section 12 is not limited to cases in which the law specified by the general rule is displaced by the law of the forum. It is perfectly possible for the most appropriate law to be the law of a country which is neither the forum nor the locus delicti. For example, if, following a road accident in Malta involving two Scottish residents, the dispute between the parties is litigated in England, the right solution

74 S 12(2).
75 [1963] 2 Lloyd's Rep 286.
76 [1971] AC 356, [1969] 2 All ER 1085.

would be to allow the claimant to recover damages for non-pecuniary losses under Scots law (by virtue of section 12) rather than to apply Maltese law to the issue (under section 11). Such cases will, however, be rare because it will be unusual for the English court to exercise jurisdiction in a case which has such strong connections with other countries and so little connection with England.

There are three fundamental issues surrounding the operation of the exception.

First, what is the relationship between section 11 and section 12? One possibility is that the relationship is intended to mirror the relationship between the double actionability rule and the common law exception. The cases decided at common law, both in England and in the United States, suggest that the law applicable under the general rule is likely to be displaced only in two types of case: first, where both parties are foreigners to the country where the tort is committed and come from the same country; secondly, where both parties are foreigners to the country where the tort is committed and, although they belong to different countries, the relevant rules of their countries are the same on the issue in question.

The position would appear to be much the same under the 1995 Act. Although the common law exception and section 12 are inspired, at least in part, by the proper law doctrine as applied to contractual situations, the analogy between contracts and torts is not always very helpful. One of the features of international contracts is that they may have numerous connections with many different countries. In determining the country with which a contract is most closely connected relevant factors include the territorial connections of the parties, the place where the contract was negotiated and concluded, and the place (or places) of performance of the contractual obligations. As regards torts which are connected with more than one country there are normally only four factors to consider: the territorial connections of the claimant and of the defendant, the place where the claimant was injured and the place where the defendant committed the wrongful act. Since in a typical case involving personal injury or property damage the claimant's injury is suffered at the place where the defendant commits the wrongful act, there are often only three connections of substance: the claimant's residence, the defendant's residence and the place of the tort. If one of the parties is resident in the country in which the tort is committed that country normally has to be regarded as more closely connected than any other. As a general rule, only if neither party is resident in the country in which the tort is committed will there be a strong argument for saying that a law other than the lex loci delicti is the most appropriate law. In

Edmunds v Simmonds[77] the claimant and the defendant, both of whom were domiciled in England, hired a car while on holiday in Spain. While the car was being driven by the defendant, the claimant was injured when, as a result of the defendant's negligence, the car hit a Spanish lorry. Garland J held that, in these circumstances, the general rule in section 11 was displaced by the exception in section 12. Given that both parties were English and the accident resulted from the defendant's lack of control, the involvement of the Spanish lorry was irrelevant. Accordingly, it was substantially more appropriate for English law to be the applicable law. In reaching this conclusion, the judge placed some reliance on *Chaplin v Boys*.

Secondly, what is the threshold for the application of the exception rather than the general rule? The fact that the general rule is most likely to be displaced in cases where neither party belongs to the country where the tort is committed does not mean that the general rule should always be displaced in such cases. Much depends on the facts of each individual case and the particular issue in question. Where, for example, an English resident is injured in a road accident in Ireland in circumstances in which the English defendant is guilty of negligence according to Irish law, but not according to English law, it is not unreasonable to suppose that Irish law, as the lex loci delicti, should determine the relevant standard of care even though both parties are English residents. It must be remembered that the 1995 Act does not allow for the law of the country identified by the general rule to be displaced simply on the ground that the tort is more closely connected with another country. Section 12 allows for the application of a law other than the law specified by section 11 only if the other law is 'substantially more appropriate'.[78] The use of the word 'substantially' indicates that the drafters did not intend that the combined operation of sections 11 and 12 should degenerate into a vague, proper law doctrine.

Thirdly, how is the applicable law under section 12 to be determined? It has been noted that, in *Chaplin v Boys*, Lord Wilberforce favoured Unites States interest analysis in his formulation of the exception to the double actionability rule. It may be questioned whether section 12 can be read as endorsing an interest analysis approach. The list of factors which the court may consider when deciding whether to apply the general rule or the exception includes factors relating to the parties, the events which constitute the tort and the circumstances or consequences of those events.[79] Section 12

77 [2001] 1 WLR 1003.
78 See *Roerig v Valiant Trawlers Ltd* [2002] EWCA Civ 21, [2002] 1 All ER 961.
79 S 12(2).

seems grounded in the more traditional 'centre of gravity' approach. Of course, in practice, the two approaches will normally point to the same result; the country in which the localising elements are most densely grouped is likely to be the country whose interests will be most affected by the application or non-application of its law. In *Babcock v Jackson* the judgment of Fuld J makes it clear that both interest analysis and a 'centre of gravity' approach led to the conclusion that New York law was the most appropriate law.[80]

What, however, would be the position under the 1995 Act in a case like *Chaplin v Boys* if the claimant were a Scottish resident rather than an English resident? Obviously, Maltese law would be the applicable law under the general rule. As in *Chaplin v Boys* itself there would be little argument in this situation for the application of Maltese law to the question of whether the claimant should recover damages for non-pecuniary losses. Is it possible to say in these circumstances that the application of either Scots law or English law, according to which the claimant is entitled to recover for such losses, is 'substantially more appropriate'? Looked at from the perspective of interest analysis, a strong case can be made out for the application of Scots law and it is at least arguable that Scots law should be applied by way of exception under section 12. Indeed, it has been suggested that whether or not the law indicated by the general rule is intended to deal with the circumstances of the particular case should be regarded as a relevant factor for the purposes of section 12.[81] However, given the way in which section 12 is drafted, the mere fact that the claimant is resident in Scotland may not be sufficient to justify the application of Scots law in preference to the law of the country in which the events constituting the tort occurred.

D Substance and procedure

The purpose of the Private International Law (Miscellaneous Provisions) Act 1995 is to abolish the double actionability rule and the common law exception (by section 10) and replace those rules with a new general rule (in section 11) and a new exception (in section 12). Nothing in the Act affects any other rules of law.[82] This general principle is fleshed out by section 14(3) which provides, inter alia, that nothing in the Act 'affects any rule of evidence,

80 [1963] 2 Lloyd's Rep 286 at 298–290. See also Lord Hodson in *Chaplin v Boys* [1971] AC 356 at 378–380.

81 Morse, 'Torts in Private International Law: A New Statutory Framework' (1996) 45 ICLQ 888 at 900, n 91.

82 S 14(1).

pleading or practice or authorises questions of procedure in any proceedings to be determined otherwise than in accordance with the law of the forum'.[83] Of course, the 1995 Act does not attempt to define what is a question of substance, which falls to be determined by the applicable law, and what is a question of procedure. This question of classification is left to the common law and other legislative provisions.[84]

The decision of the House of Lords in *Chaplin v Boys*[85] is the leading authority. It will be recalled that the issue facing the court was whether the plaintiff could recover damages for non-pecuniary losses notwithstanding the fact that Maltese law did not award damages for such losses. A minority decided that this central question was a procedural one, which was therefore governed by English law; the fact that Maltese law did not give damages for pain and suffering and loss of amenity was irrelevant. A majority decided, however, that whether the plaintiff could recover for a particular head of damage was a substantive question which had to be decided by reference to the law (or laws) governing the tort. The classification adopted by the majority is clearly right and has not been seriously questioned.

This leaves unresolved where exactly the line between substance and procedure is to be drawn. It would seem that questions of pure quantification are to be regarded as procedural. So, once it is established that the defendant is liable for the claimant's physical injuries, the precise sum of money awarded for the injuries in question is a matter for the law of the forum.[86] So, English law determines the compensation which a victim should receive for the loss of a foot or for the loss of an eye, even if a foreign law governs the substantive claim. Similarly, whether the court can award damages in a foreign currency is a procedural question. So, the English court can award damages in tort in the currency which best expresses the claimant's loss, whether or not the tort is governed by English law.[87]

A problem which has not yet been finally settled in England is whether a rule which imposes a ceiling on damages which the claimant can recover is a substantive rule which should be applied only if it forms part of the law governing the tort or a procedural rule

83 S 14(3)(b).
84 The Foreign Limitation Periods Act 1984 provides that rules in relation to the limitation of actions are to be regarded as substantive, rather than procedural.
85 [1971] AC 356, [1969] 2 All ER 1085.
86 See *Edmunds v Simmonds* [2001] 1 WLR 1003; *Hulse v Chambers* [2001] 1 WLR 2386.
87 *The Despina R* [1979] AC 685, [1979] 1 All ER 421.

which should be applied only if it forms part of the law of the forum. The preferable view is that a rule which limits damages is more analogous to a rule which denies recovery for a particular head of damage than to a rule on quantification. A rule which imposes a statutory ceiling on damages does not determine how damages are to be assessed. Since such a rule simply provides that, however damages are assessed, they shall not exceed a stipulated amount, it should be regarded as a substantive rule.

The Law Commission favoured this view,[88] which is implicit in the decision of the Supreme Court of California in *Reich v Purcell*.[89] This is also the view adopted most recently by the High Court of Australia in *John Pfeiffer Pty Ltd v Rogerson*.[90] In this case, the High Court reconsidered its earlier decision in *Stevens v Head*[91] (in which it was held that a statutory rule laying down a limit on damages is procedural).[92] The plaintiff sued his employer in the Australian Capital Territory (ACT) in relation to injuries he suffered in an accident at work in New South Wales. Damages under the law of the ACT were considerably higher than the sum payable under the Workmen's Compensation Act 1897 (NSW). The High Court decided that the relevant provision of the NSW legislation, which places a cap on damages, is a substantive rule.

A further question which the English court has yet to consider is how damages are to be determined in a case where liability is imposed under the applicable law for a tort in relation to which there is no obvious English equivalent. Up to now the double actionability rule has prevented the issue arising. Suppose, for example, that a claimant brings proceedings in England against a foreign defendant for invasion of privacy. Assuming that the substance of the claim is well founded under the (foreign) applicable law, how is the English court to determine the level of damages? Since invasion of privacy is not a tort in English law, how can there be any English procedural rules for deciding the quantum of damages that should be awarded? The English court would have to choose between either identifying the closest analogous tort under English law and approaching quantification from that perspective or applying the quantification rules of the applicable law.

88 Law Com No 193, *Choice of Law in Tort and Delict* (1990) para 3.39.
89 432 P 2d 727 (1967). See pp 256–257.
90 (2000) 172 ALR 625.
91 (1993) 176 CLR 433.
92 Cf *Caltex Singapore Pte Ltd v BP Shipping Ltd* [1996] 1 Lloyd's Rep 286 (which was influenced by *Stevens v Head* (1993) 176 CLR 433).

E Excluding the applicable law

Questions of public policy have not loomed large in tort cases governed by the common law choice of law rules. It is not difficult to see why. The effect of the double actionability rule is that no liability can be imposed unless the claim is actionable under English law. From a functional point of view, the first branch of the *Phillips v Eyre*[93] rule operates as a rule of public policy which excludes the application of any foreign rule which imposes tort liability unless there is a corresponding rule of English law. In such circumstances it is inconceivable that the rule of foreign law might be excluded on grounds of public policy.

The Private International Law (Miscellaneous Provisions) Act 1995 opens up the possibility of a defendant being found liable for a tort committed abroad, notwithstanding the fact that no liability would be imposed under English law had the events in question occurred in England. In what circumstances, if any, would it be appropriate for the English court to refuse to apply the foreign law even though it is prima facie the applicable law under section 11 (or section 12)? For example, what should be the position if a claimant commences English proceedings with a view to recovering damages for the tort of seduction allegedly committed by the defendant in Botswana? The 1995 Act provides that nothing in Part III authorises 'the application of the law of a country outside the forum as the applicable law for determining issues arising in any claim in so far as to do so ... would conflict with principles of public policy'.[94]

It is implicit in the 1995 Act that the mere fact that a foreign legal system imposes tortious liability for acts which, if committed in England, would not be actionable cannot, in itself, be a basis for excluding the foreign law. It has been observed, however, that tort is an area of private international law in which 'the courts have always displayed, and continue to display, a marked "homing" instinct in the matter of choice of law'.[95] It would be possible, though inappropriate, for the courts to nullify completely the statutory provisions by resorting to public policy as a means of denying recovery in cases where, although the applicable law imposes liability, the law of the forum does not. Public policy should be invoked rarely and only in cases where the content of the foreign law is repugnant in English eyes. It would, for example, be wrong for the court to refuse to give effect to the applicable law on grounds of

93 (1870) LR 6 QB 1.
94 S 14(3)(a)(i).
95 Carter, 'The Private International Law (Miscellaneous Provisions) Act 1995' (1996) 112 LQR 190 at 193.

public policy simply because liability under the applicable law is strict whereas English law would impose liability only in the event of the defendant's fault.

It is also provided that the effect of the 1995 Act is not to authorise the application of a foreign 'penal, revenue or other public law as would not otherwise be enforceable under the law of forum'.[96] This provision dovetails with the general principle of English private international law according to which certain types of foreign public laws will not be enforced in England.[97] Somewhat elliptically, the Act provides that it 'has effect without prejudice to the operation of any rule of law which either has effect notwithstanding the rules of private international law applicable in the particular circumstances or modifies the rules of private international law that would otherwise be so applicable'.[98] The purpose of this provision is, like article 7 of the Rome Convention,[99] to enable the court to apply relevant overriding rules.[100] However, unlike article 7, the 1995 Act does not draw a distinction between the overriding rules of the law of the forum and the overriding rules of other laws. It will be rare that this provision will have much effect other than in relation to English overriding rules. If the situation has a sufficiently close connection with another country that the overriding rules of that country's law become potentially applicable, it is likely that the law of that country will be the applicable law (by virtue of either section 11 or section 12).

V THE INTERACTION OF TORT AND CONTRACT

There are cases in which questions of both tort and contract may arise. For example, a defendant may seek to rely on a foreign contract as a defence to a tort alleged to have been committed either in England or abroad. In *Galaxias Steamship Co Ltd v Panagos Christofis*[101] the defendants were employed – under a contract of employment governed by Greek law – to work on a ship belonging to the plaintiff. While the ship was in England, the plaintiff purported to terminate their contract of employment. When the defendants refused to leave the ship, the plaintiff sued them for trespass. The defendants argued that, as a consequence of the fact that the contract of

96 S 14(3)(a)(ii).
97 See pp 563–566.
98 S 14(4).
99 See pp 227–232.
100 For consideration of 'mandatory' and 'overriding' rules see p 225.
101 (1948) 81 Ll L Rep 499. See North, 'Contract as a Tort Defence in the Conflict of Laws' (1977) 26 ICLQ 914 at 915–916.

employment had not been validly terminated, they were entitled to remain on the ship. To succeed in the action for trespass the plaintiff had to establish that the defendants' continued occupation of the ship was unlawful. The plaintiff's claim in tort, which was governed by English law, was bound to fail if the plaintiff's purported termination of the contract was not effective under Greek law, the law governing the contract. The court held that, since according to Greek law the contract had been validly brought to an end, the defendants were trespassers. This type of case is relatively straightforward since the tort question and the contract question can be segregated and the relevant choice of law rules applied to each question.

More problematical are cases in which questions of tort and contract interact. The defendant to a tort claim may, for example, set up as a defence a clause in a contract which exempts him from the liability in question. In *Sayers v International Drilling Co NV*,[102] one of the few English cases in which the interaction of contract and tort choice of law rules has arisen, the plaintiff, an English resident, and the defendant, a Dutch company, entered into a contract of employment under which the plaintiff was to work on an oil rig in Nigerian territorial waters. The contract contained a clause exempting the company from liability for any injury which the plaintiff might suffer in the course of his employment. This exemption clause was valid by Dutch law, but was rendered void in English law by section 1(3) of the Law Reform (Personal Injuries) Act 1948. No evidence was led of Nigerian law on the point. The plaintiff was injured in the course of his employment and sued the employers in tort in England. The defendant sought to rely on the exemption clause in the contract.

How should such a defence be dealt with? There are two issues to be considered: one is the validity of the exclusion clause; the other is the effect of the clause as a defence to a claim in tort. If the contractual exclusion clause is invalid under the law applicable to the contract, there is no reason why it should be given any effect to, regardless of the clause's effect according to the law governing the tort. If, however, the clause is valid according to its applicable law, it should be for the law applicable to the tort to determine whether the exclusion clause is an effective defence to the claim in tort. Assuming the exclusion clause to be valid according to the law governing the contract, if the exemption clause affords a good defence under the law applicable to the tort the action must fail; if, however, the exemption clause does not provide a defence under the law governing the tort the claimant's action should succeed.

102 [1971] 3 All ER 163, [1971] 1 WLR 1176.

Although it is clear that the validity of the exemption clause is to be decided by reference to the law applicable to the contract, there is a further question. By which country's rules should the law applicable to the contract be ascertained – by the forum's choice of law rules or by the conflicts rules of the law governing the tort?[103] This is a question on which there is no authority in the decided cases and the academic authorities are divided. Although it has been argued that the conflicts rules of the law governing the tort should determine which law governs the contract (and therefore the validity of the exemption clause),[104] the better view is that the conflicts rules of the forum should determine this question.[105]

In *Sayers v International Drilling Co NV* there is little indication that the majority of the Court of Appeal really appreciated the nature of the problems raised by the case. In a minority judgment which is not always easy to follow, Lord Denning MR decided that the contract was governed by English law, that Dutch law was the law applicable to the tort and that Dutch law should determine the issue whether the exemption clause was a defence to the action in tort. The majority approach, however, was simply to identify the law applicable to the contract. According to the majority, Dutch law – under which the exemption clause was valid – was the applicable law, from which it followed that the defendant was not liable. No reference at all was made by the majority to the choice of law rules for tort, even though the action was brought in tort. Having decided that the exemption clause was valid according to the law governing the contract, the majority ought to have gone on to ask whether the clause was an effective defence to an action in tort according to the law governing the tort.[106]

There are, however, indications in cases from other jurisdictions which adopt the better approach. In *Brodin v A/R Seljan*[107] the pursuer's husband was employed to work on a ship belonging to the defender, a Norwegian company, under a contract of employment which was governed by Norwegian law. The pursuer's husband was killed in an accident which took place on the ship while it was in

103 This is an example of the incidental question. See pp 550–554.

104 North, 'Contract as a Tort Defence in the Conflict of Laws' (1977) 26 ICLQ 914 at 927.

105 Collins, 'Interaction between Contract and Tort in the Conflict of Laws' (1967) 16 ICLQ 103 at 115.

106 See also *Coupland v Arabian Gulf Oil Co* [1983] 3 All ER 226, [1983] 1 WLR 1136. Although in this case Robert Goff LJ might be thought to lend some support to the majority view in the *Sayers* case (at 1153) the case is weak authority; any discussion of the relationship between contract and tort was obiter since, on the facts of the case, there was no contractual defence available to the defendant.

107 1973 SLT 198.

Scottish waters. When the pursuer brought proceedings in Scotland, alleging that the accident was caused by the defender's negligence, the defender sought to rely on an exclusion clause in the contract of employment. Although the clause was valid under Norwegian law, the court held that the clause was not effective to exclude the defender's liability in tort. Under Scots law the exclusion of liability was void by virtue of section 1(3) of the Law Reform (Personal Injuries) Act 1948 and Scots law, as the law governing the tort, prevailed over the law governing the contract. A similar analysis is to be found in *Canadian Pacific Rly Co v Parent*,[108] a case decided by the Privy Council on appeal from the Supreme Court of Canada. The plaintiff's husband was killed in Ontario in a rail accident which was caused by the negligence of the defendant's employees. The contract between the defendant, the rail operator, and the plaintiff's husband excluded the defendant's liability for death or personal injury. The plaintiff sued the defendant in Quebec and the defendant invoked the exclusion clause in the contract as a defence. The Privy Council held that the defendant was not liable. Although the defendant had no defence to the action under the law of Quebec, under the law of Ontario, the lex loci delicti, the terms of the contract were effective to bar the plaintiff's claim in tort.

The Private International Law (Miscellaneous Provisions) Act 1995 does not address the question of the interaction of tort and contract choice of law rules. Accordingly, the question of the relationship between contract and tort remains to be determined by the courts according to the principles to be gleaned from the earlier cases. It is to be hoped that the courts choose to follow the approach adopted in cases such as *Brodin v A/R Seljan* and *Canadian Pacific Rly Co v Parent*, rather than the oversimplistic analysis of the majority of the Court of Appeal in *Sayers v International Drilling Co NV*.

VI CHOICE OF LAW: RESTITUTION AND EQUITABLE WRONGS

A Introduction

The previous chapter and the earlier sections of this chapter consider the choice of law rules which govern contractual and tortious obligations. According to English domestic law, however, not all non-contractual obligations are tortious ones. First, liability may be imposed for breach of an equitable obligation. In English law, the term 'equitable wrong' includes breach of trust or other fiduciary

108 [1917] AC 195.

obligation, dishonest assistance in a breach of trust and breach of confidence. Secondly, liability may be based on the principle of unjust enrichment.

Within the law of restitution it is important to draw attention to a fundamental distinction. Perhaps the most significant part of the law of restitution is concerned with the identification of the circumstances in which the claimant has a claim against the defendant on the basis of unjust enrichment (as opposed to contract, tort or equitable wrong). This part of the law of restitution, sometimes referred to as 'autonomous unjust enrichment', is to be contrasted with the part of the law which is concerned with whether the claimant is entitled to restitution (rather than compensation or some other remedy) for a wrong – whether a breach of contract, tort or equitable wrong – committed by the defendant.[109] This second part of the law of restitution is known as 'restitution for wrongs'.

Depending on the facts of the case one or other aspect of the law of restitution may be relevant. For example, whether a claimant has a claim for the recovery of money mistakenly paid to the defendant has to be decided by reference to the principles of unjust enrichment. By contrast, whether the claimant can recover restitutionary damages for breach of contract is a facet of the law of restitution for wrongs. (Of course, whether or not the defendant has committed a breach of contract is not part of the law of restitution at all.)

According to the foregoing analysis, there are three choice of law issues arising out of the law of restitution and equitable wrongs. First, which law should govern causes of action based on unjust enrichment? Secondly, which law should determine liability for an equitable wrong? Thirdly, which law should determine whether the claimant is entitled to restitution for a wrong?

B Unjust enrichment: the applicable law

In the sphere of private international law, the law relating to unjust enrichment is still in its infancy. This is not altogether surprising. It is only relatively recently that the law of unjust enrichment has been recognised in English law as being based on a coherent principle.[110] It is inevitable that the development of choice of law rules in relation to claims based on unjust enrichment is lagging some way behind the development of the rules which identify the circumstances in which such causes of action arise. In the paragraphs which follow much of the discussion is somewhat speculative.

109 See Birks, *An Introduction to the Law of Restitution* (1989) chapter 1 and Birks, *Restitution – The Future* (1992) chapter 1.

110 *Lipkin Gorman v Karpnale Ltd* [1991] 2 AC 548, [1992] 4 All ER 512.

1. Characterisation

To determine whether, in any particular case, the relevant choice of law rules to be applied are the unjust enrichment rules or some other rules, the court must first classify the issue before it. This is effected according to the lex fori's scheme of classification. It should always be remembered, however, that the conceptual categories for choice of law purposes may differ from those categories as applied in entirely domestic cases.

It is possible to exaggerate the problems of classification surrounding unjust enrichment claims. As long as the distinction between autonomous unjust enrichment and restitution for wrongs is clearly maintained, it should be possible to distinguish unjust enrichment issues from both contract and tort issues. For example, a claim arising out of a void contract is, for choice of law purposes, to be regarded as an unjust enrichment claim, rather than a contractual one.[111] As regards the borderline between tort and unjust enrichment, there is no rational argument for treating 'waiver of tort' cases as anything other than tort cases for choice of law purposes.[112]

More problematic is the potential overlap between unjust enrichment and property. The problem is not made easier by the fact that there is considerable controversy as to whether proprietary claims form part of the law of restitution according to English domestic law. The most satisfactory approach is to distinguish the question of liability for unjust enrichment (which should be decided by the law governing unjust enrichment) from any question of legal and/or equitable title in relation to specific property in the hands of the defendant (which is an aspect of the law of property for conflict of laws purposes).[113]

Furthermore, potential difficulties may be posed by the traditional division between substance and procedure. One of the problems is that, in cases of autonomous unjust enrichment, the question whether the claimant has a cause of action and the question as to whether the claimant is entitled to restitution collapse into each other. The danger is that the law of unjust enrichment may be seen as an aspect of procedure. Although some of the cases seem to fall into this trap,[114] the better view is that unjust enrichment should be regarded as a substantive category for choice of law purposes.

111 It is for this reason that art 10(1)(e) of the Rome Convention (which provides that the law applicable to the contract governs the effects of nullity) was not implemented into English law: Contracts (Applicable Law) Act 1990, s 2(2).

112 Bird, 'Choice of Law' in Rose (ed), *Restitution and the Conflict of Laws* (1995) pp 75–76.

113 *Macmillan Inc v Bishopsgate Investment Trust (No 3)* [1996] 1 All ER 585, [1996] 1 WLR 387. For choice of law in relation to property see chapter 11.

114 See, for example, *Arab Monetary Fund v Hashim (No 9)* (1994) Times, 11 October; noted by Briggs, 'The International Dimension to Claims for Contribution' [1995] LMCLQ 437.

2. Choice of law rules

Although there is an increasing number of cases in which choice of law questions relating to restitution have arisen, the authorities are to a significant degree unsatisfactory. Many of the cases do not clearly draw a distinction between autonomous unjust enrichment and restitution for wrongs and the courts' discussion is often very general (or obiter).

In some cases the courts have accepted the idea that an unjust enrichment claim should be governed by its proper law. There has been 'a tendency'[115] in the cases to endorse the principle that 'the obligation to restore the benefit of an enrichment obtained at another person's expense is governed by the proper law of the obligation'.[116] How is a very open-textured proper law approach to be applied to specific cases?

Many autonomous unjust enrichment claims are for the restitution of benefits bestowed to the defendant under a contract which, for one reason or another, turns out to be ineffective. The contract may be void, frustrated or unenforceable. The obvious starting-point in these cases is the law which governed (or would have governed) the contract. The leading commentators suggest that if an unjust enrichment obligation arises in connection with a contract, the proper law of the obligation is the law applicable to the contract.[117] It follows therefore that a claim for unjust enrichment which arises out of a void contract should be governed by the law which would have governed the contract had it been valid. While some of the cases are consistent with the view that unjust enrichment claims which arise in connection with a contract are governed by the law applicable to the contract, it must be conceded that in none of them are the choice of law issues considered in depth.[118]

In situations not involving contracts, the cases give some support to the theory that the law of the place of enrichment should be the applicable law. For example, in *Chase Manhattan Bank NA v Israel-British Bank (London) Ltd*,[119] a case involving payment of money

115 Aldous LJ in *Macmillan Inc v Bishopsgate Investment Trust (No 3)* [1996] 1 All ER 585, [1996] 1 WLR 387 at 408.

116 Dicey and Morris, *The Conflict of Laws* (13th edn, 2000) p 1485. See, in particular, *Arab Monetary Fund v Hashim* [1996] 1 Lloyd's Rep 589 at 597. Cf *Baring Bros & Co Ltd v Cunninghame District Council* [1997] CLC 108 (a decision of the Court of Session).

117 Dicey and Morris, *The Conflict of Laws* (13th edn, 2000) p 1485.

118 For example, *Fibrosa Spolka Akcyjna v Fairbairn Lawson Combe Barbour Ltd* [1943] AC 32, [1942] 2 All ER 122; *Arab Bank Ltd v Barclays Bank* [1953] 2 QB 527, [1953] 2 All ER 263; *Dimskal Shipping Co SA v International Transport Workers' Federation* [1992] 2 AC 152, [1991] 4 All ER 871.

119 [1981] Ch 105, [1979] 3 All ER 1025.

under a mistake of fact, the law of New York, being the place where the money was received, was applied to the plaintiff's claim.[120] The authorities cannot, however, be regarded as conclusive. The logic of a proper law approach is to apply the law of the country with which the situation is most closely connected; if the country in which the money is received by the defendant is not, on the facts of the case, the country with which the claim is most closely connected, the law of that country should not be the applicable law.

C Equitable wrongs: the applicable law

For the purposes of the conflict of laws it may be questioned whether there should be a conceptual category 'equitable wrong' for which a choice of law rule needs to be devised. There is no requirement that the categories employed for choice of law purposes should mirror precisely the categories of domestic law.[121] The most sensible approach to a case involving an equitable wrong is to classify it, for choice of law purposes, as a case of trust, contract, restitution or tort – depending on the particular circumstances.[122]

Questions involving the administration of a trust and the personal liability of the trustees for breach of trust are governed by the law applicable to the trust.[123] As regards cases involving the breach of other fiduciary obligations (such as the obligations owed by directors to the company's shareholders) or breach of confidence, there is little direct English authority. In cases where there is a formal legal relationship between the parties (for example, between a principal and his agent or between the directors of a company and its shareholders), the applicable law should be the law governing that relationship. So, the liability of an agent for breach of fiduciary relationship should be governed by the law governing the contract between the principal and the agent.

Where, however, there is no formal relationship between the alleged wrongdoer and the claimant (for example, where a duty of confidence arises otherwise than by virtue of a contractual relationship) an equitable wrong should be treated as a tort for the purposes of the Private International Law (Miscellaneous Provisions)

120 See also *El Ajou v Dollar Land Holdings plc* [1993] 3 All ER 717; *Re Jogia (a bankrupt)* [1988] 2 All ER 328, [1988] 1 WLR 484.
121 *Re Bonacina* [1912] 2 Ch 394.
122 Compare Barnard, 'Choice of Law in Equitable Wrongs: A Comparative Analysis' [1992] CLJ 474.
123 Art 8 of the Convention on the Law Applicable to Trusts and on their Recognition, as implemented by the Recognition of Trusts Act 1987, s 1(1). See arts 6 and 7.

Act 1995.[124] The fact that, in English law, breach of confidence and dishonest assistance in a breach of trust are equitable wrongs, rather than common law torts, is little more than an accident of history.

It seems, however, that the courts are not inclined to adopt this approach. *In Grupo Torras SA v Al-Sabah (No 5)*[125] the Court of Appeal held that a claim based on conduct which English law would treat as dishonest assistance in a breach of trust falls within the scope of neither tort nor restitution choice of law rules. In the circumstances, the court applied the law of Spain, the place where the defendant performed the acts upon which the alleged liability was based. Whether the outcome of the case would have been any different if the defendant's equitable wrong had been treated as a tort for choice of law purposes is doubtful.

In *Kuwait Oil Tanker SAK v Al Bader*[126] the claimants, a number of Kuwaiti oil companies, brought proceedings against the defendants, who were members of the senior management of the first claimant. Although the case was primarily concerned with the tort of conspiracy, the claimants argued, in the alternative, that the defendants were liable as constructive trustees for breach of fiduciary duties. The Court of Appeal held that a claim based on the defendants' breach of duties, which, under English law would be regarded as fiduciary in nature, could succeed if the defendants' conduct was wrongful under Kuwaiti law (which governed the fiduciary relationship between the parties) and it would be unconscionable for the defendants to retain funds obtained in breach of these duties.

It is worth noting, however, that both of these cases were concerned with events which took place before the entry into force of Part III of the Private International Law (Miscellaneous Provisions) Act 1995. It is, therefore, possible (if unlikely) that, when confronted with facts occurring after the statutory scheme came into force, the courts might be prepared to classify equitable wrongs (other than those occurring within the context of a pre-existing legal relationship) as torts for choice of law purposes.

D Restitution for wrongs

The law of restitution for wrongs is built on the foundation of the general law of civil liability; it determines the circumstances in which the claimant is entitled to restitution as a remedy in cases where the basis of the defendant's liability is a breach of contract, a

124 For the relevant rules see pp 267–281.
125 [2001] Lloyd's Rep Bank 36.
126 [2000] 2 All ER (Comm) 271.

tort or an equitable wrong. When, for example, can the defendant be required to give up a gain made at the claimant's expense rather than simply to compensate the claimant for the loss he has suffered?

There is little or no direct English authority on this question. There is, however, a strong argument for saying that the law governing the cause of action (lex causae) should also determine whether restitution is available. It is well established that whether a claimant may recover in tort for a particular head of damage falls to be determined by the law governing the tort.[127] By analogy, whether restitutionary damages may be awarded for a particular wrong should be determined by the law governing the wrong.[128]

127 *Chaplin v Boys* [1971] AC 356, [1969] 2 All ER 1085.
128 Bird, 'Choice of Law' in Rose (ed), *Restitution and the Conflict of Laws* (1995) p 92. See, however, *Arab Monetary Fund v Hashim* [1996] 1 Lloyd's Rep 589.

Chapter 7

Arbitration

I INTRODUCTION

Parties to an international contract may make no provision for how any dispute which may arise should be resolved – or they may include a jurisdiction clause in the contract. In these cases, if the parties fail to resolve a dispute amicably, litigation is likely to follow. Whether such litigation can take place in England depends on the application of the jurisdiction rules which were considered in chapter 3.

The parties may decide, however, that a dispute should be arbitrated rather than litigated. Parties to an international contract may, for example, include in their contract an arbitration clause, which refers any dispute that may arise out of the contract to arbitration. Even if the contract does not include such a clause – or if the dispute is not contractual – the parties may, after a dispute has arisen, enter a submission agreement referring that particular dispute to arbitration.

There are various reasons why parties may choose arbitration as an alternative to litigation. Arbitration is a private process, whereas litigation takes place in public; the parties to an arbitration agreement are free to select the arbitrator (or arbitrators), whereas in litigation the parties have no choice as to the judge, who is provided by the state; in certain types of case arbitration may be thought to be cheaper or quicker than litigation.

It is important not to confuse arbitration with conciliation or mediation. Arbitration is a legal process, albeit a 'privatised' one. An arbitrator is obliged to determine the dispute by reference to rules, rather than to seek a compromise. Furthermore, the arbitral process is ultimately subject to the supervision of the courts. For example, the court will have the final say on the validity of an arbitration agreement or on the question of whether an arbitrator can be removed for lack of impartiality.

The kind of arbitration which is most likely to give rise to conflicts problems is international commercial arbitration. It is not uncommon for a commercial contract which is concluded by parties who carry on business in different countries and which has connections with more than one country to include an arbitration clause. The conflict of laws questions which arise in international commercial arbitration include the following: (i) what law governs the arbitration agreement; (ii) what law governs the arbitration proceedings; (iii) according to what law is the dispute to be decided by the arbitrators; (iv) what is the effect of an arbitration agreement on the jurisdiction of the English court; and (v) in what circumstances will a foreign arbitral award be recognised or enforced in England?

It should be noted that English law has been significantly affected by developments on the international plane. First, the New York Convention of 1958 has played a very important part in promoting arbitration as a mechanism for resolving international commercial disputes. The Convention, which provides for the enforcement of both arbitration agreements and arbitral awards, has been ratified by more than 100 states, including all Western European countries (except Iceland).[1] The second significant development is the UNCITRAL Model Law on Arbitration of 1985. The Model Law has been adopted by a number of countries (either in its entirety or with minor modifications[2]) and has set an agenda for reform even in those countries which have decided not to adopt it. The Arbitration Act 1996, which repealed the earlier legislation and provides a comprehensive statement of the principles of English arbitration law, was clearly influenced by the Model Law from the point of view of structure, style and content. Although English law retains a number of distinctive features, the 1996 Act brought English law more into line with modern international practice.[3]

II THE LAW GOVERNING AN ARBITRATION AGREEMENT

Arbitration is a consensual process; it depends on there being a legally binding agreement between the parties. Furthermore, the parties' agreement defines the limits of the arbitral tribunal's jurisdiction. Which law determines whether there is such an agreement and whether the dispute between the parties falls within its scope?

1 The New York Convention was first implemented in England by the Arbitration Act 1975.

2 See Sanders, 'Unity and Diversity in the Adoption of the Model Law' (1995) 11 Arb Int 1.

3 See Hill, 'Some Private International Law Aspects of the Arbitration Act 1996' (1997) 46 ICLQ 274.

It has already been noted that arbitration agreements are excluded from the material scope of the Rome Convention on the Law Applicable to Contractual Obligations.[4] Accordingly, the validity and construction of an arbitration agreement is governed by its proper law, as determined by common law principles. Conceptually, an arbitration agreement forms a separate contract, distinct from any broader agreement in which it is included;[5] it follows that the proper law of the arbitration agreement may be different from the law governing the substantive dispute between the parties.

Nevertheless, in the case of an arbitration clause which forms part of a substantive contract, the proper law of the arbitration agreement will normally be the law applicable to the contract as a whole. If the contract contains an express choice of law, the chosen law will also govern the arbitration clause. If the contract does not include an express choice of law, the law governing the contract (and the arbitration agreement) will normally be implied from the seat of arbitration[6] – that is, the place where the arbitration is, from a legal point of view, centred. So, if the parties agree to arbitrate their disputes in England the proper law of the arbitration agreement will normally be English law.[7] Similarly, where a submission agreement made after the dispute has arisen provides for the arbitration to be held in a particular country that will without more probably amount to an implied choice of the law of the seat to govern the arbitration agreement. If the parties fail to make an express choice of law and do not designate the seat of arbitration (from which a choice of law can be implied), the proper law of the arbitration agreement is, according to general principles, the law of the country with which it is most closely connected. Only in exceptional circumstances will this be different from the law governing the substantive contract.[8]

As will be seen, in the context of proceedings for the enforcement of an award under the New York Convention, it is possible for the award to be challenged on the basis that the arbitration agreement

4 Art 1(2)(d).

5 Arbitration Act 1996, s 7; *Harbour Assurance Co (UK) Ltd v Kansa General International Insurance Co Ltd* [1993] QB 701, [1993] 3 All ER 897.

6 See Arbitration Act 1996, s 3. The parties may choose the seat either expressly or impliedly: *ABB Lummus Global Ltd v Keppel Fels Ltd* [1999] 2 Lloyd's Rep 24. In the absence of express choice, the court should have regard only to events leading up to the point when the arbitration began (rather than to the whole history of the arbitration leading up to the award): *Dubai Islamic Bank PJSC v Paymentech Merchant Services Inc* [2001] 1 Lloyd's Rep 65.

7 *Hamlyn & Co v Talisker Distillery* [1894] AC 202; *Deutsche Schachtbau- und Tiefbohrgesellschaft mbH v Shell International Petroleum Co Ltd* [1990] 1 AC 295, [1987] 2 All ER 769; *XL Insurance Ltd v Owens Corning* [2000] 2 Lloyd's Rep 500.

8 Dicey and Morris, *The Conflict of Laws* (13th edn, 2000) pp 597–578.

is invalid.[9] In such a case, it is provided that, in the absence of choice by the parties, the validity of the arbitration agreement is governed by the law of the country in which the award is made.[10]

III THE LAW GOVERNING ARBITRATION PROCEEDINGS

The question here is which law governs the arbitration proceedings (as opposed to the arbitration agreement or the merits of the dispute between the parties). The arbitration proceedings include two elements: first, the procedure to be followed in the arbitration itself and the powers of the arbitral tribunal in relation to that procedure (the internal procedure); and secondly, the powers of the court to support and supervise the arbitration (the external procedure). Powers of support include, for example, the court's powers to appoint an arbitrator[11] and to grant an interim injunction[12] (such as a Mareva injunction freezing the respondent's assets). The most important of the court's powers of supervision is the power to set aside an award in a case where the arbitrator has exceeded his jurisdiction[13] or where there has been serious irregularity affecting the tribunal, the proceedings or the award.[14] The extent to which courts control arbitrations varies from country to country.

The rules determining which law governs the arbitration procedure have to try to satisfy two potentially conflicting objectives. On the one hand, the country in which the seat of arbitration is located has a legitimate interest in exercising a measure of control over local arbitrations to ensure that arbitration proceedings meet certain minimum standards of fairness. On the other hand, arbitration is a consensual process and the parties should, as a general rule, be free to determine for themselves how to resolve their disputes.

The Arbitration Act 1996 contains a number of provisions which seek to reconcile these competing objectives. First, the general principle is that the various provisions of the Act are prima facie applicable to an arbitration whose seat is in England.[15] So, if two foreign companies refer their dispute to arbitration in England the English court will have the power to remove an arbitrator on the

9 Art V(2)(a). See p 304.
10 Arbitration Act 1996, s 103(2)(b).
11 S 18.
12 S 44.
13 S 67.
14 S 68.
15 S 2(1).

basis of doubts as to his impartiality[16] or to set aside the award if it is obtained by fraud.[17] Most of the powers conferred by the Act are discretionary, however, and the court will have regard to the parties' connections with England when deciding whether or not to exercise its statutory powers.[18]

Secondly, the various provisions of the Act are divided into two groups: mandatory provisions and non-mandatory provisions.[19] The mandatory provisions obviously apply to all English arbitrations whatever the expressed wishes of the parties may be. Not surprisingly, the court's supervisory powers are to be found in mandatory provisions. This does not mean, however, that the powers conferred by the mandatory provisions will necessarily be exercised by the courts in all cases. As already noted, most of the court's powers – even the powers contained in the mandatory provisions – are discretionary. By contrast, the non-mandatory provisions apply only to the extent that the parties have not made their own arrangements.[20] A choice of a foreign law as the applicable law in respect of a matter provided for by a non-mandatory provision is equivalent to an agreement making provision about that matter.[21] Where, for example, parties to an English arbitration agree that the arbitration procedure should be governed by German law, all the non-mandatory provisions of the Act are displaced by the relevant German rules.

Where the seat of arbitration is abroad, as regards procedural questions, English law is prima facie irrelevant. However, certain provisions of the Act are applicable regardless of the seat of arbitration.[22] For example, the provisions relating to the staying of actions brought in breach of an arbitration clause are of universal application.[23] The court also has the power to exercise certain of its powers of support with regard to foreign arbitrations. Just as article 31 of the Brussels I Regulation authorises the English court to grant provisional and protective measures in support of legal proceedings being conducted in another member state, the Act

16 S 24(1)(a).
17 S 68(2)(g).
18 *SA Coppée-Lavalin NV v Ken-Ren Chemicals and Fertilizers Ltd* [1995] 1 AC 38, [1994] 2 All ER 449.
19 S 4 and Sch 1.
20 S 4(2) and (3). The mere fact that the parties' agreement provides that disputes should be 'submitted to the exclusive jurisdiction' of arbitrators is not sufficient to exclude the court's power to grant interim relief under s 44: *Re Q's Estate* [1999] 1 Lloyd's Rep 931.
21 S 4(5).
22 See s 2(2)–(5).
23 S 2(2).

enables the English court to exercise certain powers in support of foreign arbitration proceedings: the court may, for example, make orders in relation to the taking of the evidence of witnesses, the preservation of evidence, the sale of goods which are the subject-matter of the proceedings and the grant of interim injunctions.[24] There can, however, be no question of the court being able to set aside an award on the basis of serious irregularity in a case where the seat of arbitration is abroad, even if the parties have expressly agreed that the arbitration procedure should be governed by English law.

Because the Act permits the court to exercise some of its powers in relation to foreign arbitrations there is a danger that the English court could come into conflict with the courts of the seat of arbitration. The court should exercise caution when invited to assist a foreign arbitration; it is expressly provided that the court may refuse to exercise any power if the fact that the seat of arbitration is outside England and Wales makes it inappropriate to do so.[25] It must be remembered that, if the seat of arbitration is in country X, the court of country X is 'the natural court' to provide assistance.[26]

Legal proceedings under the 1996 Act are governed by the CPR. In order for the court to have jurisdiction, the arbitration claim form, which initiates the proceedings, must be served on the defendant in accordance with the relevant procedural rules.[27] In appropriate cases, the court will give permission to serve the defendant out of the jurisdiction.

IV THE LAW GOVERNING THE MERITS OF THE DISPUTE

Where a dispute is referred to arbitration, usually the dispute arises out of a contract. According to what rules is the arbitral tribunal to decide the dispute? It is well established that the arbitral tribunal is required to apply the choice of law rules of the law of the seat of arbitration. As far as the common law was concerned, it was generally assumed that English arbitrators were bound to apply the choice of law rules which were binding on the English courts. This rule was the consequence of the traditional English approach that

24 S 44.
25 S 2(3). See *Viking Insurance Co v Rossdale* [2002] 1 Lloyd's Rep 219.
26 Lord Mustill in *Channel Tunnel Group Ltd v Balfour Beatty Construction Ltd* [1993] AC 334 at 368.
27 CPR Pt 62, PD62. See *Vale do Rio Doce Navegaçao SA v Shanghai Bao Steel Ocean Shipping Co Ltd* [2000] 2 Lloyd's Rep 1.

awards could be reviewed by the courts on points of law, including choice of law issues.[28]

Some other countries have taken a different approach and an established feature of many foreign arbitration laws is a statutory provision which sets out the special choice of law principles to be applied by arbitrators. The Arbitration Act 1996 broke with English tradition by introducing such a provision into English law. The choice of law rules in section 46 deal with three different types of situation: first, the parties make a choice of law; secondly, the parties choose 'other considerations'; thirdly, the parties fail to make a choice.

A Choice of law

The first principle is that the arbitral tribunal shall decide the dispute 'in accordance with the law chosen by the parties as applicable to the substance of the dispute'.[29] The doctrine of renvoi is excluded.[30] It would seem that a choice of public international law would also be effective under this first principle.[31]

B Choice of 'other considerations'

Arbitration is seen by some as a mechanism for avoiding the idiosyncrasies of national laws. Why should the parties to an international contract have to submit their dispute to the substantive law of a particular country? Why should they not authorise the tribunal to decide the dispute by reference to other standards? There are various options which the parties might consider. First, if one party is English and the other French the parties might agree that the contract should be governed by principles common to English and

28 Under the Arbitration Act 1996 the court may still rule on points of law: s 69. However, the parties are free to exclude this power in the arbitration agreement; where the parties agree to arbitration in accordance with the rules of certain arbitral institutions (such as the ICC) the effect of the agreement is to exclude the right to appeal on points of law: *Arab African Energy Corpn Ltd v Olieprodukten Nederland BV* [1983] 2 Lloyd's Rep 419; *Sanghi Polyesters Ltd (India) v International Investor (KCFC) (Kuwait)* [2000] 1 Lloyd's Rep 480. Where s 69 has not been excluded, the court's power is limited to ruling on points of English law; if the applicable law is the law of another country, there can be no application under s 69: *Egmatra AG v Marco Trading Corpn* [1999] 1 Lloyd's Rep 862.

29 S 46(1)(a).

30 S 46(2).

31 *Orion Compania Espanola de Seguros v Belfort Maatschappij voor Algemene Verzekgringeen* [1962] 2 Lloyd's Rep 257.

French law[32] or the parties might agree on principles common to the law of country X and public international law. Secondly, the parties may wish to choose rules which are detached from any particular legal system. A choice of law clause may stipulate, for example, 'internationally accepted principles of law governing contractual relations' (sometimes referred to as the lex mercatoria).[33] Thirdly, the parties may wish the tribunal to decide the dispute by reference to principles of equity or fairness rather than in accordance with strict rules of law. Arbitration under an 'equity clause' is often referred to by its Latin label, arbitration *ex aequo et bono*, or by the broadly equivalent French term, *amiable composition*.

The Act permits the parties to make any of these choices. It is provided that, if the parties so agree, the arbitral tribunal shall decide the dispute 'in accordance with such other considerations as are agreed by them or determined by the tribunal'.[34]

C Absence of choice

If the parties fail to make a choice of law the Arbitration Act 1996 provides that 'the tribunal shall apply the law determined by the conflict of laws rules which it considers applicable'.[35] By virtue of this provision English arbitrators are no longer bound by the choice of law rules which are applied by the English courts. Of course, English arbitrators may, in suitable cases, apply the choice of law rules contained in the Rome Convention on the Law Applicable to Contractual Obligations, but they do not have to.

It is not uncommon for parties who have little or no connection with England to agree to arbitration in London. Indeed, the parties may choose London as the seat of arbitration precisely because it is a neutral venue. The arbitrators might in such a case choose to apply the conflicts rules which are common to the laws of both parties' countries. Where, for example, a dispute between a Singaporean claimant and a New Zealand respondent is referred to arbitration in England the tribunal might decide that the governing law is to be determined by the common law proper law doctrine, rather than by the choice of law rules to be found in the Rome Convention, on the

32 This was the choice of the parties in some of the contracts relating to the Channel Tunnel project: Redfern and Hunter, *Law and Practice of International Commercial Arbitration* (3rd edn, 1999) pp 108–109.

33 Whether the lex mercatoria really exists is not free from controversy. See, for example, Mustill, 'The New Lex Mercatoria: The First Twenty-Five Years' (1988) 4 Arb Int 86.

34 S 46(1)(b).

35 S 46(3).

basis that the proper law doctrine is applicable in both Singapore and New Zealand. The advantage of such an approach is that it reduces the chance that the outcome of the dispute will turn simply on where the arbitration happens to be held.

Although the Act gives arbitrators considerable room for manoeuvre in cases where the parties fail to make a choice, it should be noted that the statutory rules require the tribunal to adopt a traditional choice of law methodology. In the absence of choice by the parties the tribunal must, first, decide which choice of law rules are applicable and, then, apply those rules to identify the law of a country as the applicable law. The tribunal is not entitled, in the absence of choice by the parties, to ignore all choice of law rules and decide the dispute in accordance with the lex mercatoria or by reference to the arbitrator's own conceptions of what is fair; the tribunal must apply a 'law', a term which is inapt to describe principles of fairness or the lex mercatoria.[36]

D Mandatory rules

If, in a case where the parties have not designated the applicable law, the arbitrators are free in their discretion to choose conflicts rules to determine the applicable law, there is a danger that the parties will be permitted to evade mandatory rules imposed in the public interest which would have to be applied by the court if the parties' dispute were resolved by litigation. Furthermore, in cases where the parties make an express choice of law, section 46 of the Arbitration Act 1996 does not seem to make any provision for the application of the mandatory rules of a law with which the situation has a close connection, but which is not the law chosen by the parties.

The extent to which arbitrators should have regard to mandatory rules is a controversial issue.[37] The practical reality, however, is that if arbitrators fail to take into account the mandatory rules of a country which has a close connection with the situation (by virtue of being the seat of arbitration or the country in which the award will be enforced) there is a likelihood that the award will be legally ineffective. It has already been noted that, if England is the seat of

36 This view is supported by the Departmental Advisory Committee's *Report on the Arbitration Bill* (1996) p 50 (para 225). A different view is suggested, however, by the judgment of Donaldson MR in *Deutsche Schachtbau- und Tiefbohrgesellschaft mbH v Shell International Petroleum Co Ltd* [1990] 1 AC 295 at 316.

37 See Mayer, 'Mandatory Rules of Law in International Arbitration' (1986) 2 Arb Int 274; Hochstrasser, 'Choice of Law and "Foreign" Mandatory Rules' (1994) 11 J Int Arb (1) 57; Blessing, 'Mandatory Rules of Law versus Party Autonomy in International Arbitration' (1997) 14 J Int Arb (4) 23.

arbitration, a party may challenge the award on the ground of serious irregularity.[38] It is provided, for example, that the court may set aside an award which is contrary to public policy.[39] An award which is set aside by the courts of the country in which it was made is a nullity and enforcement of such an award may be refused in any country which is party to the New York Convention.[40] The New York Convention also provides that enforcement of an award may be refused on the ground that it infringes the public policy of the forum in which enforcement is sought.[41]

The possible impact of public policy may be illustrated by a simple example. Suppose that two Unites States corporations conclude an anti-competitive agreement to be performed exclusively in Europe. The agreement is void under article 81 EC but is valid under New York law, the law chosen by the parties. When a dispute arises it is referred to arbitration in England. What is the likely outcome if the English arbitrator upholds the agreement on the ground that it is valid under New York law? The answer, of course, is that the losing party will in all probability apply to have the award set aside on the ground that it infringes English public policy (which undoubtedly includes European public policy[42]). Since, in the final analysis, the whole arbitration is a waste of time and money if the arbitrator's award is not enforceable (because, for example, it violates the public policy of the law of the seat) the arbitrator must, in practice, consider the potentially relevant mandatory rules.

V THE JURISDICTIONAL EFFECT OF AN ARBITRATION AGREEMENT

What position should the courts adopt in a situation where one party to an arbitration agreement starts legal proceedings in breach of the terms of that agreement? The issues raised by this type of situation are similar to those surrounding jurisdiction agreements. One might reasonably suppose that the courts would require the parties to stick to their agreement and would stay the proceedings. One of the purposes of the New York Convention was to ensure that arbitration agreements are respected and enforced. Article II of the Convention obliges the courts of contracting states to stay legal proceedings

38 S 68.
39 S 68(2)(g).
40 Art V(1)(e).
41 Art V(2).
42 Case C-126/97 *Eco Swiss China Time Ltd v Benetton International BV* [1999] ECR I-3055.

which are brought in breach of an arbitration clause. According to the provisions of the Arbitration Act 1996 which implement article II of the Convention, the English courts are required to grant a stay of proceedings only if a number of conditions are satisfied.

First, the arbitration agreement must be 'in writing'.[43] This expression is given a broad definition; the Act extends to agreements which are evidenced in writing[44] and to cases where the parties agree otherwise than in writing to terms which are in writing.[45] It is also provided that an agreement is 'in writing' if it is recorded by any means.[46] In *Zambia Steel and Building Supplies Ltd v James Clark & Eaton Ltd*[47] an English seller offered to sell goods to a Zambian company on its standard terms and conditions, which included an English arbitration clause. The buyer orally consented to the terms and ordered goods from the seller. Subsequently, the buyer started legal proceedings in England and the seller sought a stay on the basis of the arbitration clause. A question arose as to whether the clause was 'in writing'. The Court of Appeal held that it was; where a printed clause is orally or tacitly accepted – so that it becomes a term of the contract – it satisfies the formal requirements of the English legislation.

Secondly, the legal proceedings in question must be 'in respect of a matter which under the agreement is to be referred to arbitration'.[48] The defendant does not have the right to a stay if the dispute does not fall within the arbitrator's jurisdiction. The court may have to decide, for example, whether the arbitration agreement is broad enough to cover a claim in tort brought by one party to the agreement against another. Such questions must be determined by reference to the proper law of the arbitration agreement.[49]

Thirdly, the arbitration agreement must not be 'null and void, inoperative or incapable of being performed'.[50] Whether or not the agreement is valid should also be referred to its proper law.[51]

Fourthly, the defendant in legal proceedings loses the right to a mandatory stay under the Act if he submits to the court's jurisdiction by taking a step in those proceedings to answer the substantive claim.[52] However, a party who applies for a stay but, subsequently

43 S 5.
44 S 5(2)(c).
45 S 5(4).
46 S 5(6).
47 [1986] 2 Lloyd's Rep 225. See also *Abdullah M Fahem & Co v Mareb Yemen Insurance Co* [1997] 2 Lloyd's Rep 738.
48 S 9(1).
49 See pp 292–294.
50 S 9(4).
51 See pp 292–294.
52 S 9(3). See *Patel v Patel* [2000] QB 551.

or simultaneously, invokes or accepts the court's jurisdiction conditionally on the application for a stay failing, is not to be regarded as having taken a step in the proceedings.[53]

Finally, the subject-matter of the dispute must be capable of settlement by arbitration.[54] Although the majority of commercial disputes are arbitrable, there are limits. Because of the consensual nature of arbitration, the arbitrator cannot determine certain types of dispute which have implications not only for the parties. It is not possible, for example, for an arbitrator to make an award in rem in a shipping dispute or to make a binding award winding up a company.

If these conditions are satisfied, the defendant is entitled to a stay and the fact that there would be potential advantages if the parties' dispute were considered by the court (where, for example, the dispute involves three parties, only two of whom are bound by the arbitration agreement) is irrelevant.[55] By the same token, the court cannot refuse to grant a stay on the basis that the defendant has no prospect of successfully defending the claim and it would be quicker and cheaper if the court made a summary judgment under the procedure provided by Part 24 of the CPR.[56] If there is a dispute between the parties – that is to say, where the claimant advances a claim which the defendant does not admit – the grant of a stay is mandatory.[57] It should also be noted that, even if the case is not one in which a stay is mandatory under the 1996 Act, the court may grant a stay under its inherent jurisdiction.[58]

VI THE ENFORCEMENT OF FOREIGN ARBITRAL AWARDS

A Introduction

Arbitral awards made in foreign countries may be enforced in England under one of a number of regimes: the common law, Part II of the Arbitration Act 1950 (which implements the Geneva

53 *Capital Trust Investments Ltd v Radio Design TJ AB* [2002] 2 All ER 159.
54 S 81(1)(a).
55 *Wealands v CLC Contractors Ltd* [1999] 2 Lloyd's Rep 739.
56 *Halki Shipping Corpn v Sopex Oils Ltd* [1998] 1 WLR 726. For criticism of this decision see Wallace, 'Arbitration: Another Nail in the Coffin' [1998] ICLR 371.
57 See Swinton Thomas LJ at 761. Arguably, the court should also grant a stay in a case when, whether or not the defendant admits the claim, the arbitration agreement provides that, in the particular circumstances, a dispute shall be deemed to have arisen: see *Glencore Grain Ltd v Agros Trading Co* [1999] 2 Lloyd's Rep 410.
58 *Channel Tunnel Group Ltd v Balfour Beatty Construction Ltd* [1993] AC 334.

Convention of 1927) and the Arbitration Act 1996 (which gives effect to the provisions of New York Convention of 1958). Because the New York Convention has been so widely ratified the vast majority of foreign awards fall within the scope of the 1996 Act. Part II of the 1950 Act applies only to awards made in one of the very few countries which has ratified the Geneva Convention, but not the New York Convention. The common law rules, which apply to awards made in countries which have not ratified any of the conventions, are not significantly different from the statutory rules based on the New York Convention.[59] Accordingly, the paragraphs which follow deal exclusively with enforcement under the 1996 Act.

B The scope of the Arbitration Act 1996

The Act applies only to 'New York Convention awards' and provides that an award[60] falls within the scope of the Act if it was made in pursuance of an arbitration agreement in a state which is a party to the Convention.[61] For the purposes of this principle the arbitration agreement must be an agreement in writing[62] and an award is treated as made at the seat of arbitration, regardless of where it was signed.[63] As long as, when the claimant seeks to enforce the award, the country of the seat of arbitration is a party to the Convention, the Act applies, even if the country had not yet become a party to the Convention when the arbitration agreement was concluded or when the arbitration was commenced or when the award was made.[64]

C Grounds for refusing enforcement

To resist enforcement of an award under the Arbitration Act 1996 the defendant must establish one of a number of grounds set out in the Act. These grounds are exhaustive; enforcement cannot be refused for a reason outside the legislation.[65] Even if the defendant establishes one of the grounds listed in the Act, the court retains a

59 See *Minister of Public Works of the Government of the State of Kuwait v Sir Frederick Snow & Partners* [1984] AC 426 at 434–435.

60 To qualify as an award for the purpose of the 1996 Act the decision must emanate from a body whose jurisdiction derives from the parties' agreement: *Al Midani v Al Midani* [1999] 1 Lloyd's Rep 923.

61 S 100(1).

62 S 100(2)(a).

63 Ss 53 and 100(2)(b) (reversing the much criticised decision of the House of Lords in *Hiscox v Outhwaite* [1992] 1 AC 562, [1991] 3 All ER 641).

64 *Minister of Public Works of the Government of the State of Kuwait v Sir Frederick Snow & Partners* [1984] AC 426, [1984] 1 All ER 73.

65 S 103(1). *Rosseel NV v Oriental Commercial & Shipping Co (UK) Ltd* [1991] 2 Lloyd's Rep 625.

discretion whether to order enforcement or not.[66] Where, for example, the defect on which the defendant relies is insubstantial or technical and the degree of prejudice suffered by the defendant is minor, the court is likely to order enforcement.[67] There are eight potential grounds.

First, enforcement may be refused if the person against whom the award is invoked proves that 'a party to the arbitration agreement was (under the law applicable to him) under some incapacity'.[68] Secondly, enforcement may be refused if 'the arbitration agreement was not valid under the law to which the parties subjected it or, failing any indication thereon, under the law of the country where the award was made'.[69]

Thirdly, enforcement may be refused in cases of procedural unfairness – where the person against whom the award is invoked was not given proper notice of the appointment of the arbitrator or of arbitration proceedings or was otherwise unable to present his case.[70] This provision is designed to deal with the situation where the inability to present his case results from matters outside the defendant's control; it does not provide a defence to enforcement where the defendant fails to take advantage of the opportunity provided by the arbitration procedure.[71] As a general rule, the arbitrator is given a broad discretion to fix the procedure which is most appropriate for the particular dispute which has been referred to arbitration. For example, it may be decided to conduct a 'documents-only' arbitration. The fact that the arbitrator has chosen one procedural model rather than another will not normally, in itself, provide a ground for resisting the award. The mere fact that the defendant was not permitted to present oral evidence, for example, does not without more constitute a ground for refusing to enforce the award.[72] Even where the arbitrator failed to follow the agreed procedure, the defendant is not able to rely on the natural justice defence if the procedural irregularity has been waived.[73]

Fourthly, if the award deals with matters which are not within the arbitrator's jurisdiction, enforcement may be refused.[74] If it is

66 See Paulsson, 'May or Must under the New York Convention: An Exercise in Syntax and Linguistics' (1998) 14 Arb Int 227.
67 *China Agribusiness Development Corpn v Balli Trading* [1998] 2 Lloyd's Rep 76.
68 S 103(2)(a).
69 S 103(2)(b). The proper law of an arbitration agreement is considered at pp 292–294.
70 S 103(2)(c). See *Irvani v Irvani* [2000] 1 Lloyd's Rep 412.
71 *Minmetals Germany GmbH v Ferco Steel Ltd* [1999] CLC 647.
72 *Dalmia Dairy Industries Ltd v National Bank of Pakistan* [1978] 2 Lloyd's Rep 223.
73 *Minmetals Germany GmbH v Ferco Steel Ltd* [1999] CLC 647.
74 S 103(2)(d).

possible to sever the matters which were within the terms of the submission to arbitration from the matters which were not, the court may order enforcement of the award in relation to the matters which were within the arbitrator's jurisdiction.[75]

Fifthly, if the arbitral tribunal did not follow the applicable procedural rules enforcement may be refused. The ground for refusing enforcement may be invoked if 'the composition of the tribunal or the arbitration procedure was not in accordance with the agreement of the parties or, failing such agreement, with the law of the country in which the arbitration took place'.[76] On the face of it, the arbitrator is placed in an impossible situation in a case where the procedure agreed by the parties is in conflict with the mandatory requirements of the law of the seat: if the arbitrator complies with the parties' agreement, the award may be set aside by the courts of the country in which the seat is located; if the arbitrator complies with the law of the seat, enforcement may be refused for failure to act in accordance with the parties' agreement. It should be stressed, however, that the Act sets out grounds on which an award *may* be refused. The court should not exercise its discretion to refuse enforcement in a case where an arbitrator, in order to adhere to the mandatory rules of the law of the seat, fails to respect the terms of the parties' agreement.

Sixthly, an award may be refused enforcement if it has not yet become binding on the parties (because, for example, the parties have a right to appeal to a second arbitral tribunal) or the award has been set aside by a competent authority of the country in which, or under the law of which, it was made.[77] It has been seen that the courts of the seat of arbitration have the primary role of supervising the arbitral process. If the French courts set aside an award made in France, the award is a nullity. Notwithstanding the fact that the court has discretion to order enforcement in cases where one of the defences is made out, it is not thought that an English court would exercise its discretion to enforce an award which has been set aside in the country of origin.[78] However, there have been exceptional cases in which the courts of some other countries have done so.[79]

75 S 103(4).
76 S 103(2)(e).
77 S 103(2)(f).
78 Dicey and Morris, *The Conflict of Laws* (13th edn, 2000) p 640. See also Goode, 'The Role of the Lex Loci Arbitri in International Commercial Arbitration' (2001) 17 Int Arb 19.
79 For consideration of the United States case law see Freyer, 'United States Recognition and Enforcement of Annulled Foreign Awards' (2000) 17 J Arb Int (2) 1; Wahl, 'Enforcement of Foreign Arbitral Awards Set Aside in their Country of Origin' (1999) 16 J Int Arb (4) 131. See also Petrochilos, 'Enforcing Awards Annulled in their State of Origin' (1999) 48 ICLQ 856.

The legislation also envisages the situation where parties agree to arbitrate a dispute in country X according to the procedural law of country Y. If, in such a case, the award is set aside by the courts of country Y enforcement of the award in England may be refused.

Seventhly, enforcement may be refused if it is in respect of a matter which is not capable of settlement by arbitration.[80] The legislation does not expressly indicate by which law arbitrability is to be tested. However, the relevant provision of the New York Convention states that the applicable law is the law of the country in which enforcement is sought.[81] So, if the claimant seeks to enforce in England an award which is made in Switzerland the English court may refuse enforcement on the ground that the dispute was not arbitrable under English law, even though it was arbitrable under the law of the seat.

Finally, a foreign award may be refused enforcement in England if it conflicts with English public policy.[82] The cases suggest that public policy is to be interpreted restrictively in this context. Where, for example, an award has already been challenged (unsuccessfully) in legal proceedings at the seat of arbitration, the court will not normally reinvestigate those same issues at the enforcement stage.[83] The courts have not been impressed by the suggestion that enforcement should be refused on the basis of public policy in a case where the arbitrator has decided the dispute according to the lex mercatoria[84] or through the application of non-legal criteria.[85] It has been said that enforcement should not be refused under this head unless 'there is some element of illegality or [unless] the enforcement would be clearly contrary to the public good or, possibly, [unless] enforcement would be wholly offensive to the ordinary reasonable and fully informed members of the public on whose behalf the powers of the state are exercised'.[86]

80 S 103(3).

81 Art V(2)(a).

82 S 103(3). For the purposes of this provision 'public policy' includes European Union public policy: see Case C-126/97 *Eco Swiss China Time Ltd v Benetton International BV* [1999] ECR I-3055 (a case involving a Dutch award which failed to take into account European Union competition law). For consideration of whether non-compliance with the Human Rights Act 1998 can give rise to non-enforcement of an award on grounds of public policy see Ambrose, 'Arbitration and the Human Rights Act' [2000] LMCLQ 468.

83 *Minmetals Germany GmbH v Ferco Steel Ltd* [1999] CLC 647.

84 *Deutsche Schachtbau- und Tiefbohrgesellschaft mbH v Shell International Petroleum Co Ltd* [1990] 1 AC 295, [1987] 2 All ER 769.

85 *Norske Atlas Insurance Co Ltd v London General Insurance Co Ltd* (1927) 28 Ll L Rep 104 (a case decided at common law).

86 Donaldson MR in *Deutsche Schachtbau- und Tiefbohrgesellschaft mbH v Shell International Petroleum Co Ltd* [1990] 1 AC 295 at 316.

While it is well established that awards will be refused enforcement in cases involving illegality, the precise boundaries of the English doctrine are not clear.[87] Three cases are of interest. First, in *Soleimany v Soleimany*[88] the Court of Appeal, on grounds of public policy, refused enforcement of an award (made under Jewish law) which had upheld a contract, the purpose of which was to smuggle carpets out of Iran illegally. Secondly, in *Westacre Investments Inc v Jugoimport-SDRP Holding Co Ltd*,[89] an award by Swiss arbitrators ordered the defendant to make certain payments which the claimant alleged were due under a consultancy contract. The arbitrators had rejected the defendant's argument that the contract was illegal under the law of Kuwait, where the consultancy services were to be performed. When the claimant started proceedings to enforce the award in England, the defendant sought to resist enforcement on the basis of public policy. The Court of Appeal ordered enforcement; the arbitral tribunal had rejected the defendant's argument based on illegality and, in the absence of fresh evidence which called into question the arbitrators' decision, the Court of Appeal declined to re-open the issue.[90] Thirdly, in *Omnium de Traitement et de Valorisation SA v Hilmarton Ltd*[91] the defendant declined to pay all the fees which had been agreed in a consultancy contract under which the claimant helped the defendant to secure a public works contract in Algeria. Although the Swiss arbitrator decided that the contract wittingly breached Algerian law, he ordered the defendant to pay the fees due under the contract. When the claimant sought to enforce the award in England, the defendant, relying on the *Soleimany* case, argued that enforcement would be contrary to English policy – on the basis that, if the award was enforced, the court would be indirectly enforcing a contract, the performance of which was illegal under the law of the place of performance. Although in *Soleimany v Soleimany* the Court of Appeal held that 'the interposition of an arbitration award does not isolate the successful party's claim from the illegality which gave rise to it,'[92] the judge decided that, notwithstanding the fact that the underlying contract was illegal under Algerian law, enforcement of the award was not contrary to public policy; the important point was that, as in the *Westacre* case, there was no element of corruption involved.

87 See Enonchong, 'The Enforcement of Foreign Arbitral Awards Based on Illegal Contracts' [2001] LMCLQ 495.
88 [1999] QB 785.
89 [2000] 1 QB 288.
90 See also *Soinco SACI v Novokuznetsk Aluminium Plant* [1998] 2 Lloyd's Rep 337.
91 [1999] 2 Lloyd's Rep 222.
92 [1999] QB 785 at 800.

D Staying enforcement proceedings

Once an award has been made, it is not uncommon for an unsuccessful respondent to start proceedings to challenge the award at the seat of arbitration before the successful claimant takes steps to enforce it. Where, for example, an award is made in Switzerland, what should the English court do if, when enforcement proceedings are commenced in England, there are already setting aside proceedings pending in the Swiss courts? The Arbitration Act 1996 provides that where an application for setting aside has been made to a competent authority abroad the English court may, if it considers it proper, adjourn its decision on the enforcement of the award; if enforcement is adjourned the defendant may be required to put up suitable security.[93]

The exercise of the power to adjourn enforcement proceedings requires the court to strike a delicate balance. It would be unfortunate if the English court ordered immediate enforcement only for the court of the seat to decide subsequently that the award is a nullity. If there is a serious likelihood that the award will be set aside, the prudent course is for the English court to adjourn its decision. However, the court should not order an adjournment as a matter of course. If the application for the award to be set aside is obviously hopeless, it would be wrong to deprive the successful claimant of the fruits of victory (even temporarily). The court needs to be vigilant to ensure that respondents are not permitted to exploit potential opportunities to slow down the arbitral process.

As a general rule, enforcement should be adjourned only if the respondent produces 'some summary proof that the award is tainted by a defect which is likely to cause its setting aside in the country of origin'.[94] In *Soleh Boneh International Ltd v Government of the Republic of Uganda*[95] the Court of Appeal considered that the exercise of discretion to adjourn enforcement and to order security requires a consideration of two factors. First, the court must consider the strength of the argument that the award is invalid:

> If the award is manifestly invalid, there should be an adjournment and no order for security; if it is manifestly valid, there should either be an order for immediate enforcement, or else an order for substantial security.[96]

Secondly, the court must consider the ease or difficulty of enforcement of the award, and whether it will be rendered more difficult if it is

93 S 103(5). *Dardana Ltd v Yukos Oil Co* [2002] 1 Lloyd's Rep 225.
94 Van den Berg, *The New York Arbitration Convention of 1958* (1981) pp 353–354.
95 [1993] 2 Lloyd's Rep 208.
96 Staughton LJ at 212.

delayed (for example, by the respondent removing assets from the jurisdiction).

E Recognition

Most cases concerning foreign awards involve proceedings brought by a successful claimant to enforce the award. However, a successful respondent in arbitration proceedings is entitled to rely on the award as a defence against a subsequent action by the claimant on the same cause of action.[97] The Arbitration Act 1996 provides that a New York Convention award 'shall be recognised as binding on the persons as between whom it was made, and may accordingly be relied upon by those persons by way of defence ... in any legal proceedings in England'.[98]

97 See *Dallal v Bank Mellatt* [1986] QB 441, [1986] 1 All ER 239.
98 S 101(1).

Chapter 8

Marriage

I INTRODUCTION

When the English court has to decide whether a marriage is valid, foreign elements may be involved: one or both of the spouses may be foreign, or the marriage may have been celebrated in a foreign country. This chapter considers which law applies to determine the validity of such marriages.

There are various defects which may make a marriage invalid. These and the rules that precisely define them will differ between various legal systems. For example, the question may be whether the proper formalities for the celebration of the marriage were complied with, or whether one of the spouses was below the minimum permitted age, or whether they are too closely related. On such matters, obviously, different countries have different rules.

For choice of law purposes, rules about the validity of marriage are divided into two classes: those concerned with *formal* validity and those concerned with *essential* validity. Rules of formal validity lay down the way in which a marriage must be celebrated. Rules of essential validity are concerned with the substance of the marriage relationship itself. Formal validity is governed by the law of the country where the marriage is celebrated (lex loci celebrationis), while essential validity is governed by the personal laws of the parties at the time of, or immediately after, the marriage. These propositions will be considered in detail below.

A Degrees of invalidity

There are different degrees of invalidity which can result from a defect according to different laws. In English law a marriage which is invalid may be either void ab initio or merely voidable. In the cases of a marriage within the prohibited degrees, or below the permitted age, for example, the marriage is void. Lack of consent of a party makes the marriage voidable. When a marriage is void in English law either party may apply to the court for a nullity decree, but a decree is not necessary to make the marriage void. Even without a decree, the parties are single and free to remarry. On the other hand, a marriage which is voidable is valid unless and until it is annulled by the court on the petition of one of the parties. As regards a voidable marriage, if a nullity decree is made, it does not have retrospective effect; the marriage merely ceases to exist for the future.

Foreign laws also have different kinds of invalidity, but these do not necessarily correspond to the English distinction between void and voidable marriages. Under Scots law, for example, the annulment of a voidable marriage has retrospective effect. Under a particular law there may be more than two categories of invalidity. In principle, the law which determines whether the marriage is invalid also determines the kind of invalidity and its consequences.[1] However, this must presumably be subject to the qualification that the English court can grant a decree only of a kind and form known to English law. It would follow that the kind of invalidity under the foreign law must be classified by the English court as either voidness or voidability, whichever is closer to the foreign conception.

B Classification of defects

Because there are different choice of law rules for questions of formal validity and questions of essential validity, it is necessary that any alleged defect to a marriage be classified as relating to either formalities or essentials. Until this is done, the appropriate choice of law rule cannot be applied. With most alleged defects this classification process is simple and automatic. For example, whether the requisite number of witnesses is present at the marriage ceremony obviously relates to the formalities, whereas the age at which one can marry is clearly a matter relating to capacity or essential validity. However, in respect of certain other alleged impediments, the appropriate classification may not be self-evident. In particular, problems have arisen here with regard to proxy marriages and parental consent.

1. Proxy marriages

Under English law both parties are required to be present at the marriage ceremony.[2] In some other countries, however, proxy

1 *De Reneville v De Reneville* [1948] P 100, [1948] 1 All ER 56; *Lepre v Lepre* [1965] P 52, [1963] 2 All ER 49.

2 This is implicit in the Marriage Act 1949, s 44(3), which requires both parties to make various declarations at the marriage ceremony.

marriages are permitted. In *Apt v Apt*[3] an English domiciliary executed a power of attorney authorising a friend to go through a marriage ceremony on her behalf in Argentina with an Argentinian domiciliary. If the requirement of the parties' presence at the marriage ceremony were classified as relating to the essentials of marriage, the marriage would have been held void as the English woman would have lacked capacity. It was held, however, classifying the issue according to the lex fori,[4] that the requirement of presence related to the method of giving consent, as opposed to the fact of consent (which would have been an essential requirement). It thus related to the method by which the ceremony was performed which is a matter of formal validity to be governed by Argentinian law, the lex loci celebrationis, according to which the marriage was valid.

2. Parental consent

Legal systems often provide that persons below a certain age must have the consent of their parents to marry, but of course the age below which such consent is necessary, and the consequences of failure to obtain it, differ from one law to another. Does this requirement relate to formalities or essentials? At first sight, it might seem that a requirement of parental consent relates to capacity, at any rate if the marriage is invalid without such consent, presumably because it is thought that the judgment of the person concerned is insufficiently mature. The English requirement of parental consent, however, is regarded by the English courts as a formality, not an incapacity. The main reason for this is that the absence of parental consent in English law does not normally invalidate the marriage. If the parties manage to have the marriage celebrated without it, nevertheless the marriage is normally valid. So, it is hardly possible to say that there is any incapacity involved.

It should not necessarily follow that a foreign rule about parental consent should also be classified as one of formalities if by the foreign law the absence of parental consent does affect the validity of the marriage. Nevertheless, following the general rule that classification is to be effected by the lex fori, it has been held that such a foreign rule concerns formalities and, therefore, is only to be applied if the marriage is celebrated in the foreign country concerned. *Ogden v Ogden*[5] involved a marriage which was celebrated in England between a woman domiciled in England and a man aged 19 domiciled in France. According to French law a man of that

3 [1948] P 83, [1947] 2 All ER 677.
4 See p 12.
5 [1908] P 46.

age required the consent of his parents to marry and, if such consent was not obtained, the marriage was voidable. The Court of Appeal held that the French requirement of parental consent was a formality and, accordingly, that French law, not being the lex loci celebrationis, was inapplicable. The formal validity of the marriage was tested by English law as the parties had married here. The marriage had been celebrated according to the forms required by English law and was thus held to be valid.[6]

This decision has been widely criticised, but in *Lodge v Lodge*[7] it was again accepted that the French requirement was a formality. In this case, the marriage was celebrated in Scotland between a husband domiciled in England and a wife aged 18 domiciled in France who did not have parental consent. The English court held the marriage valid under Scots law as the lex loci celebrationis, following *Ogden v Ogden*.[8]

Critics of this approach would not necessarily claim that all rules relating to parental consent should be treated as rules of capacity. In *Simonin v Mallac*[9] a couple domiciled in France celebrated their marriage in England without parental consent. The husband was 29 and the wife 22. By French law parties of those ages had to request the consent of their parents 'by a respectful and formal act'. If, however, this was refused, and continued to be refused when the request was repeated twice more at monthly intervals, then the parties were free to marry without it. The marriage was held valid. The French rule here can reasonably be regarded as one of formality, in substance analogous to a requirement of notice, unlike the rule considered in *Ogden v Ogden*, under which the parental consent could not be dispensed with.

II FORMAL VALIDITY

A The general rule

Under formal validity one is concerned with the law which governs the ceremony and other procedures required for the valid celebration

6 Another reason for the decision was that since the marriage was celebrated in England and the wife was domiciled here, then according to the rule in *Sottomayer v De Barros (No 2)* (1879) 5 PD 94 the validity of the marriage was to be tested exclusively by English law. See p 333.

7 (1963) 107 Sol Jo 437.

8 This decision could not have been reached on the basis of the rule in *Sottomayer v De Barros (No 2)*. See p 333.

9 (1860) 2 Sw & Tr 67.

of a marriage. The following matters relate to the formalities of the marriage: whether a civil ceremony or a religious ceremony is necessary, or whether either will suffice, or whether it is enough for the spouses simply to take each other as husband and wife; if a ceremony is required, what ancillary formalities as to notices and witnesses are necessary; where, when and by whom the ceremony must be conducted. Also, as already seen, issues relating to proxy marriages and parental consent are regarded as matters relating to formal validity.

Under English domestic law a failure to comply with the English formal requirements relating to a marriage ceremony will not necessarily render the marriage void. Broadly speaking, there are two types of formal requirement. Non-compliance with the first category (for example, parental consent) does not render the marriage void.[10] Thus while a marriage official may refuse to marry persons without the necessary consents, if they go through a marriage ceremony, the marriage is valid. Non-compliance with the second category (for example, that the marriage must be solemnised by a person who is a recognised marriage official) will render the marriage void – but only if both parties were aware of the irregularity at the time of the marriage ceremony.[11] The main sanction for non-compliance with the formalities of marriage is afforded by the criminal law.[12] Many other legal systems, however, are not so indulgent and a failure to comply with formal requirements will render a marriage void.

The basic rule is that formal validity is governed by the lex loci celebrationis, the law of the country where the marriage is celebrated. In *McCabe v McCabe*[13] a marriage ceremony was performed in Ghana. The parties to the marriage, an Irish and a Ghanaian domiciliary, were not present but the man had sent £100 and a bottle of gin. Relatives of both parties were present and the money was distributed among them and the gin opened to bless the marriage. It was held that the marriage was formally valid because it had complied with Akan custom which was permitted by Ghanaian law.

This rule is an application of a general principle of the conflict of laws, locus regit actum (the place governs the deed). The principle is partly one of convenience. Parties to a transaction must be free to

10 Marriage Act 1949, ss 24, 48.

11 Ss 25, 49. See, for example, *Chief Adjudication Officer v Bath* [2000] 1 FLR 8.

12 S 75; Marriage (Registrar General's Licence) Act 1970, s 16; Perjury Act 1911, s 3.

13 [1994] 1 FLR 410. See also *Pazpena de Vira v Pazpena de Vire* [2001] 1 FLR 460 where, again, neither party was present at a proxy marriage in Uruguay.

use a form which is required of or available to them. In *McCabe* it would not be reasonable to require a couple who are marrying in Ghana to use there a ceremony required by the law of their domicile if that ceremony is not available or has no legal foundation there. In most cases where both parties will be present at the marriage ceremony, local formalities are easily ascertainable; the parties can rely on local legal advice and the application of such a law would accord with their reasonable expectations.[14]

In *Berthiaume v Dastous*[15] the spouses, who were domiciled in Quebec, married in a Roman Catholic church in France. The marriage was void by French law because, owing to a mistake by the priest, it had not been preceded by a civil ceremony. Even though by the law of Quebec a religious ceremony alone was sufficient, the Privy Council (on appeal from Quebec) held the marriage void.

In relation to some legal acts, such as wills and contracts, compliance with a law other than that of the place of acting may be sufficient and in some legal systems that is true for marriages as well, at least for marriages celebrated in foreign countries. For example, compliance with the formalities of the lex loci celebrationis or the personal laws of the parties may be enough. In English law, however, compliance with the lex loci celebrationis is not only sufficient, it is also normally compulsory, there being only minor exceptions (which will be mentioned below) to the rule that the law of the place of celebration governs the formal validity of marriage. So, for example, the 'marriage' in Bali between Mick Jagger and Jerry Hall was subsequently held to be invalid because the parties (apparently contrary to their beliefs) had not complied fully with the local formal requirements.[16] The requirement that the lex loci celebrationis must be complied with cannot be explained by reference to the convenience of the parties. English law recognises that the lex loci celebrationis has a legitimate interest in ensuring that its formalities are complied with by persons marrying within its borders. The efficacy of its procedures depends on compliance by all persons marrying here. When persons marry abroad, considerations of international comity dictate that we should recognise such interests especially as English law insists on compliance with its formal requirements in respect of marriages celebrated in England.[17] If non-compliance with the formalities of the lex loci celebrationis

14 Law Com Working Paper No 89, *Private International Law: Choice of Law Rules in Marriage* (1985) para 2.36.

15 [1930] AC 79.

16 *The Times*, 14 August 1999.

17 Law Com Working Paper No 89, para 2.46.

were sanctioned it could lead to unacceptable clandestine marriages and resultant chaos in the reliability of local records.[18]

The rule extends even to the retrospective validation by the lex loci celebrationis of a marriage originally void under that law. In *Starkowski v A-G*[19] spouses domiciled in Poland celebrated their marriage in a church in Austria, without any civil ceremony. According to Austrian law, as it then stood, such a marriage was void, but five years later the marriage was retrospectively validated as a result of Austrian legislation. In the meantime, the parties had become domiciled in England, but they separated and the year after the validation of the marriage by Austrian law the wife remarried. The House of Lords had to decide whether a child of that second marriage was legitimate, which depended on the validity of that marriage, which in turn depended on whether the first marriage had been validated in the eyes of English law.

The House of Lords held that effect must be given to the retrospective validation by Austrian law, even though this involved a change in the status, without their assent, of people who at the time of the validation were domiciled in England and had no remaining connection with Austria. The good practical reason for this was that legislation retrospectively validating marriages which, through error or misconstruction of a statute, have not complied with the proper formalities is necessary from time to time in all countries. Such legislation can, of course, only practicably be enacted in the country where the marriages in question were celebrated. The courts should give effect to such legislation, for to do so will be beneficial to the great majority of the spouses concerned who celebrated their marriages in good faith and wish them to be validated. The result in *Starkowski* itself was that the second marriage was void and the child of it illegitimate.

The House of Lords left open the question whether effect would have been given to the Austrian legislation had the wife's remarriage taken place before the validation of the first marriage. That would mean not merely that the first marriage would be retrospectively validated, but that the second marriage, originally valid, would be retrospectively invalidated. It is doubtful whether the law would go as far as that.[20]

18 Hartley, 'The Policy Basis of the English Conflict of Laws of Marriage' (1972) 35 MLR 571 at 574.

19 [1954] AC 155, [1953] 2 All ER 1272.

20 In the Canadian case of *Ambrose v Ambrose* (1961) 25 DLR (2d) 1 it was held that effect should not be given to the retrospective validation of a divorce decree after a remarriage.

B Exceptions to the lex loci celebrationis rule

In certain exceptional situations the parties are exempted from compliance with the lex loci celebrationis. There are both common law and statutory exceptions.

1. Common law exceptions

In certain circumstances the parties are permitted to ignore the formalities of the lex loci celebrationis and can instead contract a 'common law marriage'. A common law marriage is one that complies with the English common law as it stood before Lord Hardwicke's Clandestine Marriages Act of 1753. All that is required is that the parties take each other as husband and wife in the presence of each other. Originally, when such marriages could still take place in England, it was held that the ceremony had to be performed by an episcopally ordained clergyman,[21] but later decisions have indicated that this requirement is not applicable to marriages celebrated abroad (which is the only place where one can celebrate a common law marriage).[22] Whether such marriages can take place only in circumstances of some urgency or where the parties are likely to remain in the foreign country for some appreciable time is an unresolved issue. In such circumstances one can understand the law adopting a flexible approach to try to uphold the validity of such marriages. However, it would be patently absurd to extend this indulgence to persons who are merely on holiday or present for a short time in the foreign country. Common law marriages may be regarded as formally valid in the following three situations.

(A) WHERE ENGLISH COMMON LAW APPLIES

In the days of the British Empire there was a rule of constitutional law that settlers took with them as much of the English common law as was applicable to local conditions.[23] This was often achieved by a capitulatory agreement providing that the Crown exercised extraterritorial jurisdiction over British subjects in a foreign country to which an Order in Council had been extended. In *Wolfenden v Wolfenden*[24] an Order in Council of 1925 applied to the province of

21 *R v Millis* (1844) 10 Cl & Fin 534.
22 *Wolfenden v Wolfenden* [1946] P 61, [1945] 2 All ER 539; *Isaac Penhas v Tan Soo Eng* [1953] AC 304. It has been suggested that the requirement of an episcopally ordained clergyman can be dispensed with only if such a person is not available (Cheshire and North, *Private International Law* (13th edn, 1999) p 715).
23 *Maclean v Cristall* (1849) 7 Notes of Cases, Supp xvii.
24 [1946] P 61, [1945] 2 All ER 539.

Hupeh in China. A common law marriage entered into there by an English and a Canadian domiciliary was recognised as valid. This is, of course, not a true exception to the lex loci celebrationis rule because in this type of case the English common law is deemed to be the local law for British subjects.

(B) INSUPERABLE DIFFICULTY IN COMPLYING WITH THE LOCAL LAW

If it is impossible (having regard, inter alia, to their religious beliefs) for the parties to comply with the form required by the law of the foreign country in which they marry, or if no form is available, then they may validly contract a common law marriage. In *Ruding v Smith*[25] a common law marriage entered into at the Cape of Good Hope was recognised. The 'insuperable difficulty' here was that the local law required the guardian of each party to consent to the marriage; the husband's guardian was in England and the wife had not had a guardian appointed after the death of her father. Another example of an 'insuperable difficulty' would be where the parties were domiciled in England and only a polygamous local form of marriage was available.[26]

(C) MARRIAGES IN COUNTRIES UNDER BELLIGERENT OCCUPATION

The exception to the lex loci celebrationis rule was extended at the end of the Second World War to marriages celebrated by members of occupying forces in Germany and Italy. In *Taczanowska v Taczanowski*[27] two Polish domiciliaries married in Italy without complying with the local Italian formalities but in a manner that satisfied the requirements of English common law. The husband was a member of the Polish occupying forces. It was held that the rationale of the general lex loci celebrationis rule is that parties marrying in a country are presumed to submit themselves to the law of that country. Such a presumption was inapplicable in cases of members of occupying forces as the conqueror could not be presumed to submit to the law of the conquered. As Italian law was inapplicable, it was held that the English common law applied and the marriage was valid. While one can have some sympathy with the court's desire to uphold the validity of such marriages, the result is nevertheless extraordinary in that the validity of a marriage contracted in Italy by two Poles who had never set foot in England was tested by reference to English law as it stood before 1753. A more intelligible approach

25 (1821) 2 Hag Con 371.
26 Law Com Working Paper No 89, para 2.23.
27 [1957] P 301, [1956] 3 All ER 457.

would be that adopted by Australian courts[28] to such marriages whereby the marriage will only be valid if there had been an insuperable difficulty in complying with the local formalities which was not the case in *Taczanowska* – unless 'insuperable difficulty' is defined so broadly as to include 'merely distasteful'. Alternatively, if the presumption of submission is the basis of the lex loci celebrationis rule, if it is rebutted it should presumably be rebutted in favour of the parties' personal law. It makes no sense to assert that if the parties have not submitted to the lex loci celebrationis they must be deemed to have submitted to the law of a country with which they have never had any connection.

Despite such criticisms, *Taczanowska* has been followed on numerous occasions.[29] Doubt still remains, however, over the precise ambit of the rule and whether it covers other persons in war zones, such as mercenaries in Angola, Red Cross members in Bosnia or armed forces in Afghanistan. Perhaps the most authoritative approach is that adopted in *Merker v Merker* which limited the *Taczanowska* rule to 'marriages within the lines of a foreign army of occupation ... or of persons in a strictly analogous situation to the members of such an army, such as members of an organised body of escaped prisoners of war'.[30] In *Merker* the court also challenged the underlying rationale of submission put forward in *Taczanowska* on the basis that if generally applied it would 'introduce anarchy in a field where order and comity are particularly required'.[31] Instead, the exception was explained on the basis that such an army of occupation or organised body of escaped prisoners of war formed an 'enclave' within which it was unreasonable to apply the local law. However, even accepting this better rationale, one is still left with the question of what law applies within this enclave and, again, it is far from clear why this should be English common law if none of the people within the enclave is in fact English.

2. *Statutory exceptions*

(A) CONSULAR MARRIAGES

The Foreign Marriage Act 1892, as amended, makes special provision for the valid solemnisation by consular officials of marriages in foreign countries where at least one of the spouses is a British citizen. Various requirements are specified in the Act. The Foreign Marriage

28 *Savenis v Savenis* [1950] SASR 309.

29 For example, *Kochanski v Kochanska* [1958] P 147, [1957] 3 All ER 142; *Preston v Preston* [1963] P 411, [1963] 2 All ER 405.

30 [1963] P 283 at 295.

31 Ibid.

Order 1970[32] provides that such marriages should not be solemnised unless the marriage officer is satisfied that insufficient facilities exist under the lex loci celebrationis and that the local authorities will not object to the solemnisation of the marriage and that the marriage will be recognised as valid by both parties' domiciliary laws.

(B) MILITARY MARRIAGES

Special provision is made under the Foreign Marriage Act 1947, as amended, for the solemnisation of military marriages in foreign countries when one of the parties is a member of HM Forces (whether navy, military or air force) serving there. This provision has been extended to the children of, and civilian personnel accompanying, such forces.[33] Such marriages are celebrated by military chaplains or other persons authorised by the commanding officer.

C Renvoi

So far it has been assumed that when the English choice of law rule directs the court to apply a foreign lex loci celebrationis this means the *domestic* law of the foreign country. However, this is one of the areas of law where the doctrine of renvoi has been considered. According to this, a reference to a foreign law involves applying that country's conflicts rules as opposed to its domestic laws.[34] In *Taczanowska v Taczanowski*,[35] as has been seen, two Polish nationals celebrated their marriage in Italy. By Italian domestic law the marriage was void, for lack of a civil ceremony. By Italian conflict of laws a marriage is formally valid if it complies with the requirements of the law of the country of which the parties are nationals. It was assumed in this case that if the marriage were formally valid by Polish law it would have been valid in English eyes, but the point was obiter, because in fact the Polish requirements had not been satisfied.

There are two different reasons why an English court might choose to have recourse to the doctrine of renvoi. First, the doctrine could lead to uniformity of result between various countries with an interest in the case. Because different countries have not only different domestic laws but also different conflicts rules, a marriage may be valid in one country and invalid in another. This

32 SI 1970/1539.
33 Foreign Marriage Act 1892, s 22, as amended.
34 See pp 14–16 and 539–550.
35 [1957] P 301, [1956] 3 All ER 457.

results in what is called a 'limping marriage'. The hardship and inconvenience which can arise from parties having the status of married persons in one country but not in another is obvious. How can this be avoided? The only sure way would be by the harmonisation, by international convention, of the conflicts rules of the different countries. Apart from this, where a particular foreign country's choice of law rule is different from the English one, the English court might be able to secure uniformity with that country by using the doctrine of renvoi and employing the foreign country's choice of law rule instead of the English one. For example, in *Taczanowska* the English and Italian conflicts rules were different. By applying the Italian conflicts rule, as opposed to the domestic Italian rule, the English court could (had it not ended up resorting to the common law marriage fiction) have ensured that a limping relationship was avoided. The difficulty with this approach, however, is that renvoi may well produce uniformity with the wrong countries. What is wanted, of course, is uniformity with the countries with which the parties at the time of litigation have a legitimate connection. There seems to be little value in obtaining uniformity of status with the law of a country in which the marriage happened to be celebrated, if that is not the country to which the parties belong. In short, given that the parties' connections with Italy were only brief, it matters little whether Italian and English law agree on the validity of the marriage.

The second main justification for utilising the doctrine of renvoi is that it provides extra flexibility. Normally, one should try to uphold the validity of a marriage where possible and if one's primary conflicts rules fail in that regard, recourse to the foreign country's conflicts rules may achieve the desired result. This was clearly the reason why the doctrine was flirted with in *Taczanowska.* Such an approach, however, is objectionable and contrary to principle.

Choice of law rules are designed to lead to the application of appropriate laws. There are strong policy reasons why formal validity of marriage is governed by the lex loci celebrationis. If these policy considerations are sound, the whole point of applying the English choice of law rule is defeated if it does no more than lead to another country's choice of law rule. If, on the other hand, the policy considerations underlying the English choice of law rule are questionable and renvoi is being resorted to as a corrective for an unduly strict conflicts rule, then one should re-examine the English rule and adopt a more flexible one. If it were felt that necessary compliance with the lex loci celebrationis is too restrictive, the rule should be reformed so that a marriage can be upheld as formally valid if it complies with the formalities of either the lex loci celebrationis or the parties' personal law. This would, of course, mean an alternative reference to the law of the parties' domicile (and not to the law of nationality as in *Taczanowska*).

The Law Commission has considered this proposal but concluded that such an alternative reference rule should not be introduced on the ground, inter alia, that the interests of the lex loci celebrationis are so strong that compliance with its formalities should be insisted upon. Considerations of international comity dictate that persons should not be permitted to evade such a law by complying with the law of their domicile instead.[36] The Law Commission felt that the necessary flexibility (and prospect of greater uniformity of result) would be best achieved by an application of the doctrine of renvoi. It has already been argued that such an approach is misconceived. These and other arguments concerning the doctrine of renvoi are further explored in chapter 12.

III ESSENTIAL VALIDITY

A Terminology

'Essential validity' covers all questions of validity other than formal validity. 'Capacity to marry' is a category within essential validity. 'Capacity to marry' ought strictly to be confined to rules which lay down that a particular class of person lacks a power to marry which other people possess (for instance, a rule that a person below a certain age may not marry). In practice, however, capacity to marry also includes cases where the reason for the invalidity is that such a marriage relationship is objectionable in the eyes of the law (for instance, rules prohibiting marriages between relatives of certain degrees or between persons of the same sex). Capacity to marry does not, however, cover the whole field of essential validity; it does not include the consent of the parties or the non-consummation of the marriage.

B The choice of law rule

1. *Introduction*

Although formal validity is governed by the law of the country where the marriage is celebrated, that law is not generally thought appropriate in the English conflict of laws to govern essential validity. While there is an argument, to be canvassed later,[37] that the

36 Law Com Working Paper No 89, paras 2.46–2.47.
37 See pp 358–360.

lex loci celebrationis does have *some* interest in the essential validity of marriages contracted within its borders, it is clear that this interest is insufficient to justify utilising the lex loci celebrationis as the primary choice of law rule here. This is because the marriage may be celebrated in a country which in other respects has no connection with the marriage or the parties. Neither of the parties may be domiciled there before the ceremony and they may not establish their home there after it.

For essential validity, therefore, it is the personal law which is important. The personal law governs those matters relating to status and personal relationships that are regarded as vital to the maintenance of the institution of marriage in a society and therefore all persons 'belonging' to that society have to comply with its rules. Any other approach would open the door to unacceptable evasion of the law with the parties simply making temporary visits to foreign countries in order to marry and thereby evade the provisions of their personal law. It was seen in chapter 2 that for most choice of law purposes a person is regarded as 'belonging' to the country of his domicile. With marriage, however, one is dealing with a relationship between two people (at least) who before the marriage might be domiciled in different countries and who after the marriage might set up a home together in another country. What is the appropriate test of belonging here? Is it where the parties each belonged before the marriage or is it where the marriage belongs? The answer to this question is far from self-evident and consequently there is some uncertainty as to the precise nature of the present English choice of law rule for essential validity of marriage. Various solutions have been adopted and suggested. Each of these will be considered in turn.

2. *Dual domicile doctrine*

According to the dual domicile doctrine, the law of each party's domicile at the date of the marriage has to be considered. For the marriage to be valid, each party must have capacity by the law of his or her domicile to contract the marriage. Suppose the English court has to determine the validity of a marriage between first cousins, one of whom at the date of the marriage is domiciled in Sweden and the other in Portugal. By Swedish law, let it be assumed, such a marriage is valid, but by Portuguese law it is within the prohibited degrees of relationship. Under the dual domicile doctrine, the marriage would be invalid.

This rule, which, as will be seen, commands most support in English law, has several advantages. In terms of principle, it is appropriate that people be governed by the law of their existing domicile. This law will usually have governed their status for a long time, if not for their whole life. The reasonable expectations of the parties are best fulfilled by an application of their existing personal law. The application of any other law (say, the law of the intended matrimonial home) will enable the parties to evade any restrictions imposed by their antenuptial domiciliary laws. As the Law Commission put it:

> The main rationale of the dual domicile rule is that a person's status is a matter of public concern to the country to which he belongs at the time of marriage; and therefore the domiciliary law of each party has an equal right to be heard. The issue of whether a valid marriage has been or may be contracted should, in principle and in logic, depend on the conditions existing at the time of marriage rather than subsequently.[38]

Another advantage claimed for the dual domicile doctrine is that it is easy to apply in prospective situations. Recourse to the other suggested tests, such as the intended matrimonial home doctrine, would involve the validity of the marriage remaining in suspense until the new home is established. Under the dual domicile doctrine the validity of the marriage can be established from the moment of marriage. Indeed, as far as marriage officials who have to decide whether the parties are capable of marrying are concerned, this is the only possible test they can apply.

There are, however, certain disadvantages associated with the dual domicile doctrine. In assessing the validity of a marriage, the most appropriate law to apply could be regarded as being the law to which the *marriage* belongs. This is the community which is most affected by the marriage. The country where the parties came from is less interested in the validity of the marriage than is the country where the marriage is based. Following this point, there can be no 'evasion' of the antenuptial domiciliary law. Evasion of the law involves evading a law which has a legitimate interest in the parties. If the married couple have left their old country and are not returning, that country of former domicile no longer has an interest in the marriage. A further objection to the dual domicile doctrine is that because both parties' antenuptial domiciliary laws have to be applied cumulatively, there is a greater chance of the marriage being declared invalid than if any single law were applied. Such an approach runs counter to the well-established policy in favour of upholding the validity of a marriage.

3. Intended matrimonial home doctrine

An alternative approach is that the law of the intended matrimonial home (sometimes called the matrimonial domicile) governs the

38 Law Com Working Paper No 89, para 3.36.

essential validity of a marriage. This test, most forcefully advocated in earlier editions of Cheshire's *Private International Law,*[39] provides a basic presumption in favour of the law of the country in which the husband is domiciled at the date of the marriage. This presumption can be rebutted if at the time of the marriage the parties intended to establish a matrimonial home in a different country and if they implemented that intention within a reasonable time. For example, in *Frankel's Estate v The Master*[40] a man, domiciled in Germany, married a woman, domiciled in Czechoslovakia. The marriage took place in Czechoslovakia. At the time of the marriage they had planned to emigrate from Europe to settle permanently in South Africa, which they did four months later. They lived in South Africa for the next 15 years until the husband died. Under the intended matrimonial home doctrine the validity of this marriage would be tested by South African law. At the date of the marriage they intended to settle there and implemented this intention within a reasonable period of time.

Cheshire's original formulation, drawing on the writings of Cook[41] and Savigny,[42] points presumptively to the law of the husband's domicile on the basis that in most cases where the parties have different domiciles they are likely to make their home in his country. This might have been empirically true 50 years ago, but can only be regarded as questionable today and, given its sexist assumption, cannot be accepted. A further explanation for the original presumption was that at the moment of marriage the wife acquired a domicile of dependence on the husband. Since the abolition of the married woman's domicile of dependence, this rationale is no longer applicable. Accordingly, the better view today is that the basic presumption must be in favour of the dual domicile doctrine. If no matrimonial home is established within a reasonable time, the validity of the marriage will be decided exclusively by the dual domicile doctrine. The issue is whether that doctrine should be displaced in clear cases in favour of the intended matrimonial home.

The main advantage of applying the intended matrimonial home doctrine is that it allows the validity of a marriage to be tested by the law of the country most affected by, and interested in, the marriage. That country forms the 'true seat' of the marriage;[43] its law is the 'proper law' of the marriage. If, for example, the issue is the validity of a marriage between cousins, it is the country where the married

39 For example, 7th edn, 1965, p 276.
40 1950 (1) SA 220 (South Africa).
41 *The Logical and Legal Bases of the Conflict of Laws* (1942) p 448.
42 *A Treatise on the Conflict of Laws* (Guthrie's translation, 1869) p 240.
43 Ibid.

cousins will live that has the most interest in the marriage. The country from which the parties came can have little interest in the matter. The other significant advantage of the doctrine is that it tends to favour the validity of marriages, in that it is necessary to have recourse only to one law.

The disadvantages attached to the doctrine are, however, formidable. First, the doctrine can be applied only retrospectively. If the parties in *Frankel's Estate* had sought advice before their marriage as to whether it would be valid, no definitive answer could have been provided as the validity of the marriage would have depended on whether they implemented their intention within a reasonable time. As noted above, this places marriage officials in a predicament. Such officials cannot operate according to the laws of a place where the parties might establish a home. As has been stated:

> Very serious practical difficulties are likely to arise if the validity of a marriage has to remain in suspense while we wait and see (for an unspecified period) whether or not the parties implement their (unexpressed) antenuptial intention to acquire another domicile. This is especially true if interests in property depend on the validity of a marriage, as, for instance, where a widow's pension ceases on her remarriage.[44]

Secondly, what if the parties leave the country of their intended matrimonial home after a limited period and establish a permanent home in another country? In such a case it is the law of the new country that is most interested in the marriage. One could not, however, continually reassess the validity of a marriage every time the parties change their home. Thirdly, there is, perhaps, a fallacy in the assumption that it is the law of the intended matrimonial home that is most interested in the marriage. Many rules on capacity to marry are designed to protect a person. For instance, the rule in English law that no marriage may be contracted until the age of 16 is designed to protect the immature. English law has a legitimate interest in ensuring its domiciliaries do not evade this prohibition. When a 13-year-old English domiciliary went through a marriage ceremony in 1996 with a Turkish domiciliary and set up a home with him in Turkey, the resultant furore indicated very clearly that English law maintained a strong interest in her welfare and the validity of her marriage.[45] Fourthly, it is highly questionable whether the application of the intended matrimonial home does accord with the reasonable expectations of the parties. Suppose two cousins domiciled in England decide to marry and set up a matrimonial

44 McClean, *Morris: The Conflict of Laws* (5th edn, 2000) p 194.
45 *The Times*, 25 January 1996, p 1.

home in Portugal. In such a case the parties would probably have relied on English legal advice that marriages between cousins are lawful; indeed, they might have been brought up their whole lives with such a belief. An application of Portuguese law which could declare their marriage void would clearly frustrate their reasonable expectations.[46] Fifthly, there are the inevitable practical problems: how can one establish what the parties intended at the time of their marriage[47] and how long is a reasonable period of time? In practice, such questions would not be unanswerable[48] – but they are certainly vaguer questions than those posed in the ascertainment of a person's domicile. Finally, over the last half century immigration patterns have shown a greater movement of people from developing countries to developed countries and from countries permitting polygamy to countries practising monogamy than vice versa.[49] Particularly with regard to age restrictions, developing countries tend to have lower age limits than developed countries.[50] Application of the intended matrimonial home test would therefore result in the invalidation of marriages which are valid according to the parties' domiciliary law. Similarly, where a couple from a country practising polygamy planned to emigrate to the United Kingdom, there would be a greater chance of their marriage being declared invalid if the intended matrimonial home doctrine were utilised.[51]

In view of these strong objections, it is submitted that if the intended matrimonial home doctrine is to be utilised at all, Cheshire's original formulation needs modification so that the dual domicile doctrine will be displaced only in exceptional cases where the marriage clearly belongs to the country of matrimonial residence. In addition to the requirements that the parties must have intended, at the time of their marriage, to make their home in the new country and have implemented this intention within a reasonable period of time, it should also be necessary that they remain in the new country for a significant period of time. If it transpires that the new home was only temporary the justifications for the application of that law are

46 Law Com Working Paper No 89, para 3.35.
47 Jaffey, *Topics in Choice of Law* (1996) p 130 argues that this should not be a requirement in most cases.
48 Ibid at pp 127–128.
49 *UN Demographic Yearbook 1996* (48th issue, 1998) pp 1076–1093.
50 As in *Mohamed v Knott* [1969] 1 QB 1, [1968] 2 All ER 563. For example, in many South American countries (Panama, Chile, Columbia, Ecuador, Paraguay and Uruguay) the age at which the parties can lawfully marry is 14 for boys and 12 for girls (*UN Demographic Yearbook 1993* (45th issue, 1995) pp 546–556).
51 Karsten, 'Capacity to Contract a Polygamous Marriage' (1973) 36 MLR 291 at 296; Davie, 'The Breaking Up of Essential Validity of Marriage Choice of Law Rules in English Conflict of Laws' (1994) 23 Anglo-Am L Rev 32 at 35.

significantly reduced. This, of course, means that the intended matrimonial home doctrine can only be applied in retrospective situations. Marriage officials, in deciding whether to allow persons to marry, or courts adjudicating on the validity of marriages in the early years will be forced to apply the dual domicile test. In *Frankel's Estate*, where the parties lived in South Africa for 15 years until the husband died, there can be no doubt that all elements of the proposed test would be satisfied and the validity of the marriage would be tested by South African law. Of course, other cases will call for finer judgment. In *Radwan v Radwan (No 2)*[52] an Egyptian domiciliary married an English domiciliary in France. At the time of the marriage they planned to settle in Egypt and implemented this intention soon thereafter. However, after five years' residence in Egypt the couple moved to England where they lived for the next 14 years until divorce proceedings were commenced. Under the proposed modified test there would need to be a determination as to whether this marriage truly belonged in Egypt sufficiently for the dual domicile doctrine to be displaced. In answering this question it is submitted that the mere length of residence in the intended matrimonial home should be important but not decisive. The test should be a qualitative rather than a purely quantitative one. If a couple marry in England and then take up an expatriate contract abroad for six years before returning to England, the case for displacing the dual domicile doctrine is not made out. This would be an English marriage with the couple living temporarily abroad. In *Radwan*, however, the couple had contemplated permanent residence in Egypt and the English woman had converted to the Islamic faith. The case for holding that this was an Egyptian marriage, whose validity should be governed by Egyptian law, is strong.

4. *Real and substantial connection*

Another possibility is that the essential validity of a marriage should be governed by the law of the country with which the marriage has its most real and substantial connection. As with the intended matrimonial home doctrine this rule is trying to connect the marriage (as opposed to either of the parties) with the country to which it 'belongs'. Normally, the country with which a marriage is most closely connected will be the country where the matrimonial home is situated.[53] It is, however, a test that provides extra flexibility in that other factors such as domicile and nationality can be taken into

52 [1973] Fam 35, [1972] 3 All ER 1026.
53 *Lawrence v Lawrence* [1985] 1 All ER 506 at 511.

consideration.[54] In *Vervaeke v Smith*[55] this test was considered (obiter) by Lord Simon in a case involving the validity of a marriage of convenience where no matrimonial home had been intended. In this case the marriage had been contracted in England. The man was an English domiciliary and the woman, while a Belgian domiciliary, was planning to become permanently resident in England and assume British nationality. The marriage was clearly most closely connected with England.

In *Vervaeke v Smith* Lord Simon indicated that the real and substantial connection test should be applied 'if not [to] all questions of essential validity, at least [to] the question of the sort of quintessential validity in issue in this appeal, the question of which law's public policy should determine the validity of the marriage'.[56] In *Lawrence v Lawrence*,[57] at first instance, Lincoln J regarded this dictum as referring to 'circumstances in which the public policy of two legal systems pulled in opposite directions'; the judge regarded the issue of capacity to remarry after a foreign divorce as one that 'directly ... involve[d] "the quintessential validity" of the marriage contract'. Such an approach is unacceptable. While the issue of a marriage of convenience can perhaps be interpreted as one of quintessential validity because the question is whether the parties intended a 'marriage', it is difficult to fathom the basis upon which any other impediment can be so classified. All prohibitions on marriage, such as lack of age or marriages within the prohibited degrees of relationship, are little more than crystallisations of public policy. Indeed, it has been suggested that marriages within the prohibited degrees and capacity to contract a polygamous marriage raise questions of quintessential validity of marriage.[58] If this is true, it would seem that all questions of capacity and consent can be so regarded, with the result that only matters such as impotence and wilful refusal would be regarded as essential rather than quintessential. Such a classification hardly seems helpful.

Further, while the real and substantial connection test has its supporters,[59] it is, in reality, a question-begging test. The question is which choice of law rule will best lead to the application of the law to which the parties and the marriage 'belong'. This test does not

54 *Indyka v Indyka* [1969] 1 AC 33, [1967] 2 All ER 689.
55 [1983] 1 AC 145 at 166.
56 Ibid.
57 [1985] 1 All ER 506 at 511.
58 Jaffey, *Introduction to the Conflict of Laws* (1988) p 37.
59 Fentiman, 'The Validity of Marriage and the Proper Law' [1985] CLJ 256; Fentiman, 'Activity in the Law of Status: Domicile, Marriage and the Law Commission' (1986) 6 OJLS 353.

answer the question, but rather 'simply restates the problem'.[60] And, as the Law Commission put it:

> It is an inherently vague and unpredictable test which would introduce an unacceptable degree of uncertainty into the law. It is a test which is difficult to apply other than through the courtroom process and it is therefore unsuitable in an area where the law's function is essentially prospective, ie, a yardstick for future planning.[61]

5. *Alternative reference test*

It has been suggested that (at least for some incapacities) a marriage should be regarded as essentially valid if it is so regarded by either the dual domicile doctrine or the intended matrimonial home test.[62] This view was supported in *Lawrence v Lawrence*.[63] This would mean that the marriage would only be invalid if it is so *both* by the law of the intended matrimonial home *and* by the law of the domicile of one or both of the parties. This approach can be justified on the basis that there is no reason to hold a marriage invalid on a ground based on the public interest (such as polygamy or prohibited degrees) if it is valid by the law of the country where the marriage relationship is to exist. However, even if it is invalid by the law of that country, the spouses' expectation that their marriage, which is unobjectionable by the standards of their own countries at the time of the marriage, will be valid should be met.

This solution was considered and rejected by the Law Commission[64] on the ground that it would be wrong to elevate the general policy in favour of upholding the validity of marriages into a general choice of law rule. The Law Commission's approach has much to commend it. Choice of law rules should be based on sound policy grounds. While there might be disagreement as to whether those policy considerations point to the antenuptial domiciliary laws of the parties or the law of the intended matrimonial home, they cannot point to both. The alternative reference test amounts to little more than an abdication of the quest for a rational choice of law rule. Further, it could necessitate proof of three different laws, which could greatly complicate and lengthen the process.

60 Davie, 'The Breaking Up of Essential Validity of Marriage Choice of Law Rules in English Conflict of Laws' (1994) 23 Anglo-Am L Rev 32 at 37.
61 Law Com Working Paper No 89, para 3.20.
62 Jaffey, 'The Essential Validity of Marriage in the English Conflict of Laws' (1978) 41 MLR 38.
63 [1985] 1 All ER 506 at 512 (at first instance by Lincoln J); [1985] 2 All ER 733 at 746 (in the Court of Appeal by Sir David Cairns).
64 Law Com Working Paper No 89, para 3.37.

6. Validity by either party's domiciliary law

Under this test a marriage would be regarded as essentially valid if it were valid under either party's antenuptial domiciliary law.[65] This proposal has the advantage that it would promote the policy in favour of validity of marriages, but has little else to commend it. As the Law Commission put it:

> If it is accepted that a person's status is a matter of public concern to the country in which he or she is domiciled at the time of marriage, then the rules of that country which are designed to protect its public interest (such as rules laying down prohibited degrees of relationship or requiring monogamy) should be given effect. The proposed rule would enable a party to evade the requirements of his domiciliary law and would also lead to limping relationships.[66]

7. A variable rule

Most of the above theories are premised on the notion that there should be one rule applying to all questions of essential validity. However, there is no reason why this should be so. It has already been seen that in *Vervaeke v Smith*[67] it was suggested that some issues, namely, those involving quintessential validity, could be dealt with differently from the remaining essentials to a valid marriage. This approach was adopted in *Radwan v Radwan (No 2)* where Cumming-Bruce J stated:

> It is arguable that it is an over-simplification of the common law to assume that the same test for purposes of choice of law applies to every kind of incapacity – non-age, affinity, prohibition of monogamous contract by virtue of an existing spouse, and capacity for polygamy. Different public and social factors are relevant to each of these types of incapacity.[68]

While this approach has met with some hostility on the ground that it leads to 'uncertainty, anarchy and ultimately injustice',[69] it is suggested that a variable test has much to commend it. As stated in *Radwan*, there are different social and policy factors underlying each incapacity. In order to determine the most appropriate choice of law rule, one should examine why a particular impediment exists and which law has the most interest in the validity of the marriage. On

65 Hartley, 'The Policy Basis of the English Conflict of Laws of Marriage' (1972) 35 MLR 571.
66 Law Com Working Paper No 89, para 3.38.
67 [1983] 1 AC 145.
68 [1973] Fam 35 at 51.
69 Cheshire and North, *Private International Law* (13th edn, 1999) p 735.

this basis, the modified intended matrimonial home rule proposed above [70] seems the more appropriate to govern incapacities which are imposed to protect the public interests of countries, rather than the interest of the parties to the marriage.[71] This is because it is the country in which the parties settle as a married couple after the marriage, rather than a country in which either of them used to live before the marriage, whose interests are affected by the existence of the marriage. An example of such an incapacity, imposed in the public interest, is the prohibition of polygamy. Another instance would be the prohibited degrees of consanguineous relationship (although, as shall be seen, this defect is in fact subject to the dual domicile rule).

The dual domicile rule seems the more appropriate for incapacities which are imposed in the interests of a party, or for his protection, such as a minimum age for marriage (although, as will be seen, there are other arguments here). The law of the country to which a party belongs at the time of the marriage seems the right one to determine what protection he requires. Another example is lack of consent where arguably it is the antenuptial domiciliary law of the non-consenting party that is most interested in protecting that party and, accordingly, reference should be made only to that law.

This functional approach will enable one to identify the most appropriate law for the purpose of the particular impediment. Such a solution is also consistent with an interest analysis approach to choice of law rules[72] whereby investigation reveals the law which has the most interest in the validity or otherwise of the marriage.[73] However, a caution must be entered here. Interest analysis can be utilised in one of two ways. First, on an issue by issue basis (or, here, an impediment by impediment basis), the interests of the respective laws can be evaluated in order to develop the most appropriate choice of law rule for the particular impediment. Secondly, in the United States interest analysis has become associated with 'rule-scepticism' whereby general choice of law rules are eschewed in favour of a case-by-case investigation of the respective state interests.[74] While this latter approach has little to commend it as it amounts to

70 See pp 327–328.

71 Jaffey, 'The Foundations of Rules for the Choice of Law' (1982) 2 OJLS 368; Jaffey, *Topics in Choice of Law* (1996) pp 3–7.

72 See pp 255–258 and 568–573. See Reed, 'Essential Validity of Marriage: The Application of Interest Analysis and Depecage to Anglo-American Choice of Law Rules' (2000) 20 NYL Sch J Int'l & Comp L 387

73 Smart, 'Interest Analysis, False Conflicts, and the Essential Validity of Marriage' (1986) 14 Anglo-Am L Rev 225.

74 See pp 568–573.

little more than a return to judicial discretion which would generate considerable uncertainty and unpredictability,[75] the former approach, as already employed in *Radwan*, is more defensible.

There can be no doubt that, to a limited extent at least, English law now adopts this variable or functional approach. For example, capacity to marry after a foreign divorce which is entitled to recognition is governed by special rules quite different from capacity to marry in other cases.[76] However, whether this approach can be said accurately to reflect the common law is a moot point. The various impediments to a valid marriage will shortly be considered and the present English law in relation to each will be analysed. At that stage an attempt will be made to reveal the underlying social and policy factors that have shaped each rule. In the light of that, the most appropriate choice of law rule, which will best serve that policy, can be exposed. Before that, however, one final general consideration needs examination.

C The role of the lex fori

There is an exception to the general choice of law rule (whatever it is), to the effect that if a marriage is celebrated in England, and one party is domiciled in England at the time of the marriage, then the validity of the marriage is governed by English law alone. Any invalidity under the law of the foreign domicile of the other party is ignored. This rule was laid down in *Sottomayer v De Barros (No 2)*,[77] in which a marriage was celebrated in England between first cousins, the husband being domiciled at the time of the marriage in England and the wife in Portugal. Even though a marriage between first cousins was prohibited by Portuguese law, the marriage was held valid under English law. The basis of the decision was that it would be unjust to an English party who celebrates in England a marriage which is valid by English law to hold the marriage void under foreign law.[78] This rule in *Sottomayer v De Barros (No 2)*, as it has become known, has been applied in cases dealing with other impediments and must now be regarded as an accepted part of the law.[79] As will be seen, however, its ambit has been somewhat limited by statute in respect of certain marriages within the prohibited degrees of affinity.[80]

75 Davie, 'The Breaking Up of Essential Validity of Marriage Choice of Law Rules in English Conflict of Laws' (1994) 23 Anglo-Am L Rev 32 at 43–44.
76 Family Law Act 1986, s 50.
77 (1879) 5 PD 94.
78 (1879) 5 PD at 104, based on a dictum in the judgment of the Court of Appeal in *Sottomayor v De Barros* (1877) 3 PD 1 at 6–7.
79 *Ogden v Ogden* [1908] P 46; *Vervaeke v Smith* [1981] 1 All ER 55 at 87 (though the point was not considered by the House of Lords on appeal: [1983] 1 AC 145).
80 Marriage (Enabling) Act 1960, s 1(3). See p 337.

This rule has been condemned as 'xenophobic'[81] and 'unworthy of a place in a respectable system of conflict of laws'[82] because it only operates in favour of an English person marrying in England, not a foreign person marrying in his own country.[83] It can also be argued that the supposed injustice to the English party marrying in England would only occur if the parties intended to settle in England (as was indeed the case in *Sottomayer v De Barros (No 2)*, although this was not the basis of the decision); if they planned to settle abroad, it is hard to see how justice could be offended if the marriage were held invalid under the foreign law.

On the other hand, it is possible to support the rule or, at least, to defend it on the basis that this type of forum preference is common in the conflict of laws.[84] Inevitably, the lex fori will adopt a role of protecting English interests, values and institutions. For instance, in relation to contract there are special provisions ensuring that English interests in protecting its consumers are not bypassed by the application of foreign laws.[85] Similarly, the doctrine of public policy will generally only be invoked when enforcement of a foreign law will have an impact in England.[86] Marriages contracted in England have a greater potential impact in England than marriages contracted abroad and, accordingly, there is a greater interest in ensuring conformity to the standards of English law. Where parties, one of whom is domiciled in England, marry in England and there is a conflict between the spouses' domiciliary laws, it is inevitable that the English court will lean in favour of the English domiciliary. In view of the fact that the English domiciliary has not stepped into the international arena by marrying abroad, such a person does not deserve to forfeit the right to rely on the law of the country to which he belongs and with which the marriage is more closely connected. The court is justified in ignoring the foreign incapacity on the ground that the English domiciliary has married in England and would reasonably expect the validity of the marriage to be judged by English law. Further, such an approach accords well with the policy of upholding the validity of marriages where possible.

However, despite these arguments, the Law Commission has concluded that 'on balance'[87] the rule in *Sottomayer v De Barros (No 2)* should be abolished. No reasons for this proposal are advanced

81 Cheshire and North, *Private International Law* (13th edn, 1999) p 731.
82 Falconbridge, *Essays on the Conflict of Laws* (1954) p 711.
83 *Re Paine* [1940] Ch 46.
84 Clarkson, 'Marriage in England: Favouring the Lex Fori' (1990) 10 LS 80.
85 See pp 235–236.
86 See pp 561–562.
87 Law Com Working Paper No 89, para 3.48.

other than that the rule is 'illogical' and 'cannot be supported from the standpoint of principle'.[88]

D The impediments

1. Prohibited degrees of relationship

While all systems of law impose restrictions on marriage between persons who are related, the precise rules vary between different countries. The prohibitions may extend not only to blood relationships (consanguinity), but also to relationships by marriage (affinity). One reason for the prohibition of marriage between blood relations is the eugenic one of reducing the risk of handicapped offspring. Other reasons for the prohibition are sociological, moral and religious. So it is the public interest, rather than the protection of the spouses themselves, that is the main object of these incapacities. One might therefore think that the intended matrimonial home rule would be the correct one here. If a woman domiciled in England marries her uncle domiciled in Egypt, such a marriage being prohibited by English but not Egyptian law, and the parties settle in Egypt after the marriage, there seems to be no good reason why English standards should be applied to invalidate the marriage. Egyptian law would seem to have the greater interest in the validity of the marriage.

However, with regard to marriages within the prohibited degrees of affinity, it is arguable that the antenuptial domiciliary laws of the parties have a sufficient interest in the marriage not to be displaced by the law of the intended matrimonial home. Such marriages are prohibited only on social and moral grounds. For example, a marriage to one's daughter-in-law is liable to create tensions within the family, particularly if her former spouse is still alive.[89] The place of pre-existing domicile has a greater interest in preventing such disruption and conflict within families than does the country to which the newly married couple moves. The same is true of marriages between stepparents and stepchildren. The rationale for such prohibitions is that such relationships amount to an abuse of the relationship and could lead to sexual exploitation.[90] Again, this is a matter primarily of interest to the antenuptial domiciliary laws of the parties.

88 Para 3.46.

89 Bromley and Lowe, *Bromley's Family Law* (9th edn, 1998) p 34. See Marriage Act 1949, s 1(5).

90 Ibid. Such a marriage can be valid if the stepchild has not been 'a child of the family in relation to the other party': Marriage Act 1949, s 1(3).

Accordingly, applying a functional approach, the interests and policies underlying these incapacities suggest that for consanguinity the intended matrimonial doctrine would be most appropriate, but for affinity the dual domicile doctrine should be applied. However, an examination of the authorities reveals that it is the dual domicile rule that applies to all the prohibited degrees. Admittedly, the only House of Lords decision on the matter leaves the question open. In *Brook v Brook*[91] the husband wished to marry the sister of his deceased wife. The intending spouses were both domiciled in England. By English law, at that time, a marriage between a man and his former wife's sister, aunt or niece (or between a woman and her former husband's brother, uncle or nephew) was prohibited, so the parties celebrated their marriage in Denmark, by whose law it was valid. They returned to live in England after the marriage. The House of Lords held the marriage void, establishing that questions of essential, as opposed to formal, validity are not to be decided by the lex loci celebrationis. Lord Campbell said:

> The essentials of the marriage depend on the lex domicilii, the law of the country in which the parties are domiciled at the time of the marriage and in which the matrimonial residence is contemplated.[92]

This leaves open the position when one or both of the parties have a different antenuptial domicile from the intended matrimonial residence.

Later cases,[93] however, with increasing explicitness, have inclined to the dual domicile test, although, at least in most cases, the result under either test would have been the same. In *Re Paine*,[94] for example, the marriage was celebrated in Germany between a man domiciled in Germany and his deceased wife's sister, who was domiciled in England. By German law such a marriage was valid, but the marriage was held invalid under English law, the judge holding that each spouse must have capacity to marry the other by the law of his or her antenuptial domicile. The parties did establish a matrimonial home in England, but this was clearly not the basis of the decision. Though there is no House of Lords case excluding the intended matrimonial home approach, and, as shall be seen, there have been judicial statements in favour of that approach in other contexts, it seems safest to say that, as the law stands, the dual domicile rule applies to prohibited degrees of relationship.

91 (1861) 9 HL Cas 193.
92 At 207.
93 *Mette v Mette* (1859) 1 Sw & Tr 416; *Sottomayor v De Barros* (1877) 3 PD 1; *Cheni v Cheni* [1965] P 85, [1962] 3 All ER 873.
94 [1940] Ch 46.

Statutory support for the dual domicile doctrine in respect of some of these incapacities is to be found in section 1(3) of the Marriage (Enabling) Act 1960. Originally, English domestic law had strict rules prohibiting marriages between relatives by marriage. These were progressively relaxed, the last step being taken by the 1960 Act, which abolished the remaining restrictions against a man marrying his divorced or deceased wife's sister, niece or aunt and a woman marrying her former husband's brother, nephew or uncle.[95] Section 1(3) contains a choice of law provision that:

> ... this section does not validate a marriage if either party to it is at the time of the marriage domiciled in a country outside Great Britain, and under the law of that country there cannot be a valid marriage between the parties.

The effect is that, as regards marriages within these degrees of affinity, the dual domicile doctrine is applicable. Accordingly, if a man marries, for example, his former wife's sister who is domiciled in a country forbidding such marriages, the marriage is void even if the intended matrimonial home was England. Section 1(3) also has the effect of excluding the *Sottomayer v De Barros (No 2)* exception. So if a man domiciled in England marries, in England, his first cousin, who is domiciled in a country by whose law the marriage is void, the marriage is valid under the *Sottomayer* exception. But if a man domiciled in England marries in England his former wife's sister, who is domiciled in a country by whose law such marriage is void, the marriage is invalid under section 1(3). There is no sense in this distinction; the point must have been overlooked in the drafting of the statute.

2. Lack of age

Countries have varying rules on the minimum age for marriage. The English rule is contained in section 2 of the Marriage Act 1949, which provides that a marriage solemnised between persons either of whom is under the age of 16 shall be void.

There is no doubt that the dual domicile rule applies here. The law which is most fitted to decide whether a young person needs protection against his own immaturity and want of judgment is the law of the country to which he belongs at the time of the marriage. As has been stated:

> Since children may develop socially and emotionally, and even physically, at different rates in different environments, it seems sensible for English

95 S 1.

> law to rely on the judgment of the law of the country to which a person belongs for the decision whether he or she is mature enough to marry.[96]

So each party must have capacity by the law of his or her antenuptial domicile. In *Mohamed v Knott*[97] a man of 26 and a girl of 13, both domiciled in Nigeria, had married each other there, and come to England four months later, where they were to live while the husband was a student. The court accepted that the marriage was valid, because the wife was old enough by Nigerian law, even though she was much too young by English law.

What is the position where an English domiciliary aged 16 or over marries a person aged under 16 who is domiciled in a country permitting marriages at the lower age? In *Pugh v Pugh*[98] a British army officer, domiciled in England, married in Austria a girl aged 15 who was domiciled in Hungary. The wife had capacity to marry under Hungarian law. On a construction of the English statutory provision – 'a marriage solemnised between persons either of whom is under the age of sixteen shall be void' – the marriage was held void as the wife was under the age of 16. This decision has attracted adverse comment: 'was it really the object of the statute to protect middle-aged English colonels from the wiles of designing Hungarian teenagers?'[99] It has also been argued that an interest analysis approach in this case would have yielded a better result.[100] The argument is that English law had no reason to invalidate the marriage as the English domiciliary was old enough to marry; Hungarian law also had no reason to invalidate the marriage as the Hungarian domiciliary was, by Hungarian law, old enough to marry. The marriage should, accordingly, have been held valid.

Such reasoning, however, fails to understand the policy rationale underlying the English prohibition. In reality, there are two policies enshrined in section 2 of the Marriage Act 1949. The first and most obvious one is that relied on by the critics of *Pugh v Pugh*, namely, that the object of the provision is to protect the immature: 'According to modern thought it is considered socially and morally wrong that persons of an age, at which we now believe them to be immature and provide for their education, should have the stresses, responsibilities and sexual freedom of marriage and the physical strain of

96 Jaffey, 'The Essential Validity of Marriage in the English Conflict of Laws' (1978) 41 MLR 38 at 46.
97 [1969] 1 QB 1, [1968] 2 All ER 563.
98 [1951] P 482, [1951] 2 All ER 680.
99 McClean, *Morris: The Conflict of Laws* (5th edn, 2000) p 200.
100 Smart, 'Interest Analysis, False Conflicts, and the Essential Validity of Marriage' (1986) 14 Anglo-Am L Rev 225 at 230, 233–234.

childbirth.'[101] As the criteria of maturity can differ from country to country, the requisite age at which a person can marry should be tested solely by reference to the allegedly immature person's antenuptial domiciliary law. However, there is a second, equally important, policy underlying the English provision, namely, that an English domiciliary of whatever age should not be permitted to contract a marriage with a child: 'Child marriages are by common consent believed to be bad for the participants and bad for the institution of marriage.'[102] English law has an interest in preventing its domiciliaries from sexually exploiting children. Such reasoning was instrumental in the introduction of laws prohibiting, inter alia, British tour operators from organising 'sex package holidays' involving children in foreign countries.[103] Viewed in the context of this second policy, the decision in *Pugh v Pugh* is justifiable. It could, however, be argued that, if this is a legitimate concern, it ought not to be limited to cases involving English domiciliaries and that marriages such as the one in *Mohamed v Knott* should not have been regarded as valid. Such an argument cannot be accepted. English law has, through section 2, laid down its criterion of a 'child' for these purposes and it is entitled to prevent its own domiciliaries from contracting child marriages with, say, Nigerian children.[104] It would, however, be improper for English law to impose its own standards on marriages involving two foreigners, domiciled in a country that regards the marriage as valid, unless the children were so young that the doctrine of public policy could be invoked to deny validity to the marriage. If such a couple were to come to England, as they did in *Mohamed v Knott*, there would, of course, be associated problems, such as whether the child was obliged to attend school and could be taken into care and whether criminal liability could be imposed if sexual intercourse took place.[105] However, the rules dealing with such issues are driven by different policy considerations and should not be allowed to determine the validity or otherwise of a marriage.

From the above, it can be seen that under the functional approach advocated earlier, rules on lack of age are primarily of interest to the

101 *Pugh v Pugh* [1951] P 482 at 492.

102 Ibid.

103 Sexual Offences (Conspiracy and Incitement) Act 1996, s 1.

104 Such a marriage would, in any event, probably be void under Nigerian law. Nigerian law permits customary marriages in some parts of Nigeria. Customary law does not fix a minimum age of marriage but such marriages are void if contracted 'between a native of Nigeria and a non-native' (Okonkwo, *Introduction to Nigerian Law* (1980) pp 290, 292). It should be noted that under Nigerian customary law, the child may, on reaching full age, resile from the marriage.

105 This last point was left open in *Mohamed v Knott* [1969] 1 QB 1 at 16 but Lord Parker CJ thought it unlikely that the police could prosecute in such a case.

law of the parties' antenuptial domiciles and, accordingly, the dual domicile doctrine is the most appropriate test to be applied. It might be argued that the purpose of a rule laying down a minimum age for marriage is not only to protect young people and to prevent child marriages, but also in the public interest to discourage unstable marriages, suggesting a role for the law of the intended matrimonial home. However, although the country in which the parties set up their home after the marriage is concerned that they should be mature enough for marriage, it can reasonably defer to the judgment of the law of the country to which each belongs before the marriage as to whether he or she is sufficiently mature.

As the rule in *Sottomayer v De Barros (No 2)*[106] has been held to apply to essential validity generally, and not merely to prohibited degrees, it would presumably apply to a case of non-age.[107] So if one party is domiciled in England, where the marriage is celebrated, then a provision of the law of the other party's domicile setting a minimum age higher than the English one would be ignored.

3. *Capacity to contract a polygamous marriage*

Some countries permit polygamous marriages, while others do not. Conflicts problems arise when the husband admittedly already has a wife according to all the possibly relevant laws, and one or more of them permit polygamy but the others do not. The topic of polygamous marriages will be dealt with further below. However, the question of capacity to enter a polygamous marriage when the husband is already validly married will be dealt with here.

It was decided in *Radwan v Radwan (No 2)*[108] that the intended matrimonial home rule applies to this aspect of capacity. In this case, the marriage was celebrated in France in Islamic form. The husband was a Muslim domiciled in Egypt who already had a wife married to him in Egypt by Islamic rites. The second wife was domiciled in England at the time of the ceremony, but the parties set up their matrimonial home in Egypt after the marriage, as they had intended at the time of the marriage. Five years later they moved to England. When the wife petitioned in the English court for a divorce, the question arose whether the marriage was valid. It was argued that it was void because under English law, the law of her antenuptial domicile, the wife lacked capacity to marry a man who was not single. However, applying Egyptian law as the law of the intended

106 See pp 333–334.
107 This point was accepted in the Singapore case of *Re Maria Hertogh* (1951) 17 MLJ 12, but, as the husband was found not to be domiciled in the forum, the rule could not be applied.
108 [1973] Fam 35, [1972] 3 All ER 1026.

matrimonial home, it was held that this was a valid polygamous marriage.

The decision has been strongly criticised,[109] mainly on the ground that it is well established that other aspects of capacity to marry are subject to the dual domicile rule. But, as seen earlier, Cumming-Bruce J in *Radwan* was careful to limit his decision to capacity to contract a polygamous marriage on the basis that different public and social factors are relevant to each type of incapacity. Accordingly, adopting the functional approach advocated above, the real issue is to determine the 'public and social factors'[110] underlying the rule on capacity to contract a polygamous marriage. One can then ascertain which choice of law rule will best give effect to that rationale. The English rule against polygamy safeguards the English institution of monogamous marriage which has traditionally been regarded as fundamental to the structure of the family in English society. It is a rule imposed to protect the public interest, rather than to protect the interests of the parties to the marriage. It follows that it is the country in which the marriage is to be located, the intended matrimonial home, that has the most interest in the validity and status of the marriage. In *Radwan* the wife's domicile in England was to cease after the marriage; she was to become an Egyptian domiciliary and polygamous marriages are lawful by Egyptian law. There seems little reason to apply the English prohibition to a marriage relationship which was intended to, and did, subsist in Egypt.[111]

Since *Radwan* was decided, section 11(d) of the Matrimonial Causes Act 1973 has come into force. This provision reads:

> A marriage celebrated after 31 July 1971 shall be void on the following grounds ...
> (d) in the case of a polygamous marriage entered into outside England and Wales that either party was at the time of the marriage domiciled in England and Wales.

109 Wade, 'Capacity to Marry: Choice of Law Rules and Polygamous Marriages' (1973) 22 ICLQ 571; Karsten, 'Capacity to Contract a Polygamous Marriage' (1973) 36 MLR 291; Pearl, 'Capacity for Polygamy' [1973] CLJ 43. The decision has been defended by Jaffey, 'The Essential Validity of Marriage in the English Conflict of Laws' (1978) 41 MLR 38 and Stone, 'Capacity for Polygamy – Judicial Rectification of Legislative Error' (1983) 13 Fam Law 76.

110 [1973] Fam 35 at 51.

111 It was argued earlier (pp 327–328) that the intended matrimonial home doctrine should only be applied in cases where the marriage did subsist in that place for a significant period of time. Whether 5 years' residence in Egypt followed by 14 years' residence in England is sufficient to conclude the marriage belonged most appropriately to Egypt is a moot point.

This provision must be read with section 14(1) of the Act, the effect of which is that section 11 does not apply if the validity of the marriage is to be determined by a foreign law. In other words, despite the reference to the domicile of a party, section 11(d) is not a conflicts rule, but a rule of English domestic law, to be applied only if, according to the common law rules of the conflict of laws, English law is the governing law. Accordingly, if *Radwan* is not followed and the dual domicile doctrine applied, any polygamous marriage contracted by a party domiciled in England will be void. However, if *Radwan* is applied, the result seems to be as follows. If the intended matrimonial home is any country other than England, section 11(d) does not come into the picture at all. The validity of the polygamous marriage is determined by the law of the foreign country in question.[112] So *Radwan* would have been decided in the same way even if the marriage had been celebrated after 31 July 1971. On the other hand, if the intended matrimonial home is England, then English law governs and section 11(d) does apply. If either of the parties is domiciled in England at the time of the marriage, it is void. If neither of the parties is domiciled in England at the time of the marriage, section 11(d) is not applicable but the same result will be reached and the marriage held void. This is because polygamous marriages are not permitted under English domestic law. This was the reason why the marriage in *Radwan*, decided before section 11(d) came into effect, would have been void under the dual domicile doctrine. Further, even if this were not the position at common law in cases where neither party was domiciled in England,[113] section 11(b) of the Matrimonial Causes Act 1973 provides that a marriage is void if 'at the time of the marriage either party was already lawfully married'. Unlike section 11(d), this is not limited to cases where either of the spouses is domiciled in England. So if England is the intended matrimonial home, the marriage will be void even if both parties are domiciled in an Islamic country when they marry.

112 This is, of course, somewhat perverse. Cumming-Bruce J in *Radwan* accepted that s 14 was enacted on the assumption that the dual domicile rule governed the question of capacity to contract a polygamous marriage (at 52).

113 This was the view adopted by Jaffey, *Introduction to the Conflict of Laws* (1988) p 32. The more orthodox position was that stated in Dicey and Morris, *The Conflict of Laws* (12th edn, 1993) p 700: 'All monogamous countries have a rule prohibiting bigamy and, though this was originally intended to apply where both marriages are in monogamous form, it could be applied without undue distortion to an actually polygamous marriage.'

4. *Capacity to marry after a foreign decree of divorce or annulment*

(A) INTRODUCTION

Here the concern is with cases where none of the potentially applicable laws permit polygamy. A monogamously married person lacks capacity to contract a second monogamous marriage until the first marriage has been dissolved or annulled. Conflicts can arise when the first marriage is dissolved or annulled and one potentially applicable law recognises the divorce or annulment but another does not. The result is that one of the parties is already married according to one of the laws but not according to another. The issue is whether that spouse has capacity to marry again or whether the second marriage would be bigamous. For example, in *Lawrence v Lawrence*[114] the wife, then domiciled in Brazil, obtained a divorce from her first husband in Nevada. The next day, in Nevada, she married the second husband, who was domiciled in England. England was also the intended matrimonial home and the parties set up home here very soon after the marriage. The wife's Nevada divorce was recognised by English law but not by Brazilian law, under which she remained married to her first husband. The wife petitioned in the English court for a nullity decree on the ground that the second marriage was bigamous. English and Brazilian law agreed that the wife did not have capacity to contract the second marriage unless she was single. The conflict arose because the two laws, taking different views as to the validity of the Nevada divorce, also took different views as to whether the wife was single when she remarried. The wife contended that her capacity to marry her second husband was governed by Brazilian law as the law of her antenuptial domicile. Since the Nevada divorce was invalid by Brazilian law she lacked capacity by that law, so the marriage was void. The trial judge, however, held that the validity of the remarriage was governed by English law, because, being the law of the intended matrimonial domicile, it was the law of the country with which the marriage had its most real and substantial connection.[115] Since the divorce was recognised by English law, the remarriage was valid. The Court of Appeal adopted a third approach. English law has its own conflicts rules on recognition of foreign divorces and under these rules the Nevada divorce was entitled to recognition. The wife was therefore a single woman at the time of her second marriage. That marriage could not be declared void on the ground of her bigamy. The English conflicts rules (as the law of the forum) should

114 [1985] Fam 106, [1985] 1 All ER 506.
115 Following Lord Simon in *Vervaeke v Smith* [1983] 1 AC 145 at 166. See pp 328–329.

not have to give way to the Brazilian conflicts rules on recognition of foreign divorces. Which of these three approaches is correct?

The underlying rationale of the prohibition against bigamous marriages is fairly self-evident. The monogamous institution of marriage could hardly be preserved if parties were allowed more than one spouse.[116] Before remarriage there needs to be a valid divorce or annulment so that the ancillary matters of property distribution, maintenance and custody of children can be resolved. While the law of the intended matrimonial home clearly has a public interest in such remarriages, it would appear that it is the law with which the *first* marriage is most closely connected that has the greater interest in ensuring that the divorce or annulment is valid and that the ancillary matters have been properly resolved and the other spouse's interests protected. The first marriage is likely to be more closely connected with the law of domicile of the party seeking to remarry than with the intended matrimonial home of the second marriage. For example, in *Padolecchia v Padolecchia*[117] the locus of the first marriage was Italy. Both parties were Italian domiciliaries. The husband obtained a divorce in Mexico and then, while still domiciled in Italy, remarried intending to establish a new matrimonial home in Denmark. The divorce was not recognised by Italian law. Simon P had no hesitation in disregarding Danish law completely and focusing on whether the parties to the first marriage were validly divorced by Italian law. Any other approach would have left the Italian wife in an impossible position. She would still have been married to her husband with the ancillary matters unresolved while her husband might, under the intended matrimonial doctrine, have been regarded as validly married to his new Danish wife.

Accordingly, it is clear that under the functional approach advocated above, the dual domicile doctrine is to be preferred to any other doctrine. But, what of the third possible approach, namely, the one adopted by the Court of Appeal in *Lawrence*? The forum, England, has its own conflicts rules on recognition of foreign divorces and annulments. Why should these be subjugated to the conflicts rules of another country? To assess the validity of this claim, it is necessary to consider more closely the tensions arising in a phenomenon known as the incidental question.

(B) THE INCIDENTAL QUESTION

An incidental question arises when one country's conflicts rules lead to a foreign law, but under that law an incidental or subsidiary

116 *Whiston v Whiston* [1998] 1 All ER 423 at 429.
117 [1968] P 314, [1967] 3 All ER 863.

question arises which can only be resolved by an application of a further conflicts rule governing that incidental question. The issue is whether that incidental question should be governed by the conflicts rule of the foreign law (the lex causae approach) or the conflicts rule of the forum (the lex fori approach).

In *Lawrence v Lawrence*[118] the question before the English court was the wife's capacity to marry the second husband. According to the general rule, explored above, this is (contrary to what the trial judge held) governed by the law of her antenuptial domicile, Brazilian law. The relevant rule of capacity of Brazilian domestic law was that only a single person can marry. In applying that rule the English court would immediately be confronted with another question: was the wife single when she married her second husband or was she still married to her first husband? This question – of the validity of the Nevada divorce – could be described as an incidental question because it arises for decision, not independently, but in the course of deciding the main question of the wife's capacity to remarry. To this incidental question the conflicts rules of England and Brazil (in this case, their rules for the recognition of foreign divorces[119]) gave different answers, the divorce being recognised in England but not in Brazil.

In deciding the incidental question, should the English court simply use its own rules for the recognition of foreign divorces (the lex fori approach) or should it use the Brazilian ones, since it is Brazilian law which governs the main question of the wife's capacity to remarry (the lex causae approach)? One could argue that it is pointless referring to Brazilian law as the antenuptial domiciliary law and then ignoring the only relevant Brazilian rules, that is, whether she was validly divorced. On the other hand, simply to say that the wife lacked capacity under Brazilian law is to conceal the fact that there are two separate questions. First, what is the relevant Brazilian domestic rule of capacity to marry? Answer: only a single person can marry. Secondly, arising from that answer, was the wife single when she remarried? This second question is a question of her status, not her capacity. There would be no logical contradiction in applying the Brazilian domestic rule of capacity that only a single person can marry and English conflicts rules to test whether she is single.

It is this latter view that is consistent with the modern English law. It is helpful, however, to distinguish two situations.

118 [1985] 1 All ER 506.
119 The recognition of foreign matrimonial decrees is dealt with in chapter 9.

(i) Divorce or annulment recognised by English law but not by law of domicile

In earlier cases,[120] the courts took it for granted that the lex causae should decide the incidental question of whether the divorce or annulment should be recognised. In *R v Brentwood Superintendent Registrar of Marriages, ex p Arias*[121] the first marriage of the husband, who was domiciled in Switzerland but a national of Italy, was dissolved by a Swiss court. This divorce was recognised in England but not in Italy. The husband wanted to remarry in England, and the question came before the Divisional Court whether he was entitled to do so. The court held that his capacity was governed by Swiss law, as the law of his antenuptial domicile. By Swiss law, since he was an Italian national, his capacity to marry was governed by Italian law.[122] As the divorce was not recognised in Italy, it followed, in the court's view, that the husband lacked capacity to marry again. In other words, the incidental question of the validity of the Swiss divorce was decided by the lex causae,[123] Swiss law. The consequence was that a single person (for that is what he was in the eyes of the English court) was not permitted to marry.

In *Perrini v Perrini*,[124] however, such reasoning was departed from and a second marriage held valid because a preceding nullity decree obtained from a New Jersey court was entitled to recognition by English law. This result was reached despite the fact that the decree was not recognised by Italian law, the law of the husband's domicile at the date of the second marriage. Similarly, as has been seen, the Court of Appeal in *Lawrence v Lawrence*[125] held that, if a divorce is recognised in England, a remarriage cannot be held void on the ground that the divorce is not recognised in some other country. In other words, the incidental question is to be decided under the conflicts rules of the lex fori.

The decision in *Lawrence v Lawrence* was confirmed by section 50 of the Family Law Act 1986. Its effect is that where a divorce or annulment has been granted by an English court, or is recognised in England, the fact that the divorce or annulment would not be recognised elsewhere shall not preclude either party to the marriage from remarrying in England or cause the remarriage of either party (wherever the remarriage takes place) to be treated as invalid in England.

120 For example, *Padolecchia v Padolecchia* [1968] P 314, [1967] 3 All ER 863.
121 [1968] 2 QB 956, [1968] 3 All ER 279.
122 The English court's application of the Swiss conflicts rule (renvoi) is discussed at pp 361–362.
123 The court did not in fact analyse the issue in this way, but simply assumed that this was the proper approach.
124 [1979] Fam 84, [1979] 2 All ER 323.
125 [1985] 1 All ER 506.

(ii) Divorce or annulment recognised by domiciliary law but not by English law

The converse situation to that in *Lawrence v Lawrence*[126] can also occur, where the divorce is not recognised by the lex fori, but is recognised by the lex causae. In the Canadian case of *Schwebel v Ungar*[127] the wife and her first husband were originally domiciled in Hungary. On their way to settle in Israel, while in Italy but still domiciled in Hungary, the husband divorced the wife under Jewish law. They then made their way to Israel, where both became domiciled, and where the divorce was recognised as valid. Some years later, the wife, still domiciled in Israel, married in Ontario a second husband who was domiciled there. The divorce obtained in Italy was not recognised in Ontario. The second husband petitioned in the Ontario court for a nullity decree on the ground that, when the wife's second marriage was celebrated, she was still married to her first husband. The Canadian courts held the remarriage valid, because, using the dual domicile rule, the wife's capacity to remarry was governed by the law of Israel, and by that law the divorce was valid, even though it was not valid by the lex fori, Ontario law. In other words, the lex causae approach was used for the incidental question.

How would such a case as *Schwebel v Ungar* be decided by an English court today? There is no statutory provision dealing with this situation, as there is for the converse case under section 50 of the Family Law Act 1986; nor does the case strictly fall within the ratio of *Lawrence*. Nevertheless, the lex fori approach seems preferable in a case such as *Schwebel v Ungar* as much as in *Lawrence*. In the latter case, the lex fori must decide the validity of the divorce to avoid the consequence that a single person is not free to marry. In a case such as *Schwebel*, the lex fori should be used to avoid the even more startling result that a person is validly and monogamously married to two spouses at the same time. This is because under the forum's own rules of recognition (to be applied when there is no main question governed by a foreign law), the first marriage still subsists, even though the second marriage has been held valid. Intractable problems in relation to succession, matrimonial relief and other matters could arise.[128] Suppose in such a case as *Schwebel*, the wife, after her second marriage had been held valid in England, became

126 [1985] 1 All ER 506.

127 (1963) 42 DLR (2d) 622; affd 48 DLR (2d) 644.

128 It is arguable that *Schwebel v Ungar* decided that in view of the position under Israeli law the divorce had to be recognised in Ontario: see Lysyk (1965) 43 Can Bar Rev 363. But if such a case arose in England, the divorce could not be recognised under the English statutory grounds, and the problem of two coexisting monogamous marriages could arise.

domiciled in England and died here intestate. The first husband would be entitled to succeed as the surviving spouse, for the divorce would not be recognised in England. What about the second husband, whose marriage had been held valid?

It thus appears that in all bigamy cases the English rules of recognition of foreign decrees are to be applied. This can be interpreted in one of two ways, both leading to the same result. First, it could be regarded as confirming the proposition that there is no single choice of law rule to be applied in all cases of capacity to marry. While the dual domicile doctrine might be applicable to some incapacities such as lack of age, and the intended matrimonial home to others such as capacity to contract a polygamous marriage, the appropriate rule to be applied here is the English rule on recognition of foreign divorces and annulments. Alternatively, it could be argued that no choice of law rule for bigamy is necessary. On the question of capacity, all the possibly applicable laws are the same: only a single person can marry. The conflict is about the status of a party – whether or not he is single. This question is to be decided by the court's own rules of recognition.

5. *Consent of the parties*

Another question of essential validity, which is not normally classified as a matter of capacity, is lack of consent. In English domestic law the effect of this defect is to make the marriage voidable rather than void.

Lack of consent relates to cases where a party maintains that he did not consent to the marriage at all, or, more likely, that his apparent consent was vitiated by some defect such as fraud, duress or mistake, or that he consented to something other than a marriage. So far as English law is concerned, section 12(c) of the Matrimonial Causes Act 1973 provides that a marriage shall be voidable if either party did not consent to it, whether in consequence of duress, mistake, unsoundness of mind or otherwise. The only types of mistake affecting the validity of a marriage under English law are mistake as to the identity of the other party and mistake as to the nature of the ceremony.[129] Marriages of convenience (where the parties have no intention of cohabiting) are thus valid on this ground under English law.[130] Conflicts of laws will arise because the precise rules differ from one legal system to another. For example, marriages of convenience are not valid by Belgian law.

129 Bromley and Lowe, *Bromley's Family Law* (9th edn, 1998) pp 92–93.

130 *Vervaeke v Smith* [1983] 1 AC 145, [1982] 2 All ER 144. Such marriages could be voidable on grounds of non-consummation. See pp 351–352.

In *Vervaeke v Smith*[131] Lord Simon in the House of Lords suggested, obiter, that whether a marriage of convenience was valid was a matter of 'quintessential validity' to be governed by the law of the country with which the marriage had its most real and substantial connection. Despite this, however, the authorities are overwhelmingly in favour of the dual domicile doctrine for all matters of consent because the issue is the protection of an aggrieved party, not the public interest of the country in which the marriage relationship will be centred. In *Szechter v Szechter*[132] the parties were domiciled in Poland, where the marriage was celebrated. The parties only entered into the marriage in order to obtain the wife's release from prison, where her personal safety was threatened. On her release, the parties made their way to England. The wife brought nullity proceedings in the English court on the ground that she had entered the marriage under duress. Simon P, holding that the matter was governed by Polish law as the law of the parties' antenuptial domicile, granted a nullity decree on the basis that the marriage was invalid for lack of consent by Polish law. The husband was thus able to remarry his original wife, whom he had divorced as part of the scheme to secure the release of the second wife.

In *Szechter* both parties were domiciled in Poland. What is the position if at the time of the marriage the parties are domiciled in different countries, whose laws give different answers to the question whether or not there was consent? No doubt if the marriage is invalid by the law of the antenuptial domicile of the party whose consent is questioned, then the marriage will be annulled, even if there was consent by the law of the other party's domicile. Suppose, however, that the wife has validly consented by the law of her domicile, but not by the law of the husband's domicile. Will the court grant a nullity decree? It can be argued that, if by the standards of her own law she has validly consented, there is no reason why the marriage should be annulled. By the same token, however, it could be said that the husband would have no cause to complain of injustice if the marriage were annulled, seeing that by the standards of his own law the wife has not consented. The answer to this difficult question is unsettled.

In *Szechter*[133] Simon P agreed obiter with the suggestion in the then current edition of Dicey and Morris[134] that 'no marriage is valid

131 [1983] 1 AC 145, [1982] 2 All ER 144.
132 [1971] P 286, [1970] 3 All ER 905.
133 [1971] P 286 at 294.
134 *The Conflict of Laws* (8th edn, 1967) p 271. In the present edition the contrary view is preferred (13th edn, 2000) p 690.

if by the law of either party's domicile one party does not consent to marry the other'. According to this, a party *can* rely on lack of consent under the law of the other party's domicile. Earlier, in *Way v Way*[135] a marriage had been celebrated in Russia between a wife domiciled there and a husband domiciled in England. The husband sought a nullity decree in the English court, one of the grounds being lack of consent: he had entered the marriage under the mistaken belief that the wife would be permitted to come to live with him in England. The judge's view seems to have been that whether the husband had consented was to be decided according to English law as the law of his own domicile. By that law the mistake was immaterial, so the marriage was not invalid for lack of consent. There is no suggestion that Russian law, the law of the wife's domicile, could be relevant to test whether the husband had consented. In *Vervaeke v Smith* a Belgian domiciliary entered into a marriage of convenience in England with an English domiciliary in order to acquire British nationality so as to be able to remain in England to carry on her trade as a prostitute. Under Belgian law such a marriage was void. In the Court of Appeal,[136] Arnold P stated that the *Sottomayer v De Barros (No 2)*[137] exception applied and the marriage was thus valid under English law. It will be recalled that this rule (or, rather, exception to the dual domicile test) applies when the parties marry in England, one of the parties is an English domiciliary and the marriage is valid by English law. Had the Dicey and Morris rule, approved in *Szechter*, been applicable, the marriage would not have been valid by English law because the *husband's* lack of consent by Belgian law would have rendered the marriage invalid. It is thus implicit in the judgment that each party's consent was tested by reference to that person's antenuptial law alone. This approach is clearly preferable in terms of policy. The rationale of applying the law of antenuptial domicile here is that a person is entitled to the protection of his own law; he does not need the protection of his spouse's law. As the Law Commission has pointed out, it is 'difficult to see why, if a party's own law considers that he has validly consented to the marriage, he should nevertheless be entitled to avoid the marriage on the basis of his lack of consent under the other party's domiciliary law'.[138]

135 [1950] P 71 at 78–79. On appeal the judge's statement on this point was assumed to be correct: *Kenward v Kenward* [1951] P 124 at 133.
136 [1981] Fam 77, [1981] 1 All ER 55.
137 (1879) 5 PD 94.
138 Law Com Working Paper No 89, para 5.23.

6. Physical impediments

Several disparate impediments (under English law) can be grouped under this heading. First, under section 12(e) of the Matrimonial Causes Act 1973, a marriage is voidable if at the time of the marriage the respondent was suffering from venereal disease in a communicable form, and under section 12(f) if at the time of the marriage the respondent was pregnant by some person other than the petitioner. As it is provided by section 13(3) that a decree shall not be granted in these situations unless the petitioner was at the time of the marriage ignorant of the facts alleged, it has been pointed out[139] that these cases are similar to ones involving lack of consent. However, even if they are not so regarded, no doubt the choice of law rule for them will be the same.

Secondly, there is the problem of non-consummation of a marriage, whether through impotence or wilful refusal to consummate the marriage. Such marriages are voidable according to English law.[140] Other countries may have different rules on the subject. For example, neither impotence nor wilful refusal may affect the validity of the marriage; or the latter may not do so, but may, or may not, be a ground for divorce.[141] Which law governs?

It was held by the Court of Appeal in *De Reneville v De Reneville* that these issues are to be decided by 'the law of the husband's domicile at the time of the marriage or (preferably ...) ... the law of the matrimonial domicile in reference to which the parties may have been supposed to enter into the bonds of marriage'.[142] This approach has been followed in subsequent cases.[143] In *Ponticelli v Ponticelli*,[144] for example, a marriage was celebrated in Italy between a wife domiciled there and a husband domiciled in England, where the parties set up their matrimonial home. The husband petitioned the English court for a nullity decree on the ground of the wife's wilful refusal to consummate the marriage. By Italian law wilful refusal was not a ground of nullity. Sachs J held that English law governed, either as the lex fori or (the view he preferred) as the lex domicilii,

139 McClean, *Morris: The Conflict of Laws* (5th edn, 2000) p 208.

140 Matrimonial Causes Act 1973, s 12(a) and (b).

141 For example, wilful refusal to consummate is a ground for divorce in Alabama (Code, s 30–2–1(a)(1)); it is not a ground for relief at all in Scotland (Dicey and Morris, *The Conflict of Laws* (13th edn, 2000) p 727).

142 [1948] P 100 at 114.

143 *Casey v Casey* [1949] P 420, [1949] 2 All ER 110; *Way v Way* [1950] P 71, [1949] 2 All ER 959. *Robert v Robert* [1947] P 164, [1947] 2 All ER 22 in which the lex loci celebrationis was held applicable, cannot stand with *De Reneville v De Reneville.*

144 [1958] P 204, [1958] 1 All ER 357.

by which he meant 'the law of the country in which the parties are domiciled at the time of the marriage, and in which the matrimonial residence is contemplated'.[145] This, he said, 'normally coincides with the law pertaining to the country of the husband's domicile at the time of the marriage'.[146] So a nullity decree was granted.

While authority is in favour of the law of the husband's domicile at the time of the marriage, or of the intended matrimonial home if that is different, it is by no means clear that this is the best rule for non-consummation. Here, as with consent, the concern is with the protection of a party from contracting a marriage that is different in nature from the one anticipated. The rule is not concerned with the public interest of the country in which the parties set up their home. Looked at in this light, a matrimonial home rule can work unjustly against the petitioner, as a variation of the facts in *Ponticelli v Ponticelli* will show. Suppose the wife is English, the husband Italian, and Italy the matrimonial home. The husband wilfully refuses to consummate the marriage, which does not give ground for annulment under Italian law. On the basis of the intended matrimonial home test, the wife would be unable to obtain an annulment in the English court. It seems only just, however, that a spouse should be able to rely on the law of the country to which she belonged before the marriage to determine that the marriage is one to which she should not be unwillingly tied. On this basis, the governing law should be that of the petitioner's domicile at the date of the marriage.[147]

7. *Same-sex marriages*

Under English law a marriage is void if the parties are not respectively male and female.[148] Until recently, this has posed little problem for the conflict of laws because the laws of all other countries were the same. However, in recent years the laws of some countries have started giving formal recognition to same-sex relationships, with the result that such relationships have legal consequences similar to those which flow from a traditional marriage between a man and a woman. For example, the Danish Registered Partnership Act 1989[149] allows homosexuals to register their relationships in a civil ceremony and grants such couples a legal status comparable to married couples. Only one of the parties needs to be a Danish citizen and

145 Citing *Brook v Brook* (1861) 9 HL Cas 193 at 207.
146 At 214.
147 Jaffey, 'The Essential Validity of Marriage in the English Conflict of Laws' (1978) 41 MLR 38.
148 Matrimonial Causes Act 1973, s 11(c).
149 Act No 372 of 7 June 1989.

permanently resident in Denmark.[150] On 1 April 2001 the Netherlands became the first country in the world to legalise same-sex marriages.[151] The potential for conflicts of laws is obvious. If an English person were to register a relationship with a Dane in Denmark, or marry a Dutch domiciliary of the same sex, the English court could be called upon to determine the validity of such a legal relationship or marriage.

Dealing first with registered partnerships, the initial question for an English court would be one of classification. Are such registered relationships to be classified as marriages or contracts? If the latter view were taken, the conflicts rules on contract would apply and there would be no issue of essential validity of marriage. In such a situation, however, it is not certain which contract rules would be applicable. The Rome Convention on the Law Applicable to Contractual Obligations does not apply to questions involving 'status' or 'rights and duties arising out of a family relationship',[152] thus suggesting that the common law should apply and the contract be governed by its proper law. On the other hand, it could be argued that if the relationship were not to be classified as a 'marriage' that must be because it is not regarded as raising an issue of status or family relationship and therefore the Rome Convention rules do apply. This whole approach, however, seems unrealistic. As will be seen,[153] the process of classification is normally effected by examining the incidents of a status, relationship or whatever, and then characterising it according to its nearest English analogue. On this basis, these registered relationships involve most of the incidents of marriage[154] and so the English court should be forced to classify it as a marriage – and would then have to assess its validity. With Dutch same-sex marriages the question of essential validity of marriage would clearly have to be determined.

150 Similar registered partnership laws have been introduced in Norway, Sweden, Iceland, Finland, Greenland, The Netherlands, Belgium, France and Germany, and in the United States by Hawaii and Vermont.

151 http://ruljis.leidenuniv.nl/user/cwaaldij/www/NHR/news.htm. For background to the new legislation see Waaldijk, 'Small Change: How the Road to Same-Sex Marriage Got Paved in the Netherlands' in Wintemute and Andenaes (eds), *Legal Recognition of Same-Sex Partnership: A Study of National, European and International Law* (2001). The legalisation of such marriages is in addition to permitting registered partnerships which, of course, may be entered into by persons of the opposite sex.

152 Art 1(2).

153 See pp 527–528.

154 See, for example, Steiner, 'The Spirit of the New French Registered Partnership Law – Promoting Autonomy and Pluralism or Weakening Marriage' (2000) 12 CFLQ 1 at 7 who argues that the French registered partnership law 'constitutes a replica of marriage'.

Of course, it could be argued that no choice of law rule need be developed because any such partnership or marriage would be regarded as contrary to public policy. In *Hyde v Hyde*[155] the classic definition of marriage was given as being 'the voluntary union for life of one man and one woman to the exclusion of all others'. Over the past 130 years this proposition has been eroded. Marriage is no longer necessarily for life; divorce is permitted. For conflict of laws purposes marriage is no longer 'to the exclusion of all others'; polygamous marriages are recognised and are not regarded as contrary to public policy.[156] Over the past decade enormous strides have been made internationally in the direction of affording legal equality to homosexuals.[157] While full equality is still a long way off in English law[158] and the prohibition on same-sex marriages in England certainly would not contravene the European Convention on Human Rights,[159] it is unlikely in today's climate that an English court would hold a registered partnership between two Danes or a marriage between two Dutch persons of the same sex to be contrary to public policy. However, it is conceded that the English court might be influenced by the nature of the issue before it. For instance, while such marriages might well be regarded as valid for purposes of the law of succession and for incapacitating the parties from marrying anyone else, it is unlikely that any such marriage would be recognised for immigration purposes.[160] Nevertheless, for at least some purposes, it is likely that English courts will have to determine whether such an English (or other foreign) domiciliary can be validly registered or married. This would have to be determined under normal choice of law rules.

Prohibitions against homosexual marriages are designed to buttress the institution of heterosexual marriage. They are not designed to protect the parties to the marriage. Accordingly, it is the country where the marriage or partnership is to be based that has the most interest in the validity of such a marriage or relationship. If an

155 (1866) LR 1 P & D 130.

156 See p 365.

157 See, for example, Wintermute and Andenaes, n 151 above.

158 In 2001 the Greater London Authority introduced measures allowing persons to register a same-sex partnership. Although such registration will have no legal effect, the hope was that it would be recognised by public bodies and be used in disputes over wills, property and succession rights (*Independent*, 6 September 2001). In January 2001 a Private Member's Civil Partnership Bill which would allow all cohabiting couples to have the same legal rights and obligations as married couples was launched.

159 *X, Y, Z v United Kingdom* [1997] 2 FLR 892.

160 Norrie, 'Reproductive Technology, Transsexualism and Homosexuality: New Problems for International Private Law' (1994) 43 ICLQ 757 at 772–774.

English domiciliary registers a partnership with a Dane in Denmark and the intended partnership home is in Denmark and, under the proposed modification suggested earlier, the parties remain in Denmark for a significant period of time, no English interests are affected and the legal consequences of such a relationship should be recognised. It follows that, as with polygamous marriages, capacity to enter a same-sex partnership or marriage should be governed by the law of the intended home and not by the dual domicile doctrine.

8. *Transsexual marriages*

Under English law, for the purposes of marriage, a person's sex is fixed at birth and so a sex-change operation has no legal effect.[161] Under the laws of many other countries, however, such marriages are recognised as valid. What is the position if an English domiciled male to female transsexual marries a male German domiciliary under whose law the marriage would be valid? It has been argued[162] that this is not a question of capacity to marry but rather one of the definition of a 'man' or 'woman'; this is a matter of status to be governed by the law of the transsexual's domicile. The better view, however, is that the validity of such marriages should be determined by the same rules governing same-sex marriages. If the parties marry in Germany intending to make their home there and implement their intention for a significant period of time, no English interests are affected. It follows that the validity of the marriage should be governed by the law of the intended matrimonial home.

9. *Other incapacities under foreign laws*

All the incapacities discussed to this point are ones known to English law. The detail might differ from country to country – for example, different degrees of consanguinity render a marriage void in different countries – but the broad incapacitating category has always been one known to English law. However, some legal systems have incapacities quite unknown to English law, for example, the prohibition on marriages of convenience under Belgian law[163] or, more importantly, the prohibition under Islamic law against Muslim women marrying non-Muslim men.[164] English law appears to adopt

161 *Corbett v Corbett* [1971] P 83; *Bellinger v Bellinger* [2001] EWCA Civ 1140, [2001] 2 FLR 1048. This has been held not to be contrary to the European Convention on Human Rights: *Cossey v United Kingdom* [1991] 2 FLR 492.
162 Norrie, above n 160.
163 *Vervaeke v Smith* [1983] 1 AC 145, [1982] 2 All ER 144.
164 Pearl, *A Textbook on Muslim Personal Law* (2nd edn, 1987) pp 50–51; Hodkinson, *Muslim Family Law Handbook* (1984) p 108.

one of two approaches to such marriages. If the foreign incapacity can be regarded as analogous to a known English incapacity, effect can be given to it under the normal rules. For example, in *Vervaeke v Smith*[165] the Belgian prohibition on marriages of convenience was regarded as being similar to the English prohibition on non-consensual marriages; the English conflicts rules on lack of consent could then be applied. If, on the other hand, the foreign prohibition cannot be regarded as equivalent to any English prohibition, academic commentators tend to regard the foreign prohibition as contrary to public policy and thus to be disregarded. For example, it is often asserted that English courts will not apply a rule of the law of domicile which prohibits marriages between members of different races, castes or religions.[166] Equally, a foreign incapacity prohibiting the guilty party to a divorce from remarrying before the innocent one has been held to be unenforceable as contrary to public policy.[167]

Public policy must, of course, be allowed its proper role here.[168] If a foreign prohibition is genuinely repugnant to English standards of morality, effect cannot be given to it. For example, under the laws of South Africa during the apartheid era, marriages between persons of different races were prohibited. It would have been unthinkable in most situations for an English court to have given those laws a seal of legitimacy by enforcing such prohibitions.[169] Similarly, if a prohibition is, in reality, penal – such as the prohibition against remarriage before the innocent party to a preceding divorce – effect ought not to be given to it. However, there can be no justification for such an approach when dealing with prohibitions against marrying a person of a different religion. Invocation of the doctrine of public policy here smacks of a chauvinistic attitude that if a prohibition is unknown to English law it must be 'wrong' in the sense of being offensive to English standards of justice, decency and morality. Such prohibitions are widely accepted in varying degrees in other countries, for example, in most Islamic countries. Other manifestations of the Islamic faith, such as polygamous marriages, are not regarded as contrary to public policy and, accordingly, there seems little reason for invoking the doctrine of public policy here.

165 [1983] 1 AC 145, [1982] 2 All ER 144.

166 Dicey and Morris, *The Conflict of Laws* (13th edn, 2000) p 688; Cheshire and North, *Private International Law* (13th edn, 1999) p 734.

167 *Scott v A-G* (1886) 11 PD 128.

168 See pp 18–19 and 555–562.

169 See, however, pp 560–561 for the view that in certain limited circumstances (where both parties had relied on the invalidity of the marriage and remarried) recognition could be afforded to such laws.

The cases relied on by the academic commentators cited above[170] do not in fact support the proposition that such prohibitions are contrary to public policy. For example, in *Chetti v Chetti*[171] a husband argued that as a Hindu domiciled in India he was incapable of marrying anyone outside his own caste or religion. This incapacity[172] was indeed ignored – but not on the ground that recognition of the incapacity would be contrary to public policy. The husband had married an English domiciliary in England and so the rule in *Sottomayer v De Barros (No 2)*[173] clearly applied. Indeed, there are dicta in this case that if the marriage had been contracted abroad, public policy could not be invoked as it would then 'be free to every judge to indulge his own feelings as to what prohibitions by foreign countries on the capacity to contract a marriage are reasonable'.[174] Other cases relied on by academic commentators[175] have concerned Cypriot members of the Greek Orthodox church or Maltese Roman Catholics who have married in England without the appropriate religious ceremony as then required by their law of domicile. These foreign 'incapacities' were indeed ignored – but, again, not on the basis that the incapacity was contrary to public policy, but rather that the type of marriage ceremony required was a matter relating to formal validity. The parties had married in England and, accordingly, only compliance with English law was necessary. In *Corbett v Corbett*[176] a Jewish wife domiciled in Palestine married a Christian in Palestine. Under Palestinian law she lacked capacity to contract such a marriage. Although the decision turned on other grounds, there is no hint in the judgment that such an incapacity could be regarded as contrary to public policy. To the contrary, Barnard J expressly stated that 'undoubtedly a marriage which one of the parties had not the capacity to contract would be regarded as a void marriage by English law'.[177]

Assuming the foreign incapacity is not regarded as contrary to public policy, it is necessary to determine the appropriate choice of law rule. Again, the most sensible approach is to explore the underlying rationale of the prohibition to ascertain the choice of law

170 See n 166.
171 [1909] P 67.
172 The evidence of Indian law was unsatisfactory and so much of the analysis was obiter (at 78–80).
173 (1879) 5 PD 94.
174 At 86.
175 *Papadopoulos v Papadopoulos* [1930] P 55; *Gray v Formosa* [1963] P 259, [1962] 3 All ER 419; *Lepre v Lepre* [1965] P 52, [1963] 2 All ER 49.
176 [1957] 1 All ER 621.
177 At 623.

rule that will best give effect to it. Continuing with the example of religious incapacities, such as the Islamic prohibition against marriages to non-Muslims, there should be a basic presumption in favour of the dual domicile doctrine. There can be little doubt that this is the correct approach where the parties continue to live in the foreign country; they might have treated the marriage as void, and perhaps remarried. If the validity of the original marriage arose in the context of an English succession, or one of the parties later came to live in England, it is hard to think that justice would be done, or moral standards preserved, by insisting on upholding the validity of the original marriage. If a foreign domiciled Muslim woman were to marry a non-Muslim English domiciliary in England, English standards of marriage for persons marrying here would, of course, be preserved under the rule in *Sottomayer v De Barros (No 2)*. More problematic is the case where the parties marry abroad but intend to establish a matrimonial home in England or in a third country which disregards the incapacity. Here, by analogy with the rules on monogamy and polygamy, it can be argued that the parties intend their marriage relationship to be a secular one and, accordingly, the marriage should be regarded as valid. It *would* be contrary to public policy to enforce a rule that effectively prevented people from changing their religion or, at least, casting off a consequence attaching to that religion. Of course, such an approach would cause problems were one of the parties later to return to their earlier place of domicile. The proposed modification to the intended matrimonial home doctrine, suggested earlier,[178] would largely solve this. The law of the intended matrimonial home would only apply in retrospective situations where the parties had established a matrimonial home in the new country for a significant period of time.

E The role of the lex loci celebrationis

Suppose the parties have capacity according to the rules so far considered. Does it matter if they lack capacity by the law of the country where the marriage is celebrated? The Law Commission has argued that the lex loci celebrationis does have a legitimate interest in not allowing its procedures to be used for the contracting of marriages which it considers void and that in the interests of international comity English law should recognise this interest.[179] Further, ignoring the lex loci celebrationis view on essential validity

178 See pp 327–328.
179 Law Com Working Paper No 89, para 3.43.

is likely to lead to limping relationships as the marriage will usually be regarded as void in the country of celebration but valid by English law.[180] However, the better view is that the lex loci celebrationis does not have a *sufficient* interest in the essentials of marriage to justify the imposition of an extra hurdle with which the parties have to comply. Neither of the parties nor the marriage relationship may have more than a transient connection with that country. It seems unjustifiable to insist on compliance with that law when the marriage will have no impact on that society. There is authority in Australia[181] and Canada[182] that capacity by the lex loci celebrationis is unnecessary. There is no direct authority in England on the point, but it seems to have been assumed in *Breen v Breen*[183] that a marriage must be valid by the law of the country of celebration. In this case two English domiciliaries married in Ireland. The husband had previously been divorced. Karminski J held that the marriage would only be valid if the divorce was recognised by Irish law. This is tantamount to saying that the parties must have capacity by the lex loci celebrationis. However, as it was concluded that the divorce would be recognised by Irish law and the marriage was thus held valid, this is a somewhat weak precedent which has been roundly condemned.[184]

If the marriage is celebrated in England, however, as far as the English court is concerned, it must be valid by English law on the ground that the English court could hardly disregard its own law on such vital matters as the minimum age, or prohibited degrees of marriage. One could not expect an English registrar to marry two homosexuals or a girl of 13 simply because such persons had capacity by their law of domicile. Of course, this amounts to a differential approach in that parties marrying in England must have capacity by the lex loci celebrationis but when marrying abroad no such capacity is required. However, this can be justified.[185] When a marriage takes place in England there is a greater potential impact here and, accordingly, the law has a greater interest in ensuring that the marriage conforms to all the standards of an English marriage. There is nothing inconsistent with general conflicts principles in

180 Ibid.
181 *Re Swan's Will* (1871) 2 VLR (IE & M) 47.
182 *Reed v Reed* (1969) 6 DLR (3d) 617. The same view was taken in a Bahamas case, *Re Hewitt's Estate* (1985), discussed by Bradshaw, 'Capacity to Marry and the Relevance of the Lex Loci Celebrationis in Commonwealth Law' (1985) 15 Anglo-Am LR 112.
183 [1964] P 144, [1961] 3 All ER 225.
184 Cheshire and North, *Private International Law* (13th edn, 1999) p 732.
185 Clarkson, 'Marriage in England: Favouring the Lex Fori' (1990) 10 LS 80.

English law, as the lex fori, effectively imposing mandatory requirements on persons marrying within the jurisdiction.[186] As the Law Commission states: 'our courts can hardly be expected to uphold the validity of marriages which their own law does not countenance'.[187]

A possible compromise approach would be that while marriage officers should rightly refuse to celebrate such marriages if the facts are known to them, nevertheless if the parties manage to have their marriage celebrated here, the marriage should not later be declared invalid on grounds of non-compliance with English law.[188] This view, however, has little to commend it and could amount to an encouragement to suppress relevant facts from marriage officers. Later proceedings can only be held in England if there is some sufficient jurisdictional link with England. If, as already argued, English law, as both the lex fori and the lex loci celebrationis, has a sufficiently legitimate interest in ensuring compliance with its standards, this should be reflected whenever the validity of the marriage is called into question.

F Renvoi

Earlier in this chapter it was seen that the English courts have occasionally considered the doctrine of renvoi when assessing the formal validity of a marriage. The rationale of such an approach was seen to be the desirability of achieving uniformity of result, thereby avoiding limping relationships, and the extra flexibility the doctrine provides in enabling courts to uphold the validity of marriages. Such a rationale could be applied to essential validity of marriages. For example, suppose the English court has to decide on the essential validity of a marriage between spouses who at the time of their marriage were domiciled in Italy, but were citizens of the United Kingdom. By Italian domestic law the marriage is void, say for lack of age. But suppose that an Italian court, applying the Italian conflicts rule, would hold that the validity of the marriage is governed by English domestic law, as the law of the nationality, by which the marriage is valid. If the English court holds the marriage void under Italian domestic law, but in Italian eyes the marriage is valid under English domestic law, there will be a limping marriage.

186 The arguments here are similar to those put forward in defence of the rule in *Sottomayer v De Barros (No 2)*. See pp 333–334.

187 Law Com Working Paper No 89, para 3.42.

188 Hartley, 'The Policy Basis of the English Conflict of Laws of Marriage' (1972) 35 MLR 571 at 577; Dicey and Morris, *The Conflict of Laws* (13th edn, 2000) p 685.

However, if the English court uses renvoi, it will decide the case exactly as the Italian court would do, applying English law to hold the marriage valid, with the result that the status of the parties will be the same in both countries.

The role of renvoi in relation to the essential validity of marriage is doubtful. The doctrine was used in *R v Brentwood Superintendent Registrar of Marriages, ex p Arias*.[189] In this case the question was the capacity of the husband, domiciled in Switzerland but a national of Italy, to remarry. The English choice of law rule indicated Swiss law as the antenuptial domiciliary law, but as under Swiss conflicts rules capacity to marry was governed by the law of nationality, the English court applied Italian law. As that law did not recognise the Swiss decree dissolving the husband's previous marriage, it was held that he lacked capacity to remarry. (This form of renvoi, where the foreign law indicated by the English conflicts rule points to a third country, is known as transmission, as distinct from remission when the foreign law points back to English law.)

This seems to be the only case in which renvoi has been used in the context of essential validity of marriage. That could in theory be explained on the basis that the question of renvoi does not arise unless the foreign country's conflicts rule points to a different law, giving a different result, from the English conflicts rule, and that has not been proved in other cases.

Is it desirable to use renvoi for essential validity of marriage? In the *Brentwood Marriage Registrar* case the doctrine enabled uniformity of decision to be achieved. The effect of the decision was that any remarriage by the husband would be void by English law, as well as by Swiss and Italian law, thus achieving uniformity of status in England and the countries of the husband's domicile and nationality. However, this uniformity was achieved at a price. The Swiss divorce in this case was entitled to recognition under English conflicts rules on recognition of foreign divorces. The husband was therefore a single man in English eyes. Utilising renvoi resulted in the English court holding that a single man was not free to remarry. The decisive law was Italian law, the law of the husband's nationality. For reasons explored in chapter 2, English law has largely rejected nationality as a connecting factor. Renvoi, all too often, simply allows nationality in through the back door. Further, renvoi may well produce uniformity with the wrong countries. What is wanted is uniformity with the countries to which the parties belong now, when the question arises. Renvoi can only produce uniformity with the country in which the party was domiciled at the time of the marriage (or soon after the

189 [1968] 2 QB 956, [1968] 3 All ER 279.

marriage, when the intended matrimonial home rule is applicable). That is of no value if he has changed his domicile since the marriage. Renvoi in such a case might even destroy a uniformity which exists with the law of the present domicile. Moreover, uniformity with the country of one spouse may be achieved at the expense of lack of uniformity with the country of the other. Finally, the use of renvoi in the *Brentwood Marriage Registrar* case was not consistent with the general policy in favour of upholding the validity of marriages. It would have resulted in the second marriage, had it been contracted, being void. Accordingly, it is very doubtful whether renvoi is worth the price, which is the sacrifice of the English choice of law rule in favour of the foreign one. As explored earlier,[190] the *Brentwood Marriage Registrar* case has since been reversed by section 50 of the Family Law Act 1986 which provides that if a foreign divorce or nullity decree is entitled to recognition under the Act the parties to that divorce are entitled validly to remarry irrespective whether their law of domicile recognises the divorce or annulment. Renvoi has thus been ousted from this particular area of law. Courts should clearly hesitate before utilising it in relation to any of the other incapacities.

IV PUBLIC POLICY

It is a general principle of the conflict of laws that a rule of foreign law which would be applicable under the ordinary choice of law rules may be disregarded if its application would be contrary to English public policy. As regards the validity of marriage, public policy will be invoked if the foreign rule is thought by the court to be grossly offensive or repugnant to English standards of justice, decency or morality. However, public policy does not insist that English standards must always prevail. Priority is often given to the interests and expectations of the spouses under a foreign law. So polygamous marriages, even if the spouses come to live in England, may be valid and effective,[191] as may marriages between persons more closely related than English law permits. Because of the danger of public policy being used as a mask for 'judicial cultural imperialism'[192] it is only when the foreign rule is so repugnant to English notions that the conscience of the court simply will not

190 See p 346.
191 See p 365.
192 Murphy, 'Rationality and Cultural Pluralism in the Non-Recognition of Foreign Marriages' (2000) 49 ICLQ 643.

permit it to apply the foreign law, that public policy will be invoked. This will seldom occur.

If the doctrine is applied, the effect will be that either a marriage is valid despite a foreign incapacity which would otherwise prevail or, conversely, a marriage which is valid under the governing foreign law is held invalid.

With respect to invalidity under the foreign law, it was argued above that the doctrine of public policy should be invoked only in rare cases where application of the foreign law would be regarded as offensive (for example, prohibitions on inter-racial marriages or where a foreign rule can be construed as penal – such as a prohibition against remarriage before the innocent party to a preceding divorce). With regard to using public policy to deny validity to a marriage which is valid under the governing foreign law, the doctrine must be used with great circumspection. As Simon J said in *Cheni v Cheni*, the test is:

> whether the marriage is so offensive to the conscience of the English court that it should refuse to give effect to the proper foreign law ... [I]n deciding the question the court will seek to exercise common sense, good manners and a reasonable tolerance.[193]

This case involved a marriage between uncle and niece which was valid by the law of the spouses' Egyptian domicile at the time of the marriage. Years later, when they came to England, the wife sought a nullity decree on the grounds that they were within the prohibited degrees under English law, contending that the Egyptian rule offended English public policy. This contention was rejected, but the judge accepted[194] that if the relationship had been such that intercourse between them would infringe the criminal law of incest, the result might have been different.

Another case which illustrates the reluctance to invoke public policy is *Mohamed v Knott*[195] in which the court upheld the validity of a marriage between a man of 26 and a girl of 13 celebrated in Nigeria, where both parties were domiciled. This result was reached despite the fact that sexual intercourse between the parties in England would have been a criminal offence and despite the fact that evidence suggested the wife had not achieved puberty at the date of the marriage.[196]

193 [1965] P 85 at 99.
194 At 97–99.
195 [1969] 1 QB 1.
196 At 4. See further, Murphy, 'Rationality and Cultural Pluralism in the Non-Recognition of Foreign Marriages' (2000) 49 ICLQ 643.

Finally, it is doubtful, for reasons argued above,[197] whether same-sex marriages would be regarded as contrary to public policy if celebrated abroad by persons domiciled in a country that permitted such marriages. It can even be argued that such a marriage, where one of the parties is an English domiciliary, would not be contrary to public policy provided the parties satisfied the modified intended matrimonial home test suggested earlier.[198]

A sphere in which public policy might well operate is that of consent. Indeed, it has been suggested[199] that any foreign rule under which a party had consented when consent was absent according to English law would be rejected on grounds of public policy. For example, a foreign rule allowing a parent to consent to a marriage when the person contracting the marriage did not consent would almost certainly be regarded as contrary to public policy.

V POLYGAMOUS MARRIAGES

A Introduction

The laws of many countries permit polygamous marriages, under which a man may have more than one wife. Islamic countries allow polygamy and in a number of African countries polygamous marriages may be celebrated under Islamic or customary law. Some laws permit a woman to have more than one husband at the same time.[200] Correctly speaking, where a man is allowed more than one wife the marriage is described as *polygynous* and where the woman may have more than one husband it is *polyandrous*. All such marriages are generically termed *polygamous* marriages.

What is the attitude of English law to polygamous marriages? In *Hyde v Hyde* marriage was defined as 'the voluntary union for life of one man and one woman to the exclusion of all others'.[201] However, part of the function of the conflict of laws is to ensure that a status or relationship created by foreign cultures and religions is respected and recognised. In view of immigration over the past half century from countries permitting polygamy, there would be grave hardship

197 See p 354.
198 See p 327.
199 Hartley, 'The Policy Basis of the English Conflict of Laws of Marriage' (1972) 35 MLR 571 at 580.
200 See generally, Majumdar, *Himalayan Polyandry: Structure, Functioning and Cultural Change: A Field Study of Jaunsar-Bawar* (1962) pp 75–77; *Guardian*, 4 March 1993, p 12.
201 (1866) LR 1 P & D 130 at 133.

if polygamous marriages were denied all recognition. Accordingly, it has long been clear that a polygamous marriage may be entitled to recognition as a valid marriage. The approach of the courts, as stated in *Mohamed v Knott*, is that 'a polygamous marriage will be recognised in England as a valid marriage unless there is some strong reason to the contrary'.[202] Formerly, however, under the rule laid down in *Hyde v Hyde*, while such marriages were entitled to recognition for most purposes, the parties were not permitted to obtain matrimonial relief in England. Although they were regarded as validly married to each other, the courts had no power to grant either spouse a divorce, a decree of judicial separation, a nullity decree or financial relief. This hardship[203] was removed by the Matrimonial Proceedings (Polygamous Marriages) Act 1972.[204] Since then polygamously married persons have been entitled to the same matrimonial relief as monogamously married persons.

Despite the general recognition of polygamous marriages, the question whether a marriage is monogamous or polygamous may still need to be answered. For example, the parties may lack capacity to enter into a marriage if it is polygamous. Other instances where the distinction is important will be discussed below.

B Classification

In order to determine whether the conflicts rules on monogamy or polygamy are applicable the marriage in question needs to be classified as monogamous or polygamous. For example, under traditional Chinese law a man was permitted only one primary wife (a tsai) but was allowed concubines (tsips) who had legal rights (for example, succession rights and their children were legitimate) and were often referred to as secondary wives. In *Lee v Lau*[205] the Privy Council, on appeal from Hong Kong, declared that the marriage to the primary wife was polygamous, despite the fact that Hong Kong law described it as monogamous. Consistent with the normal approach, this classification was effected by the lex fori. The court looked beyond the nomenclature employed by the applicable law and examined the nature and incidents of the foreign marriages or relationships and characterised them according to their nearest analogue in English law. Although the concubines or secondary wives did not have the same full legal status as the primary wife, they nevertheless had sufficient legal rights of a wife for the relationships

202 [1969] 1 QB 1 at 13–14.
203 See, for example, *Sowa v Sowa* [1961] P 70, [1960] 3 All ER 196.
204 Now s 47 of the Matrimonial Causes Act 1973.
205 [1967] P 14, [1964] 2 All ER 248.

to be regarded as polygamous marriages. Accordingly, the marriage to the primary wife was also polygamous.

How is a marriage to be classified where the husband has only one wife in fact but is permitted under his personal law to take more wives? Such marriages, known as *potentially polygamous marriages,* used to be regarded as polygamous even if the husband never took another wife. Accordingly, the conflicts rules on polygamy were applicable both to actually and potentially polygamous marriages. However, the Private International Law (Miscellaneous Provisions) Act 1995 abolished the concept of a potentially polygamous marriage if either party to the marriage is domiciled in England or Wales at the time of the marriage.[206] Thus if an English domiciled woman marries in Pakistan a man domiciled there who has no other wife, the marriage, which previously would have been regarded as potentially polygamous, will be treated as monogamous.[207] However, if neither party is domiciled in England or Wales at the time of the marriage, such marriages are still regarded as potentially polygamous and governed by the conflicts rules on polygamy.

C Law determining nature of marriage

Where a married man contracts a second marriage, it is clear that the nature of this marriage is determined by the lex loci celebrationis. For example, if a Muslim domiciled in Pakistan, who already has a wife, marries another woman by Islamic rites in Pakistan the marriage is polygamous. If the second marriage is celebrated in a country only permitting monogamous marriages, then, while the second marriage is monogamous in nature, it will be void, because a monogamous marriage cannot be validly contracted by a person who is already married.

However, if a single man marries a single woman and neither party is domiciled in England, the marriage may be monogamous or potentially polygamous. It will be potentially polygamous if the husband is free to take further wives. What law decides whether the marriage is of such a nature? Suppose the husband, a Muslim domiciled in New York, marries in Pakistan a woman domiciled in Pakistan. The marriage is celebrated by Islamic rites; by Pakistani law the husband would be free to take further wives; by New York law (let it be assumed[208]) he would not. Is the marriage potentially

206 Para 2(2) of the Schedule to the Act amending the Matrimonial Causes Act 1973, s 11(d). See p 369.
207 See p 370.
208 See n 210 below.

polygamous or monogamous? Is its nature to be decided by Pakistani law as the lex loci celebrationis or by New York law as the law of the husband's domicile?

The argument in favour of applying the law of the husband's domicile at the time of the marriage is that the question whether the nature of the marriage is such that the husband is permitted to marry another wife is a question of his capacity to be governed by the law of his domicile.[209] If this were the rule, it would mean that, if at the time of the marriage the husband was domiciled in New York, or any other monogamous country, the marriage would be monogamous.[210] If, however, he was domiciled in Pakistan, or any other country whose law permitted him to marry further wives, the marriage would be potentially polygamous. It would not matter where the marriage was celebrated.

The alternative solution is that the nature of the marriage should be governed by the law of the country where it was celebrated. On this approach, the question whether the marriage is such that the husband is free to marry again is not a question of capacity. The nature of the marriage is determined by the lex loci celebrationis. The role of the law of domicile is limited to the (important) issue of whether the marriage contracted in such a form is valid. The justification for referring to the lex loci celebrationis is that the nature of the marriage should depend on the intentions and expectations of the parties. If they go through a ceremony under which, according to the law of the country where it is celebrated, the husband is entitled to marry again, then presumably they intended the marriage to be of that nature. In *Isaac Penhas v Tan Soo Eng*,[211] a Privy Council decision on appeal from Singapore, it was held that whether a marriage was monogamous or polygamous depended on the intention of the parties. If the lex loci celebrationis permits both religious polygamous marriages and civil monogamous marriages, the parties are free to choose whichever form of marriage to which they wish to subject themselves. A fortiori, if there is only one form of marriage available, the parties must be deemed to have chosen to contract a marriage of that form and nature. On this basis, if a husband domiciled in New York marries in Pakistan by Islamic rites, the marriage is potentially polygamous.

209 This assumes the dual domicile doctrine is applicable.

210 It is a moot point whether reference should be made to the conflict of law rules, rather than the internal law, of the country concerned (see, by analogy, Dicey and Morris, *The Conflict of Laws* (13th edn, 2000) p 705). In view of the general trend against extending the use of renvoi, such a suggestion is unlikely to be accepted.

211 [1953] AC 304.

In order to assess the law's response to this issue, it is necessary to distinguish between marriages contracted in England and those contracted abroad. It is clear law that no valid polygamous marriage can take place in England. When England is the locus celebrationis the parties have to comply with the provisions of the Marriage Act 1949 under which only monogamous marriages can be contracted. In *R v Bham*[212] a Muslim man and woman went through a form of 'marriage' in accordance with Islamic rites under which the 'marriage' would have been polygamous. The 'marriage officer' was prosecuted for knowingly solemnising a marriage in an unregistered building contrary to section 75(2)(a) of the Marriage Act 1949. On appeal the defendant's conviction was quashed on the ground that the Islamic ceremony did not constitute a 'marriage'. It was a religious ceremony of no legal significance. In *Qureshi v Qureshi*[213] the husband, domiciled in Pakistan, and the wife, domiciled in India, went through an English register office marriage ceremony which was followed by a further ceremony in accordance with Islamic rites. It was common ground that the register office ceremony gave rise to a valid monogamous marriage and the subsequent religious ceremony was of no legal significance even though it would have given rise to a potentially polygamous marriage under the law of the husband's domicile. In *A-M v A-M*[214] an Islamic ceremony conducted in a flat in London was compared to a staged dramatic marriage ceremony in a soap opera: it did not constitute a 'marriage'. This rule is not hard to understand. While polygamous marriages can be recognised if they take place abroad, where the parties marry in England the link with England is stronger and the law is entitled to insist on conformity with English standards under which only monogamous marriages can be contracted.

Where the parties marry abroad, the courts for many years adopted the view that the nature of the marriage was governed by the law of the country where it was celebrated. In *Re Bethell*[215] the husband, an English domiciliary, married in Bechuanaland (as it then was) a local woman from the Baralong tribe. It was held that this was a Baralong (and hence polygamous) marriage. As the husband was an English domiciliary lacking capacity to contract a polygamous marriage, the marriage was void.

This approach caused severe hardship in many cases. By the latter half of the last century there were many persons domiciled in England whose families had originally come from the Indian

212 [1966] 1 QB 159, [1965] 3 All ER 124.
213 [1972] Fam 173, [1971] 1 All ER 325.
214 [2001] 2 FLR 6.
215 (1888) 38 Ch D 220. See also *Risk v Risk* [1951] P 50, [1950] 2 All ER 973.

subcontinent.[216] It was not uncommon for arranged marriages to persist within such families and often it would be the English domiciled husband who would return to the Indian subcontinent and there contract the arranged marriage.[217] Under the traditional approach, whereby the lex loci celebrationis determines the nature of the marriage, such marriages would be regarded as potentially polygamous in nature and therefore void on the ground that one party was domiciled in England.[218] Such an approach amounted to a 'serious interference with the customs of ethnic minority communities'[219] in this country and had many practical adverse consequences affecting the immigration status of the wife, acquisition of British nationality, social security benefits and rights of succession.[220] In an attempt to alleviate these hardships the Court of Appeal in 1982 in *Hussain v Hussain*[221] introduced a new approach. In this case the marriage was celebrated in Pakistan according to Islamic rites, the husband being domiciled in England and the wife in Pakistan. The parties set up their matrimonial home in England. In answer to the wife's petition in the English court for a judicial separation, the husband contended that the marriage was void under section 11(d) of the Matrimonial Causes Act 1973. As seen earlier,[222] section 11(d) provides that a polygamous marriage (which then included a potentially polygamous one even if one of the spouses was domiciled in England and Wales) shall be void if either party was at the time of the marriage domiciled in England. The husband argued that the marriage was void because he was domiciled in England at the time of the marriage, which was potentially polygamous under the lex loci celebrationis. The Court of Appeal, however, held that the marriage was monogamous. The court's view was that a marriage can be potentially polygamous for the purpose of section 11(d) only if one of the spouses has the capacity to marry a second spouse. Whether the husband had such capacity depended on the law of his domicile, English law, and by that law he had not. Accordingly, the marriage was monogamous and valid.

How far did *Hussain* go towards overruling the common law rule that the nature of the marriage was to be determined by the lex loci

216 Law Com No 42, paras 23–24; Figures show that from 1985 to 1995 a total of 175,630 persons from the Indian subcontinent, Iran, Iraq and Saudi Arabia were given rights to settle in the United Kingdom. Of course, it must not be assumed that all these persons were Muslims.

217 Poulter, '*Hyde v Hyde* – A Reappraisal' (1976) 25 ICLQ 475 at 504.

218 Matrimonial Causes Act 1973, s 11(d). See p 341.

219 Poulter, 'Polygamy – New Law Commission Proposals' [1983] Fam Law 72.

220 Ibid.

221 [1983] Fam 26, [1982] 3 All ER 369.

222 See p 341.

celebrationis? One view is that the decision is to be limited to cases involving an interpretation of section 11(d), that is, where one of the parties was domiciled in England and Wales at the date of the marriage.[223] However, the more widely accepted interpretation is that the *Hussain* principle applies irrespective of the husband's domicile. According to this view a marriage is monogamous if by the law of the husband's domicile at the date of the marriage he is not permitted to take a further wife. It is immaterial that the marriage is potentially polygamous by the lex loci celebrationis. The converse, however, would not apply. A marriage celebrated in a country by whose law it is monogamous is always monogamous, even if by the law of the husband's domicile at the time of the marriage he is free to take a further wife.[224] In other words, a marriage is potentially polygamous only if it is so under both the lex loci celebrationis and the law of the husband's domicile.[225] The advantage of this interpretation is that more marriages will be held to be monogamous and thus valid.

D One party domiciled in England and Wales with no existing spouse

Where one of the parties is domiciled in England and Wales the decision in *Hussain*[226] has been superseded by the Private International Law (Miscellaneous Provisions) Act 1995. The Schedule to this Act amended section 11(d) of the Matrimonial Causes Act 1973 so that where 'either party was at the time of the marriage domiciled in England and Wales ... a marriage is not polygamous if at its inception neither party has any spouse additional to the other'. A marriage which is 'not polygamous' must, logically, be monogamous. Section 5(1) of the 1995 Act spells out that such marriages are 'not void'. For English domiciliaries, this provision is wider than the principle established in *Hussain* in that it applies even if it is the wife who is domiciled in England and Wales. Under *Hussain* if an English domiciled woman married a Pakistani domiciliary (with no existing wife) in Pakistan the marriage would have been polygamous in nature and void under the old section 11(d). Under the 1995 Act, however, assuming the husband did not already have a spouse, this marriage is regarded as 'not polygamous'

223 Carter, (1982) 53 BYIL 298 at 302.
224 Compare Briggs, 'Polygamous Marriages and English Domiciliaries' (1983) 32 ICLQ 737 at 740 who suggests that the husband's domicile should be determinative in all cases.
225 Dicey and Morris, *The Conflict of Laws* (13th edn, 2000) p 696.
226 [1983] Fam 26, [1982] 3 All ER 369.

(that is, monogamous) and, assuming there were no other impediments, valid. The implications of *Hussain* were rightly described as 'sexist' in that 'the daughters of immigrant families [could not] return to marry local men whose domiciliary law permits polygamy'.[227] Under the 1995 Act such a marriage would be monogamous and valid.

Section 5(2) of the 1995 Act adds:

> This section does not affect the determination of the validity of a marriage by reference to the law of another country to the extent that it falls to be so determined in accordance with the rules of private international law.

This provision is best interpreted[228] as a reminder that the other conflicts rules relating to validity of marriage, apart from those relating to polygamy, are, of course, applicable. The marriage is only 'not void' if the alleged defect relates to lack of capacity to contract a polygamous marriage. If, however, continuing the example of the English woman marrying the Pakistani man, the parties failed to comply with the formal requirements of the locus celebrationis or if one of them lacked capacity on other grounds, for example, lack of age, the marriage is not to be declared valid on the basis of section 5(1). The normal conflicts rules governing the formalities and essentials of a marriage are still applicable.

It should be noted that these provisions of the 1995 Act are for most purposes retrospective. Accordingly, if a wife domiciled in England married an Egyptian domiciliary (without an existing wife) by Islamic rites in Egypt before the commencement of the Act, this marriage, which would have been void under the common law rules,[229] is to be regarded as valid.[230] However, such a marriage is

227 Schuz, 'When is a Polygamous Marriage Not a Polygamous Marriage' (1983) 46 MLR 653.

228 The Law Commission in its Explanatory Notes to the Draft Bill – which eventually became the 1995 Act – states that (what became) s 5(2) 'corresponds to section 14(1) of the Matrimonial Causes Act 1973' (see p 342) (Law Com No 146, Explanatory Notes to cl 1(3)). It would, however, be perverse to argue that s 5(2) similarly excludes the operation of s 5(1) and that, under the intended matrimonial home test, an English domiciliary can contract a potentially polygamous marriage. S 11(d), which is not affected by s 5(2), is clear that if one of the parties is domiciled in England, the marriage is not polygamous. Dicey and Morris, *The Conflict of Laws* (13th edn, 2000) p 705 suggests that s 5(2) means that one must refer to the conflict rules on polygamy of the law of domicile of the relevant spouse, ie, s 5(2) endorses the doctrine of renvoi. The better interpretation, however, is that the reference in s 5(2) to 'the rules of private international law' means the English rules of private international law.

229 Assuming Egyptian law is not applied as the law of the intended matrimonial home. See pp 340–341.

230 Private International Law (Miscellaneous Provisions) Act 1995, s 6(1).

not retrospectively validated if one of the parties has, before commencement of the Act, already entered into another marriage that would be valid either under the common law or under the Act[231] or if the marriage has already been annulled before commencement of the Act.[232] Further, such a marriage is not retrospectively validated for the purposes of succession, benefits, allowances or pension rights payable before commencement and tax in respect of the period before commencement.[233]

E Validity of polygamous marriages

It has been seen above that polygamous marriages are recognised as marriages for most purposes. But it is, of course, only *valid* polygamous marriages that can be recognised. In addition to the general issues of formal and essential validity which arise in relation to all marriages, there is the particular question here whether the parties have capacity to enter into a polygamous (as opposed to a monogamous) marriage. With regard to actually polygamous marriages, the rules have been explored above.[234] It was seen there that the validity of such marriages depended on whether one applied the dual domicile doctrine or followed the decision in *Radwan v Radwan (No 2)*[235] that capacity to contract a polygamous marriage is governed by the law of the intended matrimonial home. These same rules are equally applicable to potentially polygamous marriages where neither party is domiciled in England and Wales.

As regards the validity of such polygamous marriages, it is important to remember that section 14 of the Matrimonial Causes Act 1973 excludes the provisions of section 11 of the same Act when English conflicts rules refer the question of the validity of the marriage to a foreign law. Of course, according to the dual domicile doctrine, an English domiciliary cannot contract a valid actually polygamous marriage. However, if the intended matrimonial home doctrine is applied, it is possible for an English domiciled person to contract a valid actually polygamous marriage. It is not possible, however, for an English domiciliary to contract a potentially polygamous marriage because, following the entry into force of the Private International Law (Miscellaneous Provisions) Act 1995, such marriages are regarded as monogamous. There is some logic to this approach. If, for example, an English domiciled woman

231 S 6(2).
232 S 6(3)–(5).
233 S 6(6).
234 See pp 340–342.
235 [1973] Fam 35, [1972] 3 All ER 1026.

knowingly marries in Pakistan a married man domiciled there, and the parties intend to establish a permanent matrimonial home in Pakistan, she can be deemed to have submitted herself to a Pakistani marriage with all its consequences. The same cannot be said for the woman who marries a Pakistani domiciliary with no wife. Even if the husband takes another wife – as permitted by his personal law – the first wife is to be regarded as a valid monogamous spouse.

F Change in the nature of a marriage

1. Polygamy to monogamy

A marriage which at its inception is potentially polygamous may subsequently become monogamous as the result of some event or a change in the law.[236] In *Parkasho v Singh*[237] a marriage celebrated in India was at the time of its celebration potentially polygamous according to Indian law. Subsequently, the effect of the Indian Hindu Marriage Act was to debar the husband from marrying further wives. It was held that the marriage had become monogamous in the eyes of English law. Similarly, in *Ali v Ali*,[238] it was held that if the husband in a potentially polygamous marriage becomes domiciled in England (or any other monogamous country), the marriage thereby becomes monogamous. The reasoning was similar to that later used in *Hussain v Hussain*[239] in relation to the nature of the marriage at its inception. Once the husband is domiciled in England, he no longer has capacity to marry again; hence the marriage becomes by definition monogamous. It follows, as was held in *Onobrauche v Onobrauche*,[240] that if the wife, but not the husband, becomes domiciled in England, a potentially polygamous marriage will not become monogamous. An actually polygamous marriage cannot, of course, become monogamous, but there is no reason why, if there is only one wife remaining from a hitherto polygamous marriage, it should not become monogamous.

The reason why the courts were anxious in the above cases to hold that the potentially polygamous marriages had become monogamous was that unless they were monogamous the court could not have granted matrimonial relief. The question is less important following

236 *Sinha Peerage Claim* [1946] 1 All ER 348n; *Cheni v Cheni* [1965] P 85, [1962] 3 All ER 873.
237 [1968] P 233, [1967] 1 All ER 737.
238 [1968] P 564, [1966] 1 All ER 664.
239 [1983] Fam 26, [1982] 3 All ER 369. This reasoning casts some doubt on the correctness of the use of the intended matrimonial home test in *Radwan v Radwan (No 2)* [1973] Fam 35, [1972] 3 All ER 1026.
240 (1978) 8 Fam Law 107.

the entry into force of the Matrimonial Proceedings (Polygamous Marriages) Act 1972, which gave the courts power to grant matrimonial relief in respect of polygamous marriages. Nevertheless, the question can still arise (for example, in deciding whether the husband is guilty of the crime of bigamy if he remarries). Moreover, as the following discussion will show, if the husband subsequently enters a valid polygamous marriage, the first wife's legal position may be stronger if her marriage has become monogamous.

2. Monogamy to polygamy

In *A-G of Ceylon v Reid,*[241] an appeal to the Privy Council from Ceylon (as it then was), Alan and Edna Reid had contracted a valid Roman Catholic monogamous marriage. Twenty-six years later Alan Reid wished to marry one Fatima Pansy. Accordingly, he converted to the Islamic faith and three days later married her. His conviction for bigamy was quashed with the Privy Council holding, in effect, that his second marriage was a valid polygamous marriage. Similar situations can arise in cases where there has been no change of religion or domicile. In *Nabi v Heaton*[242] the husband, domiciled in Pakistan, married the first wife in England. This marriage was clearly monogamous. He then returned to Pakistan and there married a second wife under Islamic law. It was accepted without argument on appeal that the second marriage was a valid polygamous marriage. In both these cases the result was that the husband had contracted a valid monogamous marriage followed by a valid polygamous marriage. He was validly married to both wives. What is the effect in these cases of the second marriage on the first monogamous marriage? Does the first marriage retain its legal character as monogamous or have the husband's unilateral acts converted it into a polygamous one?

At first sight it seems that the nature of the initial marriage must have changed. It is a logical, legal and linguistic nonsense to assert that the husband is monogamously married to the first wife, but polygamously married to the second wife. However, while this is true from his perspective, it now seems clear than from the first wife's perspective the nature of her monogamous marriage does not change. As she had the reasonable expectation at the time of the marriage that she would be the only wife, her rights as a monogamous wife should be protected. In *A-G of Ceylon v Reid* it was accepted that while, from his perspective, Alan might be validly married to Fatima, nevertheless from his first wife's perspective he was

241 [1965] AC 720, [1965] 1 All ER 812.
242 [1981] 1 WLR 1052.

committing adultery. The same conclusion was reached in *Drammeh v Drammeh*[243] where it was held that a husband might well be validly married to his second wife, but from his first monogamous wife's point of view he was committing adultery.

The nature of the first marriage is important for several reasons. If it remains a monogamous marriage the wife, in matrimonial proceedings, can rely on her husband's intercourse with his second wife as adultery because it falls outside the monogamous relationship.[244] Such intercourse is not adultery if the first marriage is polygamous.[245] Further, the first wife's rights of succession are more likely to be protected if her marriage remains monogamous despite the husband's second valid marriage.[246] Finally, it seems clear also that the wife under a monogamous marriage will be entitled to social security benefits as such, even if there is a subsequent valid marriage.[247] Her status as a monogamous wife remains protected and is not affected by a subsequent marriage by the husband. The first marriage does not become a polygamous marriage.

G Recognition of polygamous marriages

The approach today is that a valid polygamous marriage is to be recognised unless there is some strong reason to the contrary. It will seldom be that such a reason is found. As seen above, the old rule that a polygamous marriage was not recognised for the purposes of matrimonial relief was abolished by the Matrimonial Proceedings (Polygamous Marriages) Act 1972. The initial fears that English court procedures would be difficult to adapt to polygamous marriages have proved to be largely unfounded. As shall be seen in the next chapter, English courts always apply the lex fori when granting divorces and separation orders. However, the fact that a man is polygamously married to more than one wife can be relevant to the interpretation of this lex fori. For example, a divorce can only be obtained on the ground that the marriage has irretrievably broken down and this has to be proved by establishing one of a number of stated facts such as adultery, unreasonable behaviour or desertion.[248] In *Onobrauche v Onobrauche*[249] the husband had two polygamous

243 (1970) 78 Ceylon Law Weekly 55.
244 Matrimonial Causes Act 1973, s 1(2)(a).
245 *Onobrauche v Onobrauche* (1978) 8 Fam Law 107.
246 See pp 377–378.
247 See pp 378–379.
248 Matrimonial Causes Act 1973, s 1.
249 (1978) 8 Fam Law 107.

wives. The second wife claimed that the husband had committed adultery with the first wife. This claim was rejected on the basis that sexual intercourse with a lawful wife could not amount to adultery. In *Poon v Tan*[250] it was held that marrying a second wife was unreasonable behaviour towards the first wife. This, of course, need not always be the case; much should depend on the cultural acceptability of polygamous marriages under the relevant law and the first wife's reasonable expectations. For instance, while polygamous marriages are still tolerated in India, both Indian law and culture are moving firmly against such marriages.[251] The first wife under such an Indian polygamous marriage would certainly have a plausible claim that her husband's second marriage amounted to unreasonable behaviour. Whether such a plea should be accepted from a Muslim first wife who is domiciled in Pakistan is more questionable. Polygamy is more widely practised and accepted by Muslims in Pakistan and, in marrying under Pakistani law, the wife should be deemed to have accepted the possibility of the husband taking further wives. Much, of course, will depend on all the factual circumstances. For example, in *Quoraishi v Quoraishi*[252] it was held that while it was appropriate to take foreign law into account as part of the background to the marriage, where the husband and wife were professional people who had been resident in England for ten years, the husband's taking of a second wife could be sufficient to give the first wife a 'just cause' for deserting him.[253] In matrimonial proceedings provision is made for notice to be given to other spouses and for conferring on them the right to be heard in the proceedings.[254]

It has long been established that a polygamous marriage is recognised so as to render void a subsequent monogamous marriage. For example, in *Baindail v Baindail*[255] an Indian domiciliary who had contracted a valid polygamous marriage in India came to England and married an English woman in an English register office. The second 'marriage' was annulled as being bigamous. The validity of his first polygamous marriage was thus recognised. Such second marriages are, however, only civilly bigamous. In *R v Sagoo*[256] it was held that the celebration of the subsequent marriage in such

250 (1973) 4 Fam Law 161.
251 Law Com No 42, para 37, n 91.
252 [1985] FLR 780.
253 Under the Matrimonial Causes Act 1973, s 1(2)(c) desertion is only a 'ground' for divorce if the deserting spouse has no 'just cause' for the desertion.
254 Matrimonial Causes Act 1973, s 47(4), as amended by para 2(3)(b) of the Schedule to the Private International Law (Miscellaneous Provisions) Act 1995.
255 [1946] P 122, [1946] 1 All ER 342.
256 [1975] QB 885, [1975] 2 All ER 926. See also *R v Sarwan Singh* [1962] 3 All ER 612.

a case does not render the husband liable to conviction for the crime of bigamy, unless the first polygamous marriage has in the meantime become monogamous. This rule is explicable on the basis that the criminal law is normally concerned with the punishment of blameworthy conduct. Where a person from a different cultural background, where polygamy is accepted, goes through another marriage ceremony (probably thinking it is a polygamous marriage), criminal liability and punishment seem inappropriate. With no excuse of ignorance of the law, English law is perhaps wise to achieve the same result by these circuitous means.

There is little doubt that the children of a polygamous marriage are legitimate[257] and entitled to succeed to all property in England with the possible exception of entailed interests and titles of honour that devolve with property.[258] For example, in *Bamgbose v Daniel*[259] it was held that the children of nine polygamous marriages celebrated in Nigeria between Nigerian domiciliaries were entitled to succeed to their father's property on his intestate death.

It is also clear that the spouses under polygamous marriages qualify as spouses for succession purposes.[260] In *Cheang Thye Phin v Tan Ah Loy*[261] the Privy Council endorsed the Straits Settlements' practice of dividing the widow's share equally between the surviving widows. A polygamous wife qualifies as the wife of the deceased under the Inheritance (Provision for Family and Dependants) Act 1975, enabling her to apply to court for an order for reasonable provision to be made out of her husband's estate. In *Re Sehota*[262] the husband had left the whole of his estate to the second of his two polygamous wives. The court made an order for provision to be made in favour of the first.

More problematic in these succession situations is the case where there is a monogamous wife and the husband marries a second wife polygamously. There are two views that can be adopted here. On the one hand, if the polygamous spouse were to be given, say, intestate succession rights this would in reality erode the first wife's status as a monogamous spouse. The monogamous wife should take the whole of the surviving spouse's share, to the exclusion of polygamous wives, in view of her expectation under the monogamous marriage of being the only wife. On the other hand, the result might seem

257 *Sinha Peerage Claim* [1946] 1 All ER 348n; *Baindail v Baindail* [1946] P 122 at 127–128.
258 *Sinha Peerage Claim* [1946] 1 All ER 348n.
259 [1955] AC 107, [1954] 3 All ER 263.
260 *Coleman v Shang* [1961] AC 481, [1961] 2 All ER 406.
261 [1920] AC 369. See also *Choo Eng Choon v Neo Chan Neo* (*Six Widows' Case*) (1908) 12 Straits Settlements LR 120.
262 [1978] 3 All ER 385, [1978] 1 WLR 1506.

unfair to the second wife who has contracted a valid polygamous marriage and presumably has reasonable expectations that she would receive a polygamous wife's share of her husband's estate on his intestacy. The counter-argument that she could have no such reasonable expectations because she has married a man who has a monogamous wife seems implausible as it involves imputing to her a sophisticated legal knowledge about the nature of the first marriage and its consequences.

What is the position with respect to family provision where there is a first monogamous wife and a second polygamous wife? The polygamous spouse is clearly entitled to apply for family provision because any person who has lived with the deceased in the same household 'as the husband or wife of the deceased' for two years immediately before the death of the deceased may apply for family provision.[263] But, in doing this she would be in no better position than a woman who had lived with the man outside marriage and would be entitled only to provision for maintenance as opposed to the more generous reasonable financial provision available to wives.[264] Such an approach would amount to a negation of the polygamous spouse's status as a wife. The innocent 'wife' of a void bigamous marriage is permitted to apply for family provision as a wife.[265] It would seem odd that that such a person should be favoured above a validly married polygamous spouse. Further, if the polygamous spouse divorced her husband, she would be entitled to full financial relief which would ultimately be to the detriment of the first wife. There seems no reason why she should be prejudiced by his dying rather than being divorced.

It has been held[266] that a wife under a polygamous marriage can apply to court under the Married Women's Property Act 1882 for a declaration that she is entitled to a share of certain property; an actually polygamous marriage has been recognised under the income tax legislation;[267] and polygamously married spouses are entitled to statutory protection under Part IV of the Family Law Act 1996 which deals with the family home and domestic violence.[268]

Special statutory provision is made for polygamous marriages in relation to social security benefits.[269] The effect is that a polygamous

263 Inheritance (Provision for Family and Dependants) Act 1975, s 1(1A), as introduced by the Law Reform (Succession) Act 1995, s 2(3).
264 Inheritance (Provision for Family and Dependants) Act 1975, s 1(2).
265 S 25(4).
266 *Chaudhry v Chaudhry* [1976] Fam 148, [1975] 3 All ER 687.
267 *Nabi v Heaton* [1983] 1 WLR 626.
268 S 63(5).
269 Social Security Contributions and Benefits Act 1992, ss121(1)(b), 147(5).

marriage is treated as having the same consequences as a monogamous marriage but only as regards those periods when there was in fact only one wife. So none of the wives under an actually polygamous marriage is entitled to benefits in respect of contributions paid by the husband. However, there seems no doubt that a wife under a monogamous marriage is entitled to benefits, even if the husband has subsequently contracted a valid polygamous marriage. Polygamous spouses are denied rights to a widow's pension under the state pension scheme.[270] Some special schemes, however, such as the NHS superannuation scheme, allow polygamous widows to share pension entitlements.[271] With regard to income support, the critical issue is no longer whether the parties are married, but rather whether they are partners who are members of the same household; a 'partner' is defined as including a polygamous wife.[272]

Polygamous marriages are largely denied recognition for immigration purposes if there is another wife who is, or since the marriage has been, in the United Kingdom,[273] but, ironically, such marriages are recognised for purposes of deportation.[274]

It can thus be seen that the general legal position of polygamous spouses has been considerably improved since the days of *Hyde v Hyde*.[275] It is, however, a matter of regret that there are still isolated instances where a woman who is a party to an actually polygamous marriage is not accorded full recognition as a married spouse. In the multi-cultural society of modern Britain, the few remaining discriminations are no longer acceptable.

270 See *R v Department of Health, ex p Misra* [1996] 1 FLR 129.
271 NHS (Superannuation) Amendment Regulations 1989, SI 1989/804, reg 9. See *R v Department of Health, ex p Misra* [1996] 1 FLR 129.
272 Income Support (General) Regulations 1987, SI 1987/1967, reg 2(1).
273 Immigration Act 1988, s 2(2). Home Office, *Immigration Rules* (2001) Rule 278.
274 Immigration Act 1971, s 5(4), as amended.
275 (1866) LR 1 P & D 130.

Chapter 9

Matrimonial causes

This chapter examines the jurisdiction of the English court and the choice of law process in proceedings for divorce, judicial separation and annulment of marriage and the extent to which the decrees of foreign courts in such matrimonial cases are recognised in England.[1] Finally, there is a consideration of the powers of the English court to grant financial relief and to recognise foreign maintenance orders.

I JURISDICTION OF THE ENGLISH COURT

A Introduction

At common law different jurisdictional rules applied to divorce, judicial separation and annulment of marriage. Originally, English courts would only consider granting a divorce if, at the commencement of the proceedings, the parties were domiciled in England.[2] Such an approach was unduly rigid and caused grave hardship to those who had lived in England for many years but not acquired a domicile here and to wives who, before the entry into force of the Domicile and Matrimonial Proceedings Act 1973, had a domicile of dependence on the husband who might have left England and acquired a domicile in another country. Accordingly, statutory extensions to the court's divorce jurisdiction were made for the protection of married women, enabling a wife to petition for divorce in England if her husband had been domiciled in England immediately before deserting her, or if she had been ordinarily resident in England for the three years immediately preceding her petition, wherever the parties might be domiciled at the commencement of the proceedings.[3]

1 Proceedings for presumption of death, dissolution of marriage and declarations of status are not dealt with. See Dicey and Morris, *The Conflict of Laws* (13th edn, 2000) pp 765–769.

2 *Le Mesurier v Le Mesurier* [1895] AC 517.

3 Matrimonial Causes Act 1973, s 46(1)(a), (b) (originally Matrimonial Causes Act 1937, s 13 and Law Reform (Miscellaneous Provisions) Act 1949, s 1).

The English common law jurisdictional rules in nullity cases were more complex with much depending on whether the marriage was void or voidable. Essentially, English courts exercised jurisdiction on the basis of domicile, common residence or, when the marriage was void, the fact that the marriage had been contracted in England; with decrees of judicial separation, because no change of status is involved, domicile was displaced by residence as the basic connecting factor founding jurisdiction.[4]

B Jurisdictional rules

The exclusive role of domicile having been breached, and married women having independent domiciles, new uniform grounds of jurisdiction were introduced for all three types of matrimonial proceedings by the Domicile and Matrimonial Proceedings Act 1973. These grounds were based on the policy that at least one of the parties, whether husband or wife, applicant or respondent, should have a sufficient connection with England to make it reasonable for the English court to deal with the case and likely that the divorce would be recognised in other countries. Section 5(2) provided that the English court would only have jurisdiction if at least one of the parties had been domiciled in England and Wales on the date when the proceedings were begun or had been habitually resident in England and Wales throughout the period of one year ending with that date. Section 5(3) laid down broadly similar jurisdictional rules for nullity decrees.[5]

In 1998 the Brussels II Convention[6] was signed by the member states of the European Union and (with amendments) was brought into force as an EC Regulation[7] on 1 March 2001 applying to all European Union countries except Denmark. Like the Brussels I Regulation, the new Regulation (referred to hereafter as the Brussels II Regulation) introduces uniform jurisdictional rules throughout the European Union and provides for almost automatic recognition of all matrimonial judgments granted by the courts of the member states. The Regulation is an important step in avoiding limping marriages in Europe.[8] In particular, there was a problem

4 See further, Graveson, *The Conflict of Laws* (6th edn, 1969) pp 336–346, 363–366.

5 Additionally, the court had (and still has: see n 15) jurisdiction where either of the parties has died, and at death either was domiciled in England and Wales or had been habitually resident here for the preceding year.

6 Convention on Jurisdiction and Enforcement of Judgments in Matrimonial Matters, OJ 2000 C221.

7 Council Regulation (EC) No 1347/2000, OJ 2000 L160/19.

8 Remien, 'European Private International Law, the European Community and its Emerging Area of Freedom, Security and Justice' (2001) 38 CML Rev 55 at 56.

between France and Germany in that German divorces involving a French national would not be recognised in France.[9] However, the real driving force behind the process which led to the Regulation was not so much the eradication of perceived problems regarding jurisdiction or the recognition of foreign judgments, but the promotion of European goals: 'European integration, the creation of a common judicial area, the operation of the single market and the development of European citizenship.'[10]

The Brussels II Regulation applies to civil proceedings relating to divorce, legal separation or marriage annulment.[11] While the Regulation covers non-judicial proceedings, it does not extend to purely religious procedures[12] unless they can be regarded as 'equivalent to judicial proceedings'.[13] As the Regulation largely, but not completely, replaced the 'traditional' jurisdictional rules, section 5(2) of the Domicile and Matrimonial Proceedings Act 1973 was amended[14] and provides that an English court shall have jurisdiction to entertain proceedings for divorce or judicial separation if: (a) the court has jurisdiction under the Brussels II Regulation; or (b) no court of a member state has jurisdiction under the Brussels II Regulation and either of the parties to the marriage is domiciled in England and Wales on the date when the proceedings are begun.[15]

Accordingly, the process for ascertaining whether the English court has jurisdiction is as follows. If the respondent is habitually resident in or a national of or, in the case of the United Kingdom and Ireland, 'domiciled' in, a member state the grounds of jurisdiction set out in articles 2, 5 and 6 must be applied. As against such a respondent jurisdiction can be exercised only in accordance with the Regulation. If, however, the respondent does not have one of the stipulated territorial connections with a member state the traditional rules are applicable. Under section 5(2) of the Domicile and Matrimonial Proceedings Act 1973 the only remaining traditional ground in English law is the domicile of either party. However, if it is the respondent who is domiciled in England, the Regulation must apply. So, despite the wording of section 5(2)(b) of the Domicile

9 Karsten, 'Brussels II – An English Perspective' [1998] IFL 75.

10 McGlynn, 'A Family Law for the European Union?' in Shaw (ed), *Social Law and Policy in an Evolving European Union* (2000); see also Borrás Report, OJ 1998 C221/27.

11 Art 1(1)(a).

12 Recital 9 to Council Regulation (EC) No 1347/2000, OJ 2000 L160/19.

13 Art 1(2).

14 European Communities (Matrimonial Jurisdiction and Judgments) Regulations 2001, SI 2001/310.

15 S 5(3) contains similar provisions for jurisdiction in nullity proceedings but additionally affords jurisdiction in cases where one of the parties has died. See n 5 above.

and Matrimonial Proceedings Act 1973, the traditional rules are applicable only if the applicant is domiciled in England. These provisions can now be examined in more detail.

1. Exclusive nature of jurisdiction under the Regulation

Article 7 provides that a respondent who is habitually resident in or a national of or, in the case of the United Kingdom and Ireland, 'domiciled' in a member state can be sued only in accordance with the Regulation. This means that if the respondent is, say, a Spanish national or an English domiciliary and the exclusive jurisdictional grounds of articles 2, 5 and 6 are not satisfied, an English court is not permitted to exercise jurisdiction under the traditional rules.

2. The grounds of jurisdiction under the Regulation

The basic jurisdictional rules are contained in Chapter II of the Regulation. Article 2 lists several alternative bases of jurisdiction without any order of preference. Jurisdiction lies with the courts of the member state in whose territory: (i) the spouses are habitually resident; or (ii) the spouses were last habitually resident in so far as one of them still resides there; or (iii) the respondent is habitually resident; or (iv) in the event of a joint application, either of the spouses is habitually resident; or (v) the applicant is habitually resident if he or she resided there for at least a year immediately before the application was made; or (vi) the applicant is habitually resident if he or she resided there for at least six months immediately before the application was made and is either a national of the member state in question or, in the case of the United Kingdom and Ireland, has his 'domicile'[16] there. In addition, a member state has jurisdiction if (vii) both spouses are nationals of that state or, in the case of the United Kingdom and Ireland, both spouses are 'domiciled' in that state.[17]

The premise underlying all the above jurisdictional bases is that they provide a 'real link between the party concerned and the

16 Art 2(2) provides that '"domicile" shall have the same meaning as it has under the legal systems of the United Kingdom and Ireland'. Art 2(2) of the Brussels II Convention provided that each member state had to stipulate in a declaration whether it would be applying the criterion of nationality or domicile. The Regulation, however, omitted art 2(2) of the Convention and made it clear that only the United Kingdom and Ireland could apply the criterion of domicile, with the other member states having to utilise nationality as the alternative connecting factor.

17 Two further jurisdictional bases are provided. Under art 5 the court in which proceedings are pending on the basis of art 2 shall also have jurisdiction to examine a counterclaim. Under art 6 a court of a member state which has given judgment on a legal separation shall also have jurisdiction to convert that judgment into a divorce, if the law of that member state so provides.

member state exercising jurisdiction'.[18] It is clear that habitual residence is regarded as the most appropriate connecting factor to indicate this 'real link'. Nationality and domicile are regarded as providing weaker links with a territory in that *both* spouses must have the relevant connection with the territory, a requirement not necessarily imposed when jurisdiction is based on habitual residence.

These jurisdictional criteria are more complex than the English traditional rules and could give rise to problems of interpretation. First, while the meaning of habitual residence is reasonably clear under English domestic law, the concept must, for these purposes, bear a European meaning ultimately to be determined by the Court of Justice.[19] If a different interpretation emerges, the undesirable result will be that habitual residence will bear differing meanings in different contexts. The same point can be made with regard to the fortifying connecting factor 'residence'. This is not a connecting factor generally employed in the conflict of laws but in the areas of law where it is employed is thought to bear 'different meanings in different branches of the law'.[20] Yet a further meaning of the concept and, again, one determined by the Court of Justice will emerge. As far as English courts are concerned this problem will not present itself with domicile which will not be given a European interpretation but will bear the meaning it has in the United Kingdom and Ireland. For this reason the word 'domicile' appears in inverted commas in the Regulation to indicate that it has a special meaning.[21] However, courts of other member states (except Ireland) will face such problems. For instance, if a German court is seised of a case where the jurisdictional bases in articles 2, 5 and 6 are not satisfied, before applying German traditional rules, the court would need to ensure under article 7 that, inter alia, the respondent was not domiciled in the United Kingdom with 'domicile' bearing the meaning its bears in the United Kingdom. This means that not only continental European courts, but also the Court of Justice, could find themselves exploring the intricacies of, for example, revival of domicile of origin.

The Regulation jurisdictional criteria are in many respects broader than the traditional rules. Under the traditional rules habitual residence had to have endured for at least a year prior to the commencement of the proceedings. Under the Regulation the

18 Recital 12 to Council Regulation (EC) No 1347/2000.

19 *Swaddling v Adjudication Officer* C-90/97 [1999] 2 FLR 184. See Borrás Report, OJ 1998 C221/27 para 32.

20 Dicey and Morris, *The Conflict of Laws* (13th edn, 2000) p 246; McClean, 'The Meaning of Residence' (1962) 11 ICLQ 1153.

21 Borrás Report, OJ 1998 C221/27, para 34.

respondent's habitual residence for less than a year suffices. Further, the mere residence of one party suffices provided it was the place where the spouses were last habitually resident; again, there would have been no jurisdiction under the traditional rules in such a case.

However, the Regulation rules are narrower than the traditional rules in one important respect. Unlike the position under the traditional rules, no application can be made on the basis of one spouse's domicile in England. This restriction could cause hardship. It will be recalled that in *IRC v Bullock*[22] the husband was domiciled in Nova Scotia and the wife was domiciled in England where both spouses had lived for 44 years. Let us suppose that the Bullocks went to work abroad on a three-year, fixed-term contract and became habitually resident in that country. If the marriage broke down (and assuming their habitual residence in England had been lost), Mr Bullock would not be able to apply to the English court for a divorce: the Regulation rules would not confer jurisdiction on the English court because only one spouse (Mrs Bullock) was domiciled in England; the traditional rules could not be used because that one party (the respondent) was domiciled in England.[23] The same hardship can arise even if both parties are from member states. Suppose an English domiciled husband's wife is a German national. They have homes and have lived for long periods in England and/ or Germany but, as with the above example, they spend a few years abroad becoming habitually resident in that country. In this situation the English court would not have jurisdiction: only one party is domiciled in England and so there is no jurisdiction under the Regulation; the husband cannot use the traditional rules because the wife is a German national;[24] she cannot obtain a divorce under the traditional rules because he (the respondent) is domiciled in England.[25] Further, in this example, for the same reasons, a divorce cannot be obtained in Germany either under the Regulation or under any German traditional rules. An obvious response to these examples is that if people work abroad in a country for long enough to acquire habitual residence there *and* lose habitual residence in the country of domicile or nationality then the most appropriate place for divorce is in that other country. However, this argument overlooks the fact that the country where they are working as expatriates might have strict jurisdictional criteria that they do not meet or strict grounds for divorce that they do not satisfy. Also, if they have spent a substantial portion of their marriage in, say, England, and have

22 [1976] 3 All ER 353.
23 Art 7.
24 Ibid.
25 Ibid.

their main assets here, say, a matrimonial home, most people would regard the English court as the most appropriate forum to dissolve the marriage and deal with all the consequential proprietary, financial and parental responsibility consequences. For these reasons the Brussels II Regulation has received a hostile reception by some commentators in England.[26]

3. Residual jurisdiction

Article 8 (the equivalent of articles 3 and 4 of the Brussels I Regulation) provides that where no court of a member state has jurisdiction and the respondent spouse does not come within article 7, courts of member states may avail themselves of their traditional jurisdictional rules. The Borrás Report[27] provides a full list of such residual jurisdiction rules for each of the member states. For example, if exercising its traditional jurisdictional criteria, a German court could exercise jurisdiction on the basis that one spouse was a German national when the marriage took place. In England the amended section 5(2) of the Domicile and Matrimonial Proceedings Act 1973 specifies the only remaining residual jurisdiction under the traditional rules: if either of the parties to the marriage is domiciled in England and Wales on the date when the marriage proceedings are begun. In practical terms the scope of the traditional rules is thus extremely narrow. Only when the applicant spouse is domiciled in England *and* the respondent spouse is not habitually resident in a member state nor a national of a member state (other than the United Kingdom or Ireland) nor domiciled in the United Kingdom or Ireland will the English court be able to exercise such jurisdiction.

C Staying proceedings

With such broadly-drawn jurisdictional rules it is quite possible that there could be matrimonial proceedings between the same parties pending in the court of another country at the same time as proceedings have been commenced in England (lis pendens) or, even if there are no proceedings abroad, the parties to English proceedings could be more closely connected with another country (forum non conveniens). The extent to which the English court has power to stay its proceedings (and the legal basis for doing so) depends on whether the rules set out in the Brussels II Regulation or the traditional rules apply.

26 Karsten, 'Brussels II – An English Perspective' [1998] IFL 75; Mostyn, 'Brussels II – The Impact on Forum Disputes' [2001] Fam Law 359; Gold, 'Brussels Sprouts New Matrimonial Law' (2001) 151 NLJ 451.

27 OJ 1998 C221/27.

1. Brussels II Regulation

Under the Regulation the English court may not stay its proceedings on the ground that the courts of another member state are clearly more appropriate to resolve the issue. Similarly, there is no power to issue an antisuit injunction restraining a party from pursuing proceedings in any such court. However, in situations of lis pendens, article 11(1) provides that where proceedings involving the same cause of action and between the same parties are brought before courts of different member states, the court second seised shall of its own motion stay its proceedings until such time as the jurisdiction of the court first seised is established. This is the exact counterpart of article 27 of the Brussels I Regulation.[28] So, if divorce proceedings have been commenced in France, the English court *must* stay any divorce proceeding commenced here provided the French court is the court 'first seised'.

Article 11(2) extends this rule to 'dependent actions'. These are proceedings not involving the same cause of action but must be proceedings for divorce, annulment or legal separation between the same parties. So, if a French court is first seised of proceedings for legal separation an English court *must* decline jurisdiction if divorce proceedings are commenced here. This is tighter than the analogous article 28 of the Brussels I Regulation[29] under which the court has a discretion to decline jurisdiction where there are related proceedings pending in another member state. No such discretion is afforded under article 11(2). However, in another sense article 11(2) is narrower than article 28 of the Brussels I Regulation under which 'related proceedings' can be broadly construed.[30] Article 11(2) is limited to the proceedings in both countries being for divorce, annulment or legal separation.

Although under the 1968 Brussels Convention there was no definition of when a court was 'seised', the Brussels I Regulation does provide such a definition[31] and this definition is replicated in article 11(4) of the Brussels II Regulation. According to article 11(4) a court is deemed to be seised when the document instituting the proceedings is lodged with the court or, if the document has to be served before being lodged with the court, at the time when it is received by the authority responsible for service.[32]

28 Formerly art 21 of the Brussels Convention.
29 Formerly art 22 of the Brussels Convention.
30 See p 118.
31 Art 30.
32 Provided the applicant has not subsequently failed to take the steps he was required to take to have service effected on the respondent or to have the document lodged with the court (art 11(4)).

The 'inflexibility' of this new rule has been described as 'shocking'.[33] The scenario painted is of a couple, one a Swedish national, the other an English domiciliary, who have established a matrimonial home in England and lived here for many years. The Swedish spouse could return to Sweden and be habitually resident there for six months and then commence divorce proceedings there. The spouse in England, the forum conveniens, cannot institute proceedings in England. A further scare-scenario involves a variation of the above example but this time an Irish spouse returns to Ireland, where the only ground for divorce is a four-year period of separation, and commences legal separation proceedings. The English spouse would be barred from commencing divorce proceedings in England and would have to wait four years before an Irish divorce could be obtained – raising suggestions that this could be a violation of articles 6 and 13 of the European Convention on Human Rights.[34]

On the other hand, the new provisions could be welcomed as avoiding the sometimes unseemly 'race to the finish' that can occur under the traditional rules as well as eliminating the uncertainty surrounding the operation of the discretionary doctrine of forum non conveniens. While it could be asserted that the new rules simply substitute a 'race to the start' – and are therefore likely to operate as a disincentive to mediation and conciliation[35] – the reality is that both the Swedish and Irish spouse in the above examples must have done more than simply return to their respective countries; they must have been habitually resident there for at least six months, signifying a genuine connection with that country. Where an English domiciliary returns to England and has been habitually resident here for six months, it is unlikely that many would describe it as 'shocking' for an English court to exercise jurisdiction. Further, the practical advice to the spouse left behind in England in the above scenarios is that they have a choice: they can institute proceedings in England within the six-month period or they can defend the foreign proceedings.

There is one further situation in which a stay of proceedings is mandatory. Under article 10(1) where a respondent who is habitually resident in another member state does not enter an appearance the proceedings must be stayed unless it is shown that the respondent has been able to receive the document instituting the proceedings in sufficient time to enable him to arrange for his defence, or that all necessary steps have been taken to this end. Although this does not solve the 'race to the start' problem, it does ensure that, in the two

33 Truex, 'Brussels II – Beware' [2001] Fam Law 233.
34 Mostyn, 'Brussels II – The Impact on Forum Disputes' [2001] Fam Law 359.
35 Karsten, 'Brussels II – An English Perspective' [1998] IFL 75.

scenarios above, the English spouse will be afforded a full opportunity to defend the proceedings abroad.

2. *Traditional rules*

The Domicile and Matrimonial Proceedings Act 1973 makes provision for English matrimonial proceedings to be stayed in certain circumstances when proceedings are pending in a foreign court other than one of a member state of the European Union. Such a stay of proceedings may be obligatory or discretionary.

(A) OBLIGATORY STAYS

The English court is bound to order a stay of *divorce* proceedings in the English court if, before the beginning of the trial in the English court, divorce or nullity proceedings in respect of the same marriage are continuing in another jurisdiction in the British Isles and the parties resided together in that jurisdiction when the English proceedings were begun, or, if they were not then residing together, the place where they last resided together was in that jurisdiction and either of the parties was habitually resident in that jurisdiction throughout the year ending with the date on which they last resided together before the commencement of the English proceedings.[36] It is immaterial in which court the proceedings are instituted first.

If any of these criteria is not satisfied, for example if the English proceedings are for annulment of marriage, the English action could still be stayed under the following discretionary rules.

(B) DISCRETIONARY STAYS

In cases where the English court is not bound to grant a stay, it may have a discretion to do so. There is, however, considerable uncertainty as to the circumstances in which English matrimonial proceedings may be stayed under the traditional rules contained in the Domicile and Matrimonial Proceedings Act 1973. Paragraph 9(1) of Schedule 1 to this Act provides that such discretionary powers exist in relation to any matrimonial proceedings 'other than proceedings governed by the Council Regulation'.[37] A literal interpretation of this suggests that if the English proceedings are governed by the Brussels II Regulation, the traditional rules are not applicable. Accordingly, if the English court has exercised jurisdiction under the Brussels II Regulation and there are matrimonial proceedings

36 Domicile and Matrimonial Proceedings Act 1973, s 5(6); Sch 1, paras 3(2) and 8.

37 As amended by European Communities (Matrimonial Jurisdiction and Judgments) Regulations 2001, SI 2001/310.

pending in New York, there is no power to stay the English proceedings even though New York might be a far more appropriate forum. Under this interpretation there is no room for an approach comparable to that adopted in *Re Harrods (Buenos Aires) Ltd*[38] where it was held, in a case where the court had jurisdiction under the Brussels I Convention, that proceedings could be stayed if the court of a non-contracting state was a more appropriate forum.

Notwithstanding the express wording in paragraph 9(1), it is unlikely that the above interpretation was intended by the drafters.[39] A more likely interpretation is that matrimonial proceedings 'other than proceedings governed by the Council Regulation' refers to proceedings that must be stayed under article 11 of the Brussels II Regulation. This, as seen above, refers to cases where there are proceedings pending before the courts of different member states.

If this latter interpretation were adopted (and it could well be a more attractive interpretation to the judiciary), the result would be that the traditional rules would apply to all cases where there are proceedings pending in a non-member state. Whether the English jurisdiction had been exercised under the Brussels II Regulation or the traditional rules would be irrelevant.

Under the traditional rules where, before the beginning of the trial in England in any matrimonial proceedings (not merely divorce proceedings), any proceedings in respect of the same marriage are continuing[40] in another jurisdiction (whether elsewhere in the British Isles or overseas), the court may order the English proceedings to be stayed if it appears to the court that the balance of fairness (including convenience) as between the parties to the marriage is such that it is appropriate for the proceedings in the other jurisdiction to be disposed of before further steps are taken in England.[41]

In considering the balance of fairness and convenience, the court must have regard to all the factors appearing to be relevant, including the convenience of the witnesses and any delay or expense which may result from the proceedings being stayed, or not being stayed.[42]

38 [1992] Ch 72, [1991] 4 All ER 334. See p 133.

39 The amendments to the Domicile and Matrimonial Proceedings Act 1973 (see n 14) are poorly drafted. Reference is made throughout to contracting state instead of member state. The amended s 5(2) purports to implement the Brussels II Regulation notwithstanding the fact that the Regulation is directly applicable in the member states.

40 In *R v R* [1994] 2 FLR 1036 it was implied that these statutory powers were available in cases where the foreign proceedings had been stayed. This ignores para 4(2) of the Domicile and Matrimonial Proceedings Act 1973, Sch 3, which provides that 'proceedings in a court are continuing if they are pending and not stayed'.

41 Domicile and Matrimonial Proceedings Act 1973, Sch 1, para 9(1).

42 Para 9(2).

It has already been seen[43] that at common law the English courts may stay civil proceedings on the ground that a foreign court is a more appropriate forum (forum non conveniens). In *De Dampierre v De Dampierre*[44] the House of Lords held that in applying the balance of fairness test for the staying of matrimonial proceedings under the Domicile and Matrimonial Proceedings Act 1973, the courts should have regard to the civil cases on forum non conveniens. The effect of these is that, if by reason of the factors connecting the case to the foreign court that court is clearly the more appropriate forum for the trial of the action, a stay will ordinarily be granted unless there are circumstances by reason of which justice requires that the stay should not be granted.

In *De Dampierre v De Dampierre* the parties were both French. In 1979 they moved to England, where the husband was involved in marketing cognac produced on his family estate in France. A few years later the wife set up a business in New York, where she subsequently took their child, informing her husband that she did not intend to return. The husband instituted divorce proceedings in France, and a few months later the wife instituted similar proceedings in England. The husband then applied to the English court for a stay of the English proceedings. He subsequently returned to live in France. Reversing the decision of the lower courts, the House of Lords held that a stay should be granted. The very strong factors connecting the case with France meant that, prima facie, the French court was the appropriate forum. The Court of Appeal had refused a stay on the ground that, if in the French proceedings it was found that the wife was exclusively responsible for the breakdown of the marriage, she might be refused any financial relief, except for maintenance of the child, whereas such a finding in the English court would not have that effect. The House of Lords, however, held that for the wife to be deprived of that advantage by the application of French law could not be held a substantial injustice to her, in view of the parties' connections with France. Thus the stay should be granted.

In *Butler v Butler*[45] Hobhouse LJ stated obiter that the wording of the 1973 Act was different from the test of forum non conveniens laid down in the *Spiliada* case[46] and therefore a different test was applicable. While the *Spiliada* test demands that there be another jurisdiction which is clearly or distinctly more appropriate, the 1973 Act merely lays down a criterion of 'an assessment of the balance of

43 See chapter 3.
44 [1988] AC 92, [1987] 2 All ER 1.
45 [1997] 2 All ER 822.
46 [1987] AC 460, [1986] 3 All ER 843.

fairness'. This dictum was disapproved in *S v S*[47] on the basis that the establishment of a 'clearly or distinctly' more appropriate forum was critical in assessing the 'balance of fairness'.

In considering the balance of fairness and convenience the courts have held several factors to be relevant: the locus of the marriage[48] and location of matrimonial assets; whether the English divorce decree will be recognised in the other country;[49] and the fact that the parties have contracted a prenuptial contract governed by the law of the other forum[50] – especially if the contract contains a jurisdiction clause in favour of the alternative forum.[51]

In exercising its discretion the English court ought not to be too influenced by the fact that a party will receive no, or less, financial relief in the foreign divorce proceedings. Since the *Spiliada* case the fact that the applicant is deprived of a significant advantage ought not to be given too much weight.[52] Further, the English court is empowered, when recognising a foreign matrimonial decree, to grant financial relief itself.[53] Despite this, it is clear that financial questions will continue to influence English courts in the exercise of their discretionary powers. For example, in *R v R*[54] it was not clear whether England or Sweden was the more appropriate forum but, because the wife was able to apply for property adjustment, a lump sum and periodic payments in England, whereas a Swedish court could only enforce a marriage contract providing for separation of property, it was held that justice demanded that a stay of the English proceedings be refused. In *S v S*[55] it was stated that it was relevant to take a 'general look' at the financial arrangements that would be made in the foreign court but these would only tilt the balance of fairness in favour of the English forum if they amounted to a substantial injustice. The absence of legal aid in the other country and the costs involved for an English spouse having to travel to that country can be taken into account but the weight to be attached to them will be entirely dependent on the circumstances. For example, in *Krenge v Krenge*[56] a stay of English proceedings was granted on

47 [1997] 1 WLR 1200.
48 *Krenge v Krenge* [1999] 1 FLR 969 at 981: 'the relationship between the parties "budded, blossomed and withered" in Germany.'
49 *C v C* [2001] 1 FLR 624.
50 Ibid.
51 *S v S* [1997] 1 WLR 1200.
52 See pp 125.
53 Matrimonial and Family Proceedings Act 1984. See p 434.
54 [1994] 2 FLR 1036.
55 [1997] 1 WLR 1200.
56 [1999] 1 FLR 969.

condition that the husband deposited a sum of money to meet his wife's reasonable legal and travel expenses in Germany.

The statutory provisions are additional to the inherent jurisdiction of the English court to stay an action on the basis of forum non conveniens.[57] As the statutory scheme largely reproduces the common law as explained in the *Spiliada* case, there seems little scope for the common law powers to be invoked when there are proceedings pending abroad. However, the inherent common law power could usefully be invoked in cases where there were no proceedings abroad.[58] Of course, in view of the more rigorous matrimonial jurisdictional rules there will be far less need to invoke the power than in civil and commercial cases. However, there can be cases where the concept of domicile gives the English court jurisdiction, despite there being only the most tenuous of links with England.[59] In exceptional cases the common law powers can also be invoked to restrain a party from pursuing matrimonial proceedings abroad on the basis that the proceedings there are vexatious and oppressive. In *Hemain v Hemain*[60] it was confirmed that such a power existed and was to be exercised in the same way as in civil jurisdiction cases.[61]

II CHOICE OF LAW

A Divorce and separation

It might be thought that just as the question whether a marriage was valid at its inception may be governed by a foreign law, so also in appropriate cases should the question whether there are sufficient grounds for its dissolution to be referred to a foreign law (for instance, the law of the parties' domicile at the date of the proceedings). In fact, however, when the English court has jurisdiction in divorce or separation proceedings, it applies English law exclusively to determine whether a divorce should be granted.[62]

57 Domicile and Matrimonial Proceedings Act 1973, s 5(6)(b). See *W v W* [1997] 1 FLR 257.
58 *Sealey v Callan* [1953] P 135, [1953] 1 All ER 942 (endorsing the existence of such a general power although there were, in fact, proceedings pending abroad). In *T v T* [1995] 2 FLR 660 at 665–666 the court seemed in little doubt that it had the power to stay proceedings even if the foreign proceedings had been withdrawn. See also *Butler v Butler* [1997] 2 All ER 822.
59 See, for example, *T v T* [1995] 2 FLR 660.
60 [1988] 2 FLR 388.
61 *Société Nationale Industrielle Aérospatiale v Lee Kui Jak* [1987] AC 871, [1987] 3 All ER 510. See pp 145.
62 *Zanelli v Zanelli* (1948) 64 TLR 556.

There are two main reasons for this approach. The first is historical. Originally, English courts had jurisdiction only if the parties were domiciled in England. English law, both as the lex fori and the lex domicilii, was the only conceivable law that could be applied. While the extended jurisdictional grounds today mean that the English court can grant a divorce to persons domiciled elsewhere, the rules are designed to ensure that at least one of the parties belongs here in the sense of having a genuine connection with England. Indeed, in view of the technical rules of domicile, habitual residence may denote a greater connection with England than domicile. Accordingly, it is appropriate that English law be applied. Secondly, it is often asserted that the circumstances in which a marriage should be dissolved by the English courts are very much a matter of English public policy, as reflected by English domestic law. It may be distasteful and time-consuming for English courts to have to apply sometimes 'exotic'[63] and often antiquated foreign grounds for divorce. Some 99 per cent of divorces are uncontested, with courts performing little more than a rubber-stamp function that does not involve any inquiry as to whether the grounds for divorce have been established.[64] It would be invidious to treat foreign domiciliaries differently by embarking on a full trial to ascertain whether the foreign grounds for divorce have been satisfied.

On the other hand, it has been suggested that 'if the courts take jurisdiction over "exotic foreigners" then the pass has been sold and it is arguably no more bizarre to apply their personal law to the dissolution than to apply it to the creation of their marriage'.[65] The courts in civil law countries do, to differing extents, apply foreign laws, usually the law of nationality, to determine whether divorces should be granted.[66] The result of the English courts' approach is that many of the divorces granted here will not be recognised elsewhere – particularly by the law of the parties' domicile.[67] One possible compromise could be that, rather than the application of foreign law, there should be a requirement that the divorce be recognised by the law of the parties' domicile before a divorce order can be made by the English court. Such an approach would, however, raise problems in cases where the spouses had different

63 McClean, *Morris: The Conflict of Laws* (5th edn, 2000) p 235.

64 Law Com No 170, *Facing the Future: A Discussion Paper on the Grounds for Divorce* (1988) paras 5.17, 2.8.

65 North, 'Development of Rules of Private International Law in the Field of Family Law' (1980) 166 Hag Rec 9 at 83.

66 Ibid at 78–79. See, for example, the French Civil Code, art 310, as interpreted in *Massimo Selmi v Claire Fray*, Rev Crit 1995, 117, note Gaudemet-Tallon.

67 In *Kapur v Kapur* [1984] FLR 920 at 926 such lack of recognition was dismissed as 'irrelevant'.

domiciles or, because of the artificiality associated with the concept of domicile, were domiciled in countries with which they had little real connection. Further, lack of recognition of English decrees is more likely to be based on the foreign court's rejection of the wide English jurisdictional grounds than on the English court's failure to apply the foreign law. In view of these considerations, it is not surprising that there is little pressure for reform of the present English approach that the lex fori be applied in all cases where a divorce or separation is sought in England.

B Nullity

Unlike the position in divorce cases, the governing law in nullity proceedings in the English court may well be a foreign law. The governing law will be determined by the choice of law rules which were examined in chapter 8, for example, the lex loci celebrationis if the marriage is alleged to be formally invalid, or the laws of the parties' antenuptial domiciles if the issue concerns prohibited degrees of relationship.

As was seen in chapter 8,[68] it is not only the question whether a marriage is invalid which can be governed by a foreign law. That law will also in principle determine the kind of invalidity. But the English court will presumably not grant a decree of a kind which is unknown to its laws and procedure. Thus, as English nullity decrees are designed for the annulment of void and voidable marriages in the English sense, the kind of invalidity under the governing foreign law (which might have several kinds of invalidity) must presumably be equated with either a void or voidable marriage, whichever is the nearer, and the appropriate decree granted. It is also arguable that since an annulment of a voidable marriage which operates retrospectively is unknown to English law, an English court cannot grant a decree having such effect, even if that is the consequence of the annulment of a voidable marriage by the governing law.

III RECOGNITION OF FOREIGN JUDGMENTS

Recognition of decrees of divorce, legal separation[69] and annulment are all governed by either the Brussels II Regulation or the Family

68 See p 311.
69 The Family Law Act 1986 refers to 'judicial separation' for the purpose of recognising British decrees (s 44), but refers to 'legal separation' for the purpose of recognising overseas decrees (ss 46–52). The Brussels II Regulation also refers to 'legal separation'.

Law Act 1986. However, as the implications of recognising a foreign annulment can be somewhat different, these will be dealt with separately.

A Decrees of divorce and legal separation[70]

1. Introduction

The question often arises whether a divorce granted by a foreign court is recognised as valid in England. If it is not recognised the parties, although regarded as single persons in the country where the divorce was granted and in any other country which recognises the divorce, remain married to each other in the eyes of English law (and of any other law which does not recognise the divorce). Such a marriage, which still subsists according to one or more laws, but has been dissolved according to others, is called a 'limping marriage'. The hardship and inconvenience which can result from a marital status which differs from one country to another is obvious. However, to try to avoid this by simply recognising all foreign divorces would enable a spouse to evade the requirements of the law of the country or countries with which the parties are connected by obtaining a divorce in a country with which neither has any genuine connection, but whose courts exercise divorce jurisdiction on flimsy grounds.

The rules governing the recognition of foreign divorces therefore aim to strike the right balance between being too restrictive, thus unnecessarily creating limping marriages, and being too generous, thus sanctioning divorces of convenience. It should be mentioned, however, that one of the hardships that could formerly result from the recognition of a foreign divorce has been removed. The rule used to be that once a marriage had been validly dissolved, the English court lacked power to make, for the first time, an order for financial provision in favour of a former spouse (although an existing order could be continued or varied after a divorce). This meant that an English wife, whose husband had obtained a foreign divorce which was recognised in England, could not obtain an order for financial relief in the English court, even though the foreign court had not made adequate provision for her. The courts have, however, been given power to make orders for financial provision in favour of former spouses who have an appropriate connection with England.[71]

70 For reasons of convenience discussion in the ensuing text will be limited to recognition of foreign divorces. The same rules apply to recognition of foreign legal separations.

71 Matrimonial and Family Proceedings Act 1984, s 12. See pp 434–435.

2. Historical development

Originally the principle was that it was for the courts of the domicile alone to change the status of the parties; just as the English courts would exercise divorce jurisdiction only if the spouses were domiciled in England, so also they would recognise only divorces granted by,[72] or recognised by,[73] the courts of the domicile. When the jurisdiction of the English courts was extended by statute, the recognition rules were expanded so that divorces granted in circumstances in which the English court would have exercised jurisdiction were entitled to recognition.[74] The final common law extension was that a foreign divorce could be recognised if at the commencement of the foreign proceedings there was a real and substantial connection between either of the parties and the country in which the divorce was obtained.[75] While this was certainly a generous approach, this ground of recognition was extremely vague, making the status of the parties in England uncertain, and the decision of the court difficult to predict.[76]

The Recognition of Divorces and Legal Separations Act 1971 replaced these common law rules with statutory provisions that were both reasonably generous and precise. This Act was repealed and replaced by the Family Law Act 1986 which both amended the provisions of the 1971 Act and extended the recognition rules to nullity decrees.

As seen above,[77] the Brussels II Convention was signed in 1998 and brought into force as an EC Regulation in 2001 applying to all member states except Denmark. Under this Regulation divorces, legal separations and annulments from courts of member states are entitled to almost automatic recognition throughout the European Union. Accordingly, there are now two regimes for the recognition of such divorces: the Brussels II Regulation governs judgments from the courts of member states and the 'traditional rules' contained in the Family Law Act 1986 apply in all other cases.

72 *Harvie v Farnie* (1881) 8 App Cas 43.

73 *Armitage v A–G* [1906] P 135.

74 *Travers v Holley* [1953] P 246, [1953] 2 All ER 794.

75 *Indyka v Indyka* [1969] 1 AC 33, [1967] 2 All ER 689.

76 It was then estimated that the Registrar-General of Births, Marriages and Deaths in England had to decide some 2,500 cases a year whether a marriage could be celebrated in England after a foreign divorce. After *Indyka v Indyka* this task became extremely difficult and led to a plethora of appeals to the courts. See Law Com No 34, *Hague Convention on Recognition of Divorces and Legal Separations* (1970), para 25, n 42.

77 See p 381.

3. Brussels II Regulation

(A) RECOGNITION

The Brussels II Regulation applies to 'civil proceedings'[78] which can cover non-judicial proceedings[79] which are officially recognised in the member state as being equivalent to judicial proceedings.[80] However, purely religious procedures are excluded from the scope of the Regulation. This means that divorces obtained by administrative proceedings in a member state fall within the scope of the Regulation. However, it would appear[81] that the only European Union member state that permits administrative divorce is Denmark. As Denmark chose not to participate in the Regulation this means that in practical terms the Regulation does not apply to the recognition of non-judicial divorces.

The rules here are broadly similar to those contained in the Brussels I Regulation. With commercial judgments, however, it is enforcement of the judgment that is usually critical. The Brussels II Regulation does not cover any financial matters that could be the subject of enforcement. Accordingly, with divorces, legal separations and annulments, the rules relate purely to the recognition of such judgments.[82]

Chapter III starts from the premise that a judgment falling within its scope is entitled to recognition. Under no circumstances may a foreign judgment from a member state be reviewed as to its substance.[83] Equally, the jurisdiction of the original court may not be reviewed,[84] irrespective of whether that court exercised jurisdiction under the Regulation or according to its traditional rules (if the case fell within article 8). Further, recognition may not be refused on the ground that the recognising member state would not allow the divorce on the same facts.[85]

Article 14 provides that a judgment of divorce, legal separation or annulment given in a member state shall be recognised in other member states without any special procedure being required. Unlike the Brussels I Regulation, this only covers positive decisions that do grant the decree. Negative decisions denying a decree are not entitled to recognition and so will not give rise to an issue estoppel.[86]

78 Art 1(1)(a).
79 Recital 9.
80 Art 1(2).
81 Borrás Report, OJ 1998 C221/27, para 20.A.
82 Borrás Report, OJ 1998 C221/27, para 80. The rules on enforcement apply only to judgments on the exercise of parental responsibility.
83 Art 19.
84 Art 17.
85 Art 18.
86 Kennett, 'Current Developments: Private International Law: The Brussels II Convention' (1999) 48 ICLQ 465 at 470.

The recognition of a divorce, legal separation or annulment is of particular importance for the updating of civil status records (rather than recognition by a court of law). No special procedure is required for this purpose; the mere existence of the decree from a member state is sufficient.[87] This simple provision 'will be much appreciated by European citizens ... (and) will save time and money, thus representing a considerable advance over the [Brussels I Regulation]'.[88] Another important difference from the Brussels I Regulation is that the judgment must be a final one from which no further appeal lies.[89]

Of course, a party might wish to obtain a ruling that the decree is entitled to recognition or might wish to contest the validity of the decree. The Regulation gives power to 'any interested party' to apply for a decision whether the judgment should be recognised or not.[90] The meaning of 'any interested party' is to be construed broadly under the national law of the recognising state.[91] The Borrás Report gives the example of a public prosecutor.[92] In England an 'interested party' could be the Registrar-General of Births, Marriages and Deaths who might seek a ruling prior to granting a licence permitting a party to remarry in England.

A question whether a decree should be recognised can arise incidentally in judicial proceedings: for example, in determining the validity of a subsequent marriage. Where this occurs that court may determine whether the decree should be recognised.[93]

(B) REFUSAL OF RECOGNITION

While judgments from member states (other than Denmark) are normally entitled to automatic recognition, article 15 of the Regulation provides some limited grounds for non-recognition.

First, a judgment will not be recognised if such recognition would be manifestly[94] contrary to public policy.[95] Inclusion of this ground in the Regulation is felt to be important because states are 'extremely sensitive' about family cases and the major discrepancies between laws on divorce.[96] However, this public policy ground for non-

87 Art 14(2).
88 Borrás Report, OJ 1998 C221/27, para 63.
89 Art 14(2).
90 Art 14(3).
91 Borrás Report, OJ 1998 C221/27, para 65.
92 Ibid.
93 Art 14(4).
94 See p 418 below as to whether the inclusion of the word 'manifestly' is significant.
95 Art 15(1)(a).
96 Borrás Report, OJ 1998 C221/27, para 69.

recognition will only have a limited reach. As already seen, neither the jurisdiction of the court of origin[97] nor the substance of a judgment[98] may be reviewed and recognition may not be refused on the ground that the recognising member state would not allow the divorce on the same facts.[99] Accordingly, a judgment from a state with flexible divorce laws cannot be refused recognition in a state with strict divorce laws on grounds of public policy. Despite the sensitivity of this area of law, it is likely that this basis for refusing recognition will be limited to situations where the corresponding provision of the Brussels I regime[100] has been applied, namely where the foreign decree has been obtained by fraud or where the respondent's human rights (as protected by the European Convention on Human Rights) have been infringed.[101] It seems likely that the courts will draw on the jurisprudence interpreting the comparable provisions of the Brussels I regime and tightly control the circumstances in which public policy can be used as a basis for non-recognition.[102]

Secondly, a divorce shall be refused recognition where it was given in default of appearance, if the respondent was not notified in sufficient time and in such a way as to enable a defence to be arranged.[103] This ground of non-recognition mirrors article 34(2) of the Brussels I Regulation and, again, presumably, will be interpreted in a similar manner.[104] However, like article 34(2) of the Brussels I Regulation, article 15(1)(b) contains a qualification that limits the scope of the defence. Even if the respondent was not able to arrange for his defence, the decree must be recognised if the respondent 'has accepted the judgment unequivocally'. An example of such unequivocal acceptance would be a remarriage by the respondent.[105]

Thirdly, and again mirroring the Brussels I Regulation,[106] recognition must be refused to a judgment which is irreconcilable with a judgment given in proceedings between the same parties in the member state in which recognition is sought.[107] This provision

97 Art 17.
98 Art 19.
99 Art 18.
100 Art 34(1) of the Brussels I Regulation (formerly art 27(1)of the Brussels Convention).
101 It has been suggested that divorces of same-sex marriages would come within this provision (Carnec and Chauveau, 'The Convention on Divorce Jurisdiction (Brussels II) – From Forum Shopping to Divorce Planning' [1998] IFL 73). For the reasons given at p 354 this seems unlikely.
102 See p 190.
103 Art 15(1)(b).
104 See pp 191–194.
105 Borrás Report, OJ 1998 C221/27, para 70.
106 Art 34(3).
107 Art 15(1)(c).

applies regardless of which judgment was given first.[108] There is no requirement that the two judgments relate to the same cause of action. For example, if the parties had obtained a legal separation judgment in France and a divorce in England, the French judgment would be refused recognition in England as being irreconcilable with the English divorce.[109]

Fourthly, the courts of a member state shall not recognise a judgment if it is irreconcilable with an earlier judgment given in another member state or in a non-member state between the same parties, provided the earlier judgment fulfils the conditions necessary for its recognition in the member state in which recognition is sought.[110]

Suppose, for example, that the English court is faced with a separation judgment granted by a New York court which meets the conditions for recognition under the Family Law Act 1986 and a later divorce decree from a French court which meets the conditions for recognition under the Regulation. The French divorce decree is not irreconcilable with the New York separation judgment and so can be recognised.[111] In the converse case where there is a divorce decree from New York and a legal separation judgment from France, the French judgment will not be recognised because it is irreconcilable with the New York divorce decree.

The Regulation specifically covers irreconcilable judgments from the courts of two member states.[112] The provision applies equally to the situation where, for example, there has been a Spanish separation judgment followed by a French divorce decree.

4. *The traditional rules: Family Law Act 1986*

In examining these rules it is necessary to distinguish between recognition of judicial divorces and recognition of extra-judicial divorces.

(A) JUDICIAL DIVORCES

The recognition of judicial divorces from non-member states is governed by the Family Law Act 1986. This Act draws a distinction

108 Borrás Report, OJ 1998 C221/27, para 71.

109 The result would be different if a decree of judicial separation had been obtained in England and a divorce in France. As separation 'may be considered a preliminary to divorce' (Borrás Report, OJ 1998 C221/27, para 71), the French divorce could be recognised: it would not be irreconcilable with the English judicial separation decree.

110 Art 15(1)(d).

111 See n 109.

112 See also art 34(4) of the Brussels I Regulation.

between 'British Isles divorces'[113] and 'overseas divorces'. With regard to the former, section 44(2) of the Family Law Act 1986 provides that a divorce granted by a court in any part of the British Isles is automatically entitled to recognition throughout the United Kingdom, subject to one qualification which will be mentioned below.[114] For the purpose of the recognition of divorces obtained outside the British Isles ('overseas divorces'), a distinction is drawn between divorces obtained by means of proceedings and those not 'obtained by proceedings'. The meaning of 'obtained by proceedings' is discussed later. It can safely be assumed that all overseas judicial divorces have been 'obtained by proceedings'.

The policy underlying the recognition rules is that the divorce should have been obtained in a country having an adequate connection with either of the parties. Section 46(1) of the Act provides that an overseas divorce obtained by proceedings qualifies for recognition if it is effective under the law of the country in which it was obtained, and at the date of the commencement of the proceedings either party was: (i) habitually resident in the country in which the divorce was obtained; or (ii) domiciled in that country according to English law or domiciled in that country according to the law of that country in family matters; or (iii) a national of that country.

(i) Habitual residence

If either spouse was habitually resident in the foreign country at the date of the commencement of the foreign proceedings, a divorce decree obtained in that country is, in principle, entitled to recognition. Habitual residence must be interpreted according to English law.[115] Unlike the former English traditional jurisdictional rule, the habitual residence need not have endured for any set period of time. It is not unusual for English divorce recognition rules to be more flexible than the English jurisdictional rules.[116]

(ii) Domicile

A divorce obtained in a country in which either party is domiciled, according to English law, is entitled to recognition. The common law rule, preserved in the Recognition of Divorces and Legal Separations Act 1971, that a divorce recognised by the law of the

113 The United Kingdom (consisting of England and Wales, Scotland and Northern Ireland), the Channel Islands and the Isle of Man.

114 S 51(1), (2). See p 416.

115 As to the relevance of foreign findings of fact, see pp 405–406.

116 At common law the recognition rules under *Indyka v Indyka* [1969] 1 AC 33 were more generous than the English jurisdictional rules.

parties' domicile, though not obtained in the country in which either was domiciled, was entitled to recognition was abolished by the Family Law Act 1986. One of the parties must be domiciled in the country where the divorce was obtained.

Further, however, contrary to the general rule that domicile is defined by the lex fori, a divorce can also be recognised if either party was domiciled in the foreign country according to that country's law in family matters. In *Messina v Smith*[117] the wife obtained a divorce in Nevada where she had resided for six weeks, which was sufficient for her to acquire a domicile according to Nevada law. Such a divorce would qualify for recognition.[118] In this way, provision is made for a ground of jurisdiction likely to be used by foreign courts which, although constituting a reasonable connection, coincides neither with domicile in the English sense nor with habitual residence. The domicile in the foreign country has to be 'according to the law of that country in family matters'.[119] One reason for this formulation is to provide for such federal states as Australia and Canada whose laws, while normally requiring domicile to be in a constituent state or province, have created a domicile in the composite state as a whole for the purposes of matrimonial causes.[120] So if the court of an Australian state granted a divorce on the basis that one of the parties was domiciled in Australia (as opposed to being domiciled in that state), the divorce qualifies for recognition, even though according to the English rules of domicile neither of the parties was domiciled in that state and domicile in Australia as a whole is not possible.

(iii) Nationality

A divorce obtained in the country of nationality of either party is entitled to recognition. Despite nationality not being a favoured connecting factor in English law, this provision was added as part of the price of reaching international agreement with civil law countries in the 1968 Hague Convention on Recognition of Divorces and Legal Separations. In *Torok v Torok*[121] the spouses were Hungarian nationals who came to Britain where they became naturalised subjects while retaining their Hungarian nationality. Later the husband returned to Hungary and there obtained a divorce. It was held that the divorce would, on this basis, be prima facie entitled to

117 [1971] P 322, [1971] 2 All ER 1046.
118 See Ormrod J (obiter) at 339. The comparable provision of the 1971 Act was not yet in force.
119 S 46(5).
120 See p 25.
121 [1973] 3 All ER 101, [1972] WLR 1066.

recognition.[122] It was irrelevant that the husband was also a national of another country.

(iv) Country
In the case of a state comprising law districts in which separate systems of law are in force in matters of divorce (for example, the United States), if a divorce is sought to be recognised on the basis of habitual residence or domicile in either sense, then it is the law district, not the composite state, which counts as the country.[123] So, for the recognition of a divorce obtained in Colorado, the question would be whether either party was habitually resident or domiciled in Colorado, not anywhere else in the United States. If, however, recognition of the divorce is sought on the ground of either party being a national of the country, then 'country' means the composite state, not a constituent law district[124] (for normally nationality will relate to the whole political unit). Thus a divorce obtained in Colorado will qualify for recognition if either party is a citizen of the United States.

(v) Effective under foreign law
At common law the fact that a divorce was invalid under the law of the country in which it was obtained was not necessarily an obstacle to its recognition. Under the Family Law Act 1986, however, a foreign divorce cannot be recognised on any ground unless it is effective under the law of the country in which it was obtained.[125] This means that if the divorce is not effective under that law, because for example the foreign court lacked jurisdiction under its own law to grant divorce decrees, or because of some procedural irregularity, the divorce cannot be recognised in England. For example, in *D v D*[126] the husband, a Ghanaian national, returned to Ghana and there obtained a divorce without the wife being present or notified. After hearing expert evidence of Ghanaian law, the English court concluded that, if the matter were to be appealed to the High Court of Ghana, the divorce would be set aside on the ground that there had been no voluntary submission by both parties. Accordingly, the divorce was not effective under Ghanaian law and so not entitled to recognition.

122 Recognition was, in fact, denied for other reasons.
123 Family Law Act 1986, s 49(1), (2).
124 S 49(1), (3).
125 Ss 46(1)(a) and (2)(a). This rule was first introduced by the Recognition of Divorces and Legal Separations Act 1971, s 2(b) in respect of the statutory bases of recognition.
126 [1994] 1 FLR 38.

In *Kellman v Kellman*[127] it was held that 'effective' does not necessarily mean 'valid'; 'effective' connotes a less rigorous standard than 'valid'. In this case the parties obtained a 'mail order divorce' from Guam. Both parties regarded this as a valid divorce and the husband remarried. Ten years later it transpired that the divorce might not have been valid under Guam law and so the wife attempted to have the divorce decree set aside in Guam. The Supreme Court of Guam denied her motion on grounds of equitable estoppel. Accordingly,[128] the divorce, although not 'valid', could be regarded as effective.

What is the position in relation to states comprising law districts in which different systems of law are in force? If recognition is based on habitual residence or domicile in a particular law district, the divorce must be effective under the law of that law district. For example, if a divorce were obtained in Colorado, it would need to be effective under the law of Colorado. Where recognition is sought on the ground that either party was a national of the composite state, then the requirement is that the divorce must be effective throughout the composite state.[129] In *Kellman v Kellman*,[130] where the divorce was obtained in Guam, an unincorporated territory of the United States, recognition was sought on the basis that the parties were United States nationals. It was held that the divorce had to be effective under the law of the United States. The reason, no doubt, is that if the connection which justifies the recognition is with the composite state, then the effectiveness in the country in which it was obtained should be assessed by the same yardstick.

(vi) Proof of facts relevant to recognition

For the recognition of a foreign divorce, the English court will have to decide whether a party had the required connection (habitual residence, domicile or nationality) with the foreign country. It is not essential that the foreign court should have exercised jurisdiction on one of these bases. For example, a foreign court could exercise jurisdiction on the basis of one party's presence in the country; such a divorce decree could still be recognised provided either party was in fact habitually resident or domiciled there or a national of that country. Very often, however, the foreign court will have itself exercised jurisdiction on the basis of habitual residence, domicile or nationality and in such cases, to avoid the unnecessary reopening in

127 [2000] 1 FLR 785.
128 See n 130 below.
129 S 49(1), (3).
130 [2000] 1 FLR 785.

the English court of issues already decided in the foreign court, provision is made that:

> any finding of fact made (whether expressly or by implication) in the [foreign] proceedings and on the basis of which jurisdiction was assumed in the proceedings shall –
> (a) if both parties to the marriage took part in the proceedings, be conclusive evidence of the fact found; and
> (b) in any other case, be sufficient proof of that fact unless the contrary is shown.[131]

So the foreign finding of fact relevant to jurisdiction is conclusive if the respondent as well as the petitioner took part in the proceedings (which includes even a formal appearance without any further participation), because the respondent would have had the opportunity, if so inclined, to contest the fact in the foreign court. If, however, the respondent did not appear, the foreign finding is presumed to be correct, but it is open to a party in the English proceedings to prove otherwise.

The foreign finding of fact which is conclusive, or prima facie sufficient, will often be a finding that a party was habitually resident in the foreign country, or was domiciled in that country under its law, or was a national of that country (when the foreign court's jurisdiction under its own law is based on such ground). However, it could merely be a finding of a fact which is a step towards deciding whether a ground of jurisdiction existed. For example, a finding by the foreign court that a party was present in its country at a certain time or for a certain period would be conclusive, or prima facie sufficient, proof of that fact for the purposes of the English court's decision whether the party was habitually resident in that country or domiciled there in the English sense. Of course, there is little possibility of an actual finding by the foreign court that a party was domiciled there in the English sense, for that could hardly ever be a relevant question in the foreign proceedings.

(B) EXTRA-JUDICIAL DIVORCES[132]

(i) Introduction

Although in England a marriage can be dissolved only by judicial proceedings in a court of law, this is not so in all countries. Under some foreign legal systems, the proceedings for divorce may be

131 S 48.

132 There have been no cases on extra-judicial legal separations for well over a century. See North, *The Private International Law of Matrimonial Causes in the British Isles and the Republic of Ireland* (1977) p 280. The following section is, accordingly, limited to extra-judicial divorces.

administrative rather than judicial, or the divorce may be obtained merely by the agreement of the parties or by the act of only one of them, either with or without attendant formalities. The kind of extra-judicial divorce which has most often come before the English courts is the Islamic talak. Under some traditions of classical Islamic law, the husband can divorce his wife merely be declaring three times, in writing or orally, 'I divorce you'. In some Islamic countries such a talak divorce is effective. In Pakistan, however, statute has added further requirements to the procedure. Under Jewish religious law, as applied in Israel, a consensual form of divorce may be obtained: the husband appears before the Beth Din (Rabbinical court) and executes a letter of divorce, a get, which is then delivered to the wife, either in person or by proxy, at the Beth Din. The divorce is final when she receives the document. Although the procedure takes place at the Beth Din, it is not the court which grants the divorce.

English conflict of laws rules have long accepted in principle the validity of foreign extra-judicial divorces, so long as the ordinary grounds of recognition are satisfied. At common law, the original grounds for recognition of a foreign divorce were that it should have been obtained in the country of the parties' domicile or be recognised as valid by the law of that country. On this basis, not only were talak divorces obtained in a foreign country recognised in England,[133] but even a talak divorce pronounced in England while the parties were living here was recognised on the ground that it was valid by the law of Pakistan, the country in which the parties were domiciled.[134] It was not thought contrary to public policy to recognise such divorces,[135] even if the foreign law required no formalities of any kind. However, when further grounds of recognition (habitual residence and nationality) were added by the Recognition of Divorces and Legal Separations Act 1971, they, although not confined to judicial divorces, extended only to divorces obtained by 'proceedings'. Then in 1973 it was laid down by statute[136] that in future no extra-judicial divorce obtained anywhere in the British Isles should be recognised in England; this principle was re-enacted in the Family Law Act 1986.[137]

133 *Russ v Russ* [1964] P 315, [1962] 3 All ER 193.
134 *Qureshi v Qureshi* [1972] Fam 173, [1971] 1 All ER 325. In *Har-Shefi v Har-Shefi (No 2)* [1953] P 220, [1953] 2 All ER 373, a case involving the dissolution of a marriage between Israeli domiciliaries, a Jewish religious divorce obtained by the husband's delivering a letter of divorce to the wife at a Rabbinical court in London was recognised on the ground that it was effective by the law of Israel.
135 *Qureshi v Qureshi* [1972] Fam 173, [1971] 1 All ER 325.
136 Domicile and Matrimonial Proceedings Act 1973, s 16(1).
137 In somewhat different wording: s 44(1).

At the moment,[138] the rules for recognition of extra-judicial divorces are governed by the Family Law Act 1986 under which the rules applicable depend on whether the extra-judicial divorce was obtained by means of 'proceedings' or not.

(ii) 'Proceedings'
What is the reason for having different rules of recognition for divorces obtained by proceedings and for those obtained without proceedings? Historically, the reason is that, before the Recognition of Divorces and Legal Separations Act 1971, the original and primary basis for the recognition of a divorce was that it was obtained in the country of the parties' domicile, or recognised by its law, which was the appropriate law to determine status. This principle was held to require the recognition of divorces however obtained, and the question whether there had been any proceedings was not thought material. Under the 1971 Act, the existing grounds of recognition on the basis of domicile were continued,[139] even in relation to an entirely informal non-judicial divorce, such as a bare talak.[140] The Act, however, introduced new grounds of recognition (habitual residence, nationality, domicile in the foreign sense), but only (following the Hague Convention which was being implemented) for divorces obtained by 'judicial or other proceedings'. Although the courts might conceivably have held that any act by which a divorce is obtained, including a bare talak, constituted proceedings – thus obliterating any distinction between divorces obtained by proceedings and those not so obtained – they ultimately did not do so.

The Law Commission, in its report which gave rise to the relevant part of the 1986 Act, recommended that 'other proceedings' should 'include acts which constitute the means by which a divorce ... may be obtained in [the] country and are done in compliance with the procedure required by the law of that country'.[141] This would include bare talaks. However, this recommendation was not implemented in the statute.

The Family Law Act 1986 merely states that proceedings are 'judicial or other proceedings'.[142] Accordingly, the meaning of 'other proceedings' has been a matter of judicial interpretation.

138 If a member state were to introduce non-judicial civil proceedings for divorce, the Brussels II Regulation would apply to the recognition of such divorces.
139 S 6.
140 *Chaudhary v Chaudhary* [1985] Fam 19.
141 Law Com No 137, *Recognition of Foreign Nullity Decrees and Related Matters* (1984) para 6.11.
142 Family Law Act 1986, s 54(1).

In *Quazi v Quazi*[143] the husband, a Pakistani national, had obtained a divorce by talak under the law of Pakistan. Under the 1971 Act, as under the 1986 Act, an overseas divorce was to be recognised if either spouse was a national of the country in which it was obtained, but only if the divorce had been obtained by means of judicial or other proceedings.[144] In this case, the divorce had been obtained in Pakistan under the Muslim Family Laws Ordinance 1961. This provided that the husband, after pronouncing the talak, had to send a written notice of the divorce to the chairman of an administrative body called the union council, and a copy to the wife. The chairman of the union council then had to set up an arbitration council, whose function was to try to bring about a reconciliation. The effect of the talak was suspended until 90 days after notice of the talak had been given to the official, but if within that period the husband did not revoke the talak it then became effective. The issue was whether a divorce obtained in this way had been obtained by 'proceedings'. The Court of Appeal[145] held that it had not, for it thought that the requirement of 'proceedings' meant that the efficacy of the divorce must depend in some way on the authority of the state expressed in a formal manner. A divorce obtained under the Ordinance did not satisfy this requirement, because the state could not prevent the husband from divorcing his wife if he chose not to be reconciled. This decision was reversed by the House of Lords, for it was plain to them that the pronouncement by the husband of the talak, and the giving of notice to the council and the wife, constituted 'proceedings' by means of which the divorce had been obtained.

What remained undecided was whether a 'bare' talak, that is, the mere pronouncement, orally or in writing, of a talak without any other formality – which is legally effective in some Islamic countries[146] – would amount to 'proceedings'. One view expressed in *Quazi v Quazi* was that 'any act or acts officially recognised as leading to a divorce in the country where the divorce was obtained'[147] amounted to proceedings; this would seem to include a bare talak. However, after conflicting decisions in the High Court,[148] it was held by the Court of Appeal in *Chaudhary v Chaudhary*[149] that a bare talak did

143 [1980] AC 744, [1979] 3 All ER 897.
144 Recognition of Divorces and Legal Separations Act 1971, s 2.
145 [1980] AC 744 at 784.
146 For example, Dubai (*Zaal v Zaal* (1982) 4 FLR 284); Iraq (*Sharif v Sharif* (1980) 10 Fam Law 216); Kashmir (*Re Fatima* [1986] AC 527, [1986] 2 All ER 32).
147 [1980] AC 744 at 824.
148 See cases cited in n 146 above.
149 [1985] Fam 19.

not amount to proceedings. In this case, the husband had gone from England to Kashmir to pronounce the talak three times orally. He did this before two witnesses in a mosque and reinforced it with a written document. These latter requirements are not required under the law of Kashmir under which bare talaks are permitted. Although the talak was pronounced in that part of Kashmir which is within the borders of Pakistan, the 1961 Ordinance does not extend to it and by Pakistani law the divorce was effective. As the husband was a national of Pakistan, the divorce would have qualified for recognition under the 1971 Act if it had been obtained by means of 'proceedings'. The Court of Appeal held that the divorce could not be recognised. 'Proceedings', it was held, does not include 'a private act conducted entirely by parties inter se or by one party alone' even if there are witnesses.[150] There must be 'a degree of formality and at least the involvement of some agency, whether lay or religious, of or recognised by the state as having a function that is more than simply probative'.[151] Accordingly, if the only requirement under the law of the country where the talak is pronounced is that there must be a set number of witnesses, this will not be enough to render the divorce one obtained by proceedings. It was added that what is critical is the elements required by the foreign law and whether they amount to proceedings. It is irrelevant if the parties, as in this case, go through extra solemnities not insisted upon by that law.

In *El Fadl v El Fadl*[152] the husband divorced his wife by talak in Lebanon. Under Lebanese law the husband is required to pronounce the words of the talak before two witnesses and then register the divorce before the Sharia court. Under Lebanese law some talaks are revocable while others are irrevocable. The Sharia court identified this divorce as irrevocable and recorded this fact. Even though the Sharia court has no power to grant or refuse a divorce, the fact that the process of identifying the type of talak had to be gone through and that formal declarations are taken and registered was enough to render the process 'proceedings'.

It follows from these cases that a wide range of talaks can be regarded as obtained by proceedings but there must be 'the intervention of some other body or person with a specific function to fulfil'.[153] However, 'bare talaks' where, for instance, the only legal requirement is that there be witnesses, do not qualify as 'proceedings'. The fact that not all talaks can be regarded as involving 'proceedings'

150 At 41.
151 Ibid.
152 [2000] 1 FLR 175.
153 Balcombe J in *Chaudhary v Chaudhary* [1985] Fam 19 at 46.

is further underlined by the fact that the Family Law Act 1986 expressly recognises a category of divorce that does not involve 'proceedings'. This would almost certainly include another kind of Islamic divorce, known as a khula.[154] This is a divorce by mutual consent: the wife makes a written statement that she wishes to end the marriage, and the husband accepts this in writing, in the presence of witnesses. On the tests stated in *Chaudhary v Chaudhary*, such a divorce would seem not to be obtained by proceedings.[155]

(iii) Extra-judicial divorces obtained by proceedings

If the divorce was obtained by means of 'proceedings', then the grounds of recognition are those which have already been considered: it will be recognised if either party was habitually resident or domiciled (in either the English or the foreign sense) in, or a national of, the country in which it was obtained, provided that it is effective under the law of that country. As with judicial divorces, it is not sufficient that it is recognised as valid by the laws of the parties' domiciles, if obtained elsewhere.

These rules indicate that it should be possible for English domiciliaries to obtain extra-judicial divorces in their country of nationality or habitual residence (or, indeed, in a country in which they are domiciled in that country's sense). However, it was indicated in *Chaudhary v Chaudhary*[156] that it would be contrary to public policy for English domiciliaries to go abroad and obtain a talak divorce. It is difficult to understand such reasoning. If (as in *Chaudhary*) a Muslim Pakistani national who is domiciled in England returns to his country of nationality and obtains a divorce in accordance with his religion, it hardly seems that any English interests are being sufficiently threatened to justify the invocation of the doctrine of public policy. Denying recognition in such cases amounts to little more than reintroducing the old common law rules based on domicile via the back door and ignoring the clear provisions of the 1986 Act to the effect that divorces should be recognised if obtained in the country of nationality or habitual residence – irrespective of the parties' domiciles. The real concern in *Chaudhary* appeared to be the desire to prevent English domiciliaries evading English law by travelling abroad to obtain a divorce leaving the wife destitute. This has become less of a problem since the entry into force of the Matrimonial and Family Proceedings Act 1984 under which the English court can itself make financial relief orders when recognising foreign divorces.

154 See *Quazi v Quazi* [1980] AC 744 at 820, 824.
155 Lord Scarman in *Quazi v Quazi* [1980] AC 744 at 824 had, however, thought to the contrary.
156 [1985] Fam 19 at 39–40,43–45,48.

(iv) Divorces obtained otherwise than by means of proceedings
If the extra-judicial divorce was not obtained by 'proceedings' then, according to section 46(2) of the Family Law Act 1986, it can be recognised only if it is effective under the law of the country in which it was obtained and at the date on which it was obtained:

> (b) (i) each party to the marriage was domiciled in that country; or
> (ii) either party to the marriage was domiciled in that country and the other party was domiciled in a country under whose law the divorce ... or legal separation is recognised as valid; and
> (c) neither party to the marriage was habitually resident in the United Kingdom throughout the period of one year immediately preceding that date.

For the purposes of section 46(2), 'domicile' means domicile according to either English law or the foreign law.[157]

The grounds for recognition of an extra-judicial divorce not obtained by proceedings are narrower than for a divorce, whether judicial or not, which is obtained by proceedings. It cannot be recognised on the ground that either party was habitually resident in, or a national of, the country, nor even on the ground that one of the parties was domiciled there (whether in the English or foreign sense) unless the divorce is recognised by the law of the domicile of the other party. It is not clear why, if such informal divorces are not thought fit for recognition if obtained in the country of habitual residence or nationality, they are thought fit for recognition if obtained in the country of domicile. The reason can hardly be the peculiar importance in English eyes of the domicile's view of status, because that primacy is no longer accepted in the Act's main provisions for recognition.

A literal interpretation of these provisions would suggest that an English domiciliary (in the English sense) can obtain such an extra-judicial divorce provided both parties are domiciled (in the foreign sense) in the country where the divorce was obtained.[158] For example, an English domiciliary (in the English sense) could obtain an extra-judicial divorce in Dubai which would be entitled to recognition if both parties were domiciled in Dubai according to the law of Dubai. More problematic is the case where one party is domiciled (in the foreign sense) in the country of divorce and the other is an English domiciliary (in the English sense) but is domiciled in a third country (in that country's sense) which recognises the

157 S 46(5).
158 Provided the argument above concerning the interpretation of *Chaudhary v Chaudhary* is accepted. See p 411.

divorce. For example, one party could be domiciled in Dubai according to the law of Dubai and there pronounce talak while the other party could be an English domiciliary (in the English sense) but domiciled in Sudan according to Sudanese law, which recognises the divorce. Again, a literal interpretation would dictate that, as the divorce is recognised as valid by the law of domicile (in either sense) of the other party (Sudanese law), it should be entitled to recognition in England. To assert that domicile in the English sense 'trumps' domicile in the foreign sense would involve a bold interpretation – but, given the dicta in *Chaudhary v Chaudhary*,[159] such a possibility cannot be discounted.

The reason for the additional requirement that neither party should have been habitually resident in the United Kingdom for a year immediately preceding the divorce is that if either had been so resident, then a United Kingdom court would have had jurisdiction to grant a divorce before the coming into force of the Brussels II Regulation. This was thought to be the proper avenue for the applicant in such a case to follow, even if it was not the applicant who was habitually resident in the United Kingdom.[160]

(v) Transnational divorces

A transnational divorce is one where some steps towards the divorce occur in one country and other steps are performed in another country. Suppose, for example, a husband, being a national of Pakistan, pronounces the talak in England, and then, in terms of the Pakistan Ordinance, sends notice of it to the chairman of the union council in Pakistan, with a copy to his wife there; the arbitration council is set up in Pakistan and the talak is not revoked, and so the divorce becomes effective by Pakistani law. In such cases it is important to determine where the divorce is obtained as section 44 of the Family Law Act 1986 provides that no extra-judicial divorce obtained in the British Islands shall be regarded as effective. Only 'overseas'[161] extra-judicial divorces are entitled to recognition. Or, alternatively, suppose the same husband pronounces the talak in Iraq, under whose law it would be an effective divorce and sends the appropriate notices to Pakistan. Can such transnational divorces be recognised?

To decide the effect in England of a transnational divorce it is necessary again to distinguish divorces obtained by proceedings from those obtained otherwise than by means of proceedings.

159 [1985] Fam 19.

160 Young, 'The Recognition of Extra-Judicial Divorces in the UK' (1987) 7 LS 78 at 85–86.

161 Family Law Act 1986, s 46.

a. Divorces obtained by proceedings

In *Re Fatima*[162] the husband pronounced talak in England and sent the appropriate notices to Pakistan, the country of his nationality. On an interpretation of section 3 of the Recognition of Divorces and Judicial Separations Act 1971 which required him to have been a national of Pakistan 'at the date of the institution of the proceedings in the country in which is was obtained' it was held that the 'institution of the proceedings' was inextricably linked to the 'obtaining' of the overseas divorce and, accordingly, both had to take place in the same country. The proceedings had been instituted in England; the divorce could not be recognised.[163] The wording of the Family Law Act 1986, however, is different in that it simply requires one of the parties to be habitually resident or domiciled in or a national of the overseas country at the 'date of the commencement of the proceedings'[164] and, additionally, specifies that the divorce must be 'effective under the law of the country in which it was obtained'.[165] Arguably, this could mean that if, as in *Fatima*, the husband was a national of Pakistan when he pronounced the talak (albeit in England) and the divorce was 'obtained' in Pakistan, it should be entitled to recognition. However, in *Berkovits v Grinberg*[166] it was held that transnational divorces could still not be recognised. In this case the Jewish get of divorce was written in England and then delivered to the wife in Israel, the country of both parties' nationality. Wall J accepted the expert evidence that the divorce was only final when the wife received the letter of get. However, he concluded that the word 'obtained' connoted a process rather than a single act: 'To obtain a divorce a party must go through a process, in the same way that a person obtains a university degree.'[167] The writing of the get in England was an integral part of the process. This process (the 'proceedings') had to be instituted in the same country in which the divorce was obtained. From this it follows that no transnational divorces obtained by proceedings, whether get or talak, whether initiated in England or another country, is entitled to recognition.

162 [1986] AC 527.

163 See also *Maples v Melamud* [1988] Fam 14, [1988] 1 FLR 43 where a get was executed and received by the wife in England. This divorce was clearly obtained in England. It was not a transnational divorce as the confirmation of the get by a court in Israel was not part of the process by which the divorce was obtained.

164 S 46(3)(a).

165 S 46(1)(a).

166 [1995] Fam 142.

167 At 157.

This conclusion, which has 'far-reaching implications for the Jewish community in the United Kingdom, and also for the Muslims and other communities'[168] living here, has little to commend it. Nothing in the statute dictates that the proceedings must have been commenced in the country where the divorce was obtained. To pursue Wall J's metaphor: under a modularised system a degree may be commenced at one university and obtained at another. More significantly, in policy terms, the result is that the rich who can afford to fly to Pakistan or Israel to pronounce talak or write a get can 'buy' recognition of their divorce. The ordinary person, like Mr Grinberg who complies with the laws of his religion and the country of his nationality (a recognised basis for recognition under the 1986 Act), finds himself in a limping marriage and Mrs Grinberg is placed 'in an extremely vulnerable position, and one she could hardly have anticipated or desired'.[169]

b. Divorces obtained otherwise than by means of proceedings

Such divorces can be recognised if each party is domiciled in the country where the divorce is obtained at the date on which it is obtained (or one party is domiciled there and the divorce is recognised by the other party's law of domicile).[170] As there are no proceedings to be commenced, the issue here is simpler: where is the divorce 'obtained'?

There is little direct authority on the point but it would appear that most bare talaks are obtained where they are pronounced;[171] any further steps, such as sending notice to the wife, are not an integral part of the divorce. Accordingly, such divorces can be obtained only in the country where the talak is pronounced and cannot be 'transnational'. However, it is arguable that the necessary steps for obtaining a khula could straddle more than one country. A khula would appear to be obtained where the husband accepts the wife's divorce proposal and utters the word 'khul'.[172] So, if a wife in Thailand e-mails her husband in Dubai asking for a divorce and he accepts the proposal and utters the words there, the divorce would appear to have been obtained in Dubai and if both parties are domiciled in Dubai or one of them is domiciled there and the divorce is recognised by the other party's domiciliary law, the divorce is entitled to recognition in England.

168 Reed, 'Extra-Judicial Divorces since *Berkovits*' [1996] Fam Law 100 at 103.

169 *Berkovits v Grinberg* [1995] Fam 142 at 159, citing evidence from the expert witness.

170 Family Law Act 1986, s 46(2) and s 46(3)(b).

171 *R v Registrar General of Births, Deaths and Marriages, ex p Minhas* [1977] QB 1 at 5–6; *Sulaiman v Juffali* [2002] 1 FLR 479.

172 Abdur Rahman I Doi, *Shariah: The Islamic Law* (1984) p 192.

Given the present denial of recognition to extra-judicial transnational divorces obtained by proceedings, it is odd – and little more than a quirk of statutory interpretation – that such 'bare' transnational divorces involving, if anything, less protection for the rights of wives, should so easily be entitled to recognition.

(c) REFUSAL OF RECOGNITION

The grounds on which judgments from non-member states and Denmark may be refused recognition are discretionary rather than mandatory and are contained in the Family Law Act 1986.

(i) Marriage void or previously annulled or dissolved

Under section 51(1) and (2) of the Family Law Act 1986, the court may refuse to recognise a British Isles or overseas divorce or legal separation if, at the time it was obtained, the marriage had already been annulled or dissolved by the English court, or by another court whose decree is recognised, or entitled to recognition, in England, or if the marriage was a nullity in the eyes of English conflict of laws rules even without any such decree. Obviously, a divorce cannot effectively dissolve a marriage which is void or has already been annulled or dissolved.

(ii) Divorce obtained contrary to natural justice

This ground for refusal of recognition applies only to overseas divorces and legal separations.

a. Reasonable steps for giving notice

Section 51(3)(a)(i) of the Family Law Act 1986 deals with the failure to afford a party to the marriage a proper opportunity to contest the proceedings. In the case of a divorce or legal separation obtained by proceedings, recognition may be refused if it was obtained:

> without such steps having been taken for giving notice of the proceedings to a party to the marriage as, having regard to the nature of the proceedings and all the circumstances, should reasonably have been taken.

There is no requirement that a party should actually have received notice. Sometimes the whereabouts of the respondent will be unknown to the applicant and some form of non-personal service, such as publication in a newspaper, may then be allowed. Inevitably, there will be cases where a spouse is divorced without knowing of the proceedings. However, the court may refuse recognition if in its view such steps for giving notice have not been taken as reasonably should have been taken in the circumstances. This ground for refusing recognition has been narrowly confined: there must be a 'fundamental' breach of natural justice.[173] Further, the mere fact that this provision has not been complied with is not determinative of the issue; it simply generates a discretion on the part of the English court as to whether to recognise the foreign divorce.

In *Sabbagh v Sabbagh*[174] a wife in England who received notice of her husband's initial unsuccessful application for a decree of separation in Brazil received no notice of his appeal (that was successful) which, in accordance with Brazilian law, was only published in the official gazette in Brazil – a publication 'not normally circulated in Hendon',[175] where she lived. It was held that, despite the Brazilian procedures having been properly complied with, she had not received reasonable notice. However, the court refused to exercise its discretion to refuse recognition to the decree because, in all the circumstances, she had not been prejudiced as she had already made a decision not to take part in the proceedings. In *D v D*[176] the husband, a Ghanaian national, left his wife in England and went to Ghana where he obtained a divorce from the Customary Arbitration Tribunal without informing his wife. The wife's mother was the defendant in the proceedings which can be permissible under Ghanaian law as the proper parties to the proceedings are the families themselves and not the married couple. However, it was held that the court had to apply the English concept of reasonableness, having regard to the nature of the Ghanaian proceedings. On this basis,[177] especially as the mother had objected to the lack of notice to her daughter, the court decided that reasonable steps for notifying the wife had not been taken.

b. Opportunity to take part

Section 51(3)(a)(ii) of the Family Law Act 1986 provides that a divorce or legal separation may be denied recognition if it was obtained:

> without a party to the marriage having been given (for any reason other than lack of notice) such opportunity to take part in the proceedings as, having regard to those matters, he should reasonably have been given.

An example of a case falling within this provision is *Joyce v Joyce*.[178] A wife in England had been given notice of proceedings in Quebec,

173 *B v B (Divorce: Northern Cyprus)* [2001] 3 FCR 331.
174 [1985] FLR 29.
175 At 32.
176 [1994] 1 FLR 38.
177 It was also held that the divorce was not effective under Ghanaian law. See p 404.
178 [1979] Fam 93, [1979] 2 All ER 156.

but despite letters by her English solicitors to the registrar of the court, the husband's lawyers, the Quebec Law Society and the legal aid authorities there, all stating that she wished to contest the proceedings, the case continued without her being represented, and a decree was granted to the husband in default. It was held that the wife had not been given such opportunity to take part in the proceedings as she should reasonably have been given.[179]

What is the position of a spouse in England who receives adequate notice of foreign divorce proceedings but cannot afford to travel to the foreign country to defend the action? In *Mamdani v Mamdani*[180] it was held that an inability to afford to go to the foreign country to defend proceedings and a lack of legal aid available there were relevant considerations in determining whether a spouse had been given a reasonable opportunity to take part in the proceedings. Even more weight is attached to this point if the lack of finances is attributable to the other spouse's failure to make maintenance payments.[181] However, in *Sabbagh v Sabbagh*[182] it was concluded that an impecunious wife had not been denied an opportunity to take part in the proceedings because her physical presence was not required and she had made no attempt to apply for legal aid or seek financial assistance from her family.

(iii) Public policy

Under section 51(3)(c) of the Family Law Act 1986, recognition of a divorce or legal separation, whether or not obtained by means of proceedings, may be refused if recognition 'would be manifestly contrary to public policy'. Public policy is always to be used sparingly in the conflict of laws and the word 'manifestly' emphasises that this is 'a very high hurdle to clear'.[183]

There is no closed or definitive list of the kinds of case which can offend public policy.[184] At common law it was settled that fraud in the foreign court as to the merits would not bar recognition,[185] but fraud as to the jurisdiction of the foreign court would result in

179 See also, to similar effect, *Newmarch v Newmarch* [1978] Fam 79, [1978] 1 All ER 1.
180 [1984] FLR 699.
181 *Joyce v Joyce* [1979] Fam 93, [1979] 2 All ER 156.
182 [1985] FLR 29.
183 *Kellman v Kellman* [2000] 1 FLR 785 at 798.
184 In *B v B (Divorce: Northern Cyprus)* [2001] 3 FCR 331 a divorce obtained in the Turkish Republic of Northern Cyprus was refused recognition on this ground because that country had never been recognised by the UK. However, this approach was not followed in *Emin v Yeldag (A-G and Secretary of State for Foreign and Commonwealth Affairs intervening)* [2002] Fam Law 419, where such a divorce was recognised.
185 *Bater v Bater* [1906] P 209.

recognition being refused.[186] Under the Act it would seem that fraud can be a ground for a refusal of recognition only if one party deceived the other and the foreign court.[187] In *Kendall v Kendall*[188] the husband fraudulently procured the commencement of proceedings in Bolivia purportedly by the wife without her knowledge, by getting her to sign a document which he told her was to enable her to take the children out of Bolivia, but in fact was a power of attorney in favour of Bolivian lawyers to start divorce proceedings on her behalf. A divorce was then granted, purportedly to the wife, by the Bolivian court on the basis of false evidence by witnesses that they had seen the husband assault the wife. Not surprisingly, the English court held that it would be manifestly contrary to public policy to recognise the divorce. Here the fraud was more fundamental than fraud as to the merits or as to the court's jurisdiction. The very proceedings themselves were a fraud on the wife and the Bolivian court. In *Eroglu v Eroglu*[189] the husband and wife, acting together, deceived a Turkish court into granting them a divorce on grounds of extreme incompatibility. The parties continued to live together for the next 12 years during which time children were born. The reason for this 'divorce of convenience' was that under the then Turkish law university graduates were entitled to privileged and abbreviated national service provided they were not married to a foreign national; the wife was British. It was held that recognition of this divorce was not manifestly contrary to public policy. While the Turkish court might have been deceived, neither of the parties was deceived and the motive for obtaining a divorce was 'generally irrelevant' and the discretion to refuse recognition was to be 'exercised sparingly'.[190] Thorpe J concluded that:

> Those who play games with divorce decrees expose themselves to a variety of risks and, having enjoyed the desired benefits during cohabitation, cannot reorder their status now that they have fallen out.[191]

Another situation in which recognition of a divorce may be refused is if the institution of the proceedings was the result of duress. In the common law case of *Re Meyer*[192] the parties were Germans, the husband, but not the wife, being Jewish. In 1938, when Jews were being persecuted in Germany, the husband escaped to England.

186 *Middleton v Middleton* [1967] P 62, [1966] 1 All ER 168.
187 *Eroglu Eroglu* [1994] 2 FLR 287 at 289.
188 [1977] Fam 208, [1977] 3 All ER 471.
189 [1994] 2 FLR 287.
190 At 289.
191 At 290.
192 [1971] P 298, [1971] 1 All ER 378.

The wife then divorced him in the German court, as arranged between them before he left. The necessity for the divorce was that if she remained married to a Jew, she herself would be in danger, would lose her job and her flat, and it would be difficult for her and their child to survive. After the war, the wife joined the husband in England, where they regarded themselves as still husband and wife. On the husband's death, the wife's right to a German pension as the widow of a person who had been persecuted by the Nazis depended on whether, in the view of the English court, she was still married to her husband at his death. The court granted a declaration that the German divorce was not recognised in England because it had been obtained under duress. No doubt under the Act the recognition of a divorce obtained in such circumstances would be regarded as manifestly contrary to public policy.

(iv) Discretion

Even if a foreign divorce has been obtained without reasonable steps having been taken to give a party notice of the proceedings, or without a party having been given a reasonable opportunity to take part, or if recognition would be contrary to public policy, recognition need not necessarily be refused. The court has a discretion, for the Family Law Act 1986 provides that recognition 'may be refused'.[193]

In exercising its discretion, the court will have regard to what will be just as between the spouses, and to the interests of any children of the marriage. The decision has often turned on the question of financial provision, because usually the objective of a party who contests divorce proceedings is to secure a satisfactory financial and property settlement rather than to keep the marriage going. In *Newmarch v Newmarch*[194] the wife's solicitors in England instructed solicitors in New South Wales to file an answer to the husband's case in proceedings which he had instituted there. The Australian solicitors failed to do so, and the divorce was granted in default. Although the English court held that the wife had not been given a reasonable opportunity to take part in the proceedings, it nevertheless exercised its discretion to recognise the divorce. The wife's object in wishing to contest the divorce had been to obtain adequate maintenance from her husband. As the English court would be in a position to order such maintenance[195] even if the Australian divorce was recognised, no one's interests would be served by refusing recognition.

193 S 51(3).
194 [1978] Fam 79, [1978] 1 All ER 1.
195 An English interim maintenance order which could be converted to a substantive maintenance order had been obtained by the wife prior to the Australian divorce.

On the other hand, in *Joyce v Joyce*,[196] where the wife had not been given the opportunity to take part in the Quebec proceedings, the court exercised its discretion to refuse recognition, because, as the law then stood, the wife would otherwise be deprived of the possibility of financial and property relief in the English court. As seen above, similar considerations were also taken into account in deciding whether public policy required the withholding of recognition from talak divorces. Now that the court has power to make financial orders even after the recognition of a foreign divorce obtained by proceedings, the discretion to refuse recognition, when it exists, will probably be used less frequently.

Can circumstances and events happening after the foreign divorce, perhaps even years later, be taken into account in deciding whether to refuse recognition? Suppose, for example, that in *Kendall v Kendall*,[197] in which the divorce proceedings and the decree were procured by the husband's fraud, the wife, when she learned about the divorce, had been willing to accept the situation, and even remarried on the strength of the divorce. Would the English court still refuse recognition on grounds of public policy, thus invalidating the innocent wife's remarriage in English eyes? That would be to penalise the wife for the husband's fraud. It might be argued that a divorce must in the eyes of English law be either valid or invalid at its inception; it cannot be initially invalid because of the fraud and then become valid if years later an innocent party remarries. In practice, however, no real difficulty is likely to arise from taking later events into account, for usually the status would only need to be legally determined when the question of recognition comes before the court.

There are indications in the cases that the courts will indeed take subsequent events into account. In *Hornett v Hornett*[198] the wife had obtained a divorce in France, although the husband in England had not received notice of the proceedings. Subsequently the parties had lived together again in England as husband and wife for many years, ignoring the French divorce. Eventually they parted again, and the husband wished to remarry. The court had to decide whether the French divorce was to be recognised in England, in view of the failure to give notice to the husband. In exercising its discretion to recognise it, the court took into account all the subsequent happenings. It was indicated that if recognition of the divorce would have caused injustice (for example, if the parties had had children while they were living together after the divorce, who would be

196 [1979] Fam 93, [1979] 2 All ER 156.
197 [1977] Fam 208, [1977] 3 All ER 471.
198 [1971] P 255, [1971] 1 All ER 98.

illegitimate if the divorce was recognised) recognition would have been refused. Again, in *Re Meyer*[199] it was clear that the court was moved by the wife's situation subsequent to the divorce and it was inevitable that it would exercise its discretion in a manner that would benefit her. Had the circumstances been different (for example, if it had been in the wife's interests to have the divorce recognised) the same result would not necessarily have been reached. It thus seems that subsequent events, as well as the circumstances existing at the time of the divorce itself, can be taken into account in deciding how to exercise the discretion whether or not to recognise a foreign divorce.

(v) Extra-judicial divorces

Most of the above grounds for refusing recognition of foreign divorces apply to extra-judicial divorces that are obtained by proceedings. However, the application of these rules is somewhat different.

a. Divorces obtained contrary to natural justice

Section 51(3)(a)(i) (lack of notice) and section 51(3)(a)(ii) (lack of opportunity to take part) of the Family Law Act 1986 apply only to divorces and legal separations obtained by means of proceedings. With regard to extra-judicial divorces obtained by proceedings, such as a talak obtained under the Pakistan Ordinance, it must be recalled that the question is to be judged 'having regard to the nature of the proceedings and all the circumstances'. Accordingly, it seems unlikely that recognition would be refused if the requirements of the Pakistan Ordinance were complied with. Indeed, in *D v D*[200] it was said that it was 'possible ... to envisage circumstances, albeit they would be highly unusual, in which it would be reasonable to take no steps'.[201] In *El Fadl v El Fadl*[202] it was held that whether advance notice of a talak should reasonably be given depended on the circumstances. Dealing with a Lebanese talak[203] it was held that, despite being a 'wrong' to the wife, the absence of notice ought not to lead to refusal of recognition for several reasons. First, advance notice could avail the wife nothing. Secondly, although not informed at the time of the talak, the wife had known of the divorce for many years. Thirdly, and most interestingly, as the divorce was obtained in the country where both spouses were domiciled, it was

199 [1971] P 298, [1971] 1 All ER 378.
200 [1994] 1 FLR 38.
201 At 52.
202 [2000] 1 FLR 175.
203 See p 410.

'accomplished in the forum which was the natural forum for both parties. There was no forum shopping.'[204] This is a somewhat surprising basis for the decision. The 1986 Act has specified that for divorces obtained by proceedings, the courts of the habitual residence, domicile or nationality of either party are a sufficiently appropriate forum to justify recognition. There is no warrant for elevating domicile (or the domicile of both parties) to a privileged category in interpreting the provisions of the Act.

The statutory provisions relating to natural justice do not apply to divorces obtained otherwise than by means of proceedings. It is suggested that in such cases recognition could not be refused on the grounds that no notice was given to the wife of the husband's intention to divorce her or that she was denied a reasonable opportunity to be involved in the process. The nature of such a talak is that it is a purely unilateral act.

b. Public policy

It follows from the fact that the law provides for the recognition of extra-judicial divorces that such recognition is not necessarily contrary to public policy. In *El Fadl v El Fadl*[205] the absence of notice to a wife was described as offending English sensibilities but the doctrine of public policy was to be used sparingly and accordingly 'comity between nations and belief systems requires ... that our courts should accept the conscientiously held but very different standards of another where they are applied to those who are domiciled in it'.[206]

However, while this might be the approach in relation to people domiciled in the country where the divorce was obtained and where there is 'no evidence of forum shopping',[207] it has been stated that recognition of such a divorce, obtained by an English domiciliary, is contrary to public policy.[208] As has already been argued, this approach is misguided for two reasons. First, the Family Law Act 1986 draws no distinction between divorces obtained in the country of habitual residence, domicile or nationality. It is a misunderstanding of the policy of the Act to treat persons domiciled in the other country differently from those habitually resident there or nationals of the country. Secondly, the main concern in *Chaudhary v Chaudhary* was to ensure the wife received financial relief; this could only be achieved then if the divorce were not recognised and a divorce was

204 At 189.
205 [2000] 1 FLR 175.
206 At 190.
207 At 191.
208 *Chaudhary v Chaudhary* [1985] Fam 19, [1984] 3 All ER 1017. See p 411.

instead granted by the English court. Since the English court now has power to grant such relief when recognising foreign divorces obtained by proceedings, it is unlikely that the doctrine of public policy would still be invoked.[209] However, the power of the English court to grant financial relief is limited to cases where the foreign divorce was obtained by proceedings.[210] It is possible, of course, that the expression 'proceedings' could be construed more broadly in cases where it is thought appropriate to grant financial relief.[211] However, where the foreign divorce has been obtained by means other than proceedings (for example, a bare talak), it is possible that the doctrine of public policy could still be invoked in a case involving English domiciliaries or persons with close links with England.

c. No official document for divorces obtained otherwise than by means of proceedings

With regard to divorces not obtained by means of proceedings, the court may refuse to recognise a divorce if there is no official document certifying that the divorce is effective under the law of the country in which it was obtained, or, where one of the parties was domiciled in another country when it was obtained, no official document certifying that it is valid under the law of that country.[212] An official document means one issued by a person or body appointed or recognised for the purpose under the foreign law. As the power to refuse recognition if there is no official document is discretionary, the court could still recognise the divorce if satisfied by expert evidence of its efficacy under the foreign law.[213]

(vi) Divorces obtained before the commencement of the Family Law Act 1986

The provisions of the Family Law Act 1986 apply to British Isles and overseas divorces obtained before as well as after the date of its commencement. However, a divorce obtained before that date which was recognised under the law as it then was remains entitled to such recognition, even if it would not otherwise be entitled to recognition under the Act.[214] The main cases are divorces obtained in a country in which neither party was domiciled at the date of the commencement of the proceedings, but recognised as valid by the

209 This point was recognised in *El Fadl v El Fadl* [2000] 1 FLR 175.
210 It seems to be an error that the power is limited to divorces obtained by proceedings. For the probable reason, see Poulter, 'Recognition of Foreign Divorces – The New Law' (1987) 84 *Law Society Gazette* 253 at 255.
211 *El Fadl v El Fadl* [2000] 1 FLR 175 at 191.
212 S 51(3)(b) and (4).
213 *Wicken v Wicken* [1999] Fam 224.
214 S 52.

law of the country or countries in which they were domiciled,[215] and extra-judicial divorces obtained in the British Isles before 1 January 1974 and recognised as valid by the laws of each party's domicile at the time they were obtained.[216]

B Nullity decrees

1. Grounds of recognition

Under the common law the grounds for recognition of foreign nullity decrees were, for the most part, based on the theory of equivalence: a foreign decree should be recognised if the English court in equivalent circumstances would itself have exercised jurisdiction. In addition, there was a blanket ground that a decree should be recognised if either party had a real and substantial connection with the country in question.[217]

These common law grounds for recognition were unaffected by the Recognition of Divorces and Judicial Separations Act 1971. It was, of course, undesirable and unjustifiable to have different rules for recognition of divorces and judicial separations, on the one hand, and recognition of nullity decrees, on the other. So, the Family Law Act 1986 abolished the common law rules on recognition of nullity decrees and applied the same rules to recognition of all three types of decree. Similarly, the Brussels II Regulation draws no distinction between the various decrees.

Accordingly, the grounds of recognition of foreign nullity decrees are exactly the same as those for the recognition of divorces, even to the extent of the distinction between those obtained by means of proceedings and those not so obtained. So, as with the recognition of divorces, there are now two regimes: the Brussels II Regulation governs judgments from the courts of member states (other than Denmark) and the Family Law Act 1986 applies in all other cases. However, recognition of nullity decrees can give rise to issues somewhat different from recognition of divorces.

2. The effect of recognition

The notion of recognising a foreign nullity decree, though certainly accepted by the law, is not without difficulties. If a foreign court

215 Entitled to recognition under the Recognition of Divorces and Judicial Separations Act 1971, s 6.

216 Entitled to recognition at common law prior to coming into force of Domicile and Matrimonial Proceedings Act 1973, s 16(1).

217 See, generally, Clarkson, 'Recognition of Foreign Nullity Decrees in Singapore' (1987) 8 Sing LR 166.

annuls a marriage on the ground that it is void (under whatever is the governing law according to the foreign court's conflicts rules), it may be that the marriage is also void under English conflict of laws rules. Then no difficulty arises from recognising the decree, and duplication of proceedings in England is avoided. However, it may be that the marriage is valid under English conflict of laws rules. It is well established that even in such a case the foreign decree can be recognised. Thus in *Merker v Merker*[218] a marriage was annulled by a decree of the German court on the ground that the requisite formalities under German conflict of laws rules had not been complied with. The decree was recognised, even though the marriage was formally valid under English conflicts rules. Such recognition means that, in effect, the foreign country's choice of law rules have superseded the English ones.

The reason for recognising the foreign decree in such a case is no doubt to ensure uniformity of status. If the court of a country having a reasonable connection with one of the parties has decreed that the marriage is invalid, the English court should not create a limping marriage by insisting that it is valid. That is no doubt right, so far as the future is concerned. If, however, the foreign court by its nullity decree has pronounced a marriage void ab initio, then the effect of recognising it is to render the marriage void ab initio in England. In *Salvesen (or von Lorang) v Austrian Property Administrator*[219] the effect of recognising a German decree declaring a marriage void ab initio, made 27 years after the marriage, was that the wife had not after all become an Austrian national by virtue of the marriage. If the marriage which is declared void ab initio by the foreign decree is valid by English conflicts rules, its recognition can retrospectively nullify rights which have hitherto existed in English eyes.[220]

Suppose that while still married to one wife a man marries another, and then dies intestate domiciled in England. His widow is entitled to succeed to his estate. If the first marriage is valid under English conflicts rules, it follows that the second marriage is void for bigamy. The first wife is therefore entitled to succeed, and it makes no difference that by the conflicts rules of some other country the first marriage is void, and the second valid. Is it right that the first wife should be disinherited by the husband's obtaining, after his second marriage, a decree in a foreign country declaring that, according to its conflicts rules, his first marriage was void ab initio?

218 [1963] P 283, [1962] 3 All ER 928.
219 [1927] AC 641.
220 But in *Salvesen (or von Lorang)* itself the retrospective effect of the German annulment secured for the wife a benefit which she wanted (although it seems that the marriage was in any event void under English conflicts rules).

Such a result would be avoided if the rule were adopted that the recognition of foreign nullity decrees does not operate retrospectively, and the question of the validity of the marriage as at any earlier date than the decree is to be decided by the English court according to the English conflict of laws.[221] However, given the relatively clear provisions of the Brussels II Regulation and the Family Law Act 1986, it is extremely doubtful whether such an approach is permissible. One possible solution could be to declare the foreign annulment contrary to public policy.[222] However, this would mean denying recognition to the nullity decree completely, rather than simply denying the retrospective operation of the decree.

3. *Refusal of recognition*

The grounds for refusing recognition to a nullity decree which is prima facie entitled to recognition are the same as for a divorce decree, though the different nature of the decree may lead to differences in their operation.

(A) IRRECONCILABLE WITH A PREVIOUS DECISION

A British Isles or overseas annulment may be refused recognition in England if it was granted at a time when it was irreconcilable with a decision determining the question of the subsistence or validity of the marriage of the parties previously given by a court in England, or by a court elsewhere and recognised in England.[223] So, if in English nullity proceedings it is contended that a marriage is invalid on a particular ground, but the marriage is held valid, then a subsequent foreign annulment may be refused recognition if granted on that ground. The mere fact that the marriage was valid according to English conflict of laws rules does not preclude recognition, but if the English court has actually held it to be valid, recognition may be refused.

While this ground of refusal is mandatory under the Brussels II Regulation, it is discretionary under the Family Law Act 1986. It is suggested that the discretion to refuse recognition should be exercised if the foreign decree declares void ab initio a marriage which is valid by English conflicts rules and the consequent retrospective invalidation of the marriage would alter rights or entitlements which would exist on the basis of the marriage's being valid. An example

221 Though findings of fact in the foreign court should perhaps be conclusive in the English court on the basis of issue estoppel.
222 See p 429.
223 Brussels II Regulation, art 15(1)(c); Family Law Act 1986, s 51(1).

is *Vervaeke v Smith*[224] in which the House of Lords held, before the enactment of the 1986 Act, that this ground of refusal of recognition existed at common law as an aspect of estoppel per rem judicatem.

The petitioner, a Belgian national, had married her first husband in England. It was a marriage of convenience, for it was never the parties' intention to live together as husband and wife. The husband was paid a sum of money and emigrated immediately after the marriage. The object was solely to obtain United Kingdom citizenship for the petitioner by virtue of the marriage so that she could continue her trade as a prostitute in this country. Some years later, this first marriage not having been dissolved, the petitioner married a second husband who died intestate on his wedding night. Wishing to succeed to his estate as his widow, she brought proceedings in the English court for an annulment of her first marriage on various grounds, one being lack of consent. The English court, however, dismissed the petition, holding the marriage valid. Then, after she had been habitually resident in Belgium for over a year, she obtained a decree in the Belgian court declaring the marriage void for lack of consent. The ground for the annulment was that under Belgian law, which was applicable under the Belgian conflicts rules, a marriage in which the parties never intend to cohabit is void ab initio for lack of consent. Under English law, which had been applicable according to English conflicts rules in the earlier English proceedings, such a marriage of convenience is valid.[225] When the petitioner sought a declaration in the English courts that the Belgian decree should be recognised (with the consequence that, the second marriage being valid, she could succeed to her second husband's estate), recognition was refused. One of the grounds was that under the doctrine of res judicata recognition would be incompatible with the prior English decision. The same result would clearly be reached under the 1986 Act.

(B) CONTRARY TO NATURAL JUSTICE

Under the Brussels II Regulation the same provision relating to inadequate service applies as for divorce decrees.[226] Under the Family Law Act 1986 the court has the same discretion to refuse recognition if the decree was obtained without reasonable steps having been taken to notify the respondent of the proceedings, or

224 [1983] 1 AC 145, [1982] 2 All ER 144.

225 As the parties had married in England and the first husband was an English domiciliary, the wife's incapacity under Belgian law could be disregarded under *Sottemayer v De Barros (No 2)* (1879) 5 PD 94. See p 333.

226 Art 15(1)(b).

without his being given reasonable opportunity to take part in them, as in the case of a foreign divorce.[227]

(C) PUBLIC POLICY

Recognition may be refused if it would be manifestly contrary to public policy.[228] No doubt fraud or duress would lead to refusal to the same extent as with a divorce. Under the Brussels II Regulation recognition may not be refused to an annulment because the law of the state in which recognition is sought would not allow an annulment on the same facts.[229] However, under the Family Law Act 1986 public policy may lead to a refusal to recognise a nullity decree because the foreign rule by which the marriage is invalid is objectionable. Although recognition will not normally be refused to a divorce merely because the ground of divorce is objectionable (for example, the husband's unilateral repudiation of his wife by talak), a different approach to nullity decrees may be justified by the fact that the recognition of a foreign nullity decree may have the effect of retrospectively invalidating a marriage which is valid according to English choice of law rules.

In *Gray v Formosa*[230] the husband, who was a Roman Catholic domiciled in Malta, married a woman domiciled in England at an English register office. Subsequently, the husband deserted his wife and children, leaving them without support in England, and returned to Malta. There he obtained a nullity decree, granted on the ground that under Maltese law a Roman Catholic could not validly marry except by a religious ceremony. By Maltese conflicts rules this incapacity was applicable even to a marriage celebrated in England. The Court of Appeal refused to recognise the Maltese decree on the ground that to do so would be contrary to substantial justice. The marriage was, of course, valid by English conflicts rules, under which the question whether a civil as opposed to a religious ceremony is sufficient is regarded as one of form, governed by the lex loci celebrationis. Recognition was not refused merely because the marriage was valid under English conflicts rules, but because it was:

> an intolerable injustice that a system of law should seek to impose extraterritorially, as the condition of the validity of a marriage, that it should take place according to the tenets of a particular faith.[231]

227 Family Law Act 1986, s 51(3)(a).
228 Brussels II Regulation, art 15(1)(a); Family Law Act 1986, s 51(3)(c).
229 Art 18.
230 [1963] P 259, [1962] 3 All ER 419.
231 Simon P in *Lepre v Lepre* [1965] P 52 at 64, explaining the basis of the decision in *Gray v Formosa* [1963] P 259, [1962] 3 All ER 419.

In *Gray v Formosa* it was the foreign country's conflicts rule, that the Maltese requirement of a church marriage applied to a marriage celebrated in England, which was thought objectionable. In *Vervaeke v Smith*[232] a second reason for refusing recognition to the Belgian decree was that recognition would be contrary to public policy. Here it was not the Belgian conflicts rule that was the obstacle, but the Belgian domestic rule by which a marriage under which the parties never intend to cohabit is void. By English law, on the contrary, such a marriage is valid. Lord Hailsham held that, as the English rule is one of public policy, it would be contrary to public policy to recognise the Belgian decree declaring void such a marriage which was celebrated in, and had other connections with, England. Bearing in mind the very narrow scope of the doctrine of public policy in English conflict of laws, this conclusion seems unwarranted. Given that, on the facts of the case, the doctrine of res judicata dictated that the Belgian decree should be denied recognition,[233] there was no need for the doctrine of public policy to have been invoked.

(D) DECREE INVALID UNDER THE FOREIGN LAW

At common law, if a foreign nullity decree was invalid under the law of the foreign country in which it was obtained, it would nevertheless be entitled to recognition in England if the reason for the invalidity was a mere procedural defect,[234] but not if the reason was that the court was not competent to grant a nullity decree.[235] Under the Family Law Act 1986, however, the decree can only be recognised if it is effective under the law of the country in which it was obtained.[236] It makes no difference what the basis of the invalidity is under the foreign law.

IV FINANCIAL PROVISION

A Jurisdiction of the English court

English courts have power to make orders for financial provision in three situations. First, such an order can be made ancillary to the granting of a divorce, separation or annulment. Secondly, financial provision may be ordered quite independently of other matrimonial

232 [1983] 1 AC 145, [1982] 2 All ER 144.
233 See p 428.
234 *Merker v Merker* [1963] P 283, [1962] 3 All ER 928.
235 *Papadopoulos v Papadopoulos* [1930] P 55.
236 Family Law Act 1986, s 46(1)(a), (2)(a).

proceedings in situations where the parties are still married but one spouse is failing to provide reasonable maintenance to the other spouse and/or children of the family. Thirdly, when recognising a foreign divorce, legal separation or annulment, the English court has power itself to grant financial provision to either party.

The Brussels II Regulation has no application here as it does not affect 'property consequences of the marriage, the maintenance obligation or any other ancillary measures'.[237] The jurisdictional rules explored earlier in this chapter are not affected by the Brussels I Regulation,[238] which does not apply to the 'status or legal capacity of natural persons, [and] rights in property arising out of a matrimonial relationship'.[239] However, under article 5(2) the Brussels I Regulation applies to 'matters relating to maintenance'. Accordingly, as with civil and commercial claims, the jurisdictional rules of the English court here are a blend of the English traditional rules and the Brussels I Regulation.

1. *Ancillary relief*

When the English court has jurisdiction to grant a divorce, separation or annulment, it also has jurisdiction to make an order for maintenance or other financial provision, or the adjustment of property rights as between the parties and for the benefit of the children of the marriage. These jurisdictional rules are unaffected by the Brussels I Regulation as article 5(2) confers jurisdiction on the English court if the maintenance proceedings are ancillary to 'proceedings concerning the status of a person' (that is, proceedings for divorce, annulment and, perhaps, separation) provided the English court has jurisdiction under its own rules. However, because matters of 'maintenance'[240] are within the scope of the Brussels I Regulation, the English court's ancillary jurisdiction to grant maintenance when making a divorce or separation order or granting a decree of annulment may be excluded by an agreement between the parties under article 23[241] that the courts of another member state shall have jurisdiction to determine the matter. Further, the English court will be forced to stay the ancillary proceedings if prior maintenance proceedings have been brought in the courts of another member

237 Recital 10.
238 Council Regulation (EC) No 44/2001, OJ 2001 L12/1.
239 Art 1(1).
240 Property adjustment orders and lump sum payments are regarded as relating to 'maintenance' if the purpose is to ensure the former spouse's maintenance (Case C-220/95 *van den Boogaard v Laumen* [1997] QB 759, [1997] ECR I-1147).
241 Formerly art 17 of the Brussels Convention.

state (article 27[242]) or may stay the ancillary proceedings if prior related proceedings are pending in another member state (article 28[243]).[244] The English court will not be forced to stay the main matrimonial proceedings,[245] but in such cases could exercise traditional powers to stay the action.[246]

2. Other maintenance orders

During the subsistence of a marriage the English court has power to make various orders for financial provision in favour of a spouse or child of the family. The High Court has power to order one spouse, who has failed to provide reasonable maintenance, to make periodic payments or lump sum payments to the other or to make similar payments to or for the benefit of a child. There is a further power to make a property adjustment order transferring property to the other spouse or to a child of the family. Magistrates' courts are also given powers to make financial provision for a spouse or child of the family.

The jurisdiction of the English court in such cases is as follows. If the respondent, domiciled in a member state, voluntarily appears before the English court (other than to contest jurisdiction), the English court has jurisdiction under article 24[247] of the Brussels I Regulation. If the parties, one of whom is domiciled in a member state, have agreed in terms satisfying article 23 of the Brussels I Regulation that the English court should have jurisdiction, then jurisdiction may be exercised. If the respondent is domiciled in England (in the Brussels I regime sense[248]), the English court will have jurisdiction. If the respondent is domiciled (in the Brussels I regime sense) in another member state or another part of the United Kingdom, the English court will have jurisdiction only if the petitioner (the 'maintenance creditor'[249]) is domiciled (in the Brussels I regime sense) or habitually resident in England.[250] (It is

242 Formerly art 21 of the Brussels Convention.
243 Formerly art 22 of the Brussels Convention.
244 In *D v P* [1998] 2 FLR 25 a stay was (surprisingly) granted under what is now art 28 despite there being no actual Italian proceedings underway at the time.
245 Unless the case is governed by the Brussels II Regulation.
246 See pp 389–393.
247 Formerly art 18 of the Brussels Convention.
248 Art 52; Civil Jurisdiction and Judgments Order 2001, SI 2001/3929, para 9. See pp 69–70.
249 Art 5(2). A 'maintenance creditor' includes a person applying for maintenance for the first time as well as one who has already obtained a maintenance order: Case C-295/95 *Farrell v Long* [1997] QB 842, [1997] 3 WLR 613.
250 Art 5(2) and Civil Jurisdiction and Judgments Act 1982, Sch 4, r 3(b).

a moot point whether there is much difference between domicile in the Brussels I regime sense and habitual residence.)

If none of the above provisions apply, the jurisdiction of the English court is determined by its traditional rules.[251] This depends on the court involved. In the High Court[252] the grounds of jurisdiction are that either spouse is domiciled (in the English sense) in England at the date of the application, or the applicant has been habitually resident here for a year immediately preceding the application, or the respondent is resident here at the date of the application.[253] A magistrates' court has jurisdiction if either spouse ordinarily resides within its area at the date of the application[254] and the respondent is resident in the United Kingdom.[255] But, if the respondent is resident in Scotland or Northern Ireland, the court has jurisdiction only if the applicant resides in England and the parties last ordinarily resided together as man and wife in England.[256] This jurisdiction is exercisable notwithstanding that either party is not domiciled in England.[257]

It should be noted that irrespective of the ground upon which the English court exercised jurisdiction, the provisions of articles 27 and 28 of the Brussels I Regulation are applicable so that the English proceedings must (or may) be stayed if proceedings involving the same (or a related) cause of action are pending in the courts of another member state. In *K v B*[258] the husband commenced proceedings in Italy applying for access to a child and stating he was prepared to pay maintenance to his wife. The wife commenced proceedings for maintenance in England and soon thereafter cross-petitioned in the Italian proceedings seeking maintenance. It was held that the English proceedings should not be stayed under what is now article 28 because the first Italian proceedings did not relate to the same cause of action and, with regard to the maintenance claims, the English court was the one first seised of the matter.

In addition to the English courts' jurisdiction as outlined above, there are statutes[259] which make provision, in conjunction with

251 Art 4.
252 And, in undefended cases, a divorce county court.
253 Matrimonial Causes Act 1973, s 27(2), as amended.
254 Domestic Proceedings and Magistrates' Courts Act 1978, s 30(1).
255 *Forsyth v Forsyth* [1948] P 125, [1947] 2 All ER 623.
256 Domestic Proceedings and Magistrates' Court Act 1978, s 30(3).
257 S 30(5).
258 [1994] 1 FLR 267.
259 Maintenance Orders (Facilities for Enforcement) Act 1920; Maintenance Orders (Reciprocal Enforcement) Act 1972. See further Cheshire and North, *Private International Law* (13th edn, 1999) pp 843–844.

reciprocal laws of other countries, for maintenance orders to be made in the country in which the applicant resides and then, after confirmation of the order in the court of the country in which the respondent resides, to be enforced in the latter country. Provision is also made,[260] in pursuance of a United Nations Convention, for an applicant resident in one country to make application in the court of another country with the assistance of the authorities of the former country.

3. Financial relief after a foreign decree

English courts used not to be able to make an order for financial relief after the dissolution of a marriage by a recognised foreign divorce. This caused great hardship to people living in England if the foreign court made no, or inadequate, provision for a spouse. This was remedied by Part III of the Matrimonial and Family Proceedings Act 1984 which provides that after such a divorce (or annulment or separation) obtained by judicial or other proceedings, the High Court may grant financial relief to either party who has not remarried.[261]

With regard to the English court's jurisdiction to make such an order, if the Brussels I Regulation is applicable it takes precedence over the jurisdictional rules laid down in the 1984 Act.[262] These Brussels I Regulation rules apply when the respondent has voluntarily appeared before the English court or is domiciled (in the Brussels I regime sense) in England or another member state. It is unclear whether article 23 is applicable here as it is limited to cases where there is an agreement that the courts of a member state are to have jurisdiction to settle disputes arising in connection with a 'particular legal relationship'. If the spouses have obtained a divorce or annulment (but not a separation) which is recognised in England, it is arguable that there is no longer any legal relationship between the parties rendering article 23 inoperable. However, the better view is that, just as there is a 'legal relationship' between parties to a purported commercial contract which is held to be void, so too there is a legal relationship between a maintenance creditor and a maintenance debtor even though they are no longer married.

If the Brussels I Regulation rules are not applicable, the bases of jurisdiction are laid down by section 15(1) of the 1984 Act. According to this, the English court has jurisdiction if either of the parties was domiciled (in the English sense) in England at the date

260 Maintenance Orders (Reciprocal Enforcement) Act 1972, Pt II.
261 S 12.
262 Matrimonial and Family Proceedings Act 1984, s 15(2).

of the application or at the date of the foreign decree, or if either of the parties was habitually resident in England for a year immediately preceding either of those dates, or if either or both of the parties had at the date of the application a beneficial interest in a former matrimonial home in England.

Again, irrespective of the ground upon which the English court exercised jurisdiction, the provisions of articles 27 and 28 of the Brussels I Regulation relating to the staying of actions are applicable. Of course, these provisions are unlikely to be utilised much in practice as the parties will already have obtained their divorce in the foreign country. However, it could be that a divorce had been obtained in a foreign country and one party, while attempting to have the decree recognised, seeks to obtain an order for financial relief in a member state at the same time as the other spouse is making an application under the 1984 Act. In such a situation, article 27 would apply.

Even though the above jurisdictional rules are satisfied, no application can be made without the permission of the court which must be satisfied that there is a 'substantial ground'[263] for making the application and that, having regard to all the circumstances of the case, it is appropriate for a financial order to be made.[264] The factors to be taken into account include the connections which the parties have with England and with the country where the decree was obtained or any other country; any financial benefit or relief the applicant is entitled to and is likely to receive under any agreement, foreign law or order of a foreign court; the availability of property in England in respect of which an order could be made; and the extent to which an English order is likely to be enforceable.[265]

These provisions are not designed to permit an applicant to have 'two bites at one cherry'[266] or to empower an English court to exercise jurisdiction to 'second-guess' the foreign court's financial relief orders. In *Holmes v Holmes*[267] it was stressed that the English court should be slow to interfere with the orders of a court of competent jurisdiction and that the criteria of appropriateness laid down in the *Spiliada* case[268] and in *De Dampierre*[269] are applicable in this context. In *M v M*[270] a divorce was granted in France and

263 Matrimonial and Family Proceedings Act 1984, s 13(1).
264 S 16(1).
265 S 16(2).
266 *Lamagni v Lamagni* [1995] 2 FLR 452 at 454.
267 [1989] Fam 47, [1989] 3 All ER 786.
268 [1987] AC 460, [1986] 3 All ER 843.
269 [1988] AC 92, [1987] 2 All ER 1.
270 [1994] 1 FLR 399.

financial relief obtained there, but an application for the distribution of shared property was rejected and the wife was unsuccessful on appeal in France. The wife's application for financial relief under Part III of the Matrimonial and Family Proceedings Act 1984 was rejected. She had pursued her financial rights fully before the French courts which were the courts of 'competent jurisdiction in one of our nearest neighbouring friendly states and the principles of comity' required that its orders be respected and not 'chauvinistically' judged.[271] In *Hewitson v Hewitson*[272] it was stated that even if circumstances between the parties had changed and they had cohabited subsequent to the foreign divorce, it would be 'inconsistent with the comity existing between courts of comparable jurisdiction'[273] for the English court to review or supplement the foreign order.

B Choice of law

In all matters of maintenance English courts apply the lex fori, English domestic law, to determine whether relief, and the type and extent, is available.[274] The fact that the parties are domiciled or resident abroad is irrelevant.

The extent to which the English court will be influenced by the fact that the parties are married under a foreign regime providing for a form of community of property or have entered into a marriage contract regulating their property rights is examined in chapter 11.

C Recognition and enforcement of foreign maintenance orders

A maintenance order made by a foreign court, whether ancillary to a divorce order or not, is a foreign judgment in personam thus qualifying for recognition under the rules discussed in chapter 4. However, normally such judgments can be varied by the foreign court and therefore lack the common law requirement of finality necessary for enforcement. Accordingly, several statutory regimes for the recognition and enforcement of foreign maintenance orders have been established.

271 At 407–408.
272 [1995] Fam 100, [1995] 1 All ER 472.
273 At 105.
274 In limited circumstances under the Maintenance Orders (Facilities for Enforcement) Act 1920 and the Maintenance Orders (Reciprocal Enforcement) Act 1972 it may be necessary to have recourse to foreign law. See Dicey and Morris, *The Conflict of Laws* (13th edn, 2000) p 787.

1. United Kingdom maintenance orders

Under Part II of the Maintenance Orders Act 1950 a maintenance order made in another part of the United Kingdom may be registered in an English court.

2. Foreign maintenance orders

Under the Maintenance Orders (Facilities for Enforcement) Act 1920 there is a special regime for the enforcement of Commonwealth maintenance orders applying to countries to which an Order in Council has been extended. Under Part I of the Maintenance Orders (Reciprocal Enforcement) Act 1972[275] there is a similar regime for the reciprocal enforcement of other foreign maintenance orders from countries to which an Order in Council has been extended.

3. Brussels I Regulation

Judgments from member states, providing they qualify as 'maintenance' judgments are entitled to recognition and enforcement under the Brussels I Regulation.[276] However, to the extent that the Acts of 1920 and 1972 are derived from conventions to which the United Kingdom is a party, they are not overridden by the Brussels I Regulation.[277] So, with respect to countries such as France and Germany to which the 1972 legislation applies, the maintenance creditor has a choice as to which regime to follow.

Under the Brussels I Regulation the maintenance judgment of a member state must be denied recognition if it is irreconcilable with a judgment given in a dispute between the same parties in England. For example, a French maintenance order granted to a spouse will be denied recognition if an English court has granted an order dissolving the marriage.[278]

275 As amended by the Maintenance Orders (Reciprocal Enforcement) Act 1992.

276 Similarly, maintenance judgments given by the courts of Lugano contracting states (Iceland, Norway, Poland and Switzerland) are entitled to recognition and enforcement under the Lugano Convention; Danish maintenance judgments still fall under the Brussels I Convention.

277 Art 66 (formerly art 57 of the Brussels Convention).

278 Art 34 (3). See Case 145/86 *Hoffman v Krieg* [1988] ECR 645; *Macaulay v Macaulay* [1991] 1 All ER 865, [1991] 1 WLR 179.

Chapter 10

Children

I INTRODUCTION

This chapter is concerned with the conflict of laws rules relating to 'children', that is, persons below the age of majority which is set at 18 in England. While the main thrust of legislative reforms has been child-centred with the focus being on the child's welfare as the paramount consideration, the relationship between the child and its parents is still of great importance. The crucial issues for children are who has parental responsibility for them and with whom must they live? Also, it can be important initially to determine the legal status of the child, in particular whether he is legitimate or adopted. These matters will be discussed first and then there will be an examination of the problems relating to 'custody'[1] of children.

II LEGITIMACY

A Introduction

At common law, a person was legitimate only if he was born in lawful wedlock. Accordingly, under English domestic law, children born of void marriages were illegitimate. However, in 1959 English law[2] introduced the doctrine, long accepted by many other legal systems, that a person is also legitimate if born of a putative marriage, that is, a marriage which, though void, was reasonably believed by the parties, or one of them, to be valid. This rule, which applies only where the father is domiciled in England at the date of the child's birth,[3] is now to be found in section 1 of the Legitimacy Act 1976.

1 As will be seen, this term no longer has any legal meaning in English domestic law, but is used here generically to refer to issues of residence and contact.
2 Legitimacy Act 1959, s 2.
3 Or died domiciled in England before the birth of the child: Legitimacy Act 1976, s 2(1).

The importance of the distinction between legitimacy and illegitimacy has been significantly reduced as a result of the Family Law Reform Act 1987 which avoids the use of the terms 'legitimate' and 'illegitimate' as legal terms of art. For instance, rights of succession of children are no longer influenced by their status and, indeed, are no longer even dependent on whether the parents of the child are or were married to each other.[4] The status of legitimacy and illegitimacy used to be important in determining the rights and responsibilities of the father. However, under the Children Act 1989 it is not the status of the child that matters in determining parental responsibility, but rather whether the father and mother were married to each other at the date of the child's birth.[5] Further, under the Adoption and Children Act 2002 a father of a child who is not married to the child's mother acquires parental responsibility for the child if he is registered on the child's birth certificate as the child's father or if he makes an agreement with the child's mother providing for him to have parental responsibility for the child or if a court orders that he shall have parental responsibility for the child.[6] Nevertheless, there is still some importance attached to the distinction. The reference in the Children Act 1989[7] 'to a person whose father and mother were married to each other at the time of his birth' includes the child of a putative marriage under section 1 of the Legitimacy Act 1976 and also includes any other person who is legitimate or legitimated under the English conflict of laws.[8] Further, it may still be necessary to determine the status of a person as legitimate or illegitimate for purposes of citizenship,[9] succession to a title of honour,[10] ascertaining domicile, and, perhaps,[11] rights of succession governed by foreign law.

B The choice of law rule

The choice of law rule for legitimacy is somewhat controversial. Suppose that a child is born of a marriage which is void according

4 Family Law Reform Act 1987, s 1(1). All children, whether legitimate or illegitimate, can claim as dependants under both the Inheritance (Provision for Family and Dependants) Act 1975 and the Fatal Accidents Act 1976. For an exception to these rules, see n 10 below.

5 Ss 2, 4.

6 S 108(2), amending the Children Act 1989, s 4.

7 Above, n 5.

8 Family Law Reform Act 1987, s 1(2) and (3).

9 British Nationality Act 1981, s 50(9).

10 Family Law Reform Act 1987, s 19(4): *Re Moynihan* [2000] 1 FLR 113 – not contrary to European Convention on Human Rights.

11 See pp 521–522 and 554.

to the English conflict of laws and the father is not domiciled in England at the date of the child's birth. By English domestic law such a child is illegitimate. Would it necessarily follow that the child is illegitimate in the eyes of the English court if he is domiciled in France, and by French law he is legitimate?

The natural approach would be that a person's status as legitimate or illegitimate should be determined, not necessarily by English domestic definitions, but by his personal law. So whether a person is legitimate or illegitimate at birth should be governed by the law of his domicile of origin. This, however, will not work if at his birth his parents were domiciled in different countries, because, as seen earlier, a person's domicile of origin depends on whether he is legitimate or illegitimate. Until it has been decided whether he is legitimate or illegitimate, it is not known what his domicile of origin is. To avoid the vicious circle, it has been suggested[12] that legitimacy is governed by the law of the father's domicile at the date of the birth. As shall be seen later, it is the father's domicile which is relevant to the subsequent legitimation of an illegitimate person.

This approach is, however, not consistent with the decision of the House of Lords in *Shaw v Gould*.[13] Elizabeth 'Shaw' had originally been married to Buxton. She divorced him in Scotland, at a time when Buxton was domiciled in England, and then married Shaw, who was domiciled in Scotland, where they settled. Children were born to Elizabeth by Shaw. The question for the House of Lords (on appeal from the English courts) was whether those children were entitled to property under the will of a relative of their mother's; they would be entitled only if they were legitimate. The difficulty was that Elizabeth's Scottish divorce was not recognised in England, because Buxton was domiciled in England, not Scotland. It followed that according to the English conflict of laws Elizabeth's marriage to Shaw was void for bigamy, and so the children were not born in lawful wedlock. The House of Lords accordingly held that they were illegitimate.

The possibility that the children might be legitimate by the law of their father's domicile at the date of their birth (because their parents' marriage was valid by Scots law) was not taken into account. (It would not have been possible to rely on the children's domicile of origin, because their mother remained domiciled in England, in English eyes, still being married to Buxton. So their domicile of origin could not have been decided until it had first been

12 Cheshire and North, *Private International Law* (13th edn, 1999) p 895, citing *Re Grove* (1888) 40 Ch D 216. Dicey and Morris, *The Conflict of Laws* (13th edn, 2000) p 859 regard this solution as 'quite arbitrary'.

13 (1868) LR 3 HL 55.

decided whether or not they were legitimate.) According to *Shaw v Gould*, therefore, a child is legitimate only if it was born in lawful wedlock. No inquiry is to be made into its status under any other law.

A different approach was taken by the High Court in *Re Bischoffsheim*.[14] A man and his deceased wife's sister, both then domiciled in England, married each other in New York. Subsequently, after they had become domiciled in New York, a child was born to them. The question was whether this child was legitimate so as to entitle him to succeed under a relative's will. So far as the English court was concerned, the child was not born in lawful wedlock: the validity of his parents' marriage was governed by English law, as they were domiciled in England at the time of the marriage, and by English law they were within the prohibited degrees of affinity. Nevertheless, Romer J held that the child was legitimate because, in his view, the legitimacy of a child at birth is governed by the law of his domicile of origin. This was New York, and by New York law the child was legitimate (because by New York conflicts rules the validity of his parents' marriage was governed by New York law,[15] under which it was valid). It will be seen that there was no vicious circle involved in determining the domicile of origin in this case, because both parents were domiciled in New York at the time of the birth.

It is difficult to reconcile this decision with the reasoning of the House of Lords in *Shaw v Gould*. It has been suggested,[16] however, that the two cases can stand together, in their results, though not their reasoning, if *Re Bischoffsheim* is treated as a decision that a child, even if not born in lawful wedlock, is legitimate if it is so by the law of the domicile of *each* of its parents (not just the father) at the time of its birth. This would not be inconsistent with the result of *Shaw v Gould*, for in that case the children were not legitimate by English law, the law of their mother's domicile. Such an approach is consistent with the decision in *Motala v A-G*[17] where, in the context of claims to British citizenship, the children of a void marriage in Northern Rhodesia (now Zambia) were held legitimate because they were so regarded by the law of India, the country in which they had their domicile of origin and the place where both their parents were domiciled.

When the parents have different domiciles, it would seem that it is possible for a child's legitimacy to be determined by reference to

14 [1948] Ch 79, [1947] 2 All ER 830.

15 This is an instance of an incidental question (the validity of the marriage) being decided by the conflicts rule of the law governing the main question (the child's legitimacy): see pp 550–554.

16 Dicey and Morris, *The Conflict of Laws* (13th edn, 2000) p 857 (Rule 97(2)).

17 [1990] 2 FLR 261 (revsd, on other grounds, [1992] 1 AC 281).

the father's domicile alone. In *Hashmi v Hashmi*[18] the father, who was domiciled in Pakistan, married his first wife by Islamic rites in Pakistan. He then married a second wife, who was domiciled in England, at a register office in England. This second 'marriage' was, of course, 'monogamous' but void under English conflicts rules as the husband was regarded as validly married to the first wife. However, it was held that the children born of the second 'marriage' were legitimate, because they were legitimate by the law of Pakistan, their father's domiciliary law at the time of their birth, his second marriage being a valid polygamous marriage under Pakistani law. As the children were not legitimate by the law of their mother's domicile, English law, this case, unlike *Re Bischoffsheim* and *Motola v A-G*, cannot be reconciled with *Shaw v Gould*.

It has been argued[19] that the decision in *Shaw v Gould* is to be restricted to the exceptional circumstances of the case, and that *Re Bischoffsheim*, together with the cases on legitimation,[20] justify the proposition that a person is legitimate if he is so according to the law of his father's domicile at his birth. This conclusion is fortified by the use of that criterion in relation to the doctrine of putative marriage in English law. Section 1(2) of the Legitimacy Act 1976[21] provides that the rule that the child of a void marriage is legitimate where both or either of the parents reasonably believe that the marriage is valid is only applicable if the father of the child was domiciled in England at the time of the birth of the child, or died domiciled in England before the birth. If such a child is legitimate where the father is domiciled in England, there seems little reason to deny a child the beneficial status of legitimacy where the father is domiciled in another country under whose law the child is legitimate.

III LEGITIMATION

By the laws of many countries, a person who is illegitimate by birth can be legitimated by the subsequent marriage of his parents. This was not provided for by English domestic law until 1926, but even before then the courts accepted that a legitimation by subsequent marriage under a foreign law could be recognised in England.

In this context the courts took a different approach from that adopted in *Shaw v Gould*[22] and accepted that legitimation was a matter for the personal law. The rule which was established was that

18 [1972] Fam 36, [1971] 3 All ER 1253.
19 Cheshire and North, *Private International Law* (13th edn, 1999) pp 891–894.
20 See p 443.
21 As amended by the Family Law Reform Act 1987, s 28.
22 (1868) LR 3 HL 55.

a legitimation by subsequent marriage was to be recognised in England if the subsequent marriage had the effect of legitimating the child according to both the law of the father's domicile at the date of the birth of the child and the law of his domicile at the date of the marriage.[23] The reference to the law of the father's domicile at the date of the marriage is understandable enough, for it is at that date that the status is to be changed. The explanation for the need to refer also to the law of the father's domicile at the date of the birth was that the child must have capacity by that law to be subsequently legitimated.[24] Since English domestic law did not provide for legitimation, the father's domicile in England at either date precluded legitimation.

The law was reformed by the Legitimacy Act 1926 which was replaced by the Legitimacy Act 1976, section 2 of which provides for legitimation by subsequent marriage if the father is domiciled in England at the date of the marriage. Thus legitimation was introduced into English domestic law.

Section 8(1) of the Legitimacy Act 1926 (subsequently replaced by section 3 of the 1976 Act) provides that a foreign legitimation is to be recognised if at the date of the marriage the father is domiciled in a country (other than England) by the law of which the illegitimate person became legitimated by virtue of the subsequent marriage. Reference to the law of the father's domicile at the date of the child's birth is not required.

The laws of some countries provide for legitimation in ways other than subsequent marriage, for example, by some formal act of the parent declaring the child to be legitimate. The Legitimacy Act 1976 makes no provision for the recognition of such a legitimation. In *Re Luck's Settlement Trusts*[25] the Court of Appeal held, on the analogy of the common law rule dealing with the recognition of legitimation by subsequent marriage, that a legitimation by parental acknowledgement can be recognised only if it is effective by the law of the father's domicile at the date of the child's birth as well as at the date of acknowledgement. The father, then domiciled in California, had executed a formal document acknowledging his child to be his legitimate son. Although this had the effect of legitimating the child by Californian law, it was held that it did not have that effect in England, because the father had been domiciled in England at the time of the child's birth. The decision may reasonably be criticised on the basis that it uses as an analogy a rule of the common law which not only was unsatisfactory, but which prior to the decision had been corrected by statute.

23 *Re Goodman's Trusts* (1881) 17 Ch D 266.
24 *Re Grove* (1888) 40 Ch D 216 at 232.
25 [1940] Ch 864.

IV ADOPTION

A Introduction

Adoption is a legal act that changes status; an adopted child is treated in law as the legitimate child of his adoptive parent or parents rather than the child of his natural parents. Under English domestic law only an unmarried child under the age of 19[26] may be adopted and the paramount consideration is the welfare of the child throughout his life.[27] Under some other legal systems, however, adults may be adopted and it is not necessarily the case that the adopted person is treated as the legitimate child of his adoptive parents in every respect.

Since the 1960s there has been a marked reduction in the number of adoptions in England and Wales. This is largely attributable to the increased availability of contraception and abortion and to the fact that more unmarried mothers are keeping and raising their children.[28] Perhaps because of this reduction in the number of English babies available for adoption, there has been an increase in the number of intercountry adoptions with English applicants going abroad to countries such as Korea, India, Sri Lanka, Romania and Latin American countries and bringing children back to England to adopt them.[29] Such intercountry adoptions present problems particularly when English people go abroad and, sometimes after the payment of money, bring children back to the United Kingdom with a view to adopting them here. Accordingly, the Adoption and Children Act 2002 makes it a criminal offence for a person habitually resident in the British Isles to bring into the United Kingdom a child who is habitually resident elsewhere for the purpose of adoption unless requirements prescribed by the Secretary of State are satisfied.[30]

Further problems arise when, in similar circumstances, the adoption takes place abroad. For instance, in the highly publicised

26 Adoption and Children Act 2002, s 46(9). The application for adoption must be made before the child has reached the age of 18 (s 48(4)).

27 Adoption and Children Act 2002, s 1(2).

28 Lowe and Douglas, *Bromley's Family Law* (9th edn, 1998) p 614.

29 Department of Health, *Inter-Departmental Review of Adoption Law: Discussion Paper No 4: Intercountry Adoption* (1992) para 10. For example, it has been estimated that about 4,000 Romanian children were adopted by foreigners worldwide between August 1990 and February 1991 (ibid, para 11).

30 S 82(7). Such Regulations had been brought into force under the Adoption (Intercountry Aspects) Act 1999 (now partially repealed by the 2002 Act). These requirements involved, inter alia, obtaining approval from the adoption agency that the person was suitable to be an adoptive parent (Adoption of Children from Overseas Regulations 2001, SI 2001/1251).

case of *Flintshire County Council v K*[31] an English couple, after payment of money in the United States, removed twins from California where they had been placed for adoption with another couple, took them to Arkansas and there obtained an adoption order before bringing the children back to England. Section 82 of the Adoption and Children Act 2002 now makes it a criminal offence to bring such a child back to the United Kingdom within six months of the foreign adoption if there has been no compliance with prescribed regulations.

Even if such safeguards are complied with, conflict of laws problems remain. When, and in what circumstances, should the adoption of foreign children be permitted in England and what regard should be had to the personal law of such persons? With similar intercountry adoptions becoming more common in other countries (particularly the United States, France, Sweden, the Netherlands, Italy and Switzerland[32]), and with some English applicants adopting children abroad before returning to England, the question arises as to the circumstances in which a foreign adoption will be recognised.

With regard to jurisdiction and choice of law there are two different types of case which, for the sake of convenience, will be described here as English adoptions and Convention adoptions. After a consideration of each of these, the problem of recognition of foreign adoptions will be considered.

B English adoptions

In English law adoption is effected by an order of court, so the question of jurisdiction arises. Under the Adoption and Children Act 2002 the English court has jurisdiction if the adoptive parent, or one of the adoptive parents, is domiciled in a part of the British Isles or, alternatively, if the adoptive parent or both parents have been habitually resident in a part of the British Isles for a period of not less than one year ending with the date of the application.[33] The child must have had his home with the applicant/s for a prescribed minimum period of time[34] and the adoption agency which placed the child there or the appropriate local authority must have had sufficient opportunities to visit the child and applicant/s in their

31 [2001] 2 FLR 476.
32 See n 29 above, para 10.
33 Adoption and Children Act 2002, s 48(2), (3).
34 For ten weeks if the child was placed with the applicant/s by an adoption agency or in pursuance of a High Court order (s 41(2)). In other cases longer periods are prescribed (s 41(3)–(5)).

home environment.[35] Thus, while not formally required as such, this effectively means that the child and applicant/s must have a home in England.

There is no requirement that the child be domiciled in England. This is for the pragmatic reason that the domicile of many such children might be unknown. Alternatively, they could well have domiciles of dependence on their natural parents in foreign countries and such a requirement would represent a major obstacle to the adoption of foreign children.

Under the former law as found in the Adoption Act 1976 only the domicile of the applicant/s in a part of the United Kingdom, the Channel Islands or the Isle of Man sufficed for jurisdictional purposes. This was criticised on the basis that, with the somewhat archaic rules on domicile, this meant that a person such as the propositus in *IRC v Bullock*[36] who had resided in England for 44 years, but without acquiring an English domicile, would have been unable to adopt a child here. Responding to this criticism the habitual residence of the applicant/s has been introduced as an alternative jurisdictional basis to domicile. Of course, there is still the converse problem that a person domiciled in England under the archaic rules would be permitted to adopt here even if the connections with England are tenuous. However, the requirement that the child reside with the adopter/s for a set period of time does go some way in such cases to ensuring that the child does have a home in England.

The law applied by the English court in deciding whether to make an adoption order is contained in the Adoption and Children Act 2002 which makes elaborate provision for ensuring that the adoption will be for the welfare of the child, and for the obtaining of the consent of the natural parents, or dispensing with it in exceptional circumstances. There is no question of the application of any foreign law in the making of an English adoption order. As the result of an English adoption order, the child's status in England may differ from his status elsewhere, in particular the country of his domicile before the adoption, if the English adoption is not recognised there. The result will be a 'limping child'. This could, in exceptional cases, work to the disadvantage of the child and, accordingly, it has been suggested[37] that no adoption should be granted in England unless it is in accordance with the law of the child's domicile. Some account of this view was taken, obiter, in *Re B (S) (Infant)*[38] where it was held that the question whether the adoption will be recognised in the

35 S 41(7).
36 [1976] 3 All ER 353, [1976] 1 WLR 1178.
37 Cheshire and North, *Private International Law* (13th edn, 1999) p 904.
38 [1968] Ch 204, [1967] 3 All ER 629.

country of the child's domicile may be relevant in deciding whether the adoption will be for the welfare of the child. Such a consideration is one of fact rather than law. Cases where this question will be a weighty factor are likely to be few.[39]

The parental responsibility of the natural parents in relation to the child is terminated by the adoption order.[40] Consequently, their status also is changed in English eyes, even though they may not be domiciled in or have any other connection with England, and even though the adoption may not be recognised in their domicile. It is not surprising, however, that the possible problems of differing status in different countries have been subordinated to the more pressing and immediate question of providing for the welfare of children. The best way of achieving uniformity of status in different countries, here as elsewhere in the law (for instance, in relation to divorce), is by international convention.

C Convention adoptions

In an attempt to address some of the problems considered above the Hague Convention on Protection of Children and Co-operation in Respect of Intercountry Adoptions was signed in 1993 and will be implemented in the United Kingdom by the Adoption (Intercountry Aspects) Act 1999.[41] The remainder of this chapter assumes such implementation.

This Convention, which has been ratified by 33 countries, signed by another 14 countries and acceded to by an additional 11 countries,[42] seeks to establish a system of co-operation amongst contracting states so as to promote the best interests of children and prevent the abduction, sale of, or traffic in, children.[43] The Convention applies where a child habitually resident in one contracting state has been, is being, or is to be moved to another contracting state before or after the adoption by spouses or a person habitually resident in the latter state.[44] Competent authorities in the

39 It is conceivable that the non-recognition of the adoption in a country other than that of the child's domicile might also be adverse to his welfare.

40 Adoption and Children Act 2002, s 45(2).

41 While many of the provisions of this Act no longer have any effect in England (Adoption and Children Act 2002, Sch 3, s 94), the provision giving effect to the Convention remains. An earlier Hague Convention on the Adoption of Children 1965, which was implemented in the United Kingdom by the Adoption Act 1976 (but only ratified by Austria and Switzerland) is no longer in force (Sch 3, s 87).

42 Most European countries have either ratified or signed the Convention, as have other countries such as the United States, Canada and Australia.

43 Art 1.

44 Art 2.

state of the child's habitual residence must establish that the child is adoptable and that an intercountry adoption is in the child's best interests and must ensure that all the necessary consents have been obtained.[45] Competent authorities in the receiving state must determine that the prospective adoptive parents are eligible and suited to adopt[46] and prepare detailed reports on them.[47] Provision is made for co-operation between the authorities of both states.

D Recognition of foreign adoptions

An adoption order made in Scotland or Northern Ireland is recognised and automatically has effect in England.[48] With regard to foreign adoptions, there are three routes to recognition.

1. Convention Adoptions

Adoptions made in accordance with the 1993 Hague Convention, discussed above, 'shall be recognised by operation of law in other contracting states'.[49] For example, if a French child is adopted in France by an English couple in accordance with the procedures laid down in the Convention, the French adoption order is automatically recognised in England. The only ground for refusing recognition is if the adoption is contrary to public policy.[50] Given the stringent procedural requirements under the Convention coupled with the fact that all contracting states have (or are supposed to have) broadly similar views as to the purposes of adoption, it is unlikely that this provision will be frequently invoked.

2. Overseas adoptions

As regards adoptions made outside the British Isles, the Secretary of State was empowered by the Adoption Act 1976 and is now empowered under section 85 of the Adoption and Children Act 2002 to specify adoptions, called overseas adoptions, which are to have the same effect in law as an English adoption.[51] Adoptions made under the statutory law (as opposed to the common law or

45 Art 4.
46 Art 5.
47 Art 15.
48 Adoption and Children Act 2002, ss 102–103. Under s 105 regulations will need to be made for adoption orders from the Isle of Man or the Channel Islands to have effect in England.
49 Art 23.
50 Adoption and Children Act 2002, s 87(1).
51 Adoption and Children Act 2002, s 65(1).

customary law) of many countries have been specified,[52] and are thus fully effective in England, subject to the power of a court to hold an adoption invalid on the ground that it is contrary to public policy or that the authority which purported to authorise the adoption was not competent to entertain the case.[53] Overseas adoptions are entitled to recognition without reference to whether any of the parties is domiciled in or has any other connection with the country in question.

Many countries which have been specified for this purpose are also signatories to the 1993 Hague Convention: for example, France. However, the recognition rules on overseas adoptions continue to apply if the adoption is not a 'Convention adoption'. For example, a French child might be adopted in France by an English couple but the Convention was not applicable as it was not a 'Convention adoption' because the couple were living in France and, at the time of the adoption, had no plans to move the child to England. In such a case the French adoption would be recognised as an 'overseas adoption'.

3. Recognition at common law

A foreign adoption which is neither an 'overseas adoption' (because it is not made in a specified country, or because it is made under the foreign country's common law or customary law) nor a Convention adoption may nevertheless be entitled to recognition at common law. It will then also have the same effect in law as an English adoption.[54] According to the majority of the Court of Appeal in *Re Valentine's Settlement*,[55] a foreign adoption will be recognised at common law if the adoptive parents were domiciled in the country concerned at the date of the adoption. The basis for such recognition is that questions affecting status are to be determined by the law of the domicile and that the English courts themselves exercise jurisdiction to make adoption orders on the basis of the adoptive parents' domicile.[56] Since an adopting couple may have different domiciles and the English court may make an order in favour of adoptive parents if only one of them is domiciled in the British Isles, presumably it is sufficient for the recognition of a foreign adoption at common law if one of the parents is domiciled in the foreign

52 SI 1973/19. These include the United States, many Commonwealth countries and all Western European countries.
53 Adoption and Children Act 2002, s 87(2).
54 S 65(1)(e).
55 [1965] Ch 831.
56 At 842.

country. It is also possible with the expansion of the English jurisdictional grounds in the Adoption and Children Act 2002 that a foreign adoption could be recognised if the adoptive parent has been (or both adoptive parents have been) habitually resident in the country of adoption for at least one year.

In *Re Valentine's Settlement* Lord Denning MR thought that it was also a requirement for the recognition of a foreign adoption that the child should be ordinarily resident in the country concerned, 'for it is the courts of ordinary residence which have the pre-eminent jurisdiction over the child'.[57] At that time, the residence of the child was a requirement of the jurisdiction of the English court but, as this is no longer so, it seems unlikely that the child's residence in the foreign country will be material for recognition.

Although adoption in England can be effected only by an order of court, it does not follow that a foreign adoption made in some other way cannot be recognised. On the contrary, it was accepted in *Re Wilby*[58] that an adoption made in Burma by means of a registered agreement without any court order, valid by the law of Burma where the adoptive parents were domiciled, could be recognised in England.

Recognition of a foreign adoption at common law can be refused on grounds of public policy.[59] It was emphasised in *Re Valentine's Settlement*[60] that an adoption would not be recognised if the foreign court did not apply adequate safeguards. So recognition might be refused if the court thought that the foreign law attached insufficient weight to the welfare of the child and that in the particular case recognition of the adoption would be contrary to the child's welfare.

E The effect of foreign adoptions

Under the Adoption and Children Act 2002 a recognised foreign adoption, whether a Convention adoption, an 'overseas adoption' or an adoption recognised at common law, has the same effect as an English adoption.[61] This means that even if under a foreign law an adopted child is treated as the child of its adoptive parents only for certain purposes or to a limited extent he will nevertheless generally be treated by English law as the legitimate child of his adoptive parents. Of course, if the effect of a foreign adoption fell very far short of equating an adopted child with a natural one, it is conceivable

57 At 843.
58 [1956] P 174, [1956] 1 All ER 27.
59 See, for example, *Wender v Victoria (County) Official Administrator* [1998] 7 WWR 480 in which an adoption of an adult was refused recognition on grounds of public policy.
60 [1965] Ch 831 at 843, 852.
61 S 65.

that the court would not classify the foreign 'adoption' as an adoption at all within the meaning of English law, in which case it would be incapable of recognition. However, such a course of action should be taken only in extreme circumstances. As always with classification, the object is to find the closest English analogue with the foreign status; it is not necessary that the English status, or its incidents, be identical to the foreign one.

However, with regard to Convention adoptions, section 86 of the Adoption and Children Act 2002 permits such partial adoptions to be recognised as such provided that the adoption was not a full adoption under the law of the country in which it was effected, that the relevant consents have not been given for a full adoption and that it would be more favourable to the child not to recognise the adoption as a full adoption.

As a recognised foreign adoption has the same effect as an English adoption, it follows that the succession rights of such a child are the same as a child adopted in England. Except in relation to property devolving with a title of honour[62] such children have the same succession rights as other children with respect to dispositions of property. It is commonly stated[63] that this applies only to English successions and that if the succession is governed by a foreign law, that law should determine the succession rights of an adopted child. This must be correct with respect to the *extent* to which an adopted child can succeed. For example, if the foreign law governing the succession states that adopted children cannot succeed at all, effect must be given to this. But with regard to whether a person is an adopted child capable of succeeding to whatever extent permitted by the foreign law, it will be argued in chapter 12, where the problem of the incidental question is considered more fully, that as a guiding principle it should be for English law to determine whether a person is an adopted person. For example, if Mexican law provides that an adopted person can succeed to the same extent as any other child, then it should be for English law to determine whether any particular person is an adopted person. So if X is not regarded as adopted under Mexican law but is considered adopted under English law, the English conflicts rules should prevail and X be allowed to succeed. However, this is only a guiding principle that can give way to the lex causae approach when justice so demands. An instance where this would be appropriate would be where there is no person considered adopted under English law but Y is regarded as adopted under Mexican law. In such a case the Mexican rules on adoption should prevail.

62 S 70.

63 Dicey and Morris, *The Conflict of Laws* (13th edn, 2000) p 901; Cheshire and North, *Private International Law* (13th edn, 1999) p 913.

V PARENTAL RESPONSIBILITY

A Introduction

The legal term 'custody' was abandoned in England by the Children Act 1989 and replaced by the concept of parental responsibility. Under the 1989 Act custody and access orders have been replaced by 'section 8 orders', namely residence orders (determining with whom a child is to live) and contact orders (allowing the child access to another person).[64] While the concept of parental responsibility is being increasingly adopted in other jurisdictions and in international instruments, the terms 'custody' and 'access' are still employed in many other countries and in international conventions.

The central issue for most children is the determination of where and with whom they should live. The increased mobility over the past half century has meant there is a greater possibility of the courts of more than one country having jurisdiction to determine issues relating to children. This increases the chances of a parent who has been unsuccessful in custody proceedings in one country removing the child to another country in an attempt to 'try again' and be awarded custody. Thousands of children are abducted and taken abroad by a parent every year.[65] Significant legal reforms have been effected both nationally and internationally to introduce uniform rules specifying which courts should have jurisdiction in such cases, to promote the recognition of the orders of other countries and to secure the return of abducted children to the country from which they were abducted.

B Jurisdiction

There are now two sets of rules governing the jurisdiction of the English courts: the European Regulation rules and the traditional rules.

64 Two other section 8 orders can also be made: a prohibited steps order (prohibiting a parent from taking a specified step in relation to a child such as removing the child from England or having contact with a particular person); and a specific issue order (determining a specific issue in relation to a child, for example specifying which school he should attend or ordering a parent to return a child to the jurisdiction).

65 In 1999 there were applications under the Hague Convention alone (see pp 460–474 below) involving some 1,800 children (Lowe, Armstrong and Mathias, *A Statistical Analysis of Applications made in 1999 under the Hague Convention of 25 October 1980 on the Civil Aspects of International Child Abduction*, Preliminary Document No 3, Hague Conference on Private International Law: Child Abduction (2001)).

1. European Regulation rules

Council Regulation (EC) No 1347/2000 (the Brussels II Regulation) was brought into force on 1 March 2001. As already seen,[66] this lays down detailed jurisdictional rules for the granting of a divorce, legal separation or marriage annulment for member states of the European Union. Article 3 provides that any court exercising such matrimonial jurisdiction shall have jurisdiction in a matter relating to parental responsibility over a child of both spouses where the child is habitually resident in that member state. Where, however, the child is not habitually resident in the state where the matrimonial proceedings are being conducted that state will nevertheless still have jurisdiction if the child is habitually resident in another member state and at least one of the spouses has parental responsibility in relation to the child and the jurisdiction of that court has been accepted by both spouses and is in the best interests of the child.[67] Under article 12 courts are not prevented in urgent cases from taking provisional, including protective, measures in respect of children even though the courts of another member state have jurisdiction as to the substance of the matter under the Regulation. It is likely that this provision will be narrowly interpreted.[68]

While these provisions will clearly cover many 'normal' cases, it is nevertheless, in conflict of laws situations, relatively narrow. First, there have to be matrimonial proceedings pending between the parents. Secondly, the parental responsibility issue must relate to a child of both spouses. The Regulation does not apply to increasingly common issues affecting stepchildren or non-marital children. Finally, the jurisdiction to determine an issue relating to parental responsibility does not flow automatically from the existence of the matrimonial proceedings. If the child is not habitually resident in the state where the matrimonial proceedings are pending (which can easily happen with the fairly broad matrimonial jurisdictional rules[69]), that court will only have jurisdiction if, inter alia, both spouses have accepted that jurisdiction. Where parents are living in separate countries and there is a contentious issue relating to parental responsibility of their child, such agreement could be difficult to secure.

Within a month of the Brussels II Regulation coming into force, the European Commission published a proposal to extend Brussels II to cover all decisions relating to parental responsibility within member states. This is sometimes referred to as the proposed

66 Above, pp 381–389.
67 Art 3(2). For the rules on the staying of such proceedings, see pp 387–389 above.
68 *A v L (Jurisdiction: Brussels II)* [2002] Fam Law 241.
69 See pp 383–386 above.

Brussels IIA Regulation.[70] At the same time discussions commenced on a French initiative on rights of access.[71] These proposals were adopted in January 2002 by the Economic and Social Committee[72] and in May 2002 the EU Commission announced a proposal for a Council Regulation that would replace the Brussels II Regulation and consolidate its provisions with the Brussels IIA proposals and the French initiative on rights of access.[73]

Under this revised Brussels II Regulation the expectation[74] is that generally jurisdiction will be based on the habitual residence of the child. Where, however, the child changes his habitual residence after the courts of his former habitual residence have given a judgment relating to parental responsibility, these original courts will retain jurisdiction for six months provided one of the holders of parental responsibility is habitually resident there unless that person accepts the jurisdiction of the courts of the state of new habitual residence.[75] This latter provision is aimed at providing continuity. Where the habitual residence of a child is altered, the court that was closest to the child prior to the relocation continues to have jurisdiction; this also relieves the left-behind holder of parental responsibility from having to commence litigation in an unfamiliar setting.[76]

These basic rules are displaced in cases of prorogation of jurisdiction where all holders of parental responsibility accept the jurisdiction of the courts of a member state and the child has a substantial connection with the state and jurisdiction is in the best interests of the child.[77] Where the child's habitual residence cannot

70 *Proposal for a Council Regulation on Jurisdiciton and the Recognition and Enforcement of Judgments in Matters of Parental Responsibility* (COM (2001) 505 final, 2001/0204 (CNS), OJ C332E, 27/11/2.

71 *Initiative of the French Republic with a view to adopting a Council Regulation on the Mutual Enforcement of Judgments on Rights of Access to Children*, OJ 2000 C234/7.

72 *Opinion of the Economic and Social Committee on the 'Proposal for a Council Regulation on jurisdiciton and the recognition and enforcement of judgments in matters of parental responsibility'* OJ 2002 C 80/41.

73 EU Institutions Press Releases, *Commission proposes EU-wide recognition of family law rulings to tackle child abducion* IP/02/654, 03/05/2002.

74 The ensuing text draws on the proposals contianed in Brussels IIA which are expected to form the core of the consolidated Regulation. References to specific article numbers have been omitted as they are certain to be altered in the revised Regulation.

75 Where the move to the new state is 'wrongful', special provisions on child abduction apply and are discussed below at pp 475–476.

76 Explanatory Memorandum to art 4 of the current Brussels IIA proposal.

77 There can also be a prorogation of jurisdiction in the context of a matrimonial proceedings under the present art 3(2) of the Brussels II Regulation.

be established and no other court of a member state has jurisdiction under the above rules, the courts of the member state where the child is present shall have jurisdiction. In urgent cases courts of a member state may take provisional measures for a period not exceeding one month to protect a child present there even though the courts of another member state have jurisdiction as to the substance of the matter.

Although the basic rules are structured to try to ensure that the court with the closest link with the child is afforded jurisdiction, there is a recognition that in rare cases the courts of another member state might be more appropriate. Accordingly, it is proposed that a forum non conveniens discretion be exercised in exceptional cases: the courts having jurisdiction as to the substance of the matter may, where this in the best interests of the child, transfer the case to the courts of the member state of the former habitual residence of the child or of the habitual residence of a holder of parental responsibility. As with the other Brussels Regulations, provision is made for lis pendens: the court second seized shall of its own motion stay its proceedings until such time as the jurisdiction of the court first seized is established.

2. *Traditional rules*

When brought into force the revised Brussels II Regulation rules will cover the vast majority of cases. Nevertheless, there will still be room for the application of the traditional rules.[78] The revised Brussels II Regulation will provide for member states to determine jurisdiction by their own laws where no court of a member state has jurisdiction described above. The English court has jurisdiction under traditional rules in the following situations.

(A) MATRIMONIAL PROCEEDINGS

In most cases the English court will exercise jurisdiction under the revised Brussels II Regulation and so the parental responsibility rules under that Regulation will apply. However, there could well be residual cases where the English court exercises jurisdiction under

78 These rules, contained in the Family Law Act 1986, have been amended to take account of the Brussels II Regulation (European Communities (Matrimonial Jurisdiction and Judgments) Regulations 2001, SI 2001/310). See Lowe, 'The Family Law Act 1986 – A Critique' [2002] Fam Law 39. Further amendment will be required prior to the revised Brussels II Regulation coming into force. This section anticipates such amendments and is, accordingly, somewhat speculative.

its traditional rules[79] and the child does not satisfy the revised Brussels II jurisdictional criteria.

In such situations where the English court has jurisdiction in proceedings for divorce, nullity or separation, it also has jurisdiction to make an order in respect of any child of the family.[80] This jurisdiction may be invoked even though a child's connections with England are minimal or non-existent. However, in such cases where it is concluded that the matter could be more appropriately dealt with outside England, the English court is given a discretion to direct that no order be made in those proceedings.[81]

(B) PRESENCE

At present the English court has jurisdiction to make a section 8 order if at the date of the application the child is present in England[82] provided the child is not habitually resident in another part of the United Kingdom[83] and provided no matrimonial proceedings are continuing in Scotland or Northern Ireland.[84] When the revised Brussels II Regulation is brought into effect it is probable that this rule will be altered to allow the English court to exercise jurisdiction on the basis that the child is present in England provided no member state has jurisdiction by virtue of the revised Brussels II rules and the child is habitually resident in a non-member state.[85]

(C) EMERGENCY JURISDICTION

At present the English court has jurisdiction over a child who is present in England if 'the court considers that the immediate exercise of its powers is necessary for his protection'.[86] Jurisdiction may be exercised on this basis even though the child is habitually resident or matrimonial proceedings are continuing in another part of the United Kingdom. A fortiori, the habitual residence of the child in another jurisdiction outside the United Kingdom will not preclude the English court from assuming jurisdiction. When the revised Brussels II Regulation is brought into force, this rule will

79 See p 386.
80 Family Law Act 1986, s 2A. This includes stepchildren and others who are legally deemed to be a 'child of the family'. See Herring, *Family Law* (2001) p 281.
81 Family Law Act 1986, s 2A(4).
82 Ss 2(2), 3.
83 S 3(1)(b).
84 S 3(2).
85 If the habitual residence of the child cannot be ascertained in such a situation, jurisdiction on the basis of presence may be assumed under the revised Brussels II Regulation.
86 Family Law Act 1986, s 2(3)(b).

need to be limited to cases where no other court of a member state has jurisdiction as to the substance of the matter.[87]

(D) DECLINING JURISDICTION AND STAYING PROCEEDINGS

An English court may decline jurisdiction if the matter has already been determined in proceedings outside England.[88]

An English court may stay proceedings if it appears that proceedings with respect to the same matters are continuing outside England or that it would be more appropriate for those matters to be determined in proceedings outside England.[89] In short, this means that the doctrine of forum non conveniens as laid down in the *Spiliada* case[90] and *De Dampierre v De Dampierre*[91] is applicable.[92] In *Re S (Residence Order: Forum Conveniens)*[93] it was held that, in the context of the application of the *Spiliada* doctrine, the welfare of the child is an important, but not the paramount, consideration. Choosing between international jurisdictions is not 'a question with respect to the upbringing of a child' within the meaning of section 1(1)(a) of the Children Act 1989.

(E) THE 1996 HAGUE CONVENTION

The United Kingdom government had wished to ratify the Hague Convention on Jurisdiction, Applicable Law, Recognition, Enforcement and Co-operation in respect of Parental Responsibility and Measures for the Protection of Children (1996). However, under European Union law individual member states may no longer ratify the Convention on their own[94] and so the UK opted-in to the proposed Brussels IIA Regulation which contains provisions broadly similar to the Hague Convention. However, since then the European Commission has published a proposal for a Council Decision authorising member states to sign the 1996 Hague Convention.[95] In

87 Where the courts of another member state have jurisdiction, the present proposed art 9 of the Brussels IIA Regulation limits emergency jurisdiction to a period not exceeding one month. It is likely that the revised Brussels II Regulation will contain a similar provision.

88 S 5(1).

89 S 5(2).

90 [1987] AC 460, [1986] 3 All ER 843.

91 [1988] AC 92, [1987] 2 All ER 1.

92 *Re S (Stay of Proceedings)* [1993] 2 FLR 912.

93 [1995] 1 FLR 314 at 325.

94 See Karsten, 'The Draft EU Regulation on Parental Responsibility' [2001] Fam Law 885. See also Clive, 'The 1996 Hague Convention – A Proposal for Simplification' [2002] Fam Law 131.

95 COM(2001) 680 final.

addition, negotiations are to be opened for accession to the Hague Convention by the Community as a whole. The Hague Convention produces a regime similar to the revised Brussels II Regulation and, if or when it comes into effect within the UK (or throughout the Community), it will apply in English proceedings involving children habitually resident in non-member states.

C Choice of law

When the English court has jurisdiction to make a section 8 order, there is no question of choice of law. The matter is governed by English law under which the court, in deciding any question as to the custody or upbringing of a child, must regard the welfare of the child as the 'paramount consideration'.[96]

D Recognition of foreign orders; child abduction

1. Introduction

At common law foreign custody orders were never entitled to recognition or enforcement in England. Such orders are not final and are always subject to review.[97] Accordingly, while foreign orders might well carry weight in the English court's decision as to what order it should make, the overriding consideration was the welfare of the child.

Such an approach inevitably encouraged disgruntled parents who had been deprived of custody in one country to abduct their child, take him to another country, such as England, and try to obtain an award of custody. For example, in *McKee v McKee*[98] a Californian court awarded custody to the mother (the father had previously had custody). The father abducted the child and took him to Ontario where he was awarded custody, a decision confirmed by the Privy Council.

Abductions of this nature can be extremely harmful to children in disrupting their normal patterns of life, severing their relationships with others and, perhaps, involving a move to a country whose culture, language and educational system are alien to them. Such abductions pose a major problem as the normal judicial process for

96 Children Act 1989, s 1(1). Under the 1996 Hague Convention issues in relation to the attribution or extinction of parental responsibility are governed by the law of the state of the habitual residence of the child (art 16).
97 *McKee v McKee* [1951] AC 352 at 364.
98 Ibid.

resolving custody disputes is frustrated. This problem is exacerbated when 'in every country, there is a tendency to think that it must be within the child's best interest to be brought up there rather than elsewhere'.[99]

There have been several responses to this increasing problem of parents removing children across international boundaries. The Child Abduction Act 1984 makes it a criminal offence for a 'connected person' to remove (or attempt to remove) a child under the age of 16 from the United Kingdom without the appropriate consents of any other person having parental responsibility over the child.[100] The criminal law is, however, not the most appropriate mechanism for solving parental disputes over children. At civil law a prohibited steps order under section 8 of the Children Act 1989 can be obtained prohibiting a parent from removing a child from the jurisdiction. Alternatively, a child can be made a ward of court, the effect of which is to prohibit anyone removing him from the country.

These remedies are, of course, limited to trying to prevent the removal of children from England and Wales. The conflict of laws has to take a broader sweep and resolve issues where children have already been removed from one country to another whether in breach of a custody order or not.

At the national level (with regard to parental responsibility disputes between different parts of the United Kingdom) a solution was effected by Part I of the Family Law Act 1986. The approach adopted, as with the Brussels regime, was to tackle the problem by introducing uniform jurisdictional rules and providing for the almost automatic recognition of all such orders in other parts of the United Kingdom.

At the European level, the European Convention on Recognition and Enforcement of Decisions concerning Custody of Children and on the Restoration of Custody of Children (1980) was implemented in England by the Child Abduction and Custody Act 1985. This European Convention applied only where there had been a custody decision by the courts of a contracting state; the child need not have been improperly abducted. For parental responsibility orders made pursuant to matrimonial proceedings (probably the vast majority of such orders), the European Convention was superseded by the Brussels II Regulation.[101] This in turn will be superseded by the

99 Shirley Summerskill, *Hansard* (HC) vol 946, col 1849.

100 S 1.

101 This Regulation takes precedence over the European Convention (art 37). It only applies to parental responsibility orders affecting the children of both spouses. The European Convention continued to apply to stepchildren and other 'children of the family'.

revised Brussels II Regulation which apples to all civil proceedings relating to parental responsibility, whether these are made pursuant to matrimonial proceedings or not. The result will be that the European Convention will apply only to those contracting states that are not member states bound by the revised Brussels II Regulation.[102]

The other major international development was the Hague Convention on the Civil Aspects of International Child Abduction (1980) which was implemented by the Child Abduction and Custody Act 1985. The Hague Convention applies whether or not there has been a custody order, but applies only in cases where there has been a wrongful abduction of a child from a contracting state in which he is habitually resident. This Convention will also be significantly altered, in relation to children abducted between European Union member states, by the revised Brussels II Regulation.

Finally, in cases falling outside the scope of the Hague Convention and the revised Brussels II Regulation, the common law continues to apply. The remainder of this chapter will be devoted to an examination of these three mechanisms relating to child abduction and the recognition of parental responsibility orders.

2. *Hague Child Abduction Convention*

(A) INTRODUCTION

The Hague Convention on the Civil Aspects of International Child Abduction of 1980 was implemented by the Child Abduction and Custody Act 1985. There are 69 states that have either ratified or acceded to this Convention with the list increasing annually.

The Hague Convention applies only where a child has been 'wrongfully' removed from one contracting state to another or, while initially properly removed from a contracting state, has been 'wrongfully' retained in another contracting state. It applies irrespective of whether a custody order has been made. The object of the Convention is to ensure that children are returned promptly

102 Cyprus, Denmark, Iceland, Liechtenstein, Malta, Norway, Poland and Switzerland. For a discussion of the rules of this European Convention as still applied to these countries, see the 1997 edition of this book at pp 430–432.

to the country of their habitual residence;[103] it is for the courts of that country to resolve custody disputes. This rule of prompt return could be viewed as a manifestation of an underlying forum conveniens principle. The natural forum for the determination of custody disputes is the country of the child's habitual residence. Such a view is, however, only partially true. Given the ease with which habitual residence may be acquired,[104] there may well be situations where the country of habitual residence would not be the forum conveniens for the resolution of such issues.[105] The real object of the Hague Convention is to deter potential abductors from removing children from the country of their habitual residence.[106] Ensuring the almost automatic return of the child (with limited exceptions) is seen as beneficial to the interests of children (in the sense of promoting continuity and stability of family relationships) and as the best way of deterring potential abductors.

This principle of prompt return can conflict with the established family law principle that justice, with respect to children, must be individualised to promote the welfare of the particular child. While, as shall be seen, there are exceptions under the Hague Convention, the fact is that in some cases children will be sent to the country of their habitual residence when that will not serve their welfare. As stated in *W v W (Child Abduction: Acquiescence)*: 'the object of stability for the mass of children may have to be achieved at the price of tears in some individual cases'.[107] In *Re L (Abduction: Pending Criminal Proceedings)* it was stated that even though an order to return children would not promote their welfare, nevertheless such an order would contribute 'in a very small way to the welfare of those numerous other children who live in the contracting states across the world and whose parents would be deterred from abducting them'.[108]

The Hague Convention was constructed around the paradigm of an abductor, who was a non-custodial parent, snatching the child from the primary carer and removing the child to another country so as to be able to have sole custody of the child. However, now in 72 per cent of cases the abductor is the primary carer: 'the parent who has always looked after the children, upon whom the children

103 Art 1(a).
104 See pp 50–56.
105 Schuz, 'The Hague Child Abduction Convention: Family Law and Private International Law' (1995) 44 ICLQ 771 at 786–791.
106 *Re A (Abduction: Custody Rights) (No 2)* [1993] Fam 1 at 13.
107 [1993] 2 FLR 211 at 220.
108 [1999] 1 FLR 433 at 442.

rely for all their basic needs, and with whom their main security lies'.[109] In such cases the natural forum for resolution of custody disputes might not necessarily be the country of the child's habitual residence. Further, there is a real chance that if the child is returned, the courts of that country could well allow the primary carer and the children to leave lawfully[110] making the order to return an 'empty gesture'.[111] Accordingly, there have been suggestions that when applying the exceptions, mentioned above, the threshold should be lower and different when dealing with primary carers.[112] While such views are receiving some judicial acknowledgment,[113] the prevailing view is that, while the profile of abductors might have changed, the Hague Convention has not been modified and should be applied as it stands.[114]

(B) INTERNATIONAL ABDUCTION

The Hague Convention effectively defines an international abduction[115] as a wrongful 'removal or retention' of a child under the age of 16 from a contracting state in which he is habitually resident.[116] The meaning of habitual residence has already been examined.[117] What is meant by a 'wrongful removal or retention'?

(i) Wrongful: in breach of rights of custody

A removal or retention is wrongful if it is in 'breach of rights of custody'[118] existing in the country of the child's habitual residence immediately before the removal or retention. Article 3(a) provides that whether such rights of custody exist is to be determined 'under the law of the state in which the child was habitually resident'. Article 15 permits the courts to which the child has been abducted to seek a decision from the authorities of the state of the child's habitual residence that the removal or retention was wrongful. It has been argued that, as there is no specific provision that this be a reference to the internal law of that country, as is usual in Hague

109 *TB v JB (Abduction: Grave Risk of Harm)* [2001] 2 FLR 515 at 527, per Hale LJ. Hale, 'The View from Court 45' (1999) 11 CFLQ 377.
110 Ibid.
111 Freeman, 'Primary Carers and the Hague Child Abduction Convention' [2001] IFL 140.
112 Ibid.
113 Hale LJ dissenting in *TB v JB (Abduction: Grave Risk of Harm)* [2001] 2 FLR 515 at 530.
114 Arden LJ at 544.
115 The term 'abduction' only appears in the title to the Convention.
116 Arts 3 and 4.
117 See pp 50–56.
118 Art 3.

Conventions, this leaves room for the application of the doctrine of renvoi.[119] However, no English court has ever considered this possibility[120] and, in view of the problems associated with renvoi,[121] it is unlikely they will ever do so. Further, while the existence of rights attributed to a person is a matter for the foreign law, it is for English law (or the law of any other requested state) to determine whether these rights are 'rights of custody' within the Convention[122] and, accordingly, a decision under article 15 is 'not determinative'.[123] Indeed, as shall be seen, the Hague Convention adopts an 'autonomous meaning' of rights of custody in article 5(a). It must be noted, however, that a consequence of this approach is that a child could be returned to a country that did not regard the removal as wrongful so that there would be no restriction on the same person lawfully taking the child abroad again.[124] For example, in *Re D (Abduction: Custodial Rights)*[125] the argument that under the law of Zimbabwe the separation of the parents vested all custody rights in the mother was dismissed with the court ruling that it was applying the law relating to the Hague Convention 'as applied by the English courts'.[126] If this were really the position under Zimbabwean law[127] there would be little to be gained in sending the child back to Zimbabwe.

Irrespective of the foreign law, article 5(a) provides that 'rights of custody' include the right to care for a child and, in particular, the right to determine the child's place of residence.[128] It includes rights which would have been exercised by a person had the child not been removed.[129] However, a mere right to be consulted before a child is removed, but without a power to veto the removal, does not amount to 'rights of custody'.[130] In *Re B (Abduction)*[131] it was held that such

119 Beaumont and McEleavy, *The Hague Convention on International Child Abduction* (1999) p 46.
120 Ibid, p 47.
121 See Ch 12.
122 *Re F (Abduction: Custody Rights Abroad)* [1995] Fam 224, [1995] 3 All ER 641.
123 *Practice Note (Hague Convention: Application by Fathers without Parental Responsibility)* [1998] 1 FLR 491.
124 Beaumont and McEleavy, *The Hague Convention on International Child Abduction* (1999) p 62.
125 [1999] 2 FLR 626.
126 At 629.
127 This was doubted by the court. Further, although 'not binding' a declaration of wrongful removal under art 15 had been obtained from the High Court in Zimbabwe.
128 Art 5(a).
129 *Re F (Abduction: Custody Rights Abroad)* [1995] Fam 224, [1995] 3 All ER 641.
130 *Re V-B (Abduction: Custodial Rights)* [1999] 2 FLR 192.
131 [1995] 2 FCR 505 at 517.

rights vested in a person who was actually exercising the responsibilities of a parent or guardian if this position was likely to be upheld by the courts of the child's habitual residence. This was (controversially) extended in *Re O (Child Abduction: Custody Rights)*[132] to the factual day-to-day carer of a child. In this case a child was returned to Germany to her grandparents with whom she had been living. Cazalet J was clearly influenced by both the fact that Germany was the forum conveniens – 'this case has Germany stamped all over' – and the fact that the child's welfare would be best served by a return to Germany. In less clear-cut cases it might not be so easy to establish that a mere de facto carer has acquired 'rights of custody'.

It has been decided that rights of custody can be acquired after the removal of the child from a country. In *Re S (Custody: Habitual Residence)*[133] relatives removed a child from England to Ireland the day after his mother died. This removal was not wrongful as the unmarried father had no 'rights of custody'. Two days later an English court granted him interim care and control of the child. It was held by the House of Lords that he thereby acquired 'rights of custody' and the retention of the child in Ireland from that date (or from when the relatives were served with notice of the order) was wrongful. This decision reveals a potential clash between the twin policies underlying the Convention. While England might well have been the appropriate forum, it is hard to see how the policy of deterring abductions is furthered if, at the time of the removal, there were no rights of custody vested in any person.

A removal or retention is wrongful even if the taker is unaware of the wrongfulness of his actions.[134] Again, this is hardly compatible with the policy of deterring abductions, but is a necessary rule on the pragmatic ground that too many parents would claim they were unaware of the wrongfulness of their actions; this would result in protracted litigation and delays to the prompt return of children and, if such arguments were accepted, destroy the underlying policy of the Convention.

'Rights of custody' may vest in a person, several persons jointly, or an institution or other body.[135] For instance, in *Re JS (Private International Adoption)*[136] rights of custody were regarded as vested in a foreign adoption agency and in *Re H (Abduction: Rights of Custody)*[137] it was decided that these rights vested in a court to whom an application for guardianship of a child had been made.

132 [1997] 2 FLR 702.
133 [1998] AC 750, [1998] 1 FLR 122.
134 *C v C (Child Abduction)* [1992] 1 FLR 163.
135 Art 3(a).
136 [2000] 2 FLR 638.
137 [2000] 2 AC 291.

Rights of custody may arise by operation of law or by reason of a judicial or administrative decision or as a result of a legally binding agreement.[138] This covers, for instance, custody awards that are made in Scandinavian countries by administrative authorities. It also caters for the increasing trend towards private regulation of custody matters: for example, a legally binding separation agreement between parents establishing arrangements for the shared custody of their children.

(ii) Removal or retention

The terms 'removal' and 'retention' are mutually exclusive; there cannot be a removal and a retention in the same case.[139] A removal occurs when a child is taken across the frontier of the state of his habitual residence; a retention occurs when a child is kept in a country beyond the lawful period of time he was permitted to be there (for example, when he is not returned after a specified period of access). A wrongful retention can occur when a person makes a firm decision not to return the child to his country of habitual residence, even if that decision is made at a time when the child is lawfully in another country.[140] It has been held that a retention is not a continuing state of affairs that lasts as long as the child is kept in the country. It is a single event which occurs as soon as the child is not returned[141] and therefore it is the wrongfulness of the retention at that time, and the habitual residence of the child at that moment, that is crucial under the Convention. However, as seen above, in *Re S (Custody: Habitual Residence)*[142] a retention that was not initially wrongful was held to become wrongful at a later stage. This suggests that an innocent retention is a continuing state of affairs until it becomes wrongful.

(C) ROLE OF THE CENTRAL AUTHORITY

The Convention provides for the appointment of a Central Authority in each contracting state,[143] whose functions include taking steps to

138 Art 3.
139 *Re H (Abduction: Custody Rights)* [1991] 2 AC 476, [1991] 1 All ER 836.
140 *Re AZ (Abduction: Acquiescence)* [1993] 1 FLR 682.
141 Ibid.
142 [1998] AC 750, [1998] 1 FLR 122.
143 In the United Kingdom the functions of the Central Authority are in England and Wales and Northern Ireland discharged by the Official Solicitor acting on behalf of the Lord Chancellor; in Scotland it is the Secretary of State for Scotland who has this responsibility (Child Abduction and Custody Act 1985, s 3(1)).

find abducted children, trying to secure their voluntary return,[144] and, if that fails, initiating or facilitating the institution of proceedings for their return.[145] A person seeking the return of a child under the Convention will normally make an application through the Central Authority of the country in which the child is habitually resident or of any other contracting state, which will transmit it to the Authority in the state where the child is believed to be.[146]

A parent of an abducted child is not obliged to use the Central Authority of the country of the child's habitual residence. An application may be made directly to the Central Authority of the country to which the child has been taken. However, the speed with which the Central Authority is able to act, coupled with the expertise it has built up and the fact that its services are free,[147] makes private action a less attractive option.[148]

(D) DUTY TO RETURN

The basic rule is that if proceedings for the return of the child are brought in any contracting state in which the child is present, the court must order the prompt return of the child.[149] Such judicial returns in 1999 took an average of 87 days across contracting states with judicial returns from England taking an average of 58 days.[150]

In all disputes relating to children, particularly younger children, time is of the essence. Accordingly, the Convention distinguishes between cases where the application for a return is made within one year of the wrongful removal or retention and those where the application is made after a year. Where the application is made within one year of the wrongful removal or retention the court 'shall order the return of the child forthwith'[151] unless one of the exceptional grounds under article 13, discussed below, is made out. In cases where more than a year has elapsed since the wrongful removal or retention, the return of the child must still normally be ordered

144 There was a voluntary return in 18 per cent of cases in 1999 across contracting states (Lowe, Armstrong and Mathias, *A Statistical Analysis of Applications made in 1999 under the Hague Convention of 25 October 1980 on the Civil Aspects of International Child Abduction*, Preliminary Document No 3, Hague Conference on Private International Law: Child Abduction (2001)). See Armstrong (2002) 51 ICLQ 305.

145 Art 7.

146 Arts 8 and 9.

147 Art 26.

148 See, generally, Bruch, 'The Central Authority's Role under the Hague Child Abduction Convention: A Friend in Deed' (1994) 28 FLQ 35.

149 Art 12.

150 Lowe et al, above n 144.

151 Art 12.

(unless one of the exceptional grounds under article 13, discussed below, is made out). In these cases, however, the child might be so well established and settled in the new country that the potential harm in sending him back outweighs the broader goal of deterring abduction. Accordingly, article 12 provides that the child need not be ordered to return if 'it is demonstrated that the child is now settled in its new environment'. In *Re M (Abduction: Acquiescence)*[152] it was held that weight must be given to emotional and psychological settlement as well as to physical settlement. The danger of a provision such as this is that it could encourage abductors to keep a child hidden for longer periods of time. Accordingly, it has been held that a year living in hiding cannot lead to a 'settled life'.[153]

(E) EXCEPTIONAL GROUNDS FOR REFUSING TO ORDER RETURN OF CHILD (ARTICLE 13)

The basic rule that there is a duty to return prevails over the normal welfare test applied in custody disputes. Returning children promptly is seen as promoting the welfare of children generally and it is this consideration, rather than the interests of a specific child, that is central to the Hague Convention.[154] However, as a compromise to those who were concerned at the abandonment of the welfare principle, provision is made for exceptional grounds for refusing to order the return of a child. In all cases, whether the child has been in the new country for more or less than a year, article 13 lists several exceptional grounds which, if established, allows the court a discretion whether to order a return or not. In *Re O (Abduction: Consent and Acquiescence)*[155] it was stressed that there is a two-stage process: (i) one of the exceptional grounds must be established; (ii) if so, the court has a discretion, it may refuse to order the return of the child. In exercising this discretion it was held in *H v H (Abduction: Acquiescence)*[156] that the following factors should be considered: (a) the comparative suitability of the forum to determine the child's future in the substantive proceedings; (b) the likely outcome (in whichever forum) of the substantive proceedings; (c) the consequences of acquiescence, with particular reference to the extent to which a child may have become settled in the requested

152 [1996] 1 FLR 315 at 321.

153 *Re H (Abduction: Child of 16)* [2000] 2 FLR 51.

154 See, for example, Lord Denning in the House of Lords opposing an amendment to treat the welfare of the child as the paramount consideration: 'the first and paramount consideration is to return the child who has been wrongfully taken away' (*Hansard* (HL) 1985, vol 461, col 1156).

155 [1997] 1 FLR 924.

156 [1996] 2 FLR 570 at 574.

state; (d) the situation which would await the absconding parent and the child if compelled to return; (e) the anticipated emotional effect upon the child of an immediate return (a factor to be treated as significant but not paramount); and (f) the extent to which the purpose and underlying philosophy of the Hague Convention would be at risk of frustration if a return order were to be refused.

It is in this context that the real tension between the welfare principle and the policy of deterring abduction is exposed. One approach has been that the welfare of the child is an important but not the paramount consideration; the child should generally be promptly returned to the country of his habitual residence which will normally be the forum conveniens, the jurisdiction most appropriate to determine the issue.[157] An alternative approach is that once the discretion has been generated, 'the gate is unlocked'[158] and the welfare test is predominant, with the goals of the Convention being a relevant, but subsidiary, consideration.[159] This should be particularly true in those cases (now the clear majority) when the abductor is the primary carer of the child.[160] Despite some recent support,[161] this latter approach seems to have been on the wane with the comments of Butler-Sloss LJ best summing up the current attitude that English courts are 'rightly sceptical of attempts by many abducting parents to invoke the provisions of article 13 to try to stave off the almost inevitable requirement to return the child. The welfare of the child who has been abducted is generally seen as best served by returning him to the jurisdiction of his habitual residence'.[162] In 1999 in only 10 per cent of cases was an application for the return of a child refused or rejected across contracting states.[163]

Under article 13 the court may refuse to order the return of the child if one of the following grounds is established. The burden is on the party seeking to prevent the return to establish that a ground is

157 *C v C (Abduction: Rights of Custody)* [1989] 1 WLR 654 at 661; *V v B (Abduction)* [1991] 1 FLR 266 at 273; *Re L (Abduction: Pending Criminal Proceedings)* [1999] 1 FLR 433 at 441; *Re R (Abduction: Consent)* [1999] 1 FLR 828 at 836.

158 Schuz, 'The Hague Child Abduction Convention: Family Law and Private International Law' (1995) 44 ICLQ 771 at 775.

159 *Re A (Abduction: Custody Rights) (No 2)* [1993] Fam 1, [1993] 1 All ER 272; *A v A (Child Abduction)* [1993] 2 FLR 225. See Caldwell, 'Child Welfare Defences in Child Abduction Cases – Some Recent Developments' (2001) 13 CFLQ 121.

160 See p 461 above.

161 Hale LJ dissenting in *TB v JB (Abduction: Grave Risk of Harm)* [2001] 2 FLR 515.

162 *Re P (Abduction: Minor's Views)* [1998] 2 FLR 825 at 827.

163 Lowe et al, above n 144.

made out and to persuade the court to exercise its discretion not to order a return.[164]

(i) Custody rights not actually exercised

The child need not be returned if the person, institution or body having care of the child was not actually exercising the custody rights at the time of the removal or retention. It is, of course, unlikely that a person who is voluntarily not exercising custody rights over a child would seek a return of the child. A parent who has secretly moved children to prevent the other parent exercising such rights cannot utilise this ground.[165] Research reveals that there were no cases in 1999 across contracting states where this ground was used as a basis for refusing to order the return of a child.[166]

(ii) Consent or acquiescence

The child need not be returned if the person, institution or body having care of the child had consented to, or subsequently acquiesced in, the removal or retention.[167] Consent need not be express and may be inferred from conduct, but the evidence of such consent needs to be 'clear and cogent'[168] but need not be in writing.[169] Consent may be negated by fraud[170] or non-disclosure of material facts,[171] but a mere reluctance to see the child leaving does not of itself negate consent.[172]

A definition of acquiescence was provided in *W v W (Child Abduction: Acquiescence)*: 'Acquiescence means acceptance. It may be active arising from express words or conduct, or passive arising by inference from silence or inactivity.'[173] Typically, it will occur when a person having custody rights does nothing after the child has been wrongfully removed or retained. The House of Lords has held that whether or not there is acquiescence is a subjective test. What matters is the actual state of mind of the wronged parent and not whether the other parent believed there was acquiescence. However, where the words or actions of the wronged parent clearly showed, and led the other parent to believe, that he was not going to assert

164 *Re L (Abduction: Pending Criminal Proceedings)* [1999] 1 FLR 433.
165 *TB v JB (Abduction: Grave Risk of Harm)* [2001] 2 FLR 515.
166 Lowe et al, above, n 144.
167 Art 13(a).
168 *Re C (Abduction: Consent)* [1996] 1 FLR 414 at 419; *Re R (Abduction: Consent)* [1999] 1 FLR 828.
169 *Re K (Abduction: Consent)* [1997] 2 FLR 212
170 *Re B (Abduction)* [1994] 2 FLR 249.
171 *T v T (Abduction: Consent)* [1999] 2 FLR 912.
172 *Re M (Abduction) (Consent: Acquiescence)* [1999] 1 FLR 171.
173 [1993] 2 FLR 211 at 217.

his rights, justice requires that the wronged parent be deemed to have acquiesced.[174]

Whether there is acquiescence is a question of fact.[175] Negotiations between the parents do not amount to acquiescence.[176] The acquiescence must be real in the sense that the person acquiescing must be aware that he or she has a general right of objection, but it is not necessary to have a precise knowledge of legal rights and remedies such as those under the Hague Convention.[177]

Delay in seeking the return of a child is evidence of acquiescence,[178] but may be negated by an explanation, for example, that wrong legal advice was given.[179] It was emphasised in *Re AZ (Abduction: Acquiescence)*[180] that the courts should be slow to infer acquiescence from conduct and that a mere acceptance that the child should stay in the new country 'for a matter of days or a week or two' does not amount to acquiescence. In *Re R (Abduction)*[181] it was held that waiting for four months for the outcome of foreign proceedings did not amount to acquiescence.[182] It will be difficult to establish acquiescence if the abductor has hidden the child from the wronged parent.[183]

(iii) Grave risk

The child need not be returned if there is 'a grave risk that his or her return would expose the child to physical or psychological harm or otherwise place the child in an intolerable situation'.[184] In many cases where a child is living with a parent, albeit one that has abducted him, it could cause some psychological harm to uproot and send him back to the country of his habitual residence. It has been held that there must be more than this general psychological harm and unhappiness to be associated with a transfer of care.[185] The damaging features of the child's family life must generally have existed immediately prior to the wrongful abduction and been the motivation for the departure.[186]

174 *Re H (Abduction: Acquiescence)* [1998] AC 72.
175 Ibid.
176 *Re I (Abduction: Acquiescence)* [1999] 1 FLR 778.
177 *W v W (Child Abduction: Acquiescence)* [1993] 2 FLR 211.
178 Ibid.
179 *Re S (Abduction: Acquiescence)* [1994] 1 FLR 819.
180 [1993] 1 FLR 682.
181 [1994] 1 FLR 190.
182 In *W v W (Child Abduction: Acquiescence)* [1993] 2 FLR 211 it was held that inactivity for ten months did amount to acquiescence.
183 *Re H (Abduction: Child of 16)* [2000] 2 FLR 51.
184 Art 13(b).
185 *P v P (Child Abduction)* [1992] 1 FLR 155.
186 *Re C (Abduction: Grave Risk of Physical or Psychological Harm)* [1999] 2 FLR 478 at 487–488.

Research suggests that 70 per cent of abductors are women and that a high proportion of those may be mothers escaping the father's abuse and violence.[187] To prevent this provision destroying the policy of the Convention[188] by allowing the welfare test to be predominant, it is provided that the risks to the child must be *grave* and place the child in an *intolerable* situation. There must be a risk of 'substantial' harm or other intolerability.[189] The intolerable situation must be 'something extreme'[190] and there needs to be 'clear and compelling' evidence of the grave risk.[191] As these proceedings are of a summary nature, the standard of proof is set at a 'high hurdle'.[192] The grave risk must be to the child. Evidence of general violence will not suffice unless that violence would expose the child to a grave risk of psychological harm.[193]

Two examples show the reluctance of the English courts to find that this exception has been established. First, in *TB v JB (Abduction: Grave Risk of Harm)*[194] children were ordered to return to New Zealand despite the mother's second husband being an abusive and unpredictable person who had allegedly raped her and maltreated both her and the children. A majority in the Court of Appeal accepted that the New Zealand authorities would take the necessary protective measures. The mother was not permitted to rely on her fear of her husband which made her unwilling to seek such protection as a factor relevant to the risk. Similarly, in *Re M (Abduction: Intolerable Situation)*[195] a child was ordered back to Norway despite the mother's claim that there was a risk of physical harm from the father who was about to be released from prison for murdering a man with whom he believed she had been having an affair. The court accepted that the Norwegian authorities would be able to offer various forms of protection.

On the other hand, examples of where a return has been refused on this ground include a case where the child would have had to live with his father who had previously mistreated him and the child would have found this disturbing,[196] and a case where the return of

187 Lowe and Perry, 'International Child Abduction – The English Experience' (1999) 48 ICLQ 127.
188 This is by far the most common ground for refusing to order a return of children: 26% of cases in 1999 (Lowe et al, above n 144.)
189 *Re A (Abduction)* [1988] 1 FLR 365 at 372.
190 *Re N (Abduction)* [1991] 1 FLR 413 at 419. See also *Re HB (Child's Objections)* [1997] 1 FLR 392 at 396–397.
191 *Re C (Abduction: Grave Risk of Psychological Harm)* [1999] 1 FLR 1145 at 1154.
192 Laws LJ in *TB v JB (Abduction: Grave Risk of Harm)* [2001] 2 FLR 515 at 546.
193 *Re R (Abduction: Consent)* [1999] 1 FCR 87.
194 [2001] 2 FLR 515.
195 [2000] 1 FLR 930.
196 *Re F (Abduction: Rights of Custody Abroad)* [1995] Fam 224, [1995] 3 All ER 641.

one child, separating him from his siblings, would have had a disastrous effect upon him.[197]

(iv) Objection of children

A return may be refused if the child objects to being returned and has attained an age and degree of maturity at which it is appropriate to take account of his views.[198] It is not possible to state any particular age at which the child's views are to be taken into account.[199] Much depends on the extent to which the objections are clear and reasoned.[200] While the views of children as young as seven years old have, on occasion, been taken into account,[201] the objections of children aged 13 to 16 are most likely to be accepted.[202] While concern has been expressed that too much weight has been placed on the wishes of children thereby frustrating the objective of the Convention,[203] the evidence shows that some 78 per cent of abducted children are under the age of ten and their objections were a reason for refusal to return only in under three per cent of cases where the child was not returned.[204] Nevertheless, this issue again forces to the fore the central dilemma between the welfare principle (under which the child's wishes should always be taken into account) and the forum conveniens principle (the country of the child's habitual residence is normally the most appropriate forum to determine issues relating to custody). Of course, the views of children are never decisive; if the child is old and mature enough for his views to be taken into account, this does no more than generate a discretion to refuse to order a return.[205]

(F) PROTECTION OF ACCESS RIGHTS

The main purpose at the time of the drafting of the Hague Convention was to secure the return of a child that has been wrongfully removed

197 *B v K (Child Abduction)* [1993] 1 FCR 382; *Ontario Court v M and M (Abduction: Children's Objections)* [1997] 1 FLR 475.

198 Art 13.

199 *Re R (Child Abduction: Acquiescence)* [1995] 1 FLR 716; *Re P (Abduction: Minor's Views)* [1998] 2 FLR 825.

200 *Re T (Abduction: Child's Objections to Return)* [2000] 2 FLR 192.

201 *B v K (Child Abduction)* [1993] 1 FCR 382.

202 Lowe et al, above n 144.

203 Lord Chancellor's Department, *Consultation on Child Abduction: Review of the Hague Convention* (1996) p 2.

204 Lowe et al, above n 144.

205 *Re* S *(Abduction: Acquiescence)* [1994] 1 FLR 819. In *Re HB (Abduction: Children's Objections)* [1997] 1 FLR 392 two children aged 13 and 11 were ordered to return to the country from which they had been abducted despite both making a 'very dramatic objection to returning' (at 398) and one of them saying he would kill his stepfather if returned.

from (or retained outside) his country of habitual residence. In short, the paradigm was the protection of the custodial rights of the parent with whom the child lived. A related problem, however, occurs when a parent having 'rights of custody' removes a child from the country of habitual residence thereby denying the other parent rights of access that he might possess or have been granted. Such a removal is wrongful[206] but the Hague Convention has no clear legal provisions to enforce such rights. However, article 21 obliges the Central Authority of each contracting state 'to promote the peaceful enjoyment of access rights' and to take steps to remove obstacles to the exercise of such rights. This creates no rights in private law that a parent can directly enforce.[207] At most, it places a public law duty on the Central Authority who may initiate proceedings to protect access rights. However, there is no obligation to commence such proceedings and no clear principles are laid down to guide the courts. Under article 21 it is the duty of the Central Authority to provide the applicant with English solicitors who can institute proceedings under the Children Act 1989.[208] In such proceedings the welfare principle will prevail.[209]

As already seen, however, the real position today is that some 72 per cent of abductors are primary carers and therefore the parent in the country of habitual residence only had rights of access. Since the drafting of the Hague Convention there has been an 'evolution in child-care provision which has seen traditional classifications like custody and access replaced with wider, more inclusive concepts such as parental rights and responsibilities'.[210] This means that many parents with only 'rights of access' now qualify as having 'rights of custody' and, instead of bringing access applications, can seek the return of the child under the rules discussed above. This trend is borne out by the evidence. In 1999 84 per cent of applications under the Hague Convention were for the return of the child while only 16 per cent were access applications.[211]

It has been questioned whether it is appropriate that a father, with a right of custody over a child by virtue of having a right of veto over

206 *B v B (Access: Jurisdiction)* [1988] 2 FLR 6; *C v C (Child Abduction)* [1992] 1 FLR 163.

207 *Re G (Enforcement of Access Abroad)* [1993] 3 All ER 657, [1993] 1 FLR 669.

208 *Re T (Practice Note)* [1993] 3 All ER 127n, [1993] 1 WLR 1461.

209 See, generally, Lowe, 'Problems Relating to Access Disputes under the Hague Convention on International Child Abduction' (1994) 8 Int J of Law and the Family 374.

210 Beaumont and McEleavy, *The Hague Convention on International Child Abduction* (1999) p 213.

211 Lowe et al, above n 144.

the removal of the child from the jurisdiction, should be able to apply for the return of a child that he only sees on Sunday afternoons.[212] Such changed social realities behind the pattern of international abductions have lead increasingly to calls for reform of the Hague Convention.[213] Indeed, a 1996 Hague Convention has been drafted but has not yet been ratified by the United Kingdom.[214]

3. *The revised Brussels II Regulation*

As already seen,[215] this Regulation will apply to all civil proceedings relating to parental responsibility. This includes decisions on rights of access.[216] The main focus of the Regulation is on securing uniform jurisdictional rules throughout the European Union. All judgments will then be entitled to automatic recognition and enforcement in other member states.

As is the position under the current Chapter III of the Brussels II Regulation, this means that recognition and enforcement will be automatic without any special procedure being required.[217] There can be no review of the jurisdiction of the court of origin[218] and under no circumstances may a judgment be reviewed as to its substance.[219] It would appear that, unlike the position with regard to recognition of matrimonial decisions where only positive decisions can be recognised, the revised Regulaiton will cover all parental responsibility orders, whether positive or negative.[220]

The other important relevant provisions that will be incorporated are the grounds for non-recognition in article 15(2) of the Brussels II Regulation. The effect of these is that a judgment relating to parental responsibility shall not be recognised: (a) if such recognition is manifestly contrary to the public policy of the member state in which recognition is sought taking into account the best interests of the child; (b) if it was given, except in case of urgency, without the child having an opportunity to be heard, in violation of fundamental

212 Beaumont and McEleavy, *The Hague Convention on International Child Abduction* (1999) p 213.
213 Ibid pp 213–215; Freeman, 'Primary Carers and the Hague Child Abduction Convention' [2001] IFL 140.
214 See p 457.
215 See p 454.
216 Recital 6 to the current proposed Brussels IIA Regulation. The revised Brussels II Regulation will incorporate the French initiative on rights of access: see above n 71.
217 Brussels II, art 14.
218 Brussels II, art 17.
219 Brussels II, art 19.
220 Lowe, 'New International Conventions Affecting the Law Relating to Children – A Cause for Concern?' [2001] IFL 171.

principles of procedure of the member state in which recognition is sought; (c) where it was given in default of appearance, if the person in default was not served with the documentation in sufficient time and in such a way as to enable a defence to be arranged, unless that person accepted the judgment unequivocally; (d) where a judgment infringes a person's parental responsibility, if that person was not given an opportunity to be heard; (e) if it is irreconcilable with a later judgment relating to parental responsibility given in the member state in which recognition is sought or given in another member state or the non-member state of the habitual residence of the child provided these later judgments are entitled to recognition in the member state in which recognition is sought. This last ground for non-recognition departs from the more usual rule that earlier judgments prevail.[221] The rationale for this approach is presumably related to the fact that children's circumstances can change so speedily; with 'time being of the essence' in all matters relating to children, it is the latest judgment that is most likely to reflect the current situation.

Unlike the recognition of matrimonial decrees, where the issue of enforcement does not arise, special provision will be made for the enforcement of parental responsibility orders.[222]

The most striking innovations of the current Brussels IIA proposals (and likely to be incorporated into the revised Brussels II Regulation) are the provisions on child abduction which modify the operation of the Hague Convention in cases of abductions between member states. It is provided that the courts of the country to which the child has been abducted may no longer refuse to order the return of the child on the basis of the exceptions in article 13 of the Hague Convention. Because it is assumed that the courts of all member states are equally able to protect children, there must be an immediate return of the child except in the very limited circumstances discussed below.

These rules for the automatic return of children only apply in cases where there has been a wrongful removal or retention. Under the current Brussels IIA proposals, this is defined in terms substantially similar to the Hague Convention[223] but instead of the Hague Convention's terminology of 'in breach of rights of custody' it uses the more modern formulation of 'in breach of rights of parental responsibility'. In such cases there can be no refusal to return the child on the Hague Convention grounds that there is a

221 Brussels I Regulation, art 34(4), Brussels II Regulation, art 15(1)(d).

222 Brussels II Regulation, arts 21–31.

223 While art 5(4) simply provides for a 'breach of rights of parental responsibility', art 2 states that the holder of parental responsibility means 'any natural or legal person having parental responsibility over a child by judgment or by operation of law'.

grave risk that the return would expose the child to physical or psychological harm or otherwise place the child in an intolerable situation. Equally there can be no refusal based on the child's objections. It is hoped that the removal of these 'exceptions' to the rule of prompt return will provide an added deterrent against abductions.[224]

Under the current Brussels IIA proposals, which are likely to be included in the revised Brussels II Regulation, there are, however, two situations where the rule of prompt return does not apply. First, the rule on acquiescence in the Hague Convention has been somewhat clarified. The child need not be returned if he has acquired a habitual residence in the new state and each holder of parental responsibility has acquiesced in the removal or retention or the child has resided in that new state for at least a year after the holder of parental responsibility has or should have had knowledge of the whereabouts of the child and has not lodged a request for return within that period and if the child is settled in the new environment.[225] Secondly, the power to take provisional measures to protect a child in urgent cases is preserved. It will be recalled, however, that such provisional measures can only last for a maximum period of one month.[226] Such limited protection is unlikely to satisfy those who advocate the application of the welfare principle in such cases. Nevertheless, as far as returns between member states are concerned, it is the forum conveniens principle of prompt return that has prevailed.

4. *The common law*

In cases falling outside the scope of the Hague Convention or the revised Brussels II Regulation, the common law rules continue to apply. This means that the welfare principle prevails over the principle of prompt return.[227] However, the English courts have tended to hold that the welfare of the child is best served by having custodial issues determined in the country of habitual residence[228] and that it is appropriate to proceed by analogy with the Hague Convention.[229] Of course, the exact provisions of the Convention, for example, those in article 13, are not to be applied literally as this

224 Explanatory Memorandum to the Brussels IIA proposals, para 9.
225 Art 5(2).
226 Above, p 455.
227 *Re P (Abduction)* [1996] 3 FCR 233.
228 *Re Z (Abduction: Non-Convention Country)* [1999] 1 FLR 1270.
229 *Re F (Abduction: Custody Rights)* [1991] Fam 25, [1990] 3 All ER 87; *Re M (Abduction: Peremptory Return Orders)* [1996] 1 FLR 478.

would undermine the welfare principle.[230] Proceeding by analogy with the Hague Convention in all cases has been criticised[231] on the ground that while all contracting states to the Hague Convention base their decisions relating to the upbringing of children on the principle that the welfare of the child is paramount, this is not necessarily true of some other countries which might award custody on other criteria, such as the gender of the parent. Such thinking was echoed in *Re JA (Child Abduction: Non-Convention Country)*[232] where it was held that, before ordering the return of a child, the court should be satisfied that the foreign court would apply the welfare principle. This approach, reminiscent of 'we do it best' chauvinism, should be treated with caution. In *Osman v Elasha*[233] the Court of Appeal held that it was not appropriate for the English courts to examine the family law regime of Sudan. While courts there would resolve disputes according to Islamic law in a manner that was different from the approach of the English courts, this would nevertheless be done within the context of Sudanese custom and culture which was familiar and acceptable to the practising Muslim family involved.

In view of this approach and, given the ever-increasing number of countries that are contracting states to the Hague Convention, the importance of the common law rules is considerably reduced and no further consideration will be given to them.

230 *Re P (Abduction: Non-Convention Country)* [1997] Fam 45.
231 Beevers, Child Abduction – Welfare or Comity' [1996] Fam Law 365.
232 [1998] 1 FLR 231.
233 [2000] Fam 62.

Chapter 11

Property

This chapter considers the choice of law rules for the transfer of property. The rules are structured round a number of distinctions. First, a distinction has to be drawn between movables and immovables. As regards movables, a further distinction is drawn between tangibles and intangibles. Secondly, the law distinguishes between cases involving the transfer of property on death and cases where property is transferred inter vivos. Thirdly, transfers which arise as a result of marriage should be distinguished from other types of transfer.

I MOVABLES AND IMMOVABLES

The English conflict of laws, like other systems, draws a distinction between movable and immovable property. The main reason for making the distinction is that immovable property, which comprises land and things attached to or growing on the land, is subject to the control of the authorities where it is situated to a much greater extent than movable property which can be physically removed from one country to another. As a result different choice of law rules have been developed for movable and immovable property.

The traditional English distinction between realty and personalty is not used for choice of law purposes for a number of reasons. First, the distinction between realty and personalty is known only to those legal systems which are derived from the English common law. Secondly, it is the factual difference between movables and immovables – rather than the more technical and artificial distinction between real property and personal property – which justifies the application of different choice of law rules. So, for conflicts purposes, property in England – as well as elsewhere – must be classified as either movable or immovable. Normally, there will be no dispute whether property is movable or immovable, for the distinction is largely factual. However, in borderline cases different laws may take different views as to whether particular property is movable or immovable. It is well established that the classification of property as either movable or immovable should be made according to the law of the country in which the property is situated (lex situs).[1]

As regards property situated in England an interest in land will, generally speaking, be classified as an immovable even if, according to English domestic law, the interest is regarded as personalty. In *Freke v Lord Carbery*,[2] for example, a testator died domiciled in Ireland, leaving a leasehold house in England. A question arose as to whether the validity of the disposition should be governed by English or Irish law. If the property were regarded as immovable, English law, as the lex situs, governed; if the property were classified as movable, Irish law, as the law of the testator's domicile, applied. The court decided that, even though English law traditionally classifies leases as personal property, for choice of law purposes the property in question was to be classified as immovable. So, the validity of the disposition was governed by English law, according to which it was invalid.

In *Re Berchtold*[3] the deceased died intestate while domiciled in Hungary. At his death he was entitled to an interest in freehold land in England which, under his father's will, was subject to a trust for sale, but which had not been sold. If the deceased's interest in the land was immovable, succession to it would be governed by English law as the lex situs; if the interest was regarded as movable, Hungarian law, being the law of the testator's domicile, would govern. It was argued that, according to English law as it then stood, the deceased's interest under the trust for sale was regarded as personalty (by virtue of the doctrine of conversion) and that it should be treated as movable property for choice of law purposes.[4] It was held, however, that the deceased's interest should be classified as immovable property. The doctrine of conversion was not relevant to the question of how the deceased's interest should be classified. However, once it was decided that the property was immovable, English domestic law (which then included the doctrine of conversion) determined who was entitled to the deceased's interest.

Where the property in question is situated abroad, classification is to be effected by the relevant foreign law. So, even though property situated in country X is by English notions immovable, the English court should classify it as movable if that is the classification

1 *Re Berchtold* [1923] 1 Ch 192 at 199; *Re Cutliffe's Will Trusts* [1940] Ch 565 at 571.
2 (1873) LR 16 Eq 461.
3 [1923] 1 Ch 192.
4 In the context of trusts of land the doctrine of conversion has been abolished by the Trusts of Land and Appointment of Trustees Act 1996, s 3. Under the 1996 Act an interest under a trust of land – even an expressly created trust for sale – is to be regarded as realty, rather than personalty.

according to the law of country X.[5] Similarly, if the situs is abroad, property which according to English law is regarded as movable must be treated as immovable if the lex situs classifies the property as immovable. In *Ex p Rucker*[6] the deeds to a plantation in Antigua were lodged with the petitioner by way of equitable mortgage in 1831 (before slavery was abolished in British colonies). When the petitioner applied for sale of the plantation, including the slaves who worked on it, a question arose as to whether or not the slaves were part of the land. The court held that they were, since that was the position under the law of Antigua at that time.

The distinction between tangible movables and intangible movables essentially mirrors the traditional English distinction between choses in possession and choses in action. It is clear that the rules relating to tangible movables apply to things such as motorcars, paintings and commodities. It is equally clear that the rules relating to intangible movables apply to interests such as debts, shares, patents,[7] trade marks and copyright. Property questions become potentially muddied, however, in cases where title to an intangible interest (such as shares in a company) is represented by tangible documents (such as share certificates). It is important to distinguish the question of who is entitled to possession of the share certificates from the question of who is entitled to the shares themselves. In *Williams v Colonial Bank*[8] share certificates (representing shares in a New York company) were deposited with the defendant bank in England. Bowen LJ formulated the issue facing the court in the following terms:

> The key to this case is whether the defendants have a right to hold these pieces of paper, these certificates. What the effect upon their ulterior rights in America would be if we were to declare that they were entitled to these pieces of paper is another question.[9]

II TRANSFERS INTER VIVOS

Which law determines whether a given act, transaction or event transfers title to property or other proprietary rights from one person

5 *Re Hoyles* [1911] 1 Ch 179.
6 (1834) 3 LJ Bcy 104.
7 Somewhat elliptically the United Kingdom legislation provides that a patent is 'personal property (without being a thing in action)': Patents Act 1977, s 30(1).
8 (1888) 38 Ch D 388.
9 At 408. See also *Macmillan Inc v Bishopsgate Investment Trust plc (No 3)* [1996] 1 All ER 585, [1996] 1 WLR 387.

to another? Title to property is often transferred in consequence of a contract, but the law which governs the contract is not necessarily the one which determines whether and when title passes in pursuance of it. It is vital to distinguish contractual questions from proprietary ones. In the case of a contract for the sale of goods, for example, if the contract is valid by its applicable law, the buyer will acquire a contractual right to receive delivery of the goods to the extent provided for by the applicable law. However, it is not necessarily the law governing the contract which determines whether title to the goods passes. Whether the buyer has title to the goods is to be determined by the law governing the transfer of movables. Immovables, tangible movables and intangible movables will be dealt with in turn.[10]

A Immovables

The general rule is that questions as to the transfer of proprietary rights in immovables are governed by the lex situs.[11] So, if the property in question is situated in England, English domestic law will be applicable. This is no doubt the proper approach as regards the material and formal validity of the transfer (for example, rules requiring the execution of a deed or rules requiring registration of the transfer in a public register). Although it has been questioned whether questions of capacity should also be subjected to the lex situs,[12] the authorities suggest that capacity to transfer immovable property (or to take such a transfer) is also governed by the lex situs.[13]

There will be few cases where the question will arise as to the law governing the transfer of a foreign immovable in view of the fact that, as has been seen,[14] it is only in rare situations that the English court has jurisdiction in such a case. One case, where the question of title arose incidentally, is *Adams v Clutterbuck*[15] in which a document executed in England conveyed shooting rights over certain moorland in Scotland. The conveyance was not formally valid under English

10 This chapter deals primarily with the voluntary transfer of property. For problems concerning involuntary assignment (for example, on the appointment of a receiver by secured creditors) see Dicey and Morris, *The Conflict of Laws* (13th edn, 2000) pp 989–1005, 1151–1160, 1183–1188.

11 *Earl Nelson v Lord Bridport* (1845) 8 Beav 527; *Norton v Florence Land and Public Works Co* (1877) 7 Ch D 332.

12 See Jaffey, *Introduction to the Conflict of Laws* (1987) p 211.

13 *Bank of Africa Ltd v Cohen* [1909] 2 Ch 129.

14 See pp 73–75 and 135–137.

15 (1883) 10 QBD 403.

law, because the document was not under seal, but it was valid by Scots law. It was held that Scots law applied.

One rationale for the application of the lex situs to questions of title to immovable property is that the property is under the close control of the authorities of the country where the property is situated. Accordingly, there is an argument for saying that the application of the lex situs should involve not simply consideration of the domestic law of the situs, but also its choice of law rules. That is to say, title to immovables is one of the areas in which the doctrine of renvoi might be regarded as playing a useful role. Where, for example, a question of title to land in Russia arises incidentally in English proceedings there is an argument for saying that the English court should seek to decide the question as a Russian court would do.

There are, however, also arguments against the application of the doctrine of renvoi.[16] Since the purpose of a choice of law rule is to identify the law which, from the perspective of English private international law, is the most appropriate one, it is not obvious that the English court should refuse to apply the lex situs simply on the basis that the courts of the country in which the immovable property is situated would apply the law of another country. Furthermore, it should not be assumed that an English judgment which is based on the application of the lex situs would not be recognised or enforced by the courts of the situs if those courts would have applied the law of another country to the issue in question.

It is also important to keep the issue of renvoi in proportion. The doctrine of renvoi is potentially relevant only if the foreign choice of law rule is different from the English rule. In a case involving title to immovable property the doctrine of renvoi cannot have any application if, according to the conflicts rules of the country in which the property is situated, title to immovable property is governed by the lex situs.

In all cases involving proprietary questions, the transfer of title must be distinguished from any contract in pursuance of which title has been transferred. A question concerning the contract is to be decided by the law applicable to the contract which may, but will not necessarily, be the lex situs.[17] Moreover, the English court may well exercise jurisdiction in a dispute over such a contract.[18] So, in *Re Smith*[19] the deceased, who had been domiciled and resident in England, had made a contract in England with his sisters by which

16 See pp 548–550.
17 See pp 203–224.
18 See pp 73 and 136.
19 [1916] 2 Ch 206.

he charged his interest in certain land in Dominica in their favour as security for money which he owed them. He also undertook in the contract to execute a legal mortgage over the land, but never did so. On his death the question arose as to the sisters' rights in relation to the land. By the law of Dominica, the lex situs, the contract was not effective itself to create a mortgage, because the requisite formalities for the creation of a mortgage had not been complied with. It was held, however, that the validity and effect of the contract was governed by English law, under which, the deceased having become bound to execute a mortgage, the executors were ordered to take the necessary steps to do so.

If, however, the enforcement of a contract to transfer a proprietary interest in an immovable under a contract which is valid by its proper law would be impossible under the lex situs, the court could hardly make an order for such enforcement. In *Bank of Africa Ltd v Cohen*[20] a contract was made in England between the plaintiff, an English bank, and the defendant, who was domiciled and resident in England. Under the terms of the contract, the defendant undertook to execute a mortgage over land which she owned in South Africa as security for money advanced to her husband. When the defendant failed to execute the mortgage the plaintiff sought a decree of specific performance from the English court. Under South African law a married woman lacked capacity to stand surety for her husband unless she expressly and voluntarily renounced the benefits of certain laws, which the defendant had not done. It was held that the wife's capacity to make the contract was governed by South African law, as the lex situs. As she lacked capacity under that law, a decree of specific performance was refused.

The reasoning of the decision may be criticised on the ground that there is no obvious reason why the choice of law rules for capacity to make a contract with regard to an immovable should be different from the choice of law rules for capacity to make any other contract. Rather than determining the defendant's capacity by reference to South African law, the lex situs, the law governing this question should have been English law, the law of the country with which the contract was most closely connected and in which the defendant was domiciled and resident.[21] According to English law the defendant had full capacity. This does not mean, however, that the decision not to grant a decree of specific performance cannot be justified. It is a well accepted maxim of equity that equity does not act in vain; it would have been futile for the court to compel the defendant to renounce the benefits of South African law given that

20 [1909] 2 Ch 129.
21 See pp 243–245.

by the lex situs the renouncing of the benefits would not be effective unless it was voluntary.

B Tangible movables

Which law should govern the transfer of tangible movables inter vivos? The various theories that have been suggested include the lex situs, the law of the transferor's domicile and the proper law of the transfer. As between the parties to a contract whose object is to pass title, it might be reasonable for questions of title to be governed by the law applicable to the contract. However, questions of title do not arise only as between the parties to a contract; often they involve third parties.[22] For example, the question whether title passed in pursuance of a sale of stolen goods will usually arise between the buyer and the original owner, rather than between the buyer and the seller who stole the goods. Similarly, the extent to which a seller may effectively retain title to goods which he has delivered to a buyer is likely to arise, not between the seller and the buyer, but between the seller and the buyer's creditors or a subsequent buyer.

The rule is that the transfer of a movable is governed by the lex situs, the law of the country where the movable is situated at the time of the alleged transfer.[23] The lex situs determines whether a given act or event does or does not transfer proprietary rights and to what extent.[24] The reason is that a person who acquires goods, or rights in goods, should be able to rely on any title which he obtains according to the law of the country where the goods are when he acquires them and to rely on that law for the retention of title he obtains. As Staughton LJ said in *Macmillan Inc v Bishopsgate Investment Trust plc (No 3)*:

> A purchaser ought to satisfy himself that he obtains good title by the law prevailing where the chattel is ... but should not be required to do more than that. And an owner, if he does not wish to be deprived of his property by some eccentric rule of foreign law, can at least do his best to ensure that it does not leave the safety of his own country.[25]

22 For the argument that choice of law rules developed in the context of three-party cases should not necessarily apply in two-party cases see Bridge, 'English Conflicts Rules for Transfers of Movables: A Contract-based Approach?' in Bridge and Stevens (eds), *Cross-Border Security and Insolvency* (2001) p 123.

23 *Cammell v Sewell* (1860) 5 H & N 728. See also *Gotha City v Sotheby's (No 2)* (1998) Times, 8 October; *Glencore International AG v Metro Trading International Inc* [2001] 1 Lloyd's Rep 284.

24 It may be that under the lex situs title will not pass in pursuance of a contract unless the contract is valid, which will have to be tested by the law applicable to the contract.

25 [1996] 1 WLR 387 at 400.

Where the situs of goods remains constant the application of the lex situs is unlikely to present many problems. In *Inglis v Robertson*,[26] for example, an English buyer of whisky which was stored in a warehouse in Scotland received a delivery order from the Scottish seller and endorsed it to the English plaintiff by way of security. Under English law the plaintiff obtained an interest in the goods, but by Scots law he did not. It was held that Scots law applied and therefore that the plaintiff acquired no interest.

The potential problems increase in cases where the situs of the property in question changes. The leading case is *Cammell v Sewell*.[27] Timber belonging to the plaintiff was shipped from Russia to England. While the timber was in transit the ship carrying it was wrecked and the cargo was sold to the defendant in Norway. Under Norwegian law, but not English law, the defendant acquired title to the goods. The plaintiff claimed the goods when the defendant subsequently brought them to England. It was held that the title acquired by the defendant while the goods were in Norway prevailed.

In *Winkworth v Christie, Manson and Woods Ltd*[28] works of art of the plaintiff were stolen from him in England and taken to Italy, where the second defendant bought them in good faith. The second defendant later sent them back to England to be sold by auction by the first defendant. The plaintiff brought proceedings against the defendants in England for, inter alia, a declaration that the works of art had at all material times been his property. The success of the action depended on whether English or Italian law should be applied to determine whether or not title to the goods had passed to the second defendant as a result of the sale to him in Italy. By English law title would not have passed; by Italian law it would because the buyer was in good faith at the time of the delivery of the goods to him. Slade J held, following *Cammell v Sewell*, that Italian law, as the law of the country where the goods were situated at the time of the delivery, governed the question. The lex situs rule was held to apply even though this meant that the plaintiff was deprived of his title under English law of goods removed from England without his consent and even though the goods were once again situated in England at the time of the proceedings. Any argument based on hardship to the original owner in such circumstances was counterbalanced by the interests of innocent purchasers: 'commercial convenience may be said imperatively to demand that proprietary rights to movables shall generally be determined by the lex situs.'[29]

26 [1898] AC 616.
27 (1860) 5 H & N 728.
28 [1980] Ch 496, [1980] 1 All ER 1121.
29 Slade J at 512.

Once title has passed as the result of a transaction under the lex situs, it is immaterial that the movable property is removed to another country under whose law title did not pass. So, in *Winkworth v Christie, Manson and Woods Ltd* the second defendant was held to have retained any title he acquired under Italian law even after the goods were sent back to England. Similarly, if title does not pass as a result of a transaction under the lex situs, it will make no difference that the movable is then taken to another country under whose law it did pass, until some event occurs when the goods are in that country by virtue of which title passes according to the law of that country. Consider, for example, the following situation: X steals goods from C in England and takes them to New York, where he sells them to Y. Under the laws of England and New York Y does not acquire title. If Y then takes the goods to France Y still cannot to be regarded as acquiring title to the goods even if Y has title under French law. If, however, while the goods are in France Y sells the goods to Z and under French law Z acquires title, the English court will recognise Z's title even if the goods are subsequently brought to England.

The proposition that the lex situs governs the transfer of title to movables may be misleading unless it is understood to mean that the relevant rule of the lex situs is applied to decide the question. In *Winkworth v Christie, Manson and Woods Ltd* the first defendant had sold some of the goods by auction in England before the proceedings were brought. Suppose the question were raised whether title passed to the buyer under that sale. One would obviously reach the wrong result by reasoning that the question whether title passed was governed by English law because the goods were in England at the time of the auction and by concluding that title did not pass because under English law the plaintiff retained his title to the stolen goods notwithstanding the subsequent sales. The right approach is to say that, because the auction took place in England, the relevant rule of English law as to the passing of title is applicable. That rule is that title will pass in the circumstances in question only if the second defendant had title to the goods. That raises the incidental question whether the second defendant had obtained title under his purchase in Italy.[30] According to the English conflicts rules that incidental question is governed by Italian law, under which the second defendant did acquire title. Therefore, title passed to the buyer at the auction.

The same considerations would apply in the converse case, where title does not pass under the foreign law, but it would under English law. Suppose a seller, A, sells and delivers goods to a buyer, B, in Germany. The contract contains a clause which is effective under

30 For further consideration of the incidental question see pp 550–554.

German law to retain title to the goods in A and to preclude B from reselling them until the price is paid; under English law, however, title would pass on delivery. B brings the goods to England and, before paying the price, sells and delivers them to C who buys in good faith. Does title pass to C? At the time when C acquired the goods they were in England, so the relevant rules of English domestic law must be applied. One such rule is that title will pass if the seller has title. That raises the question whether B had title which, according to the English choice of law rule, must be decided by German law as the lex situs at the time when B purchased the goods. B did not acquire title and his mere bringing of the goods to England does not alter the position. C therefore does not obtain title on the basis that his seller had title. Another rule of English domestic law is that where a buyer who obtains possession of the goods with the consent of the seller delivers the goods under a sale to a person receiving them in good faith, the latter obtains good title even though the former did not have title.[31] Title would pass under this rule for at the relevant time the goods were in England and the application of the rule accepts that B did not obtain title under the purchase from A.[32]

It would seem that the lex situs rule is not applicable in all circumstances. In *Winkworth v Christie, Manson and Woods Ltd*[33] it was accepted that there might be some exceptions to the general rule. First, '[i]f the goods are in transit, and their situs is casual or not known, a transfer which is valid and effective by its proper law will be valid and effective in England'.[34] Secondly, the English court may decline to recognise the effect of the lex situs if it is considered to be contrary to English public policy. Where, for example, property is expropriated by a foreign government, in certain circumstances, the expropriatory legislation may not be recognised as being effective to confer title on the government.[35] Similarly, where a buyer purchases stolen goods abroad knowing them to be stolen – and therefore does not act in good faith – the English court might consider that it would be contrary to public policy to recognise a title obtained in such circumstances under the lex situs. Thirdly, the lex situs will yield in the face of any English statute which,

31 Sale of Goods Act 1979, s 25(1).

32 Based on *Century Credit Corpn v Richard* (1962) 34 DLR (2d) 291. There are many United States cases dealing with such problems which have not arisen in the English courts. See Morris, 'The Transfer of Chattels in the Conflict of Laws' (1945) 22 BYIL 232; Davis, 'Conditional Sales and Chattel Mortgages in the Conflict of Laws' (1964) 13 ICLQ 53.

33 [1980] Ch 496, [1980] 1 All ER 1121.

34 Slade J at 501 (citing Dicey and Morris, *The Conflict of Laws* (9th edn, 1973) p 539).

35 See p 564.

according to its proper interpretation, has an overriding effect.[36] The importance of these apparent exceptions should not be exaggerated; there are very few reported cases which illustrate their application.

It has been suggested that the doctrine of renvoi should be applied to movables.[37] The arguments in favour of the doctrine are not convincing[38] and there is no reported case in which it has been applied to the question of title to movables. Moreover, the main argument which is used to support the application of renvoi in relation to immovables – namely, that the property is under the control of the authorities in the foreign country – cannot realistically be applied to movables. Movables are not amenable to public control in the same way as immovables, precisely because they are movable. When a case comes before the English court involving the transfer of a movable which took place abroad, the likelihood is that the movable has since been brought to England, so that the control of the foreign authorities does not arise. It will also be the case that, to the extent that the parties relied upon the law of the situs, reliance would have been placed on its domestic law (rather than on its choice of law rules).

C Intangible movables[39]

1. Introduction

It has been seen that, as a general rule, the transfer of immovables and tangible movables is governed by the lex situs. The rationale for this choice of law rule has already been considered and its application, while not without its complications, is facilitated by the fact that the situs of immovables and tangible movables is in most cases easy to determine. Intangibles give rise to different problems as a consequence of which the merits of applying the lex situs rule may be questioned. Although it is not unreasonable to attribute a situs to certain types of intangible (for example, France is clearly the situs of a French patent; New York is the situs of shares in a New York corporation), as regards other types of property, such as a debt, the allocation of a situs is rather artificial.[40]

36 For consideration of overriding rules in the contractual context see pp 228–232.

37 Dicey and Morris, *The Conflict of Laws* (13th edn, 2000) p 966. The point was left open in *Winkworth v Christie, Manson and Woods Ltd* [1980] Ch 496 at 514.

38 See pp 543–550.

39 See Moshinsky, 'The Assignment of Debts in the Conflict of Laws' (1992) 108 LQR 591.

40 Rogerson, 'The Situs of Debts in the Conflict of Laws – Illogical, Artificial and Misleading' [1990] CLJ 441.

There are two points which should be borne in mind in cases involving the assignment of intangibles. First, as with all property transactions, it is vital to distinguish contractual issues from proprietary ones. One must not fall into the trap of assuming that where an assignment of an intangible is effected by contract, the only question to consider is the validity of the contract. Secondly, in cases involving the assignment of certain types of intangible (in particular, debts) there are two transactions to consider: the first is the transaction which creates the relationship between the debtor and the creditor; the second is the assignment by the creditor to the assignee.

2. *The situs of intangibles*

The law artificially ascribes a situs to intangibles. The basic rule is that an intangible is situated where it is properly recoverable or can be enforced. As regards an intangible which is territorially limited (such as a patent), the situs is obviously the territory in question. Where the intangible arises out of a debtor's obligation to pay a sum of money the general rule is that the situs is where the debtor resides, because that is where the debt is properly recoverable.[41] If the debtor resides in more than one country the situs of the debt is the place where the creditor has stipulated that the debt is to be paid.[42] If it has not been stipulated where the debt is to be paid, the debt is situated in the country where it would be paid in the normal course of business.[43]

3. *Choice of law rules*

The question of which law governs the transfer of intangible movables is uncertain. Many of the common law authorities are old and inconsistent. To some extent the confusion in the case law is generated by the courts' failure to distinguish clearly contractual questions from proprietary ones. A degree of certainty, at least as regards some issues, has been injected by article 12 of the Rome Convention on the Law Applicable to Contractual Obligations.

In the discussion which follows three issues will be considered: first, which law governs whether or not a particular intangible is assignable; secondly, which law governs the contractual questions arising out of an assignment between the assignor and the assignee;

41 *New York Life Insurance Co v Public Trustee* [1924] 2 Ch 101.

42 *Jabbour v Custodian of Israeli Absentee's Property* [1954] 1 All ER 145, [1954] 1 WLR 139; *Kwok Chi Leung Karl v Estate Duty Comrs* [1988] 1 WLR 1035.

43 *Power Curber International Ltd v National Bank of Kuwait SAK* [1981] 3 All ER 607, [1981] 1 WLR 1233.

and thirdly, which law governs 'proprietary' questions (whether between the assignor and the assignee or, if the intangible is assigned more than once, between competing assignees or, in cases involving debts, between the assignee and the debtor)?

(A) ASSIGNABILITY

Whether a particular intangible is capable of being assigned is to be regarded as an aspect of the law under which the interest in question is created. Where, for example, a right arises under a contract which is governed by English law, it is logical to look to English law to determine whether the right can be assigned. This is the solution adopted by the Rome Convention on the Law Applicable to Contractual Obligations. Article 12(2) provides that '[t]he law governing the right to which the assignment relates shall determine its assignability'.

The Rome Convention applies only to contracts falling within its scope. There are two types of case which are governed by the common law. First, a debt may arise out of a contract or other legal relationship which is not within the Convention's scope. For example, the Convention does not apply to maintenance obligations or to wills.[44] It has been suggested by writers that, at common law, the question whether a debt is capable of being assigned is governed by the proper law of the debt – that is, the law governing the contract or other transaction which created the debt.[45] There are various reasons in favour of this suggestion: there is some authority to support it;[46] it is sound from the point of view of principle; and it avoids arbitrary distinctions between cases governed by the Rome Convention and those governed by the common law. Secondly, some types of intangible, such as intellectual property rights, do not arise out of transactions at all. The assignability of such rights should be determined by the lex situs (which will inevitably be the law under which the right was created). So, whether United States copyright is assignable is a question to be answered by reference to United States law and German law determines the assignability of a German registered trade mark.

(B) THE VALIDITY OF THE ASSIGNMENT: CONTRACTUAL QUESTIONS

The voluntary assignment of an intangible will be effected either by contract or by gift. Accordingly, the rights and obligations of the

44 Art 1(2)(b).
45 Dicey and Morris, *The Conflict of Laws* (13th edn, 2000) p 977; Cheshire and North, *Private International Law* (13th edn, 1999) p 961.
46 *Campbell Connelly & Co Ltd v Noble* [1963] 1 All ER 237, [1963] 1 WLR 252.

assignor and the assignee will fall to be determined by the law applicable to the transaction between the parties. The vast majority of such transactions fall within the scope of the Rome Convention and the applicable law will be determined by the choice of law rules contained in the Convention. Article 12(1) provides that '[t]he mutual obligations of assignor and assignee under a voluntary assignment of a right against another person ... shall be governed by the law which under this Convention applies to the contract between the assignor and the assignee'. If the parties make a choice of law, the chosen law governs;[47] if they have not made a choice, the law of the country with which the contract is most closely connected applies.[48] In cases involving a dispute arising out of the transfer of an intangible, one or more of the Convention's provisions dealing with material validity,[49] formal validity,[50] capacity[51] and the scope of the applicable law[52] may be relevant.[53]

It must be remembered that the Rome Convention's scope is limited. Certain types of contract and certain types of contractual question fall outside the Convention. For example, some contracts of insurance are not governed by the Convention[54] and, subject to article 11, questions of contractual capacity are governed by the common law choice of law rules. Contracts of assignment to which the common law applies will be governed by their proper law (which in most cases will be the law which would be the applicable law under the Convention's rules).

(C) THE EFFECT OF THE ASSIGNMENT: 'PROPRIETARY' QUESTIONS

So far, consideration has been given only to contractual issues as between the assignor and the assignee. Which law should govern 'proprietary' questions? Broadly speaking, there are three issues to consider. First, which law determines whether an assignee has title to the intangible which is the subject-matter of the assignment? Secondly, if an intangible, which is assignable by the law under which it was created, is the subject of successive assignments, each valid by its governing law, which law determines the priority between the assignees? Thirdly, in cases involving debts, which law determines whether or not the assignee is able to enforce the debt

47 Art 3.
48 Art 4.
49 Art 8.
50 Art 9.
51 Art 11.
52 Art 10.
53 For a full discussion of the Convention see chapter 5.
54 Art 1(3).

against the debtor? Although these questions arise in different factual contexts each raises essentially the same issue and there is an argument for saying that the same choice of law rule should apply to each.

As a matter of principle the law which governs the contract of assignment is not necessarily the law which should govern 'proprietary' questions – in particular, those which involve third parties. Where, for example, X, by a contract governed by English law, purports to assign United States copyright to Y, whether Y becomes the owner of the copyright should not be determined by English law. Indeed, the fact that the law governing the contract of assignment cannot apply as such to proprietary issues is obvious from cases which raise priority questions. If X assigns a debt to Y under a contract governed by Italian law and then assigns the same debt to Z under a contract governed by German law, it makes no sense to try to determine whether Y or Z has priority by reference to the law applicable to the contracts of assignment. Nevertheless, in a case involving the assignment of a debt, it seems that the entire relationship between the assignor and the assignee is governed by the law governing the contract of assignment.[55] Accordingly, the applicable law identified by article 12(1) of the Rome Convention determines, for example, whether, and at what point, the subject-matter of the assignment should be regarded as forming part of the assignee's estate.

From a policy point of view what is required is a choice of law rule which promotes stability in proprietary relations. Accordingly, the choice of law rule should use a single connecting factor which is unlikely to be transient. Essentially, there are two options: the lex situs or the law under which the interest was created. Of course, the law under which the interest was created will in many cases also be the lex situs. This will normally be the case, for example, where the subject-matter of the dispute is an intellectual property right which is territorially limited (such as a registered patent or trade mark) or where the property in question comprises shares in a company. However, in a case involving the assignment of a contract debt, the lex situs may well be different from the law under which the interest was created. Where, for example, an English bank makes a loan to a French company under a contract governed by English law, which specifies Paris as the place of repayment, the situs of the debt is France, but the debt arises out of a transaction governed by English law. If the bank assigns the debt to a German bank, should French law (the lex situs) or English law (the law under which the interest

55 *Raiffeisen Zentralbank Österreich AG v Five Star General Trading LLC* [2001] EWCA Civ 68, [2001] QB 825.

was created) determine whether the German bank can enforce the debt against the French company?

(i) The general principle

Some commentators support the application of the lex situs.[56] Notwithstanding the problems of ascribing a situs to interests which have no physical existence, since the lex situs governs questions of title to immovables and tangible movables, there is an obvious attraction to applying the lex situs to proprietary questions concerning intangibles. *Macmillan Inc v Bishopsgate Investment Trust plc (No 3)*[57] involved competing claims to shares in a company which was incorporated in New York, although the transactions on which the parties' claims were based had been effected in London. The Court of Appeal held that the issue as to who has title to shares in a company should be decided by the lex situs. Auld LJ said:

> [T]here is authority and much to be said for treating issues of priority of ownership of shares in a corporation according to the lex situs of those shares. That will normally be the country where the register is kept, usually but not always the country of incorporation.[58]

The lex situs, being the law under which the right was created, is equally applicable to proprietary questions in cases involving the assignment of intellectual property rights such as patents, trade marks and copyright.[59] Indeed, in *Macmillan Inc v Bishopsgate Investment Trust plc (No 3)* Auld LJ expressed the view that '[i]n general, disputes about the ownership of land and of tangible and intangible movables are governed by the lex situs'.[60]

The implication of the application of the lex situs to proprietary questions is that an assignee under a contract of assignment which is valid according to its applicable law may, nevertheless, be unable to claim title to the intangible in question. If, for example, the transaction does not comply with the formal requirements of the lex situs, but does comply with the formal requirements of the law governing the contract, the assignee will acquire contractual rights against the assignor but will not become the legal owner of the intangible. Similarly, the assignee should not be able to claim title if he lacks capacity under the lex situs. The cases suggest, however, that a person's capacity to make or receive an assignment of an intangible is governed either by the law of that person's domicile or

56 Collier, *Conflict of Laws* (3rd edn, 2001) pp 256–257.
57 [1996] 1 WLR 387.
58 At 411.
59 *Campbell Connelly & Co Ltd v Noble* [1963] 1 WLR 252.
60 [1996] 1 WLR 387 at 410.

by the law of the place of acting.[61] Such a rule, if it exists, has little to recommend it. The authorities may be criticised on the basis that they fail to distinguish proprietary questions from contractual ones and it is doubtful whether they would be followed today.

(ii) Debts

Although there is English authority for the proposition that, in cases involving the assignment of debts, it is inappropriate to characterise issues involving the relationship between the assignee and the debtor as 'proprietary' as opposed to 'contractual',[62] 'there is no doubt that the terminology of the assignability of debts lends a proprietary flavour to the transaction in question'.[63] Notwithstanding this 'proprietary flavour', it may be questioned whether the lex situs should apply to issues arising out of the assignment of a simple debt. First, it is in relation to debts that the allocation of a situs is most artificial. Secondly, one of the problems with the application of the lex situs to cases involving the assignment of debts is that it may generate uncertainty. Because the debtor's residence may change, the situs is not a connecting factor which promotes stability in legal relations.

In cases falling within the material scope of the Rome Convention, article 12(2) provides that the law governing the right to which the assignment relates shall determine the relationship between the assignee and the debtor and the conditions under which the assignment can be invoked against the debtor. So, where a debt due under a contract governed by English law is assigned by the creditor to an assignee by means of a contract governed by French law, the fact that, under French law, the assignee cannot enforce the debt (because notification of the assignment has not been made to the relevant person) is irrelevant; as long as the contract of assignment is valid according to its applicable law (as determined by article 12(1)), English law – as the law governing the right to which the assignment relates – determines whether or not the assignee can recover from the debtor.[64]

As regards cases not falling within the scope of the Rome Convention, the authorities are inconclusive. Some support for the application of the lex situs may be derived from *Re Maudslay*.[65]

61 *Lee v Abdy* (1886) 17 QBD 309; *Republica de Guatemala v Nunez* [1927] 1 KB 669.
62 See Mance LJ in *Raiffeisen Zentralbank Österreich AG v Five Star General Trading LLC* [2001] EWCA Civ 68, [2001] QB 825 at 842.
63 Dicey and Morris, *The Conflict of Laws* (13th edn, 2000) p 983.
64 *Raiffeisen Zentralbank Österreich AG v Five Star General Trading LLC* [2001] EWCA Civ 68, [2001] QB 825.
65 [1900] 1 Ch 602.

However, there is a good argument – both in terms of authority and policy – for the application of the law under which the interest was created (which, in the case of contract debts, is the law applicable to the contract out of which the debt arises). First, *Le Feuvre v Sullivan*[66] and *Kelly v Selwyn*,[67] may be read as supporting this argument.[68] Secondly, the law under which the interest was created is a less transient and therefore more appropriate connecting factor than the situs of the debt. Finally, the application, at common law, of the law under which the interest was created avoids arbitrary distinctions between cases falling within the scope of the Rome Convention and those falling outside its scope.

D Governmental expropriation of property

The general principle that the transfer of title is governed by the lex situs applies equally when the transfer is the result of expropriation by a state under a decree or other legislation. If the property is in the territory of the state at the time when the transfer is alleged to have occurred, then effect will be given to it,[69] subject to the doctrines of public policy and the non-enforcement of foreign penal laws.[70] It would seem, however, that effect will not be given to an extra-territorial expropriation.[71] Where, for example, the government of state A purports to expropriate by legislation property which is situated in state B the application of the lex situs rule means that the legislative action of state A will not be recognised as effective by the English court.

III MATRIMONIAL PROPERTY

A Introduction

Different countries have different rules about the effect of a marriage on the property of the spouses. Some countries have systems of community of property, under which, to varying extents, the spouses jointly own the property which each separately owned before the

66 (1855) 10 Moo PCC 1.
67 [1905] 2 Ch 117.
68 Cheshire and North, *Private International Law* (13th edn, 1999) pp 961–962.
69 *Aksionairnoye Obschestvo AM Luther v James Sagor & Co* [1921] 3 KB 532; *Princess Olga Paley v Weisz* [1929] 1 KB 718; *Williams & Humbert Ltd v W & H Trade Marks (Jersey) Ltd* [1986] AC 368, [1985] 2 All ER 208.
70 See pp 555–564.
71 *Bank voor Handel en Scheepvaart NV v Slatford* [1953] 1 QB 248, [1952] 2 All ER 956.

marriage, and which each acquires after the marriage. For example, until recently under Roman-Dutch law in South Africa, upon marriage all property already owned by the parties fell into a community of property as did all property acquired during the subsistence of the marriage. The more usual civil law model is that only property acquired during the subsistence of the marriage falls into the community, although even here there are variations. For example, under German law the property of the spouses remains their separate property during the marriage but on termination of the marriage, a 'deferred community' comes into existence.[72] Under these community of property regimes, on the death of one of the spouses the surviving spouse already owns his or her share of the property and does not have to inherit it by way of succession. Similarly, on divorce a spouse can assert his or her rights to a share of the community and does not have to apply to the court for a transfer of any of that property as part of a divorce settlement. Of course, in many countries the surviving spouse will additionally have succession rights in relation to the deceased's share of the community and a divorcing spouse can request extra financial provision out of the other's portion of the community.

Other systems, including English law, provide for the separate ownership of property by spouses. Marriage has no effect upon either the antenuptial or postnuptial assets of the spouses. (A spouse may acquire a beneficial interest in the matrimonial home under the rules relating to resulting and constructive trusts; these rules operate, however, quite independently of marriage and apply equally to two friends who purchase a house together.) Under English law, when a spouse dies intestate, the other spouse has fixed rights of inheritance, but has no such rights when the deceased spouse makes a will disinheriting the survivor. In such cases, the disinherited spouse can make an application for family provision under the Inheritance (Provision for Family and Dependants) Act 1975, as amended. When a divorce is obtained in England the court order may take the form of a financial provision order or a property adjustment order whereby one spouse is required to pay money or transfer property to the other spouse from his or her separate assets. In making these orders the court exercises a discretion with the safeguarding of the welfare of any children being the first consideration.

Under most systems of community of property there is provision for antenuptial marriage contracts, by which the parties make express arrangements for their property after the marriage, perhaps

72 See generally, Kiralfy (ed), *Comparative Law of Matrimonial Property* (1972) and Rheinstein and Glendon, *International Encyclopaedia of Comparative Law*, Vol IV, *Persons and Family* (1980) chapter 4.

altering the system which would otherwise prevail. The basic system of community of property applies only in the absence of such a contract. In South Africa, for example, such antenuptial contracts, which have to be notarially executed, were common. In other countries, such as Germany, there are statutory alternatives to the basic property regime which the parties may adopt by agreement. In England such antenuptial contracts are not legally enforceable[73] but, depending on the context, they may be taken into account as a factor in the exercise of any judicial discretion. For example, in *S v S*[74] the existence of an antenuptial contract with a jurisdiction clause in favour of New York 'weighed heavily' on the judge in exercising a discretion to stay English proceedings.[75]

There is clearly much scope for conflict of laws problems in this area. If a German domiciliary marries an English domiciliary, is the marriage in community of property or not? If it were in community and the parties subsequently obtained a divorce in England or one of them died domiciled in England, what account would be taken of this fact in the exercise of the court's discretionary powers to grant financial relief and in the rules of succession? If the parties had contracted a German antenuptial contract, to what extent would this regulate their proprietary regime and affect the court's discretionary powers on divorce or affect the rights of the survivor on the death of his or her spouse?

In 2002 the Commission of the European Union commenced work on the harmonisation of the conflict of law rules on matrimonial property regimes and financial provision laws, for both married and unmarried couples, of the European Union member states with a view to the introduction of a Brussels III Regulation. Work on the compilation of a report outlining the laws of the 15 member states has commenced and will be presented to the Commission in November 2002.

B Movable property

1. *The applicable law*

The traditional rule is that the effect of the marriage on movable property is governed by the law of the husband's domicile at the date

73 *N v N* [1999] 2 FLR 745.
74 [1997] 1 WLR 1200; see also *C v C* [2001] 1 FLR 624.
75 For the relevance of such contracts in divorce proceedings, see pp 507–509. The government has published proposals to allow legally enforceable antenuptial contracts in certain circumstances (Home Office, *Supporting Families: A Consultation Document*, 1998).

of the marriage.[76] At the time this rule was established, the wife took the husband's domicile on marriage, so her domicile necessarily became the same as his at the date of the marriage. So, if at the time of the marriage the husband was domiciled in England, where the regime is separation of property, while the wife was domiciled in a country where community of property prevailed, then under this rule the English system would apply.

However, a strong case can be mounted that this traditional rule in favour of the husband's law at the date of the marriage should be reformulated so that the governing law will be that of the 'matrimonial domicile'.[77] There are two reasons for making this claim. First, there has long been authority that the application of the husband's domicile at the date of the marriage is no more than a presumption which, in clear cases, can be rebutted in favour of the matrimonial domicile, that is, the intended matrimonial home. In *Re Egerton's Will Trusts*[78] a man domiciled in England married a woman domiciled in France; the parties intended to settle in France, but they did not in fact move there until two years after the marriage. On the husband's death, the wife contended that the marriage had been in community of property under French law, the law of the intended matrimonial home. It was held that the marriage was governed by English law as the law of the husband's domicile at the time of the marriage. Roxburgh J, however, accepted that in exceptional cases some law other than that of the husband's domicile might govern as the result of the agreement of the parties, either express or inferred from their conduct. If the spouses set up their domicile in a new country immediately after the marriage, an agreement that their proprietary rights should be governed by the law of that country might be inferred, but would not necessarily be so. That would depend on the circumstances. In the present case, although the parties intended to settle in France, there was no evidence that they had intended the effects of the marriage on their property to be governed by French law and, accordingly, the basic presumption in favour of the law of the husband's domicile at the date of the marriage applied.

There are fewer objections to the application of the law of the intended matrimonial home here than to its use as a choice of law rule to determine the essential validity of a marriage. While this test will always generate more uncertainty than a domicile rule, it follows from *Re Egerton's Will Trusts* that it will be only in clear, very exceptional circumstances that a conclusion will be reached not

76 *Re Martin* [1900] P 211.
77 Dicey and Morris, *The Conflict of Laws* (13th edn, 2000) p 1066 (Rule 148).
78 [1956] Ch 593, [1956] 2 All ER 817.

only that, at the date of the marriage, the parties intended to establish a matrimonial home in a new country and that they did so shortly thereafter, but also that an inference can be drawn that they intended to subject themselves to the proprietary regime of that new country. Further, the problems associated with trying to apply the matrimonial domicile test to the essential validity of a marriage in prospective situations[79] are not likely to arise in cases involving disputes over matrimonial property. Marriage officials do not need to know the proprietary consequences of a marriage. Also, the parties themselves will generally not need to know at the date of the marriage to which proprietary regime the marriage will be subject. If the parties are concerned about the matter, they can draw up an antenuptial marriage contract. In almost all cases it will only be later in the marriage – on death, divorce or insolvency – that a determination will need to be made. If the parties are allowed to regulate the proprietary consequences of their marriage expressly by contract, there seems little reason why they should not be permitted to do so impliedly. The other main problem with the application of the intended matrimonial home doctrine to determine the essential validity of a marriage is that the parties may in later years move to a different country with which the marriage is then most closely connected. Clearly one cannot continually reassess the validity of a marriage every time the parties move country. This problem does not arise in relation to matrimonial property because there is no reason why the proprietary consequences of a marriage should remain immutable. When spouses become domiciled in a new country, the laws of that country could be held to be applicable with respect to any assets acquired after that date.

The second reason for suggesting that the traditional rule in favour of the husband's domiciliary law be displaced in favour of an application of the law of the matrimonial domicile is that the former rule was established at a time when, on marriage, a woman necessarily acquired a domicile of dependence on her husband. Since the Domicile and Matrimonial Proceedings Act 1973 this is no longer the case and so, when the parties are domiciled in different countries at the date of the marriage, there is no reason to favour the husband's law. One of the reasons for the abolition of the married woman's domicile of dependence was that the rule was sexist. Abolition of the basic rule but a retention of its manifestations and applications would be a pyrrhic victory for women's rights and could well be contrary to the European Convention on Human Rights.[80] Accordingly, in cases where the parties are domiciled in separate

79 See p 326.
80 Art 14 and art 1 of the Protocol.

countries, it has been suggested that the applicable law should be that of 'the country with which the parties and the marriage have the closest connection'.[81] This more flexible test would subsume the exception established in *Re Egerton's Will Trusts* so as to become a general choice of law rule in favour of the law of the 'matrimonial domicile'.

2. Mutability or immutability

A controversial question is whether the proprietary regime fixed by the law of the matrimonial domicile at the time of the marriage will change if the parties subsequently change their domicile. Is the original regime mutable or immutable according to English conflict of laws rules? Suppose, for instance, the parties were married under a regime of community of property, but later move to a country where the system is separation of property. Will their property thereafter be held in community or separately?

In *De Nicols v Curlier*[82] the parties were both domiciled in France when they married there. Because they did not make any antenuptial contract, they were deemed by French law to have agreed that their marriage should be in community of property. Subsequently they became domiciled in England, where the husband made a large fortune. On his death, the wife claimed to be entitled to half the estate by virtue of the community of property, so that the husband's will could operate only on the other half. It was held that the community of property continued despite the change of domicile.

While this case seems to suggest that the doctrine of immutability prevails, it has been argued that this is not necessarily so, because the basis of the decision was that by French law the parties were deemed to have agreed that their property should be held in community. As an express marriage contract will continue despite a change of domicile, unless and until the parties cancel or alter it by a subsequent valid contract, the position should be the same with an implied contract, as in *De Nicols v Curlier*. Therefore the original proprietary regime should continue despite a change of domicile. Indeed, the same reasoning should arguably apply in a case where the law governing at the time of the marriage offers a choice of regimes, whether or not by that law the regime which operates in the absence of an express choice is regarded as having been impliedly agreed.[83]

81 Dicey and Morris, *The Conflict of Laws* (13th edn, 2000) p 1069.
82 [1900] AC 21.
83 It has been said that there is always a marriage contract, for when there is no actual agreement one is presumed: Goldberg, 'The Assignment of Property on Marriage' (1970) 19 ICLQ 557. But it seems artificial to say that in English law parties choose separation of property.

Since the parties could have excluded the basic regime, it is not unreasonable to suppose that their joint decision not to should be capable of alteration only by their subsequent agreement. There seems no reason why their acquisition of a domicile in a country having a different regime should be treated as such an agreement.

Does the doctrine of immutability apply even if the original matrimonial regime cannot be regarded as having been agreed between the parties? A case which may seem to be in favour of mutability is *Lashley v Hog*,[84] where the change of domicile after marriage was from England to Scotland. On the husband's death, the wife having predeceased him, it was claimed that the wife's estate was entitled to a third share of the husband's property under Scots law. The House of Lords held that the wife's estate was so entitled, even though no such right existed under English law, the law of the matrimonial domicile at the time of the marriage. However, the better view[85] is that the basis of the decision was that the wife's claim to a third share under Scots law was a right of succession, governed by Scots law as the law of the deceased's domicile at his death. If so, it does not follow that the proprietary regime of the marriage changed when the parties became domiciled in Scotland.

It is clear that a full doctrine of mutability, in the sense that assets already acquired before the change of domicile become subject to the matrimonial regime of the new domicile, is unacceptable. Take the example of a couple married under South African community of property. All assets acquired by either spouse became jointly owned. If they later became domiciled in England, they already each owned their share of the community. It would be 'quite unintelligible'[86] to assert that a change of domicile can have the effect of changing the ownership of property. This was particularly true before the Domicile and Matrimonial Proceedings Act 1973 when the change of common domicile could have been effected unilaterally by the husband's act. However, these arguments are limited to vested rights acquired before the parties' change of domicile. The rule has been advocated[87] that, where there is no express or implied antenuptial contract, a common change of domicile by the spouses should not affect rights already acquired under the previous regime, but property acquired after the change of domicile should be governed by the regime determined by the new domicile. This change in matrimonial

84 (1804) 4 Pat 581.

85 Goldberg, 'The Assignment of Property on Marriage' (1970) 19 ICLQ 557 at 580–584; Cheshire and North, *Private International Law* (13th edn, 1999) p 1020.

86 *De Nicols v Curlier* [1900] AC 21 at 27.

87 Cheshire and North, *Private International Law* (13th edn, 1999) pp 1020–1021.

property regime should be permitted only where both spouses move to the new country and it is clear that the law of the new country is the law with which the parties and the marriage have the closest connection. In the case where one spouse deserts the other and alone acquires a new domicile elsewhere, the nature of the proprietary regime should remain unaltered. However, it must be conceded that such an approach is not without difficulties. If a married couple domiciled in England settle in a new country, where the regime is community of property, should their property thereafter be held in community regardless of their wishes? While the new country may allow spouses to contract out of community of property, it may not make provision for doing so after the marriage.

C Immovable property

The central question in relation to immovables is whether the law of the matrimonial domicile (or the law of the husband's domicile at the date of the marriage) is displaced by the lex situs as the governing law. In *Welch v Tennent*[88] the House of Lords, on appeal from Scotland, held that the lex situs governed. In this case the husband and wife were domiciled in Scotland. After the marriage the wife sold land which she owned in England and paid the proceeds to her husband. She later claimed she was entitled under Scots law to reclaim these proceeds. It was held, however, that the rights of the spouses in relation to immovable property were governed by English law as the lex situs. Accordingly, the husband was allowed to keep the proceeds.

On the other hand, in *Re De Nicols*,[89] which was concerned with the same marriage as *De Nicols v Curlier*, the French couple, having married in France, came to England and purchased property here. It was held that this property was subject to the community of property regime of French law and was not subject to English law, the lex situs. While this case can be distinguished on the ground that the basis of the decision was that there was an implied contract between the parties, it would clearly be preferable to allow this issue to be determined by the law of the matrimonial domicile rather than the lex situs. Application of the lex situs rule, as in *Welch v Tennent*, can lead to an estate being 'juridically fragmented'.[90] If a couple own immovable property in several countries, each property could be subject to different matrimonial property regimes. If an English couple were to purchase a holiday home in France or Spain, it would

88 [1891] AC 639.
89 [1900] 2 Ch 410.
90 Dicey and Morris, *The Conflict of Laws* (13th edn, 2000) p 1073.

hardly be in accordance with their reasonable expectations that such property be held in community of property. Although the precise basis of the decision is unclear, the decision in *Chiwell v Carlyon*[91] provides support for the application of the law of the matrimonial domicile. In this case a husband and wife married under the South African regime of community of property and later acquired land in England. It was concluded that the rights in this property were to be governed by South African law and not by English law as the lex situs.

One way of reconciling the above authorities (although a less satisfactory solution than applying the law of the matrimonial domicile) would be to draw a distinction between foreign immovables and immovables in England. *Welch v Tennent* would be consistent with the general rule that so far as foreign immovables are concerned, the governing law should be the lex situs. However, as regards immovables situated in England (which was the situation in both *Re De Nicols* and *Chiwell v Carlyon*) there seems no reason why the law of the matrimonial domicile should not govern, so long as the kinds of interests provided for by that law are not prohibited by English law.

D Antenuptial contracts

Intending spouses may enter into a marriage settlement or other antenuptial contract regulating their proprietary rights. Some legal systems enable the parties to choose between alternative proprietary regimes by an antenuptial contract. For example, they may be free by such a contract to exclude community of property, which would be the regime in the absence of any agreement. Alternatively, they may construct their own system of community of property. Where the regime is one of separation of property, as in England, there may be settlements of property on the spouses and children. The cases discussed below are all concerned with such settlements. The present position in English law with regard to antenuptial contracts providing for either separation or community of property is that while they are unenforceable as such they are factors to be taken into consideration, the weight to be attached to them depending on the context.[92]

The validity and effect of an antenuptial contract is governed by the law governing the contract. The Rome Convention on the Law Applicable to Contractual Obligations, implemented by the

91 (1897) 14 SC 61 (Cape of Good Hope). See Cheshire and North, *Private International Law* (13th edn, 1999) pp 1023–1024.

92 See p 497 above and p 507 below.

Contracts (Applicable Law) Act 1990, is not applicable because article 1(2)(b) excludes contractual obligations relating to 'rights in property arising out of a matrimonial relationship'. Accordingly, the common law rules are applicable. Under these, a contract is governed by its proper law. This law may be chosen, expressly or impliedly, by the parties. Failing this, the proper law of a contract is the law with which the contract is most closely connected.[93] The factors used to establish the law of closest connection will, of course, not be the same as in commercial contracts. In particular, the law of the matrimonial domicile will often be the most important factor in the ascertainment of the proper law.[94]

Various issues may arise in relation to antenuptial contracts. These need separate consideration.

1. Capacity

Although the rules relating to capacity to make a commercial contract are not definitely settled, the better view is that a person should be regarded as having capacity if he has capacity either by the law of the country with which the contract is most closely connected or by the law of his domicile.[95] The reason why a person cannot rely on an incapacity by the law of his domicile alone in commercial cases is that it may be unfair on the other party, who may have no reason to know where he is domiciled. This ignorance is, of course, much less likely to exist in the case of a contract entered into between intending spouses in contemplation of their marriage and, accordingly, although the point is controversial, it is arguable that a person's capacity to make an antenuptial contract is governed by the law of his or her domicile at the date of the marriage, rather than the proper law of the contract.[96] However, if by the law of the domicile at the date of the marriage a contract made by a minor is invalid unless ratified after reaching majority, then the power to ratify it (or revoke such ratification) will be governed by the law of the person's domicile at the date of the purported ratification (or revocation).

The authorities,[97] though indecisive, tend to support the above view. In *Cooper v Cooper*[98] the wife at the time of the marriage was

93 See p 198.
94 *Re Fitzgerald* [1904] 1 Ch 573 at 587.
95 See p 244.
96 Contra Dicey and Morris, *The Conflict of Laws* (13th edn, 2000) pp 1076–1078; Cheshire and North, *Private International Law* (13th edn, 1999) p 1025.
97 See also *Re Cooke's Trusts* (1887) 56 LJ Ch 637.
98 (1888) 13 App Cas 88.

under 21. She was domiciled in Ireland and the husband in Scotland, which was the intended matrimonial home. Before the marriage, the parties made a settlement under which the wife waived certain claims under Scots law that she would otherwise have against her husband's estate on his death. On the husband's death, the question arose whether the wife could repudiate the contract on the ground that she had lacked capacity to make it. The House of Lords held that her capacity was governed by Irish law, as the law of her domicile at the time of the marriage (or, alternatively, as the law of the country where the contract was made). Under that law, the contract was invalid unless she ratified it after attaining majority, and her failure to avoid the contract within a reasonable period of attaining her majority would be treated as ratification. However, she became domiciled in Scotland on the marriage, and by Scots law any ratification of the contract was revocable by her as being a donation between spouses. As she had revoked the contract while domiciled in Scotland it was not binding on her.

In *Viditz v O'Hagan*[99] the wife was under 21 and domiciled in Ireland. She married a man domiciled in Austria, where they settled after the marriage. Before the marriage they had entered into a marriage settlement by which the wife settled property on trust for herself, her husband and the children of the marriage. Subsequently, while domiciled in Austria, the spouses executed a document by which they purported to revoke the marriage settlement and brought proceedings in the English court for a declaration that the revocation was valid. By Irish law the settlement, if valid, would have been irrevocable, but by Austrian law it remained revocable. It was held that the wife's capacity to make the contract was governed by Irish law, as the law of her domicile at the time she made it. As seen above, under that law the contract was not binding unless she affirmed it after coming of age, and if she did nothing within a reasonable time she would be presumed to have affirmed it. But on the marriage she became domiciled in Austria, by the law of which the contract could not be ratified so as to become irrevocable. Thus the revocation was held to be valid.

2. *Formal validity*

It seems that an antenuptial contract will be formally valid if it complies with the requirements of either the proper law[100] or the law of the country where it is made.[101]

99 [1900] 2 Ch 87.
100 *Van Grutten v Digby* (1862) 31 Beav 561.
101 *Guépratte v Young* (1851) 4 De G & Sm 217.

3. Essential validity and construction

The essential validity and construction of an antenuptial contract are governed by its proper law. Where there is no express or implied choice, the proper law will be the law of the country with which the contract is most closely connected. In the ascertainment of such law it has been stated that there is a 'presumption'[102] in favour of the law of the matrimonial domicile. In *Duke of Marlborough v A-G*[103] at the time of the marriage the wife was domiciled in New York and the husband in England. The proper law of a marriage settlement by which the wife's father, also domiciled in New York, settled United States investments was held to be English law. The important factors were that England was the intended matrimonial domicile, the settlement was drafted in English form, it included phrases which had significance only in relation to English law, and provision was made for an application to be made to the English court under the Infant Settlement Act 1855 (as the wife was a minor).

However, even if the law of the matrimonial domicile presumptively indicates the proper law, it is a presumption that can be rebutted by other factors and circumstances. For example, in *Re Bankes*[104] an Italian domiciliary married an English-domiciled woman. The parties settled in Italy after the marriage. By a contract in English form made in Italy before the marriage, the wife settled property she owned in England, and property she might acquire after the marriage, on certain trusts. The question arose whether certain legacies to the wife were subject to the settlement. The wife contended that the settlement was governed by Italian law, by which it was invalid, as it violated the legal order of succession. It was held, however, that English law was the proper law. The presumption in favour of Italian law, as the law of the matrimonial domicile, was rebutted in view of the English form of the contract, the fact that it was valid by English law, and that the property was English and owned by a woman who, at the time of the contract, was domiciled in England.

E Matrimonial property rights and succession

When spouses are married in community of property, on the death of one of them, the survivor will be entitled to half the joint estate by virtue of the community. This can be taken into account in the provision which the law of the country concerned makes for any

102 Cheshire and North, *Private International Law* (13th edn, 1999) p 1029.
103 [1945] Ch 78, [1945] 1 All ER 165.
104 [1902] 2 Ch 333.

share in the deceased's half to which a surviving spouse is entitled on intestacy. Anomalies can occur when parties, married in community, move to a country where separation of property is the rule, and one of them dies intestate domiciled in the new country. That country's rules of intestate succession will not take into account the possibility of the survivor taking half the joint estate before any question arises as to the succession to the deceased's half. The consequence may be that the survivor will inherit a large share in the deceased's half of the estate as well as taking his own half, thereby receiving considerably more than he would if the spouses had always been domiciled in either the original or the new country, at the expense of the children or other relatives entitled on intestacy.[105] However, it must be recalled that with respect to persons dying domiciled in England, dependants of the deceased can apply for family provision under the Inheritance (Provision for Family and Dependants) Act 1975, as amended.

Problems arising from the interaction of matrimonial property regimes and succession rules would be avoided if the doctrine of mutability applied. But that in turn could deprive the survivor of half the property which would have been held in community under the original law if the deceased made a will leaving all or much of his property away from the survivor. Again, however, the Inheritance (Provision for Family and Dependants) Act 1975, as amended, can provide the necessary corrective. A truly satisfactory solution can be achieved only if the rules of intestate succession of the new country make special provision for people formerly domiciled in countries having community regimes.

F Matrimonial property rights and divorce

Under the Matrimonial Causes Act 1973, as amended, the English court has a broad discretion to make orders for financial relief and property adjustment orders whereby one spouse is ordered to transfer property to another. In exercising this discretion English courts appear to pay little or no attention to the fact that the parties might be married in community of property or might have drawn up an antenuptial contract regulating the proprietary consequences of their marriage. In *N v N*[106] an antenuptial contract providing for steps to be taken in the event of divorce was regarded as contrary to public policy because it undermined the concept of marriage as a life-long union. In *F v F*[107] the husband and wife were German

105 *Beaudoin v Trudel* [1937] 1 DLR 216.
106 [1999] 2 FLR 745.
107 [1995] 2 FLR 45.

domiciliaries who married in Germany having drawn up a German antenuptial contract. The parties moved to England where the husband later petitioned for divorce. In an application by the wife for maintenance pending suit, the husband sought to rely on the German antenuptial contract, the effect of which would have been to provide the wife with a sum restricted to the equivalent of the pension of a German judge (the wife was a law graduate). This argument was peremptorily swept aside by Thorpe J, who was not even prepared to hear expert evidence on the effect of such a contract under German law on the basis that:

> In this jurisdiction [antenuptial contracts] must be of very limited significance. The rights and responsibilities of those whose financial affairs are regulated by statute cannot be much influenced by contractual terms which were devised for the control and limitation of standards that are intended to be of universal application throughout our society.[108]

Such an approach is understandable on the facts of the case. The husband had property worth millions of pounds and, had effect been given to the antenuptial contract, the wife would have received only a fraction of her entitlement under English law. Further, there were suggestions of undue influence at the time of contracting. However, where the basic proprietary regime or antenuptial contract has provided for a system of community of property, there must be a strong argument that the English courts ought to give effect to it, at least as a starting-point in the exercise of its discretion. The fact that the wife, for example, already owns half the property under the community regime, would not, of course, preclude the court from exercising its discretionary powers to grant her financial provision or property from the husband's share of the community. However, simply to dismiss antenuptial contracts – and the proprietary regimes of other countries under which the parties married – as being of 'limited significance' can hardly accord with the parties' reasonable expectations of how their proprietary affairs will be regulated. Antenuptial contracts are widely employed throughout the world. It is absurd to regard them 'as fit only to facilitate the serial marriages of Hollywood moguls'.[109] Community of property regimes and antenuptial contracts might be 'strange' to English lawyers, but it is precisely to deal with 'different' foreign laws that the conflict of laws exists.

A more promising tone was adopted in *S v S*[110] where it was stated (obiter) that as antenuptial contracts were regarded as legally

108 At 66.
109 Conway, 'Premarital Contracts' (1995) 145 NLJ 1200.
110 [1997] 1 WLR 1200.

enforceable in the United States and in the European Community, 'there will come a case' where they will 'prove influential or even crucial'.[111] It is to be hoped that such an approach, displaying a clearer understanding of the function of the conflict of laws, will be followed.

IV SUCCESSION

A Introduction

The only person entitled to deal with the property of a deceased person is a personal representative who has been appointed by a grant of representation as an executor (where appointed by a will) or an administrator (where a testamentary appointment fails or the deceased dies intestate). In theory there are no limits to the English court's power to make a grant of representation. However, the court has a discretion to grant representation and will not normally do so unless the deceased has left property in England or there are other good reasons for the making of such a grant, for example, because the testator died domiciled in England and a foreign court, where the assets are situated, requires such a grant before it will allow the personal representative to deal with the estate in that foreign country.[112] It has already been seen that where the deceased has left property in England, the court may also deal with the entitlement to immovable property abroad, as an exception to the normal rule about jurisdiction over foreign immovables.[113]

The personal representative must first collect all the assets and then clear the estate by paying all debts and taxes and must then distribute the remaining estate among the beneficiaries under the will or according to the rules of intestacy. This chapter does not deal with the administration of the estate (for example, payment of debts). This is regarded as a matter of procedure and, consistent with the general rule, is governed by English law, the lex fori. The concern in this chapter is with the distribution of the estate of a deceased person among the beneficiaries, either under a will or on intestacy.

The discussion of the choice of law rules for succession will deal separately with testate and intestate succession. Within each of these categories it is again necessary to distinguish between the rules relating to movable and immovable property. In 1988 the Hague

111 At 1203. See also, *M v M (Prenuptual Agreement)* [2002] 1 FLR 654.
112 Dicey and Morris, *The Conflict of Laws* (13th edn, 2000) p 1007.
113 See pp 136–137.

Conference on Private International Law adopted a draft Convention on the Law Applicable to Succession to the Estates of Deceased Persons.[114] Under this Convention most questions of succession would be governed by a single law, normally the law of the deceased's habitual residence at death. No distinction would be drawn between testate and intestate succession or between movables and immovables. This Convention has not been implemented in the United Kingdom.

In 2002 the Commission of the European Union commenced work on the harmonisation of the conflict of laws rules relating to wills and succession with a view to the introduction of a Brussels IV Regulation. Work commenced on a report outlining the law of the 15 member states; this report will be presented to the Commission in late 2002.

B Wills

1. Movables

(A) INTRODUCTION

Like a contract, a will expresses the intentions of the person who makes it, and the different issues which may arise are similar to those considered in the chapter on contracts. One difference, however, is that a will is made at one time but takes effect at another, so connecting factors at two different times may be relevant. The governing law for a contract is the law of the country with which it is most closely connected, unless the parties expressly or impliedly intend a different law. The country with which a will is most closely connected is the place of domicile of the testator, for that is the country to which the beneficiaries are likely to, and the testator is deemed to, belong, and in which all or some of the estate is likely to be situated. As shall be seen, for some issues it is the domicile of the testator at death that counts, while for others it is the testator's domicile at the date of making the will. As for the testator intending a different law, this is effective only in respect of non-mandatory rules of succession, such as those governing the construction of wills. With respect to mandatory rules, such as those governing essential validity, the testator is unable to evade the provisions of the law to which he is deemed to belong by choosing another law to govern the will.

114 See Lord Chancellor's Department, *Hague Convention on Succession: Consultation Paper* (1990).

(B) CAPACITY

The concern here is with issues such as whether the testator was old enough to make a will and whether his mental state was such as to preclude him from doing so. While it is appropriate that the law of the country to which the testator belongs should determine his capacity,[115] it has not yet been decided whether the relevant domicile is that at the date of making the will or at the date of the testator's death. The former view seems preferable,[116] first, because it refers to the law of the testator's country at the time of the legal act in question, and, secondly, because it avoids the invalidation of a hitherto valid will, as the result of a change in the testator's domicile.

The question can also arise of the capacity of a legatee to take under a will. While it seems that in principle this should be governed by the law of the legatee's domicile at the date when he claims the legacy,[117] it has been held that it is sufficient if the legatee has capacity either under that law or under the law of the testator's domicile at the date of his death.[118] However, in exceptional cases, the interests of the testator's domiciliary law in the issue may be so great that it alone should determine whether the legatee has capacity to take under a will. For example, if a foreign domiciled legatee murdered an English domiciled testator, the English rule disqualifying the beneficiary from taking under the will would almost certainly be applied irrespective of the law of the beneficiary's domicile.[119]

(C) FORMAL VALIDITY

The choice of law rules for the formal validity of a will are contained in the Wills Act 1963, which gives effect to the Hague Convention on the Conflict of Laws Relating to the Form of Testamentary Dispositions of 1961.[120] The policy of the Convention and the 1963 Act is to ensure uniformity of decision in different countries and to uphold the formal validity of a will wherever possible. There is little point in invalidating a will on purely formal grounds if the testator has complied with a law with which he has a connection. Accordingly, section 1 of the 1963 Act provides that a will is formally valid if the

115 *Re Lewal's Settlement Trusts* [1918] 2 Ch 391; *Re Fuld's Estate (No 3)* [1968] P 675, [1965] 3 All ER 776.

116 Cheshire and North, *Private International Law* (13th edn, 1999) pp 838–839; Dicey and Morris, *The Conflict of Laws* (13th edn, 2000) pp 1029–1030.

117 *Re Schnapper* [1928] Ch 420.

118 *Re Hellmann's Will* (1866) LR 2 Eq 363.

119 Miller, *International Aspects of Succession* (2000) p 164.

120 Cmnd 1729. See also the Fourth Report of the Private International Law Committee, 1958 (Cmnd 491).

testator complies with any of seven possible laws: the laws of the territory of his domicile, habitual residence or nationality at the time of executing the will or at the time of his death, and the law of the place where the will was executed. Moreover, further possibilities are added, for if the will was executed on board a vessel or aircraft, it is in addition sufficient if the execution of the will conformed to the internal law in force in the territory with which, having regard to its registration and other relevant circumstances, the vessel or aircraft may be taken to have been most closely connected.[121] Also, it is sufficient if the will complied with the formalities of any of the possible laws at the time of execution or at a subsequent time if that law is altered with retrospective effect.[122]

(D) ESSENTIAL VALIDITY

Rules of essential validity are those concerned with matters such as whether the testator is obliged to leave a certain proportion of his estate to particular relatives and whether certain kinds of gifts are invalid, for example, as infringing a rule against perpetuities. Where the issue is the protection of relatives against disinheritance, the appropriate law to govern essential validity is the law of the country to which the testator belongs (and to which the relatives will also normally belong). Where the issue is whether the will should be rendered invalid by a rule designed to protect the public interest, the law of the country whose interests are most likely to be affected by the disposition should apply. In either case, this law is normally the law of the testator's domicile at the date of his death. Accordingly, matters of essential validity of a will disposing of movables are governed by the law of the testator's domicile at his death.[123]

For example, if a testator dies domiciled in France leaving his estate to friends and failing to leave to his wife and children the share to which they are entitled under French law, this will is essentially valid only with respect to that portion of the estate which remains after the wife and children have received their statutory portions. If the testator had died domiciled in England, under whose law relatives are not entitled to any fixed share of the estate, the whole will would be essentially valid and the entire estate would pass to the friends. However, it should be borne in mind in such cases that certain dependants of the deceased can apply for family provision under the Inheritance (Provision for Family and Dependants) Act 1975, as amended by the Law Reform (Succession) Act 1995. This

121 Wills Act 1963, s 2(1)(a).
122 S 6(3).
123 *Re Annesley* [1926] Ch 692; *Re Ross* [1930] 1 Ch 377.

power to grant family provision is limited to cases where the testator died domiciled in England.[124] It follows that if the testator had died domiciled in a country under whose law complete freedom of testation is permitted, members of the family living in England could be disinherited and left destitute.

It would appear, however, that not all questions of essential validity are exclusively subject to the law of the testator's domicile at death. Where that law invalidates a disposition because it infringes a rule against perpetuities or accumulations, it ought not to be applied if the subject-matter of the disposition is situated, and is to be administered, in another country. If, for example, an English testator leaves foreign property for a purpose which is not charitable under English law but is charitable under the law of the country where the property is located, there is no reason why English law should be applied to render the disposition invalid. The issue in such a case should be governed by the lex situs. To apply the testator's domiciliary law would be to invalidate dispositions which are not capable of infringing the public interest which the invalidating rule was designed to protect or advance (such as ensuring the marketability of property in the country concerned). This approach is supported by the old case of *Fordyce v Bridges*.[125] The will of the testator, who died domiciled in England, contained a bequest of movable property on trust to sell and use the money to buy land in Scotland according to certain limitations which infringed the English rule against perpetuities, but were valid by Scots law. The gift was held valid.

(E) CONSTRUCTION

Which law should govern questions of interpretation such as what the testator meant by words which he used like 'next-of-kin'[126] and what the testator would have intended when an event occurs, such as the death of a legatee before the death of the testator, for which no provision is made in the will? In such cases the domestic rules of construction of the potentially applicable laws are non-mandatory rules; they are not rules which override the testator's intention, but rather they help to ascertain his intention when it is obscure, or they fill gaps in his expressed intention. So, the governing law should be the law intended by the testator. This is normally presumed to be the law of the testator's domicile at the time he made the will (as opposed to the law of domicile at the date of death), for, unless there is strong indication to the contrary, it is only reasonable to suppose

124 S 1(1).
125 (1848) 2 Ph 497.
126 *Re Fergusson's Will* [1902] 1 Ch 483.

that he was making his will by reference to the law of his own country at the date of making the will.[127]

In *Re Cunnington*[128] the testator, originally domiciled in England, had become domiciled in France. He made his will in England, in English form and language, bequeathing his residuary estate to ten legatees, all of whom were English. Two of the legatees died before the testator. By English law their shares would go as on intestacy, while by French law they would be divided among the surviving legatees. It was held that French law governed, a decision which shows that the presumption that the testator intended the law of his domicile to govern is a strong one, for there were weighty indications pointing to English law. But the presumption is not irrebuttable. In *Re Price*,[129] for example, it was held that a particular disposition in a will made by a testatrix domiciled in France was made with reference to English law. This was because the testatrix had specified that her will was to be 'considered in England the same as in France'.

(F) REVOCATION

There are various ways in which it may be claimed that a will, or a provision in a will, has been revoked. If it is alleged that the will has been revoked (whether expressly or impliedly) by a subsequent will, the issues will be as to the validity or construction of the later will, which have been discussed above. If the question is as to the formal validity of the subsequent will, then section 2(1)(c) of the Wills Act 1963 provides that it is sufficient if the subsequent will complies with any law which the revoked will might have complied with, in addition to any law with which the subsequent will may comply.

There is no English authority as to the law which governs the question whether a will is revoked by destroying it. Should this question be governed by the law of the testator's domicile at the date of the purported revocation or at the date of death? The better view is that this should be governed by the law of the testator's domicile at the time of the purported revocation. If the revocation is effective under that law, the will ceases to exist and therefore there is no will upon which the later domiciliary law can operate.[130] If the revocation is ineffective under the testator's then domiciliary law, the will should not be retrospectively revoked by a change of domicile

127 Wills Act 1963, s 4 provides that the 'construction of a will shall not be altered by reason of any change in the testator's domicile after the execution of the will'.
128 [1924] 1 Ch 68.
129 [1900] 1 Ch 442.
130 Dicey and Morris, *The Conflict of Laws* (13th edn, 2000) p 1050.

because no revoking act has taken place at the time the testator was subject to the new domiciliary law.[131]

Under English law, but not under the laws of many other legal systems, a will is revoked by the subsequent marriage of the testator. What is the position if a man domiciled in France makes a will, then acquires an English domicile and marries, and finally dies domiciled in Scotland? (Under French and Scots law marriage does not revoke a will.) In *Re Martin*[132] it was held that this issue was to be classified as a matter of matrimonial property (and not succession) to be governed by the law of the husband's domicile at the date of the marriage.[133] Accordingly, in the above example, the will would be revoked. *Re Martin* was, however, decided at a time when a wife automatically acquired her husband's domicile on marriage. Since the Domicile and Matrimonial Proceedings Act 1973 came into operation this is no longer the case. Thus, altering the above example to one in which a French domiciled woman makes a will and then, while still domiciled in France, marries an English domiciliary, the authority of *Re Martin* would prima facie suggest that her will is revoked. Such a position is surely now untenable. It has been suggested that the question whether a will is revoked by subsequent marriage should now be reclassified as a separate conflicts category being governed in all cases by the law of the testator's domicile at the date of the marriage.[134] Alternatively, if it is still to be classified as a matter of matrimonial property it must be subject to the proposed new choice of law rule for this category, namely, the law of the country with which the parties and the marriage have their closest connection.[135]

2. *Immovable property*

To what extent are the choice of law rules for wills different in relation to the disposition of immovable property? Does the lex situs govern all issues here? There are two reasons why questions relating to immovable property may be subjected to the lex situs. One is that the property is under the control of the authorities of the country where it is situated, and a decision different from that which would be given by the court of that country may not have any effect. This reason only applies to foreign land. The other reason, which applies

131 Mann, (1954) 31 BYIL 231. Cf Miller, *International Aspects of Succession* (2000) pp 191–192.
132 [1900] P 211.
133 See p 497.
134 Dicey and Morris, *The Conflict of Laws* (13th edn, 2000) p 1051, n 83.
135 See p 500.

to immovable property in England, is that the interests of the country where the land is situated may be affected by the disposition of the land. Whether this is so, however, depends on the nature of the domestic rules in question.

Because the rationale underlying the application of the lex situs rule depends on whether the property is situated in England or not, it is convenient to explore the two situations separately.

(A) ENGLISH IMMOVABLES

Many questions relating to the disposition by will of immovables situated in England will be governed by English domestic law, as the lex situs. However, as the land is situated here and under the control of English authorities who will clearly follow any English court decision, the main rationale for the application of the lex situs does not apply and thus a more flexible approach can be adopted.

(i) Capacity

There is no authority as to the law governing capacity to make a will disposing of immovables in England. As English interests can scarcely be affected by whether or not a testator domiciled abroad has power to dispose of property by will (assuming that the disposition would be essentially valid by English law), there seems no reason why the law of the testator's domicile should not govern, as with movables.[136]

(ii) Formal validity

Under the Wills Act 1963, the provisions relating to the formal validity of wills disposing of immovable property are the same as for movables, except that, in addition, compliance with the lex situs is sufficient.[137]

(iii) Essential validity

The essential validity of a will disposing of immovable property has been held to be governed by the lex situs, English law. For example, in *Freke v Lord Carbery*[138] a disposition by a testator domiciled in Ireland of a leasehold house in England was held invalid under the English Accumulations Act 1800, although the gift was valid by

136 This view is not supported by either Dicey and Morris, *The Conflict of Laws* (13th edn, 2000) p 1030 or Cheshire and North, *Private International Law* (13th edn, 1999) p 1001; both state that this issue would be governed by the lex situs.

137 S 2(1)(b).

138 (1873) LR 16 Eq 461.

Irish law. Similarly, the questions of what estates can be created, and with what incidents, will be governed by English law in relation to English land.[139]

(iv) Construction

The construction of a gift by will of immovables in England is not necessarily governed by English law. Here, if no mandatory rules of English law are in issue, the interests of England are not involved, so, as with movables, the intention of the testator is to be ascertained, or gaps in his provisions are to be filled, by the law intended by him. This will normally be presumed to be the law which he would reasonably expect to apply, namely, the law of his domicile at the date of making the will.[140] This is illustrated (in relation to the Scottish conflict of laws) by the Scottish case of *Studd v Cook*[141] in which a testator, domiciled in England, by his will devised land in Scotland. The effect of the disposition by English law was to give the beneficiary a life interest, but by Scots law a fee simple. The House of Lords (on appeal from the Scottish court) held that the English construction was to be applied. Of course, when the English court is dealing with English land, the essential validity of the disposition will be governed by English law, which may mean that the disposition as construed by the law of the domicile has to be accommodated to what is legally possible by English law.[142]

(v) Revocation

There seems no reason why the rules determining which law governs revocation of a will of English immovables should not be the same as for movables because English interests are not especially involved in relation to that question, merely because the property is English land. This is certainly true where it is claimed that a will is revoked by a later will. However, with regard to revocation by destruction, it was held in the United States case of *Re Barrie's Estate*[143] that whether a will had been revoked by writing 'void' across it was to be determined by the lex situs. As regards revocation by subsequent marriage it has been held by the English court[144] that the will of a testator domiciled in Scotland at the date of the marriage and disposing of land in England was revoked by his subsequent marriage under English law even though the marriage did not have that effect

139 *Re Miller* [1914] 1 Ch 511.
140 *Philipson-Stow v IRC* [1961] AC 727, [1960] 3 All ER 814.
141 (1883) 8 App Cas 577.
142 *Re Miller* [1914] 1 Ch 511.
143 240 Iowa 431, 35 NW 2d 658 (1949).
144 *Re Earl Caithness* (1891) 7 TLR 354.

by Scots law. The decision was, however, not followed by the New South Wales court in *Re Micallef's Estate*[145] in relation to land in New South Wales (whose law has the same rule as English law). The reasons were that the law of New South Wales could have no interest in imposing its rule on a testator domiciled in another country, and that in any event the rule is not one of succession but of matrimonial property, which is governed by the law of the domicile at the date of the marriage.

(B) FOREIGN IMMOVABLES

The reason why the lex situs should govern wills of foreign land is not merely that the foreign country's interests may be affected, but that the land is under the control of the authorities there. If the English court is to make any decision about the entitlement to such land it should therefore be in line with the decision which would be made by the foreign court, thereby reducing the likelihood that the matter will be disposed of differently by the foreign court. So the lex situs should apply.

Although this reasoning should logically extend to all issues which might arise in relation to foreign immovables, the lex situs does not in fact govern all such issues.

(i) Capacity

Even if in the case of English land the law of the domicile should govern, for foreign land there is a strong case that the governing law should be whatever domestic law would be applied by the court of the situs. There is little point applying the law of domicile if that law would not be applied by the lex situs.

(ii) Formal validity

The position in relation to formal validity is regulated by the Wills Act 1963 and the relevant provisions are the same as those applicable to land situated in England.

(iii) Essential validity

It is well settled that the essential validity of the will is governed by the lex situs.[146]

(iv) Construction

So far as the construction of the will is concerned, the authority that the governing law is the law intended by the testator, normally

145 [1977] 2 NSWLR 929.
146 *Re Ross* [1930] 1 Ch 377.

presumed to be the law of the testator's domicile at the time of making the will, rather than the lex situs, is not confined to English immovables.[147] However, the fundamental question here is simply one of ascertaining the intention of the testator and it may be that the presumption may be more easily rebutted in favour of the lex situs, especially if the testator uses technical language only known to the lex situs. Similarly, if a construction of a will according to the law of domicile would be illegal or impossible to give effect to under the lex situs, then the canons of construction of the lex situs must apply.[148]

(v) Revocation

As regards revocation of wills of foreign immovables, there seems no reason in principle why the rules should not be the same as for revocation of wills of English immovables and this is almost certainly the position with revocation by subsequent will and revocation by marriage. However, with regard to revocation by destruction the arguments for an application of the lex situs are, as with all issues relating to land abroad, stronger here and, accordingly, it is more likely that the United States decision of *Re Barrie's Estate*,[149] would be followed and the lex situs applied to determine the effect of the destruction of a will.[150]

C Intestate succession

1. Movables

The law which governs the disposition of a person's movable property on his death, to the extent not validly disposed of by will, is the law of the deceased's domicile at his death.[151] It is appropriate that the matter be determined by the law of the country to which the deceased belongs. A person may reasonably expect that the law of that country will apply and, in not making a will, he may be presumed to be content that his property devolve in accordance with its intestacy rules.

2. Immovables

Intestate succession to immovable property, whether situated in England or a foreign country, is governed by the lex situs.[152] This no

147 *Philipson-Stow v IRC* [1961] AC 727, [1960] 3 All ER 814.
148 Ibid.
149 240 Iowa 431, 35 NW 2d 658 (1949). See p 517.
150 Dicey and Morris, *The Conflict of Laws* (13th edn, 2000) p 1049, n 69.
151 *Re Collens* [1986] Ch 505, [1986] 1 All ER 611.
152 Ibid.

doubt is the right approach in those exceptional cases when the English court is willing to determine the entitlement to land situated abroad. However, there seems little reason why English domestic law should govern the intestate succession of land in England left by a person who died domiciled elsewhere. English interests are not affected by the way the property is divided amongst the deceased's relatives and, if the law of domicile is the appropriate law for movables, it is equally so for immovables. It is unsatisfactory that the different kinds of property of a deceased should be distributed according to different regimes, which can lead to results not contemplated by either law.[153]

D Renvoi in succession cases

When succession to immovable property in a foreign country is governed by the lex situs, this is traditionally regarded as meaning the whole law of the situs, including its conflicts rules, so that the domestic law to be applied by the English court is that which would be applied by the foreign court,[154] which, in a case of intestate succession for example, might be the law of the nationality.

The doctrine of renvoi has also been used in relation to succession to movables.[155] The justification for this is not that the property is in the control of the foreign authority (indeed, it will probably be in England), but that it may produce uniformity of distribution of the deceased's property, whether determined by the English court or the foreign court, in respect of property in either country. In chapter 12 it is argued that the doctrine of renvoi is inappropriate in such cases. Effectively, it involves the English court sacrificing its own notions of the appropriate governing law for the sake of uniformity. However, whatever view one adopts in relation to renvoi, one thing seems certain: it is not desirable to use renvoi when the governing law is the law of the domicile at the date of making the will (as opposed to the date of death), as is the case with the construction of a will, at any rate if the deceased changed his domicile after making the will. For then uniformity would be achieved with the wrong country, perhaps at the expense of uniformity with the domicile at death.

The Wills Act 1963 expressly refers to the 'internal law' of the relevant countries, which is defined in relation to any country as 'the law which would apply in a case where no question of the law in force

153 Ibid.
154 *Re Ross* [1930] 1 Ch 377.
155 *Re Annesley* [1926] Ch 692; *Re Ross* [1930] 1 Ch 377; *Re O'Keefe* [1940] Ch 124, [1940] 1 All ER 216.

in any other territory or state arose'.[156] Thus renvoi is excluded for formal validity[157] (even in respect of immovable property). Uniformity can be hoped for here to the extent that other countries adopt the international convention which was implemented by the 1963 Act.

The problem of renvoi is discussed more fully in chapter 12.

E The incidental question

When English conflicts rules lead to the application of the domestic law of a foreign country, an incidental question may arise which itself requires the application of a conflicts rule for its solution. The problem is whether the incidental question is to be decided by the English conflicts rules (lex fori) or by those of the foreign country whose domestic law governs the main question (lex causae).[158] Suppose, for example, a succession is governed by Mexican law and under Mexican law the wife and legitimate children of the deceased are entitled to succeed. The question may arise as to whether a particular claimant is the surviving wife of the deceased, which depends on whether her marriage to the deceased was valid; or the question may arise as to whether a particular child is legitimate. Are the English or Mexican conflicts rules as to the validity of the marriage or the legitimacy of the child to be applied by the English court?

The tendency of the courts has been to apply the conflicts rules of the lex causae to decide the incidental question, often, however, without any express discussion of the problem. It is possible to support using the lex causae as a general rule in the field of succession, for otherwise the application of the foreign domestic rule may be an empty gesture. If the English court applies the foreign rule of succession, say that the surviving spouse or legitimate child of the deceased is entitled to succeed, it might seem only reasonable for it to accept the foreign country's view as to who the spouse or

156 S 6(1).

157 At common law the doctrine of renvoi was applied to formal validity (*Re Fuld's Estate (No 3)* [1968] P 675, [1965] 3 All ER 776). As there is nothing in the Act which abolishes the common law rule that formal validity is governed by the law of the testator's domicile at death or the application of renvoi in that connection, it has been argued that renvoi may be applied in such cases (Dicey and Morris, *The Conflict of Laws* (13th edn, 2000) p 1034; Cheshire and North, *Private International Law* (13th edn, 1999) p 990). Such a view seems implausible as the Act specifically provides that the testator's law of domicile at the date of death is one of the bases governing formal validity.

158 There has been a great deal of academic debate of this topic. See, for example, Gotlieb, 'The Incidental Question Revisited – Theory and Practice in the Conflict of Laws' (1977) 26 ICLQ 734.

legitimate child is. Why allow the foreign law to determine the class of persons entitled to succeed, but not the members of the class?

Such little authority as there is supports the view that in the field of succession an incidental question is to be decided by the conflicts rules of the lex causae.[159] In *Re Johnson*[160] an intestate succession was governed under English conflicts rules by the law of Malta. By Maltese law, the next-of-kin were entitled to succeed, but who the next-of-kin were depended on whether or not the deceased was legitimate. He had not been born in lawful wedlock and, although he had been legitimated by subsequent marriage according to Maltese conflicts rules, he had not been legitimated under the English conflicts rules.[161] It was held that the next-of-kin were to be determined under Maltese law on the basis that he had been legitimated. Similarly in *Haque v Haque*[162] an Australian court was concerned with a succession governed by Indian law, under which the legitimate children of the deceased were entitled to succeed. It was held that a child could succeed who, although illegitimate under the Australian rules, was legitimate under Indian conflicts rules (being the child of a marriage which was void for bigamy under Australian conflicts rules, but which was a valid polygamous marriage under Indian choice of law rules).

However, despite these authorities, it is argued in chapter 12 that the better view is that the lex fori approach should normally be applied. As that argument depends on an understanding of the rationale of choice of law rules and of the relationship between renvoi and the incidental question, discussion of that view will not be rehearsed at this stage.

159 *Baindail v Baindail* [1946] P 122 at 127–128.
160 [1903] 1 Ch 821.
161 Because although his father had been domiciled in Malta (which provided for legitimation by subsequent marriage) at the time of the marriage, he had been domiciled in England at the time of the birth. See p 443.
162 (1962) 108 CLR 230.

Chapter 12

The choice of law process revisited

In chapter 1 an overview of the conflicts process was provided. In that chapter central issues relating to jurisdiction, choice of law and recognition and enforcement of foreign judgments were raised and an outline of the mechanics of the choice of law process was sketched. Most of these issues have been developed to varying extents in the ensuing chapters and nothing further need to be said of some of them, in particular the jurisdictional rules and rules relating to recognition and enforcement of foreign judgments. However, it is appropriate in this concluding chapter to return to some of the issues involved in the choice of law process and to subject them to closer examination.

I CLASSIFICATION

A Introduction

The problems of classification (or characterisation) have already been encountered, both in chapter 1 and in the discussion of the choice of law rules on various subjects: for example, the question whether rules requiring parental consent to marry are to be classified as rules of capacity to marry or rules of formal validity,[1] and the question whether the right to recover compensation for non-pecuniary loss is a matter of substance or procedure.[2] Classification has been the subject of a great deal of academic discussion.[3] There are various kinds of problems of classification which can arise, and, indeed, one of the main points of academic disagreement in a particular case may

1 See pp 312–313.
2 See p 278.
3 See Dicey and Morris, *The Conflict of Laws* (13th edn, 2000) pp 33–45; Cheshire and North, *Private International Law* (13th edn, 1999) pp 35–45; Falconbridge, *Selected Essays on the Conflict of Laws* (2nd edn, 1954); Robertson, *Characterization in the Conflict of Laws* (1940).

be over what it is that has to be characterised: the facts, the cause of action, the legal issue, rules of domestic law or rules of foreign law.[4] It will be argued that this is something of a dispute over form rather than substance. However, before developing that argument, it is necessary to return to basics and to recall how the problem of classification arises.

B The problem as illustrated by *Ogden v Ogden*

As has been seen throughout this book, the conflict of laws remains a highly compartmentalised area of law. In order that a choice of law rule can be utilised, it is necessary that the issue between the parties be allocated to a precise legal category. For example, if the dispute relates to whether a will is revoked by a subsequent marriage, one has to determine whether this is an issue relating to matrimonial property or succession. If it is the former, the applicable law is the law of the matrimonial domicile (or law of the husband's domicile at the date of the marriage). If it is the latter, the relevant choice of law rule refers to the law of the deceased's domicile at the date of death (for movables). If both these laws and English law characterise the issue in the same way, there is no problem. But if these laws are not in agreement on this point, the problem arises: by whose law should this classification be effected? Traditionally, the answer is that it is for the lex fori, English law, to determine this categorisation and, continuing the above example, the matter would be classified as relating to matrimonial property[5] and the appropriate choice of law rule can be attached; one is then referred to the applicable law.

Take, for example, the case of *Ogden v Ogden*,[6] which concerned a French domiciliary who married in England without obtaining his parents' consent. It will be recalled that there are two choice of law rules governing validity of marriage: the first is that capacity to marry is governed by the domiciliary laws of the spouses at the date of the marriage;[7] the second is that the formal validity of a marriage is governed by the law of the country in which the marriage is celebrated. The first choice of law rule means that if the English

4 See, for example, *Macmillan Inc v Bishopsgate Investment Trust plc (No 3)* [1996] 1 WLR 387 where there are references to classifying the 'issue', 'the question in this action', 'the relevant rule of law' and a 'judicial concept or category'. See, further, Forsyth, 'Characterisation Revisited: An Essay in the Theory and Practice of the English Conflict of Laws' (1998) 114 LQR 141.

5 *Re Martin* [1900] P 211.

6 [1908] P 46. See pp 312–313.

7 For the sake of simplicity it will be assumed that this is the correct choice of law rule governing capacity to marry (rather than the intended matrimonial home doctrine).

court has to determine the validity of a marriage, then any rules of the laws of the parties' domiciles which are rules of capacity to marry must be applied. Similarly, the second choice of law rule means that any rules of the law of the country in which the marriage was celebrated which are rules of formal validity are to be applied. In *Ogden v Ogden* the fact that the man had not obtained his parents' consent rendered the marriage voidable under French law. This presented a problem of classification. Was the French rule one of capacity, in which case it would be applicable?[8] Or was it a rule of formality, in which case it would not be applicable? The English court classified it as a rule of formal validity, which meant that it was not to be applied, for the marriage had been celebrated in England.

This case demonstrates the illusory nature of the dispute whether it is facts or legal rules that are being classified. One approach is to assert that the facts of this case had to be classified into one of the two legal categories as relating to either capacity or formal validity. Having categorised the facts as raising the legal issue of formal validity, the court was able to apply the appropriate choice of law rule. The parties married in England by which law the man did not need parental consent and, accordingly, the marriage was declared valid. The other approach is that the only live issue in this case was the French rule that a man of his age needed parental consent without which the marriage was voidable. The court had to classify this French rule as relating to capacity (in which case it would have been applicable) or to formalities (in which case it was not applicable). The court adopted the latter approach and the marriage was valid. It made no difference which approach was adopted. In essence, the English court was having to classify the legal issue and whether the relevant rule (the one relating to parental consent) fell within that legal categorisation. It makes no difference whether the categorisation of the issue preceded the determination of whether the French rule came within that category, or whether it was the classification of the French rule that determined the category. The outcome, and the process by which that outcome was achieved, is the same. It is the failure to grasp this simple point that has generated much of the confusion surrounding this problem.

C The solutions

In *Ogden v Ogden*[9] the legal issue was classified by the lex fori, English law. An alternative approach could have been to classify the

8 Were it not for the rule in *Sottomayer v De Barros (No 2)* (1879) 5 PD 94 (an alternative basis for the decision in *Ogden v Ogden*).
9 [1908] P 46.

rule according to the potentially applicable lex causae, French law, which regarded the rule as one relating to capacity and, therefore, one that would have been applicable had the French classification been employed. How should the court classify a legal issue or rule? Various theories have been advanced by writers, while the courts have used differing approaches without expressly espousing any particular theory.

1. The lex fori

One solution, as in *Ogden v Ogden*,[10] is that classification should always be effected according to the lex fori. This means that for conflicts purposes English domestic rules will be classified in the same way as they are in domestic law, and foreign domestic rules are to be classified in the same way as the equivalent English domestic rules. In English domestic law the rule that a minor requires parental consent for marriage is classified as a rule of formalities, and in *Ogden v Ogden* the court assumed that the equivalent French rule should be classified in the same way. The main advantage of this approach, apart from simplicity and predictability, is that it enables the English court to maintain control over its own conflicts rules; otherwise, it 'would no longer be master in its own home'.[11] To apply any other law presupposes that it is an applicable law (that is what the words 'lex causae' signify). It is impossible to be referred to a foreign lex causae other than by means of a choice of law rule and choice of law rules can only be attached to legal categories. It follows that this initial categorisation can only be effected by the lex fori because at that stage one does not know what the lex causae is. However, this rationale does not stand up to close analysis. In *Ogden v Ogden* there were only two possible applicable laws, English law and French law, and the reason that French law was a possibly applicable law was because of the English conflict of laws rule that capacity is governed by the law of domicile. If, for example, the French domiciliary had been a German national and habitually resident in Italy, the laws of Germany and Italy would not have been potentially applicable laws because there is no English choice of law rule that any aspect of validity of marriage is governed by the law of nationality or habitual residence. In short, the issue could have been classified by French law without the English court 'losing control' over its conflicts rules.

There are two main disadvantages to the lex fori approach. First, purporting to apply a foreign law, but ignoring its classifications, can

10 [1908] P 46.
11 Dicey and Morris, *The Conflict of Laws* (13th edn, 2000) p 35.

result in applying a distorted law that is effectively the law of nowhere. Imagine if the laws of England and France in *Ogden v Ogden* had been reversed so that lack of parental consent was regarded as a matter of capacity by English law and a matter of formal validity by French law. Classification by the lex fori would result in the French rule being construed as relating to capacity and hence applicable, thereby invalidating the marriage, despite the fact that by French law itself its rule would not have been applicable on the facts. It is argued that it is pointless purporting to apply a foreign law, unless it is applied in toto, including its classification rules. This argument, however, is premised on the assumption that application of a foreign law actually means applying the law as it would be applied by the foreign court. This, however, is rarely the case. Whenever the doctrine of renvoi is not applied there is a risk that the law being applied is not the same as would actually be applied by the foreign court and, as shall be examined shortly, there are good reasons for rejecting the doctrine of renvoi.

The second claimed disadvantage to the lex fori approach is that the similarity between the foreign and the English rule may be superficial and misleading, for the nature, purpose and effects of the foreign rule may be quite different from those of the English rule. That was so in *Ogden v Ogden* for under English law, if a party marries without parental consent, the marriage is nevertheless valid, while by French law the marriage was voidable. This difference might well require different classification for conflicts purposes. Further, the English court will often be called upon to classify legal rules, issues or institutions that have no analogy in English law. For example, English law has no obvious counterpart to the continental regimes of community of property, to registered same-sex partnerships, to the adoption of adults, to legitimation by acknowledgement, to children who are neither legitimate nor illegitimate as under New Zealand law, to legally binding agreements not supported by consideration and so on. The short answer to this last point is that one of the main functions of the conflict of laws is to deal legally with just such situations that do not exist in English law; foreign legal concepts cannot be disregarded just because they are unknown to English law. Accordingly, following the lex fori approach, the English court simply identifies the nearest English analogue to the foreign provision. For example, cases involving foreign domiciliaries who have married in community of property are classified as matters of matrimonial law or implied contract; cases involving registered same-sex partnerships should be classified as marriages rather than contract. Such classifications are effected, not by following the nomenclature adopted by the foreign law, but by examining the incidents of the status or legal relationship to ascertain its nearest English counterpart.[12] For example, the reason that Danish same-sex partnerships should be regarded as marriages for conflicts purposes is that, although not described as marriages under Danish law, they entail most of the incidents of a marriage and therefore approximate a marriage more closely than a contract.

2. The lex causae

The alternative theory is that classification should be according to the lex causae, which means that a domestic rule should be classified according to the law of which it is a part. The English court should classify a French rule as it is classified in French law, not in the way the equivalent English rule is classified by English law. If the English court has to decide the validity of the marriage of a person who at the time of the marriage was domiciled in France, then the English court must apply all rules which French law regards as rules of capacity. The court did not do this in *Ogden v Ogden*,[13] where the rule about parental consent was classified by French law as one of capacity.

A case in which the English court did follow the lex causae approach is *Re Maldonado's Estate*.[14] The deceased died intestate, domiciled in Spain, leaving movable property in England. She left no next-of-kin. In these circumstances, by English law, the Crown was entitled to the property as bona vacantia, while by Spanish law the Spanish state was entitled to it. Many countries have the rule that if a person dies intestate leaving no relatives entitled to succeed to his estate, then the property goes to the state. But the rule is classified differently in different systems. In some systems it is regarded as a rule of succession, the state succeeding to the property as intestate heir in the same way as an individual. In other systems the rule that the property goes to the state is regarded not as a rule of succession but of property law, under which the state is entitled to seize ownerless property. Such a right of the state to take ownerless property is called the ius regale.

There were two choice of law rules to be considered in *Re Maldonado*. One was that intestate succession to movables is governed by the law of the country in which the deceased was domiciled at her death. The other was that the acquisition of title to movable property otherwise than by succession (including the right to seize ownerless property) is governed by the law of the country

12 See, for example, *National Bank of Greece and Athens SA v Metliss* [1958] AC 509, [1957] 3 All ER 608; *Adams v National Bank of Greece and Athens SA* [1961] AC 255, [1960] 2 All ER 421. These cases are discussed fully in Dicey and Morris, *The Conflict of Laws* (13th edn, 2000) pp 40–42.

13 [1908] P 46.

14 [1954] P 223, [1953] 2 All ER 300.

where the property is situated. If the Spanish rule under which the state was entitled to the property was classified as a rule of succession, then it would be applicable because the deceased died domiciled in Spain. If, however, it was classified as a rule of property law, then it would not be applied, for the property was in England, not Spain. In that situation the Crown would take the estate. The evidence showed that by Spanish law the state's right to the estate was regarded as a right of succession. The court held that as the succession was governed by Spanish law, all rules which, according to Spanish law, were rules of succession should be applied by the English court. In other words, it followed the lex causae approach. The consequence was that the Spanish state took the estate. In other cases[15] where, according to the foreign law which governed the succession, the state's right to the property was an ius regale, not a right of succession, the English estates of intestates who died without next-of-kin were awarded to the Crown.

Another case where classification was effected according to the lex causae was *Re Cohn*.[16] In this case a mother and daughter were both killed in an air-raid in London in 1941. By the mother's will the daughter succeeded to the mother's estate if the daughter had survived the mother. It could not, however, be ascertained whether either had survived the other, both having been killed by the same bomb. As the mother had been domiciled in Germany at the time of her death, the succession to her estate was governed by German law. Under English law, as provided by section 184 of the Law of Property Act 1925, under such circumstances 'such deaths shall be presumed to have occurred in order of seniority, and accordingly the younger shall be deemed to have survived the elder'. According to German law, however, there was a provision that if it could not be proved which had died first, it was presumed that they died simultaneously. Which presumption was applicable?

The court first examined the English provision and rejected the view that the presumption was a rule of procedure, in which case it would have had to apply, following the general rule that all questions of procedure are governed by the lex fori. It was not part of the law of evidence of the lex fori which assisted in the resolution of the factual question of who died first; rather it was a substantive rule of succession, in effect laying down who should be entitled to succeed to a deceased person's estate when it was unknown whether or not some other person had survived her. The court then examined the German presumption to ascertain whether it was a rule of evidence (in which case it would not have been applicable) or a rule of

15 *Re Barnett's Trusts* [1902] 1 Ch 847; *Re Musurus's Estate* [1936] 2 All ER 1666.
16 [1945] Ch 5.

succession (which would be applicable). This classification was effected according to the lex causae. Construing the provision according to its location in the German Civil Code, it was concluded that it was a rule of succession which could be applied. Accordingly, the daughter did not take under the will.

This case highlights one of the problems with this approach to classification. If the German rule had been found to be a rule of evidence (as it could easily have been as the English court went no further than examining where the provision appeared in the German Civil Code), it could not have been applied. As the English rule was also not applicable, the result would have been an impasse with neither law applicable. Similarly, there would have been a problem had the court decided that the English presumption was procedural, but the German one was substantive. In this situation both laws would have been potentially applicable although in such cases there can be little doubt that the English procedural rule would have trumped the foreign substantive provision.

It is clear that, in addition to the above problems, classification according to the lex causae does not necessarily produce a satisfactory result. Suppose a Roman Catholic man domiciled in Malta married (before 1975[17]) a woman domiciled in Scotland in a register office in England. By Maltese law the marriage was void because the husband, being a Roman Catholic, could only validly marry in a Catholic church. If the Maltese rule were classified as a rule of formalities, the Maltese invalidity would be immaterial, because the marriage was celebrated in England, not Malta. Maltese law, however, classified its rule as one of essential validity rather than form. If the English court classified the rule in that way the marriage would be void, because Maltese law would be applicable under the relevant English choice of law rule. It is clear, however, that the English court would consider the marriage valid,[18] and rightly so. The English conflicts rule that formalities of marriage are governed by the lex loci celebrationis is surely designed precisely to deal with such questions as whether a marriage must be celebrated in a church. If the English court were to accept the Maltese classification of its rule as one of essential validity, it would be contradicting the policy of its own conflicts rule.

It is by no means clear that the lex causae approach was the correct one in *Re Maldonado*. Is it sensible that in such cases the question whether the Crown or the foreign state takes the property should depend on how the foreign law chooses to label its rule? The

17 Maltese law on this point was altered by the Marriage Act 1975, s 18.
18 *Gray v Formosa* [1963] P 259, [1962] 3 All ER 419.

facts of the situation and the issue to be decided are the same whatever the foreign classification, so the same choice of law rule should apply, however the foreign law chooses to classify its rule.[19] Why should the outcome in *Re Cohn* have depended on the location of the presumption in the German Civil Code?

3. *The better view*[20]

The reason why the court has to classify issues is to decide within which category a choice of law rule falls. The problem then is for the court to ascertain the scope of its own choice of law rule. Like all rules, choice of law rules are expressed in general terms, so their meaning may have to be elucidated to decide the particular case. In a case like *Ogden v Ogden*,[21] the problem really is to decide what sorts of domestic rule come within the meaning of 'capacity' in the choice of law rule that capacity to marry is governed by the law of the domicile, and what sorts of domestic rule come within the meaning of 'formalities' in the choice of law rule that formal validity is governed by the lex loci celebrationis.

There is nothing peculiar to the conflict of laws in this need to determine the scope of a rule of law and to interpret it to see whether it extends to a doubtful case. The same has to be done with rules of contract, tort or any other area of law in hard cases. The main difference is that the subject-matter of domestic rules of contract or tort is facts, so the question is whether the particular facts fall within the rule in question. The subject-matter of choice of law rules is not facts but rules of domestic law, so the question is whether the domestic rule in question falls within the scope of the choice of law rule.

How then is the court to determine the scope of its choice of law rules in novel cases in order to decide within which of them the domestic rule in question comes? As when determining the scope of any other rule, it should seek out the reason or policy behind the possibly relevant choice of law rules and on that basis decide which is the appropriate one for the instant case. For example, suppose that the reason for the choice of law rule for capacity to marry is that the laws of the countries to which the parties belong are the

19 The better approach would be to classify all the domestic rules as ones of property. It has been held that the Crown's right to take the estate under the Administration of Estates Act 1925 is a right of succession: *Re Mitchell* [1954] Ch 525, [1954] 2 All ER 246; but it must also be an ius regale for conflicts purposes, otherwise no state might be entitled to the property.

20 This approach is similar to that of Lipstein, 'Conflict of Laws 1921–1971: The Way Ahead' [1972B] CLJ 67 at 77–83.

21 [1908] P 46.

appropriate ones to decide whether the marriage relationship in question is permissible (because those are the countries whose laws are most fitted to determine whether an intending spouse has sufficient judgment or maturity), while the reason for the choice of law rule for formal validity is that if the marriage relationship is permissible, the law most appropriate to determine how it should be celebrated is the law of the country where it is celebrated. Then should it not follow that the French rule in *Ogden v Ogden* requiring parental consent for a valid marriage should have been treated as a rule of capacity? Similarly, the former Maltese rule that a Roman Catholic could only validly marry by a ceremony conducted by a priest should be treated as a rule of formalities, however it might have been classified by Maltese law.

It might indeed be found in a particular case that the domestic rule in question does not fit comfortably within the reason or policy behind any existing choice of law rule; then a new one will have to be formulated, on the basis of the more general principles underlying choice of law. The various legal categories recognised by the law are 'man-made, not natural. They have no inherent value, beyond their purpose in assisting to select the most appropriate law.'[22] For example, it was earlier argued that the most suitable solution to the problem of determining which law decides whether a will is revoked by marriage would be by the creation of a separate conflicts category for this issue.[23]

In determining the scope of substantive rules of domestic law to see whether the facts of the particular case fall within them, it is of course first necessary that the facts should have been correctly ascertained if the right result is to be reached. Similarly, when determining the scope of choice of law rules to see whether particular domestic rules fall within their reason or policy, it is necessary that the true nature and effect of those domestic rules be ascertained. For example, if the French rule about parental consent in *Ogden v Ogden* should have been classified as one of capacity, it does not follow that the different French rule about such consent which was at issue in *Simonin v Mallac*[24] was also a rule of capacity. In the latter case, the relevant rule provided that the marriage was ultimately permissible without consent if consent had been formally requested and refused three times.[25] Such a rule can reasonably be regarded as being concerned with the manner of celebrating a permissible marriage

22 Mance LJ in *Raiffeisen Zentralbank Österreich AG v Five Star General Trading LLC* [2001] EWCA Civ 68, [2001] QB 825 at 840.
23 See p 515.
24 (1860) 2 Sw & Tr 67.
25 See p 313.

relationship. In ascertaining the true nature and effects of the domestic rules, English or foreign, their classification within the laws to which they belong will be helpful. However, such classification cannot be conclusive, because after the nature and effect of the domestic rules has been determined, the question still remains whether they fall within the meaning of the English choice of law rule.

D English law

The English courts have generally not bothered themselves with the difficult issues raised in the preceding sections and, with notable exceptions such as *Re Maldonado*[26] and *Re Cohn*,[27] have tended to classify all issues according to the lex fori. Recent dicta, however, have started emphasising that 'the conflict of laws does not depend (like a game or even an election) upon the application of rigid rules, but upon a search for appropriate principles to meet particular situations'[28] and that while classification is to be effected by the lex fori this process must be undertaken in a 'broad internationalist spirit'.[29]

Throughout this book numerous examples of such classifications have been encountered: the requirement of parental consent,[30] laws permitting proxy marriages[31] and laws insisting on religious ceremonies for marriages[32] have all been classified as relating to formal validity of marriage; whether parties can lawfully contract marriages of convenience[33] and the effect of impotence and wilful refusal to consummate a marriage[34] have been held to be matters affecting the essential validity of a marriage; marriages where a man is permitted one primary wife and several secondary wives or concubines (who have some, but lesser, legal rights) have been classified as polygamous marriages;[35] whether a will is revoked by marriage has been classed as a matter of matrimonial property;[36] agreements not supported by consideration that are contractually binding by the law governing the agreement have been classified as

26 [1954] P 223, [1953] 2 All ER 300.
27 [1945] Ch 5.
28 See n 22 at 841.
29 Ibid at 840.
30 *Ogden v Ogden*[1908] P 46; *Simonin v Mallac* (1860) 2 Sw & Tr 67.
31 *Apt v Apt* [1948] P 83, [1947] 2 All ER 677.
32 *Gray v Formosa* [1963] P 259, [1962] 3 All ER 419.
33 *Vervaeke v Smith* [1981] Fam 77, [1981] 1 All ER 55.
34 *De Reneville v De Reneville* [1948] P 100, [1948] 1 All ER 56.
35 *Lee v Lau* [1967] P 14, [1964] 2 All ER 248.
36 *Re Martin* [1900] P 211.

contracts;[37] a tortious claim to which a contractual defence is raised has been classified as a matter of contract;[38] whether a bona fide purchase of shares provides a defence to a claim for restitution is a matter of property in shares;[39] whether one spouse is liable to another in tort has been held in the United States to be a matter of status and not tort;[40] whether a cause of action survives against the estate of a deceased tortfeasor has been treated in the United States as a matter relating to the administration of an estate and not as a matter of tort.[41] The problem of classification has also been addressed occasionally by statute. Section 3 of the Wills Act 1963 provides that any requirements of a foreign law that certain types of testator must observe special formalities and that some types of witnesses must possess certain qualifications are to be treated as formal requirements. Whether a claim is barred by lapse of time is classified by section 1 of the Foreign Limitation Periods Act 1984 as substantive rather than procedural. Section 9(2) of the Private International Law (Miscellaneous Provisions) Act 1995 provides that the characterisation of whether an issue relates to tort is a matter for the courts of the forum.

A few notable exceptions to the lex fori rule exist in English law. First, it is well established that whether property is movable or immovable is to be determined by the lex situs.[42] Secondly, whether a matter relates to contract or tort for the purposes of article 5(1) and (3) of the Brussels regime is to be determined by European law as opposed to domestic English law.[43] Thirdly, for the purposes of the Rome Convention it would appear that the term 'contractual obligations', used to define the scope of the Convention, should also be given a community meaning.[44] It follows that an issue could be construed as contractual by European law and thus within the ambit of the Rome Convention, despite the fact that under domestic English law, it might be construed as tortious.[45] These latter two rules are not true exceptions in that European law is, of course, part

37 *Re Bonacina* [1912] 2 Ch 394. This would still be the case under the Rome Convention, art 1(1). See Ch 5.

38 The majority view in *Sayers v International Drilling Co NV* [1971] 3 All ER 163, [1971] 1 WLR 1176.

39 *Macmillan Inc v Bishopsgate Investment Trust plc (No 3)* [1996] 1 WLR 387.

40 *Haumschild v Continental Casualty Co* 7 Wis 2d 130, 95 NW 2d 814 (1959).

41 *Grant v McAuliffe* 41 Cal 2d 859 (1953).

42 *Re Hoyles* [1911] 1 Ch 179.

43 Case 9/87 *SPRL Arcado v SA Haviland* [1988] ECR 1539; Case 189/87 *Kalfelis v Bankhaus Schröder, Münchmeyer, Hengst & Co* [1988] ECR 5565.

44 See p 200.

45 If the English court construed the issue as relating to tort under s 9(2) of the Private International Law (Miscellaneous Provisions) Act 1995, the claimant would have a choice whether to pursue the claim in tort or contract.

of English law. Further exceptions relating to the classification of matters as substantive and procedural exist; these will be examined separately.

E Classification of connecting factors

Consistent with the general rule, connecting factors are also generally classified by the lex fori. For example, when it is necessary to decide whether a person is domiciled or habitually resident in Texas, it is the English interpretation of domicile[46] and habitual residence[47] that is employed. This is because no foreign law becomes potentially applicable until there has been a reference to it by an English choice of law rule with an English connecting factor. For instance, there might be a dispute as to whether a person is domiciled in Texas or California. Clearly, neither of these laws could be permitted to determine the outcome as they might both, under their respective laws, conclude that the person was domiciled there. The whole point of choice of law rules is to lead to the application of the appropriate law as determined by English law.

There are, however, a few exceptions to this well-established rule. For example, a foreign divorce, separation and annulment can be recognised if either party was domiciled in the foreign country according to that country's conception of domicile in family matters.[48] In order to determine whether a person is domiciled in another contracting state for the purposes of the Brussels regime, the English court must apply the law of that state.[49] Finally, in determining the place of performance of a contractual obligation for the purposes of article 5(1)(a) of the Brussels I Regulation, it is the law governing the contract rather than the lex fori that is applicable.[50]

F Substance and procedure

As a general rule questions of procedure are governed by the lex fori, English law. The reason for the rule is that it would not be practicable for the English court to use foreign procedures to try a dispute simply because, for example, a contract was governed by French law. So the method of trial is determined by English law, and

46 *Re Annesley* [1926] Ch 692.

47 *Re A (Abduction: Habitual Residence)* [1996] 1 All ER 24 at 31; *Re B (Child Abduction: Habitual Residence)* [1994] 2 FLR 915 at 918.

48 Family Law Act 1986, s 46(5).

49 Art 59(2) of the Brussels I Regulation.

50 Case 12/76 *Industrie Tessili Italiana Como v Dunlop AG* [1976] ECR 1473; Case C-288/92 *Custom Made Commercial Ltd v Stawa Metallbau GmbH* [1994] ECR 1-2913.

English rules of evidence are applicable, whatever law governs the substance of the dispute. However, in certain contexts the distinction between substance and procedure is far from clear-cut and English courts, either because of considerations of convenience or through a desire to avoid the application of a foreign law in a particular situation, used to be somewhat over-expansive in their interpretation of procedural rules with the result that doubtful cases were classified as procedural. However, as the following examples show, English law is now adopting a more balanced approach.

1. The Statute of Frauds

Under section 4 of the Statute of Frauds (1677) actions could not be brought on certain contracts in the absence of a written agreement or other document signed by the party being sued. This statute applies now only to contracts of guarantee. In *Leroux v Brown*[51] it was held that the provisions of the statute are procedural and therefore applicable to contracts governed by a foreign law. The case concerned an oral contract of employment entered into in France between an English employer and a French employee, whose employment was to be in France. This oral contract was formally valid by French law. When the employee sued to enforce the contract in the English court, the employer relied on section 4 of the Statute of Frauds, under which, because the employment was to last more than a year, 'no action shall be brought upon any agreement ... unless the agreement ... or some memorandum or note thereof, shall be in writing, and signed by the party to be charged therewith'.

If this statutory provision had been regarded as a rule of formal validity, it would not have been applicable because the formal validity of the contract was governed by French law. The English court, however, held it to be a rule of procedure, because the effect of the statute was not to make the contract void, but only to prevent a party from bringing an action on a valid contract. It is hard to see why that should bring the statute within the policy of the English choice of law rule, for it was in no way impracticable to apply the French rule that the oral contract was enforceable. A more cogent consideration would be that the purpose of the Statute of Frauds was to eliminate the fraud or uncertainty which may arise when a claim has to be decided on the basis of conflicting oral evidence. So the rule is one of evidence, and it is generally proper that the court should stick to its own rules of proof. This argument seems outweighed, however, by the policy behind the choice of law rule for formal validity, that it should be sufficient for parties making their

51 (1852) 12 CB 801.

contract in a particular country to comply with the local requirements of form, including the need for writing. Parties making a contract in France, perhaps to be performed in France and having no connections with England, should not have to comply with an English statute merely on the off chance that an action may have to be brought in England. This is indeed now the position under the Rome Convention which provides that a contract is formally valid if it complies with, inter alia, the law governing the contract or the law of the country where it was concluded.[52] Article 14(2) provides that a contract may be proved by any mode of proof recognised by the law governing the formal validity of the contract, provided that such mode of proof can be administered by the forum. Accordingly, if a similar issue as in *Leroux v Brown* were to arise today in relation to a French contract of guarantee, the mode of proof (that is, whether the contract needs to be in writing) could[53] now be governed by French law, the law governing the formal validity of the contract.[54]

2. *Statutes of limitation*

A similar approach to that in *Leroux v Brown*[55] used to be taken by the courts to statutes of limitation, that is laws laying down periods within which claims of various kinds could be brought. Very often the effect of such a law is that the expiry of the period only bars the remedy, but does not extinguish the right, which may still be relied upon in some other way, for instance to support a lien. Where the statute of limitation, whether English or foreign, merely barred the remedy, it was classified by the English courts as procedural. This meant, for instance, that a contract could be enforced in England if not barred by the English statute, even though it was governed by a foreign law under which the claim was time-barred.[56] The converse also applied.[57]

These common law rules were replaced by the Foreign Limitation Periods Act 1984 which provides that where any matter is governed by the law of a foreign country, then that country's law on limitation shall apply irrespective whether it classifies the rule as substantive or

52 Art 9(1), (2).

53 The matter cannot be regarded as settled. Art 14(2) provides that this law 'may' be applied as an alternative to the lex fori. It does not say that it must be applied.

54 Even before the Contracts (Applicable Law) Act 1990, it is possible that an English court might have departed from the approach adopted in *Leroux v Brown* as was done in the Californian case of *Bernkrant v Fowler* 360 P 2d 906 (1961). Compare *Monterosso Shipping Co Ltd v International Transport Workers' Federation, The Rosso* [1982] 3 All ER 841 at 846.

55 (1852) 12 CB 801.

56 *Huber v Steiner* (1835) 2 Bing NC 202.

57 *British Linen Co v Drummond* (1830) 10 B & C 903.

procedural,[58] except where application of the foreign law would conflict with public policy.[59] A rule will conflict with public policy, inter alia, to the extent that its application would cause undue hardship to a party.[60]

3. Remedies and damages

In relation to both contracts[61] and torts,[62] the nature of the remedy is a question of procedure so that, for example, it is for English law to determine whether specific performance or an injunction or only damages shall be granted.

As regards damages, it has been seen that questions of substance – such as remoteness of damage[63] and the kind of loss recoverable (for example, non-pecuniary as well as pecuniary)[64] – are governed by the lex causae. For example in *Chaplin v Boys*[65] a majority of the House of Lords concluded that whether a particular head of damage (pain and suffering) could be claimed was a substantive matter to be determined by the lex causae. On the other hand, questions of procedure – such as the measure or quantification of damages[66] – are governed by the lex fori, English law. For example, in *Chaplin v Boys* the question of how much money should be awarded for pain and suffering was determined by English principles of quantification.[67]

It is, however, often difficult to distinguish sharply between substance and procedure here. For example, a rule imposing a ceiling on damages in tort was held by a majority of the High Court of Australia in *Stevens v Head*[68] to be a procedural rule of quantification. More recently, the same court in *John Pfeiffer Pty Ltd v Rogerson*[69] held that a rule which places a cap on damages is a substantive rule. This latter view has been favoured by the Law Commission on the basis that it is more analogous to one denying recovery for a particular head of damage.[70] With regard to contract,

58 S 1(1).
59 S 2(1).
60 S 2(2).
61 Rome Convention, art 1(2)(h).
62 Private International Law (Miscellaneous Provisions) Act 1995, s 14(3)(b).
63 *D'Almeida Araujo (J) Lda v Sir Frederick Becker & Co Ltd* [1953] 2 QB 329, [1953] 2 All ER 288.
64 *Chaplin v Boys* [1971] AC 356, [1969] 2 All ER 1085.
65 Ibid.
66 *Coupland v Arabian Gulf Petroleum Co* [1983] 2 All ER 434, [1983] 1 WLR 1136.
67 The same approach was adopted in relation to Pt III of the Private International Law (Miscellaneous Provisions) Act 1995 in *Edmunds v Simmonds* [2001] 1 WLR 1003.
68 (1993) 67 ALJR 343.
69 (2000) 172 ALR 625. See p 279.
70 Law Commission No 193, *Choice of Law in Tort and Delict* (1990) para 3.39.

the Rome Convention provides that the consequences of breach 'including the assessment of damages in so far as it is governed by rules of law' is a substantive matter governed by the applicable law provided it is 'within the limits of the powers conferred on the court by its procedural law'.[71] While it has been suggested that this may lead to 'a more nuanced approach to quantification',[72] the precise effect of this provision is, as yet, untested. One view is that the assessment of damages is always 'governed by rules of law' and thus the issue of quantification is now, under this provision, always a matter of substantive law to be governed by the applicable law.[73] An alternative view is that one of the 'limits' imposed by the court of the forum 'by its procedural law' is the rule that questions of quantification are procedural to be governed by the lex fori and thus the distinction here between issues of substance (remoteness and recoverable heads) and procedure (quantification of damage) is unaffected by the Rome Convention.[74] It has been suggested that the phrase 'in so far as it is governed by rules of law' refers only to certain rules of the applicable law such as those limiting the amount of damages or rules governing contractual pre-estimates of damage.[75]

II RENVOI

A Introduction

Whatever the rationale of choice of law rules, the result is that in many cases there will be a reference to a foreign law. While this will usually be taken to mean the foreign domestic rules, it has already been seen that this need not necessarily be so and that the reference could be to the foreign law in its entirety, including its choice of law rules. This raises the problem of renvoi.

Under the doctrine of renvoi the English court treats the reference to a foreign law in the English choice of law rule as a reference to the conflict of laws rules of the foreign law, and not merely to its domestic law. So, for example, the choice of law rule that intestate succession to movable property is governed by the law of the deceased's domicile at the date of his death refers to the conflicts rules of that law, not its domestic rules. The potential problem of renvoi only arises if the foreign country's choice of law rule is

71 Art 10(1)(c).
72 Stone, *The Conflict of Laws* (1995) p 391.
73 Collier, *Conflict of Laws* (3rd edn, 2001) pp 65–69.
74 Dicey and Morris, *The Conflict of Laws* (13th edn, 2000) p 1264.
75 Ibid. See, further, p 251.

different from the English one. If the English rules refer to South African law as the law of domicile and South African conflicts rules would refer to South African domestic law as the law of domicile, there is no problem and there would be no point in either party pleading that the South African conflicts rules should be taken into account.

B Approaches to renvoi

There are several approaches that can be adopted when there is a difference between the English and the relevant country's choice of law rules. The English court can either 'reject renvoi' and simply apply the domestic rules of the foreign country or it can take account of the foreign country's conflicts rules. If the latter course is adopted, this can be done in one of two ways: either by applying 'partial' or 'single' renvoi, on the one hand, or by applying 'total' or 'double' renvoi (also known as the 'foreign court theory'), on the other.

1. Rejection of renvoi

If the doctrine of renvoi is rejected, when an English conflicts rule refers a matter to a foreign law, this is taken to mean the domestic, non-conflicts rules of that country. For example, if a person dies intestate domiciled in Mexico, the English conflicts rule is clear that the beneficial distribution of the person's movable property should be governed by Mexican law as the law of domicile at the date of death. If renvoi is rejected, this means that the domestic rules of Mexican intestacy law will be applied (for example, that the estate should be divided in set proportions between the surviving spouse and the children of the marriage). The fact that a Mexican court might regard this as a conflict of laws case and refer the matter to another law is disregarded.

2. Partial renvoi

Under partial or single renvoi, the English court takes account of the conflicts rules of the country indicated by the English choice of law rule and applies the domestic law of the country referred to by that foreign choice of law rule. For example, suppose the English court has to decide who is entitled to movable property left in England by an intestate who died domiciled in Mexico, but who was a citizen of the United Kingdom. According to the English choice of law rule, the succession is governed by the law of the deceased's domicile, Mexican law. By Mexican choice of law rules, let it be supposed, intestate succession is governed by the law of the deceased's nationality at the date of his death, which is (let it be assumed for the moment[76]) English law. If, in these circumstances, the English court were to 'accept the remission' back to English law and apply English domestic law, without any further consideration of what the Mexican court would do in such a case, then it would be following the doctrine of partial renvoi. This doctrine is used in some civil law countries.

3. Total renvoi

Under total renvoi, also known as double renvoi or the foreign court theory of renvoi, the English court deals with the case in the same way as it would be dealt with by the court of the foreign country referred to by the English choice of law rule. The English judge has to 'don the mantle' of the foreign judge and try to decide the case exactly as the foreign judge would decide it. This means applying not only the foreign country's choice of law rule, but also its doctrine of renvoi and thus applying whatever domestic law it would apply. In the above example, where a citizen of the United Kingdom died domiciled in Mexico, the English choice of law rule refers to Mexican law. The English court, under total renvoi, applies not only the Mexican choice of law rule that the succession is governed by the law of the nationality, English law, but also the Mexican rule relating to renvoi. So if Mexican law adopts the doctrine of partial renvoi (or 'accepts the renvoi'), that is, if the Mexican court would take its choice of law rule to refer to English conflict of laws rules, and would accordingly apply Mexican domestic law, then that is what the English court would do. If, however, Mexico rejects the doctrine of renvoi, so that its court would take its choice of law rule to refer to English domestic law, then the English court would apply English domestic law.[77]

The operation of total renvoi is well illustrated by two succession cases. In *Re Annesley*[78] the testatrix, a British subject, died domiciled in France. The English court had to decide who was entitled to movable property she left in England. Her will was valid by English domestic law, but invalid by French domestic law to the extent that she had failed to leave two-thirds of her property to her children. Under the English choice of law rule, the essential validity of the will was governed by French law as the law of her domicile at her death. Russell J took this to mean that he must decide the case as a French court would decide it. By French choice of law rules, the succession

76 English law is not necessarily the law of the nationality of a citizen of the United Kingdom. This is one of the difficulties raised by renvoi. See p 549.

77 For a consideration of the problems that would result if Mexican law were to adopt total renvoi, see p 549.

78 [1926] Ch 692.

was governed by English law. But would a French court simply apply English domestic law (that is, reject renvoi), or would it 'accept the renvoi' (that is, use partial renvoi) and thus apply French domestic law? The experts on French law disagreed on this question, but it was held that the better view was that the French court would accept the renvoi. Accordingly, French domestic law was applied.

In the other case, *Re Ross*,[79] the deceased was a British subject who died domiciled in Italy, leaving movable property in England, and movable and immovable property in Italy. The will was valid by English law but invalid by Italian domestic law. The English choice of law rules pointed to Italian law (as the law of the domicile in relation to the movables and the lex situs in relation to the immovables). The Italian choice of law rule referred back to English law for both classes of property. In this case, however, the evidence was that the Italian court would reject the doctrine of renvoi and would simply apply English domestic law. Accordingly, English domestic law was applicable.

To the extent that renvoi is adopted in the English conflict of laws it seems to take the form of total, rather than partial, renvoi. It is true that in some cases where renvoi has been used there has been no mention of the foreign country's rules of renvoi, but that can be explained in one case[80] on the basis that the foreign choice of law rule referred to the law of a second foreign country (transmission), as opposed to pointing back to England (remission), and the conflicts rule of the second foreign country was the same as that of the first. In such a case, a choice between total and partial renvoi does not arise. Of other cases[81] it could be argued that in the absence of evidence that a foreign country uses renvoi, it is to be assumed that it does not (when, again, the result will be the same whether the English court uses total or partial renvoi).

C Application of renvoi in English law

It must be stressed at the outset that the doctrine of renvoi is not used in the vast majority of cases. It can only possibly be utilised if one party to the litigation expressly pleads it. Because of the cost and difficulty involved in proving foreign countries' choice of law rules and their rules on renvoi, this is seldom done. Nevertheless, the doctrine has been applied in English law. In particular, renvoi has

79 [1930] 1 Ch 377.

80 *R v Brentwood Superintendent Registrar of Marriages, ex p Arias* [1968] 2 QB 956, [1968] 3 All ER 279.

81 For example, *Taczanowska v Taczanowski* [1957] P 301, [1956] 3 All ER 457.

been applied to questions of intestate succession[82] and essential validity of wills.[83] So far as marriage is concerned, there is one case[84] in which renvoi was applied to capacity to marry after a foreign divorce. Further, there is some authority[85] that if a marriage is not formally valid by the domestic law of the country in which it was celebrated, it will suffice if it is valid under the conflicts rules of that country. Renvoi has been applied in one case of legitimation by subsequent marriage at common law.[86] It is generally accepted that renvoi should apply to cases involving the title to immovable property[87] and, possibly, in cases involving title to movables.[88]

The doctrine of renvoi has traditionally not been applied in commercial areas of law.[89] Its use has been outlawed by statute in the fields of both contract[90] and tort.[91]

D Advantages of renvoi

There are several alleged advantages to the application of renvoi. First, it is claimed that it is self-defeating to purport to apply a foreign law unless one applies the solution that would actually be applied by the courts of the foreign country. If a British person dies intestate domiciled in Mexico leaving a movable estate in England, one is applying the law of 'nowhere' if one applies Mexican domestic law and ignores the fact that a Mexican court would (let it be assumed) not itself apply Mexican law, but would treat the case as a conflicts case and apply English law. According to this argument, the doctrine of partial renvoi is as objectionable as rejecting renvoi because under partial renvoi one is simply assuming (without

82 *Re O'Keefe* [1940] Ch 124, [1940] 1 All ER 216.

83 *Re Annesley* [1926] Ch 692; *Re Ross* [1930] 1 Ch 377.

84 *R v Brentwood Superintendent Registrar of Marriages, ex p Arias* [1968] 2 QB 956, [1968] 3 All ER 279.

85 *Taczanowska v Taczanowski* [1957] P 301, [1956] 3 All ER 457.

86 *Re Askew* [1930] 2 Ch 259.

87 *Re Ross* [1930] 1 Ch 377.

88 *Glencore International AG v Metro Trading International Inc* [2001] 1 Lloyd's Rep 284 at 297.

89 For example, in matters relating to insurance, sale of movables, mortgages, negotiable instruments, partnerships and dissolution of foreign companies (Cheshire and North, *Private International Law* (13th edn, 1999) p 64) and matters concerning title to shares in a company (*Macmillan Inc v Bishopsgate Investment Trust plc (No 3)* [1996] 1 WLR 387 at 399).

90 Rome Convention, art 15. The doctrine was not applicable at common law: *Re United Railways of Havana and Regla Warehouses Ltd* [1960] Ch 52, [1959] 1 All ER 214; *Amin Rasheed Shipping Corpn v Kuwait Insurance Co* [1984] AC 50, [1983] 2 All ER 884.

91 Private International Law (Miscellaneous Provisions) Act 1995, s 9(5). The doctrine was not applicable at common law: *M'Elroy v M'Allister* 1949 SC 110.

investigation) that the foreign court would reject renvoi and apply the domestic law of the country to which its conflicts rules refer.

This so-called justification of renvoi is, however, somewhat flawed. The most significant objection is the assumption that application of a foreign law means applying the solution that a foreign court would actually apply. This is misconceived and misunderstands the nature and purpose of choice of law rules. Further, it is naïve to assert that an English court ever 'really' applies foreign law. The reality is that English rules on classification, the non-applicability of foreign procedural rules and the doctrine of public policy all ensure that often foreign law is not applied in its totality as it would be applied by the foreign court.

Secondly, it is claimed that in some situations renvoi will protect the reasonable expectations of the parties.[92] For example, if the parties to a contract stipulate that the French courts should have jurisdiction, it is clear they must have wanted a French court to hear the issue and that they would expect that that court would apply French law including its rules of the conflict of laws.[93] Such a jurisdiction clause will usually be regarded as an implied choice of law.[94] Accordingly, if an English court were exercising jurisdiction in such a case, the application of French law should include French conflicts rules. However, a better solution to this problem is achieved through jurisdiction rules. If there is a jurisdiction clause in favour of France, English courts should normally stay any proceedings here in favour of the French courts.[95] If, however, the English court does exercise jurisdiction in such a situation, this will normally be because both parties to the litigation have submitted to the jurisdiction of the English courts. Such a submission must be deemed to include an acceptance of English choice of law rules which do not include renvoi in cases of contract.

The doctrine of renvoi could be said to protect the reasonable expectations of the parties in some cases of transmission[96] where, for example, both parties to a marriage are domiciled in country X but are nationals of country Y. They are within the prohibited degrees of relationship under the domestic law of X, but not under the domestic law of Y. The conflicts rules of both X and Y refer the essential validity of the marriage to the law of the nationality, so the courts of both countries would regard the marriage as valid. It is claimed that it would defeat the parties' reasonable expectations if

92 Anton, *Private International Law* (1967) p 58.
93 Briggs, 'In Praise and Defence of Renvoi' (1998) 47 ICLQ 877at 881.
94 See pp 206–209.
95 See Ch 3.
96 Dicey and Morris, *The Conflict of Laws* (13th edn, 1999) pp 75–76.

the validity of their marriage later came within the purview of English courts and it was held to be void under the domestic law of X. However, this argument again misconceives the nature of choice of law rules. The English choice of law rule that the essential validity of marriage is governed by the law of domicile assumes the parties would 'reasonably expect' the law of their domicile (their 'home') to govern such matters – and not the law of their nationality. Further, if by the time the question arose in England the parties had become domiciled in, and nationals of, country Z, whose courts would hold the marriage void, the consequence of the English court holding the marriage valid would be to create a limping marriage, and perhaps defeat the parties' present expectations. Nor would this argument for renvoi apply if under the conflicts rules of Y, the law of the domicile governed, or if the parties were domiciled in different countries with different conflicts rules.

Thirdly, it is often stated[97] that the principal reason for resorting to total renvoi is to achieve uniformity of decision of the case, irrespective of the country in whose court it is brought. If the English court decides the case in exactly the same way as the court of a foreign country would decide it, by using the foreign country's conflicts rules, including its rules of renvoi, then uniformity with that country results. And if that country is the one with which, apart from England, the case and the parties are most closely connected, then a good deal has been achieved. Thus in *Re Annesley*[98] and *Re Ross*,[99] the deceased's property in England and in France and Italy respectively was distributed according to the same domestic law. In *R v Brentwood Marriage Registrar, ex p Arias*[100] the effect of using renvoi was that the husband's status was the same in England, Switzerland (where he was domiciled) and Italy (of which he was a citizen).

However, choice of law rules are designed to select the domestic law which is appropriate (whether in terms of public or private interests). Their main purpose cannot be to achieve uniformity by choosing the conflicts rules of some other country to select the appropriate domestic law. If that were the function of the choice of law rules of all countries, then, of course, no domestic law could be found to apply to the case at all. Further, a vicious circle would result if the country to which the English choice of law rule referred also used total renvoi. The doctrine can only work if the other country either does not accept the doctrine of renvoi at all, or uses partial renvoi.

97 Jaffey, *Introduction to the Conflict of Laws* (1988) pp 262–263.
98 [1926] Ch 692.
99 [1930] 1 Ch 377.
100 [1968] 2 QB 956, [1968] 3 All ER 279. See pp 346 and 361–362.

The quest for uniformity of outcome presupposes that there be uniformity between the 'right' countries. However, renvoi could achieve uniformity between the 'wrong' countries. For example, using renvoi in the field of marriage could bring about uniformity of status between countries to which the person concerned no longer belongs, perhaps even removing a uniformity with countries with which he is now connected. This would occur in a marriage case where the domicile or nationality of the parties has changed since the marriage. If uniformity were the overriding objective in a marriage case, the proper course would be to apply the conflicts rules of the countries with which the parties are connected by domicile and nationality at the time of the English proceedings, whenever those rules are all in agreement. Such an approach would require a substantial revision of choice of law rules, and their rationale, as presently understood.

Fourthly, it is argued that renvoi can operate as a deterrent to forum shopping. There would be little point in forum shopping in England if the English courts were to apply the more appropriate foreign law as it would be applied by the foreign court.[101] There are two obvious responses to this argument. First, people do not forum shop primarily to ensure a certain law is applied. Rather, they are seeking procedural or other advantages associated with the operation of the legal system in the chosen country. Secondly, the most obvious mechanism to prevent forum shopping is through the development of a doctrine of forum non conveniens; this has occurred in England as a result of the landmark decision in the *Spiliada* case.[102]

Fifthly, there is an argument for total renvoi in cases concerning title to immovable property situated abroad. The choice of law rule that title to immovable property is governed by the lex situs is based not merely on the view that the domestic law of the situs is normally the appropriate law to govern the matter, but also on the fact that the property is under the control of the authorities of the situs, without whose concurrence an English judgment on the title can be of no effect. It is for this reason that the English courts do not normally exercise jurisdiction in such a case.[103] In the exceptional cases where they will exercise jurisdiction, for example, when the court is administering an estate which, in addition to the foreign immovable, includes property in England,[104] the possibility of the decision being

101 Briggs, 'In Praise and Defence of Renvoi' (1998) 47 ICLQ 877 at 881.
102 See p 120 et seq.
103 See p 135.
104 As in *Re Ross* [1930] 1 Ch 377.

nugatory in the foreign country is reduced if the case is decided according to the same domestic law that the court of the situs would apply. While there is some force to this argument, it is possible to overstate the importance of applying the lex situs as the foreign court would apply it on the ground that the property is ultimately subject to the control of the authorities of that country. This argument presupposes that foreign courts would never recognise English judgments that did not apply the foreign law in exactly the same way as the foreign court would have done. Such a premise is clearly misconceived. Indeed, the lex situs rule for intestate succession to immovables has been abandoned in most civil law countries[105] and the draft Hague Convention on the Law Applicable to Succession to the Estates of Deceased Persons of 1988 similarly suggests the abandonment of the lex situs rule for immovables. If the lex situs rule itself is being abandoned, at least for some purposes, it is difficult to take too seriously the claims of total renvoi in those fields where the lex situs rule still prevails.

Finally, and possibly most significantly, the doctrine of renvoi can be utilised as a convenient expedient to avoid the application of a foreign law that would lead to an undesirable result. Indeed, it was such thinking that was behind the introduction of renvoi in English law in *Collier v Rivaz*.[106] In this case the court was concerned with the formal validity of a will and six codicils made by a British person domiciled in Belgium. Under the strict conflicts rule then in existence, formal validity of wills was governed exclusively by the law of domicile of the testator at the date of death. The will and two of the codicils complied with domestic Belgian law and accordingly were held to be formally valid. The remaining four codicils were not formally valid by Belgian domestic law, but, desirous of upholding their validity, Sir Herbert Jenner applied the Belgian conflicts rule which referred the matter to English law[107] under which they were valid. Of course, little can be said in support of this approach[108] where the court had its cake and ate it by applying renvoi to certain testamentary instruments and rejecting renvoi in respect of others so as to ensure that all were ultimately valid. Nevertheless, it demonstrates how the doctrine can be a useful tool in enabling courts to reach what they perceive to be a just result. Another similar example can be seen in the approach adopted in *Taczanowska*

105 Dicey and Morris, *The Conflict of Laws* (13th edn, 2000) p 1027.
106 (1841) 2 Curt 855.
107 According to Belgian law the testator was domiciled in England. This decision was before nationality became a widely accepted connecting factor in civil law countries.
108 *Collier v Rivaz* was disapproved in *Bremer v Freeman* (1857) 10 Moo PCC 306.

v Taczanowski.[109] The parties in this case, two Polish domiciliaries and nationals, married in Italy at the end of the Second World War without complying with the Italian formalities of marriage. The English choice of law rule here referred to the lex loci celebrationis. On discovering that the marriage was formally invalid under Italian domestic law, Karminski J attempted to uphold the validity of the marriage by having recourse to the doctrine of renvoi and applying the Italian conflicts rule that formal validity of a marriage is governed by the law of the parties' nationality. However, this endeavour was in vain as it transpired that the marriage was also formally invalid by Polish law. Determined to achieve his objective, Karminski J then, as we have seen,[110] fell back on the fiction that the parties had contracted a valid English common law marriage. Again, it was clear that the court was determined to uphold the formal validity of this marriage and the doctrine of renvoi was seen as one means of enabling the 'just' result to be achieved.

E Disadvantages of renvoi

As can be seen from the above, none of the arguments in favour of renvoi are capable of withstanding close analysis. Additionally, strong arguments can be advanced against application of the doctrine.

Renvoi involves the English court applying the conflicts rules of a foreign country in preference to its own. An English choice of law rule, for instance that succession to movable property is governed by the law of the domicile, is designed to select the domestic law that is regarded by the English conflict of laws as appropriate for the cases covered by the rule. For reasons already examined, English law regards the law of a person's domicile – as opposed to the law of nationality – as best reflecting the law to which that person belongs. Application of the doctrine of renvoi will often amount to nothing less than the substitution of nationality for domicile as the appropriate connecting factor. The rule that intestate succession to movables is governed by the law of domicile was developed on the assumption that application of the law of a person's 'home' would best accord with the reasonable expectations of the deceased. He might have refrained from making a will because he was content that his property should devolve in accordance with the local rules governing intestate succession.[111] Application of the domestic law of some other country would defeat the reasonable expectations of the person and amounts to a negation of the policy underlying the English conflicts rule.

109 [1957] P 301, [1956] 3 All ER 457.
110 See pp 318–319.
111 Cheshire and North, *Private International Law* (12th edn, 1992) p 58.

Further, there are practical difficulties involved in the application of renvoi. One arises when the conflicts rule of the foreign country refers to the law of the nationality, and the person concerned is a national of the United Kingdom or the United States or some other state consisting of more than one country in the conflicts sense. The foreign law may be deficient or uncertain in its rules prescribing which is the domestic law to be applied in such a case.[112] In such cases there has been an alarming tendency by the English courts to assume that the national law of a British person is either the law of his domicile of origin[113] or that it must mean English law.[114] Either assumption is patent nonsense and results in the application of a law that might not have been indicated by either the English or the foreign conflicts rule. Also, difficulties have been experienced in the English court in deciding what the foreign country's rules of renvoi are (as, of course, has to be done under total renvoi), especially when the question is unsettled in the foreign country itself.[115] The result is unpredictability of outcome and, at times, the application of an absurd and unrealistic law. For example, in *Re O'Keefe*[116] the result was that the intestate succession to the movable estate of an Italian domiciliary was governed by the law of the Republic of Ireland, a country which the deceased had only once briefly visited and which had only come into political existence while she was living in Italy. Finally, the doctrine of total renvoi can, of course, only apply if the foreign country either rejects renvoi or applies partial renvoi. If it also applies total renvoi, the English court would have to attempt to resolve the case as the foreign court would do, only to discover that the foreign court would try to decide the case as the English court would do. The result would be stalemate. It is difficult to justify a doctrine whose existence is premised on the assumption that no other country in the world adopts it.[117]

In view of the above objections, it can only be hoped that the doctrine of renvoi is fast approaching its sell-by date. Accordingly, it is particularly unfortunate that the Law Commission[118] has not chosen roundly to condemn the doctrine and that the English

112 See, for example, *Re O'Keefe* [1940] Ch 124, [1940] 1 All ER 216.
113 Ibid.
114 *Re Ross* [1930] 1 Ch 377; *Re Askew* [1930] 2 Ch 259.
115 *Re Annesley* [1926] Ch 692; *Re Duke of Wellington* [1947] Ch 506, [1947] 2 All ER 854.
116 [1940] Ch 124, [1940] 1 All ER 216.
117 Lorenzen, 'The Qualification, Classification, or Characterization Problem in the Conflict of Laws' (1941) 50 YLJ 743 at 753.
118 See, for example, Law Com Working Paper No 89, *Choice of Law Rules in Marriage* (1985) para 3.39.

judiciary has seen fit to continue to make reference to the doctrine[119] even when it has not been pleaded.[120]

III THE INCIDENTAL QUESTION

A Introduction

The problem of the incidental question has already been encountered and the cases considering the doctrine have been subjected to analysis.[121] All that will be attempted in this section is an evaluation of how the solutions to the problem of the incidental question fit in with the rationale of choice of law rules and how such solutions connect with the doctrine of renvoi and the criticisms of that doctrine.

When English choice of law rules refer to a foreign law, an incidental question may arise which could be resolved by a different English conflicts rule or by the foreign law. For example, English conflicts rules could refer a matter of succession to Mexican law and under Mexican law the property could devolve to the legitimate children of the deceased. The main issue is one of succession. Whether the children are legitimate is an incidental question. How is this incidental question to be answered? English law has choice of law rules relating to legitimacy, but so too does Mexican law. If they both agree on the issue, there is no problem. However, if they disagree, the question is whether the law governing the main issue should also govern the incidental question (the lex causae approach), or whether the English conflicts rules should themselves govern the incidental question (the lex fori approach).

Examples of incidental questions include the status of a person as married or single, legitimate or illegitimate, adopted or not adopted. Another example is where, under the foreign law applicable in a tort case, an exemption clause in a contract is a good defence so long as the contract is valid. The validity of the contract is then an incidental question. It could be governed by the law governing the main issue of tort (the lex causae approach), or by English conflicts rules on the validity of contracts (the lex fori approach).

B Relationship to renvoi

The problems and arguments concerning the incidental question are similar to those raised and canvassed in relation to renvoi. Adopting

119 See, for example, Lord Scarman in *Quazi v Quazi* [1980] AC 744 at 824.
120 *Vervaeke v Smith* [1981] 1 All ER 55 at 87, CA.
121 See pp 344–348, 450–451 and 521–522.

the lex causae approach can be seen as similar to applying the doctrine of renvoi; one is striving to achieve the same solution as the foreign court. It can be argued, as with renvoi, that it is pointless referring to Mexican law which, in the above example, would allow the property to devolve only to legitimate children if we ignore the Mexican rules on who are actually legitimate children. If English conflicts rules are allowed to determine who is legitimate, this could be allowing persons to succeed to property who would not be so entitled under Mexican law. On the other hand, adopting the lex fori approach can be likened to rejecting renvoi; one is not seeking an illusory uniformity of result but, rather, giving full effect to the English choice of law rules. English conflicts rules on succession allow Mexican law to make the basic determination as to what class of persons are to succeed. English law has conflicts rules on legitimacy and these should not be displaced by the Mexican rules which could employ a connecting factor such as nationality which has been rejected by English law.

It is important to stress, however, that the parallel between renvoi and the lex causae approach to the incidental question is not exact. First, it need not be the choice of law rules of the foreign country that govern the incidental question. It could be the domestic law of the foreign country. Secondly, if it were the conflicts rules of the foreign country that governed the incidental question, the English authorities to date have not treated such rules in the same manner as when applying renvoi. In particular, there has been no attempt to apply total renvoi and deal with the incidental question in whatever way the foreign court would do. Similarly, the analogy between rejection of renvoi and the lex fori solution to the incidental question is imprecise. The argument for rejection of renvoi is that it allows full scope to be given to the English conflicts rule bearing in mind that that rule was shaped by policy considerations which were designed to lead to the domestic law of the foreign country. When the problem of the incidental question presents itself, one could give full effect to the English choice of law rule governing the main issue (by rejecting renvoi) even though one allowed the lex causae to govern the incidental question. The real issue is whether the English conflicts rule governing the incidental question should be displaced in such a manner.

C The solution

The view widely accepted today is that there is no general rule applicable to all types of case.[122] Instead, there needs to be an

122 Gottlieb, 'The Incidental Question Revisited – Theory and Practice in the Conflict of Laws' (1977) 26 ICLQ 734; Dicey and Morris, *The Conflict of Laws* (13th edn, 2000) pp 46–47.

examination and weighing of the relative strengths of the policies underlying each English conflicts rule[123] and a consideration of the practical consequences of each approach in the particular case.[124] Such a solution, however, leads inevitably to uncertainty and lack of predictability and raises the familiar problem of how the relative policies of conflicts rules are to be established and then measured against each other.[125] Accordingly, it is suggested that a better way forward would be acceptance of a general guiding principle applicable in most situations – but one that would give way to a different approach where policy or justice clearly demands such a result. Following this, it is submitted that the lex fori approach should normally be applied, but that in clear cases this could be displaced by the lex causae approach. Discussion of this solution will be restricted to two areas, namely capacity to marry after a preceding divorce or annulment, and succession.

1. Capacity to marry after a preceding divorce or annulment

In some cases the main question will be that of capacity to marry, but an incidental question can arise as to whether one of the parties, who has previously obtained a divorce or nullity decree, is single. For example, in *Lawrence v Lawrence*[126] the question was the validity of the remarriage of a woman whose previous marriage had been dissolved in Nevada. Her capacity to remarry was governed by the law of Brazil, where she was domiciled.[127] The Nevada divorce was recognised in England, but not in Brazil. In deciding whether she lacked capacity to remarry under Brazilian law, on the ground that she was already married, should the English court apply the Brazilian rules for the recognition of foreign divorces or the English ones? The Court of Appeal held that the English rules of recognition were to be applied (the lex fori approach), with the result that the remarriage was valid. This avoided the undesirable consequence of a person who was single in English eyes lacking the power to marry. Such an approach is clearly preferable to the lex causae solution adopted in *R v Brentwood Superintendent Registrar of Marriages, ex p Arias*[128] where the husband, domiciled in Switzerland, divorced his Swiss domiciled wife in Switzerland. The husband came to England and

123 Stone, *The Conflict of Laws* (1995) p 399.
124 Dicey and Morris, *The Conflict of Laws* (13th edn, 2000) p 47.
125 See pp 255–258 and 568–573.
126 [1985] Fam 106, [1985] 1 All ER 506. See p 343.
127 Assuming that capacity to remarry is governed by the law of the antenuptial domicile: see the discussion in chapter 8.
128 [1968] 2 QB 956, [1968] 3 All ER 279. See p 346.

wished to marry again. When the registrar refused to marry them, an order was sought in the English court requiring the registrar to perform the marriage ceremony. The main question was the husband's capacity to marry; this was prima facie governed by Swiss law. However, using renvoi, it was held that this included Swiss conflicts rules. The man was an Italian national and it was concluded that a Swiss court would determine his capacity to remarry by Italian law. The incidental question was the recognition of the preceding divorce which would determine whether he was single. The English court adopted the lex causae approach and held that the incidental question had to be governed by Swiss law (which referred the issue to Italian law) under which the divorce was not recognised and, accordingly, the man was not free to remarry. Such a decision is difficult to support. Under English conflicts rules the man was validly divorced and free to remarry. Why should these rules be ignored in favour of the lex causae's conflicts rules? In effect, the man's capacity to remarry was being determined by Italian law, the law of his nationality – a connecting factor rejected by English law for this purpose. The first wife, being not only a Swiss domiciliary but also a Swiss national, had in fact already remarried. The husband was left abandoned in a legal 'no man's land'. He was not married to his first wife under either English or Swiss law (the only relevant laws from an English perspective), but he was unable to remarry. Accordingly, section 50 of the Family Law Act 1986 has adopted the lex fori approach. Under this provision if a divorce or annulment is recognised under the Act, a remarriage cannot be held invalid on the ground that the decree is not recognised by some other law.

The lex fori approach can also be supported in the converse situation in which the divorce is not recognised in England, but is recognised by the lex causae. This avoids the unfortunate implications of the decision of the Canadian court in *Schwebel v Ungar*[129] where the application of the recognition rules of the lex causae led to a remarriage being held valid. This produced the result that a person was validly and monogamously married to two spouses at the same time (for in the eyes of the Canadian courts the first marriage still subsisted, even though the second marriage was held valid). Intractable problems in relation to succession, matrimonial relief and in other areas could follow from this approach. Such problems would be avoided by allowing the incidental question to be decided by the lex fori.

129 (1963) 42 DLR (2d) 622. See p 347.

2. Succession

When a succession is governed by a foreign law and under that law property devolves to a spouse or legitimate children of the deceased, an incidental question can arise as to whether a person is indeed a spouse or legitimate child of the deceased. It was seen earlier that there is judicial support here for the view that the lex causae should also govern the incidental question.[130]

Such an approach should not, however, be accepted in all cases. For example, suppose that in a succession governed by Mexican law the issue arises as to whether a woman was the wife of the deceased. The parties could be validly married under English law and have lived for years in England. It would be extremely unfortunate if the Mexican rules on the validity of this marriage were allowed to prevail with the result that the 'wife' (by English law) were excluded from the succession. The same argument applies where the incidental question is a person's legitimacy. If a person is regarded as legitimate by English conflicts rules, there seems no justification for excluding him from a succession simply because Mexican law has different rules on legitimacy. Such a person might even, in separate proceedings, have obtained a declaration of legitimacy,[131] the effect of which would be practically meaningless were the lex causae approach to be adopted.

However, as indicated above, there can be situations where the lex fori approach should give way to the lex causae approach. For example, if there is no spouse or legitimate child under English conflicts rules, but there is such a person under Mexican law, policy dictates that they be allowed to succeed.

Of course, problems arise if X is a spouse or legitimate child under Mexican law and Y is a spouse or legitimate child under English conflicts rules. In such cases, the English rules should not be expected to give way to the Mexican rules and Y should be entitled to succeed. If Y were a wife under English law, she would be entitled to maintenance, family provision, a divorce and so on from the English courts. The lex fori approach, while perhaps sacrificing uniformity of result, does nevertheless achieve 'internal harmony'[132] within English law.

130 *Re Johnson* [1903] 1 Ch 821; *Haque v Haque* (1962) 108 CLR 230. See pp 521–522.

131 Family Law Act 1986, s 56 (as substituted by the Family Law Reform Act 1987, s 22).

132 Dicey and Morris, *The Conflict of Laws* (13th edn, 2000) p 46.

IV EXCLUSION OF FOREIGN LAW

A Public policy

1. Introduction

A foreign rule which would normally be applicable, or a foreign judgment or decree which would normally be enforced or recognised, will not be given effect if to do so would be contrary to English public policy. Such a law or judgment is disregarded: 'It is as though it did not exist.'[133] The doctrine of public policy is most likely to be encountered in relation to the essential validity of marriages,[134] the validity and enforcement of contracts,[135] matters relating to tort after the Private International Law (Miscellaneous Provisions) Act 1995,[136] the recognition of foreign matrimonial decrees[137] and the recognition and enforcement of other foreign judgments.[138] It is appropriate, however, to make a few general observations about the application of the doctrine.

One general point needs to be made by way of introduction. The doctrine of public policy, its ambit and extent, and the manner in which it is to be applied has been entirely the creation of the common law. However, as the conflict of laws has been increasingly regulated by statute the doctrine of public policy has been enshrined in such legislation and in EC Regulations.[139] These statutes, however, do not define the concept whose meaning and role must be ascertained from the common law. Sometimes, drawing on international conventions, statutes have stipulated that the doctrine can be invoked only where a foreign law or judgment is 'manifestly contrary to public policy'.[140] It has been held that the inclusion of the word 'manifestly' means that this is 'a very high hurdle to clear'.[141]

2. Limited scope of doctrine

The doctrine of public policy is used relatively sparingly in the English conflict of laws, especially in comparison with the laws of

133 *Kuwait Airways Corpn v Iraqi Airways Co (No 3)* [2001] 1 Lloyd's Rep 161.
134 See pp 362–364.
135 See pp 232–234.
136 See pp 280–281.
137 See pp 418–420.
138 See pp 177, 190–191.
139 For example, Brussels I Regulation: Council Regulation (EC) No 44/2001, art 34(1); Private International Law (Miscellaneous Provisions) Act 1995, s 14(3)(a)(i).
140 Family Law Act 1986, s 51(3)(c); Contracts (Applicable Law) Act 1990, Sch 1, art 16.
141 *Kellman v Kellman* [2000] 1 FLR 785 at 798.

some foreign countries such as France and Germany.[142] There are several reasons for this.

First, many English choice of law rules have a 'forum-oriented bias'[143] with the result that English law is the applicable law and consequently there is no scope for the application of public policy. For example, the English choice of law rule in matters relating to divorce, judicial separation, maintenance, adoption and parental responsibility is that the lex fori applies. Any issue classified as procedural is automatically subject to English law and, as seen, the English courts have, at times, adopted a rather broad view as to what constitutes a matter of procedure.

Secondly, and in similar vein, many choice of law rules are structured in such a manner as to give English law ultimate 'control' and prevent the unfettered application of foreign law. In tort, before the entry into force of the Private International Law (Miscellaneous Provisions) Act 1995, the effect of the rule in *Phillips v Eyre*[144] was that no liability could be imposed unless the claim was actionable under English law. In essential validity of marriage, the rule in *Sottomayer v De Barros (No 2)*[145] ensures the displacement of the normal dual domicile doctrine in favour of English law when the parties marry in England and one of them is an English domiciliary. Further, the use of English overriding rules, for example, those relating to exemption clauses in the Unfair Contract Terms Act 1977,[146] ensure that an otherwise applicable foreign law is not applied.

Thirdly, there are many conflicts rules which, while framed in different terms, are either performing the same function as a doctrine of public policy or, alternatively, can be regarded as crystallisations of public policy. For example, the rule that a foreign judgment will not be recognised if insufficient notice of the foreign proceedings was given or if no reasonable opportunity to take part in the proceedings was provided[147] is regarded as a rule requiring natural justice as a prerequisite to the recognition of a foreign judgment. Were such a rule not in existence, resort to the residual doctrine of public policy would be necessary. Similarly, the rule that a foreign commercial judgment obtained by fraud will not be

142 Dicey and Morris, *The Conflict of Laws* (13th edn, 2000) p 82.
143 Carter, 'The Role of Public Policy in English Conflict of Laws' (1993) 42 ICLQ 1 at 3.
144 (1870) LR 6 QB 1.
145 (1879) 5 PD 94.
146 Rome Convention, art 7(2).
147 Family Law Act 1986, s 51(3)(a); the same rule applies to recognition of commercial judgments under the traditional rules: *Adams v Cape Industries plc* [1990] Ch 433, [1991] 1 All ER 929.

recognised or enforced[148] can be regarded as a crystallisation of public policy. Under the Brussels regime, which does not expressly deal with the problem of judgments procured by fraud, the extent that such judgments may be denied recognition or enforcement depends upon the application of the doctrine of public policy.[149]

Fourthly, there is recognition by the English judiciary that public policy is an 'unruly horse'[150] and that '[c]are must be taken to ensure that this animal is not allowed to wreak havoc in international pastures'.[151] Many foreign laws are different and even strange to English eyes but 'those who live in legal glass houses, however well constructed, should perhaps not be over-astute to throw stones at the laws of other countries'.[152] Accordingly, a distinction is drawn between domestic public policy and international public policy. Transactions which offend purely local (English) interests are not necessarily to be regarded as contrary to public policy when set on an international stage and having no direct impact upon, or posing no direct threat to, English institutions. In *Addison v Brown*[153] a maintenance agreement ousting the jurisdiction of the Californian court was recognised despite the fact that a similar agreement to oust the jurisdiction of the English court would have been void. Similarly, while it is clear that no talak divorce can take place in England[154] as this would offend local public policy by enabling the parties to circumvent the protections afforded by the English courts, foreign talaks, khulas and gets are entitled to recognition.[155]

Finally, but not unrelated to the previous point, it has been argued[156] that the growing acceptance by the English judiciary of international comity has led to a corresponding decline in the use of public policy to exclude the normally applicable foreign law. Increasingly, 'judicial chauvinism has been replaced by judicial comity'[157] with the result that using public policy is regarded as

148 *Owens Bank Ltd v Bracco* [1992] 2 AC 443, [1991] 4 All ER 833. See p 176.
149 *Interdesco SA v Nullifire Ltd* [1992] 1 Lloyd's Rep 180.
150 Lord Hodson in *Chaplin v Boys* [1971] AC 356 at 378.
151 Carter, 'The Role of Public Policy in English Private International Law' (1993) 42 ICLQ 1 at 3.
152 Sachs J in *R v Brentwood Superintendent of Marriages, ex p Arias* [1968] 3 WLR 531 at 537.
153 [1954] 2 All ER 213, [1954] 1 WLR 779.
154 Family Law Act 1986, s 44(1).
155 See p 407.
156 Enonchong, 'Public Policy in the Conflict of Laws: A Chinese Wall Around Little England? (1996) 45 ICLQ 633. Enonchong does not assert that comity is the basis of the conflict of laws, but rather that considerations of comity have led the English judiciary to become more internationalist in its approach.
157 Lord Diplock in *The Abidin Daver* [1984] AC 398 at 411–412.

'being discourteous to the foreign state whose law is excluded. It is like throwing stones at your neighbour's house'.[158]

Perhaps conscious of such considerations English judges have, at times, chosen to 'speak with forked tongues' and, while avoiding all reference to public policy as such, have refused to apply a foreign law or recognise a foreign judgment on the ground that it offends English notions of 'substantial justice'.[159] This discretion was mainly used in the field of recognition of foreign divorces and nullity decrees.[160] For example, in *Gray v Formosa*[161] a Maltese nullity decree granted on the ground that the parties had not married in a Roman Catholic church was refused recognition as offending English notions of substantial justice. This discretion to refuse recognition, in relation to such matrimonial decrees, has been abolished by the Family Law Act 1986,[162] which provides that recognition of the decree can be refused only if recognition would be 'manifestly contrary to public policy'. It is unfortunate that in relation to commercial judgments the Court of Appeal should have chosen to revive the doctrine of 'substantial justice' in *Adams v Cape Industries plc.*[163] In this case it was decided that a process whereby the amount of the plaintiffs' damages was averaged – with the plaintiffs being placed by their lawyers in four bands according to the seriousness of their injuries – rather than assessed following a judicial investigation into the injuries sustained by each plaintiff, offended English notions of substantial justice. No explanation of the relationship between public policy and substantial justice was provided. Given the fact that over the past century the ambit of public policy has been rigorously circumscribed, and that a new discretionary power based on substantial justice could be broad and unlimited, it is to be hoped that the difference between public policy and substantial justice is simply one of nomenclature.

3. *Scope of doctrine*

There seem to be two classes of case (which sometimes overlap) in which public policy may be invoked by the court. In the one class the foreign rule is not applied, or the foreign judgment not recognised

158 Enonchong, 'Public Policy in the Conflict of Laws: A Chinese Wall Around Little England?' (1996) 45 ICLQ 633 at 653.
159 *Pemberton v Hughes* [1899] 1 Ch 781 at 790.
160 See, for example, *Middleton v Middleton* [1967] P 62 at 69–70; *Lepre v Lepre* [1965] P 52, [1963] 2 All ER 49.
161 [1963] P 259, [1962] 3 All ER 419.
162 S 51(3)(a).
163 [1990] Ch 433, [1991] 1 All ER 929. See pp 174–175.

or enforced, because to do so in the circumstances of the case would offend fundamental English ideas of morality, decency, human liberty or justice. In the other class of case, public policy is invoked because the case falls within the scope of an English rule whose purpose is to protect the public interest.

(A) CONTRARY TO ENGLISH CONCEPTS OF MORALITY, DECENCY, HUMAN LIBERTY OR JUSTICE

A foreign law will not be applied and a foreign contract, status, transaction or foreign judgment will not be recognised or enforced if it is regarded as repugnant to fundamental English concepts of morality, decency, human liberty or justice. Examples include the refusal to enforce rules prohibiting marriages between people of different races;[164] a rule prohibiting the guilty party to a divorce from remarrying before the innocent party does so;[165] a rule upholding a contractual promise by a wife to repay money stolen by her husband as the price for not bringing a criminal prosecution against the latter;[166] the refusal to recognise or enforce judgments obtained by fraud[167] or duress;[168] the refusal to recognise a foreign maintenance agreement entitling a child to receive maintenance after minority;[169] and the refusal to recognise an extra-judicial divorce when the marriage had substantial connections with England and recognition would mean that the wife would have been deprived of the financial relief to which she would be entitled under English law.[170] In the sphere of government expropriation of property, effect will not be given to 'foreign confiscatory laws which, by reason of their being discriminatory on grounds of race, religion or the like, constitute so grave an infringement of human rights that they ought not to be recognised as laws at all'[171] (for example, Nazi laws providing for the confiscation of the property of Jews[172]). Similarly, foreign confiscatory orders that are in breach of clearly established principles of international law are regarded as contrary to English public policy.[173]

164 See p 363.
165 *Scott v A-G* (1886) 11 PD 128.
166 *Kaufman v Gerson* [1904] 1 KB 591.
167 *Kendall v Kendall* [1977] Fam 208, [1977] 3 All ER 471.
168 *Kaufman v Gerson* [1904] 1 KB 591.
169 *Re Macartney* [1921] 1 Ch 522.
170 *Chaudhary v Chaudhary* [1985] Fam 19.
171 *Williams & Humbert Ltd v W & H Trade Marks (Jersey) Ltd* [1986] AC 368 at 379.
172 *Oppenheimer v Cattermole* [1976] AC 249 at 278, 282.
173 *Kuwait Airways Corpn v Iraqi Airways Co* [2001] 1 Lloyd's Rep 161. In this case Iraqi decrees confiscating Kuwaiti planes in breach of principles of public international law were held to be contrary to English public policy.

Cases of a similar kind, not usually described in terms of public policy, are those in which the English court enforces an obligation relating to foreign land arising from 'a fiduciary relationship or fraud, or other conduct which, in the view of the Court of Equity in this country, would be unconscionable'.[174] In such cases, overriding effect is given to English rules relating to fraud, the abuse of fiduciary relationships and other unconscionable conduct. In effect, public policy dictates the application of English rules even if the lex situs would normally be the governing law.

In all the above cases the doctrine of public policy can generally be invoked even if no English interests are affected. For example, the contract for the sale of a slave would today be regarded as so offensive that no English court would enforce it even if all connections in the case were with a foreign country. However, there are two possible qualifications to this proposition. First, transactions could be regarded as broadly immoral, but not so repugnant as to justify the application of public policy. In effect, they are regarded as 'quasi-immoral'. In such cases public policy will only be applied if the transaction is also regarded as immoral by another directly affected country. For example, in *Lemenda Trading Co Ltd v African Middle East Petroleum Co Ltd*[175] a contract (governed by English law) that the claimant would use influence with the minister in charge of oil companies in Qatar to procure renewal of a supply contract was described by Phillips J as 'contrary to ... general principles of morality'[176] but it was 'questionable whether the moral principles involved [were] so weighty'[177] as to justify a refusal to enforce the agreement unless the agreement was also contrary to public policy and unenforceable under the law of Qatar.

Secondly, even in seemingly obvious cases, it does not necessarily follow that public policy would be invoked irrespective of the context in which the issue arose. Public policy is not a 'hard edged concept'.[178] Take the example of the laws that existed in South Africa during the apartheid era prohibiting marriages between persons of different races. Suppose two South African domiciliaries of different races married in South Africa and then, the marriage having later broken down, they relied on the nullity of the marriage under South African law and remarried. It would be surprising if the English court, when called upon to assess the validity of either

174 *Deschamps v Miller* [1908] 1 Ch 856 at 863.
175 [1988] QB 448.
176 At 461.
177 Ibid.
178 Brooke LJ in *Kuwait Airways Corpn v Iraqi Airways Co* [2001] 1 Lloyd's Rep 161 at 214.

party's second marriage, were to use public policy to uphold the validity of the first marriage with the result that the second marriage would be void. It has been suggested that in such cases there could be an 'intermediate type of foreign law which, although intrinsically repugnant, cannot always be treated as unacceptably so'.[179] Justice in the particular case can override principled objections to a foreign law. A similar approach (albeit in reverse, justifying the invocation of public policy) can be discerned in cases concerning the recognition of foreign divorces where the doctrine of public policy tends to be used only where justice in the particular case so demands.[180] Most of the family law cases where public policy in the guise of substantial justice has been used are also explicable on a similar basis. For example, in *Gray v Formosa*,[181] where the Maltese nullity decree granted on the ground that the parties had not married in a Roman Catholic church was denied recognition, it was clear that the court was strongly influenced by the injustice that would be caused to the parties were the decree to be recognised and the fact that such recognition would have entailed recognising that a marriage contracted in an English register office was void.

(B) ENGLISH INTERESTS THREATENED

The second class of case includes the application to contracts governed by a foreign law of English domestic rules which invalidate contractual provisions in order to protect the English public interest, for example, a rule invalidating a clause in restraint of trade.[182] If the contract in question will tend to damage the English public interest in the way in which the rule is designed to prevent, it will be held invalid even though it is valid by its foreign applicable law. The English interest here is, of course, only the protection of free trade in England and therefore it is only contracts restraining free trade in England that will be held contrary to public policy. Similarly, in *Trendex Trading Corpn v Crédit Suisse*[183] a champertous assignment of an English cause of action was regarded as void. There can be little doubt that a champertous contract relating to litigation in a country where champerty is lawful would be regarded as valid.[184] In *Saxby*

179 Carter, 'The Role of Public Policy in English Conflict of Laws' (1993) 42 ICLQ 1 at 4.
180 See, for example, *Joyce v Joyce* [1979] Fam 93, [1979] 2 All ER 156.
181 [1963] P 259, [1962] 3 All ER 419.
182 *Rousillon v Rousillon* (1880) 14 Ch D 351.
183 [1982] AC 679, [1981] 3 All ER 520. See also *Grell v Levy* (1864) 16 CBNS 73.
184 Dicey and Morris, *The Conflict of Laws* (13th edn, 2000) p 84.

v Fulton[185] a contract for the loan of money to be used for gambling in Monte Carlo was enforced; were the gambling to have taken place in England, the contract would have been unenforceable. Another instance falling in this class is the refusal of the House of Lords in *Vervaeke v Smith*[186] to recognise a Belgian decree annulling a marriage on the ground that the parties never intended to cohabit because, inter alia, the English rule that such a marriage is valid is one of public policy and the marriage in question had substantial connections with England. Had all the connections of the parties been with Belgium in this case, doubtless a different result would have been reached. This approach ought to be adopted in relation to same-sex marriages or registered partnerships. Where both parties are foreign domiciliaries who marry and live abroad, there are no English interests affected and therefore as with foreign polygamous marriages, there is no justification for invocation of the doctrine of public policy.[187] This argument could even be extended to cases involving an English domiciliary provided the parties marry and establish a permanent home abroad.

Included in this category of situations are those where a transaction threatens the national interests of the United Kingdom and its good relations with other states. Examples include the rule which prohibits trading with the enemy[188] and the refusal to enforce a contract to import liquor contrary to a friendly country's prohibition laws[189] or to export prohibited commodities.[190]

Public policy is not the only means available to the court to protect a litigant from the inappropriate application of a foreign law. The English court has power to issue an injunction restraining a party from instituting or continuing proceedings in a foreign country.[191] Foreign proceedings will not normally be restrained if the claimant would have no remedy for his cause of action if he sued in the English court. However, an injunction may be granted in such a case if the bringing of the foreign action is unconscionable, for example, where an English claimant brings proceedings against an English defendant in a foreign court, in which he has a cause of action which he would not have in the English court, in respect of acts which were done entirely in England and must have been intended to be governed by English law.[192]

185 [1909] 2 KB 208.
186 [1983] 1 AC 145, [1982] 2 All ER 144.
187 See pp 354–355.
188 *Dynamite Act v Rio Tinto Co Ltd* [1918] AC 260.
189 *Foster v Driscoll* [1929] 1 KB 470.
190 *Regazzoni v KC Sethia (1944) Ltd* [1958] AC 301, [1957] 3 All ER 286.
191 See pp 143–149.
192 *Midland Bank plc v Laker Airways Ltd* [1986] QB 689, [1986] 1 All ER 526.

B Penal laws

In certain circumstances effect may be given to foreign penal laws as part of the lex causae governing a legal transaction. For example, an English court will not enforce a contract that is illegal by the law governing the contract. However, the English court will not *enforce*, whether directly or indirectly, a foreign penal law[193] as this would amount to recognising 'an assertion of sovereign authority by one state within the territory of another'.[194] In *Re State of Norway's Application (Nos 1 and 2)*[195] it was indicated that the English court has no jurisdiction to assist such an assertion of authority; in effect the English court is declining jurisdiction in such cases.

Whether a foreign law is penal is, consistent with the general principle, to be determined by English law, the lex fori.[196] A penal law means a law under which a fine or other pecuniary penalty is recoverable, or property forfeited, for a crime or other breach of the public law, at the instance of the state or someone representing the public.[197] The court will also not enforce a foreign judgment in respect of such a penalty. In *United States v Inkley*[198] an action was brought by the United States government for the enforcement in England of a Florida judgment. The defendant had been released on bail in Florida, having given an appearance bond, and then absconded. Although the Florida judgment was a civil one, the Court of Appeal refused to enforce it on the basis that the purpose of the judgment was to enforce the criminal law of Florida.[199] Three criteria were laid down to determine whether a foreign law or judgment was penal and/or public: the party in whose favour the right was created; the purpose of the foreign law; and the general context of the case. Here, all these considerations, despite the 'civil clothing'[200] pointed to the Florida judgment being one aimed at enforcing the criminal law.

The English courts have, at times, adopted an unfortunately wide interpretation of what constitutes a penal matter. In a series of cases it was decided that a foreign status which entailed incapacities upon the person was to be regarded as penal with the consequence that no

193 *Huntington v Attrill* [1893] AC 150.
194 *Government of India v Taylor* [1955] AC 491 at 511.
195 [1990] 1 AC 723, [1989] 1 All ER 745.
196 *United States v Inkley* [1989] QB 255 at 265.
197 *Huntington v Attrill* [1893] AC 150 at 155–158.
198 [1989] QB 255.
199 It was indicated, in the alternative, that this was a 'public law' which was similarly not enforceable (at 264). See pp 565–566.
200 At 266.

effect was to be given to any of the incapacities. *Worms v De Valdor*[201] and *Re Selot's Trusts*[202] both concerned persons declared prodigals in France. An order of prodigality involves the appointment of a person who is empowered to control the spending, and in certain respects manage the affairs, of a spendthrift. The prodigal is therefore, to an extent, disqualified from managing his own affairs. These disqualifications were regarded as being penal in nature. Similarly, in *Re Langley's Settlement Trusts*[203] it was held that an order declaring a person suffering from multiple sclerosis to be incompetent to manage certain of his affairs and appointing his wife to do so on his behalf was penal. These cases have been roundly condemned[204] on the basis that the foreign orders were designed to protect the person concerned rather than punish him. These cases represent unfortunate instances of the English court adopting a somewhat chauvinistic response that if a status is unknown to English law, there must be something objectionable about it. It is to be hoped that these decisions will not be followed.

A wide view of what constitutes a penal matter may lead to a refusal to give effect to a foreign state's expropriation of property, even though the property was situated in that state at the relevant time, if it was not actually taken into the state's possession before removal from the state's territory. In *A-G of New Zealand v Ortiz*[205] a New Zealand statute provided that historic articles exported from New Zealand without the permission of the government should be forfeited to the Crown. Such an article was exported contrary to the statute, and the New Zealand government, relying on the statute, sought to recover it in English proceedings. It was held that on its true construction, the effect of the statute was that an article was only forfeited when seized, so that in the present case no title to the article had ever passed to the New Zealand government on which an action could be founded for its recovery. However, it was held obiter in the Court of Appeal[206] that, even if the effect of the Act had been that title passed to the New Zealand state before the article left New Zealand, nevertheless the action in the English court must fail. The forfeiture under the statute was a penalty to the state for the contravention of a public law, and the action was therefore one to enforce a foreign penal law.

201 (1880) 49 LJ Ch 261.
202 [1902] 1 Ch 488.
203 [1961] 1 All ER 78, [1961] 1 WLR 41; affd [1962] Ch 541, [1961] 3 All ER 803.
204 For example, Cheshire and North, *Private International Law* (13th edn, 1999) pp 129–130.
205 [1984] AC 1, [1982] 3 All ER 432.
206 By Ackner and O'Connor LJJ; for Lord Denning's approach, see p 566. This aspect was not considered by the House of Lords.

C Revenue laws

The position with regard to revenue laws is similar to that affecting penal laws. Such laws can be recognised as valid rules of the law of the country in question, to be applied if that law is the lex causae under the ordinary English conflicts rules. So if a contract is governed by the law of X and is invalid by that law because it contravenes a revenue law of X, it will be held invalid by the English court (unless to apply the foreign law would be contrary to public policy).

However, as with penal laws, it is a well-established principle that the English court will not enforce a foreign revenue law.[207] The reason why the English courts will not enforce foreign revenue laws is simply that they 'do not sit to collect taxes for another country'.[208] Accordingly, the public authorities of a foreign country cannot recover in the English court any sort of tax or duty payable under its laws. Nor will a foreign revenue law be enforced indirectly, for example, by allowing the foreign government to recover property in England over which it claims a lien in respect of the owner's liability to unpaid tax (unless the property had actually previously been taken into possession by the foreign government in its own territory).[209] For example, in *QRS1 ApS v Frandsen*[210] it was held that a claim by the liquidator of Danish companies against the controlling shareholder of the companies was an unenforceable revenue claim because the only creditor was the Danish revenue authorities. Where, however, there are other creditors, in addition to the revenue authorities of a country, this principle will not apply.[211] Again, it is for English law, as the lex fori, to determine whether an issue relates to 'revenue law'.[212]

D Public laws

As with penal and revenue laws, enforcement of a foreign country's public laws would amount to an assertion of sovereign authority over another state and so English courts have no power to entertain proceedings for the enforcement of a public law of a foreign state. The scope of this doctrine is, however, somewhat uncertain.

207 *Government of India v Taylor* [1955] AC 491, [1955] 1 All ER 292.
208 *Regazzoni v K C Sethia (1944) Ltd* [1956] 2 QB 490 at 515.
209 *Brokaw v Seatrain UK Ltd* [1971] 2 QB 476, [1971] 2 All ER 98.
210 [1999] 1 WLR 2169.
211 Smart, 'The Rule against Foreign Revenue Laws' (2000) 116 LQR 360 discussing the unreported case of *Teletalk Mobil Engineers v Jyske Bank* (1998).
212 For a full list of such matters see Dicey and Morris, *The Conflict of Laws* (13th edn, 2000) pp 93–94.

In *A-G of New Zealand v Ortiz*[213] Lord Denning, rather than classifying the New Zealand statute as penal, stated obiter that the New Zealand government's claim would fail as its statute was a public law. In *Re State of Norway's Application (Nos 1 and 2)*[214] the House of Lords accepted that there was a category of 'other public laws' which might not be revenue or penal laws but which, for similar reasons, were not enforceable in England.[215]

In the Australian case of *A-G (UK) v Heinemann Publishers Australia Pty Ltd (No 2)*[216] the High Court dismissed an action brought by the United Kingdom to restrain publication of the book *Spycatcher*, written by a former member of the British security services, on the ground that the claim arose out of acts of the British government seeking to exercise powers relating to the protection of national security. It was accepted that the court should not enforce foreign public laws.[217]

V RATIONALE OF CHOICE OF LAW RULES[218]

A Introduction

This section briefly explores the reasons which underlie choice of law rules. Obviously a court should not apply a rule of foreign law instead of its own without good reasons. The discussion which follows considers what those good reasons may be, for choice of law rules must be based on them. If good reasons cannot be found for choice of law rules they should be dispensed with altogether.

Broadly speaking, the reason for applying a foreign law rather than English law will normally be to serve the interests of the parties to the case and/or to protect or advance the interests of a foreign country. It is hard to conceive of a good reason for applying a foreign law which does not in the end come down to these. It is unusual for English courts to consider explicitly the underlying rationale for the application of choice of law rules (though their United States

213 [1984] AC 1, [1982] 3 All ER 432.
214 [1990] 1 AC 723, [1989] 1 All ER 745.
215 See also *United States of America v Inkley* [1989] QB 255, [1988] 3 All ER 144. For a list of such 'public laws' see Dicey and Morris, *The Conflict of Laws* (13th edn, 2000) p 99.
216 (1988) 165 CLR 30.
217 A different approach was adopted in New Zealand in relation to the same book in *A-G for the United Kingdom v Wellington Newspapers Ltd* [1988] 1 NZLR 129 where it was indicated obiter that the duty of confidentiality between the author and the British government could be enforced.
218 See Jaffey, *Topics in Choice of Law* (1996) chapter 1.

counterparts have been more forthcoming). In the discussion which follows attention is focused on academic writers, who have developed theoretical perspectives on the choice of law process.

Many theories and approaches have been advocated by scholars in the United States.[219] Generally they share the view that the construction of legal rules in the light of their policy is important in determining their applicability in conflicts cases. One approach has been to suggest choice-influencing factors which are relevant to the decision as to which law to apply.[220] The American Restatement (Second) lists the following 'factors relevant to the choice of the applicable rule of law':

(a) the needs of interstate and international systems;
(b) the relevant policies of the forum;
(c) the relevant policies of other interested states and the relative interests of those states in the determination of the particular issue;
(d) the protection of justified expectations;
(e) the basic policies underlying the particular field of law;
(f) certainty, predictability and uniformity of result; and
(g) ease in the determination and application of the law to be applied.[221]

This list of factors provides a useful starting point since it draws attention to the fact that the underlying rationale of choice of law rules involves two aspects: first, a 'public' aspect which considers the interests of the countries involved; secondly, a 'private' dimension which reflects the interests of the parties and the justice of the case. The first aspect is reflected in particular by factors (b) and (c); the second aspect by factors (d), (f) and (g).

Some commentators have suggested other considerations which might be relevant in the choice of law process. For example, it has been proposed that one 'choice influencing consideration' should be the application of the better law.[222] Not surprisingly, this approach has been widely criticised on the basis that it would generate uncertainty and come perilously close to a rejection of the binding force of legal rules. If a particular legal rule is applied not because a choice of law rule directs its application – nor because, on its true construction, it is applicable – but because the court likes it, why

219 For a survey see McClean, *Morris: The Conflict of Laws* (5th edn, 2000) chapter 23.
220 See, for example, Cheatham and Reese, 'Choice of the Applicable Law' (1952) 52 Col L Rev 959.
221 Restatement (Second) of the Conflict of Laws, s 6(2).
222 Leflar, McDougall III and Felix, *American Conflicts Law* (4th edn, 1988) p 729.

should the court not be free to invent a new rule which it thinks is even better than any actual rule? As far as English legal theory is concerned, the position is that, subject to the doctrine of public policy, under which a foreign rule may be rejected if it is grossly repugnant to the standards of justice of the forum, the court is not permitted to apply the law of country X rather than the law of country Y simply on the basis that the standards of justice of country X are thought to be superior. Having said that, it would be hard to deny that there are many instances where the courts seem prepared to manipulate the relevant choice of law rules in a way which leads to the application of the law which, from the courts' perspective, is the better law. Some of the tort cases decided by reference to the common law choice of law rules may be explained by the courts' implicit desire to apply the law of the forum rather than a foreign law which the court perceives to be unjust.[223]

B Interest analysis

1. Deducing the applicability of a legal rule from its policy

An approach to choice of law problems which is attractive at first sight is to try to glean from the legal rule itself the extent to which it is applicable in a particular case having foreign elements by construing it according to its purpose or policy. This approach, which has been taken furthest in the governmental interest analysis of Brainerd Currie,[224] has attracted a number of disciples, especially in the United States. Governmental interest analysis has been particularly influential in multistate tort cases. The basic method is to start with an examination of the policies underlying the laws which might conceivably apply to the particular facts of the case. In a tort case, for example, the competing laws may include the lex fori, the lex loci delicti and the laws of the countries with which the parties are closely connected.

If, on investigating the policy of a rule, it is found that, having regard to the foreign elements, the facts of the case do not fall within the scope of that policy, there is no point in applying that rule. The rule should be applied only in cases for which it was designed. If the case does fall within the policy of the rule – and to apply the rule will advance the policy – there is a reason to apply it. Depending on whether or not the policy of the rule of a particular country calls for its application to the facts of the case, it is said that the country has

223 See, for example, *Chaplin v Boys* [1971] AC 356 and the discussion by Fawcett, 'Policy Considerations in Tort Choice of Law' (1984) 47 MLR 650.

224 *Selected Essays in the Conflict of Laws* (1963).

– or does not have – an interest in its rule being applied. The premise of this approach is that a country has an interest that the policies underlying its legal rules should be advanced. According to this analysis, France has an interest in the application of French consumer protection rules to a dispute arising out of a contract involving a French consumer.

The application of this method may lead to the conclusion that, on the facts of the particular case, only one country has an interest in its rule being applied. In this situation, which is known as a 'false conflict', governmental interest analysis requires the application of the law of that country. Where, for example, a married couple from country X are involved in a road accident in country Y, it is not unreasonable to conclude that only country X has an interest in the question whether the wife can sue her husband for injuries caused by his negligence. However, it is also possible that the particular facts of the case fall within the scope of the policy of two or more of the competing laws, an example of a 'true conflict'. For example, a 'marriage of convenience' contracted by a woman domiciled in Belgium, under whose law the marriage is void, and a man domiciled in England, under whose law the marriage is valid, gives rise to a true conflict. In this type of case some basis has to be found for choosing between the competing laws. Which country's policy is to be preferred?

Currie's view was that if one of the countries having an interest is the forum – and the apparent conflict cannot be eliminated by a moderate and restrained interpretation of the competing laws – the law of the forum must be applied. This approach does not solve the problem when the forum is 'disinterested' and the conflict is between the laws of two other countries (though in many cases where the forum is disinterested one would expect the case to have an insufficiently strong connection with the forum to justify the exercise of jurisdiction). An alternative view is that the strengths of the conflicting interests should be weighed.[225] According to the 'comparative impairment' approach[226] the court should seek 'to determine which state's interest would be more impaired if its policy were subordinated to the policy of the other state'.[227]

The most valuable feature of governmental interest analysis as a method is that it avoids the pointless application of a legal rule when the purpose of the rule would not be served by applying it. Suppose

225 See, for example, Von Mehren and Trautman, *The Law of Multistate Problems: Cases and Materials on Conflict of Laws* (1965) pp 76–77, 341–342, 376–378.
226 Baxter, 'Choice of Law and the Federal System' (1963) 16 Stan LR 1.
227 *Bernhard v Harrah's Club* 546 P 2d 719 (1976); *Offshore Rental Co Inc v Continental Oil Co* 583 P 2d 721 (1978).

a rule of country X makes void a provision in a contract under which an employee agrees with his employer not to compete with his employer after the end of the employment. If the only purpose of that rule is to promote competition in country X there would seem little point in applying the rule to a restraint of trade provision which is to operate in country Y, not country X. If by the law of country Y the provision is valid it would be sensible to apply the rule of country Y. A choice of law rule which led to the application of the law of country X, simply because that law was the law applicable to the contract, would seem defective.

2. The limits of interest analysis

Taken to its logical conclusion, interest analysis leads to the view that choice of law rules are unnecessary. The methodology of interest analysis is premised on the notion that the sphere of application of any rule of law can be determined by reference to its policy. Interest analysis postulates that a conflict of laws can be resolved by a consideration of the strength of the competing policies. As far as English law is concerned, it has never been seriously suggested that choice of law rules can be dispensed with. Nevertheless, there seems little doubt that the content of our choice of law rules is, to a certain extent, determined by the policy considerations which are articulated by interest analysis theorists. Traditional choice of law rules are not abstractly plucked out of the air; they are shaped by various influences and concerns. The idea that a particular transaction, relationship or event should be governed by the law of the country with which it is most closely connected is explicable, at least in part, by the fact that the country of closest connection is the country which is likely, from the point of view of policy, to have the greatest interest.

While many would concede that governmental interest analysis can make a positive contribution towards an understanding of important issues in choice of law, few would seek to maintain that the theory is not subject to limits. A central problem is that the policy of a rule will not always give clear guidance as to its applicability in a case having foreign connections. It may well do so when the purpose, or one of the purposes, of a rule is to protect or advance the interests of the public generally, or a section of the public. For example, as has been seen, a rule of the law of country X may invalidate a particular contract in order to protect the public interest in some way. It will then often be possible to work out what connections the contract must have with country X if it is to fall within the policy of the rule. So, if the purpose of the rule is to deter the doing of certain acts, then very likely a contract will not fall within the purpose of the rule if no such act is to be done under the contract in country X. In such a case it can well be accepted that country X has no interest in having its rule applied. Similarly, the purpose of a rule which makes a marriage invalid may be to protect the public interest. This may well be the case, for example, with a rule which prohibits polygamy. If the public interest in question can be affected only if the matrimonial home is in the country concerned, this may be an argument for preferring an intended matrimonial home doctrine to a dual domicile doctrine.[228]

However, many rules of private law are not primarily designed to protect the public interest, whether by deterring harmful conduct or encouraging useful conduct or otherwise. Their function is to decide disputes between people, arising out of their relationships with each other or the effects of the conduct of one or another. Their purpose is to do justice between people, in the sense of producing a fair and reasonable solution to the dispute. But a rule's purpose in doing justice between parties to a dispute can tell us nothing about its applicability in a case having foreign elements. It makes little sense to ask whether a country has – or does not have – an interest in the application of its rule when the policy of the rule is to do justice between the parties. The only answer would be that the rule is intended to be applied to disputes in that country's courts, unless its choice of law rules direct that another country's standards of justice should be applied. The problem is simply that different countries have different concepts of what is the just solution in a particular case. The traditional function of choice of law rules is to indicate to the court in what circumstances, in view of the foreign connections, it should prefer the standards of justice of another country to its own.

Recognition of the fact that not all rules of private law are designed to protect the public interest does not invalidate interest analysis. It does entail the conclusion, however, that interest analysis cannot solve all choice of law problems. Nevertheless, sometimes Unites States courts and writers have tried to avoid the difficulty posed by the fact that many rules of private law have no obvious public dimension by treating a rule whose purpose is really to achieve a just solution between parties to a dispute as one whose purpose is to protect claimants or defendants in such cases. Then it may be held that the country in question has – or does not have – an interest in its rule being applied, depending on whether the claimant or the defendant, as the case may be, does or does not belong to the country.

In *Reich v Purcell*,[229] for example, the plaintiff's wife was killed in Missouri as a result of the negligent driving of the defendant. The

228 See p 341.
229 432 P 2d 727 (1967).

plaintiff and his wife came from Ohio; the defendant was Californian. The plaintiff sued for damages in California. A Missouri statute limited the damages in a wrongful death action to $25,000, but under the laws of Ohio and California the plaintiff was entitled to his full loss of $55,000. The court held that Missouri had no interest in the application of its statute, for the concern of Missouri law was to avoid imposing excessive financial burdens on Missouri defendants. Ohio, however, had an interest in the application of its law, whose policy afforded full compensation for injured parties, because the plaintiff resided in Ohio. California, the policy of whose law was the same as Ohio's, had no interest in the application of its law, for the injured party was not a Californian. Accordingly, the law of Ohio was applied.

In another Californian case, *Offshore Rental Co Inc v Continental Oil Co*,[230] a 'key' employee of a Californian company was injured in Louisiana by the negligence of the Louisiana defendant. Under Californian law an employer had a cause of action against a person who negligently injured his key employee. Under the law of Louisiana the employer had no such cause of action. The court held that the policy of the Californian rule was to protect Californian employers from loss arising from such injury and that the opposite Louisiana rule was to protect negligent tortfeasors acting within Louisiana's borders from the financial hardships which would be caused by the imposition of legal liability in such a case. So, both California and Louisiana had an interest in the application of its rule. The court decided in favour of the application of law of Louisiana on the basis of the comparative impairment theory.

While the results achieved in these cases are not difficult to defend, the process of reasoning is more questionable. It might be suggested that the whole approach to the rules in question is fallacious. The basis of the court's analysis seems in the end to be little more than that each rule under consideration is more favourable to one party than is the corresponding rule of another country. To maintain that the concern of a law which limits damages to $25,000 is to protect defendants from excessive financial burdens is only plausible if the comparison is with laws which do not limit damages. In comparison with laws allowing even less than $25,000 to be recovered, it would make little sense to say that the concern of the Missouri law was to protect defendants. Of course, a country which previously allowed full recovery of damages may pass a statute which limits damages to a certain amount. In such a case the purpose of the legislation may well be to protect defendants from excessive financial burdens. However, it is quite another matter to say that the purpose of the

230 583 P 2d 721 (1978).

resulting law, as amended, is to protect defendants. The true position is that the purpose of the new law, like that of the previous law, is to provide a just solution between the parties. It is simply that the perception of what is just in such a case has changed, the balance having been tilted more towards the defendant.

Another example of this approach is to hold that a policy of a 'guest statute', under which a driver is not liable for negligently injuring a gratuitous passenger – either at all or unless the driver was guilty of more than ordinary negligence – is to protect the driver from being ungratefully imposed upon by his guest.[231] However, a law which provides that a driver is not liable unless he was guilty of gross negligence could scarcely be regarded as being concerned to protect drivers if the comparison was with a rule by which the driver was not liable even for such negligence. And, as we have seen, it would be beside the point to show that the purpose of introducing the guest statute in the first place was to amend the law to make it more favourable than it had been for drivers.

The effect of the interest analysis approach in cases such as *Reich v Purcell* seems to be that a country has an interest in its law being applied when it favours a party belonging to that country, but not when it is against him (or when the law favours a party who belongs to another country). Why should that be so?

A more plausible analysis seems to be that a country can have an interest in its rule being applied only if a policy of that rule is to protect the public or a section of the public. It is only such a rule that can by its construction give any guidance to its applicability in a conflicts context. If the public purpose of such a rule will not be served by its application, having regard to the foreign elements, and the rule has no other purpose, then there is no point in applying it. If, however, the attainment of the object of the rule does require it to be applied there is a prima facie case for the application of the rule. It may be questioned, however, whether the mere fact that the public purpose of a foreign rule will be advanced by its application should necessarily mean that the rule must be applied – even if no other country's public interest can be affected. Considerations of justice between the parties may come into the picture; the 'private' dimension must also be considered.

C Principles of conflicts justice

It was said at the beginning of this discussion that the reason for applying a foreign rather than an English rule is likely to be to advance either the interests of a foreign country or the interests of

231 *Neumeier v Kuehner* 286 NE 2d 454 (1972).

the litigants. For some theorists the notion that the choice of law process should focus on public interests adopts the wrong starting point. For them, the fundamental principle is that 'concern for the interests of individuals as opposed to those of the state is the main preoccupation and justification of private international law'.[232] Even if one accepts that interest analysis can illuminate aspects of the choice of law process, the idea that choice of law disputes can be resolved simply by reference to public interests is controversial; the ascription of public purposes to certain types of rules is, at best, highly artificial. So, the question arises: if choice of law rules are shaped, at least in part, by reference to the interests of the parties, what are the principles which underpin those rules?

One of the most important factors underlying choice of law rules must be the desire to achieve justice between the parties. Of course, the actual standards of justice which will decide each issue will be those of one or more systems of law. But which? The problem is that different legal systems have different standards of justice. The principles of justice that are relevant to choice of law are those which enable a decision to be made as to which country's (or countries') standards of justice should be applied to a case having given foreign connections. These are principles of conflicts justice[233] or of justice at the choice of law level.[234] There is no exhaustive list of such principles and the decided cases rarely refer to them explicitly. The principles which are considered below are based to a significant extent on what the courts have done, rather than on what they have said.

1. *Giving effect to the parties' intentions*

One of the principles which underlies the whole of private law is the principle of party autonomy. Such autonomy is not unfettered; it may be limited by policy considerations (such as the public interest in a system of free competition). Nevertheless, party autonomy is a reasonable starting point in the conflict of laws, just as it is in other areas of private law.[235]

The desire to give effect to the common intention of the parties, unless there is good reason to the contrary, supports the rule that parties should be free to choose the law applicable to a contract.

232 Vischer, 'General Course on Private International Law' (1992) 232 Hag Rec 9 at 31.

233 Kegel, *International Encyclopedia of Comparative Law*, Vol III, *Private International Law* (1986) chapter 3, pp 14–15.

234 For a fuller discussion see Jaffey, 'The Foundations of Rules for the Choice of Law' (1982) 2 OJLS 368.

235 See Nygh, *Autonomy in International Contracts* (1999); Harris, 'Contractual Freedom in the Conflict of Laws' (2000) 20 OJLS 247.

There are, of course, problems of deciding how far the chosen law should prevail over the mandatory rules of another country, designed to protect its public interest.[236]

Related to the principle of party autonomy is the principle (sometimes referred to as the favor validatis) that when parties freely enter legal transactions or create legal relationships such transactions and relationships should normally be effective.[237] It is recognised, for example, that choice of law rules should normally seek to uphold the validity of marriages.[238] Of course, systems of law contain rules which are designed to render certain transactions and relationships invalid and these rules cannot simply be ignored. However, such rules should not be applied – thereby invalidating a particular transaction or relationship – unless, in the light of the territorial connections of the facts and the parties, there is a sufficient ground for doing so. An invalidating rule should not be applied if the case does not come within its purpose. Even if the case does come within the purpose of the rule, it does not follow that the public interest of the country concerned must necessarily prevail over the interests of the parties. A balance has to be struck between the public interest of the country concerned and the private interests of the parties.

2. *Giving effect to the parties' legitimate expectations*

One of the choice-influencing factors of the American Restatement is the protection of justified expectations. Once it is accepted that a particular expectation is likely to have existed and that it was legitimate (and it may be reasonable to assume that it did exist if it would be legitimate), it is sensible for choice of law rules to give effect to such expectations. The principle that effect should be given to the legitimate expectations of the parties is not unconnected to the principle of party autonomy. Where, for example, parties make a choice of law the expressed will of the parties is a clear indication of their expectations. However, the principle of giving effect to reasonable expectations goes further than simply respecting the parties' express intentions.

The proper law approach – which seeks to identify the law with which a particular transaction or legal relationship is most closely connected – is, to some extent, inspired by consideration of legitimate expectations: 'In many cases the closest connection will be clearly centred in one particular country and the application of its law will

236 See pp 224–234.
237 See Ehrenzweig, 'Contracts in the Conflict of Laws' (1959) 59 Col LR 973 at 988.
238 See p 324.

most readily meet the expectations of the parties.'[239] Similar thinking explains two other trends which can be gleaned from the cases.

(A) 'QUASI-DOMESTIC' CASES

A party is normally entitled to rely on his own law in a case where the facts are domestic to his own country (but for the fact that the other party is a foreigner). For example, a person who is injured in his own country will not normally be deprived of his remedy merely because the person who caused the injury happens to be a foreigner. It is the defendant, rather than the claimant, who has entered the international arena and the claimant may reasonably expect his law to govern. Similarly, a person who acts in his own country and there causes injury to a claimant for which he is not liable by his own law, is not normally held liable merely because the claimant happens to be a foreigner. In such a case the situation is, from the defendant's point of view, a domestic one.

The principle that a party should normally be able to rely on his own law in a case where the facts are domestic to his own country is one of the reasons why, as a general rule, liability in tort is normally governed by the lex loci delicti. Usually, at least one of the parties belongs to the country where the events occur. Even if neither party belongs to the locus delicti, the principle of legitimate expectations may indicate that a defendant whose conduct was deliberate should be able to rely on the fact that it was not actionable by the law of the country where he acted. This principle may also explain why the courts will uphold a marriage under the rule in *Sottomayer v De Barros (No 2)*[240] even though the marriage is void under the domiciliary law of one of the parties.[241]

(B) THE LAW OF THE PARTIES

Where parties to a dispute come from different countries it is inevitable that their rights and obligations will be determined by a law which is foreign to at least one of them. Where, however, both parties belong to the same country there is an argument for applying the law of that country on the basis that the application of that law would meet their reasonable expectations. Cases such as *Chaplin v Boys*[242] and *Johnson v Coventry Churchill International Ltd*[243] are

239 Nygh, 'The Reasonable Expectations of the Parties as a Guide to the Choice of Law in Contract and in Tort' (1995) 251 Hag Rec 269 at 332.

240 (1879) 5 PD 94.

241 See pp 333–335.

242 [1971] AC 356, [1969] 2 All ER 1085.

243 [1992] 3 All ER 14.

classic instances involving foreign torts in which the lex loci delicti was displaced in favour of the law of the country to which both parties belonged. Of course, the lex loci delicti will not necessarily be displaced in cases where both parties belong to the same country; the public interest of the country where the conduct occurs – for example, to deter harmful conduct within its borders – may take priority.

3. *Certainty and predictability*

It is widely accepted that certainty and predictability are desirable aims for choice of law rules; they are among the choice-influencing factors of the American Restatement. It is in the interests of the parties to a transaction or relationship that the governing law should be readily ascertainable without recourse to litigation. This can be achieved only by definite and precise choice of law rules. Certainty and predictability cannot be achieved by dispensing with choice of law rules.

D Balancing public interests and principles of conflicts justice

It was seen above that it is a purpose of some legal rules to protect or advance the public interest. Such rules include, for example, rules which invalidate marriages or contractual provisions in the public interest. No doubt also it is the purpose (though probably not the only purpose) of some tort rules to protect the public interest by deterring harmful conduct. On the other hand, it has also been seen that many rules of private law are not designed to protect the public interest and that one of the functions of choice of law rules is to protect the interests of the parties. In many cases the interests of countries (to the extent that they are relevant) and principles of conflicts justice coincide. For example, in a case where country X is the only country which has a public interest and the parties belong to country X there are few arguments for the application of a law other than the law of country X. *Babcock v Jackson*[244] was not a hard case. All the arguments pointed towards the application of New York law: both the parties came from New York and, although the accident in which the plaintiff was injured occurred in Ontario, the public interest of Ontario did not require the application of the rule of Ontario law according to which a gratuitous passenger was barred from recovering damages from a negligent driver.

244 12 NY 2d 473 (1963). See pp 255–256.

Where the interests of the parties and principles of conflicts justice diverge (for example, where the public interest of country X requires the application of the law of country X, but the parties' intention – or legitimate expectation – is that the law of country Y should be applied) potential problems arise. Of course, it is inevitable that the conflicts rules of a country will give full scope to its own rules which protect the public interest. Each country has 'interests asserted either directly on its own behalf, such as the protection of its currency or security, or on behalf of those members of the community who need protection, such as consumers and employees'.[245] It is only to be expected that an English court will allow English interests to prevail over any conflicting interests of the parties. From this point of view it is not difficult to understand the rule that – notwithstanding the principle that the law should seek to uphold marriages rather than invalidate them – a valid polygamous marriage cannot be contracted in England.

What is the appropriate solution where the country which has a public interest is not the forum? Should the English court seek to advance the public interest of a foreign country, even if that means that the foreign country's interest takes priority over principles of conflicts justice which are designed to achieve a just solution between litigants? There is no simple answer to these questions.

The intractable nature of the problem is illustrated by article 7(1) of the Rome Convention on the Law Applicable to Contractual Obligations, which provides:

> When applying under this Convention the law of a country, effect may be given to the mandatory rules of the law of another country with which the situation has a close connection, if and in so far as, under the law of the latter country, those rules must be applied whatever the law applicable to the contract. In considering whether to give effect to these mandatory rules, regard shall be had to their nature and purpose and to the consequences of their application or non-application.[246]

This provision allows for the public interests of foreign countries (as expressed in mandatory rules) to be given priority over principles of conflicts justice (notably, the principle that the parties' intentions should be respected). The effect of article 7(1) is not that the interest of a foreign country necessarily takes precedence over the intentions (or expectations) of the parties; it all depends on the circumstances. Where, for example, a contract is invalid according to a rule of

245 Nygh, 'The Reasonable Expectations of the Parties as a Guide to the Choice of Law in Contract and in Tort' (1995) 251 Hag Rec 269 at 376.

246 This provision has not been implemented into English law: Contracts (Applicable Law) Act 1990, s 2(2). See pp 227–228.

country X which is intended to protect the public interest, it would not necessarily be right to apply the rule to a contract – even though it falls within the policy of the rule – if the party who would suffer loss from the invalidation of the contract did not belong to country X and the contract's connections with X were not such that it could reasonably have been anticipated that the contract might be affected by its law. Even in those countries where article 7(1) has been implemented, it is likely that it will be relied upon – so as to give effect to the public interests of a country which is not the forum and whose law is not the applicable law – only rarely.

A provision such as article 7(1) may be thought to be founded on principles of comity[247] or – to use the words of the American Restatement – the needs of the international system. If the courts of country Y are prepared to promote the public interests of country X in cases where the situation has a close connection with country X, the courts of country X may be more prepared to promote the public interests of country Y in cases where the situation has a close connection with country Y.

E Concluding comments

United States approaches have not been very influential in the English courts, with the notable exception of the speech of Lord Wilberforce in *Chaplin v Boys*.[248] It is doubtful whether interest analysis as such will find much favour in the English courts, which remain wedded to the 'classical method', which requires the court to classify the issue in question and apply the relevant choice of law rule. Even as regards choice of law in tort – the area in which interest analysis has been most widely employed in the United States – the common law rules which were approved in *Chaplin v Boys* have been abolished by legislation[249] and the statutory rules which replaced them bear little influence of interest analysis. Nevertheless, a close examination of English choice of law rules reveals that they have been shaped by the need to accommodate competing public and private interests.

247 While the old theory that comity is the main foundation of the conflict of laws is no longer accepted, its role cannot be excluded altogether. See Enonchong, 'Public Policy in the Conflict of Laws: A Chinese Wall Around Little England?' (1996) 45 ICLQ 633.

248 [1971] AC 356, [1969] 2 All ER 1085.

249 Private International Law (Miscellaneous Provisions) Act 1995, s 10.

Index